Perverse Titillation

Perverse Titillation

*The Exploitation Cinema
of Italy, Spain and France,
1960–1980*

DANNY SHIPKA

McFarland & Company, Inc., Publishers
Jefferson, North Carolina, and London

LIBRARY OF CONGRESS CATALOGUING-IN-PUBLICATION DATA

Shipka, Danny, 1967–
Perverse titillation : the exploitation cinema of Italy, Spain and France, 1960–1980 / Danny Shipka.
      p.   cm.
Includes bibliographical references and index.

ISBN 978-0-7864-4888-3
softcover : 50# alkaline paper

1. Exploitation films—Italy—History and criticism.
2. Exploitation films—Spain—History and criticism.
3. Exploitation films—France—History and criticism.
4. Motion pictures—Europe—History—20th century.
5. Sensationalism in motion pictures. I. Title.
PN1995.9.S284S55   2011   791.43'655—dc22   2011015583

BRITISH LIBRARY CATALOGUING DATA ARE AVAILABLE

© 2011 Danny Shipka. All rights reserved

No part of this book may be reproduced or transmitted in any form or by any means, electronic or mechanical, including photocopying or recording, or by any information storage and retrieval system, without permission in writing from the publisher.

On the cover: Details of poster art from the 1971 films *The Bird with the Crystal Plumage* (hand with knife) and *Requiem for a Vampire* (women). Front cover design by Mark Berry (www.hot-cherry.co.uk)

Manufactured in the United States of America

McFarland & Company, Inc., Publishers
Box 611, Jefferson, North Carolina 28640
www.mcfarlandpub.com

To all of those who have received grief
for their entertainment choices and
who see the study of weird and wacky films
as important to understanding our popular culture

Acknowledgments

Books like this one are a collaborative effort between the people you love and the filmmakers you admire. I'd be remiss in not thanking people like Dr. Bernell Tripp, Dr. Jennifer Robinson, Dr. Lisa Duke-Cornell and Dr. Mark Reid for showing their support during the initial stages of this work. It's rare to find people who are not only professional but have the open mind and strong stomach to look at this subject matter with a clear eye.

I am very fortunate to have had two wonderful parents that have supported me throughout this process as well as my life. This work would not have been possible had both my mother and father not allowed me to watch all those cheesy and, let's be honest, quite disturbing horror movies when I was younger, never knowing that one day I'd be writing about them. I'd also like to thank my friend Debbie Jones, a true original, who has stood by my side for 30 years watching and loving these movies too, and her wonderful opposite, Dr. Nadia Ramoutar, who wouldn't be caught dead watching any of these films but still supporting me with her spirit, humor and strength.

Finally, I'd like to thank Dr. Steve Smethers for his support, intelligence and love throughout this process and throughout my life. I would not be the person I am today without his strength and his generosity.

Table of Contents

Acknowledgments vi
Preface 1
Introduction: The Eurocult Phenomenon 5

1. Italy 19
2. Spain 171
3. France 261

A Euro-Conclusion 310
Chapter Notes 315
Bibliography 325
Index 331

Preface

I was talking to my childhood friend Debbie the other night in one of those typical midnight calls when it seems it's the only time available to have a conversation. We talked about everything under the sun before the talk inevitably turned to movies. Being almost as much a horror film lover as I, she lamented to me that there was just "nothing scary out. All the stuff these kids watch is so stupid." As the mother of three girls in their late teens and early 20s, she probably had seen it all, so I said "Hey, have you seen *The Human Centipede* [2010] yet?" She had not and I gleefully related the major plot points of the heartwarming tale that had a mad scientist sewing together 3 people via their anus-to-mouth. After her initial "That's just messed [only she didn't use the word 'messed'] up," she came back, "Who could think that stuff [again, I'm selectively editing] up?" I told her it was European and made by a Dutch filmmaker, to which she xenophobically replied, "Of course, that figures ... [after a long pause] ... so can I pick it up anywhere, and oh yeah ... when are you going to send me that [French] film *Martyrs* [2007] you keep talking about?" After I hung up, I realized that nothing has really changed in the last 25 years when she and I would ride our bikes to the local video store and rent movies like *Beyond the Darkness* (*Buio omega*, 1979) and the *Gates of Hell* (*Paura nella città dei morti viventi*, 1980) and were completely grossed out and fascinated by European exploitation films. I called her up again last night and asked why we watched all those scary and nasty movies when we were growing up and her response was typical Debbie: "Oh, Dan, we were just bored, we didn't have anything better to do. It was freaky shit [you're getting the idea she's impossible to edit] and we LOVED it," she said with a giggle.

She was right: we did love it. When I was a kid, I would get teased mercilessly that I was a "monster freak." Kids (especially my brothers and sister) could be very mean, but truth be told, I didn't mind; I loved monster movies. Maybe I get it from my Dad, who used to love to watch the old Universal horror films of Dracula, Frankenstein, the Mummy, etc., and consequently made a fan out of me. As a baby boomer, he and my mom (and later us kids) would go to the drive-in and enjoy all those harmless scary movies that always seemed to be playing. I begged and pleaded with them to take me to see more "adult" scary movies like *Beyond the Door* (*Che sei?*, 1974), an Italian film, though I didn't know it at the time, that made millions ripping off *The Exorcist* (1973), to which I got a firm no. (I don't mean to imply that my parents wouldn't go see the films for themselves. Quite the contrary: often my enthusiasm for a film would send them off to see it, always to return to tell me it "wasn't very good," as if to lessen my pain.) George Romero's *Night of the Living Dead* (1968) was the film that solidified my love for the genre at the ripe old age of 9. The *TV Guide* said it was perhaps the scariest movie ever (well, up to 1975) and that was enough for me. It was a Saturday night and as usual the aunts and uncles were over and no, we couldn't watch it on our big (25-inch ... we thought we had it so good!) color TV. So me and my cousins hunkered down with the lights off to watch this film on the tiny 10-inch black and white rabbit-eared TV, and lo and behold, it scared the hell out of me. The monsters in the film were people, people that looked suspiciously like members of my family. No one survived, the hero was shot, and when the zombies ate people they actually showed it. I was completely traumatized and I loved every minute of it! (For years after that movie, I would always scope out my surroundings to look for places to hide if and when zombies happen to attack us.) For me it was like a roller coaster, the thrill taking me to places that couldn't be reached from the *Brady Bunch* land that I lived in.

I figured out there was a God when cable TV and the VCR were introduced just as puberty hit. It was the era of the slasher film and films like *Halloween* (1978), *Friday the 13th* (1980) and *My Bloody Valentine* (1982) were the rage, and though I was too young to go to the movies to see them (damn MPAA) we would count the days until they were released on video so we could rent them at the local video store. Cable was great because as a teenage boy I could now watch other programming that appealed to a different need in me: sex. It was hormone-popping time and cable was right there to make sure the transition into manhood was filled with as many erotic images as possible. The first "dirty" movie I saw was Radley Metzger's classic *The Lickerish Quartet* (1970), which was very softcore, very classy with only 4 sex-scenes wrapped around a deliriously complex and interesting plot. The sexual images were very artistically shot and the film, as all Metzger's films are, was one of "class." Soon, cable stations began playing a plethora of these types including Metzger's other classics *Camille 2000* (1969) and *Score* (1972), along with films like the Jaeckin's *The Story of O* (1974), *Emmanuelle* (1974), and of course her exploitive cinematic rip-off Black Emanuelle that gave this author his initial ideas about sexuality. What I didn't understand at the time was that practically all of these films came from Europe and they were to have a tremendous influence on me. These Eurocult films were classy, erotic, and very different from the American sex film, which was trashy, bland and usually comedic.

If European erotic films were one pleasure as a teenager, European horror was quite another. I can remember Debbie and me riding our bikes to the first video store in Dolton, Illinois (south side of Chicago). The store had about 50 titles! Some of them were classics like Argento's *Bird with the Crystal Plumage* (*L'uccello dalle piume di cristallo*, 1970) and Fulci's *Zombie* (*Zombi*, 1979). We didn't know the difference between European and American horror by the titles (those pesky video companies would always try to homogenize the covers); we just knew we loved them, the gorier the better. As more titles became available and the technology really took off, video companies seemed to find a way to release everything available. It was great for me as I could pick and choose anything I wanted to watch and watch it anytime (as long as the money held out and no one was home because, of course, no one in my family wanted to watch "that stuff"). It was then I began to notice that European horror and exploitation films were somehow better. The American horror film really seemed to be kind of shallow to me. It was very mechanical (killer stalks couple, couple has sex, couple dies horrifically) and rather boring. I understood American culture and I guess that I didn't find the things that scared most Americans that frightening. European horror was different. I wasn't aware of the culture so I was always caught off guard when the plot would unfold. The different perspective put me at disadvantage so I felt more vulnerable as a viewer, never knowing what to expect or how it would be portrayed on the screen.

European exploitation films were always revelatory to me. The genre never censored itself (though governments often tried to) nor shied away from topics that American filmmakers wouldn't touch with a 10-foot pole. Issues of necrophilia, bestiality, incest, schizophrenia, along with good old-fashioned, rape, murder and some pretty blasphemous portrayals of religion were subjects which Italian, Spanish and French exploitation filmmakers gleefully covered trying to find subject matter that would get people into movie theaters.

Recalling all of this now, it is fascinating to me that people could look at my growing up and wonder why I'm not a serial killer. Did these movies have a profound effect on me? Yes. Did they shape my outlook on the world? Yes, in some respects, especially with regards to sexuality. But I'm not a violent person. Never have been. I see horror and exploitation for what it is: entertainment. One of the reasons that certain mass media theories like Entertainment or Catharsis resonate strongly with me is that they pretty much encompass my reason for enjoying the genre. Do I see women and minority groups being denigrated in these via a strong white male hegemonic gaze? You bet, but in reality I saw that when I was 12 and I wondered to my mom why women don't make horror films (I still haven't gotten a firm answer on that, by the way). Do I see that these films perhaps could have a negative effect on someone whose support system is weak? Sure, I can see that as well. I think so many factors go into a person's social makeup that it's hard to just pinpoint one or two factors. But one thing I think is important is that we study this phenomenon. For too long academic scholars and historians have shied away from looking at this subject matter because they didn't see much relevance. Looking back we now see that these films hold a wealth of social and political culture I'm glad those days are coming to an end with the recent onslaught of new, thought-provoking research on the subject. It is my hope that this overview of the phenomenon will spur future interest in what I call Eurocult films.

So now the "monster freak" has come out of the proverbial closet. I embrace my love and devotion to the genre for all its strengths and weaknesses as I embrace the wackiness of some its components. Yes, the acting is often bad in these films (and yes, the dubbing is usually worse). Yes, they often go too far beyond the realms of good taste. Yes, the music is funky, as is the fashion. But I unabashedly love these films. We all have a little "monster freak" in us and it is my hope that this book will help give some much-needed respect to those who are not afraid to indulge in their perverse titillations.

Introduction:
The Eurocult Phenomenon

The European film industry has had an indelible effect on both world cinema and popular culture. Works by such filmmakers as Fellini, Goddard, Bergman, Rossellini, Truffault and Antonioni are considered classics by film scholars and critics and are respected worldwide for their cinematic genius. They've also influenced culture and reflected the times in which they were made. With their socially provocative themes—whether it's the tearing down of neo-realism of *L'avventura* (Italy, 1960), or *Jules et Jim* (France, 1962), the turning point in the battle of censorship and self-expression as showcased in *La dolce vita* (Italy, 1960) or breaking down the barriers of sensuality and opening up new, more adult styles of entertainment, which was accomplished in *Jag är nyfiken — en film i gult* (*I Am Curious, Yellow*, Sweden, 1967)—European films have brought a unique and refreshing perspective that Hollywood and other international film companies could not have duplicated in the mid–1960s and 1970s.

These critically acclaimed "highbrow" films have been universally hailed by critics and scholars alike and accepted as pioneering examples of "quality" cinema. However, these "quality" films were not the only examples of European cinema that were saturating the U.S. market. During the socially turbulent times of the '60s and '70s, another type of European film was being introduced to world moviegoers, the Euro-horror and exploitation, or "Eurocult," film. Images of horrific monsters, decaying zombies, bloodthirsty werewolves, sadistic Nazi frauleins, naughty lesbian nuns and the occasional dwarf filled the screens to the delight and shock of many fans. Any fan of Eurocult knows that these films were not known for their acting prowess, nor were they possessed with budgets that would allow for grander storytelling. Instead they relied on shocking and titillating audiences with as much nudity and violence as they could handle, all the while setting this mayhem in the best locations that Europe had to offer. These scandalous films would become as popular as the "highbrow" art films of new wave European filmmakers, many times outperforming them at the box office, and have proven to have a long-lasting legacy that continues to affect today's moviegoing audience.

Between 1960 and 1980, Eurocult movies saturated both international theaters and American drive-ins and local theaters. The sheer number of these films and their availability have had a huge influence on a new generation of modern filmmakers, including Quentin Tarantino (*Kill Bill, vols. 1 & 2,* 2003, 2004; *Grindhouse,* 2007), Brian De Palma (*Dressed to Kill,* 1980; *Blow Out,* 1981), David Cronenberg (*Dead Ringers,* 1988), William Freidkin (*The Exorcist,* 1973), Zalman King (*The Red Shoe Diaries,* 1992), Martin Scorsese (*Shutter Island,*

The Only Thing More Terrifying Than The Last 12 Minutes Of This Film Are The First 92.

SUSPIRIA

Once You've Seen It You Will Never Again Feel Safe In The Dark

RELEASED BY INTERNATIONAL CLASSICS INC.

2010) and Ridley Scott (*Alien*, 1979), as well as international filmmakers Guillermo Del Toro (*Pan's Labyrinth*, 2006) and Jaume Balagueró (*REC*, 2007), all of whom have incorporated aspects of European horror and exploitation in their films. The work of these directors and many others who contribute their own brand of cinematic homage within their films is perhaps one of the reasons for the recent explosion of interest in this genre. In addition, with the advent of new media technologies like DVD and Blu-Ray, Eurocult films are enjoying a renaissance, with films long unseen now available in unedited, original versions, released and sold in special editions that are both popular and profitable. Films such as Just Jaeckin's *Histoire d'O* (1974), Dario Argento's *Suspiria* (1976), and Lucio Fulci's *Zombi* (1979), as well as such lesser-known films as *La casa dalle finestre che ridono* (known in the United States as *The House with Laughing Windows*, 1976), *La novia ensangrentada* (*The Blood-Spattered Bride*, 1972) and *Mais ne nous délivrez pas du mal* (*Do Not Deliver Us from Evil*, 1971) are currently lining the shelves of American video stores alongside top Hollywood titles.

The time period between 1960 and 1980 was one of great social change in and around Europe as well as the rest of the world. Many of these social changes were reflected in the changes of censorship standards that had governed the film industries for decades. European film producers also reacted to these changing social mores by creating a myriad of different types of exploitation movies that reflected the attitudes of this turbulent time. For example, Italian murder mysteries with strong sexual and violent themes, called "gialli," became popular worldwide and comprised a subgenre that included more than 200 films. These films, the precursor to the American slasher movies, focused on the exploitative aspects of social life and reflected a discontent with Italian society.[1] Spanish and Italian cannibal films and their zombie counterparts were also big exports. These films, which were also some of the most violent films in the entire exploitation genre, reflected an increasingly globalized world in which people's xenophobia was exploited as well as their fear of being consumed by a culture that was not theirs, along with the standard lethargy of consumerism. In addition to zombies and slashers, Spain and Italy produced a staggering number of "nunsploitation" films, which featured nuns indulging in sinful—and often murderous—acts, as well as "devil possession" films, which all signified discontent with traditional religious institutions.[2] Spain produced a series of movies utilizing the familiar monsters of the '30s (Frankenstein, the Wolfman, etc.) that were modernized and reflected the failings of everyday men and in the process gave rise to some subversive criticism of the dictatorship of the ruling Franco regime. France incorporated strong doses of sexuality and eroticism into their exploitation films to take their place in the Eurocult field while playing down the hard-core violence they abhorred.[3] As a result of all this change, local film industries were able to take countries' new social norms and export them to a mass audience, changing the way that many non-Europeans view violence and sexuality.

Hidden within the shocking and controversial subject matter of exploitation films of the '60s and '70s were a patchwork of important ideals and issues that resonated with worldwide audiences. These films explored themes which included the mistrust of the rising women's movement (*Flavia, la monaca musulmana*, 1974; *Emanuelle nera*, 1975), technological advances (*Les Raisins de la mort*, 1978; *Il gatto a nove code*, 1971), mistrust between the hippie culture and authority (*Una lucertola con la pelle di donna*, 1971; *Non si deve*

Opposite: The U.S. poster for *Suspiria* (1978). International Classics is actually 20th Century–Fox, which was too embarrassed by the material to release it under their own moniker.

profanare il sonno dei morti, 1974), marriage (*Il rosso segno della follia*, 1968; *La novia ensangrentada* 1972), cultural imperialism (*Mondo cane*, 1962; *Cannibal Holocaust*, 1980), child abuse (*Mais ne nous délivrez pas du mal*, 1971; *Non si sevizia un paperino*, 1971), race relations (*Africa addio*, 1971; *Emanuelle e gli ultimi cannibali*, 1977), sexual freedom (*Emmanuelle*, 1974; *Histoire d'O*, 1974), homosexuality (*Quattro mosche di velluto grigio*, 1972; *Profondo rosso*, 1975) and war (*Apocalypse domani*, 1980). In addition, Eurocult films brought out subjects that weren't being discussed in the mainstream by delving into areas such as incest (*Eugenie, The Story of Her Journey into Perversion*, 1969), necrophilia (*L'orribile segreto del Dr. Hichcock*, 1962) and bestiality (*Emanuelle in America*, 1976; *Emanuelle perché violenza alle donne*, 1972).

Why Study Eurocult?

Last week I was talking to some colleagues and graduate students about a film I had just watched. In the film an evil female Nazi officer (who of course, was the epitome of sexy; after all, this is Eurocult) during World War II was attaching electrodes to the female genitalia of her patients before throwing them into a cage with a Neanderthal man who would rape them and kill them (yes, for all you Eurocult fans it was *S.S. Hell Camp*, 1974). In my glee in describing the film, I failed to notice one student looking at me with a disgusted look on her face. In a haughty tone this student said, "How is this important? I'm sorry, but I don't see the relevance." I laughed, since it was an argument I've heard pretty much most of my life. I said, "To you it may not be, but to the tens of millions of people who grew up and loved these types of films, to the countries and industries who invested their time and resources in them as well as their cultural identities, to the distributors who still manage to make money even today from these films, it has relevance to them." The student's response was something along the lines of "Well, it's still disgusting." To which I smiled from ear to ear and said, "Yep, I love it!"

Film has been an integral part of the world's mass media structure. Since its inception, film, along with radio and television, has allowed countries to develop a sense of identity. Cinematic texts allow filmmakers to explore their cultural identities and reinforce notions of nationality, gender, sexuality, and ethnicity.[4] It is through film that we can see historical social and political perspectives of those immersed in the era. The rise of European exploitation films in the mid-'60s to late '70s gave America and other parts of the world a social and cultural snapshot of the issues and trends that were consciously and subconsciously permeating Europe during that time.

Eurocult films were distinctly tied into political, social, and economical events of the '60s and '70s. Whether it was censorship battles with the devoutly fascist Franco regime in Spain or dealing with a more socially liberal country like France, Eurocult proliferated in these chaotic times. The fall of the Hays code in Hollywood and social and political events that shaped this era, including Vietnam, racial issues, and the Kennedy assassination, began to desensitize audiences in the United States. Their hunger for new and provocative material matched the themes being explored in Eurocult films.

Most movie historians look at the '60s as being the decade in which a liberating international perspective was challenging and enriching the cinematic landscape. French New Wave auteurs like Godard, Chabrol and Truffaut, Italian masters Fellini and Antonioni, Sweden's Bergman, and Poland's Polanski have long been cited as pioneers and visionaries whose works are considered positive representations of what is "good" in modern cinema.

Eurocult, however, is largely forgotten in these discussions. Whether it's the unsavory glorification of violent themes or the use of graphic and often perverse sexuality in uncomfortable situations, the Eurocult film seems to have been ignored in any discussion of impact, style, or quality. This book posits that the genre deserves serious reevaluation in terms of its impact on mass culture and its unique style and production.

The overarching assumption of this book is that Eurocult films are one of the first examples of a modern mass-communication and mass-cultural environment that relied on increasing globalization to facilitate its success. The assembly-line productions of these films stretched across both physical and cultural borders, creating global partnerships that in many ways were a reflection of the changing social, political and economic landscape. In their introduction to *Horror International* (2005), Schneider and Williams make the case that the new "global economy" has made it increasingly difficult to distinguish exclusive national and sociocultural parameters.[5] This book purports that the phenomenon had occurred some 40-odd years earlier in the exploitation genre.

In addition, Eurocult had a role in the social history of American society. These films, along with their American exploitation counterparts, filled the drive-ins and theaters in a particular time in American history. Understanding their reception and popularity is important in creating an accurate representation of the American cultural landscape of the '60s and '70s. This book looks at the history of European exploitation films from 3 of the most prolific filmmaking countries in Europe: Italy, Spain and France. The films are laid out in chronological order from 1960 to 1980.

Mario Bava's fun *Gli orrori del castello di Norimberga* (1971), which took advantage of the changing social times yet still retained a classic Gothic feel. The film was a welcome success for American International Pictures in the U.S. under the name *Baron Blood*.

It is important to establish the definition of what constitutes an exploitation film. Exploitation films can run the gamut from action movies and crime dramas to sex pictures. For purposes of this study, an exploitation film is any film that typically sacrifices the traditional notions of artistic merit for a more sensationalistic display, often featuring excessive sex, violence, and gore. In many cases these films' success relied not on the quality of their content, but on the ability of audiences to be drawn in by the advertising of the film. This definition encompasses a large variety of films that have violence as a commonality. Therefore films with large budgets and/or legitimate literary sources like Just Jaeckin's *Histoire d'O* (*The Story of O*, 1974) can still be considered exploitation because the violence portrayed in the film is on an equitable level with other exploitation films.

The films and classifications included are from traditionally non–English-speaking, mainland, free European countries. Films of an exploitative nature from Great Britain are not included. Though an argument can be made that some films (for example, Hammer's output in the '60s and '70s and the Pete Walker films from the early '70s) qualify under the definition of exploitation, they are not a part of this book for a couple of reasons. First, English and American film productions are inexorably linked in terms of history, language, and themes, so much so that in my opinion the two industries can be considered interchangeable. The cognitive dissonance that accompanies the viewing of Eurocult films dissipates severely with familiarity. Eurocult, by nature, skews the audiences by bending the traditional narrative models normally associated with horror. In addition, it deconstructs sexual, racial, and gender identities that allow audiences to adopt multiple viewing positions and experiment with differing subject positions.[6]

Political events such as the assassination of John F. Kennedy in November of 1963, the worldwide acceptance of television and such social endeavors like summer trips to Europe all helped bring about a transformation in the American cultural landscape in the early '60s. By 1960, the American audience was ready for new forms of entertainment, which could not originate, due to both government and religious restrictions, in the stale homogenous environment of the United States, but instead, outside the country's borders. The start of the "British Invasion" a few years later (with rise of the Beatles and the Rolling Stones, as well as the newfound popularity of such European themed pop-culture like Ian Fleming's *Goldfinger*) opened the floodgates for European exploitation film and allowed them to flourish. By 1964, the amount of European exploitation cult films that were being released increased exponentially. Seminal works in the genre such as Bava's classic *Sei donne per l'assassino* (*Blood and Black Lace*, 1964), Franco's *El secreto del Dr. Orloff* (1964), and the American release of Freda's *L'orribile segreto del Dr. Hichcock* (*The Horrible Secret of Dr. Hichcock*, 1961), all showcase the popularity of the genre within this historical timeframe.

Nineteen eighty marked a turning point in mass communications as well. The advent of the VCR made it possible for people to watch their favorite films without leaving their homes.[7] Theaters and drive-ins that once were the lifeblood of European exploitation distribution waned in popularity. Obscure favorites such as *L'uccello dalle piume di cristallo* (*Bird with the Crystal Plumage*, 1970), and *Le Viol du vampire* (*The Rape of the Vampire*, 1968), as well as adult exploitations like *Emmanuelle* (1974), could be rented or bought alongside Hollywood blockbusters at any given time. With the exception of a short, intense spurt in the early '80s, European exploitation production dropped off significantly in that decade. This trend continues today with European exploitation films being distributed directly to DVD after their initial foreign run. No longer is it possible with any frequency (with the exception of the larger cities where an occasional showing is scheduled) to see European exploitation in theaters.[8]

Special mention must be made about the films themselves and the methodology of their examination. Any one version of a Eurocult film rarely stands as a completed work. Different versions, with different titles and varying degrees of violence, nudity and sexuality, may exist for a film depending on the country in which it was shown. For example, *La noche del terror ciego* (1971) was released in a censored form (minus overt sexuality and violence) in Spain. In Germany, the sex scenes and violence were added back in, while the rest of the world edited the films to the social taste of the country.[9] To grasp this, it is important to understand the intricacies of foreign distribution, which played a huge part in the success of Eurocult from its onset. This extraordinarily complex, multinational exercise arose from the need to make films as palatable as possible to the widest variety of audience tastes and as a way of recouping financial risks associated with production and international distribution. Foreign producers making horror films in the late '50s had to produce their works from a cultural standpoint that was widely applicable.[10]

The usual template for these films productions began with financing. This would be obtained from a differing number of distributors in different countries. Each distributor would then have its own individual rights over a particular film in its respective country. In order to help facilitate success, distributors would pressure or force filmmakers to cast those stars that would appeal to their particular countries' audiences.[11] A good example of this would be the film *Maison de rendez-vous* (*French Sex Murders*, 1972), which had French, German, Italian, and Spanish involvement in its production. Its lead actors were a who's-who of popular and fading actors in Europe at the time, including Barbara Bouchet (France), Anita Ekberg, Robert Sacchi, Rosalba Neri (Italy), and Howard Vernon (Spain), who all play suspects in a murder mystery that's solved by a Humphrey Bogart–impersonating actor (no, I'm not kidding, though I wish I were). In order to fully maximize the roles of those actors that had homegrown appeal, distributors in each country would be allowed to re-cut the film in a way that showcased them to better advantage. Also these distributors were allowed to change the titles as they saw fit; *Maison* itself had a varying number of titles and running times, including *Casa d'Appuntamento* (Italy, 81 minutes), *Meurte dans la 17e avenue* (France, 84 minutes) and *French Sex Murders* (U.S., 90 minutes).[12]

The fluidity of these films can be traced to their production. In Europe, with money tight, films had to be rush-produced in order to capitalize on a current trend. Ian McCulloch, British actor and star of several Italian Eurocult favorites in the late '70s, commented, "These films were almost in profit before a frame was shot. They were pre-sold all over the world on a title, storyboards, poster artwork, and synopsis."[13] He added, "Everything is sold ... they know before the camera rolls that they will make a profit. It may not be very much but they know they have covered all their costs. They will sell the film to South America and all places that are easy to sell to, and in the difficult markets they will do deals."[14] These distribution deals that are made can have a radical impact on the presentation of the film. For example, American and British distributors often bartered for rights to change the content of a film. In the early days of Eurocult, these rights were given freely so that the filmmakers could gain a profit. This meant that portions of the movie, usually the violent parts, were often eliminated, having a disastrous effect on the story, or worse, extra footage would be shot, occasionally by those having nothing to do with the original production, to soften up the material. For example, Mario Bava's first three films, *La maschera del demonio* (*Black Sunday*, 1960), *La raggaza che sapeva troppo* (*The Girl Who Knew Too*

Much, 1962) and *I tre volti della paura* (*Black Sabbath*, 1963), were entirely rescored, edited, and changed from their initial conception for American audiences, resulting in the films' having a drastically different tone from their original form.[15] As the '60s progressed into the '70s and public acceptance of hard-core pornography began to grow around the world, distributors would take this liberty even farther: they would film hard-core shots and splice them in into a film, giving audiences the impression that their favorite actor and actress were actually participating in hardcore sex! Though this probably didn't sit well with the actors, and truth be told many of them probably didn't know it until many years later, there were very few contracts that stipulated it couldn't be done.

The restructuring of films for international audiences resulted in what is probably one of the major complaints about the genre: dubbing. Poor dubbing can ruin any film but it seems to have a particular affinity for ruining many a Eurocult classic. The same laissez-faire attitude that distributors had with the handling of other aspects of each film also went into the dubbing. It just wasn't that big of a deal to get it precisely right. The practice of recording voices that do not belong to the original actors grew out of necessity. European filmmakers in the '60s and even as late as the early '70s never shot their films with live sound. Complete redubs of the entire script, along with sounds, etc., were placed within the movie after it was shot by the countries that were showing the film.[16] There was a plus side to this, though: since film producers didn't have to worry whether an actor could speak a particular language, they could cast anyone they wanted in their films. Because of this multinational approach, actors would frequently find themselves acting with those who were speaking their own lines in another language, meaning that American actors would say their lines in English, while Italian actors would say their lines in Italian. Catriona MacColl, star of Lucio Fulci's *L'aldilà* (*The Beyond*, 1981) commented on the difficulties of these situations for the actors: "I'm trying to remember the name of this actor, charming man ... but his English wasn't very good with all due respect and he tried to learn the lines in English and I can't quite remember what came out but it was quite difficult. It was quite difficult for me to keep a straight face with him sometimes because he would come out with some hysterically funny lines that were between English and Italian."[17] If the scene required 4 different actors it's more than possible that the scene was being in acted in 4 different languages. And just because a certain actor could speak more than one language didn't necessarily guarantee that it would be his voice that the audience would finally hear. Actors with distinctive voices like Boris Karloff and Christopher Lee were often dubbed by native speakers, highly diminishing their performances. A good example would be Karloff in Mario Bava's original Italian version of *I tre volti della paura* (*Black Sabbath*, 1963) in which the Italian dubbing sounds nothing like the Karloff international audiences know. After having some bad experiences, British actor Christopher Lee, who was fluent in many languages, had it built into his contract that he would do the dubbing.

So with the blurring of nationalities in terms of production and directors crossing borders, and the sheer variety of different versions of films, movies in the study will be examined using a number of criteria. The majority of these fall within the time parameters of the study, 1960 to 1980. A small number of seminal works prior to this time period are examined in order to gain historical precedent. Movies were classified as belonging to a

Opposite: The very serious giallo, *Una lucertola con la pella di donna* (*Lizard in a Woman's Skin*, 1971), gets a marketing markover from U.S. distributors who try to pass the film off as a killer bat movie!

particular country if either the director and/or majority of the production staff originated from area and brought their own perspective to a film (ex. Jess Franco). Care was taken to find the longest cut of a film available, though hard-core inserts weren't examined unless specifically filmed by the director himself during filming. Films that were not shot using live sound will be examined in the language spoken by a majority of the cast, and those recorded with live sound will be viewed in their native languages. Any and all comments from directors, actors, and production personnel accompanying the film will also be examined, and critical evaluation of the films will be consulted when available. The point of the pinpointing the exact language, running time, and best transfer is to find those elements in which the true expression of the filmmaker's ideas are communicated.

The first chapter looks at the history of the Italian horror and exploitation film from its inception in the late '50s to the advent of home video in 1980. Italy, especially from the autumn of 1969 onwards, was a dangerous place and the negativity and angst of the times are reflected in the exploitation films of the period.[18] The chapter shows that the Italian horror and exploitation film industry, though born out of duplication of U.S./British themes in the '50s, perfected new original subgenres successful enough to be copied in turn by the U.S. By isolating and defining each subgenre within the category of Italian horror/exploitation cinema and by looking at many of the popular auteurs involved (Mario Bava, Dario Argento, Lucio Fulci, etc.), the chapter will show a film industry that had a fluid, cyclical relationship with the Hollywood and British film industries. This relationship allowed Italian filmmakers to copy particular genre styles from established studios, apply their own distinct styles, and profit, only to lose out again when Hollywood took back these changes and mass-produced them. The chapter will look at the beginning of the Italian exploitation film industry in terms of its early history and style. Beginning with Ricardo Freda's *I vampiri* (1956) and Mario Bava's *La maschera del demonio* (*Black Sunday*, 1960), this section discusses the Italian pioneers of the genre and examines the political/social/economic events in order to understand the popularity and acceptance of the genre around the world.

The Gothic, with its atmospheric sets and evocative lighting, closely mirrors the English Gothic dramas of the '30s through the '50s. The giallo, which are vicious, sexualized murder mysteries that take their name from pulp crime detective novels popularized in Italy, will be discussed. Zombie, cannibal, and mondo films, a mainstay of Italian exploitation, from the worldwide success of *Mondo cane* (1962) to *Zombi* (1979), represent a subgenre that walks the line between cinéma vérité and obscenity. The Catholic Church's residence within the borders of Italy and its permeating influence shapes the next subgenre, nunsploitation/devil possession. The final subgenre will be a look at Italian erotic films such as the *Black Emanuelle* films that blur the line between sexuality and exploitation. Each one of these subgenres will receive its own history, social/critical effects, and patterns of influence.

Intermixed within this section will be a more in-depth examination of those auteurs that have defined the Italian exploitation industry. These filmmakers—Mario Bava (1914–1980), Lucio Fulci (1927–1996), Sergio Martino (1938–), and Dario Argento (1940–)—often crossed the lines between subgenres and it is important to state their importance to the overall genre.

The second chapter will deal with the Spanish exploitation film industry. Spending the better part of the '60s dealing with the declining, repressive Franco regime, Spain was responsible for some of the most popular and provocative exploitation films in the genre. The early history of the genre will be explored, focusing on the local traditions of horror and drama, themes important in the development of exploitation. The chapter will also look at both the government and religious factions that sought to repress the genre's unsavory themes. As film censorship abated in Spain in the late '60s, several subgenres solidified. Like neighboring Italy, Spain is heavily Catholic, and the Spanish "religious exploitation" film used a variety of symbolism to weave tales of religion gone wrong. The Spanish "zombie and blind dead" subgenre differed greatly from Italian films relating to this genre in its mix of history and sexual politics. Spain was also responsible for updating the "classic" monster tales (the Frankenstein monster, Dracula and the Wolf Man), presenting the characters with a more exploitative, nationalistic bent. Intermixed within this section will be an examination of those auteurs—Jacinto Molina (1934–2009), Jess Franco (1930–), and Amando de Ossorio (1918–2001)—that have defined the Spanish exploitation industry.

The third chapter will look at France. Unlike their Italian neighbors, the French film industry had an aversion to the overt horror and violence of traditional exploitation, shifting its exploitative gaze to the erotic and the violence committed to the physical body. Early history and style will be examined at the beginning of the French exploitation film industry. Beginning with Buñuel's dreamy *Un Chien andalou* (1929) up to Franju's *Les Yeux sans visage* (1959), this section will discuss the French pioneers of the genre, as well as look at the political/social/economic events prior to 1960 that affected the genre. The next section will look in-depth at the subgenres that make up French exploitation. Though not as diverse as other European film industries, French exploitation concentrated on the violent aspects of human sexuality. Their obsession with the vampire is a result of this. Infused with an erotic charge and taking precedent from earlier traditional works (for example, La Fanu's *Carmilla*), the French embraced various undead motifs. Another popular subgenre would be the erotic subjugation films. Whether taking their inspiration from the popular French cartoon strips of the time (such as Crepax's *Valentina*) or popular literature (such as Reage's *Histoire d'O*), these sadomasochistic male fantasies were immensely popular in the '70s. Intermixed within this section will be an examination of those French auteurs—Jean Rollin (1938–), Just Jaeckin (1940–), and Mario Mercier (1948–)—that have defined the French exploitation industry.

This book is a meant to be survey of the Eurocult phenomenon that experienced its greatest success between 1960 and 1980 using the 3 most prolific countries that produced it: Italy, Spain and France. While examples of Eurocult from an individual-country perspective have been featured in the popular press, this topic has never been explored from a larger continental perspective and has largely been avoided until very recently by academic researchers. Moreover, few scholars have attempted the task of tying all these countries together into one cohesive structure. That doesn't mean some wonderful works have not been done in the field looking at individual aspects. Scholar Tim Lucas's work on Mario Bava in his mammoth *All the Colors of the Dark* (2007) is a superlative investigation of the director's life and work and ranks in my mind as one of the best books ever written on film in general, let alone Eurocult, while *Immoral Tales* (1995), by Pete Tombs and Cathal Tohill, was certainly a guiding light and inspiration.

The work here is twofold. First, it is meant to take a closer look at those films the Italian, Spanish and French film industries. Second, it's meant to be a primer for those who don't know much about these films or the artists that created them. When writing a book like this the question always arises: should the author take the firm scholarly approach, exploring themes and history outside the confines of what is actually on celluloid ("Boring," says the casual Eurocult fan), or should he take the approach of a fan who loves these films and wants to share in spreading the fun ("You prove nothing," says the academic)? My

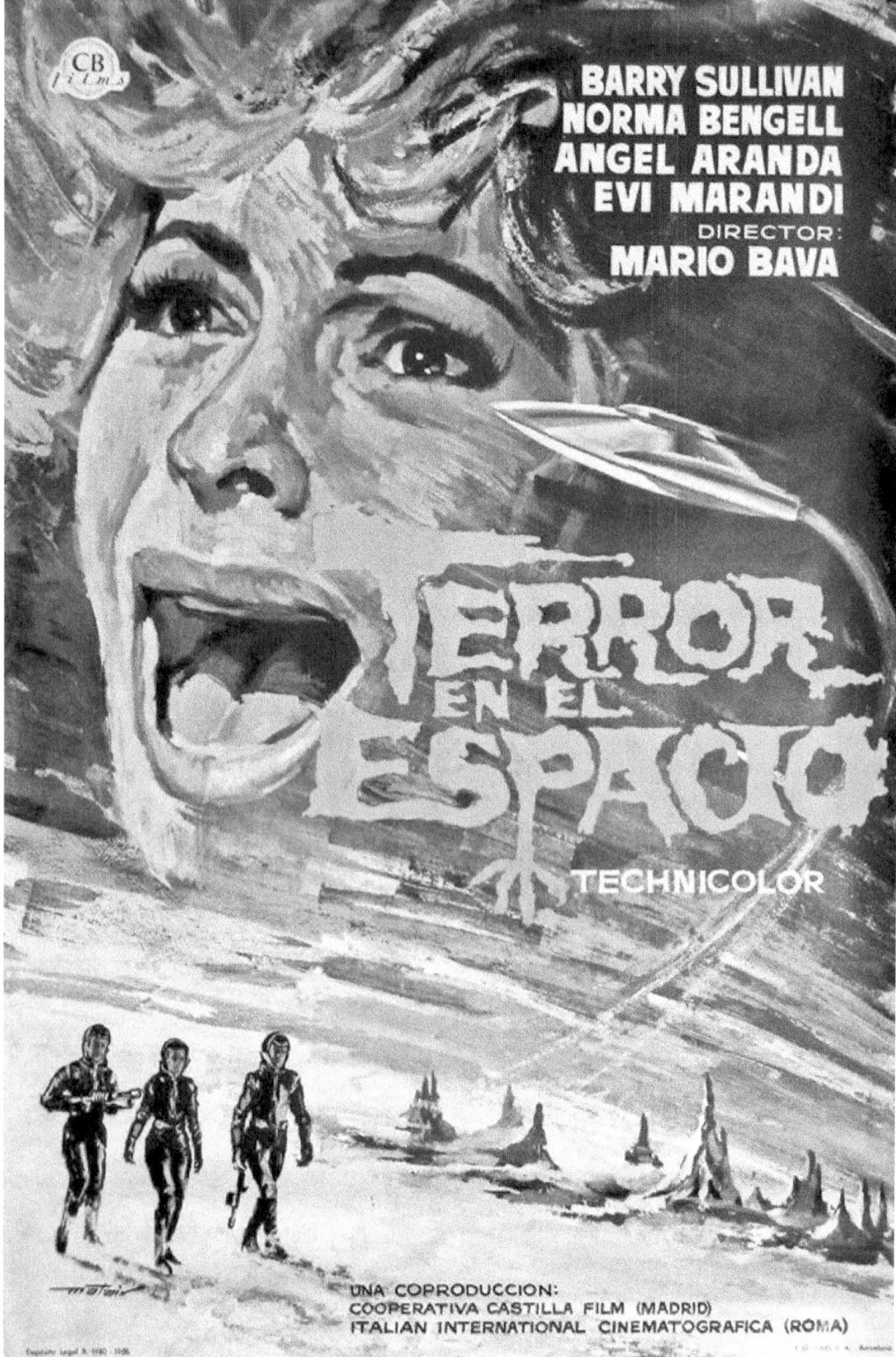

thought is, let's do both! I think it's quite possible when dealing with subjects like, for example, women having sexual affairs with the severed heads of their lovers (Lamberto Bava's *Macabro*, 1980) or doctors who can only make love to their wives if they're dead (Ricardo Freda's *L'orribile segreto del Dr. Hichcock*, 1964), to look at it from a myriad of perspectives. So that's what I set out to do. The book is laid out with each chapter representing a different country. It is here that we take a close look at the phenomenon of Eurocult from a more academic standpoint. At the end of each section is a filmography with a little synopsis of many of the major, and some not-so-major, films within each subgenre, as well as my two cents about the subject matter. One of the reasons that Eurocult is so popular even in today's market is that it offers viewers, especially American viewers, the element of surprise. We develop a natural dissonance or resistance to products developed in our own countries, which results in a comfortable pattern in which we view film. Eurocult breaks this down because the perspective of the filmmakers is different, throwing the viewers into situations they couldn't foresee. I'm not going to be the spoiler with these synopses, since certain subgenres are predicated on the art of surprise (gialli especially: don't even watch the theatrical trailers before you watch one, as many times they give away important information!), so you're better off not knowing until you watch. No matter how disgusting, repellent or subversive, Eurocult films are meant to be enjoyed and I use the filmography to have a bit of fun.

Now for the absolute hard-core Eurocult fan there is bound to be some griping about the films not included. "But where's *La endemoniada* (*Demon Witch Child*, 1974) or *The Visitor* (1979)?" "How can you possibly talk about Eurocult and not talk about *Il medaglione insanguinato* (*The Night Child*, 1975)?" "And what about the other European countries? Germany, Greece, Sweden produced some great exploitation; why not include them?" The truth is I tried to fit as many films as possible into this book but only commented on those that I have actually seen or that fit within the parameters of exploitation. A film like *Il medaglione*, which was extremely enjoyable, just isn't exploitation; it's more straight-ahead horror, which doesn't always translate into exploitation. Just because there's a few shots of Joanna Cassidy's breasts in a very tepid love scene doesn't mean it's out-and-out exploitation. *La endemoniada*, on the other hand, is most definitely exploitation, and it looks like a blast, but unfortunately no copy was available for me to see while I was writing this. As for the other countries, you bet, there is a lot of exploitation left to cover and perhaps a future volume is justified to explore those wonders.

For now, though, it's time to explore the country that was the most prolific of any country producing Eurocult: Italy. Fasten your seat belts and don't forget your barf bag!

Opposite: Mario Bava's ***Terrore nello spazio*** (***Planet of the Vampires***, 1965) is a good example of how Italian directors were always looking for new environments to exploit.

CHAPTER 1

Italy

> We Europeans have a cultural past that the Americans don't possess, and I think the right thing would be for us to deal with our stories and they with theirs. Instead, we have this desperate attempt to imitate American cinema, which cheapens our cinema.
> —Italian exploitation director Michele Soavi[1]

If European exploitation films were to have a central geographic point, that center would be Italy. No one country in Europe has had more of an output and influence on the genre than Italian filmmakers and producers.[2] Beginning in 1956 with the Riccardo Freda/Mario Bava chiller *I vampiri*, the Italian horror film, with its lurid, exploitative narratives, lasted well over 30 years before its demise in the late '80s. The genre, which began solely as a way of copying American and British themes and productions, quickly turned out some of the most original and evocative films of the '60s and '70s. It was during that time the Italian production of Eurocult was among the most popular in all of Europe.[3] As the sixties progressed and censorship began to lessen, the films from Italy began to become more sexualized and violent. These films would have a strong impact on generations of established filmmakers including Quentin Tarantino (*Kill Bill, vols. 1 & 2*, 2003, 2004) and Bob Clark (*Black Christmas*, 1974), as well as Eli Roth (*Hostel*, 2005) and James Wan (*Saw*, 2004), who have all incorporated aspects of Italian horror and exploitation in their films. Classic films such as Dario Argento's *Suspiria* (1976), Lucio Fulci's *Zombi* (1979), and Mario Bava's *Sei donne per l'assassino* (*Blood and Black Lace*, 1964), as well as films like *Che sei?* (*Beyond the Door*, 1974), *Cosa avete fatto a Solange?* (*What Have You Done to Solange?*, 1971), and the *Black Emanuelle* films, have created such a resonating impression that techniques utilized in these films (camera shots, music, use of color) have become commonplace in today's media market in commercials (*Universal Studio's Orlando Nights of Horrors*), television programs (*The Sopranos*) and music videos (Marilyn Manson).

Differing from their American counterparts, Italian horror films are not composed of franchised monsters like the Universal films of the '30s and '40s as well as the British and Spanish exploitative markets of the '60's and '70's, but encompass a wide range of different subgenres or "filone" (Italian for genre) within the horror and exploitation realm. Gothic horror stories like Bava's *La maschera del demonio* (*The Mask of Satan*, 1960) and Caiano's *Amanti d'oltretomba* (*Nightmare Castle*, 1965) focused on lighting and atmospheric sets to transport their viewers into a creepy narrative similar to that of *Frankenstein* (1931) or *The Wolf Man* (1942), but the adult themes and violence in these films all stem from a cultural sensibility that was Italy's own.[4]

Gothic movies were not the only type of horror and exploitation in which the Italians excelled. During a time when censorship and social battles were raging around the world, Italy produced a mind-boggling number of different types of film, each more extreme than the last.[5] Murder mysteries based on popular Italian pulp novels with strong sexual and violent themes, called gialli, became popular worldwide and started a subgenre that included well over 200 films. These films, the precursor to the American slasher film, had a tendency to focus on the exploitative aspects of social life and reflected a discontent with Italian society. Cannibal films and their zombie film counterparts were also big Italian exports. These films reflected the times which saw an increasingly nihilistic, xenophobic society mistrustful of differing societies and cultures, as well as reflecting a growing devotion to mass consumerism.[6] The '60s and '70s also signaled a time of growing unrest with religion. Growing out of the iconography of the Roman Catholic Church, the Italians many times chose to shock by portraying their most respected institutions as oppressive, patriarchal systems where basic human rights were denied, or at worst where the environments were little more than dens of sin conducive to abuse. Nunsploitation films involving nuns indulging in sinful acts of sexuality and violence, were just as popular as sexually exploitative films, such as the *Black Emanuelle* films, that called into question gender roles and the role of marriage and sexuality in society. These films saw often female protagonists on an endless search for sexual fulfillment in stories where no man, woman or animal was beyond their sexual longings.

Italy also produced some of the finest auteurs of the Eurocult genre. No two were more prolific than Mario Bava and Dario Argento. Mario Bava worked on the first-ever Italian horror film, *I vampiri* (*The Devil's Commandment*, 1956) and has since become a legend in the annals of Italian cinema.[7] With low budgets, Bava designed evocative sets and focused on atmospheric aspects of fear to achieve some the best examples of the genre. Films such as *I tre volti della paura* (*Black Sabbath*, 1963), with its Gothic countryside complete with fog and dark shadows, where vampire Boris Karloff snatches his grandson off to make him one of the undead, to *Terrore nello spazio* (*Planet of the Vampires*, 1965), with its deserted barren planet awash in green and red lights, showcased Bava at his best with a minimal amount of budget.[8] Dario Argento continued the Bava tradition in the '70s. Becoming the master of the giallo with films such as *L'uccello dalle piume di cristallo* (*The Bird with the Crystal Plumage*, 1970) and *Profondo rosso* (*Deep Red*, 1975), Argento quickly moved on to more stylized ghost stories in vein of Bava.[9] His *Suspiria* (1976) is considered one the scariest movies of all time due, in part, to the in-your-face violence, jarring rock score and intricate writing.[10] Audiences in an Argento film felt like they couldn't escape the nightmare until the credits rolled.

The proliferation of exploitation movies out of Italy was due primarily to the popularity and fluidity of the Italian film industry after World War II. Exploitation prior to the '50s was nonexistent, as both Mussolini's and subsequent government prohibition of horror films, which are often the staple of exploitation, as well as the aftereffects of a terrible war, contributed to a lack of interest by both the industry and audiences.[11] Things began change as the postwar economy began infuse life back into the Italian film industry. By 1950 the industry was back and enjoyed a huge economic and artistic boom that lasted for decades. From the 92 films produced in 1950 to over 200 films a year throughout the '60s, Italy was on the forefront of the changing world cinema environment. The neorealism movement, which started after World War II with such Italian auteurs as DeSica, had begun to move away from the Italian sociological struggle that was essential to its plots. In its stead Italian film began to use more conventional themes that appealed to a more worldwide audience.

Better sets, conventional fictional structures and themes, and the inclusion of international actors all contributed to the increasing international success of Italian films.[12] This success, along with aid from the Marshall Plan, which sought to build back the Italian economy, translated into a welcome influx of cash as money from the government started flowing, leading to greater employment opportunities for Italian citizens. Due to the increase in production, more studio personnel were needed to fill the demand, resulting in a large immigration of workers into Rome from other areas of Italy, most especially the south.[13] The influx of new perspectives that the immigrants brought added a more broadly nationalistic feeling to the industry and was the first step into creating a product that would have greater outreach outside the borders of Italy.

In addition to economics, the social upheavals of the '50s in Italy also had a large role in the burgeoning success of their film industry. Writers and directors were taking advantage of relaxed media censorship as Italian politics moved to a more centrist position. No longer satisfied with sanitized images that did not resemble real life, the public tastes began to change, requiring more radical narratives than those films in the produced in '40s or even the popular American films which were still fairly conventional by design.[14] Though full censorship laws in Italy would not be relaxed until 1968, sexuality and especially violence began creeping into Italian films a decade or so earlier.[15]

Violence is often an overriding theme in many Italian movies. Films of gangsters and crime, lurid murder mysteries and battlefield action all proved to be big hits with Italian audiences and paved the way for the natural progression into exploitation. The Italian filmmaker's penchant for violence and violent drama may have its roots in the psyche of Italians. Luigi Barzini, in his book *The Italians* (1964), expressed a belief that the social culture and mindset that permeates Italy is violent by nature. He writes, "Italians fear sudden and violent death. Italy is a bloodstained country. Almost everyday of the year jealous husbands kill their adulterous wives and their lovers, about as many wives kill their adulterous husbands and their mistresses. "Barzini goes on, detailing many scenarios that have rivaled situations in Italian exploitation cinema. He explains, "The world of vice also demands their daily victims, streetwalkers are found dead with silk stockings wound tied around their necks or knives stuck in their ribs on their unmade beds or country lanes. Fatherly homosexuals are found in public parks with their heads smashed in and their pockets turned out. On deserted beaches, naked call girls are found at dawn in a few inches of water. Even when violent death is not lurking in the shadows, Italians must be alert and move with circumspection."[16] All of these sentiments were echoed by Italian filmmaker and horror auteur Lucio Fulci who stated, "Violence IS Italian art."[17]

Italians have a propensity of transforming their social deviants into monsters, which stems back to the earliest of the Italian literary tradition. Italy's ties to classical mythology, where mortals and demigods were consistently embroiled in battles with monsters, are a starting point in describing how the country has dealt with changing social landscapes throughout its history. Representations of monstrosity have been key to understanding the dominant traditions of thought in Italy. Reconceived monsters throughout each period of Italian history have signified major changes in the evolution of Italian art and philosophy.[18] The "monsters" that came out of Italy in the period from 1956 to 1980 go a long way toward explaining the particular thoughts, explicitly and subliminally, of a cultural group on such sociological subjects as gender relations, religion, globalization, politics and family issues. How the Italians dealt with these "monsters" also goes a long way in explaining how the culture was able to adapt to the perceived threats to its way of life.

I vampiri: *Italian Genre Beginnings*

> Seeing an Italian name, they [Italians] all made ugly faces because they found the very idea preposterous. They were of the opinion that Italians didn't know how to make these kinds of films.
> — Italian producer Ricardo Freda[19]

The 1950s were a productive and prosperous period for European cinema. Audiences continued to grow, domestic industries were beginning to recapture much of the box office that Hollywood had stolen, and television, which had radically changed the film industry in America, had been slow to make an impact.[20] In 1955 (the first year for television in Italy), ticket sales equaled $819 million, the highest ever in the history of Italian cinema. Additionally, the number of films that were produced in Italy grew as well, from 25 in 1945 to 204 in 1954. These films helped combat the deluge of American products that had been in distribution in Italy. Box office from domestic features grew from 13 percent in 1945 to almost 50 percent by the end of the '50s.[21]

The proliferation of the Italian film industry signified a new growth potential allowing filmmakers to explore new subjects and genres. Riccardo Freda's *I vampiri* (*The Devil's Commandment*, 1956) was one of those films that broke away from the fantasy films and big-screen spectacles that Italians gravitated to.[22] The country's first Gothic horror film, *I Vampiri* established all the constructs for the Gothic film, and though the producers wouldn't realize it until much later, the film actually set in motion the entire Eurocult phenomenon. It was Freda and his friend, cinematographer Mario Bava, who came up with the idea of directing a horror film. The idea was intriguing to Italian producers but also made them nervous, as Italy had no history when it came to producing films of this sort.[23] They had been banned under the fascist regime of the '30s and '40s, and their lurid, violent content still caused censors some sense of nervousness well into the '50s. American horror films (usually courtesy of Universal Studios) had been playing throughout Europe with varying degrees of success. Freda decided he wanted to outdo the Americans by delivering an Italian horror film. Recalled Freda, "They asked if I had anything prepared. I said no, but I could cook something up by the next day. When I returned I brought my treatment — not written out on paper, but recorded on tape! I did the sound effects also, even the creakings of the door; it was very amusing!"[24] Though the recorded treatment impressed the producers, they were still not certain that a film of this type could be successfully produced in Italy. Taking a gamble, Freda made an outlandish bet with producers that, one, he could pass the script with the censors, and two, that he could shoot the film in 12 days! Producers took that bet and money was made available for the production.

I Vampiri set the standard for visual style that would be the foundation for most Italian Gothic films of this nature. Freda, a former art critic, wisely chose his friend Mario Bava, whose visual style stemmed from his love of photography and special effects, as his cinematographer for the film. He knew that Bava would be able to create the perfect atmosphere to tell his story of Gisele (Gianna Maria Canale), a beautiful aristocrat who is desperately in love with the son of her great lover, and who must use blood in order to keep herself young. It was Bava, with Freda's blessing, who, knowing the film would rely heavily on special lighting to showcase the aging of Gisele, decided to shoot the film in black and white

Opposite: The Italian poster of the first true horror film from Italy, *I vampiri* (*The Devil's Commandment*, 1956), plays up the Gothic atmosphere of the film.

in order to the facilitate the special effects as well as keep the budget down. Even though he had a limited budget, Bava was able to translate his love of Gothic literature to the screen, helping him create the eerie, decaying castle of Gisele via shadows, fog, framing and some well-produced cobwebs—in short, atmosphere.[25] Along with this atmosphere come the subliminal political messages that are usually found imbedded within the great traditions of Gothic narratives. Gisele's castle, for example, stands for the dark, dank air of a dead aristocratic class, which is in keeping with her aged appearance. It is only when she is transformed into a younger, more attractive woman that her surroundings become like a coffin, trapping her. In Bava's world the aristocracy is the foundation of culture, but that foundation is built on deceit, cheating (as Gisele does with her youth) and evil. All of this is tied to the physical environment that he creates. This atmosphere underscored the European Gothic motif that would become a part of one of the most successful of the Italian horror movies from the late '50s to the mid–'60s. From this film on, all Gothic horror films coming out of Italy, whether color or black and white, would employ this foggy, dark and dead atmosphere.

Unfortunately for Freda, the bet he made with producers failed. While able to secure approval from Italian censors, Freda was having trouble with the shooting, and after 10 days, he had only half the film completed. Bava recalled, "Freda knew his job well. He was gifted, but his behavior was unbelievable.... Just imagine: he would only walk onto the set after the next scene had been completely blocked and rehearsed! He would sit down in his chair, turn his back to the cast and shout, 'Roll 'em!' After the take was finished, he would return to me and ask if everything was okay!" When asked for an extension on filming the producers said no, reminding Freda of his bet, to which the director threw a fit and stormed off the set. He was replaced by Bava, who shot the rest of the film in the remaining two days![26]

Though *I vampiri* set the benchmark for the upcoming genre of Italian Gothic as well as the Italian exploitation film, it was not a box-office success. In both Italy and France, the film was met with complete ambivalence. Many factors can be attributed to its tepid reception, including relative uninterest in the subject matter, the lack of true star power (though Canale was a bankable star), and poor marketing, but the film's failure at the box office is most likely due to Italian reluctance to accept a domestic interpretation of the horror genre. Freda explained: "Italians will only accept fettuccine from their fellow countrymen! They would stop and look [at the marquee]: *I vampiri* ... *I vampiri*... This seemed to intrigue them, but then at the last moment they saw the name Freda. Their reaction was automatic: Freda!? Seeing an Italian name, they all made ugly faces because they found the very idea preposterous."[27]

The lack of box office for *I vampiri* resulted in little interest for producers to make adult horror films. Freda understood that for a film to even earn back its initial investment it had to be sold to the widest possible market. For his next horror picture, *Caltiki—Il mostro immortale* (*Caltiki—The Immortal Monster*, 1959), a fun science fiction film that plays like a cross between Britain's *The Quatermass Experiment* (1955) and America's *The Blob* (1958), Freda decided to use Anglicized pseudonyms to give the appearance that the film was English. He believed that this would alleviate the fear native Italians had about their own actors in the genre, and more importantly, would help sell the film to other

Opposite: The Blob meets *The Ruins* as the Freda/Bava funfest *Caltiki—Il mostro immortale* (1959) makes its way to U.S. shores.

markets, including the United States.[28] Freda was beginning to catch on to certain business practices that would eventually help in getting Eurocult films shown throughout the world. He was discovering the murky world of foreign distribution.

A Word About Foreign Distribution

> Let's face it, in Italy horror films never made a lire. I always made money in the U.S.
>
> — Italian director Mario Bava[29]

To understand the reason for Anglicizing names in Italian (or, for that matter, any other European language) it is important to understand the intricacies of foreign distribution. The need to make films palatable to the widest possible audiences was seen as a way of recouping financial risks from production. From the beginning, foreign distribution played an integral part in the success of Eurocult. If a foreign producer wanted to make a horror film in the late '50s, he had to make it from a cultural standpoint that was widely applicable. In Italy, with money tight, films had to be rush-produced in order to capitalize on a current trend. Ian McCulloch, British actor and star of several Italian horror films (*Zombi 2*, 1979; *Alien Contamination*, 1980) talked about the impact these deals had: "These films were almost in profit before a frame was shot. They were pre-sold all over the world on a title, storyboards, poster artwork, and synopsis."[30] In a later interview he elaborated on the process, "Everything is sold.... They know before the camera rolls that they will make a profit. It may not be very much but they know they have covered all their costs. They will sell the film to South America and all places that are easy to sell to, and in the difficult markets they will do deals."[31]

Scriptwriters for these films were also at the whim of these distribution deals. Dardano Sacchetti (*Zombi 2*, 1979; *Paura nella città dei morti viventi*, 1980) relates, "For most of my screenplays I learned who the director was only a week before the film went into production. De Angelis [producer of many Italian exploitation films] would attend MIFED [the Milan-based confab for film distribution] and would ask me, 'Could you write a few lines, two, five lines, an idea about an adventure movie, western, mystery or porno?' He would have someone draw some posters then he we would attend MIFED and display the posters in his stand. When the foreign buyers stopped by the stand, he would tell them that the movies were in production. Then, if the foreign buyers said we are interested in this one, he would call me on the phone and tell me, 'Write immediately the mystery, or the porn movie.'"[32]

These distribution deals had a radical impact on the presentation of the film. Many times American and British distributors would barter for rights to change content. In the early days of Italian horror, these rights were given freely so that the filmmakers could make a profit. Many times violent portions of the movies were eliminated with a disastrous effect on the story. Even worse, extra footage would be shot to soften up the material. For example, Mario Bava's first three films, *La maschera del demonio* (*The Mask of Satan*, 1960), *La ragazza che sapeva troppo* (*The Girl Who Knew Too Much*, 1962) and *I tre volti della paura* (*Black Sabbath*, 1963) were entirely rescored, edited and changed from their initial conception in many of the countries they played.[33]

Ironically, changes such as anglicized names didn't always translate into box-office acceptance in Italy. As film historian Tim Lucas points out, *Caltiki — Il mostro immortale* (*Caltiki — The Immortal Monster*, 1959) with its anglicized names, did a quarter of a million lire less than the disappointing *I vampiri* (1956).[34] It seems that Italians at that point in time simply were not interested in horror movies wherever they were perceived to have been produced. *Caltiki*'s anglicized names did make it easier to sell to overseas markets, though. This cross-continental distribution scheme paid off for producers as the film was able to recoup its original cost plus profit by the end of its run.

The frenzied distribution deals that were made in the '60s and '70s have come back to haunt modern-day DVD and Blu-Ray distributors. Films were bought and sold at such a pace in those earlier decades, with films changing titles, lengths and distributors at the drop of a hat, that the true owners of the original copyrights have become obscured. Many modern distributors have found it virtually impossible to uncover who legitimately holds the rights to these films as most Eurocult of the period had a variety of different international companies involved in the deals with each believing they had the right to license these films. As the rights traded hands throughout the decades, actual ownership has become murkier, with many foreign companies either demanding more remuneration, or worse, stopping the release entirely and throwing the DVD/Blu-Ray company into court. Dark Sky Films found out the hard way when they tried to release a definitive version of Mario Bava's *Operazione paura* (*Kill Baby Kill*, 1966) in 2007. Believing they had secured the rights from the true owners of the film, they proceeded to buy the licensing rights to release the film in the United States. As the release date neared, the company was sued by Italian producer Alfredo Leone, who believed that he owned the rights to the film and had recently sold the film to rival DVD company Anchor Bay Entertainment. The court sided with Leone and Anchor Bay. Dark Sky Films, who had already pressed the DVDs and given them out to retailers, were then forced to cancel the release, costing the company thousands of dollars. Court cases and a very tangled web of distribution owners may signal a decline in future releases of Eurocult. On a web blog, historian Tim Lucas laments:

> The state of classic Italian cinema, especially the popular cinema of the '50s through the '80s, is seriously endangered because the rights issues have become so hopelessly tangled. This is how any one film might now have two, three or four different companies/individuals claiming rights to it. And whoever has the best elements has no more guarantee than anyone else of holding the bona fide chain of title. With this jungle of red tape attached to these films, best elements not necessarily guaranteed, the potential return on any release of these films being limited to begin with, and court costs also a possibility, it could well be that fewer domestic DVD companies will risk this kind of release.[35]

Another disturbing outcome of the tangled nature of Eurocult is that audiences may only have access to certain cuts of the films. For example, Turner Classic Movie (TCM) channel's version of *La maschera del demonio* (*The Mask of Satan*, aka *Black Sunday*, 1960) in the early 2000s featured a wide array of differing edits that dramatically altered the style and narration of the film. The changes were due to copyright issues that producer Alfred Leone needed in order to update some of the public domain material within the film. Reviled by supporters of the film, the version may be the only available copy that certain audiences might see and does not reflect Bava's initial vision for the film.

Both Freda and Bava were about to understand the intricacies of foreign distribution soon as both were about to experience phenomenon success with the first successful exploitation filone in which both helped to create, the Italian Gothic.

When the Germans were looking for a Dracula-themed film to distribute in their country, they simply took Mario Bava's seminal ghost story *Operazione paura* (*Kill, Baby Kill*, 1966) and changed the title, though the film had nothing to do with Dracula.

Filmography

Caltiki — Il mostro immortale, aka *Caltiki — The Immortal Monster* (U.S.), *Caltiki — Le monstre immortel* (France). Dir. Riccardo Freda (with an assist from Mario Bava). Italy/France, 1959. Starring: John Merivale, Didi Perego, Gérard Herter and Daniela Rocca.

What happens when you mix *The Blob* (1958) with a little bit of the British Quatermass series (*X: The Unknown*, 1956) and throw in some *The Ruins* (2009) while you're at it? You get Caltiki, a god that resembles a giant piece of protoplasm and comes out of a Mayan ruin to terrorize Mexico City (aka Rome). Actually a lot of fun is to be had as our blob god grows to huge proportions thanks to some spare radioactivity and begins infecting or engulfing those it comes into contact. Romantic triangles involving pouty Italian actresses, madness and amputations all mark what is widely considered to be Mario Bava's first true directing job. He acquits himself nicely and you will too IF you manage to find a copy of this, as they are not easy to come by.

I vampiri, aka *The Devil's Commandment* (U.S.), *Les Vampires* (FR). Prod. Massimo DeRita. Dir. Riccardo Freda (with an assist from Mario Bava). Italy, 1956. Image Entertainment, 78 min. Image DVD. Starring: Gianna Maria Canale, Carlo D'Angelo, Dario Michaelis and Wandisa Guida.

The perfect introduction to Eurocult! Gisselle du Grand (Canale) is a rich, selfish, murderous bloodsucker who would like to keep her looks as long possible, especially to attract the son of her great lover. Unfortunately for her, he's not interested and even less so when he finds out that lack of blood can age her ... quickly. Freda and Bava's cinematic touch set the stage for the entire Italian Gothic genre with their masterful filming of cobwebs, creaking doors, and decay, along with some great lighting (you wouldn't expect less from a Bava film). A little ponderous and talky at times but the Gothic motif, the alluring beauty that was Canale and some incredible makeup and lighting effects make this a worthy first step into exploitation. The transformation of Canale from beauty to crone still manages to amaze over 50 years later. If you can find a copy of the U.S. version *(The Devil's Commandment)* you'll be treated to over 10 minutes of inserted footage that make absolutely no sense nor bear any relationship to the original story, though Al Lewis (Grandpa Munster) does make a brief appearance as a dirty old man.

Werewolf in a Girls' Dormitory, aka *Lycanthropus* (IT). Prod. Guido Giambartolomei. Dir. Paolo Heusch. Italy/Austria, 1962. Retromedia DVD, 83 min. Starring: Barbara Lass, Carl Schell, Curt Lowens and Maurice Marsac.

With a name like *Werewolf in a Girls' Dormitory*, how can you go wrong? Schell is the new teacher/doctor with a shady past at a local European reform school where the girls excel in interpersonal relationships and biology. The school is run by a shady director (Lowens) and the grounds are littered with suspects, any one of whom may or may not be a werewolf. Fusing together streams of the Gothic (which was popular at the time), the giallo (which was just getting going) and the Universal monster movies, *Werewolf* is an interesting film in that instead of ripping off (which is the whole purpose of Eurocult) something like Hammer's *Curse of the Werewolf* (1960), which had brought new perspective to the werewolf film, it chooses to go with the more traditional, silly American standard route. An interesting film historically, it still won't convert any fans to genre with its slow pace and bad dubbing (in the U.S. version). If you can find a copy with the teen song "The Ghoul in School," snatch it up ... it's camp heaven!

The '60s: A Return to Gothic

> Hauntingly, beautiful, imaginative and startling as a dream, it remains my favorite Italian horror film.
> — Horror author Ramsey Campbell commenting on
> *La maschera del demonio* (*The Mask of Satan*, 1960)[36]

The late '50s and early '60s found American and British horror filmmakers immersed in Cold War imagination.[37] The nuclear age had caught the fancy of the general public and

By the late 1950s, Eurocult films were already making it to U.S. shores. ***L'amante del vampiro*** (*Vampire and the Ballerina*, 1960) was one of the first.

they were demanding stories that went along with the mysteries of science that the new age brought. Television pushed the American teen out of the house and into area drive-ins and local theaters, and the films that were shown in this new social setting reflected the fun and rebelliousness of the teenage audience.[38] Serious horror films were few and far between. For every serious horror film like *Psycho* (1960) or *Peeping Tom* (1961) there were 10 lower-budget films with names such as *I Was a Teenage Frankenstein* (1957), *The Amazing Transparent Man* (1960), *Attack of the 50 Foot Woman* (1959) and *King Kong vs. Godzilla* (1963).

In Italy, things were different. Showing a lack of interest in horror and only a passing interest in science fiction, Italians gravitated toward lowbrow comedies that had been a staple in the country since the beginning of its film industry. Using this comedic template formula made it easier for Italians to subtly bring in other types of genre, and that included horror. One of the first examples of this was *Tempi duri per i vampiri* (*Uncle Was a Vampire*, 1959), which starred Christopher Lee, fresh off his success in Britain's *Horror of Dracula* (1958) for Hammer Films. This harmless film is played for laughs as Lee vamps the popular Italian character Toto (Renato Rascel), which leads up to the standard villain chasing pretty damsels in distress to comedic effect. Silly stuff, though it is nice to see a badly dubbed Lee poking fun at his vampire stereotype, something he seldom did as he quickly tired of the many Dracula movies he played throughout the '60s and '70s.[39] *Il mio amico Jekyll* (1960) finds Raimondo Vianello inventing a machine that is able to change him into a handsome schoolteacher (Ugo Tognazzi) with hilarious consequences.[40] If comedy wasn't the focus for these watered-down horrors, then sex certainly was. For example, *L'amante del vampiro* (*The Vampire and the Ballerina*, 1960) played up the sexual implications, as the vampires in these films were portrayed as the most aggressive love makers and crudely sexual as they put the bite on their unclad female victims.[41] Also playing up the sexual aspect was Piero Regnoli's *L'ultima preda del vampiro* (*The Playgirls and the Vampire*, 1960) in which a group of buxom striptease dancers are stuck in a castle inhabited by a vampire (Walter Brandi). The dancers represent the typical stereotype of a burlesque dancer. Dumb, overly endowed, and with a penchant for screaming, they're showcased in various stages of undress as they perform their titillating dance numbers during at the most inopportune times.[42] These films seem to point out the difficulty that Italians had in finding an identity for their horror and exploitation films. By watering down the elements of terror with well-known and popular forms of entertainment in Italy, whether comedy or sex, Italian filmmakers showed their unwillingness to commit to true horror pictures. As mentioned before, the reason can probably be traced to the Italian population's still reeling from the atrocities of World War II and unprepared to be taken to a place of horror and despair in their exploitation films. This would soon change in 1960, when a popular form of literature re-emerged as a celluloid confection and the Gothic Italian horror film became popular with worldwide audiences.

The term Gothic was used originally to denote the architecture of Western Europe from the 12th to the 16th century. In the early 19th century the term came to be used to describe a particular style of literary writing that focused on supernatural fiction especially geared toward the grotesque. These works were usually laden with a heavy, gloomy atmosphere, accentuated by eerie castles on hilltops, cobwebbed tombs and vaults, flickering candlelight and an underlying repressed sexuality. Gothic literature was often considered barbarous and crude, yet the genre enjoyed widespread popularity throughout the 19th and 20th centuries. It is this crudeness and excess that makes Gothic the perfect genre for exploitation. Examples such as Walpole's *The Castle of Otranto* (1764), Shelley's *Frankenstein*,

5 PLAYGIRLS WALKED INNOCENTLY INTO HIS ARMS
...only to meet the devil in the flesh!

An unusual story of unnatural love and desire ...so bold, so shocking —it must be shown to ADULTS ONLY!

She knew... when she felt his lips on her, that there was no other man for her... if this was a man!

"THE Playgirls AND THE Vampire"

A Richard Gordon Presentation
A Fanfare Films Release

or the Modern Prometheus (1818), and Du Maurier's *Rebecca* (1938) each evoke an unnatural attachment to the past, which is an underlying theme within the literature. In addition, Gothic also suggests that reality may be broader and more tangled than most tend to think. In both literature and film this is achieved through supernatural elements or through ambiguity over whether what one is experiencing is a dream or reality.[43]

The spooky, traditional Gothic horror films of Italy came about from the success of Great Britain's Hammer horror films of the late '50s. What Hammer did and did so well was to take the classic monster (e.g., Dracula, Frankenstein, the Mummy, etc.) movies that were so successful for America's Universal Studios and update them using more sensuality and blood while retaining the Gothic environments of the original stories. The success of these films, including *The Curse of Frankenstein* (1957), *Horror of Dracula* (1958), *Revenge of Frankenstein* (1958) and *The Mummy* (1959), proved to be a formula that Italians could use to transform and exploit. By adapting Gothic style and infusing it with more gore and sex, lower-budget Italian filmmakers began to see a way in which they could reap the financial benefit of these lurid subject matters.

The success of these British films was not lost on Mario Bava (1914–1980). After finishing the directing responsibilities for Italy's first horror film *I vampiri* (*The Devil's Commandment*, 1956) and *Caltiki — Il mostro immortale* (*Caltiki — The Immortal Monster*, 1959), as well as working on popular Italian action films like *Le fatiche di ercole* (*Hercules*, 1958) with Steve Reeves, Bava was given the go-ahead to produce his own film. His love of fantasy as well as his affinity for special effects had him focusing on the horror genre. The trick was to find a quality story that could appeal to Bava's nature and to an audience on which the film's success would rest. Two competing ideas vied for Bava's attention. The first was Ukrainian author Nikolai Gogol's ghost story *The Vij* (1842), which concerned three seminary students returning home for summer break and subjected to torments of an old witch. Bava, a voracious reader, had previously read the story to his children at bedtime, scaring them senseless. The second was the popularity of the first Dracula film that Britain's Hammer Films had produced, *Horror of Dracula* (released in Italy as *Dracula, il vampiro* in 1958). Bava specifically responded to Britain's Hammer Films: "As *Dracula* had just been released, I thought I would make a horror movie myself."[44] Combining the story elements of Gogol's tale with the cinematic style of the Dracula film, Bava developed a four-page treatment that modernized the narrative, mixing in not only witchcraft but vampirism and eroticism as well. Handing off the script to several other screenwriters and gaining the trust of producers, Bava went about the task of completing his Gothic masterpiece.

Released on August 11, 1960, in Italy, Bava's original film *La maschera del demonio* (*The Mask of Satan*, 1960) was an instant classic and began the popular cycle of Italian Gothic/horror movies.[45] The story was fairly simple. Accused of witchcraft in early 1600s, Princess Asa (Barbara Steele) and her accomplice Prince Javutich (Arturo Dominici) are violently put to death before the local townspeople in a Moldavian forest. Before she dies, Asa curses the town and the future generations of their offspring. Two hundred years later, Dr. Kruvajan (Andrea Checchi) and his young assistant Andrej Gorobec (John Richardson), traveling across the country, stumble upon the tomb of Asa. Removing the Mask of Satan (painfully) from her corpse's face, the duo sets loose Asa, who proceeds to haunt her look-alike descen-

Opposite: Since horror was not a popular genre in Italy at the time, sex was often introduced into a film to attract an audience, as in *L'ultima preda del Vampiro* (*The Playgirls and the Vampire*, 1960).

Italian poster for Mario Bava's seminal shocker *La maschera del demonio* (1960), which shocked audiences around the world.

dant, Princess Katia (again played by Steele), as well her father (Ivo Garrani) and brother (Enrico Olivieri).

With its simple plot (which would be recycled many times throughout the Italian Gothic golden age), stunning black and white visuals, and its daring approach to exploring adult themes, *La maschera* is considered by critics to be a classic. Bava concocts an atmosphere that is both reminiscent of the American Universal horror films of the '30s and '40s and evocative of a new '60s sensibility.[46] One need only look at the ruins of Asa's crumbling castle estate in *La Maschera* and compare them to Bela Lugosi's castle in *Dracula* to see the similarity in decay and atmosphere. Asa's first appearance in black eerily mirrors that of Gloria Holden's in *Dracula's Daughter* (1936), and the local town could have come right out of the Universal backlot of *Frankenstein* (1931) or *The Wolf Man* (1941). With *La maschera*, Bava was able to create a film that would appeal to a variety of cultures as a fairy tale for adults with its mystic, faraway castles, fog-shrouded forests, ghosts and hidden adult sexuality.[47] Though it may have looked like a quaint Universal horror film, the difference between *La maschera* and the Universal films was the overt violence and sex. Playing to a 1960s sensibility, *La maschera* graphically illustrated what was only hinted at by Universal. From its opening scenes, in which the evil witch Asa is chained to a tree, branded and forcibly made to wear the steel-spiked Mask of Satan, to her overtly sexual resurrection halfway through the film, *La maschera* basked in a changing social culture in both Italy and certain parts of mainland Europe that were more tolerant of sex and violence, as a result creating a new template for Italian exploitation. Now international audiences around the world could see varying degrees of blood pouring out of spiked heads, corpses graphically decomposing, victims brutally attacked, and their throats being ripped out by the myriad of ghostly perpetrators. Bava seemed to revel in his ability to bring some great gore effects into the film, especially with the resurrection of Asa as she goes from skeleton to sex bomb. He would go on to use a variety of gore elements time and time again in such Gothic period horror films such as *I tre volti della paura* (*Black Sabbath*, 1963), *Operazione paura* (*Kill Baby Kill*, 1966) and *Lisa e il diavolo* (*Lisa and the Devil*, 1973)

Ironically, as good as the film was, Bava had some of the same trouble he'd experienced earlier with Freda on *I vampiri* (1956) in that Italians themselves weren't all that interested in the product. The film reportedly earned a meager 140 million lire ($87,000) in Italy upon its initial release, which just about covered its production costs.[48] It was the foreign distribution deals that made the film a cult classic, granting it more exposure and garnering an eager multinational audience intent on seeing something new that would both shock and disgust them. In the United States, the rights of the film were bought up by American International Pictures (AIP), who proceeded to give the film a total makeover, complete with a new title, *Black Sunday* (1961), bad dubbing, and a remixed musical score by Les Baxter. In addition, the producers incorporated enough ballyhoo to secure audience interest. With a lurid marketing campaign centered on Barbara Steele's eyes, cards with fake incantations to ward off evil, and the imposition of their own age rating for the film ("because it would be harmful to young and impressionable minds, it is restricted to only those over 14 years of age"), AIP bet that American audiences was ready to take their first full view of an Italian horror film. They were right, and their gamble paid off as the film became the biggest grosser in young company's repertoire. The result in Great Britain was decidedly opposite, as the film was a non-starter. British censors were appalled by the overt violence of the film as well as uncomfortable with the lurid sexuality that permeated it. Though retitled *The Mask of Satan*, the film was banned outright until mid–1968.[49]

The U.S. poster for *La maschera* wisely plays up the presence of Barbara Steele, who gave many youngsters nightmares throughout the '60s.

Arriving on the scene just after Franju's *Les Yeux sans visage* (*Eyes Without a Face*, 1959) and prior to Jess Franco's *Gritos en la noche* (*The Awful Dr. Orlof*, 1961), *La maschera* was one of the three seminal films that opened the door to a new brand of exploitation film. What *La maschera* had over the other two was Bava's introduction of the ideal Gothic heroine, Barbara Steele. Her luminous looks combined with a glacial personality set the standard for heroines in the Italian Gothic/horror movie as Steele's cult reputation in Italian Gothic borders on legendary today. Reviewer Gary Johnson said of Steele, "Without Barbara Steele, Italian horror might have been very different. Her face evoked both beautiful and demonic features—instantly suggesting a dual and possibly dangerous power of character."[50] From *La maschera* onwards, Gothic heroines strived to imitate Steele's characteristics. Reserved, sexually repressed yet wildly exciting, these female characters were the backbone of almost all Italian Gothic. If Steele wasn't available, producers would choose from a variety of international actresses that fit the Steele mold. Many of them, like Daliah Lavi (*Il frusta e il corpo*, 1963), Riki Dialina (*I tre volti della paura*, 1963) and Fabienne Dalí (*Operazione paura*, 1966), look so much like Steele that it's possible to forget that they aren't.

Steele's characters frequently suggested a hidden strength masked in a subservient veneer, very much in keeping with the modern social mores that were prevalent not only in the early 1960s but had historical literary precedent within the Gothic novel. Gothic literature has traditionally had a strong association with women as both readers and writers; the latter include Ann Radcliffe, Mary Shelley and Joyce Carol Oates, to name a few.[51] Infused in Gothic literature are strong female characters who work out solutions within the narrative. This is not to say that these female characters were trailblazing a new female sensibility to modern audiences. On the contrary, the women of the Gothic period still were firmly entrenched within a male stereotype of how women should behave. Steele herself lamented the status of the characters amid a filmmaking process controlled by men, saying, "The women that I played were usually very powerful women and they suffered for it. You saw these powerful women, usually adulteresses, full of lust and greed, playing out all this repressed stuff, and in the end I always seemed to get it. There was always this sort of morality play, this sort of final pay-off, and that was very consoling to everybody. Because the dark goddess can't just go on wreaking hubris and havoc ad infinitum, she gets her comeuppance, too."[52]

Though dismayed perhaps by a misogynistic environment, Steele would go on to star in some of the most successful Italian Gothic/horror films of sixties. These films, including Freda's *L'orribile segreto del Dr. Hichcock* (1962) and Margheriti's *I lunghi capelli della morte* (*The Long Hair of Death*, 1964), all play on the same themes of repression and subjugation. Each features Steele as either the unfortunate heroine or wicked temptress in situations she cannot control.

Another classic Gothic film released in 1960 was the evocative Italian/French coproduction *Il mulino delle donne di pietra* (*The Mill of the Stone Women*). Capitalizing on Hammer's success with color, the film was one of the first Gothics to be shot that way. It also set about changing the setting usually associated with Gothic. In *Il mulino* it was not the eerie castles of Italy and Eastern Europe that were home to terror, but an old Dutch windmill on the fjords of Denmark.[53] The windmill plays double duty as both a laboratory for Professor Wahl (German actor Wolfgang Preiss) and as a moving wax museum showcasing some of the most infamous women in history, such as Joan of Arc, Anne Boleyn, etc. Wahl's ailing daughter Elfi (another Steele look-alike, Scilla Gabel) has developed a condition in which any overt emotional activity causes her blood to harden, resulting in

PIERRE BRICE
SCILLA GABEL
LIANA ORFEI · MARCO GUGLIELMI
HERBERT BOEHME · OLGA SOLBELLI
DANY CARREL en
EL MOLINO DE LAS MUJERES DE PIEDRA
Dirección GIORGIO FERRONI
(IL MULINO DELLE DONNE DI PIETRA)
EASTMANCOLOR

her becoming a statue. This is remedied by Wahl, who, with the help of the disbarred surgeon Bolem (Herbert Böhme), supplies Elfi with frequent transfusions which require the young women in town to give up all their blood. Anyone who's seen *House of Wax* (1953) knows exactly where the wax mannequins come from. Elfi serves the typical Gothic female narrative. Throughout the film, she is seen as deprived sexually, needy and suffering through both emotional and physical pain. Her demise always seems ensured and is brought about by her love of Hans (Pierre Brice), the young hero of the piece. There is no sympathy for Elfi as she happily submits Hans's fiancée (Dany Carrel) to torture after being spurned by Hans.

The change in setting allows for greater international audience participation. By transferring to a locale that is familiar with the northern European audience while retaining the Gothic format popular in Italy, filmmakers opened up the market for the film, ensuring more return on their investment. Directed by Giorgio Ferroni, the film is a veritable hodgepodge of international themes and impressions. With its Dutch setting, French and German actors and Italian director, the film floats across the screen like an international hallucinogenic nightmare. The old mill functions like an old-time camera, turning and cranking slowly, menacingly, as statues of beautiful young women decorate the mill's walls from inside.[54] The clumsy manner in which the statues move is quite unsettling, since it looks as if they could topple over anytime, revealing the secrets of the mill. Along with the implied violence, the film doesn't shy away from sex, both overtly and covertly. Elfi's seduction of Hans is erotically charged but graphically chaste, which is interesting, as the director is not afraid to throw the audience brief glimpses of Carrel's breast during her torture scene (this is Italian Gothic so there *always* has to be a torture scene!). The nudity is significant because it is the first of its type, along with Jesus Franco's Spanish *Gritos en la noche* (*The Awful Dr. Orloff*, 1960), to push the boundaries of sexuality in exploitation films and was far ahead of what American exploitation filmmakers were doing in the United States at the time.[55]

The Italian Gothic/horror movie of the early 1960s prospered in an era of enforced censorship. These films were nothing more than period ghost stories, giving each film a pleasantly old-fashioned feeling that could be appreciated by worldwide viewers. Though the subject matters were decidedly adult, the execution was still steeped in a traditional, Hollywood/religious/governmental code.[56] This meant that while the subject matter of these films often dealt with modern issues such as sexual longing, unhealthy family relationships, and violent death, they were still rooted in suppression. Though some brief glimpses of nudity and overt violence were beginning to creep in, early Gothic audiences members had to decipher these perversions for themselves. Perversity was played in an audience member's mind, as opposed to having the action on the screen. This way filmmakers could tackle perverse issues like masochism by showing one crack of the whip and a slightly pleased smile on a face and let the audience fill in the rest.

One glaring example of a Gothic steeped in adult, depraved behavior was Riccardo Freda's sumptuously colored *L'orribile segreto del Dr. Hichcock* (*The Horrible Dr. Hichcock*) in 1962. Having already familiarized himself, though abortively, with the genre in *I vampiri* (1956), Riccardo Freda's return to gothic drama was a heady study in adult perversion. Filmed in only 8 days (he should have made a bet with these film producers), the film has

Opposite: Leaving the Gothic castle behind, *Il mulino delle donne di pietra* (*House of the Stone Women*, 1960) instead opts for a creaky windmill.

The candle of his lust burnt brightest in the shadow of the grave!
THE HORRIBLE DR. HICHCOCK
HIS SECRET WAS A COFFIN NAMED DESIRE!
BARBARA STEELE · ROBERT FLEMYNG
with MONTGOMERY GLENN · TERESA FITZGERALD · HARRIET WHITE
TECHNICOLOR
A SIGMA III PRESENTATION
plus THE AWFUL DR. ORLOF
with HOWARD VERNON · CONRADO SANMARTIN · DIANA LORYS

anesthesiologist Dr. Hichcock (English actor Robert Flemyng in a wonderful nod to macabre director Alfred Hitchcock) giving new meaning to date rape drugging. He finds himself sexually aroused by necrophilia after accidentally killing his first wife via an overdose of a new anesthetic. The rest of the film finds Hichcock trying to subdue his lust for corpses. Soon, though, his fetish gets the best of him as he fondles and, in one tense scene, nearly kisses the cadaver in his turn-of-the-century practice. Meanwhile, his new wife (Barbara Steele) is none pleased with being entombed in a coffin and haunted by her predecessor, whose spirit is out for revenge.[57]

From the opening scene in which our intrepid doctor opens up a recently buried casket and proceeds to molest a corpse, audiences knew they were in for something a little different. The main plot, Flemyng's dealing with his necrophilia, is one that has never been considered appropriate material for any film regardless of the genre. Italian filmmakers, though, were quick to capitalize on the lurid subject matter via some memorable examples, including Aristide Massaccesi's *Buio omega* (1979), Lamberto Bava's *Macabro* (1980), and Armando Crispino's *Macchie solari* (1973). While it is fascinating that a film about the frustrated passions of a necrophiliac could find an audience in 1962, it is even more interesting that there was no major outcry from religious and concerned parents over the film. This may be explained by the way these international horror and exploitation films were officially ignored on every cultural level back in the early '60s, with local television censors not bothering to view the films before they were shown. This lack of attention contributed to the viewing pleasure of every boy or girl in the '60s and '70s who happened to watch these movies on local TV stations. The thrill of seeing something forbidden in the privacy of one's home without drawing the attention of everyone in the family is a situation many scholars and fans of Eurocult can attest to.[58] The Italian Gothic films frequently escaped detection under the TV censors' scissors as the violence and sexuality were only hinted at and left to the perversity of the audience member to explore. Though seldom clipped for TV, the film did not escape the censors of the United States or Great Britain on its initial release. The scenes of Flemyng fondling the bodies of dead women were cut from both countries' prints. These edits didn't lessen the impact on the film as audiences could still read between the lines, understand exactly what the director was intimating. As modern director Joe Dante (*Gremlins, Innerspace*), a lover himself of Gothic horror films, explained, "Even though a lot of these films were re-edited before they got to America, it was very difficult to take out all the undertones of necrophilia and lesbianism."[59]

Freda's follow-up to *L'orribile segreto*, *Lo spettro* (*The Ghost*) in 1963 is often looked upon as a sequel/remake of the previous film. Working with the same themes of drugs, murder and illicit sex, the film once again sees Barbara Steele this time as the malefic Margereta, who kills her doctor husband (in some prints the character is called Dr. Hichcock) with the help of her lover.[60] Again the traditional Gothic themes of murder and sexual affairs are at the center of the film. As is typical of the subgenre, there's no happy ending as the doctor, who was only faking his death, injects Ms. Steele with a paralyzing drug only to discover too late that she has previously poisoned his celebratory drink. This seals his fate, making the last thing he sees her twisted grin, all played out in an atmospheric Gothic setting.[61] There are quite a few subtle differences between Freda's and Bava's Gothic films.

Opposite: Parents dropping their kids off to see *L'orribile segreto del Dr. Hichcock* (*The Horrible Dr. Hichcock*, 1964) would probably not be too happy to discover that the good doctor practiced necrophilia.

Freda's Gothics are less joyous, taking a much more literal approach, as opposed to Bava's more literary stance, which contributes a sense of nostalgia.

Freda and Bava were not the only Italians working with the Gothic subgenre. Antonio Margheriti (1930–2002), previously noted for his Italian science fiction films, began his output of influential Gothic horror films with the classic *Danza macabra* (*Castle of Blood*) in 1962.[62] Different from Freda's Gothic films, which were examples of psychological neurosis with an emphasis on characterization, Margheriti's style of Gothic was more in line with Bava's, concentrating firmly on setting. A huge fan of black and white photography, Margheriti wrapped his early Gothics with all the trappings common to the genre, including those mist-covered haunted houses full of shadowy rooms of decay. Bright grays and whites punctuated his cinematic landscapes that '60s audiences seemed to gravitate to.

Shot in 15 days, *Danza macabra* arose out of the success not only of Bava's and Freda's Gothics, but of Roger Corman's version of Edgar Allan Poe's *Pit and the Pendulum* (*Il pozzo e il pendolo*, 1961), which was a success in Italy. Looking for a formula that would mimic Poe's story, *Danza* concerns a young writer (George Rivière) who tracks down a fictionalized Edgar Allan Poe in a tavern. Making a wager with Poe and his friends that he can spend the night in a local haunted castle, he arrives only to be haunted by the Blackwood family, including Elizabeth Blackwood (Barbara Steele).[63] As the evening wears on, the house begins teeming with life and our writer begins to realize that the Blackwood family seems to have a sinister plan in store for him.[64] Filmed in evocative black and white utilizing a three-camera system that allowed for a quick production, the film is standard Gothic fare, with its notoriety stemming from a graphic (for its time) lesbian scene between Steele and actress Margrete Robsahm, as well as a nude scene from Sylvia Sorente. These scenes were considered quite shocking not only for audiences in the early sixties but also for the actresses contracted to play them. Speaking to Michel Caen of the French magazine *Midi-Minuit Fantastique*, Barbara Steele lamented the difficulties in shooting such provocative material. Speaking of the lesbian scene between her and Robsahm, she remarked, "That scene was terrible. My costar didn't want to kiss me ... she said she couldn't kiss a woman. Margheriti was furious. He told her to just pretend she was kissing her Ugo [her husband, actor Ugo Tognazzi] and not Barbara! I don't know what it looked like on the screen; I never saw the picture."[65] The introduction of these sexual scenes begins to show how the traditional Gothic motif was looking to up the exploitation factor in order to secure an audience and how more displays of sexuality, especially involving pretty women, would be necessary to keep the ever-changing international audience interested.

After directing a variety of science fiction and Hercules films, Margheriti returned to the genre again in 1963 with *I lunghi capelli della morte* (*The Long Hair of Death*). Again using the traditional black and white format that worked well for *Danza macabra*, and once again calling upon Barbara Steele to play the lead role, Margheriti created a thinly written but visually beautiful Gothic. Unfortunately, by the mid–'60s, the plots for these Gothic horror stories were becoming stale with international movie audiences. While the Gothic visual style is fairly easy to replicate, there seemed to be a limit to the situations that writers could put characters in. With the typical plot line featuring the female witch burned at the stake only to exact her revenge on future generations, *I lunghi* seems suspiciously similar to the previous Gothics that came before it. Steele seems to be channeling all her previous Gothic characters into one role with nowhere left to go. By the movie's release in 1964, audiences were looking to push the envelope a little further.

Margheriti's next picture, 1964's *La vergine di Norimberga* (*The Virgin of Nuremberg*,

Another one of the many classic Barbara Steele Gothics of the mid–'60s.

aka *Horror Castle*) began to mirror the changes audiences wanted and amped up the exploitative aspects. Shot in bright Eastman Color, *La vergine* had all the trappings of a Gothic, gloomy castle, a beautiful woman in distress, and a suspicious husband and staff, and added a graphically violent component. Though the modern '60s audiences (and hence distributors) were demanding color, Margheriti was not thrilled with this change, citing, "The most frightening way of presenting blood on the screen is by using black and white photography, as it registers more effectively on the viewer's subconscious."[66] But audiences wanted color and violence, and movie distributors wanted movies that would sell. *La vergine* revolves around a former Nazi (Mirko Valentin), whose face was removed during the war, and who long to relive the glory days of the Third Reich, haunting a newlywed couple (France's Georges Rivière and Italy's Rosana Podesta) in their own castle. Within the castle is the requisite torture chamber in which our Nazi works out his frustration on local victims. His female victims are subjected to such things as having a cage with a rat in it tied to their heads (so as to be able to gnaw its dinner) or having their eyes pierced with spikes from an Iron Maiden (the virgin of the title). All of this shown in blood-red color, to the international audience's delight.[67] Margheriti helps to ensure international buy-in by hiring English actor Christopher Lee to play the part of the loyal, disfigured servant to our young couple. Riding high on such Gothic roles as Dracula, Frankenstein's monster and the Mummy in Great Britain's Hammer Films, Lee gives the film star power, but his presence adds to the complexity of the soundtrack. *La vergine* is one worst examples of Eurocult dubbing. As mentioned before, the standard practice of most European cinema at the time was to record without a live soundtrack. This made the dubbing process much easier and allowed actors from around the world to perform their scenes in their own native tongues. With DVD/Blu-Ray, audiences can watch the film via their favorite dub. The advantage of this is that if a group of actors were speaking the same language, such as Italian, the Italian dub would be much preferable since it would mimic the lip movement. *La vergine* is problematic because it is obvious that no one is speaking the same language in the film. Lee is speaking English, Rivière French, Podesta Italian, etc., so regardless of which audio version is chosen something sounds and looks "off," distracting viewers. After *La vergine*, Margheriti departed the Gothic subgenre genre for a variety of others, including spy, fantasy, and most importantly for exploitation lovers, gialli.

After his first foray into gialli with *La ragazza che sapeva troppo* in 1962, Mario Bava returned in 1963 to the Gothic format with his anthology *I tre volti della paura* (*The Three Faces of Fear*, aka *Black Sabbath*) and the sexually charged *La frusto e il corpo* (*The Whip and the Body*). For the first time within this subgenre Bava used color, which he had begun to perfect on such films as *Ercole al centro della terra* (1961) and *Gli invasori* (1961), and forever dispelled the notion that Gothic is best realized in black and white. Both of these films also incorporated more blatant adult themes than ever before. Incest, rape, sadomasochism and violent death are all plot points included in these films. With the first (in the Italian version; second in the United States) story of *I tre volti* being a giallo, Bava saves his Gothic mojo for *The Wurdulak*, a classic Gothic vampire story, and *La goccia d'acqua*, which is one of the most terrifying (for this author, at least) ghost stories produced. Filmed as a color companion piece to *La maschera del demonio* (1960), *The Wurdulak* has Bava painting the ultimate Gothic landscape in its damp, foggy, cold and—most important—isolated

Opposite: Spanish poster for Mario Bava's terrifying anthology ***I tre volti della paura*** (***Black Sabbath***, 1963).

LAS TRES CARAS DEL MIEDO
BORIS KARLOFF
MARK DAMON
SUSY ANDERSEN
MICHELE MERCIER
LIDIA ALFONSI
Director:
MARIO BAVA
COLOR

environment. It is here he takes the story of a young man (American actor Mark Damon) who is thrown into an extended family's struggle against vampirism. Placing the story in a secluded Eastern Europe cottage at the turn of the century, Bava sees the vampire as a completely incestuous character. In Bava's world, vampires can only feast on those they love the most, in this case, family members. The male head of the household, Gorka (Boris Karloff), returns to his family as a vampire and quickly takes a shine to the youngest boy of the house. The scenes of Gorka holding the young boy by the fire with a gleam of blood lust in his eye border on lewd.[68] Not afraid to showcase his nihilism, Bava ends the story on a downbeat note with each family member being killed and turned into a vampire. Bava effectively throws everything in the Gothic kitchen sink at audiences. Howling dogs, decaying landscapes wrapped in shadows and fog, evil superstitions and beautiful fragile women all add to the disquieting atmosphere of dread that helps Bava exploit his story and create possibly one of the best vampire stories in cinema. *The Wurdulak* is a 1963 snapshot of the conflict between old and new generations of Italians wrapped in a Gothic cloak. The machismo and paternalistic style that is a staple of Italian culture is on full display here. Gorka runs his house with absolute authority and is feared even before he becomes a vampire. The two sons and daughter seemingly long to start their own lives but are unable to break the grasp of the family bonds which eventually kill them. These family bonds, the most salient theme in Italian Gothic, subconsciously show that it is the traditional family structure that will proliferate in Italian society and not the rebellious new generation. In short, you can never escape your family even though they will suck you dry.

Though *The Wurdulak* was intended to be the middle story of the trilogy of *I tre volti*, American distributors thought the story, perhaps because of Karloff, the strongest and picked it to end the film. After viewing it, though, they realized they had ended the movie with evil winning out over good.[69] Worried that this would be too intense for a 1963 teenage audience, the distributors insisted on a lighter ending which had Boris Karloff, as narrator, riding an obvious fake horse and having stage hands run trees by him to showcase that the film was an illusion.[70]

What passed as the final story in the European version of the film in *I tre volti* was called *La goccia d'acqua* (*The Drop of Water*). Inspired by a short story from Chekov, *A Drop of Water* is widely considered to be one the scariest short stories ever filmed.[71] Again working with the conflict between the young and old, Bava pulls out all the colorful, atmospheric stops on this story of a young nurse (Jacqueline Pierreux) who steals a ring of a dead medium, only to find her spirit is not as dead as her body. Bava utilizes all the decay motifs that go along with the Gothic subgenre along with a terrific tour de force set of the medium's huge home. It is here in this decrepit, dead place, filled with cobwebs and wild cats that one would associate with a crypt, that Bava paints the reality vs. illusion subtext with the morally bankrupt young character whose greed is her downfall. Whether it was a reflection of the turbulent social changes of the '60s or his own proclivities, Bava's main characters were often representations of a flawed society. These characters often contributed to the violent situations in which they were immersed. Whether it was *Sei donne per l'assassino* (*Blood and Black Lace*, 1964), *Il rosso segno della follia* (*Hatchet for the Honeymoon*, 1969), *Cinque bambole per la luna d'agosto* (*Five Dolls for an August Moon*, 1970), or *Ecologia del delitto* (*Twitch of the Death Nerve*, 1971), Bava frequently did little to encourage audience sympathy for his characters' actions. Most of his main characters are unaffected by matters of conscience. They are consumed by greed or nurture unhealthy neuroses, which essentially results in their downfall by the end of the film, allowing the guilt of their actions to magnify the horror that is going on around them. In an interview given in 1972, Bava related thoughts about his fascination with these characters, saying, "I'm especially interested in stories that focus on one person: if I could, I would only tell these stories. What interests me is the fear experienced by a person alone in their room. It is then that everything around him starts to move menacingly around, and we realize that the only true 'monsters' are the ones we carry within ourselves."[72]

Bava's best example of this was his other film from 1963, the superlative *La frusta e il corpo* (*The Whip and the Body*), which again pitted the old and new generations of an established aristocratic family against each other. A deeply disturbing, sexually provocative film which relies on a heavy Gothic influence, *La frusta* deals with the psychosexual and dysfunctional sexual maladies that plague a wealthy family in the twentieth century. At the heart of the picture is a woman, Nevenka, played by Israeli Daliah Lavi, who must deal with her intense sexual and emotional attraction to her evil masochistic brother-in-law Kurt (Christopher Lee). Upon his return home from exile, he immediately seizes on Nevenka's attraction and savagely beats her with a whip, then rapes her, much to her liking. When Kurt is killed, his ghost seemingly haunts Nevenka, romancing her and beating her. Unfortunately for Nevenka her quest to understand and deal with her perverse sexuality may only end up with her destroying herself.[73] Though perhaps unintended, Bava's

Sadomasochism makes its appearance in Bava's *La frusta e il corpo* (*The Whip and the Body*, 1963), which was banned in many countries for its content.

exploration of themes of deviant sexuality and eventual catharsis causes the audience to evaluate their own thoughts on the subject. Throughout the film, Bava seems to have a strong sympathy for Nevenka. Beautiful, quiet, caring, everything one would expect from a traditional Italian wife, she has an angelic demeanor marred by the guilt she feels for her sadomasochistic attraction to her brother-in-law. Bava realizes she does not live in a time or place that would accept this type of behavior, let alone allow for a female to experience sexual pleasure, and therefore she would have to pay the price with guilt and eventual madness. It is very easy to see, in a heavily Catholic society like Italy in the early '60s, how such a conclusion could still be reached. Though there is no nudity or explicit sexual scenes, *La frusta* was Bava's most frequently banned film, having been forbidden in a number of countries and forbidden to young viewers in Italy.[74] The film was brought to the Italian courts in November 1963 for "immorality" by a Roman Catholic who was perhaps a little too traumatized by the subject matter. The resulting court case did little to garner audience attention. The film did very little in box office receipts in Italy ($45,000), only making back half its production costs. By early '64 the producer of the film was exonerated and the film then moved out of the European continent and into the hands of English-speaking countries, ensuring a profit.

Because of Christopher Lee's presence in the film, Britain snapped it up for its audience. Unfortunately, the British censors were none too fond of the sadomasochistic story line and sought huge cuts. Retitling it *Night Is the Phantom* (1964), British censors edited out the whipping and the looks of ecstasy from Lavi. For the U.S audience, who were also not used to such deviant sexual fetishes being on display in public, the film underwent extensive editing to eliminate the whipping scenes, rendering the film incomprehensible. Shelved for two years, the film was released in the United States strangely titled *What!*, which may be what audiences on both sides of the Atlantic were asking after seeing their respective edited editions.

The Gothic horror film began to peter out by the mid–'60s. Films like Mario Ciano's *Amanti d'oltretomba* (*Nightmare Castle, The Faceless Monster,* 1965) and Lucianno Ricci's *Il castello dei morti vivi* (*Castle of the Living Dead,* 1964) were the stylish last gasps of the genre. These films relied heavily on formula, with producers either concentrating on the perverse sexuality to sell the film, or on the international cast. *Il castello* in particular plays up the multicultural nature of these Italian productions in the mid–'60s. Starring actors from Britain (Christopher Lee), Canada (Donald Sutherland), France (Philippe Leroy), Italy (Gaia Germani) and Yugoslavia (Mirko Valentin), the movie was designed to appeal to the widest possible audience, ensuring success due the audience familiarity.[75]

After remounting the giallo in 1964 with *Sei donne per l'assassino* and infusing a bit of Gothic style to his science fiction thriller *Terrore nello spazio* (*Planet of the Vampires,* 1965), Mario Bava returned to his Gothic roots with *Operazione paura* (*Kill, Baby, Kill*) in 1966. Cited by critics as "one of the most thrilling ghost films in the entire Italian horror cinema," *Operazione* downplays the sex and violence while playing up the supernatural dread that is key to the Gothic motif.[76]

Operazione paura has been looked at as the last film in great Gothic cycle of Italian horror.[77] This time Bava downplays the internal family struggle that is prevalent in his early Gothics and goes for class rebellion. Quiet, without much of the exploitative elements that were occurring in Italian cinema in the mid–'60s, *Operazione* tells the story of a young doctor (Giacomo Rossi-Stuart) who is summoned to investigate how townspeople are being driven to terrible acts of suicide by the mere glimpse of a ghost of a young girl (Valerio

Marketing gothic was as simple as throwing a lot of cobwebs in the photograph, as evidenced in the Italian poster for Bava's *Operazione paura* (*Kill, Baby, Kill*, 1966).

Valeri, who ironically is a young boy dressed in the film as a girl), who was none too happy to have been run over by a horse during a village festival. Filmed in shadows and an array of green and red colors, which was Bava's specialty, the film has a look that belies the ultra-low budget that he had to work with. As is typical of films of this sort, money promised isn't always money delivered. Halfway through the filming, producers ran out of the money needed to complete the film. Instead of shutting down, cast and crew, out of respect for Bava as well as a decent script, agreed to work for free to finish the film. Even with the budget limitations, Bava was able, as was his forte, to create a mystical, ominous wonderland replete with the requisite black cats, fog, half-lit figures and ancient decrepit buildings that added a noir-ish atmosphere and contributed to the supernatural aspects of the plot.[78]

Operazione paura's release in 1966 marked the end of the traditional Gothic period in Italian filmmaking. Though the film was very successful, owing in part to its infinitesimal budget as well as to its short running time (83 minutes, which meant distributors could sell it fairly cheaply to drive-in's as an extra feature), it turned out to be the swan song for the Italian Gothic. The increasing lack of censorship continued in the late '60s, when it became permissible to show the things (expressed sexuality, overt violence) that were only hinted at in films of these types.[79] The Gothic, with its traditional vs. modern animosity, seemed passé, especially with stories set at the turn of the century, and the subject matter seemed squarely rooted in the past in a time when moviegoers were searching for something a little more modern.

By the late '60s it was the younger generation that was winning the culture wars and dictating to film producers what they would pay to see. In an attempt to try to please the market both Mario Bava and Antonio Margheriti returned to Gothic in the early '70s. Both found that mixing contemporary storylines and characters with the Gothic motif was somewhat troubling.

Hoping to update his *Danza macabra* (1962) to a more modern audience, Antonio Margheriti directed the remake, *Nella stretta morsa del ragno*, in 1971. Shooting in color with a strong cast, Margheriti expressed misgivings about the project, expressing his preference for the original. But exploitation filmmaking is often at the mercy of the producers who are willing to pay for directorial services. Italy had very few "star" directors that commanded big salaries; most directors had to take whatever was offered to them so they could keep bread on the table. This is why able artists like Margheriti worked on legitimate material like the original *Danza* as well as on movies like the woeful *Jaws* redo, *Killer Fish* (1978). Margheriti is honest in his assessment of *Nella stretta*, saying, "The second was made at the express request of the producer, the same as had produced *Danza macabra*." When asked about the main flaws of the film, he expressed the problem that a Gothic had in the '70s cinematic landscape: "First of all, the fact that color was used, which made the blood red, the use of Cinemascope and, worst of all, the fact that the actors all overshadowed the story."[80]

Margheriti's second attempt at Gothic in the 1970s was *Seven Deaths in the Cat's Eye* (1973). Fusing both the giallo and Gothic together, Margheriti compiled an international cast, including the French couple of the moment, Jane Birkin and musician Serge Gainesborg. The story of a beautiful young girl (Birkin) who returns to the ancestral castle only to find a sadistic murderer roaming the grounds was typical Gothic fare. Unfortunately, the elements that had worked in the sixties — the castles, family relatives all seeking money from the dead castle's patriarch, a beautiful woman in distress — were far too quaint for the hip '70s audience. In addition, the mixture between Gothic and giallo is a blend of genres that are not altogether compatible. Gothic films thrive on implied violence and repression, while gialli are exercises in explicit sex and violence. In order to satisfy the audience, Margheriti uses the tenets of the Gothic only with regards to atmosphere. The rest of the film, from its liberal use of pink blood to the requisite "shocking" identity of the killer, all played into the constructs of the giallo.

After a six-year absence, Mario Bava returned to the subgenre with *Gli orrori del castello di Norimberga* (*Baron Blood*, 1971) an attempt to throw a very modern mini-skirted Elke Sommer into the gloomy Gothic castle motif. In the film she works as a graduate student overseeing the restoration of an impressive Austrian castle aptly titled Schloss des Teufels (Castle of Devils, and with a name like that you know it isn't going to be Disneyland) when she and the young American descendant of the castle's ancient family (Antonio Cantáfora) aren't out raising his sadistic, faceless ancestor from the grave. The resulting mayhem includes spiked caskets, hanging corpses, severed heads on spears and Ms. Sommer screaming hers off. Bava's penchant for exploring the continuing division between the generations picks up where he left off from *Operazione paura* (1966) seven years earlier. Here, though, without the constraints of turn-of-the-century characters, the division between traditional and modern is jarring. The resulting years show the widening divide between the corrupt, old culture, as represented via Joseph Cotten, and the new, hip, selfish one. While Bava seems to have some sympathy for his young characters, he doesn't seem to give them much credit, exploiting their naiveté as selfish foolishness. Ms. Sommers represents the worst of this. Her Eva is posited as a strong, intelligent woman, yet she spends the entire run of the picture in an abject state of fear, running around in the world's shortest miniskirt. By this time in his career Bava was pretty much disillusioned by all members of society. It is only with the very young that he holds any optimism for the future. In *Baron Blood*, it is young Gretchen (Eurocult favorite Nicoletta Elmi) who is able to see through evil Alfred Becker (Joseph Cotten) when others can't, even guessing the final piece of the puzzle that will destroy him. This trust in children was a little more subtle than in Bava's previous film, the seminal giallo *Ecologia del delitto* (*Bay of Blood*, 1972) in which the children of the movie brutally murdered their scheming parents as karmic reward for their wrongdoing.

Seen as a throwback to the Italian horrors to the early-to-mid-sixties, *Baron Blood* became a box office hit in America.[81] Somewhat predictable, with the usual international representation of actors (German Elke Sommer, American Joseph Cotten, Spanish Antonio Cantáfora), *Baron Blood* surprises because of its focus on the violence. Fritz's (Luciano Pigozzi) death via spiked coffin sets the stage for some fairly gruesome goings-on. Audiences were now accustomed to seeing the spikes penetrate skin, and Bava obliges. Bava's Baron is shown to be a grotesque with a face that resembles some very overcooked lasagna. Added to the mix is the obvious sexuality of Elke Sommer, allowing the film to veer into the exploitative realm that the original Italian Gothic helped to create. Now in order to find success with an audience, Gothic filmmakers had to include explicit elements of blood, gore and sexuality at the expense of subtlety.[82]

The worldwide success of *Baron Blood* in 1971 persuaded producer Alfredo Leone to offer Bava the chance to produce any film he wanted with total artistic control. Never offered this before, Bava had his pick of genres from which he could choose, but set about making a Gothic horror tale that surrealistically moved between the traditional aspects of the Gothic genre and the modern ones. The result of this is the classic Gothic *Lisa e il diavolo* (*Lisa and the Devil*, 1972).[83] Fresh from *Baron Blood* the year before, Elke Sommer stars as Lisa, a young American traveling in Spain. She finds herself lost within the medieval town of

Gothic experienced a brief renaissance in the early '70s thanks to the international success of ***Baron Blood*** in 1971.

Toledo and soon ends up in a vast country estate inhabited by a senile blind woman (Alida Valli), her necrophiliac son (Alesso Orano) and a lollipop-sucking Telly Savalas, who doubles as both the butler and the Devil. Bava deliberately sets the film up as a non-linear exercise in which Lisa finds herself stuck in a nightmarish world while the Devil plays out a Gothic scenario with her and a few other dysfunctional guests who have come along for the ride.[84] The film hits all the machinations of a traditional Gothic with images of raw sexuality combined with adult themes like necrophilia to create a dreamy world where fantasy and reality are intertwined.

But, differentiating this work from many of the other films of the era, Bava valiantly tries to stay away from the exploitative aspects of the storyline and almost succeeds. His use of nudity with actresses Sommers and Sylva Koscina is artfully done and never lurid, while the bludgeoning death of Koscina isn't taken as far as compatriots like Fulci or Masseccesi would have. Like a bad dream that never ends, *Lisa* benefits from the beautiful cinematography typical of a Bava film, along with strong performances and an adherence to a completely non-linear style of narrative that forces viewers to forget simple little things like time (one never knows in what time frame the film is set) and common sense. In many respects it represents the pinnacle of the modern Gothic as it easily creates a fantasy world of suppression and desire, yet laces it with modern touches of violence and sex.

Unfortunately, *Lisa e il diavolo* (1973) was perhaps a bit too ephemeral for an early 1970s audience who were now used to straight narratives and flowing gore. Bava and producer Leone had big hopes for their artistic masterpiece and though the film was well received at the 1973 Venice Film Festival, foreign distributors showed absolutely no interest in distributing it. Producer Leone commented on the baffling lack of interest: "We had a tremendous turn-out for the first screening. No one left the theater. We had additional screenings also to packed houses but there were no buyers. The best offer I had at the time was $6,000 for the Far East—for the ENTIRE Far East, can you imagine?"[85]

What Bava and Leone perhaps failed to see is that the audience for Italian Gothics had been siphoned off by the multitude of subgenres coming out of Europe at the time. *Lisa* is outdated and almost quaint in the era of fellow Italian Dario Argento's bloody modern thrillers, Lucio Fulci's graphic indictment of religion, and Spaniard Jess Franco's overt sexuality that was being flung at audiences. Consequently, the film in its original form disappeared for over two years. Not wanting to lose his one-million-dollar investment, Leone had no choice but to completely remount the film (with an assist from Bava) into a subgenre that was popular. Since the devil was involved, it must have made sense to him to combine the Bava's Gothic masterpiece with the devil-possession angle popularized by the international success of *The Exorcist* in 1973. As a result, he completely pulled apart *Lisa* and inserted some of the most exploitative material in the Bava canon (think Elke Sommer vomiting up green frogs) and retitled it *La casa dell'esorcismo* (*The House of Exorcism*, which will be discussed in the devil-possession chapter). The resulting film so offended Bava that he had his name removed from it.[86]

With the exception of these few films in the '70s, the Italian Gothic horror film was in deep slumber after the mid-'60s. Audiences had moved on from the subliminal thrills that Gothics provided to the more visual and graphic. The Italian Gothic would experience a slight resurgence in the early 1980s with a number of films from Italian filmmaker Lucio Fulci, like *Paura nella città dei morti viventi* (*City of the Living Dead*, 1980), *Black Cat* (1981), *L'aldilà* (*The Beyond*, 1981), and *Quella villa accanto al cimitero* (*The House by the Cemetery*, 1982). These films, though, were Gothic only in atmosphere as they were definitely not about suppression but about true exploitation. They often merged the zombie, giallo and cannibal genres, giving audiences around the world the extreme violence and gore they craved.

Gothic films played an important role in the development of European exploitation. They bridged the gap between traditional storylines and modern-day sensibilities. They allowed the first examinations of such themes as perverse sexuality to seep into the consciousness of moviegoers in the guise of a literary form that audiences felt comfortable with. Through the success of Gothic films, Eurocult filmmakers could begin to branch out to other forms of exploitation that were each more explicit than the last. They served their purpose as an initial starting point for the abundance of Italian horror/exploitation films that would follow for the next few decades. In describing these films, Italian writer Giovanni Simonelli sums up the genre: "In these movies, what you see is what you get. They were not meant to be artistic, they were just meant to be entertaining. They served their purpose and they all did well."[87]

Filmography

Baron Blood, aka *Gli orrori del castello di Norimberga*. Prod. Alfredo Leone. Dir. Mario Bava. Italy/Germany, 1971. Image Entertainment, 100 min. DVD. Starring: Elke Sommer, Joseph Cotten, Massimo Girotti, Antonio Cantafora and Rada Rassimov.

Poor Elke Sommer: no one takes her very seriously. She's working on getting her PhD by restoring an old Austrian castle (one with the name Castle of Devils) and terrible things keep happening to her. Maybe it's because she's a woman, or maybe her mini (let's just say nonexistent) skirt belies her intelligence, or maybe it's because the new guy she met, who happens to be a descendant of the castle's ancient family, decided they should invoke a curse which, oops, brings back Baron Blood, a not so nice, not so pretty, sadist who likes to murder the cast and chase her around the foggy streets of Austria. Personally, I think it's because she spends every second of the film screaming her head off like an idiot. Director Bava moves the Gothic motif into the '70s and creates a fun picture that everyone can enjoy. He sets up a great scenario using the Korneuburg Castle to great effect, as well as pretty nifty lighting shots, especially during the good Baron's chase of Miss Sommer through mist-covered streets. A hit for its time, in which Bava showed that the Gothic could indeed have a home in the '70s if the violence was ratcheted up to suit the audience's tastes. We get some heads on sticks here, a hanging, and — playing off the spiked-mask theme from his classic *Black Sunday*— a spiked coffin that spells a holey doom for one of our cast members.

Black Sabbath, aka *I tre volti della paura*. Prod. Paolo Mercuri. Dir. Mario Bava. Italy, 1963. Image Entertainment, 92 min. DVD. Starring: Boris Karloff, Mark Damon, Michèle Mercier and Jacqueline Pierreux.

A tour de force on every level and Mario Bava's most assured film! Using the anthology format, he creates three absolutely brilliant, though entirely different, short stories that are as shocking and engaging as they were 50 years ago. Depending on what print you see (I say stick with the European print, though the dubbing of Karloff is bad) the opening story, *The Telephone*, is the perfect set-up to the giallo. Tense, colorful, with the strong undercurrent of seediness (his lesbian subplot is revelatory), Bava works the suspense to unbearable levels and makes the story sexy and interesting. Truth be told, the American version, in which Frank is a ghost, works as well, though the true motivations of characters are blunted. The middle story, *The Wurdalak*, is quite simply one of the best vampire stories ever and a reminder that Karloff was really an incredibly malevolent presence when he had the right material. Moody, evocative and downright spooky, vampire Karloff comes home to vampirize the ones he loves the most, his family! Finally, *The Drop of Water*, with its moral judgment call and ghostly environment of a woman who unwisely decides to steal a ring from the finger of a dead psychic and pays dearly, gave me nightmares for years after viewing it as a child. This is a Top 5 choice for anyone wishing to explore the Eurocult genre. Don't miss it!

Black Sunday, aka *La maschera del demonio* (IT), *The Mask of Satan* (GB). Prod. Massimo De Rita. Dir. Mario Bava. Italy, 1960. Image Entertainment, 87 min. DVD. Starring: Barbara Steele, John Richardson, Andrea Checchi and Aurturo Dominici.

Simply a classic and a great jumping-in point for those interested in the Eurocult subgenre. Take a Universal horror movie, add some adult themes and throw in some fairly explicit violence and you have a true turning point for horror/exploitation cinema as Steele steals the show and cements her reputation as one of the leading ladies of Eurocult, playing the double role of Princess Vajda, a truly evil but admittedly sexy witch, and her virtuous descendant Katia, with an amazing duality. The definition of a truly atmospheric horror film, *Black Sunday* revels in undercurrents of violence and sexuality. Surprisingly for the time, and much to delight of fans, this violence spills out onto the screen with the fun of watching bugs crawl all over Steele's dead face or watching blood shoot out of her as the spiked Mask of Satan (which is what the film was called in Britain) is pounded into her. This is the first, not last, great example of the wonders that Bava could do with a low budget and an imagination. Though at times the movie does seem bogged down in the middle by dialogue, Bava keeps the audience into it by creating some of the most evocative atmospheric in the genre. Another don't-miss!

Castle of Blood, aka *Danza macabra*. Prod. Marco Vicario. Dir. Antonio Margheriti. Italy/France, 1964. Synapse Films, 89 min. DVD. Starring: Barbara Steele, Georges Rivière, Margrete Robsahm and Arturo Dominici.

Margheriti's ode to Edgar Allan Poe is great to watch but not so much to enjoy. The story is interesting enough, with a man challenged to spend the night in a haunted house and his subsequent help by ghost Steele to escape, but the film meanders and seems much longer than its 89-minute (European cut) running time. Heavy on black and white atmosphere and shot in two weeks, the film does have some fun for exploitation fans as it flirts with lesbianism and has a rather overt sexuality, including some tasteful nudity. The presence of Steele helps, as her evocative energy lifts every movie she's in. For Gothic lovers this is treat; for everyone else....

City of the Living Dead, aka *Paura nella città dei morti viventi* (IT), *Gates of Hell* (U.S.). Prod. Fabrizio De Angelis. Dir. Lucio Fulci. Italy, 1980. Blue Underground, 93 min. DVD/Blu-Ray. Starring: Catroina MacColl, Christopher George, Carlo De Mejo, Janet Agren and Giovanni Lombardo Radice.

Though many Fulci fans dismiss this as one of his weakest modern Gothics, I couldn't disagree more. Fulci's rip-roaring sequel to *Zombie* (1979) has always been one of my favorites! C'mon, where else can you see a woman throw herself up ... literally? Sure, the story doesn't make any sense under any type of examination and the ending is the epitome of lame, but for sheer atmosphere and set pieces this is one of Fulci's strongest films. From the buried-alive sequence (which could NOT have been fun for MacColl), to flying maggots and Radice's ... um ... drilling, the film, which fuses both the zombie and Gothic elements together, is like a very bad dream in which nothing is out of the realm of possibility. But that's its brilliance in that it's just one disgusting set piece after another. Gothic films succeed because of their atmosphere, and Fulci's city (okay, it's more like a very small Southern town), in its mixture of wind, sand and fog, is the perfect setting for all the mashed-up brains and worms that Fulci serves up. There's no hidden agenda, no moral message; Fulci's sole purpose is to scare, entertain and most definitely gross out. What more could a Eurocult fan want? The film was released without a rating, giving itself a self-imposed "adults only" classification, so bring the barf bag. The Blue Underground Blu-Ray sports an amazing transfer that legitimizes Fulci's vision and allows crystal clear viewing of all the copious amounts of blood and gore.

The Ghost, aka *Lo spettro* (IT). Prod. Luigi Carpenteriri. Dir. Riccardo Freda. Italy, 1963. Retromedia, 97 min. DVD. Starring: Barbara Steele, Peter Baldwin, Elio Jotta and Harriet Medin.

Freda followed up his immensely successful *Horrible Dr. Hichcock* with this mediocre Gothic that has Steele as the baddie as she tries, with the help of her lover, to poison her husband (Steele never married well in any of her Gothics). She thinks that it works, but he's faking, and spends the rest of the movie haunting her, driving her mad. The ending is truly ghastly as he poisons her with a paralyzing drug with the purpose of killing her slowly, but Steele, being Steele, has the last laugh. While it is great to see Steele in Technicolor, the film suffers from a been-there-done-that mentality that signals the staleness that was beginning to creep into the subgenre.

Horrible Dr. Hichcock, aka *L'orribile segreto del Dr. Hitchcock*. Prod. Emmano Denato. Dir. Riccardo Freda. Italy, 1962. 88 min. Starring: Barbara Steele, Robert Flemyng, Silvano Tranquilli and Harriet Medin.

Along with *Black Sunday, The Horrible Dr. Hichcock* stands out as one of the seminal Italian Gothics. Kudos to Freda, who was brave enough to give audiences, albeit somewhat subliminally as it was the early '60s, the story of a doctor (Flemyng) who can only reach sexual satisfaction with dead women. This fetish causes him to inject the ones he loves with a serum rendering them immobile while he performs his lustful duty. This doesn't go over with the first wife so well, especially after he inadvertently kills her (thus making her the perfect playmate for him), and even less with the second wife (Steele), who's not so much into it. But you can't keep a good doctor down, and Hichcock is determined to get what he wants. Colorfully filmed with a distinct "yuck" feeling; it's amazing that Freda was allowed to get away with so much. There is still not a decent version of the film available in the United States on DVD or Blu-Ray at the time of this writing. This is definitely one film that deserves the full digital treatment. It would be great to have a new audience see how Freda subtly got away with things that would be graphically shown in such necrophilia classics as *Macabre* (1980) and *Buio Omega* (1980) 20 years later.

Kill, Baby, Kill, aka *Operazione paura* (IT), *Curse of the Living Dead* (U.S.). Prod. Luciano Catenacci. Dir. Mario Bava. Italy, 1966. Anchor Bay Entertainment, 87 min. DVD. Starring: Giacomo Rossi-Stuart, Erika Blanc, Fabienne Dali and Piero Lulli.

Mario Bava's ultra-low budget ghost story is a favorite of his many admirers. There is a lot to admire as Bava takes his budgetary constraints and produces a compact ghost story that has some genuine jolts as well as a pretty memorable ghost. Dr. Eswai (Rossi-Stuart) is called into a small village to investigate the multiple deaths of its citizens. Performing an autopsy (with the help of biology student and newcomer in town Erika Blanc) he's shocked to discover that each of the victims has a gold coin embedded in his heart. It's worse than he thinks, as the townsfolk are being driven to suicide by the terrifying ghost of a young girl whose mere glance will cause one to want to kill himself. *Kill, Baby, Kill* is not a perfect film, as there are some pretty significant plot holes, undeveloped characters, and a quick, unsatisfying ending, probably due to the budget issues that Bava experienced during filming. The film is not a total write-off, though, in large part because of its visual style. Bava creates an amazing dreamlike Gothic environment (later used to better effect with *Lisa and the Devil*) where it's possible our little ghost girl can pop out at any time. Blanc and Rossi-Stuart make an attractive pair and the very quick running time prevents boredom.

Lisa and the Devil, aka *Lisa e il diavolo*. Prod. Alfredo Leone. Dir. Mario Bava. Italy, 1973. Image Entertainment, 95 min. DVD. Starring: Elke Sommer, Telly Savalas, Alida Valli, Sylva Koscina and Gabrielle Tinti.

Magical, eerie, and ephemeral, Bava's "lost" film has been resurrected in the last 10 years to the rejoicing of critics, and it's no wonder, as the film ranks among his very best. American tourist Lisa (Elke Sommer, a long way from her annoying turn in *Baron Blood*) finds herself suddenly lost in a strange town. As she tries to find her way back to her tour group she keeps running into the malevolent Telly Savalas. She eventually ends up in a large mansion with a group of people who are equally lost. The house is being served by lollipop-sucking Savalas (before *Kojak*), who serves a strange young man prone to necrophilia and his blind mother (Valli). Things get a little crazy when the people Lisa arrived with begin to have adulterous affairs and commit murder. To be honest, it really doesn't matter what the plot is because that's not Bava's point. Bava is evoking a nightmare and succeeds in building this dreamlike environment without any attention to logic or linear narrative. All the performances add to the mystical nature of the film, especially Savalas, whose Devil is a whimsical treat. The ending is quite a jolt, too! If you are looking for fun exploitation,

Lisa is not your ticket: this is not a film you watch with large groups of people, but a private film to be enjoyed when one wants to escape the real world. For a fun public showing, you might want to choose the bastardized version of *Lisa* called *The House of Exorcism*, which cuts the film to shreds and inserts some wonderfully perverse devil possession footage of Sommer projectile vomiting, climbing walls like a spider and telling the local preacher to "fuck off." Now *that's* fun!

Mill of the Stone Women, aka *Il mulino delle donne di pietra*. Prod. Giampaolo Bigazzi. Dir. Girgia Ferrani. France/Italy, 1960. Mondo Macabro, 96 min. DVD Starring: Pierre Brice, Scilla Gabel, Wolfgang Preiss and Dany Carrel.

Who said you couldn't set a Gothic in windmill? Ferrani moves the conventional Gothic to more Flemish settings in this colorful, though long exploitation classic. Using themes from such popular films as *House of Wax* (1953) and *Horrors in the Black Museum* (1959) and fusing it with traditional Gothic, he comes up with a very adult story that was in many ways ahead of its time. Young writer Hans (Brice) comes to town to work for the brilliant though troubled Dr. Bohlm, who happens to reside in a windmill that doubles as a waxworks showcasing all the most infamous women in history. The good doc also has a beautiful, reclusive Barbara Steele look-alike daughter (Gabel) whose personality is, well ... stony. Soon it becomes apparent that all is not well in Flanders: local girls are disappearing, the waxworks figures look strangely familiar, and ... well, you know the rest. The color photography is quite well done and the film does benefit from the change of scenery (after all, how many old castles can you set a story in?), but it's a long-winded affair that suffers severely from lagging in the middle part. Most interesting is the casual nudity of Hans's fiancée (Carrel) during her torture scene, which that must have served as inspiration for some of Jess Franco's early films.

Monster of Venice, aka *Il mostro di venezia* (IT), *The Embalmer* (U.S.). Prod. Christian Marvel. Dir. Dino Tavella. Italy/Germany/France, 1964. Retromedia, 77 min. DVD. Starring: Maureen Brown, Luigi Martocci, Luciano Gasper and Anita Todesco.

Monster of Venice is an insignificant film that plays more like a German Krimi or even a giallo than a Gothic horror film. The exploitation factor is high as a skull-mask-wearing killer stalks the Venice catacombs to find women so he can retain their perfection by embalming them (he must be some generational relative of Dr. Hichcock or Dr. Bohlm). A young writer, Andreas (Martocci), tries to alert the police to no avail just as the lunch wagon arrives for our killer in the guise of a troupe of beautiful "dancers" (as strippers were referred to in the '60s). A short running time, and some fun visuals (especially all the embalmed statues lined in a row), are about the only thing to recommend in the film.

Nightmare Castle, aka *Amanti d'oltretomba* (IT), *Faceless Monster* (U.S.). Prod. Carlo Caiano. Dir. Mario Caiano. Italy, 1965. Severin, 104 min. DVD. Starring: Barbara Steele, Paul Müeller, Helga Liné and Laurence Clift.

When I was five or six, I remember being haunted by a black and white movie in which all I could recollect was that a woman and her boyfriend were chained up to a wall and tortured by her husband. The look of horror and defiance on the woman's face scared the daylights out of me and traumatized me for many years. Cut to 35 years and many thousands of movies later: reviewing the movie again, I realized that it was indeed Barbara Steele who was behind all the trauma (I was sure she lived in my bedroom closet!) and *Nightmare Castle* was the film. With my much older eyes, the film stands as a middling-to-good representation of the Gothic subgenre, with Steele in a dual role, lots of hidden/repressed sexuality and some occasional jolts. By this time in the subgenre, the plots of these films were becoming interchangeable and the first whiff of staleness was becoming evident. Still, Severin's uncut, much-improved DVD transfer is a definite must-have for those who like a good adult Gothic. Just keep it out of the hands of the very young!

Playgirls and the Vampire, aka *L'ultima preda del vampiro*. Prod. Tiziano Longo. Dir. Piero Regnoli. Italian/German, 1960. Image Entertainment, 80 min. DVD. Starring: Walter Brandi, Lyla Rocco, Maria Givovanni and Alfredo Rizzo.

Here we go! With a title like this you know exactly what you're in for. A group of fairly talentless showgirls (no, this far too early for Elizabeth Berkley, but think what fun that would have been) find themselves stranded in a castle (bad storm, of course) that has a secret laboratory in the basement. As payment for the hospitality, the castle's owner (Brandi) and rest of us in the audience are "treated" to the girls' obvious talents in the form of some truly bad burlesque numbers. Much to the chagrin of everyone, Brandi's ancestor, a 200-year-old vampire, arrives and takes a shine to one of the "dancers" who reminds him of a long-lost love (I bet that relationship was a fun one, too!). Wackiness ensues, with the audience being the loser. Banal, exploitative fun where the only thing missing is a pole.

Seven Deaths in the Cat's Eye, aka *La morte negli occhi del gatto* (IT). Prod. Luigi Nannerini. Dir. Antonio Margheriti. Italy/France, 1973. Blue Underground, 95 min. Starring: Jane Birkin, Serge Gainsbourg, Anton Diffring and Venantino Venantini.

A strange film, *Seven Deaths* never knows exactly what it wants to be. Is it a Gothic? Is it a giallo? Is it an ape-gone-wild thriller? (No, I wasn't making that up.) The strangeness is compounded by the sight of our favorite early-'70s couple, Birkin (tell me you just didn't hear "Je T'Aime … Moi Non Plus" in your mind) and Gainsbourg, appearing in this "Agatha Christie meets Mario Bava"-type thriller. Birkin plays a young girl who returns to a Scottish castle to find her family dysfunctional and later her mother dead. With the help of the very French Gainsbourg (playing an inspector in Scotland, and yes, the dubbing is that bad!) they find the true perpetrator responsible for the murder. Did I tell you there's a vicious runaway ape in the film? That was a warning. The film is well put-together, though, with the requisite dark cobwebbed halls and Gothic motif, and the killings are somewhat inventive and bloody. The ending is predictable (if you've seen many of the Italian gialli of the '70s, it won't surprise), but some fun is to be had. Production values are high enough to warrant a viewing.

Slaughter of the Vampires, aka *La strage dei vampiri* (IT), *Curse of the Blood Ghouls* (U.S.). Prod. Dino Sant'Ambrogio. Dir. Roberto Mauri. Italy, 1962. Retromedi, 80 min. DVD. Starring: Walter Brandi, Graziella Granata, Dieter Eppler and Luigi Batzella.

Poor Brandi: after having to fight his 200-year-old vampire relative while being made to watch a group of talentless "dancers" perform their routines in *Playgirls and the Vampire* (1960), he is now in the put-upon position of having to save his wife from one of the campiest vampires in history. Yep, it seems this vamp has eyes for Granata, the Barbara Steele look-alike (there was a definite pattern in these Gothic films), and is determined to get her. It's up to Brandi, with the help of Batzella, to bring on the slaughter of the title, though if you're looking for slaughter, you're going to be disappointed. The film is hoot thanks to some of the most outlandish dubbing ever, making the film appear more like an MST3K episode than a serious thriller.

Virgin of Nuremberg, aka *La vergine di Norimberga* (IT), *Horror Castle* (U.S.). Prod. Marco Vicario. Dir. Antonio Margheriti. Italy, 1963. Shriek Show, 90 min. DVD. Starring: Christopher Lee, Rossana Podestà, Georges Rivière, and Jim Dolen.

Margheriti lays on the sadism in this tale of a young newlywed who discovers horrible things are going on in her husband's castle (don't these women do any sort of checking before they marry these guys?). The mansion, it seems, has a torture chamber that is still in good torturing order as she discovers the eyeless corpse of a woman in the Iron Maiden (the Virgin of the title). Things go downhill from there as the Punisher arrives, a red-hooded figure who likes to devise sadistic punishments like strapping live hungry rats to people's heads. Who could the Punisher be? Could it be her husband? Could it be Christopher Lee, the scarred servant? You'll have to wade through about 85 minutes to find out, but the wade is worth it, especially if you like cold violence, as Margheriti pushes the limits with his tortures, all in living color.

The Whip and the Body, aka *La frusta e il corpo* (IT), *What!* (U.S.). Prod. Frederico Natale. Dir. Mario Bava. Italy/France, 1963. VCI, 88 min. DVD. Starring: Christopher Lee, Daliah Lavi, Tony Kendell and Harriet Medin.

A fascinating yet serious look at a sadomasochistic relationship and the mental damage it causes. This is Mario Bava's most sexual film, even more than *Quante volte … quella notte* (1968) or *Lisa and the Devil* (1973), though there is absolutely no nudity or sexual contact! Nevenka Menliff (Lavi in a tour de force performance) is a young, proper, married woman attracted to her brother-law's (Christopher Lee) sadism and sexual mojo. One day he whips her mercilessly (in a scene that still packs a punch), knowing that it will bring pleasure. It does, and sets up a spiral of events as her guilt gets the better of her. Worse, a killer is roaming the halls, and soon the bodies start piling up. Bava piles on the Gothic setting in order to aid the whole atmosphere of suppression. The entire environment is suffocating, which only compounds Neveka's angst about her sexual fetish. This is not one of those fun S&M movies. It explores some serious issues and is executed flawlessly. The music may be a little (okay, it's a lot) over the top and dramatic, but this is one Gothic that deserves to be seen.

It's a Mondo World

> Perhaps the most devious and irresponsible filmmakers who have ever lived.
> — Pauline Kael, author and film critic[88]

Mixing the seamier aspects of life with the increasing violence around the world, the popular mondo film, with its pseudo-documentary style of filmmaking, wasn't interested in exploiting individuals, instead setting its sights on exploiting entire cultures. Emerging at roughly the same time as the Gothic Italian horror film, the popularity of mondos can be traced to increasing globalization and the social effect (positive or negative) it had on world populations via such issues as immigration. In addition, the rise of new media technologies, such as worldwide acceptance of television as a popular medium, helped facilitate the success of a subgenre that still exists in today's hyper-media environment. With the worldwide success of the first mondo film, *Mondo cane* (*A Dog's Life*) in 1962, the subgenre caused a firestorm of controversy and was the precursor for such 1980s gross-out video favorites as *Faces of Death* (1978) and *Faces of Death II* (1981).[89] Looking at the myriad of choices on television today, from reality-based TV shows to 24/7 documentary channels that go out of their way to shock, it is easy to see the mark this brand of Eurocult films has left on the world.

Simply put, mondo films are "shock" documentaries. Take any cultural anomaly, from tribal rituals to a particular culture's view on sexuality, and the mondo film was there to exploit it. Its subject matter is the proverbial car accident and its audience those passersby. Using standard documentary film techniques, mondos gleefully focus on grimy and seamier aspects to society and present a distinctly hegemonic Western point of view. Their lofty ambition was ostensibly to educate audiences about differing social cultures around the world, but in almost all cases they were nothing more than crass exploitation that took advantage of people's fear and distrust of the rapid globalization that was taking place during the '60s and '70s. What makes the mondo film interesting is that it was able to be as reprehensible as each individual country that distributed the film wanted it to be. That's because the entire tone of a mondo film is wrapped up in the narrative. The pictures tell the story but the narration gives it context. Every country was allowed to record its own narration, which could downplay or magnify the cultural differences to suit the taste (i.e., bias) of a particular country. For example, if Italians have an issue with images that seem sacrilegious, the narration will go out of its way to condemn them, while the same scene might not even register shock with an English translation. Therefore Italian mondo films are the perfect vehicle for societies around the world to gawk and feel superior to other cultures.

The popularity of the Italian mondo film in the '60s can be explained by a variety of factors. Most importantly, audiences interest in these films was rooted in the increasing globalization that was taking place. In the 1960s, European immigration patterns began to change, and Italy was on the forefront of a transformation of its work force. Prior to this shift, the pre- and postwar conditions that plagued the defeated country resulted in more people (both workers and their families) leaving Italy than entering. By the early '60s this trend began to reverse, as Italian men, working outside the country, were effected by those other countries grappling with their own immigration issues. The result was that many countries began restricting the number of visas issued to family members due to housing shortages. Consequently, Italian men often stayed outside Italy for shorter periods, and each time they returned, they would bring stories to their families about their time spent dealing with other cultures.

As important as this outside migration was, incoming immigration was also a major issue in Italy. A large influx of immigrants from places like Asia, Africa and Latin America were beginning to settle on Italian shores, bringing with them their own cultures and social ways. For several years the scale of the influx of non–European immigrants was difficult to assess, as no policy existed either to measure or to control it. By the early '70s the immigration issue had a profound impact on the Italian population. In 1972, for example, Italy for the first time registered more people entering the country than leaving.[90] All of this had helped fuel an interest, albeit it not always so positive, in how people around world behaved. Italians, as well as people in other parts of the world, went to mondo movies for not only curiosity's sake but to reinforce their own ideas on ethnicity and find solace that many of their worst fears about other cultures were confirmed by what they saw on the screen.

Immigration wasn't the only factor in the mondo films' success in the '60s. Television also played a major role. Italy had lagged behind Western Europe in adopting television: it was the last major nation in Europe without a color TV system, and it only had two channels which, combined, broadcast only 11 hours of material each day. Regardless, Italians were as fascinated as the rest of Europe and the United States by stories from far-off lands being reported. As television began its ascension as a provider of news around the world, filmmakers who found themselves competing with the new medium sought to produce a product that people couldn't get on their TV screens. The answer for many was the mondo film, which served the public's imagination by offering up some of the most salacious aspects of international culture that even the most liberal of European televisions would not air.

Finally, and most importantly, mondo films were able to overcome some of the barriers of censorship that studio films couldn't. Under the guise of "educational" and "hard-core journalism," mondo could explore such themes as cannibalism, white slavery, animal killings and sexual rituals by showing that they were real and not a concoction of a filmmaker's imagination. This "accuracy" helped these films get by most countries' censorship boards, while religious boards often turned a blind eye to the salacious aspects of mondo if the films presented other religious groups in such a way as to make their own look superior. In areas of sexuality, Europe and the United States were both home to some serious censorship laws in the early '60s, as it was still illegal to show sexually graphic material in films. While mondo was not pornographic in terms of sex, it was able to give audiences something that would only be hinted at in mainstream films. This forbidden subject matter was, of course, eagerly accepted by worldwide audiences who came out in droves to see the nudity and forbidden sexual practices of other cultures.

Prior to the explosion of mondo films in the early '60s, Italians enjoyed a variety of documentaries that served to showcase some of the beautiful locales across the world. These films were benign by nature and meant for the entire family. Many of Italy's popular directors like Rossellini, who enjoyed popular success in 1958 with his documentary on India for Italian television, produced these glimpses into a world far removed from those things happening inside the country. The popularity of these "exotic documentaries" brought audiences into the theaters, and once public tastes changed, "exotic" mixed with "erotic" and the mondo film was born.[91] Though many mondo filmmakers eschewed the idea that they were creating exploitation films, these films clearly fit within the parameters. Even from their inception they were posited as sensationalist exposés involving sex, violence and drug-related subjects and often sacrificed notions of artistic merit for a more sensationalist, shocking approach. Often these films were about a topic in which a moviegoing audience had some interest—for example, prostitution, drugs or even historical movements like the Nazi Party or civil rights—and the Mondo allowed further exploration of these often taboo topics.[92] Though posited under the guise of being educational, films like *Mondo cane* (1962) and its sequels *Mondo cane 2* (1964), *Women of the World* (1963), and *Africa addio* (1964) served as true exploitation under the guise of documentary filmmaking. In order to be truly educational these films would have had to maintain a neutral tone and remain relatively free from bias. This was never accomplished: mondo films had little respect for the outside cultures they documented, which was mainly demonstrated in the moralizing audio commentary and the attention paid to the nudity and overt sexuality. As the '60s wore on, mondo films quickly lost what little educational appeal they had and became a strictly adults-only genre, exploiting their subjects for sensation.[93]

These films had lofty ambitions on the inception of the subgenre. Pioneers of the mondo film, Italian filmmakers Gualtiero Jacopetti, Paolo Cavara and Franco Prosperi, looked to bring a domestic perspective to the "weird and wonderful" customs of the global population.[94] Attempting to showcase both modern and tribal cultures around the world, Jacopetti believed that his love of both film and journalism contributed to his particular style in telling a story. He was also a modern filmmaker who was never comfortable working with established Italian filmmaking styles, as he related: "Italian neorealism never convinced me, quite frankly. As a documentarist, I saw neorealism as artificial. I was a professional journalist. What I realized, and it didn't take long, was that cinema provided me an immense wealth of photos, of frames, and at the same time a sound track to transfer my text into spoken words. I realized that this was the perfect medium to tell the facts of life."[95]

It is these "facts of life" that were both fascinating and shocking about Jacopetti's and Prosperi's films. Jacopetti had himself always been partial to adult material, beginning his career with documentaries about the adult European nightlife. The first of these, *Il mondo di notte* (*Nights of the World*, 1959), basically consisted of filming at the local strip clubs and local cabarets. For the film, Jacopetti was sent by producers around the world for what were in the '50s the most famous forms of adult entertainment, cancan and burlesque shows. Over time he became more interested in the social aspect of these environments, becoming fascinated by who went to these shows and how the performances affected local society more than he was by nudity or the sexuality of what was happening on stage. These first forays into the adult-themed mondo films were very reminiscent of the "nudie-cutie" and nudist films that were extremely popular in the United States in the late '50s and early '60s.[96] Both of these types of film, like the mondo, relied on the "reality" aspect of the subject matter to draw an audience and placate local censors.

Jacopetti's partner, Franco Prosperi, was a naturalist filmmaker with degrees in natural

Distributors tried to play up the "artistic" aspects of *Mondo cane* (1962) and play down the negative aspects of the cultures that the film exploits.

science, biology, and theology. He began shooting documentaries when he realized they would be more financially lucrative than shooting scientific films. In 1961 he teamed with Jacopetti to create their biggest hit and the catalyst for the subgenre, *Mondo cane*.[97] Translated as "A Dog's Life," *Mondo cane* was initially designed to show the different aspects of love (human, animal, etc.) around the world. Realizing that documentaries are usually flattering, over-polished affairs, Jacopetti wanted to try his hand at what he called an "anti-documentary," which would show the world in a real light. Looking at the film as a "very long newsreel," Jacopetti and Prosperi jetted around the world to showcase the oddities of human life. The film contains a variety of different socio-cultural rituals and taboos, some more shocking than others, including neutral subjects such as a happy bevy of buxom Aussie lifeguards, or a group of naked women using their bodies to paint a blue canvas, intermixed with more horrifying scenes of Chinese peasants eating cats and dogs in Hong Kong, cattle mutilation, and the "house of death" (a place where elderly are left to die) in Singapore.[98] This hodgepodge of stories allowed international audiences to sample from a "buffet" of alien, foreign cultures as well as experience a variety of different cultural taboos that they had never seen before.

Though lurid in subject matter, all of this was put together in the most professional way possible. There is no doubt as to Jacopetti and Prosperi's talent as filmmakers, as the film is a virtual rainbow of vibrant colors and amazing cinematography. What *Mondo cane* does, though, is basically reinforce every negative stereotype imaginable. Do you believe they eat cats in Asia? This film will happily confirm that fact. Aren't all the people in New Guinea savages? Of course; just look at the way they kill their livestock, let alone how they dress. Are all Germans drunk? Jacopetti and Prosperi gleefully and playfully portray the German people as alcoholics: their sojourn in Hamburg, during what must have been Oktoberfest, is filled with disturbing images of a population completely taken over by substance abuse. All of these scenes would be palatable as a snapshot of some of the unfortunate negatives of any particular society, but the completely inappropriate narration takes the film's xenophobia to uncomfortable levels. Much like a carnival sideshow barker, *Mondo cane* (1962) revels in the "gawk." With glee and an all-too-often leering attitude, the narration, regardless of the language it is presented in, encourages its audience not to empathize with its subjects but to ridicule, to laugh at them. The theme song, an optimistic instrumental titled "More," was so popular around the world that it received an Oscar nomination for best original song, and is played throughout the proceedings to add levity as well. It's hard to take religious flagellation as seriously if there is cute Top 40 pop number playing in the background.[99]

Jacopetti, Cavara and Prosperi were optimistic that the world's film critics would see this as an important work. Most didn't. Released in 1962, *Mondo cane* received a few smatterings of praise, notably Bosley Crowther with the *New York Times* and *Variety*, but most critics around the world called the film vulgar and pornographic. Composer Riz Ortolani responded to criticism: "The critics were not kind to them. They attacked them for many reasons, said they were porn directors because there were these black women showing their breasts. This made audiences from modern Western societies more eager to see the film, causing it to be a smash hit. The fact is we took advantage of the little knowledge the public had of the world at large back then."[100] Critical response aside, the film and its lurid subject matter was a top box-office hit around the world. At a time when Italian artists of screen (Sophia Loren et al.) and music (the song "Al di là" was high atop the pop charts in 1962, with versions by both Italian Emilio Pericoli and Italian-American Connie Francis) were having huge success in the United States and pushing the boundaries of what could be shown on theater screens, *Mondo cane* cashed in on the audience's thirst for the new and different.

The success of *Mondo cane* propelled its producers to create a sequel. With a plethora of unused material from the initial shoot, they decided to use it for *Mondo cane 2* (*Mondo pazzo*, 1964). "It was about commercial money," said Jacopetti in a 2003 interview. "I knew it was going to be old hat, a rehash, so I didn't have the same enthusiasm that I had with *Mondo cane*."[101] *Mondo cane 2* continued giving audiences the same wide array of "gawking" subjects, from Asian peasants eating burritos made of living ants, religious hysteria in Europe and cross-dressing policemen in the United States. One of the most shocking segments was the suicide of a monk in Saigon. Europeans and Americans had heard stories of monks setting themselves on fire in protest but had never actually seen it. *Mondo cane 2* provided the avenue to view such controversial material, but with one big caveat that audiences were not aware of: many of the scenes were faked. Beginning with this film, several of the events that Jacopetti and Prosperi showed were faked for maximum entertainment. From the moment they made the decision to supplement real events with faked ones, mondo film producers began to walk the line between true documentaries and faked reality-based entertainment, which is problematic since audiences at the time were completely unaware of the trickery. In the early '60s, television and magazines like *National Geographic* only opened up the public minds on international cultures to a small degree and had not prepared the general public intellectually to see these re-enactments for what they were. Mondo film producers happily recreated many exploitive events for maximum thrills, duping audiences into believing what they were seeing was real. Because the deception was never uncovered, they could continue to push the envelope in simulations, resulting in more outlandish acts of violence and sex that were more legend than actual fact. This ploy makes it difficult for modern scholars to examine the film from the standpoint that there's no way to ascertain which stunts are faked and which ones are genuine. Perhaps owing to the more theatrical narrative, *Mondo cane 2* (1963) was only a moderate success as compared to the original. Prosperi himself attributed this to the lack of originality. Though he argued that the elements that defined the genre had been used up already, he and Jacopetti were more than happy to continue the mondo trend on even more controversial subjects, as it was clear '60s audiences around the world would line up to see any new mondo movie that showed Buddhist monks set on fire or young Asian children eating a burrito made of raw ants.[102]

While filming some extra scenes for *Mondo cane 2* (1964), Prosperi and Jacopetti began work on *La donna nel mondo* (*Women of the World*, 1963). The collaboration between Prosperi, Jacopetti and feminist author Oriana Fallaci took an exploitative yet lighthearted look at women throughout societies around the world. Prostitutes in Hamburg, lesbians in Paris, and half-clad female natives from Africa were all put under the mondo spotlight. Though it could be argued that the film had a feminist voice ascribed to it, the results would make any modern-day feminist or gay rights activist blanch. From the opening credits, in which we get the view of a shapely woman's derrière as she walks through the airport intercut with a group of nuns, it's obvious this movie is for men with a decidedly male gaze, as the film is not interested in getting inside the psyches of these women but in seeing their faults. While the practice of placing female Israelis in combat may have been new to worldwide

Opposite: After the success of ***Mondo cane*** (1962), producers were more apt to highlight the exploitive aspects of their marketing approaches.

UNBELIEVABLE! INCREDIBLE!
—YET EVERY LIVING SCENE IS REAL!

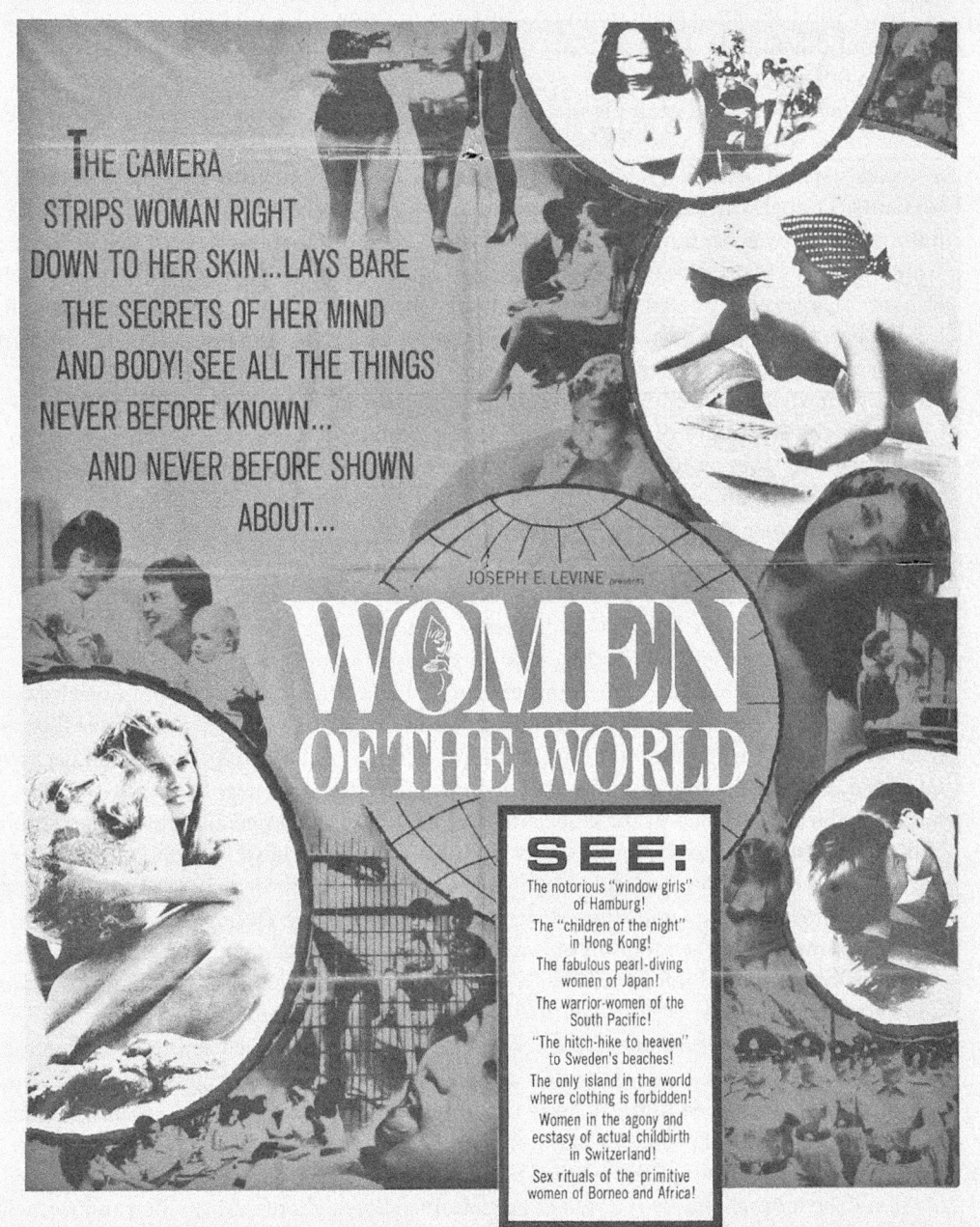

The camera strips woman right down to her skin...lays bare the secrets of her mind and body! See all the things never before known... and never before shown about...

JOSEPH E. LEVINE presents

WOMEN OF THE WORLD

SEE:

The notorious "window girls" of Hamburg!

The "children of the night" in Hong Kong!

The fabulous pearl-diving women of Japan!

The warrior-women of the South Pacific!

"The hitch-hike to heaven" to Sweden's beaches!

The only island in the world where clothing is forbidden!

Women in the agony and ecstasy of actual childbirth in Switzerland!

Sex rituals of the primitive women of Borneo and Africa!

TECHNICOLOR® As viewed by PETER USTINOV Directed by GUALTIERO JACOPETTI and (in alphabetical order) by PAOLO CAVARA • FRANCO PROSPERI
Photography by ANTONIO CLIMATI and BENITO FRATTARI • Produced by Cineriz • An Embassy Pictures Release

audiences in 1963, it is not taken seriously in *La donna*, which takes care to mock them with a condescending male narration (in some English prints the narration is performed by Academy Award winner Peter Ustinov!). Since this is a mondo film, special attention is made to show them changing their clothes in their tents. Add to the mix African bigamy, worldwide birthing practices, archaic plastic surgery techniques and a variety of half-nude girls and you have an exploitation film that does nothing but proliferate stereotypes. The women of this mondo world are only meant to be looked at and the audience (males) is made to feel superior to them.

La donna is a good example of a mondo film in which the soundtrack that a viewer listens to gives clues to a particular society's bias. Being a film about "womanhood" with a strong focus on sexuality, it's no surprise that the film happily turns its camera to homosexuality. Though still considered a criminal activity on mainland Europe in the early '60s, homosexuality was beginning to creep toward acceptance far more than in Britain or the United States. This is demonstrated in the film by the particularly offensive way in which lesbians and gays are treated in the English dub. Focusing on a seemingly normal Parisian lesbian bar, the English narrator condescendingly ridicules the more masculinized women and comments about the "underlying sadness" of their lifestyle. As if to offer a complementary viewpoint, the film then jumps to a gay bar, and, because this is exploitation, highlights an assortment of feminized men who would make Liberace blush. Our homophobic narrator goes on to say that it is because of a lack of female company that these guys overcompensate their own femininity. As the narrator says, "Woman is always present in the hermit, eunuch and the chaste and more than ever ... [in the most bitter of tones] ... THEM!" The shot then moves to a closeup of a young homosexual. The Italian dub completely eschews most of the anti-gay rhetoric, instead focusing on the amusing dynamic of the groups. There is no "underlying sadness," and while the "hermit" quote is used, the Italian version stops before including homosexual men in the category.

By 1964, mondo films were being produced with large frequency from a variety of countries around the world. All of these films followed the same documentary-style format with worldwide settings not found in traditional fictionalized films. As the market became saturated, budgets for mondo films dropped. Any film producer now could take a camera out to the farthest reaches of the globe and film anything he wanted and put the narration of his choice to entertain the audience. By the mid–'60s, the pretense of mondo films' offering anything educational had faded with films, like *Mondo Bizarro* (1966), *Mondo Teeno* (*Teenage Rebellion*, 1967) and Russ Meyer's *Mondo Topless* (1967), only interested in titillation, helping secure the mondo film's reputation as a sleazy genre.

This branding did not sit well with Jacopetti, who believed that the original *Mondo Cane* was a piece of art: "People confused *Mondo Cane* with all that ugly, vulgar junk."[103] Following *La donna nel mondo* (1963), Prosperi and Jacopetti looked to inject the mondo with more substance, and spent the next couple of years filming the highly political *Africa addio* (1966). *Africa* tried to break away from standard mondo format and focus on some of the pressing political problems that were occurring in Africa at the time. Gaining inspiration from a friend whose letter warned of the changes going on in Africa, Jacopetti wanted the film to be journalistically relevant as he examined the plight of African men and women who were caught in the post-colonial power grab of the '60s.[104] Showcasing (in the explicit style of mondo films) the brutality of burgeoning political dictatorships in Africa as the British government returned their colonies back to home rule, the filmmakers spent three years getting all the controversial footage that they needed. The beatings, animal killings,

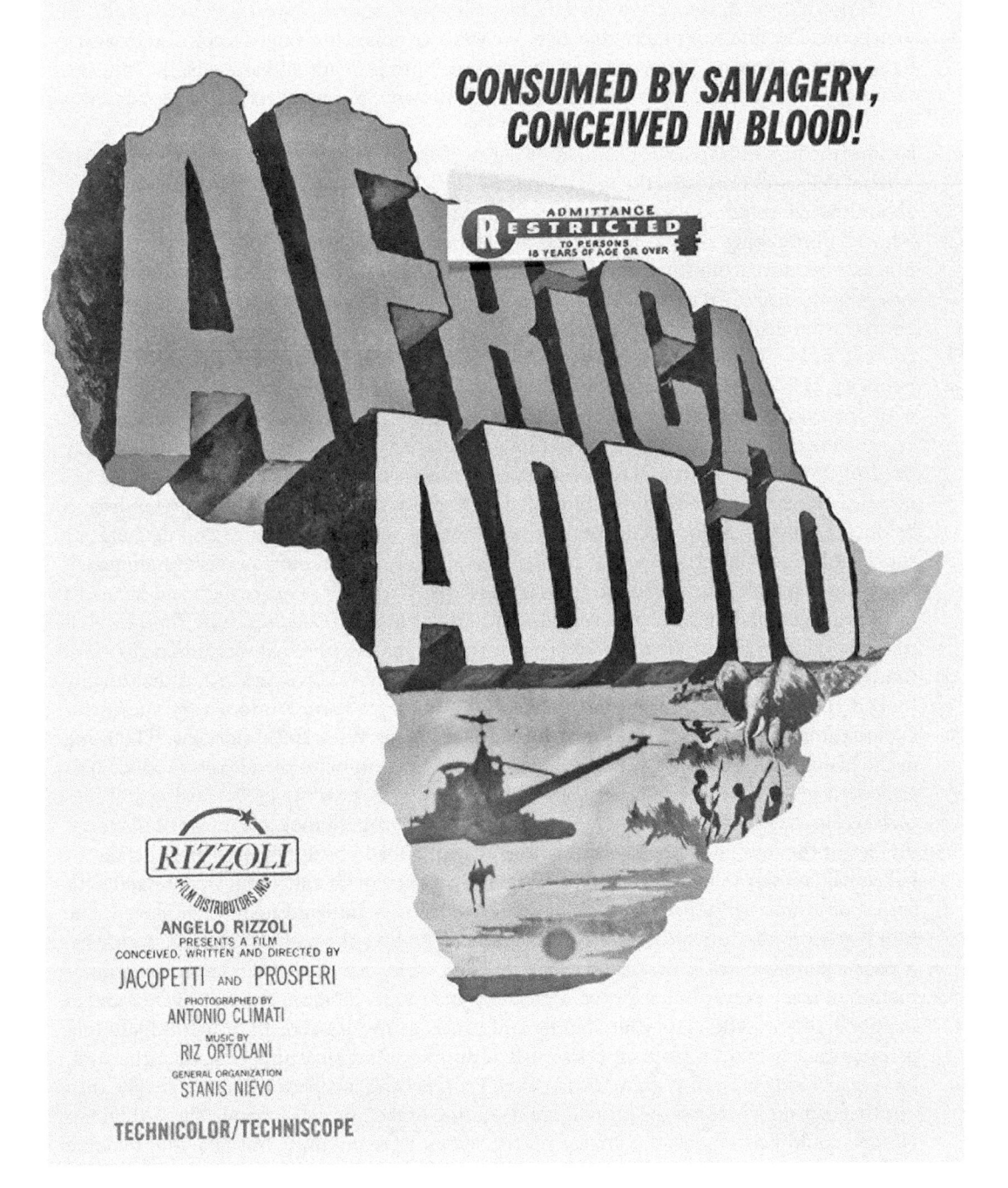

Africa addio (1966) was an attempt to infuse a more political ideology into the mondo subgenre.

rape and mass murder, including scenes of tremendous brutality that one would expect in a mondo film, were all included, adding to the controversial subject matter of the film. Again, though, the producers' proclivities for staging or faking events came under scrutiny. Naturally many who saw the film wondered whether Prosperi and Jacopetti had a natural bias. Both filmmakers were pro-colonialist and were against Britain's leaving the Africans to their own devices. Jacopetti denied the bias allegation, stating, "We didn't have a political viewpoint. The film was totally objective. We were witnesses to a tragedy, political meaning left aside."[105] Showing gruesome violence towards both humans and animals, the film was met with a storm of controversy wherever it was shown. So controversial and negative was Jacopetti's and Prosperi's condemnation of the events in Africa that the motion picture became the first film to have a complaint registered against it at the United Nations as five African delegates protested the movie's release. U.S. critical reaction to the film was favorable, although some critics (the *New York Times*, for example) saw Jacopetti's and Prosperi's "shock" filmmaking style as a "reckless and dangerous."[106] The political outcry from the film and pressure from some governmental agencies around the world to suppress the true extent of the upheaval in Africa caused the film to undergo extensive editing or be pulled entirely from distribution. In the United States the film was shorn of 45 minutes of political content and re-released as *Africa Blood and Guts* in 1970.[107] In typical exploitation-style publicity, U.S. distributor Jerry Gross hired out-of-work black actors and outfitted them with grass skirts and spears, stationing them in the lobbies of some New York theaters![108]

By the end of the '60s, the mondo film's popularity waned as movie audiences quickly tired of the subject matter. The loosening of censorship around the world allowed for fictional recreations of cultures in films that were allowed to exploit without pretending to be documentaries. Mondo films became synonymous with tacky, bizarre and deliberately shocking forms of entertainment that catered to an ever smaller, more perverse audience.[109] The relative un-interest in Mondo films in the early '70s didn't stop Prosperi and Jacopetti from producing their most controversial work, *Addio zio Tom* (*Goodbye Uncle Tom*) in 1971. After the controversy of *Africa addio*, the pair tried to make a film that was anti-racist. "We thought why don't we do *Mandingo* [the infamous 1957 novel by Kyle Onstatt that luridly looked at slavery in the antebellum South and was later turned into a very successful exploitation film in 1975] as a documentary?" said Prosperi in a 2003 interview.[110] Looking at the history of slavery in America, the producers came up with the idea to produce it as a modern news-style documentary but with an audience from the 1800s! Fusing real historical characters with slavery literature, Prosperi and Jacopetti took advantage of the racial divides of the '60s and '70s to create a film that offended absolutely everyone. Scenes of naked men on slave ships forced to live in their own excrement and vomit were mixed with scenes of idiotic white people relishing the violence they inflicted upon their slaves. The film is so over-the-top and exploitive, it is difficult to take the political message seriously. A good example of this is the final scene of the film, which may have been meant as an affirmation of black power but achieved high camp instead. A modern-day Nat Turner enters the home of a middle-class white family and proceeds to massacre all of them, including picking up a baby in a playpen (obviously a dummy) and smashing it against the wall, leaving a bloody mess.[111] With *Addio zio Tom*, Prosperi and Jacopetti went too far. The thin line that had audiences buying into the reality nature of the films was completely obliterated. No one could believe that the images on the screen were anything but fake due to some really bad acting, bad makeup effects and completely over-the-top narratives that were devoid of subtlety. The film only works as an example of cinematic karmic justice: the U.S.

film industry had traditionally exploited other cultures in their films, so here was an example of someone doing the same to them. Years after its premiere Prosperi himself realized the extreme nature of the film: "As for the film, it is difficult to watch, understandably so. Perhaps we went too far. It's our own fault."[112]

Though the mondo film faded from the theatrical landscape in the '70s, it experienced a renaissance of sorts in the early '80s via videotape. Films like *Faces of Death* (1978) and its many sequels, as well as titles like *Ultime grida dalla savana* (*Savage Man, Savage Beast*, 1975), all followed the template that Jacopetti and Prosperi created. The mondo film had two lasting effects on Eurocult as well as on global media in general. First, the subgenre morphed itself into the cannibal film (see the cannibal and zombie film chapter) in the early '70s, which fictionalized the narrative but retained its xenophobic and violent nature. Secondly and just as important, the lingering influence of the mondo film is evident in the plethora of today's shock television documentaries and reality shows. Some mondo scholars like Mark Goodall maintain that "fans of sleazy, mindless movies" like the mondo have moved on to other forms of visual entertainment. Looking at such programming as *When Animals Attack!* (FOX), *Anthony Bourdain No Reservations* (Travel), *Real Alien Autopsy* (FOX), *Big Brother* (any edition), *Fear Factor* (NBC), *Survivor* (CBS), or even *Flavor of Love* (VH-1) and *Real Housewives of* "wherever" (Bravo), it is easy to see the connection of the mondo film to this type of entertainment. Each program shows people doing things within an unfamiliar cultural setting. Audiences are riveted, entertained and often mildly disgusted by these programs' content, sharing the same feelings that they got from mondo films of the past. As the world becomes ever smaller due to globalization, as audiences continue to work out their biases, distrust and xenophobia, and as long as the proliferation of global media structures have the channels in which to broadcast, there will always be some form of the mondo film to "gawk" at.

Filmography

Africa addio, aka *Africa, Blood and Guts* (U.S.). Prod. Angelo Rizzoli. Dir. Gualtiero Jacopetti and Franco Prosperi. Italy, 1966. Blue Underground, 128 min. DVD documentary.

Wow, I hate Mondo films. There, I said it. No other subgenre fills me with such revulsion. Maybe it's my mass communication education or my master's in international studies, maybe it's because I'm so sick of watching reality television and pseudo-documentaries that take prefabricated situations and pass them off as legitimate with a majority of audiences believing what they see. Don't know, but I do know whenever I see one I usually feel manipulated right from the first frame. *Addio* doesn't make me feel better. The subject matter behind the film is an important one as it looks at the problems within Africa in the '60s as the last vestiges of British colonialism retreat and new governments take over. Jacopetti and Prosperi, who are talented filmmakers, take a decidedly pro-colonialism stance, which results in a complete skewering of events. Consequently, we're treated to hangings, shootings, rapes, and other extreme atrocities that portray the chaos in Africa as a result of the British leaving. Just to drive home the filmmakers' point about Africa's being savage, we're also treated to some obnoxious footage of animal slaughter. Though our intrepid filmmakers supposedly spent a good deal of time making the film (obviously setting up some of the fabricated scenes), there is still a lot of stock footage used to back up their biased claims. Two versions exist on DVD, the theatrical and longer directors' cut. It's completely up to you to decide how much torture you want to bear.

Goodbye Uncle Tom, aka *Addio zio Tom*. Prod. and Dir. Gualtiero Jacopetti and Franco Prosperi. Italy, 1971. Blue Underground, 123 min. DVD. Pseudo-documentary.

Disgusting, repellent, obscene, unethical: these are the words that Eurocult fans look for when selecting that perfect movie to watch. Within the context of a fictional narrative they can actually be positive qualities, but in the case of pseudo-documentaries like *Africa addio* they actually work in the negative. Lucky for us, *Goodbye Uncle Tom* is SO over-the-top, SO outrageous and completely politically incorrect that it's hard to take any of it seriously, except to ponder how screwed up it is. This film is probably at the nadir of the mondo canon (and that's saying something), but it's nevertheless fascinating in how willing it is to shock us. A "recreation" of the history of American intolerance is given the ultimate in exploitation treatment here as we see feces-covered and diseased (of course naked as well) slaves being transported to America, where they are sold by very bad actors with very bad Southern accents to plantations. From there we have the usual sex-slave scenes and torture followed by a doctor telling us it's okay to make slaves out of blacks because "they don't have feelings." The film ends with a modern-day black man throwing a white baby against the wall. Makes *Mandingo* (1975) look like *Roots* (1978)! If you've already decided to watch this, then why not go all the way and view the longer uncut version?

Mondo cane. Prod. and Dir. Paolo Carvara. Italy, 1962. Blue Underground, 105 min. DVD. Documentary.

Well, folks, here it is: the internationally successful film that started the mondo craze (and provided the fodder for the cannibal movie), as well as spawning our modern-day fascination with perverse pseudo-documentaries and reality television. Actually, it's a great-looking film that's colorful and in many respects fun. And with the Oscar-nominated theme song blaring out at 1-minute intervals, *Mondo cane* does indeed make for a great time capsule of the early '60s. Of course, for all the protests to the contrary, this is still a masterfully made exploitation film that looks to exploit the international cultures it purports to love. So prepare yourself for some drunken Germans, dog-eating Chinese, buxom Australians, gored bullfighting Spaniards, and a host of other stereotypes that will make you glad to be who you are. The tamest of all the mondo films, this is probably the film you go to if you want an introduction into the subgenre.

Mondo cane 2. Prod. Mario Maffei and Giorgio Cecchini. Dir. Gualtiero Jacopetti and Franco Prosperi. Italy, 1964. Blue Underground, 95 min. DVD. Pseudo-documentary.

Jacopetti and Prosperi's sequel to the amazingly popular *Mondo cane* (many of the sequences of the sequel are unused portions from the first film) carries on the tradition of reinforcing stereotypes, though it likes to think its aim is higher. Actually the film is a bit of a letdown from the previous entry as the dearth of good stories becomes apparent. Obviously the filmmakers understood that this subgenre had a short shelf life and looked to inject a little more drama by "staging" some of the action. So now, instead of cute little vignettes about dog-eating Chinese and overfeminized homosexuals, we are treated to monks setting themselves on fire (fake) as well other atrocities in order to dupe the audience into thinking that this is reality. After this film, Prosperi and Jacopetti brought us the "serious" *Africa addio* (1966), which really plumbed the bottom of the subgenre.

Women of the World, aka *La donna nel mondo*. Prod. and Dir. Gualtiero Jacopetti, Franco Prosperi and Paola Cavara. Italy, 1963. Blue Underground, 108 min. DVD. Documentary.

Finally, a mondo film with a feminist perspective in mind! Yeah, right. With the help of feminist writer Oriana Fallaci, Cavara, Jacopetti and Prosperi create yet another highly exploitative piece of work that stereotypes women in just as negative a light as their previous mondo films depicted foreign cultures. Looking at the customs of women around the world, the film is a colorful travelogue (the filmmakers really do know how to make an attractive film) focusing on such gender-empowering subjects as topless sunbathing, prostitution and nightclub singing. It would be more believable if we had concentrated more on the gun-toting female Israeli soldiers marching instead of watching them changing their clothes. At least this one doesn't have nuns setting themselves on fire. A male-gaze dream!

The Color of Fear: The Italian Giallo

> Horror by nature is the emotion of pure revelation. Terror by the same standards is that of fearful anticipation.
> —Italian director Dario Argento[113]

Arriving at the same time as the mondo film, the filmed version of the popular giallo murder mysteries from Italy began its ascent into the imagination of audiences around the world. While the mondo film focused on a "real" way of life via a documentary-style film, the giallo was a purely fictional concoction whose success was connected to the rising wave of violence that was sweeping throughout Italy in the late '60s and early '70s. These films, like the lurid murder mystery books that preceded them, focused on the unseemly in modern Italian society. Resonant with some of the social issues that were occurring in religion, family structures and changing sexual mores, the giallo enjoyed phenomenal success around the world, with more than 250 gialli produced in a 20-year period. The subgenre was also the forefather of the American "slasher" film with movies like *Halloween* (1978), *Friday the 13th* (1980), *Prom Night* (1981) and *Dressed to Kill* (1980), all carrying over elements that were derivative of the giallo. Murder, gore and kinky sexual betrayal are the underlying themes, mixed within an intricate story plot that would give most mystery fans whiplash. While some scholars (Koven) can give pinpoint analysis of the subgenre, for our purposes here just think Agatha Christie with leather gloves and a very sharp razor, or maybe a "slasher" film with a plot, and you have the basis for a subgenre that still retains its popularity with both Eurocult fans and audiences worldwide.[114]

When the Italian publishing company Mondadori published their first giallo *La strana morte del signor Benson* (*The Strange Death of Mr. Benson*) in 1929, little did they know that it would be the starting point for a genre that would last in popularity for over 70 years.[115] Distinguished by their yellow covers (*giallo* means yellow in Italian), these small paperbacks began as Italian translations of popular mysteries by the likes of Edgar Wallace and Agatha Christie. Before long Italian authors began to develop their own narratives that copied liberally from both the Sherlock Holmes and Edgar Allan Poe styles of storytelling, and within the narratives contained lurid descriptions of violence and sexuality under the guise of a complex murder mystery.[116] A giallo film usually involves an assailant who preys on beautiful, sexualized women. The killer, of undistinguishable gender, would only be seen in quick shots wearing black clothing (usually leather) and gloves, and would use sharp butcher knives, razors, ropes and other innovative tools instead of the usual guns to murder their victims, which often highlighted the sadism that was the cornerstone to these films. If violence was the cornerstone, then sexuality and deceit were the foundation, as perverse forms of sexuality often led to blackmail, neurosis, extramarital affairs and murder. Women in these films were complete sexual objects and they often paid for their trespasses. Homosexuality, or fear of it, was often highlighted, as were dysfunctional families whose emotional abuse often adversely affected the protagonist. Many of the titles of gialli were as convoluted as the plots with producers rushing to compete with each other for the most outlandish titles. Due to the success of Italian Dario Argento's "animal" trilogy, most took on a bizarre animal motif in their titles. So in the early '70s it was not uncommon to see films with animal titles like, *L'iguana dalla lingua di fuoco* (*The Iguana with the Tongue of Fire*, 1971), *Quattro mosche di velluto grigio* (*Four Flies on Grey Velvet*, 1972), *Una lucertola con la pelle di donna* (*Lizard in a Woman's Skin*, 1971), and *La coda dello scorpione* (*The Case of the Scor-*

pion's Tail, 1971). Outside the animal realm were such long-winded titles as *Le foto proibite di una signora per bene* (*Forbidden Photos of a Lady Above Suspicion*, 1970) or the tongue-twisting *Il tuo vizio è una stanza chiusa e solo io ne ho la chiave* (*Your Vice Is a Locked Room and Only I Have the Key*, 1972). These titles often reinforced an unsure perspective of reality that was present within the films, which often contained nightmare and dream sequences within the story to highlight the fantasy and horror aspects and gave viewers the distorted perspective on reality that the titles convey.[117]

Early gialli novels were the equivalent of U.S. pulp fiction and enjoyed immense popularity in Italy from the '30s through the '50s. They were never meant to be taken as high art but as an entertaining pleasure. Their allure was that they focused on subjects that were resonant with the Italian working class, who were the main audience for the books. By the late '50s television and newspapers played a major role in aiding the popularity of the subgenre as crime rose and the subsequent reporting became more prolific, with such issues such as incest, adultery, pedophilia and rape gaining more exposure and entering the public sphere. By the late '60s, the Italian population was reading about these issues in newspapers and watching them every day on television. The giallo was just another way to process the chaos that seemed to be going on outside in the world beyond their doors.

Jumping from print to film proved difficult for the giallo. Mussolini was no fan and the Italian Fascist government saw the giallo as a corrupting influence promoting the worst kinds of criminal behavior. Not wishing to incur the wrath of the government, most filmmakers shied away from the subgenre. After Mussolini's death the subgenre was considered unfilmable based on lurid subject matter as sex and sexualized violence were only hinted at in movies due to censorship and the profound influence of the Catholic Church. The exploitative devices that most readers found enjoyable in a giallo would be rendered muted had filmmakers attempted to recreate the narratives from the paperbacks.

By the early '60s things began to change. Filmmakers began to push the boundaries of censorship with their portrayals of sexual violence. Alfred Hitchcock enjoyed tremendous worldwide success in the late '50s exposing audiences to deceit and perverted, sexualized murder in such films as *Rear Window* (1954) and *Vertigo* (1958). *Psycho* (1960), certainly giallo-esque, pushed the envelope just a little more with its graphic shower murder of Janet Leigh and the confused sexual hang-ups of Anthony Perkins. By 1962, with loosening censorship and a general public predisposed to love the material, the giallo was ready to slice its way through a worldwide audience.

Fresh from his success with *La maschera del demonio* (*Black Sunday*) in 1960, Italian auteur Mario Bava began to examine the genre in which he had the most success. Though a lover of classic Russian literature, Bava used his time after *La maschera* to discover the more pop-culture mystery and horror stories that were in Mondadori's catalogue. In 1962, he wrote and directed what many around the world consider the first giallo, *La ragazza che sapeva troppo* (*The Girl Who Knew Too Much*). A black and white parody of sorts of the popular films of Alfred Hitchcock, even mirroring the name of the Hitchcock film *The Man Who Knew Too Much* (1956) *La ragazza* tells the story of a young American tourist Nora Davis (Letícia Román), who becomes embroiled in a violent murder mystery. Arriving in Rome to visit an ailing aunt, Nora's first day in Italy sees her given drugs at the airport, her aunt dying, and her witnessing of a brutal murder that lands her in the hospital. With the help of young Dr. Bassi (American actor John Saxon), Nora slowly figures out the mystery of what she experienced, but not before her life is again placed in danger. The film has all the classical plot devices of a typical giallo with its shadowy, atmospheric visuals, confusing red herrings, a beautiful young woman brought to the edge of insanity by situations she does not understand, drug use (omitted in the U.S. prints[118]), and more attention paid to lurid violence than your standard Hollywood fare, thus setting up all the elements that would play out for the rest of the genre.[119]

Not the first crime drama from Italy by any means, *La ragazza* was greeted by many around the world, especially the French, as something new and innovative. Film critics at the time commented that the film comes across as Hitchcock "all'italiana."[120] Author Gary Needham believes that this "Italian-ness," which is at the heart of most gialli, is representative of Italy selling itself to the rest of the world. This is a good argument, as the standard giallo usually posits the main character as a foreigner coming to Italy to experience some form of Italian culture, whether it be business or pleasure. The obsession with travel and tourism all marked a newly emerging European jet set, with Italy, a country rich in style and fashion and historic sites, rivaling France in the world's social market.[121] All of the elements that were associated with Italy are found in *La ragazza*. From its hip Italian theme song, "Fiore," to famous Roman landmarks such Piazza de Spagna, the film could be a travelogue for all things Italian. Of course the dichotomy is that all the beauty in Italy is mirrored by its violence, and as the '60s and '70s continued, the violence of the giallo became more graphic and the dichotomy more clearly exposed. The irony of the giallo is that gives worldwide audiences dueling impressions of the country. On the one hand these films say "Come visit'" on the other, "Bring your razor ... you're going to need it!"

Surprisingly for all the self-assurance Bava shows in *La ragazza*, he was not enthused about making the film. Confessing to Italian director Luigi Cozzi, Bava remarked, "I didn't feel like directing, but I needed the money, so I did it. It was supposed to be a romantic thriller, but the very idea seemed absurd to me. Such a thing might have worked with Kim Novak and James Stewart, but I had ... never mind — I don't remember who they were! I started filming seriously, though, as if it were a truly macabre story and somehow it worked out. It was actually somewhat successful."[122]

The "somewhat successful" *La ragazza* set up the giallo template. After that film, Bava reinvented the giallo in color for the first story of his 1963 film *I tre volti della paura* (*Black Sabbath*). Dealing specifically with overt and hidden sexuality, the story moved beyond the cute trappings of *La ragazza* and provided the sexual angle the genre employed for the next two decades. In the first story, *Il telefono* (*The Telephone*), Michèle Mercier plays Rosy, a fashionable young woman with a questionable past, who is terrorized by phone calls made to her apartment. Believing they are coming from her incarcerated former lover, she calls a female friend Mary (Lidia Alfonsi) over to comfort her. It is soon apparent Mary is a jealous, predatory lesbian who had an affair with Rosy and is the source of (most) of the obscene phone calls. Unfortunately for Mary, Rosy's boyfriend did escape from jail and looks to settle an old debt with all involved.

Bava's first color foray into the giallo is everything you come to expect from the genre. Sexy, leering, and tense, the story utilizes every trick in the giallo handbook to expose beautiful people not acting so beautiful. The only three characters in story are a beautiful bisexual ex-prostitute (maybe?), a predatory masculine lesbian and a murderous criminal, typical for the subgenre. In fact, it is the various subversive sexual narratives that are the focal point. Mercier is lovingly exploited throughout the story. She spends most of the story draped in a towel or her sexy negligee, as Bava uses his camera to showcase a sexualized, seemingly independent woman being driven over the brink by the two people who love her. The lesbian aspect of the story is fairly typical of the time period, with Mary being portrayed

One of the first films in the giallo subgenre, *La ragazza che sapeva troppo* (*The Girl Who Knew Too Much*, 1962).

as too hard, overcome by her jealousy of Rosy, to be sympathetic. Certainly there can be no reconciliation and her death at the hands of Rosy's boyfriend is played out obviously as the only fitting end of such a clandestine relationship.[123]

All of the sexuality, drug use and violent murder in both *La ragazza* and *I tre volti* were too much for censors around the world. Even with the tongue-in-cheek narrative of *La ragazza* many of the unsavory aspects were cut for the American print. American International Pictures (AIP, who had distributed *La maschera* as *Black Sunday* the year before) had held the picture back a year and made some major edits that changed the complexity of the film. Released under the name *The Evil Eye*, the film was entirely rescored by Les Baxter, the name of the main character was changed, the drug use was eliminated, and most importantly, the comic, romantic aspects of the movie were reinstated from scenes left on the cutting room floor. It's ironic that the romantic aspect that Bava had thought so "absurd" would be the main plot point of the American version. *I tre volti* received just as much tinkering from both U.S. and international censors. Most of the lesbian subplot had to go for AIP (who joined forces with Galatea and Emmepi Film of Rome in Italy and Societé Cinématographique Lyre of Paris to produce the film), who feared that the American audience, especially the teen market, would be stunned or perhaps not understand such subject matter. Exercising their right to edit the story, AIP producers succeeded in taking out all hints of the lesbian relationship, re-dubbing the dialogue to make Rosy and Mary friends as opposed to lovers. The crime aspect of the film, essential to all gialli, was also changed to incorporate a more supernatural element, with Rosy's criminal ex-lover Frank (Milo Quesada) not an escapee from prison, but a ghost coming back for a little (or in this case a lot of) revenge![124] The changes in these two films again point up how pliable Eurocult films were, completely mix-and-matchable to whatever culture they where shown in. Simple changes to the soundtrack along with some added footage, in some cases not filmed by the original director, could change the entire dynamic of a piece. In most cases, and Bava was definitely one, these changes meant little to the directors themselves. Most looked at the subgenre as only a job. If a film was a financial success in another country with different footage, great: it could be the springboard for more work in Italy, or, as in the case of Bava, the offer to work in the United States, which would bring in more money and prestige.

By 1963, the filmed giallo had a received tongue-in-cheek, albeit stylish, adaptation in Mario Bava's *La ragazza* as well as a short story in *I tre volti*. For his next foray into the subgenre Bava would exploit both the full use of color photography and the increasing acceptance of graphic violence in film. He went for the throat and the resulting film, *Sei donne per l'assassino* (*Blood and Black Lace*, 1964) is considered on the finest examples of the genre and one of the most violent. Commencing filming the day of JFK's assassination (November 22, 1963), *Sei donne*'s violent, sexually exploitive material foreshadows the extensive changes about to take place in world cinema.[125] The plot of *Sei donne* amps up the sadism and ties in one of the most resonant themes of most gialli: making the rich and beautiful suffer, violently. Bava was never particularly fond of the upper class in his films and here posits a particularly brutal, faceless (due to a pantyhose mask), leather-clad assailant stalking and murdering beautiful models right before the introduction of the fall line of an oh-so-posh haute couture fashion house. Utilizing some extraordinary techniques such as branding victims with a hot iron, drowning, and good old-fashioned strangulation, the assailant runs through the entire cast of models and business associates of Christiana's (Eva Bartok) in search of a diary that contains scandalous information about everyone. Bava fills his first full-length giallo with an assortment of sordid characters. There's Frank

Look deep into "THE EVIL EYE" to the twilight world of the Supernatural!

AMERICAN INTERNATIONAL
presents

JOHN SAXON
AND **LETICIA ROMAN**
STARRING IN

THE EVIL EYE

What does it want...what will satisfy its cravings??
...only the dead know
and those they choose to tell!

WITH **VALENTINA CORTESA** — Directed by MARIO BAVA · A GALATEA-CORONET PRODUCTION

(American Dante Di Paolo), the cocaine-addicted antiques dealer, whose gigolo talents have him pursued by two enabling models, Isabella (Francesca Ungarno) and Nicole (Adrana Gorini); beautiful model Peggy (American Mary Arden) who likes to keep the fact that she had an abortion secret; epileptic drug addict Mark (Massimo Righi), who not-so-secretly loves Peggy; and Max (Cameron Mitchell), whose business practices are unethical, to say the least. As with many gialli, there are very few sympathetic characters to root for. Consequently, Bava happily subjects the entire cast to some pretty intense sadism before dispatching each in death scenes that are shocking even for today's modern audiences. It is very easy with *Sei donne* to see where the inspiration for slasher films originated as the faceless stalker hunts down and kills the pretty models using a variety of weapons. The fact that Bava was filming in Technicolor also gave the violence a very real effect. Bava uses the camera to literally put the audience in the action to witness the violence first hand. The customary camera, instead of pulling away during the violent acts as was customary, lingers graphically with each death.

There are many who accuse the giallo of being completely misogynistic. Well ... it is. It's an exploitation subgenre and by nature will bring in elements that are designed to shock and titillate. giallo, once it moved past its recreation of Agatha Christie–type stories, was always posited as male fantasy entertainment and its representation on film amped up that aspect. An argument can be made that it was Bava who cemented this portrayal of misogyny in the subgenre, but that may be an easy answer to a complex issue. There is no doubt that it is the women of *Sei donne*, with their perfectly coiffed early–'60s beehive hairdos and couture, who are brutalized the most, and Bava sets up this construct from the opening kill. He seems to relish making each model suffer a completely different graphic death. Isabella's death in the first 10 minutes of the film is a good example. Exquisitely filmed in shadow with only a spotlight to show off her red rain jacket, she is hunted down by her masked assailant. Just when we think she's safe, the killer jumps out and strangles her for a full 10 seconds. The camera never cuts away during the attack as Isabella violently shakes and tries to ward off her attacker. Victorious, the assailant then drags her body slowly across the grass. Even more ghastly, the death of Peggy by burning her face off with a hot furnace showcased that filmed gialli could now gave a visual image to the misogyny of the novels, leaving no room for argument about its viewpoint. But putting the blame on Bava for the savagery is problematic. Everyone in Bava's gialli is corrupt. Not only women, but men and an occasional child are also made to suffer because of their own absence of morality. Bava makes no distinction between the sexes. The problem lies in the portrayal. Italian men were not apt to objectify their own gender with anything that was close to leering. Sure, they may have had their problems—money issues, drug addiction, etc.—but they were still shown often as virile men who could seduce the most glamorous of women regardless of these problems. Women, on the other hand, were co-modified. They were meant to be representative of their role in Italian society, and that was to be beautiful, alluring, and sexual without overdoing it. What Bava showed in *Sei donne* and with future gialli such as *Ecologia del delitto* (*Bay of Blood*, 1972) was that society itself was damaged and that evil people, regardless of gender, would get exactly what they deserved. Giallo filmmakers of late '60s and early '70s, and especially slasher producers, dropped these thought-provoking concepts in favor of something that was even more exploitative and violent. Without the intellectu-

Opposite: American International Pictures wasn't sure what to do with *La ragazza*, so they marketed the film with a distinctly American perspective, changing many aspects of the original film.

A FASHION HOUSE OF GLAMOROUS MODELS... BECOMES A TERROR HOUSE OF BLOOD!!

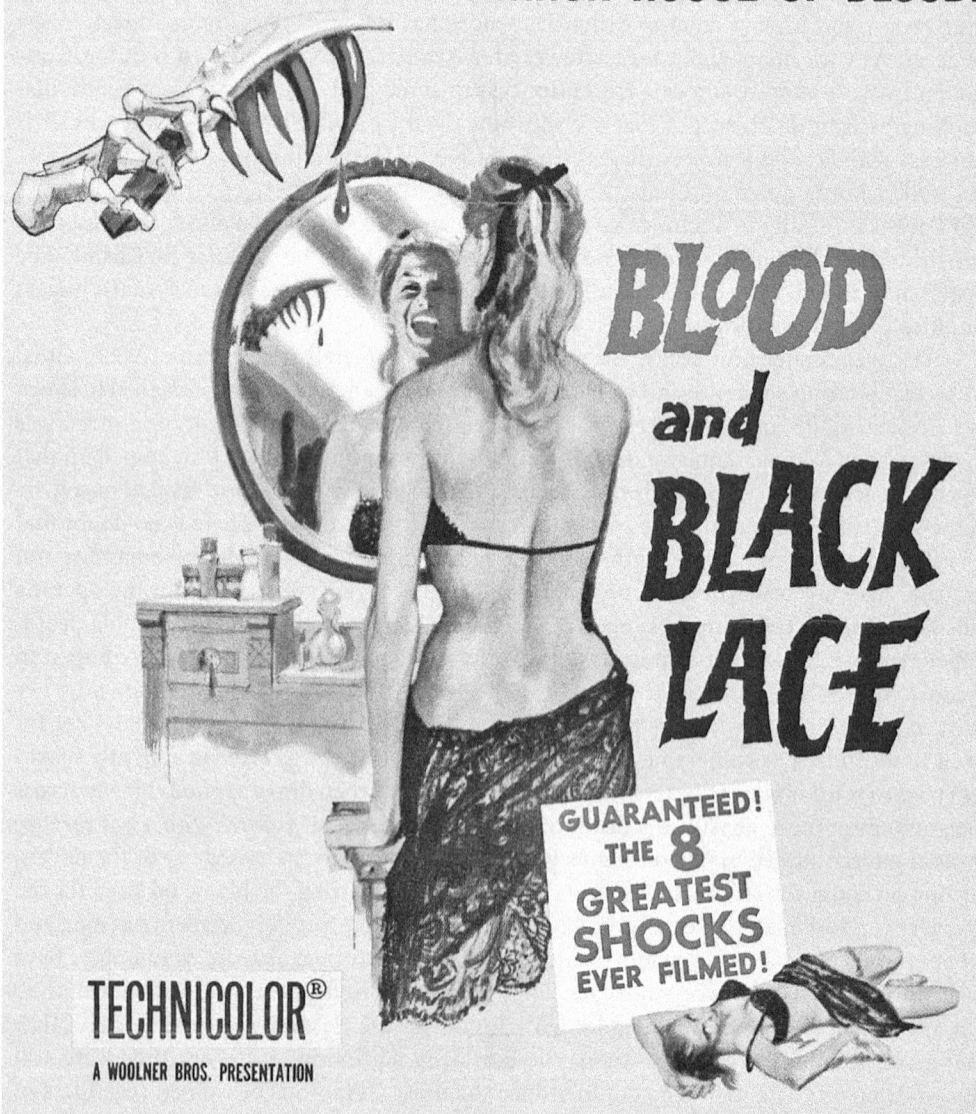

BLOOD and BLACK LACE

GUARANTEED! THE 8 GREATEST SHOCKS EVER FILMED!

TECHNICOLOR®

A WOOLNER BROS. PRESENTATION

starring CAMERON MITCHELL · EVA BARTOK AND THE 30 MOST GLAMOROUS GIRLS IN THE WORLD!

Produced by Alfred Mirabel · Directed by MARIO BAVA

Opposite: Though preceded by *La ragazza* two years prior, *Sei donne per l'assassino* (*Blood and Black Lace*, 1964) is considered the classic giallo that sets up the template for the next two decades. *Above:* Ironically, the U.S. poster for *Sei donne per l'assassino* (1964) mirrors the Italian books from which the giallo derived.

alism that was the undercurrent of the Bava gialli, the films were left with only the exploitation.

Though viewed as a classic today, *Sei donne per l'assassino* (1964) was not a big box-office success in any market. After its premiere, the giallo seemed to languish until the late '60s. It was in 1968, in a time of much social unrest within Europe, that the subgenre was re-introduced, exploding across theaters in Italy and around the world. Suddenly, gialli began springing up everywhere aided by the dismantling of censorship laws in late '60s that allowed more nudity, sexual situations and graphic violence to be shown. In addition, new social concerns involving a rising crime rate, sexual violence, and globalization created an atmosphere of fear in Italy, resulting in a variety of violent plots that played out in gialli. Issues such as tourism, exoticism, hybridity and foreignness were all incorporated into the giallo. Looking at Italian cinema in the late '60s and early '70s, it seems that the textuality of most screenplays point up the problems that Italians had with their national identities. Gialli was no exception. The hero/heroines of the genre are often foreigners in Italy or play Italian but on vacation. Whether it's London (*Tutti i colori del buio*, aka *All the Colors of the Dark*, 1972), Dublin (*L'iguana dalla lingua di fuoco*, aka *The Iguana with a Tongue of Fire*, 1971), or Haiti (*Al tropico del cancro*, aka *Death in Haiti*, 1972), the giallo uses the uneasiness of the period to promote violence and mayhem. When the giallo narrative takes a place in Italy it often becomes a nostalgic homage to the country, as in Bava's *Ecologia del delitto* (*Twitch of the Death Nerve*, 1972) or Lenzi's *I corpi presentano tracce di violenza carnale* (*Torso*, 1974), which promote "Italianness" through a foregrounding of identifiable tourist spots that often take up half the narrative.[126]

As the filmed giallo became more popular, Hollywood stars such as Carroll Baker (*Giant*, 1956; *Baby Doll*, 1956) and Farley Granger (*Strangers on a Train*, 1954) frequently crossed the ocean to appear in them.[127] Baker began the second stage of her career in Umberto Lenzi's *Orgasmo* (*Paranoia*, 1968), playing a woman who involves herself in a deadly threesome after her husband's death. The film plays up all the exploitative aspects of sexuality that were more permissible in the late '60s, offering audiences several nude scenes with the 38-year-old Baker. Baker and Lenzi would reteam for more films in the next two years, including *Cosí dolci ... cosí perversa* (*So Sweet ... So Perverse*, 1969) and *Paranoia* (*A Quiet Place to Kill*, 1969).[128] Each of these films would exploit Baker's persona, having her appear in a variety of nude scenes, something very few Hollywood actors were doing at the time.[129]

Though they would be followed by classic gialli from Sergio Martino and Umberto Lenzi, it was Mario Bava and Italian auteur Dario Argento who made the giallo subgenre popular with worldwide audiences. More murder mystery than actual giallo, Bava's 1970 entry *Cinque bambole per la luna d'agosto* (*Five Dolls for an August Moon*) seemed like a step backward from his earlier entries and the productions of the new giallo filmmakers. With no blood or leather stalker to speak of, the story of a group of people in an isolated nouveau beach house plays more like an adaptation of Agatha Christie's *10 Little Indians* with a psychedelic cast (including gialli stalwart Edwige Fenech, who would go on to be the classic heroine in a number of gialli in the '70s, dancing in her bikini) than a modern-day giallo. More successful, *Ecologia del delitto* (*Twitch of the Death Nerve*, 1971) builds on the template Bava began in *Sei donne*, foregoing any subtlety that was apparent in his earlier gialli, and opts for explicit gore and violence. Cited by critics, along with Sergio Martino's *Torso* (1973), as the modern precursor to the American "slasher" film, *Ecologia* predates the *Friday the 13th* films by nine years. The entire plot of the movie revolves around piling one innovative murder after another in what is the first "body count" movie. Similar to *Sei donne*, *Ecologia* is filled with the worst kind of people. Money-grubbing Renata (ex–Bond girl Claudine Auger) and Alberto (Luigi Pistilli), who want the inheritance of the murdered Countess Donati (Isa Miranda), lead off the list of baddies, which also includes an alcoholic psychic (Laura Betti), a cranky fisherman (Claudio Volonté), a business mercenary (Chris Avram) and his scheming secretary (Anna Maria Rosati). Throw in four horny teenagers out to have a good time and you have the makings of a giallo classic. Bava is again moralizing here, playing the film as a black comedy, embracing the notion of "man as destroyer." It's clear that he is both amused and repelled by his characters. Overall the film stands as a comment on the declining morals of European society, with all of Bava's characters, including the children, shown as capable of the most despicable acts without conscious reason or morality, and he makes each of them suffer mercilessly. There's a reason that *Ecologia* is looked at as one of the first body count films, as our killer(s) utilize every trick in the book to kill off the main characters, from a machete in the head, decapitation, strangulation, hanging, and in a particularly nifty scene, harpooning two people together as they have sex.[130] Unlike the later slasher films, it is not sexuality that is basis for destruction per se but the innate greed people are capable of. With one exception, no one makes it out alive in Bava's world because no one is redeemable. It is only the future generation or the young children that he sees as worthy of any redemption, but this being a giallo, as well as a Bava film, that redemption comes with a cost.

At the same that Bava was exploring the lack of morals in Italian society, new Italian filmmaker Dario Argento (1940–) was experiencing his first taste of

Typical Italian marketing for Mario Bava's minor *Cinque bambole per la luna d'agosto* (*Five Dolls for an August Moon*, 1970).

worldwide success with a modern, hip and deadly brand of giallo. Argento was the son of Italian producer Salvatore Argento and his wife, film photographer Elda Luxardo, and from birth was influenced by Italy's film community. Not wanting to be directly involved in the making of films, he began his career as a film critic. This exposure to a variety of films, along with his upbringing, helped shape his ideas on what makes a quality film and the types of films he was most interested in. By the late '60s Argento began writing screenplays, most notably for Sergio Leone's *Once Upon a Time in the West* in 1968. Though he initially had no interest in directing, he was often dismayed by liberties that directors took with his scripts and began to seriously think about directing his own works. Beginning in 1970, with the commencement of his "animal" trilogy, Argento began earning his reputation as the "Italian Hitchcock" by critics around the world.[131] His first film, the giallo *L'uccello dalle piume di cristallo* (*Bird with the Crystal Plumage*, 1970), was a smashing international success of which critics said "out–Hitchcock-ed, Hitchcock."[132] A reworking of Fredric Brown's novel *The Screaming Mimi* with a dash of *La ragazza che sapeva troppo* (1962) thrown in, written by Argento, *L'uccello* concerns a young American writer (Tony Musante) who witnesses an attack on a woman in an art gallery in Rome. Coerced by the police to aid the investigation, our hero inadvertently puts himself and his English girlfriend (Suzy Kendall) right in the path of the serial killer.[133] The film borrows all the clichés of the subgenre, e.g., red herrings and sexualized violence with a misogynistic tone, but adds a freshness that only a new, young writer/director could bring. Looking closely at *L'uccello*, the perspective of the new, younger generation of 1970s youth begins to make its appearance. Much like *Easy Rider* (1969), which gave a resonant, independent voice to a new generation of U.S. filmmakers and transformed the tradi-

Left and opposite: Two examples of Italian marketing for Dario Argento's seminal giallo *L'uccello dalle piume di cristallo* (*The Bird with the Crystal Plumage*, 1969).

Titanus
TONY MUSANTE · SUZY KENDALL · ENRICO MARIA SALERNO
IN UN FILM SCRITTO E DIRETTO DA
DARIO ARGENTO
L'UCCELLO DALLE PIUME DI CRISTALLO
CON
EVA RENZI · UMBERTO RAHO · RAF VALENTI · GIUSEPPE CASTELLANO
ROSA TOROS · FULVIO MINGOZZI · KAREN VALENTI · OMAR BONARO · WERNER PETERS · CARLA MANCINI (C.S.C.) · BRUNO ERBA · ANNAMARIA SPOGLI
E CON LA PARTECIPAZIONE DI MARIO ADORF
MUSICA DI ENNIO MORRICONE
EDIZIONI MUSICALI: BIXIO SAM—MILANO
CROMOSCOPE DELLA TECNOSTAMPA
UNA COPRODUZIONE ITALO-TEDESCA: SEDA SPETTACOLI S.p.A. (ROMA) C.C.C. FILM G.M.B.H. (BERLINO)
REALIZZATA DA SALVATORE ARGENTO

tional Hollywood establishment, *L'uccello* marks the beginning of a decade in which the quaintness of previous Italian filmmakers would be replaced by those who gave a gritty, graphic exploration of a society that's no longer safe. Where Bava's gialli always had an air of quaintness about them, Argento's were cool, modern and hip. Both employed graphic violence, but Bava's was more theatrical and over-the-top, while Argento's seemed all too real, rooted in headlines of the day which made them all the more terrifying. In the murder sequences, Argento isn't interested in novelty; he instead goes for the straight kill, nothing but leather and a sharp knife or razor here. This simplicity allows him to focus on the pure sexual violence that is the root of gialli. Though he solidly disputes the charge that his gialli are misogynistic (Argento: "I love women"), it's a bit of a hard sell in *L'uccello*. There are only two main female characters and both are problematic. Julia (Kendall) is, no surprise, a beautiful model. Throughout the first half of the film she projects an air of strength and sexuality, mixed with the occasional neediness. Her confrontation with the killer, though, has her completely losing whatever strength she possessed. It's strictly woman-in-danger territory here as she falls apart, locked in her apartment while the killer tries to knife his/her way in. Art dealer Monica Ranieri (Eva Renzi) also doesn't hold up as a good example of a well-rounded character. Moody, nervous and sullen (with good reason!), she seems completely dependent upon her husband for everything. Add to the film two other female characters, one butchered in her nightgown (in a scene edited in many international editions), the other slashed in an elevator, and you don't have the makings of a feminist tale. The argument can be made that while it's clear that Argento likes these characters and was not trying to exploit them, he was dealing with stereotypes that permeated Italy at the time. As the decade wore on, though, Argento began to eschew traditional female stereotypes and present stronger, more multi-dimensional characters, such as Suzy Banyon in *Suspiria* (1976).

L'uccello was picked up by UMC Pictures for U.S. distribution and became a surprising success in the summer of 1970. Italians were not impressed in the film's initial release, but positive word-of-mouth kept the film from leaving cinemas, and soon the film was at the top of the Italian charts. Surprisingly for such a self-assured performance, Argento was not keen on directing the film that he had written, but not wanting to see his work edited by filmmakers that did not understand his perspective, he took the reins himself. Said Argento, "I did think the script was a magnificent piece of writing, mainly because no one had paid me to do it. I had just written it for myself to see if I could do justice to a noir-type thriller set in Italy. It was an uncommon genre at the time but I followed my heart and went with the flow. Uppermost in my mind was that if I didn't want my screenplay ruined I would have to bite the bullet."[134]

Argento's directing style was similar to that of Bava's in terms of his use of color, but the similarities end there. Argento's style of filmmaking is a much more "in your face" modern technique with its quick edits, use of loud, electronic music, and graphic violence. The photography by Vittorio Storraro, the music by Ennio Morricone, and a tightly written script by Argento all provided the blueprint for a smashing success in the international market. It became the first part of Argento's "animal trilogy," which also included *Il gatto a nove code* (*Cat o' Nine Tales*, 1971) and *Quattro mosche di velluto grigio* (*Four Flies on Grey Velvet*, 1972). All three of these films showcased the internationalization of the giallo as each film starred popular young or established American actors of the time (Karl Malden, James Franciscus, Tony Musante, Michael Brandon), a move to make distributors happy by widening the appeal of the films.[135] What made these films, as well as Argento's other classic giallo of the '70s, *Profondo rosso* (*Deep Red*, 1975), unique was that they represented the new style of gritty filmmaking that was occurring in cinema in early '70s.[136] This style focused on modern settings and conversations, taking out the fantasy aspects of earlier genre films. Characters in these gialli were real people like family members, lovers and friends, who were thrust into terrible situations. The horror in the story was inherent in the horrors of everyday. As Europeans, as well as the rest of the world, opened their newspapers, they realized too well how the world was changing and Argento's gialli reflected their fears back at them.

Il gatto a nove code (*Cat o' Nine Tails*, 1971), Argento's second animal trilogy film, carried on the idea of gialli construct of a masked, gloved killer but added a scientific component. In the film, reporter Carlo Giordani (James Franciscus), with the help of a blind crossword puzzle creator and his niece (Karl Malden, Cinzia de Carolis), track down a killer who has a rare genetic anomaly that causes schizophrenia.[137] Though some critics criticized the film for being more science fiction than actual horror, it showcased Argento's mistrust of the advances in medicine and psychotherapy that were occurring around the world in early '70s.[138] Long before there was *CSI*, Argento was using the latest gadgetry to help his protagonists in their murder investigations. In *L'uccello* it was a large room-sized computer complete with dot-matrix printer that gave police a composite of the killer. In the film that follows *Il gatto*, *Quattro mosche di velluto grigio* (*Four Flies on Grey Velvet*, 1972), the special laser detectives use is the key point in solving the crime (and in understanding the importance of the odd name for the film). The interest Argento has in technology ensures that he is looking forward, thus making his gialli relevant. With its look at genetics and DNA, *Il gatto* still holds its scientific punch 40 years later, even as the film plays down its exploitative pedigree, instead opting for a more intricate thriller feel. Perhaps because of its less violent nature (not to worry, exploitation fans: there are enough men falling down elevator shafts or under trains to keep you happy), it was not as successful as *L'uccello* in Italy. It managed, however, to obtain worldwide distribution, including the United States, where the casting of Malden and Franciscus helped sell the film, ensuring there would be another Argento giallo.

Argento's third film in his "animal trilogy" *Quattro mosche di velluto grigio* (*Four Flies on Grey Velvet*, 1972) continues down the same scientific path began in *Il gatto*. Rock musician Roberto Tobias (Michael Brandon) and his increasingly agitated wife Nina (Mimsy Farmer) endure blackmail from a psychopath who took some damning photos of Roberto in an intense situation. As the photos begin to turn up in and around his daily haunts, those closest to him begin dying. The title comes from a police test on the eyeball of a murdered victim done with a laser, supposing that a killer's image is retained on the retina of the victim's eye as the last thing he sees. In *Quattro mosche* the image on the eye of the last victim looks like ... four flies on grey velvet. The scientific explanation doesn't stop the violence and adult themes from coming, though. Heads are cut off and women are slashed with large knives and thrown (graphically) down flights of stairs, all to the tune of Ennio Morricone's synthesized rock score. Argento once again explores possible incestuous relationships, this device also having been used in *Il gatto a nove code* the year before, to explain some of the mayhem. At the time of filming, Argento's first marriage was coming to an end, and this is manifested itself in the agitated relationship between Roberto and Nina the film. Never at any time does the audience get the feeling that these two people belong together or that Roberto is even capable of a monogamous relationship. This was the era of free love and Roberto's rock lifestyle certainly contributes to his amorous feelings for all the females in the cast.

Argento's second giallo, *Il gatto a nove code* (*Cat o' Nine Tails*, 1971), wasn't as successful as *L'uccello*, though it did obtain international distribution.

The final film in Dario Argento's "animal trilogy" found him fascinated with technology, using it to solve the convoluted plot he cooks up.

The most interesting character of the film is that of gay private detective Arrosio. *Quattro mosche* was one of the first to unashamedly feature a homosexual character in a heroic role.[139] Argento had played around with gay characters in both his previous films, from the overly flamboyant antiques dealer who gives Tony Musante his first clue in *L'uccello dalle piume di cristallo* (1970) to the murderous schizopath in *Il gatto a nove code* (1971), but never gave them hero status. As played by Jean-Pierre Marielle, the character mirrors the increasingly moderate society that Italy was becoming in the early '70s. Though stereotyped by today's standards (effeminate, funny, alone, etc.), the role is played with dignity and is integral to the story. Argento's openness to a homosexual character was a result of his rebellion against the confines of Italian society. Prior to *Quattro mosche*, Argento wanted to make a giallo with a homosexual character much like the Tony Musante's character in *L'uccello dalle piume di cristallo* (1970), saying, "I thought it would be an interesting milieu to explore but, of course, everyone thought such an idea would spell box office disaster. I wanted Arrosio to be a social rebel because I was also rebellious. I felt as persecuted by the critics as most gays did by society in general at the time so I could sympathize."[140] Though groundbreaking in its approach, adding a main homosexual character that was not a villain did not catch on with other Italian producers. The rest of the '70s gialli depicted gays as victims who were made to suffer because of their orientation, or as perpetrators of crime because of their "obvious" psychosis. Even Argento would fall into that trap later with his seminal *Profondo rosso* (*Deep Red*, 1975) and *Tenebrae* (1982).

While immensely popular in Italy, *Quattro mosche* was a flop everywhere else, which may show that audiences were becoming less accepting of "highbrow" gialli and more interested in those that focused mainly on sex.[141] Argento's early gialli, though violent and realistic, were not draped in gore. All the films in the "animal trilogy" were rated PG (Both *L'uccello* and *Il gatto* were rated GP, which stood for General Public before the PG rating took it over) and were acceptable to most audiences. Argento himself was tiring of the genre, relating, "It occurred to me that I should change my style around 1972. If I brought the horror thriller back into style, I now wanted to distance myself from it. Everywhere I looked there were pale imitations of my work with catchpenny titles that evoked my success."[142]

Argento had good reason to be wary. His success motivated an Italian industry already steeped in the art of imitation to crank out a mind-numbing number of gialli in the early '70s. These films were directed and produced by some of Italy's best talent, all trying to "out–Argento, Argento."

Lucio Fulci (1927–1996) began his ascent into Eurocult realm with a slew of top-quality gialli in beginning in 1969. Previously known as a sex comedy and spaghetti western director, Fulci tackled the giallo four times in the late '60s and early '70s with *Una sull'altra* (*One on Top of the Other*, 1969) *Una lucertola con la pelle di donna* (*Lizard in a Woman's Skin*, 1971), *Non si sevizia un paperino* (*Don't Torture a Duckling*, 1972) and *Sette note in nero* (*The Psychic*, 1977). In these films, a far cry from his later excessive gross-out horrors of *Zombi* (1979) and *L'aldilà* (*The Beyond*, 1980), Fulci managed to put his finger on the free sexuality that permeated the culture at the time and the repercussions that came along with it, especially its effects on the deep psyches of the repressed. The first of these, *Una sull'altra*, was released less than a year before Argento's *L'uccello* and plays like an Italian version of Hitchcock's *Vertigo* (1958), borrowing many of the elements of that classic and mixing them in with more permissive examples of nudity and sex. Watching the film today it isn't difficult to see where producers got the idea for *Basic Instinct* (1992, which itself could definitely be considered a giallo), as the film focuses on the deception of an adulterous San Francisco doctor (Jean Sorel) whose asthmatic wife (Marissa Mell) mysteriously dies. Later he is stunned to discover that a local stripper/prostitute looks exactly like his dead wife (Mell again, sporting the same blonde wig she used in Bava's *Diabolik* in 1967). From there the deception begins, set to a wildly played jazz score by Riz Ortolani, via visits to strip clubs, run-ins with "johns," and blackmail. Though he made it less of a giallo than a detective story, Fulci was not afraid to exploit the seedier aspects of the setting which was the foundation of '70s gialli. San Francisco in 1969 was still the cradle of the hippie and "free love" movement, making it the perfect background in which Fulci could exploit his characters, using both the titillation of Mell's striptease on a motorbike and the soft-core photography provided by Sorel's mistress (Elsa Martinelli) to transport audiences into an environment they wouldn't ordinarily be in.

Both heterosexual and homosexual angst are the root of the problems in *Una lucertola con la pelle di donna* (*Lizard in a Woman's Skin*, 1971), with Brazilian beauty Florinda Bolkan walking the tightrope between sanity and madness. Her attraction to her bisexual neighbor (Swedish Anita Strindberg) sets off a murderous hallucinatory rampage.[143] The movie then becomes a series of dream sequences that would make

Lucio Fulci's *Una sull'altra* (*Perversion Story*, 1969) was actually released prior to Argento's *L'uccello* and showed that he was just as capable of exploiting the new generation's progressive attitudes.

Freud blush as Bolkan must grapple with her orientation. Though many actresses of the time were asked to perform (or were cajoled into performing) lesbian love scenes that were only meant to exploit, Bolkan found the idea of playing a woman with a considerable amount of inner turmoil about her sexual orientation very appealing. Discussing the role and the lesbian aspects of the film, she said, "In fact I have never played anybody as disposed of, to be sexually and evilly treated as that woman, it had a lot of attraction. The mind of Fulci was to create an ambiance that gave the idea of the erotic side only that but the bad, the nastiness that a woman can produce by being sweet yet sexually driven. At that period, no one talked about it, it was taboo to talk about that. Especially because it was two women, we had seen things on men but never two women." French costar Jean Sorell agreed with the controversial aspects of the plot line, relating, "Now this is perfectly normal but back then these were the first movies which were sexually explicit where you could see love scenes, where homosexuality was addressed. You could often see them in detective movies, which were somewhat erotic. All this is completely related to a period of Italian filmmaking."[144]

For audiences, it wasn't just the sight of Bolkan and Strindberg enjoying windblown hallucinating sex that they remembered, but the shocking gore effects that Fulci and special effects creator Carlo Rambaldi devised. In one scene, Carol (Bolkan), believing that she is being pursued, runs into a room where she sees four eviscerated coyotes hanging from being on a life support machine. So realistic were these effects that Fulci and Rambaldi were taken court by animal rights activists and the sequence was edited out of most foreign versions.[145] All of this proves that Fulci was not afraid to go all the way to titillate and shock his audiences. Unlike Bava, who was never comfortable with showing graphic sexuality, or Argento, who simply preferred to focus on plot, Fulci revels in the new acceptance of onscreen carnality. Interestingly, American producers decided to focus on the horror aspects when releasing Fulci's films in the States. Retitling the film *Schizoid*, with the catchphrase "Biting, Gnawing Terror Claws at your Brain," and taking advantage of one small scene in which Carol is stuck in an empty building and attacked by bats, the marketing firm chose not to concentrate on the film's psychosexual angle, instead promoting it as, no kidding, a killer bat movie!

Fulci's next film would not even receive a U.S. release as very little could be done to make light of *Non si sevizia un paperino* (*Don't Torture a Duckling*, 1972). This time Fulci not only deals with sexual repression but places it within the context of religion. Like Bava he populates his films with people who have deep neuroses, the list of suspects including the village idiot (Vito Passeri), a woman purporting to be a witch (Florinda Bolkan), and a drug addict (Barbara Bouchet) who has granted some of the local (young) boys sexual favors. The killer, though, turns out to be someone (it's a giallo, so you'll have to see it yourself to figure it out) who strangled the boys to rescue them from the horrors of their own sexuality.[146] *Non si sevizia* is one of those films that could only be made in the '70s. A very graphic, uncomfortable seduction of a young boy (no more than 11) by the naked Bouchet in the opening 20 minutes ensures that this is one film that won't receive a remake anytime. But Fulci is trying to do something important here by contrasting old, traditional Italy with its newer counterpart. This contrast is seen during the credits of the film with a shot of a newly built superhighway cutting through the Italian landscape. Sleek and impressive, it looks strangely out of place in the rural countryside, just as the new generation of Italian culture looks to the traditional established one. A favorite of Fulci's, *Non si sevizia* also points out the discrepancies in Italian society involving sexuality. It contrasts a

The success of Dario Argento's *L'uccello dalle piume di cristallo* (*The Bird with the Crystal Plumage*, 1969) opened the floodgates for a slew of animal-themed gialli such as Fulci's *Una lucertola con la pelle di donna* (*Lizard in a Woman's Skin*, 1971).

repressed, murderous member of a revered profession with a liberated, manipulative female preying on boys' inexperience, highlighting the varying degrees of tolerance afforded to different perverse acts in Italian society. The dichotomy Fulci creates is seen insofar as the early sexual experiences of the young boys with the older woman is portrayed as fun with an air of nostalgia, while the "professional" is portrayed as deviant, due not to the homicidal impulses, but the homosexual ones that are seemingly prevalent.[147] Exploitation fans looking for leather-bound killers slashing naked women in the shower might be a little disappointed with the goings-on in *Non si sevizia*, but Fulci being Fulci, he ensures that a couple of violent set pieces remain, most notably the whipping of Maciara (Bolken) by the local townspeople, as well as the killer's demise by falling off a cliff, where we graphically see his head smashing into each and every rock.

Fulci was not the only director in Italy focusing on sexual repression. Sergio Martino (1938–) made his genre debut utilizing the same themes, beginning in 1970 with *Lo strano vizio della Signora Wardh* (*The Strange Vice of Mrs. Wardh*). Starring Algerian beauty Edwige Fenech as a woman being driven insane by an unknown perpetrator, the film combines an eerie, melancholy score by Nora Orlandi with outright exploitation.[148] The first 10 minutes of film pretty much encapsulate Martino's giallo style. In the opening credits, our intrepid killer is out searching for local prostitutes, finding one, he then proceeds to slash her with a razor blade. Five minutes later we're treated to a scene where Mrs. Wardh (Fenech) is raped during a rainstorm by Jean (Ivan Rassimov), her sadomasochistic lover. Martino, like Lucio Fulci, doesn't shy away from sex. His rape has an alarming sensuality about it as Fenech's clothes are ripped away during a downpour in high erotic fashion; later, Jean covers her in broken glass and makes love to her. A strange and gripping film, *Lo strano* foreshadows many of Martino's later masterpieces, delivering a tight and compelling storyline that features a nifty twist finale that somehow still manages to hold water. Fenech, who starred a year earlier in Bava's giallo *Cinque bambole per la luna d'agosto* (*Five Dolls for an August Moon*, 1969), became such a strong presence in these films that she has come to be regarded by many fans as the ultimate giallo heroine. Though the violence level in *Lo strano* is comparatively mild compared to the others in the genre, the film does contain the requisite throat-slashing of the naked woman in the shower and the underlying seediness of the plot, along with generous helpings of Fenech nude, to keep the exploitation audience happy.[149]

Martino's next two films, *La coda dello scorpione* (*The Case of the Scorpions Tail*, 1971) and *Il tuo vizio è una stanza chiusa e solo io ne ho la chiave* (*Your Vice Is a Locked Room and Only I Have the Key*, 1972) continued the tormenting of young beautiful women (Anita Strindberg and Edwige Fenech) by their cheating spouses/lovers. Even more so than *Lo strano*, which looked at personal infidelity and inner demons, these films explore the increasing xenophobia occurring in Europe. In *Il tuo vizio*, characters discuss the subject of the "integration of Europe," which was inaugurated by a relaxation of Catholic standards, encouraging an open-door policy toward tourism and cultural exchange. This resulted in the introduction of more British, French, German and American products into Europe, which was advantageous for consumers but not so much for local businesses. One character (Luigi Pistilli) laments that these exchanges by outsiders are "poison," as Martino showcases the increasing xenophobia dominating the Italian mindset.[150] This xenophobia is almost always manifested in ambiguity, which is the trademark of the giallo. Without a clear idea as to the identity of the killer, the characters and audiences must suspect everyone, believing that anything outside their own personage is capable of evil deeds.

Martino's final two films in the genre, *Tutti i colori del buio* (*All the Colors of the Dark*, 1972) and *I corpi presentano tracce di violenza carnale* (*Torso*, 1974), show the increasingly malefic and violent direction the giallo was taking. Due to oversaturation, the giallo storyline was starting to show signs of repetition and producers were looking for ways in which give the genre new life. *Tutti i colori* concerns a young couple (George Hilton, Edwige Fenech) who are trying to overcome their recent miscarriage due to an automobile accident. Finding herself hounded by a devil's cult, Jane (Fenech), increasingly becomes unstable, which flings her from one violent situation to the next. The introduction of a satanic cult came as a result of the popularity of Roman Polanski's *Rosemary's Baby* (1968) and gives Martino the ability to transcend the giallo constraints and film Jane's nightmares as both kinky and scarily hallucinatory.[151] With *I corpi*, Martino, like Bava's *Ecologia del delitto* (1971) created the template for the modern "slasher" film. Using a stunning musical score by Maurizio De Angelis and Guido that mixes sultry jazz, suspense music and rock, *I corpi* begins as a giallo but plays out as a woman-in-danger scenario imperative in such "slasher" movies as *Halloween* (1978) and *Friday the 13th* (1980). Martino was influenced by real-life events in Italy involving a man who murdered women, cut them into bits, and left his father to tidy up his mess.[152] In the film, local college women are being killed by a sexual perpetrator. When four of the students decide to leave the town on vacation, they realize that the killer has followed them. After dispatching three of the girls, the murderer turns his attention to the only one left (Suzy Kendall). Thus begins a cat-and-mouse game between the virtuous girl and cold-blooded killer. The perpetrator turns out to be (again) someone from an esteemed profession exacting revenge on those who secretly taped him/her having an adulterous ménage à trois.[153]

Less violent yet no less erotic were the gialli of Luciano Ercoli (1925—). His first giallo, *Le foto proibite di una signora per bene* (*Forbidden Photos of a Lady Above Suspicion*, 1970), defined Erocoli's style. With their mixture of detective stories with lots of overt sexuality, Ercoli's films focused on the deceptive relationships between heterosexual spouses and lovers. In his films, he utilizes the nightmare of being threatened by one's own sexual partner.[154] In *Le foto*, Minou (Dagmar Lassander) is sexually blackmailed by a sadistic stranger who proceeds to tell her that her husband is a murderer. Increasingly unstable and addicted to tranquilizers, she finds out the truth: that her husband (Pier Paolo Capponi) is trying to murder her for her insurance money. Helping her to understand what is happening is her bisexual free-spirited friend, played by Ercoli's real wife Susan Scott (aka Nieves Navarro, who appeared in other exploitation throughout the seventies including *Emanuelle e gli ultimi cannibale* in 1978) and *Tutti i colori del buio*, 1972). Deception from men is key to Erocoli's work, helping to explain the strong female characters he infuses into his films. In *Le foto*, Scott's character, the sexually liberated, independent Dominique, is portrayed in direct opposition to Minou or any of the typical female characters of the time. She is neither a victim nor villain but an intelligent, sexually strong character who manages to figure out the plot and diffuses it.

Ercoli's *La morte cammina con i tacchi alti* (*Death Walks in High Heels*, 1971) and *La morte accarezza a mezzanotte* (*Death Walks at Midnight*, 1972) carry on with the same themes. Both films again feature Scott, as a tough, independent woman who is inevitably deceived by her lovers. This deception either results in sudden death (*La morte cammina*) or in abusive violence (*La morte accarezza*).[155] Regardless of her characters' outcomes, Scott imbues the characters with a new-found strength that mirrors the attainment of equality for women in the early '70s. Though there was some positive movement in women's roles

Enter...
if you dare
the bizarre
world of the
psychosexual
mind.

Joseph Brenner Associates Inc.
presents a
Carlo Ponti production

TORSO

starring **SUZY KENDALL**
with Tina Aumont/John Richardson/Carla Brait/Luc Merenda
Directed by Sergio Martino • Produced by Antonio Cervi
Distributed by Joseph Brenner Associates, Inc.

R RESTRICTED

IN TECHNICOLOR

To preserve the
surprise ending,
no one admitted
during last
10 minutes.

with these characters it must be stated that it always came with a price. It must be remembered that these are gialli and often the main female character must endure some form of punishment before coming to any happy conclusion. In Ercoli's case, his attention to strong female characters could be tied to his fascination with "Fumetti," which is a form of Italian cartoon. Fumettis typically have stronger women's leads, but these women must go through a myriad of life-changing events. Whatever their inspiration, Ercoli's female leads are often a refreshing change of pace from the screaming, unbalanced women that populated Argento's and Martino's early gialli.

By the mid-'70s the oversaturation of titles had exhausted audiences and the perceived originality in gialli began to disappear. As a result, audience attendance began to drop and producers began looking at other genres to make a profit. Ironically, it was at this time that Dario Argento returned to giallo to give the world one of the seminal examples of the subgenre, *Profondo rosso* (*Deep Red*) in 1975. Blurring the boundaries between a thriller and a horror film, Argento amped up the leather and reworked the classic structure of the giallo and gave audiences a rich, thought-provoking story that both fascinated and terrified. Explained Argento: "I came back to the giallo with all my love, with all my being, with all my desire and it sublimated itself in the form of the most complex story I've ever written."[156] Typical gialli of the time gave short shrift to the psychological motives behind the protagonist's actions. *Profondo* explores a new psychological perspective, giving the film a multitude of layers in which audiences can discover a variety of different meanings. Utilizing all types of mental neuroses including alcoholism, homosexual/transgender angst, mother complex, inadequacy and dementia, Argento gives the audience a number of rationales that the killer can choose from.[157]

Starring David Hemmings (in a sort of reprisal of his role from Antonioni's *Blow Up*, 1966) and Argento's partner at the time, Daria Nicolodi, *Profondo rosso* improves on some of the same devices used in his previous *L'uccello dalle piume di cristallo* (*Bird with the Crystal Plumage*, 1970), that of a man witnessing a brutal murder, in this case that of a German psychic, and his subsequent involvement in the investigation. With an electronic score by the Goblins and a completely different technique of filming involving the use of color, composition and framing, Argento created a film which many critics call his "crowning achievement."[158] The violence in the film is much more graphic than in his previous gialli, an obvious appeal to a mid-'70s audience. Helga's (Macha Méril) death at the hands of the killer via butcher's cleaver and Carlo's (Gabriele Lavia) dragging death are all filmed unflinchingly in close-up with a large amount of red, spurting blood. Again, Argento goes to the tried-and-true giallo theme of ambiguity. In his world, mother, lover, brother or child could be a possible murderer. By setting up a plot in which everyone is capable of violence, Argento forces the audience to keep an emotional distance from his characters, which in turn allows them to process the events logically. And what are they processing? Pretty much everything in Freud's dictionary of neurosis. In the typical world of the giallo, everyone is ugly on the inside, which is why the characters are made to suffer, but Argento is doing something different here. It is self-loathing that is the motivation behind most of the cast's actions, not an inherent ugliness. With the exception of one character who is "slightly" unbalanced, the cast are victims of their own self-esteem. Whether it's Marc (Hemmings), who seems to missing some emotional component to his personality; Gianna

Opposite: One of the first films to signal the arrival of the "slasher" film, *Torso* (1973) used sexualized violence and a masked killer to enthrall audiences.

LA MORTE CAMMINA CON I TACCHI ALTI

la CINERIZ presenta

CON **FRANK WOLFF** — **SUSAN SCOTT** — **SIMON ANDREU**

CARLO GENTILI · FABRIZIO MORESCO · J.M. MARTIN · GEORGE RIGAUD · LUCIANO ROSSI

E CON LA PARTECIPAZIONE DI **CLAUDIE LANGE** | REGIA DI **LUCIANO ERCOLI** | UN FILM PRODOTTO DA LUCIANO ERCOLI E ALBERTO PUGLIESE
PER LA CINECOMPANY, Roma — C.C. ATLANTIDA, Madrid

TECHNOCHROME

CINERIZ

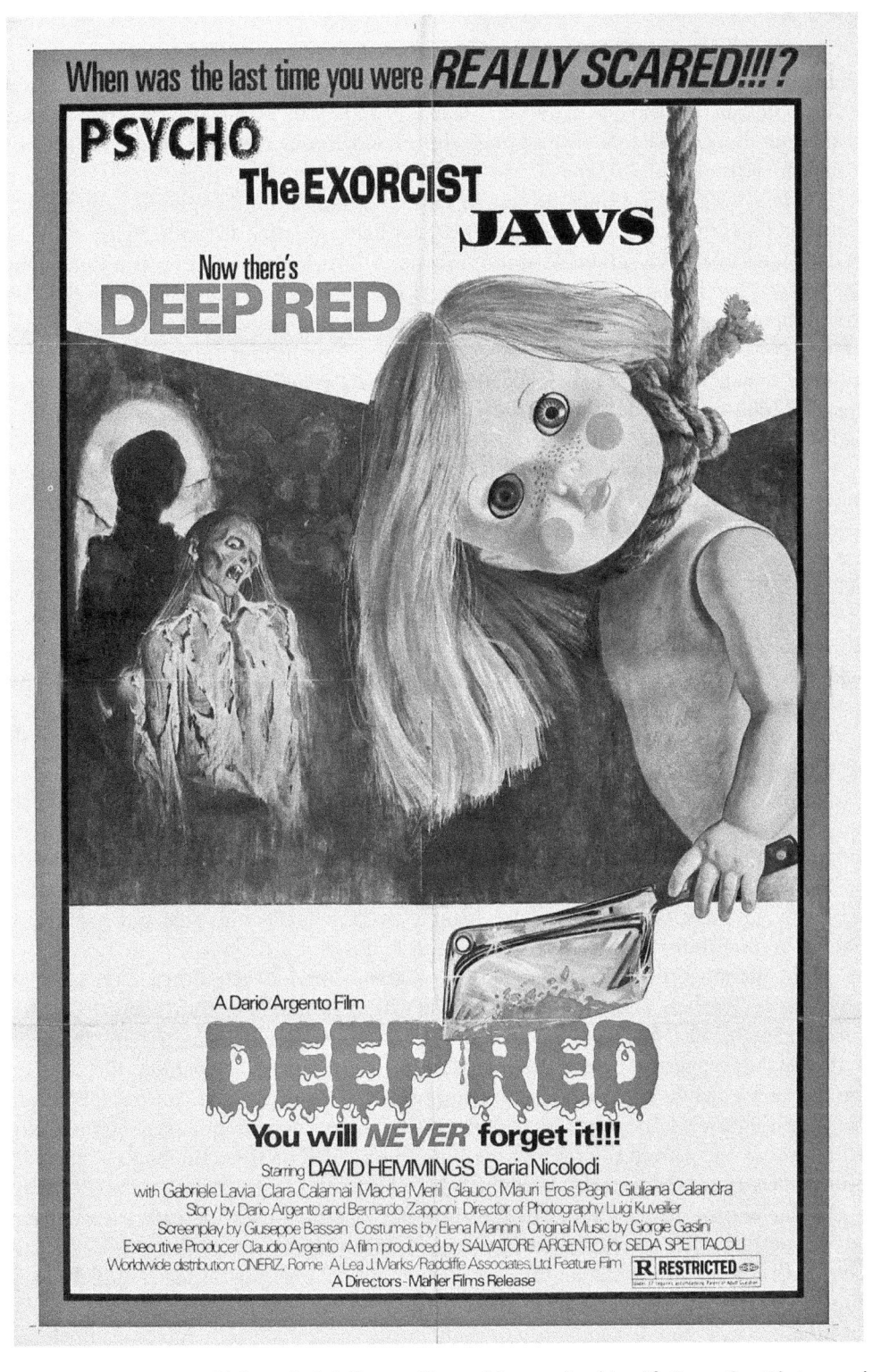

Opposite: Luciano Ercoli's brand of giallo usually saw him putting his wife Susan Scott into a variety of deadly situations. *Above:* American distributors put *Profondo rosso* (*Deep Red*, 1975) on a par with *Jaws, The Exorcist* and *Psycho*. Little did they know that in Eurocult circles *Profondo* is regarded as such.

(Nicolodi), who overcompensates her insecurity about her job with humor; or Carlo, who descends into alcoholism due to his homosexuality and mother issues, it's clear that Argento cares about these characters. Instead of gleefully condemning them, he makes us pity them in their final minutes.

Profondo rosso was a huge success in Italy as well as around the world, especially in countries like Japan, where a new audience was being exposed to gialli. Released in the United States in a much-edited 98-minute version (the original being over two hours long, which is way too long for the drive-in market), and renamed in some places with the great exploitation title *The Hatchet Murders*, the film went on to do respectable box office. Though it may have given the subgenre critical acclaim and acceptance, it did not result in a huge influx of new gialli. In fact, the gialli released after *Profondo rosso* did not try to attain Argento's high-minded ideals, but more often than not mimicked films like Andrea Bianchi's *Nude per l'assassino* (*Strip Nude for Your Killer*, 1975).

A fun exercise in exploitation, *Nude* is the bridge from giallo to slasher with a connect-the-dots plot that begins with a botched abortion, followed by a male castration scene, followed by a steam room seduction, and finally by some nude modeling — and that's in the first 15 minutes! The film has all the components that late-'70s audiences were looking for, including violent stabbings that seem to go on forever, a bevy of naked women (including Edwidge Fenech, who is seemingly slumming it here after the her stint in Sergio Martino's gialli) as well as naked men (Nino Castelnuovo, also a far cry from *The Umbrellas of Cherbourg*, 1964) a leather-clad killer who now wears a sleek black motorcycle helmet (which is very "slasher-esque" and allows him to breathe heavily all over the soundtrack), all set to some amazing bump-and-grind music straight out of a '70s porno. Set in and around the home of what has to be most celebrated profession in gialli, a photographer's studio, *Nude* has only reason for existence: to showcase beautiful, naked women running around the house before being viciously killed. No pretext of a psychological motivation is given; the film is only meant to titillate, which shows how far the subgenre had sunk by the end of the '70s. So low was the opinion of the screenwriter Massimo Felisatti of this little gem that he happily gave story credit to director Bianchi so as to "deflect his role and not have to bear full responsibility" for the events onscreen.

Though thoughtful artists like Dario Argento would periodically return to the subgenre in 1982 with *Tenebrae* and as recently as 2003 with *Il cartaio* (*The Card Player*), *Ti piace Hitchcock?* (*Do You Like Hitchcock?*) in 2005, and the self-titled *Giallo* in 2009, the giallo pretty much disappeared by the late '70s while its lobotomized companion, the "slasher" film, ascended thanks to American film such as John Carpenter's *Halloween* (1978) and Sean Cunningham's *Friday the 13th* (1980), which employed techniques synonymous with gialli filmmaking. American critics at the time commented on the uniqueness of the POV shots that Carpenter incorporated into his tale of a faceless killer's return to a small Illinois town. Whether the critics forgot or simply did not take the time to actually view some of the exploitation gialli that were coming out of Italy, the fact remains that this device had been applied in numerous Italian thrillers throughout the previous decade. Popular horror films like *Friday the 13th* (1980) and any of its sequels also owe a great debt to the giallo. The ambiguity of the killer's identity in slashers are a pure giallo construct, as is the imaginative violence. If one looks at the 10-year difference between the giallo *Ecologia del delitto* (*Bay of Blood*, 1971) with the slasher film *Friday the 13th Part 2* (1981), such striking similarities can be seen (including the infamous skewering of two people having sex) that it is surprising that copyright infringement cases weren't brought against American producers.

The über-sleazy *Nude per l'assassino* (*Strip Nude for Your Killer*, 1978) gets a marketing push that matches the film's exploitation content.

The use of music and soundtrack noise in both subgenres is a defining component as well and very much mirror each other. Listening to the eerie sing-song theme in *Lo strano vizio della Signora Wardh* (*The Strange Vice of Mrs. Wardh* 1970), one could easily make assumptions as to where American director Wes Craven may have gotten the idea for the musical theme to *Nightmare on Elm Street* (1983); and the sound effect of our heavy-breathing, motorcycle helmet–wearing killer in *Nude per l'assassino* (*Strip Nude for Your Killer*, 1975) sounds exactly like the killer miner in *My Bloody Valentine* (1981).

Many critics and scholars have looked at the slasher subgenre as the originators of graphic, almost pornographic, gore. This isn't necessarily so, as the slasher genre didn't originate pornographic gore; it simply improved on the special effects of the giallo. What American filmmakers did, though, was to eliminate the intricate plots of the giallo, which left viewers with a very one-dimensional type of film devoted solely to emotional responses. The best of gialli makes you think; the slasher makes you feel. Gialli, with its emphasis on the mystery and resolution, provided graphic violence that was offset by the weight of the story. Without the benefit of a good narrative, all that was left for the audiences of slasher films was the violence, and by the late '70s it seemed that these audiences no longer wanted the convoluted stories that the giallo offered.

The giallo provided both Italian audiences and the world with an entertaining yet disturbing view of the modern world. One of the reasons for the subgenre's success was that it gave audiences a cathartic outlet with which to deal with the ever-surging and ever-increasing media coverage of violence that was plaguing the world in the '60s and '70s. Never at any time in history were crimes, especially sex crimes, being so openly reported, and the giallo was there to take advantage of that. In addition, the subgenre offered audiences a complex look at people and their hidden motivations. Though earlier films may have hinted at the complexity of the human condition, never had taboo subjects such as sexuality and neurosis been so graphically portrayed. Whether it was incest, infidelity, sexual repression, orientation issues, or just good old mental illness, the giallo lovingly exploited it and audiences responded enthusiastically. By the middle '70s, audiences were ready to move on. Censorship had pretty much become a thing of the past, and an "anything goes" type of atmosphere permeated the worldwide film industry. A new group of films had influenced the popular culture and the Italians were more than ready to duplicate that success worldwide.

Filmography

All the Colors of the Dark, aka *Tutti i colori del buio*. (IT) Prod. Mino Loy and Luciano Martino. Dir. Sergio Martino. Italy/Spain, 1972. Shriek Show, 91 min. DVD. Starring: Edwige Fenech, George Hilton, Ivan Rassimov and Nieves Navarro.

Sergio Martino made some fantastic gialli in the early '70s and this is one of the best. Working a little witchcraft mojo in with the standard giallo, he creates a fun story about a woman (Fenech) who loses her unborn baby in a car crash, then, as if that weren't enough, finds herself pursued by a killer with ties to a local coven. All of this trauma leads her to begin hallucinating about dead dogs and orgies. Fenech is in charge here with her enigmatic personality and willingness to do anything for a film (I can't see Meryl Streep drinking a chalice of dog's blood in her movies anytime soon) paying off as she makes her character sympathetic. A stellar cast of Eurocult's finest (Rassimov, Navarro who would be her own giallo heroine soon, and Hilton) all contribute to this *Rosemary's Baby*-meets-every-giallo-you've-ever-known classic.

Autopsy, aka *Macchie solari*. (IT), *The Victim* (U.S.). Prod. Leonardo Pescarolo. Dir. Armando Crispino. Italy, 1973. Blue Underground, 100 min. DVD. Starring: Mimsy Farmer, Ray Lovelock, Barry Primus and Carlo Cattaneo.

Poor Mimsy Farmer! It's not been her summer. Solar flares are contributing to a rash of suicides around Rome, her boyfriend (Lovelock) is an ass and can't understand why she is frigid, her father is a male whore, and she keeps seeing dead bodies from the morgue where she works, having sex. What else can she do but lose her mind? Soon new bodies start to appear and she is forced, along with a priest (American Barry Primus) to get it together and solve the crime. Overlong, with a lot of scenes of Farmer freaking out, making *Autopsy* a so-so bet for that Friday night party movie viewing. The sex is plentiful and fairly graphic, plus it's called *Autopsy* for a reason, but there's a lot of lull in the meantime. Farmer is an interesting actress in that most of the characters she played in the '70s (e.g., *Four Flies on Grey Velvet* and *Perfume of the Lady in Black*) aren't all that enjoyable to watch, yet there's something about her that makes them enigmatic. *Autopsy* only reinforces that.

The Bird with the Crystal Plumage, aka *L'uccello dalle piume di cristallo*. Prod. Salvatore Argento. Dir. Dario Argento. Italy, 1970. Blue Underground, 96 min. DVD/Blu-Ray. Starring: Tony Musante, Suzy Kendall, Eva Renzi, Reggie Nalder and Enrico Maria Salerno.

This is the film that jump-started the entire wave of gialli in the '70s, and with good reason: it's brilliant. Though not the first in the giallo canon, Dario Argento's first film is a self-assured masterpiece that is worthy of many viewings. The story is simple: Sam (Musante) is witness to an attack in an art gallery in Rome, where there has been a rash of murders lately. As he tries to piece together exactly what he saw, the killer goes after him and his girlfriend (Kendall). The simplicity of the plot belies the intricacy of its unfolding as Argento piles on one red (ironic) herring after another, as well as shocking us with some fairly sexualized violence (amazingly, the film was rated PG when released in the U.S.). The jazzy score adds to the proceedings, as do some very solid performances by Musante (who reportedly did not get along well with Argento during filming) and Renzi. Suzy Kendall also hits the right notes, but her paralysis of fear toward the end is a bit much. If you're going to stab someone through the keyhole, don't scream the whole way through! This is one of the first Eurocult films released on Blu-Ray and the upgrade is remarkable, accentuating Argento's style and color palette. A definite must-see.

Black Belly of the Tarantula, aka *La tarantola dal ventre nero*. Prod. Marcello Danon. Dir. Paolo Carva. Italy/Germany, 1971. Blue Underground, 98 min. DVD. Starring: Giancarlo Giannini, Barbara Bach, Claudine Auger and Barbara Bouchet.

A great cast highlights this rather standard giallo as Giannini investigates the murders of some beautiful women connected to a local high-end salon (because, of course, it's always the rich who get it in gialli!). And you know what you can expect when the plot takes place in a salon: that's right, lots of scenes with naked women getting massaged. The film opens with the lovely Barbara Bouchet experiencing the joys and sufferings of a doozy, all set to the strumming of some very bad Eurocult music. The women are being killed via an injected poison that (no surprise) keeps them conscious but immobilized just like the venom of a tarantula. Hopefully Giannini can figure it out before the wife of the salon owner gets the poison treatment too. It takes him awhile but he eventually puts it together. Not a bad little film; a little draggy in the middle, but the amazing cast full of ex–Bond girls will help pass the time quickly.

Blood and Black Lace, aka *Sei donne per l'assassino*. Prod. Massimo Patrizi. Dir. Mario Bava. Italy, 1964. VCI, 90 min. DVD. Starring: Cameron Mitchell, Eva Bartok, Thomas Reiner and Mary Arden.

Christina's Haute Couture is experiencing something a little worse than a recession. The new fall line is about to be introduced and models keep dropping dead. It seems there's a black-trenchcoated, faceless murderer prowling around viciously killing (and it's pretty vicious) these models of questionable virtue. Though it followed Bava's *The Girl Who Knew Too Much* (1962) by a couple of years, this film is the first true example of a giallo and it works on nearly every level. Ultra-violent for its time period, the furnace burning and graphic drowning being prime examples,

Blood becomes the template for all subsequent gialli. *Blood* has all the constructs of the subgenre: a violent masked killer in leather, beautiful but completely sexualized women with secrets (they're top fashion models for Christ's sakes!), drug addiction and blackmail. Bava utilizes each one to its maximum potential creating a fun, exciting movie that stands the test of time. If you're not familiar with the subgenre you might want to start here, but beware: there's a large number of transfers and versions out there on the marketplace, all of differing quality. Perhaps one day we'll see a Blu-Ray version of this classic because it definitely warrants it!

Bloodstained Shadow, aka *Solamente nero* (IT). Prod. and Dir. Antonio Bido. Italy, 1978. Blue Underground, 109 min. DVD. Starring: Lino Capolicchio, Stefania Casini, Craig Hill and Massimo Serato.

This late entry into the giallo subgenre suffers from a genuine lack of originality. Stefano (Capolicchio), a young teacher with reoccurring nightmares, goes back to Venice to visit his brother, a local priest (Hill). Soon, though, he's watching a medium get murdered and playing detective before anyone else dies (hint: they do die). When he's not out sleuthing, he's trying to romance a young art student (*Suspiria* star Casini, who appears nude) who may hold the clue to his nightmares. If you're a fan of complicated gialli then *Bloodstained* won't offend. There's enough titillation to keep exploitation film lovers happy, though there are better examples in the giallo canon.

Case of the Bloody Iris, aka *Perchè quelle strane gocce di sangue sul corpo di Jennifer?* (IT) *What Are All These Strange Drops of Blood on Jennifer?* (U.S.). Prod. Luciano Martino. Dir. Anthony Ascott. Italy/Spain, 1972. Anchor Bay Entertainment, 94 min. DVD. Starring: Edwige Fenech, George Hilton, Annabella Incontrera and Paola Quattrini.

A wonderfully sleazy low-budget giallo, complete with Edwige Fenech and a flower cult orgy! Fenech's relationship woes continue in this film as she plays an ex-stripper turned model (isn't that the way it always works in these films?) who was previously married to the leader of a hippie commune that likes its flowers (I'm really not kidding). Fenech's husband, spouting all sorts of nonsense about "free love" straight out of an *Emmanuelle* film, wants her back so he can share her sexually with the commune. Meanwhile, all her stripper/model friends, including one who likes to get men up on stage so she can beat the hell out of them, are getting slashed up in elevators. You can't make this stuff up! *Case of the Bloody Iris* is one of those films that make you happy to be a Eurocult fan. See it today!

The Case of the Scorpion's Tail, aka *La coda dello scorpione*. Prod. Luciano Martino. Dir. Sergio Martino. Italy/Spain, 1971. No Shame Films, 90 min. DVD. Starring: George Hilton, Anita Strindberg, Janine Reynaud, Ida Galli and Luigi Pistilli.

Scorpion's Tail is a dense, plodding mystery that does deliver once you get through the convoluted plot. There are so many twists and turns in the plot is would be a great disservice to give too much away, so bare minimum here. Galli stars as a woman who unexpectedly comes into a large sum of money. Whenever that happens in a giallo you know people are going to die, and die they do. giallo regulars George Hilton and Anita Strindberg are on hand to try to solve the mystery, along with *Succubus* (1968) temptress Janine Reynaud. What's great about Martino's gialli is that he always likes to throw you a curve ball somewhere in the plot that completely changes the complexity of the film. *Scorpion's Tail* is no different. Not as exploitative as his work with Edwidge Fenech, this is still an interesting tale that deserves a viewing.

Cat o' Nine Tales, aka *Il gatto a nove code*. Prod. Salvatore Argento. Dir. Dario Argento. Italy, 1971. Anchor Bay Entertainment, 112 min. DVD. Starring: James Franciscus, Karl Malden, Catherine Spaak and Rada Rassimov.

The Terzi Institute is doing some wonderful work in the field of genetics, pinpointing the causes of such things as schizophrenia. Unfortunately, the work is too wonderful and someone a little schizoid is taking it too personally, resulting in death for several members of the cast. Newspaper reporter Franciscus, with the help of a blind crossword puzzle ace (Malden) and his "eyes," little girl sidekick Lori (Cinzia de Carolis), try to solve the crimes before they themselves are victims.

Argento's second giallo is a fun-filled romp that adds a little more complexity to the narrative than his previous *Bird with the Crystal Plumage* (1969). The film seems much more "Americanized" than most gialli, probably owing to Franciscus and Malden's appearance. It also may be why the film plays more like a straight detective story with some giallo touches than the other way around. Still, the plot is tight (and convoluted, but hey, it's a giallo), it's well acted, and Argento shows even more skill behind the camera as he happily throws people down elevator shafts, throws people into trains, and has the badly wigged Catherine Spaak take off her clothes. For those who dislike gialli for their hard-core violence, *Cat* may be a good compromise, as it keeps the violence down in favor of some terrific performances and an interesting plot. Argento would complete his "animal trilogy" the next year with *Four Flies on Grey Velvet* (1972).

Cold Eyes of Fear, aka *Gli occhi freddi della paura* (IT). Prod. José Frade. Dir. Enzo Castellari. Italy/Spain, 1971. Image Entertainment, 91 min. DVD. Starring: Frank Wolff, Giovanna Ralli, Fernando Rey and Karin Schubert.

Cold Eyes was one of the first gialli to be produced after the initial success of Dario Argento's *The Bird with the Crystal Plumage* (1969). Consequently it seems that the film was designed to be a thriller that incorporated some giallo constructs when that subgenre became lucrative. Fans of either genre were probably disappointed, though there is some fun here. An opening protracted "staged" rape, some swinging London settings and the fun of watching Ralli wander around evading a gang member intent on killing a judge (Rey) is pretty much all the film has to offer. There are plenty of action-packed, gore-soaked gialli to watch, but this is not one of them.

Death Walks at Midnight, aka *La morte accarezza a mezzanotte*. Prod. and Dir. Luciano Ercoli. Italy/Spain, 1972. No Shame Films, 102 min. DVD. Starring: Nieves Navarro, Simón Andreu, Carlo Gentili and Pietro Marellanza.

Death Walks in High Heels, aka *La morte cammina con i tacchi alti*. Prod. and Dir. Luciano Ercoli. Italy/Spain, 1971. No Shame Films, 108 min. DVD. Starring: Nieves Navarro, Frank Wolff, Simón Andreu and Carlo Gentili.

Death Walks both *in High Heels* and *at Midnight* as a group of very enjoyable gialli made by producer Ercoli and starring his wife Navarro (who performed under the name Susan Scott). It's obvious that these are star vehicles for Navarro and she handles herself admirably in some very stylish films. *High Heels* finds our heroine as a stripper/dancer (no, Erocoli was not afraid to exploit his wife's, um, talents in these films) whose thief father winds up dead. Soon Navarro is running to the coast with Wolff to escape the murderer, who has now set his sights on her. I can't tell you much more so as not to spoil any of the surprises (and there are a lot!), but this one will definitely keep you guessing from beginning to end.

Midnight finds Navarro as a fashion editor (she's obviously moved up the job chain from the last film) who experiments with drugs and finds herself witnessing a murder. Since she was so stoned, she can't remember what happened, and she becomes justifiably annoyed when the murderer turns his attention to her. Though it's not as fun as *High Heels*, Ercoli still manages to keep the action going, ending the film with a spectacular rooftop assault. Both films work because of Navarro; she makes a beguiling heroine who is not only sexy but strong as well. It's a shame she was not utilized in many more gialli (as was, say, Edwige Fenech), as she acquits herself nicely in the subgenre.

Deep Red, aka *Profondo rosso*. Prod. Salvatore Argento. Dir. Dario Argento. Italy, 1975. Anchor Bay Entertainment, 127 min. DVD. Starring: David Hemmings, Daria Nicolodi, Gabriele Lavia and Macha Méril.

Dario Argento's fourth giallo and his most seminal one. All the elements that went into his "animal trilogy" (*Bird with the Crystal Plumage*, 1970; *Cat o' Nine Tails*, 1971; and *Four Flies on Grey Velvet*, 1972) come together for a violent, if somewhat overlong classic. No surprises in the basic plot here as a musician (*Blow Up*'s David Hemmings) sees the brutal murder (let's just say meat cleaver) of a German psychic who, unfortunately for her, guessed the identity of a certifiable maniac. Soon the killer is after him and the only person to help is a goofy news reporter (Nicolodi).

Everything clicks here as Argento fills the film with an eccentric list of suspects and characters, including Hemmings's alcoholic homosexual friend (Lavia), his ex-actress scary-looking mother, a little girl (Eurocult favorite Nicholetta Elmi) who likes to stick pins in live lizards, and the father who beats her up for it. At its heart the film is about families, which is driven home by the wonderfully nostalgic Eurocult Christmas recreation that Argento opens the film with. The violence is ramped up as well, with blood spurting from everywhere via meat cleavers, scaldings, and a great shot of an actor being dragged around by a garbage truck and hitting every curb on the street until someone mercifully pops his head with a car. For all of the praise heaped on it by fans and critics alike, the film does have two major faults: its length, 127 minutes, pretty much ensures there's going to be a lot more talk than action, and the Nicolodi character comes off as more annoying than cute. Regardless, this is a classic and should be at the top of everyone's list who's interested in the giallo and in Eurocult in general.

Don't Torture a Duckling, aka *Non si sevizia un paperino*. Prod. Renato Jaboni. Dir. Lucio Fulci. Italy, 1972. Anchor Bay Entertainment, 102 min. DVD. Starring: Florinda Bolkan, Barbara Bouchet, Tomas Milian and Irene Papas.

Those who only know Lucio Fulci's work from *Zombie* (1979) or *The Beyond* (1981) might be surprised to know that he created some of the most professional, thought-provoking gialli produced. *Don't Torture a Duckling* downplays a lot of the excesses that would be a staple of his later films, yet still retains a decidedly lurid atmosphere. Teenage boys in a small Italian town are turning up dead, so a reporter from Rome (Milian) comes to investigate. What he finds is a town resembling something of an Italian version of Harper Valley PTA with a long list of suspects that includes a peeping Tom, a drug-addicted pedophile, a self-proclaimed Gypsy, and a rather intense priest. The name of the game here is repression, sin and guilt as Fulci takes an unflinching look at the politics of small-town Italian life, and what he finds isn't pretty. This being Fulci, though, you can expect some bursts of violence like a rather intense whipping as well as slow-motion close-ups of a man's head being bashed against rocks as he falls to his death. Don't worry, he deserved it. Thought-provoking and original, this is a good chance to see Fulci's work before the gore overtook his career.

Fifth Cord, aka *Giornata nera per l'ariete* (IT). Prod. Manolo Bolgnini. Dir. Luigi Bazzoni. Italy, 1971. Blue Underground, 93 min. DVD. Starring: Franco Nero, Silvia Monte, Pamela Tiffin, Ira von Fürstenberg and Rossella Falk.

This story of a J & B swigging journalist (yes, I know, there's a journalist in every giallo) is high up on a lot of critics' lists as a classic. I'm not sure I'd go that far, but it is engaging. Our journalist (Nero) is attacked on his way home from a swinging New Year's Eve party. Soon, the guests of the party start losing their fingers as a leather-glove-wearing psychopath begins murdering them, leaving behind a leather glove and a finger. The film is definitely tense (Falk's demise, as the paraplegic Sophia, is particularly stressful) as well as subliminally sleazy, with its live sex shows, implications about child pornography, and some frequent nudity from Ms. Tiffin. Nero makes an engaging hero, but the film sometimes collapses under the weight of its story. Gialli are known for their convoluted plots, but this one seems to take it to the extreme. Good? Yes. A classic? You be the judge.

Five Dolls for an August Moon, aka *Cinque bambole per la luna d'agosto*. Prod. Luigi Alessi. Dir. Mario Bava. Italy/Germany, 1969. Image Entertainment, 78 min. DVD. Starring: William Berger, Ira von Fürstenberg, Edwige Fenech and Ely Galleani.

Many fans, including Bava himself, have often been quite critical of *Five Dolls*. It's no masterpiece, for sure, but I've always had a soft spot for this psychedelic *Ten Little Indians* remake/rip-off with its hippie sensibilities and soon-to-be giallo superstar, Algerian beauty Fenech, bouncing around in her form-fitting '60s wear. It's back to the beach for Bava as he tells the standard story of a bunch of not-so-nice people staying at a very swinging art deco house on the shores of what looks like a very cold beach (similar to his *The Whip and the Body*; in fact, same beach, new house). Though he literally had two days to prepare for filming (the original director dropped out), Bava was able to throw in his own style on a number of scenes, especially the way he handled the body disposal (think bubble wrap and a freezer). This is not a film in which a lot of blood is shed and the short running time is a mercy, especially with the convoluted finale. Nevertheless if you're feeling funky and want to see a great international cast being overtly serious, *Five Dolls* might be for you.

Forbidden Photos of a Lady Above Suspicion, aka *Le foto proibite di una signora per bene*. Prod. Alberto Pugliese and Luciano Ercoli. Dir. Luciano Ercoli. Italy/Spain, 1970. Blue Underground, 86 min. DVD. Starring: Dagmar Lassander, Pier Paolo Capponi, Nieves Navarro and Símon Andreu.

There's something about the presence of Dagmar Lassander in a film that alerts you that there's going to be some good-natured sleaze. The always-engaging German actress seemed to gravitate to roles that heightened her sexuality yet gave her some decent material to act slightly over-the-top, from Bava's *Hatchet for a Honeymoon* (1969) to *The Frightened Woman* (*Femina ridens*, 1969). *Forbidden* adds to that as a fun little film that has enough sleaze in it to make most exploitation fans happy. If you notice I didn't use the word giallo, and that's because the film, while having many traits in common with the subgenre, doesn't really classify as such. It's more a sex-thriller, but who cares? Just enjoy Dagmar entering the valley of the dolls after being blackmailed by a photographer (Andreu) who purports to have pics of her husband killing his business partner. For some reason she begins an affair with the guy, which causes even worse repercussions and causes her to think she's losing her mind. Even her bisexual, porno-loving best friend (Navarro, having a great time here), who is worried about her, tries to help. Good music by Ennio Morricone, as well as able cinematography, make this a pleasant (the violence is turned way down here) time waster to enjoy.

Four Flies on Grey Velvet, aka *Quattro mosche di velluto grigio* (IT). Prod. Salvatore Argento. Dir. Dario Argento. Italy/U.S., 1972. MYA, 98 min. DVD. Starring: Michael Brandon, Mimsy Farmer, Jean-Pierre Marielle and Marissa Fabbri.

Argento's third giallo in as many years shows some staleness beginning to creep into his formula. There's really nothing new here within the confines of the giallo as rock musician and sort-of jerk Roberto (Brandon) mistakenly believes he's murdered someone and is blackmailed for it by a vicious killer. Though the narrative is familiar, Argento throws enough stylistic twists and turns to make the film an enjoyable experience. The inclusion of a gay hero private eye (Marielle) as well as the assorted oddball characters is a just another example of how Argento is not afraid to mix up convention. Mimsy Farmer, star of numerous Eurocult films, is used to good effect here as the "suffering" wife. Argento's unraveling of the murderer is rather far-fetched (hint: it has something to do with the title) but the killings are inventive and fairly gruesome for the early '70s, involving poison, the requisite stabbings, and a well-done slow-motion decapitation. Argento deservedly spent a couple of years off the genre, returning with the seminal *Profondo rosso* (*Deep Red*) in 1975.

French Sex Murders, aka *Maison de rendez-vous* (FR), *Casa d'appuntamento* (IT). Prod. Dick Randell. Dir. Ferdinado Merighi. Italy, 1972. Mondo Macabro, 90 min. DVD. Starring: Anita Ekberg, Rosalba Neri, Howard Vernon and Barbara Bouchet.

Another great international cast highlights this ridiculous film. Anita Ekberg as a high-class madam: check. Nasty killings of prostitutes: check. A list of suspects all having something lurid in their past: you betcha. This should be a great film, right? Did I also mention that the hero is a Bogart-looking, Bogart-talking detective that spends the whole movie imitating Bogart? Yep. Fail.

The Girl Who Knew Too Much, aka *La ragazza che sapeva troppo* (IT), The Evil Eye (U.S.). Prod. Lionella Santi. Dir. Mario Bava. Italy, 1962. Image Entertainment, 88 min. DVD. Starring: John Saxon, Leticia Román, Valentina Cortese and Titti Tomaino.

Some may argue this is the first true filmed giallo, and it's a smash. While the rest of the world was swooning over *Rome Adventure* (1962) or listening to Connie Francis sing a slew of Italian hits, Mario Bava was showing us the other side of Italy, creating the giallo subgenre in the process. Bava plays the film with tongue firmly in cheek (for an even more comedy-tinged version, try finding a copy of the U.S. version *The Evil Eye*, which plays up the comedy), but there's a lot of surprising adult content here that grounds the film and forces you to take it seriously. American Nora Davis (Román) is not having what one would call a good trip to Italy. On her first day there she's unknowingly given drugs at the airport, her grandmother dies, she sees a woman brutally murdered and the police thinks she's nuts. Not exactly a story out of Fodor's Travel Guide. With the assistance of Dr. Bassi (American actor John Saxon), she sets out to find out what happened before she herself is a victim. Not overtly violent (though the first murder is rather intense for 1962), the film retains an underlying perversity that's accented by Bava's masterful use of the camera. Bava had always thought the story of *The Girl* was silly, which is why he concentrated on the technical aspects; in any case, we as viewers are the beneficiaries, as the film is draped in beautiful black and white shadows, contrasts and tones. This is also one of the only examples of Bava's gialli in which we get characters we can actually care about. Román is a delight with her big expressive eyes, and her relationship with Saxon, though played for laughs, is appealing. A definite must-see, even if only for the blistering Italian theme song, "Furore," which will be stuck in your head for days!

Hatchet for the Honeymoon, aka *Il rosso segno della follia* (IT). Prod. Manuel Cano. Dir. Mario Bava. Italy/Spain, 1968. Image Entertainment, 86 min. DVD. Starring: Stephen Forsyth, Dagmar Lassander, Laura Betti and Femi Benussi.

Not a giallo by any stretch (we know who the killer is in the first five minutes), this is a transition film for Bava from his Gothic style of filmmaking he had been employing to a more modern-day approach. I'm not sure he felt that comfortable with the film, as it's a very disjointed affair, perhaps due the fact that the production ran out of money halfway through and he didn't finish it until six months or so later. John Harrington (Forsyth) designs wedding dresses and kills beautiful women at night. Obviously working out some issues (my bet is sexual orientation issues, by the way that Forsyth plays the part), he then murders his shrewish wife (Betti) and takes up with our favorite Dagmar Lassander. Unfortunately for him, Betti's none too pleased about being dead and decides to haunt him. It all has to do with childhood trauma (obviously) and is not one of Bava's best films.

The House with Laughing Windows, aka *La case dalle finestre che ridono* (IT). Prod. Antonio Avati. Dir. Pupi Avanti. Italy, 1976. Image Entertainment, 106 min. DVD. Starring: Lino Capolicchio, Francesca Marciano, Gianni Cavina and Guilio Pizzirani.

A strangely worded title for a strange movie. *House* is a — okay, let's be honest — a VERY slow-moving film about a young painter who is hired to finish work on a fresco for a church in a small Italian town. Well, wouldn't you know the town has some secrets, and in a refreshing twist they actually want to share them with our young newcomer. The only problem is they keep dying before they can actually say something. It seems that the painter who was hired previously went crazy and died, prompting an investigation by our new artist. Though there is some pretty violent stuff here — the opening stabbing and the finale, for example — this is not a film that will make most exploitation film buffs happy (go rent *Strip Nude for Your Killer!*), but true lovers of Italian cinema will find something of value in the film. Though it may be too talky, its portrayal of small-town Italian life is very interesting and the performances are solid. Many critics regard this as a classic. It's not, but it is a very professional piece of art.

The Killer Must Kill Again, aka *L'assassino è costretto ad uccidere ancora* (IT). Prod. Umberto Lenzi. Dir. Luigi Cozzi. Italy, 1975. Mondo Macabro. DVD. Starring: George Hilton, Femi Bunussi, Cristina Galbo and Antoine Saint-John.

Playing like a cross between the television show *Dexter* (2009) and Hitchcock's *Strangers on a Train* (1954), Cozzi's giallo adds some new twists to the standard giallo formula. George Hilton, obviously tired of playing the good guy in every giallo he's been in, decides he wants to murder his silly wife after watching a psycho killer dumping a body in the water. Blackmailing the assailant into committing the murder, he begins his fun, single lifestyle. But this being a giallo means that the body is probably going to disappear, the police are going to be suspicious, some beautiful women are going to become involved and the killer is going to, yes, kill again. *Killer* is a nice joy ride that keeps audiences guessing. There's a rather graphic rape involved (actually, the rape isn't as graphic as the consensual sex that Cozzi juxtaposes over it), as well as the usual "tie-up-and torture," all of which make the film perfect for Eurocult fans looking for a little suspense.

Lizard in a Woman's Skin, aka *Una lucertola con la pelle di donna* (IT), *Schizoid* (U.S.). Prod. Edmondo Amati. Dir. Lucio Fulci. Italy/Spain/France, 1971. Shriek Show, 95 min. DVD. Starring: Florinda Bolkan, Jean Sorel, Stanley Baker and Anita Strindberg.

Another top-notch giallo from Lucio Fulci! Carol Hammond (Bolkan in an amazing performance) thinks she is losing her mind. The bored housewife of an adulterous husband (Sorel) has been having some pretty intense lesbian dreams (we're talking slow-motion, with the wind machine cranked on high, blowing through their hair, lesbian dreams!) about her free-loving neighbor (Strindberg). These lurid sexual dreams soon turn to murder, both real and imagined, as Carol begins to become unraveled. *Lizard* takes on the subjects of sexual frigidity as well as sexual orientation and delivers a thought-provoking, completely enjoyable film that is both well acted and beautifully photographed (with London as the backdrop). The sex, especially in the dream sequences, is fairly graphic and the drug use is prolific. The film is infamous for its dog evisceration scene, which is often cut out of many prints. It's a good, if fake, shot that adds to the depiction of the character's mental state. A definite don't-miss. The original U.S. poster made the film look like a killer bat movie!

My Dear Killer, aka *Mio caro assasino*. Prod. and Dir. Tonino Valeri. Italy/Spain, 1971. Shriek Show, 102 min. DVD. Starring: George Hilton, William Berger, Patty Shepard and Piero Lulli.

George Hilton is at it again. In what was his five millionth appearance in a giallo, he plays a police inspector who must figure why an ex–insurance investigator was killed in a quarry. Of course, he is five steps behind the killer and the killer is pretty good at erasing the evidence *and* people with some nifty things like buzz saws. A relatively benign film released at the time the subgenre was truly flooding the market.

One on Top of the Other, aka *Una sull'altra* (IT), *Perversion Story*. Prod. Edmondo Amati. Dir. Lucio Fulci. Italy/France/Spain, 1969. Severin, 103 min. DVD. Starring: Jean Sorel, Marisa Mell, Elsa Martinelli, Faith Domergue and John Ireland.

One on Top of the Other was released at roughly the same time as Argento's *Bird with the Crystal Plumage* (1970) and showed that Fulci was more than able to compete with him in the giallo arena. Of course the film in many respects is a rip-off of Hitchcock's *Vertigo* (1958), with its San Francisco setting and female protagonist who spends a lot of time changing disguises, but Fulci puts his own spin on the film, concocting a fun, if convoluted plot. Unhappily married doctor Dumurrier (Sorel) hatches a plan to kill his sickly harpy of a wife (Marisa Mell). After she konks, the good doctor believes he sees her again as a blonde stripper (Mell again, this time wearing the same blonde wig she wore in Mario Bava's *Diabolik* (1967), who uses a motorcycle in her "dance" routine. Of course, he becomes infatuated with her and the sexual hijinks begin until the investigators show up wondering what really happened to the original Ms. Dumurrier. *One on Top* predates the exciting thrillers of the '80s and '90s like *Basic Instinct* (1991) and *Body of Evidence* (1992) that used sexuality and obsession as the doorway to some pretty heinous violent acts. The film is well acted especially by Mell, who passes between her two roles with ease. The jazzy soundtrack is also fun, giving the film a hip sound (the soundtrack is available as an extra on the Severin DVD!), while Fulci makes the most out of his San Francisco settings.

Seven Blood Stained Orchids, aka *Sette orchidee macchiate di rosso*. Prod. Horst Wendlandt. Dir. Umberto Lenzi. Italy/Germany, 1972. Shriek Show, 92 min. DVD. Starring: Antonio Sabato, Uschi Glas, Pier Paolo Capponi, Marissa Mell and Rossella Falk.

Lenzi's 1972 giallo is a middling attempt that plays up all the constructs of the giallo. After his new bride (Glas) is attacked on a train during their honeymoon, fashion designer Mario (Sabato), along with the police, decide to let the assailant believe she is dead. See, there's been a rash of murders in Rome with a killer who likes to leave heart-shaped crescents with his victims, and this leather-wearing killer is good with all sorts of things like scalpels, power drills and knives. This doesn't bode well for our funky early–'70s couple, who need to figure out their connection to the killer before he decides to come calling again. Rather dull in spots, the film is enlivened by some fun sleaze involving hippies, prostitutes and orgies (not necessarily in that order!). In addition, the violence is solid with yet another giallo elevator slashing, as well as the typical "let's murder the prostitute in cornfield" routine. All-in-all a very average affair that still doesn't seem like a waste of time.

Short Night of Glass Dolls, aka *La corta notte delle bambole di vetro* (IT). Prod. Enzo Doria. Dir. Aldo Lado. Italy/Germany/Spain, 1971. Anchor Bay Entertainment, 97 min. DVD. Starring: Jean Sorel, Barbara Bach, Ingrid Thulin and Mario Adorf.

The mark of a great giallo is that it ropes you in with a great set-up and keeps you there by throwing in some shocking surprises that reinforce the tension. *Short Night* stars giallo regular Jean Sorel (*One on Top of the Other*, 1969; *Lizard in a Woman's Skin*, 1971) as—what else?—a reporter who is rushed to the hospital after being murdered. Yep, he's dead, or so everyone thinks, as the rest of the movie has Sorel (as narrator) trying to put the pieces as to how he arrived in such a condition. The usual giallo hijinks ensue, with hippies, cult orgies, lots of red herrings, some poison and an occasional butterfly (you'll see) thrown into the mix. An engaging cast, including Barbara Bach (Mrs. Ringo Starr) and Ingrid Thulin, round out what is an enjoyable, tense and well-acted giallo that grabs you from the beginning and doesn't let go.

Slaughter Hotel, aka *La bestia uccide a sangue freddo* (IT), *Asylum Erotica* (GB). Prod. Tiziano Longo and Armando Novelli. Dir. Fernado Di Leo. Italy, 1971. Shriek Show, 95 min. DVD. Starring: Klaus Kinski, Margaret Lee, Rosalba Neri and Jane Garret.

Ha, now this is fun! Get a bunch of whack jobs in an asylum run by Club Med who are prone to masturbation and perverse sexual impulses, add in a killer who likes to spy before slicing, throw in crazy German actor Klaus Kinski for good measure, and you've got the ingredients for a mindless but vastly entertaining giallo. Foregoing most of the plot elements that make up a giallo, Slaughter prefers to linger on the sex as "residents" like Rosalba Neri, who has some incestuous desires she needs to be cured of, are forced to take cold showers as punishment (yep, it's that type of movie!), or on nurses who have sex with their patients as therapy. This is a no-brainer that is bound to satisfy after a long day at work. The plot? Who cares? You'll forget about it before the movie is over. Just enjoy the campiness of the screenplay and watching the actors try to overplay each other.

Spasmo. Prod. Ugo Tucci. Dir. Umberto Lenzi. Italy/Germany, 1972. Shriek Show, 94 min. DVD. Starring: Robert Hoffman, Suzy Kendall, Ivan Rassimov and Adolfo Lastretti.

Spasmo is a maddening, disjointed affair that makes absolutely no logical sense, has very little bloodshed and nudity (surprising, since this is a Lenzi film), and is about as close to a bad LSD trip as you can get. For those who like their mind melds without the chemicals, this film is for you. The Spanish spent the entire '70s making films that resembled bad dreams in their narratives, *Spasmo* is as close as the Italians got. The story plays like a bad episode of *Twin Peaks* as rich kid Hoffman meets amnesiac Kendall, culminating in a cross-country chase that involves a lot of strange characters as well as a bunch of stabbed female mannequins hanging from trees. Mercifully, Lenzi does a bit of explaining at the end and is able to wrap his story up, but it's quite a ride up to that point. Ably produced, *Spasmo* is not without merit, as it looks good and everyone in the cast is game to act as bizarrely as possible, but you've been warned: this film should only be watched when your brain is craving a mental margarita.

The Strange Vice of Mrs. Wardh, aka *Lo strano vizio della Signora Wardh* (IT). Prod. Luciano Martino. Dir. Sergio Martino. Italy/Spain, 1970. No Shame Films, 94 min. DVD. Starring: Edwige Fenech, George Hilton, Ivan Rassimov and Conchita Airoldi.

A classic giallo that is as exciting as it is sexy! Martino's first giallo has Fenech starring as the beautiful, unhappy wife of a diplomat. Haunted by thoughts of her sado-masochistic ex-boyfriend (Rassimov), who was prone to raping her in rainstorms (in a very eerily shot scene that is both sexy and terrifying), as well enjoying using broken glass during sex (!), she embarks on an affair with subgenre regular George Hilton. It's never a good thing to cheat in a giallo, and soon enough the blackmailing, stabbing and deception begin in earnest. *Vice* works not only because of the stylish direction of Martino, but because of Fenech herself, who successfully performs a role that is both cruel and sympathetic. She knowingly cheats on her husband for no apparent reason, yet her presence is such that we care what happens to her. In addition to the strong production values, the use of music is key here and Martino creates an atmosphere of dread as his little sing-song plays throughout the film. With a lot of nude Fenech and some pretty intense murders, *Vice* is a must-see in the giallo canon!

Strip Nude for Your Killer, aka *Nude per l'assassino* (IT). Prod and Dir. Andrea Bianchi. Italy, 1975. Blue Underground, 98 min. DVD. Starring: Edwige Fenech, Nino Castelnuovo, Femi Benussi and Solvi Stubing.

Ahh: *Strip Nude for Your Killer*. You couldn't ask for a better title for one of the sleaziest gialli out there. Bianchi, who would give us the infamous zombie film *Burial Ground* ("*Mama!*," 1981), a few years later, doesn't disappoint. By the mid–'70s the giallo was pretty much thematically bankrupt (Argento's *Deep Red* being the exception) and producers were looking for something to spice up the subgenre. Bianchi found it all right, in sex! The first four scenes in the film should tell you what you're in for:

1. A graphic botched abortion scene (cut from many prints).
2. Opening Credits with the very best in vintage '70s porn music, boom-chicka-boom.
3. A doctor getting his penis sliced off by a motorcycle-helmeted, leather-wearing assailant.
4. Our hero photographer (Castelnuovo) picking a girl up in the local gym, telling her he's going to make her a model, then having sex with her in public sauna, all in the span of four minutes!

I could go on and on throughout the entire film, but why deprive you the pleasure of seeing Fenech and Castelnuovo trying to thwart the plans of the penis-hating killer? The film is the perfect bridge to the American slasher film, as the plot is definitely dumbed down to the barest minimum and violence and sex played up. You won't care who the killer is (and to me it was a bit of a stretch), but that's okay. This is definitely the film you want to watch with some friends who are looking for some of the cheesiest, most politically incorrect, most violent films in the giallo canon.

Torso, aka *I corpi presentano tracce di violenza carnale* (IT), *Carnal Violence* (GB). Prod. Carlo Ponti. Dir. Sergio Martino. Italy/France, 1973. Anchor Bay Entertainment, 92 min. DVD. Starring: John Richardson, Suzy Kendall, Tina Aumont and Luc Merenda.

Torso is a bit of a switch for Sergio Martino, who had given some very effective gialli like *The Strange Vice of Mrs. Wardh* (1970) and *Case of the Scorpion's Tail* (1971). A precursor to John Carpenter's *Halloween* (1978) and *Friday the 13th* (1980), the film plays up the violence to the extreme and is much more like a horror film than a straight giallo. A rash of killings in Rome has some of the local university students worried. A group of girls (led by Kendall, who spent the majority of the early '70s screaming her head off in a variety of gialli) decide to pack their troubles up and go to the country home of one of the girls. From there the fun begins! This is a savage giallo that pulls no punches. The violence is extreme and the sex (as evidenced by the ménage à trois in the opening credits) graphic. The joy of Eurocult films is that you never know what is going to happen as they don't follow a cookie-cutter template. Martino doesn't disappoint, throwing a curve ball halfway through the film that totally resets it. Fun, graphic and totally engaging, *Torso* may not be a great giallo but it is a great slasher film!

Twitch of the Death Nerve, aka *Ecologia del delitto* (IT), *Bay of Blood*, *Last House on the Left Part 2* (U.S.). Prod. Giuseppe Zaccariello. Dir. Mario Bava. 1971. Image Entertainment, 90 min. DVD. Starring: Claudine Auger, Laura Betti and Luigi Pistilli.

A seminal giallo and Bava's most over-the-top film! A laundry list of the most God-awful people, including murderous relatives, money-grubbing businessmen, horny teenagers, bad parents and a psychic or two, converge on a lake and are murdered off one-by-one in the most inventive ways. Though the basic plot is fairly simple, there's nothing simple about the way that Bava executes it with all the twists and turns in the film. He's clearly having a good time here, working out his issues with the moral character of people. Whatever he doesn't like, he kills, and in the most graphic of ways: *Twitch* is one of the first body count movies (à la *Friday the 13th*, 1980), with the cast getting slaughtered via hangings, drownings, shootings, decapitations, the occasional skewer while having sex, and a machete to the head for good measure. Bava doesn't flinch from the violence; in fact, he seems to revel in it as each murder is more outlandish than the last, and they're all done in a rather comic style. A great cast, all of whom seem game to go along with Bava's tongue-in-cheek approach, add to the proceedings. If you want to see where the slasher film originated (or at least got a lot of its ideas), look no further than here.

What Have They Done to Your Daughters?, aka *La polizia chiede aiuto* (IT). Prod. Horst Wendlandt. Dir. Massimo Dallamano. Italy/Germany, 1974. Arrow DVD. Starring: Farley Granger, Giovanna Ralli, Mario Adorf and Franco Fabrizi.

What Have You Done to Solange?, aka *Cosa avete fatto a Solange?* (IT). Prod. Horst Wendlandt. Dir. Massimo Dallamano. Italy/Germany, 1972. Shriek Show, 103 min. DVD. Starring: Fabio Testi, Cristina Galbo, Camille Keaton and Karin Baal.

Dallamano's two gialli are some of the most interesting and intense in the subgenre. Working with themes like abortion and underage prostitution, he takes a serious approach to the subgenre, creating situations that will stay long after you've finished the films. In *Solange*, girls' school teacher Testi just can't seem to keep his hands off the young students. When the girl he's trifling with swears she's witnessed a murder, then is later murdered herself, the married man fears their affair will be exposed. The police get him figured out, and soon he is forced — with the help of his much-too-forgiving wife (Baal)—to figure out who is doing the killing. Their investigation exposes that the girls of the school aren't the precious little darlings they appear to be, and one girl, Solange, holds the secret to the whole thing. One of the most satisfying gialli of its day, the film combines the right amount of sleaze and story to carry the audience through all the twists and turns with an emotionally satisfying ending.

Daughters was released two years later and while not exactly a giallo (more like a police thriller in the vein of the *Prime Suspect* series), like *Solange* it still manages to pack a punch. The death by hanging of a 15-year-old girl prompts an investigation by young female district attorney (a nice change of pace, as gialli are usually male-dominated) and the police, who discover that the young girl might be part of a teenage prostitution ring. Adding to the complexity of the investigation is a leather-wearing motorcycling maniac who's determined to destroy the evidence of the case before the police get to it. *Daughters* doesn't hold as much of a grip as *Solange* as it's too focused on the police protocol, but it's an intense, gritty film that deserves to be seen.

Who Saw Her Die?, aka *Chi l'ha vista morire?* (IT). Prod. Enzio Doria. Dir. Aldo Lado. Italy/German/France, 1972. Anchor Bay Entertainment, 94 min. DVD. Starring: George Lazenby, Anita Strindberg, Adolfo Celi and Nicoletta Elmi.

Before Nicolas Roeg was mining the ghost child haunts of Venice in his classic *Don't Look Now* (1973), Italian Lado was doing the same thing a year earlier. Starring former James Bond George Lazenby, *Who* begins with a young girl's murder at a ski resort by a black-veiled assailant. Many years later, Lazenby's daughter suffers the same fate in Venice as she is mysteriously drowned by the same black-veiled character. Soon the ex-wife (Anita Strindberg) arrives and the intense investigation is on to find the killer. Aldo takes the high road through most of the film, eliminating a lot of the extreme gore and sex, but still manages to create an aura of uneasiness with his Venetian locales just as Roeg did a year later. Lazenby makes an engaging hero far removed from the Bond heroics of *On Her Majesty's Secret Service* (1969), and Eurocult favorite Nicoletta Elmi as the young daughter always manages to send a chill down my spine.

Your Vice Is a Locked Room and Only I Have the Key, aka *Il tuo vizio è una stanza chiusa e solo io ne ho la chiave* (IT), *Excite Me* (U.S.). Prod. Luciano Martino. Dir. Sergio Martino. Italy, 1972. No Shame Films, 92 min. DVD. Starring: Edwige Fenech, Anita Strindberg, Luigi Pistili and Ivan Rassimov.

In what has to be the longest title (it's even longer in Italian!) ever for a giallo, Martino creates another solid story that is slightly different from its predecessors. Though his muse Fenech is in the starring role, it is actually Anita Strindberg who's on display here, telling the story of an unhappily married couple (Strindberg and Pistili, and let's just say Kathleen Turner and Michael Douglas were more content in *The War of the Roses*, 1989) who allow hippies into their sprawling house to do their drugs and have orgies. The husband also uses this time to publicly abuse his wife and maid to make up for the fact he's a washed-up writer. Well, the maid ends up dead, and worse, his mistress as well, and he becomes the number-one suspect by the police. Adding to his troubles, his sexual dynamo of a niece (Fenech) comes to visit, and soon the cast is immersed in deception and violence. Martino takes a page out of Bava's book and presents a giallo in which there are very few characters to care about. Strindberg is the closest we get to compassion, but her insistence and willingness to take her husband's abuse is a real downer. It's great to see Fenech (in shorter hair) playing against type, but the less said about that the better. Not as satisfying as *The Strange Vice of Mrs. Wardh* (1970) or as scary as his next film *Torso* (1973), *Vice* is still a solid shocker worthy of a view, as long as you don't have to keep repeating the title.

Italy in the '70s: Sex and Sadism

> You know everything changes, everything ages, everything needs to renew itself, you always need to go hunting for something new.... And in Italy, the horror genre, like the giallo genre, does not know how to renew itself.
> —Italian film director Michele Soavi when asked about state of horror film production in Italy during the 1970s and 1980s[159]

Italy in the early '70s was a very different place from what it had been a decade earlier. Not only was the country in the midst of a recession, but negative social and political unrest was making Italy a violent place to live and work. Issues such as organized crime, drugs, terrorism, etc., began to resonate and swell in the country, contributing to an overall malaise in Italian businesses, including the film industry. By the late '60s, Italy was beginning to feel the effects of this stagnant economy.[160] The "Hot Autumn of 69" saw a proliferation of strikes, factory occupations, and mass demonstrations throughout northern Italy. Most of the work stoppages were unofficial, led by workers' factory committees or militant leftist groups rather than by the (party-linked) trade unions. The protests were not only about pay and work-related matters but also about conditions outside the factories, such as housing, transport, and pensions. As the '70s began, the situation worsened: bankruptcies increased, inflation hit twenty percent, and unemployment skyrocketed. This led to some extremely violent forms of unrest within the Italian population. Factions from the far right, who were behind a bombing that killed 16 people in Piazza Fontana in Milan in 1969, as well as Piazza della Loggia bombing in Brescia five years later, warred against those on the left, composed of disaffected intellectuals from Northern universities, creating fear within the populace.[161] All of these issues helped form a general wave of political and student protests that resonated around the country.[162]

The film landscape was changing as well. The late '60s and early '70s was a period of re-imaging for filmmakers around the world. The social mood brought on by violence in Italy, student protests in Paris, the controversies over Vietnam and Watergate in the United States, immigration issues, and the establishment of ratings systems such as the MPAA ratings code had changed the nature of films. This manifested itself in the United States in the dismantling of studios and the turning away from big blockbuster films (e.g., *The Sound of Music*, 1965) to smaller, more independent films that appealed to the social consciousness (e.g., *Easy Rider*, 1969).[163] Given this new environment of freedom, the period also signified the re-emergence of the American horror film. Basically stagnant for two decades, the genre was able to reinvent itself to become a parable about these events. Films such as Polanski's *Rosemary's Baby* (1968), Romero's *Night of the Living Dead* (1968), Craven's *Last House on the Left* (1972), and Friedkin's *The Exorcist* (1973) not only proved to strike a chord in audiences around the world, they were to have a profound impact on the Italian film industry. In the '70s, European cinema, including Italy, was experiencing a general decline. The drop in attendance in Italy was close to catastrophic. From 1976 to 1979, ticket revenues fell from 514 million to 276 million lire.[164] The cause of this was a deep neglect by the state, both institutionally and financially, as well as the proliferation of private television stations that successfully competed against filmmakers by churning out derivative product.

Italian horror/exploitation film producers in search of a profit went back to the tried and true behavior they exhibited in the late '50s. They created niches (i.e., rip-offs) that were adapted from the easiest, most audience-tested, most successful products available. With the popular resurgence of horror and a historical foundation for making horror films in the Gothic and giallo styles, Italian filmmakers had an obvious avenue of subject matter to exploit. In addition, with Italy experiencing an uprise in violence and complete transformation of its social and culture proclivities, producers knew they would have audience identification, thereby allowing them to tailor these subgenres to their most exploitative possibilities. The Italian exploitation films of the '70s appealed to basest of entertainment choices and showcased pornographic (both soft and hard) representations of sex and violence. The cannibal, zombie, nunsploitation and violent sex subgenres were among the most exploitive in the world for their time. They gave willing audiences around the world something even more violent than they could get in their living rooms, and though they echoed lofty political themes such as consumerism, globalization, religious freedom, and women's rights, they did so in way that was so subtle and hidden under all the sex and violence, we're only now — after viewing these films 30 years later — beginning to understand how society and culture shaped this much-maligned industry.

We Will Eat You: The Cannibal and Zombie Film

> This was not your daddy's favorite cannibal movie, this was an ass-kicking flick, the proudly repugnant progeny of collective fears.
> —Author Jim Van Beeber, describing his first viewing of *Cannibal ferox* (1983)[165]

The Italian zombie and cannibal film are two of the most successful subgenres in Italian exploitation. Cannibal films have their origins distinctly from the mondo films of early and mid–'60s and are distinctly Italian, while the zombie film is a liberal borrowing from the successful films by American director George Romero. Both rely on extreme gore, nudity and the collective fears of the world society as devices to not only shock an audience but to go out of their way to offend it. Films such as *Cannibal Holocaust* (1980) grossed over $2 million in Italy alone before being shut down by the courts, while Lucio Fulci's *Zombi* (*Zombie*, 1979) played to packed movie theaters around the world. At the pinnacle of their success these subgenres represented an "anything goes" mindset in that they were not afraid to push any button in order to gross out their audience. Whether it was the gut-munching, intestine-pulling style of the zombie film with its themes of death and disease, or the complete obliteration of all things non–Western in the cannibal film, these exploitation films brought the goods, so to speak, in pushing the violence to almost obscene proportions.

Cannibal films arose from the Italian shock mondo documentaries of the 1960s. Mondo films, like *Mondo cane* (1962) and *La donna nel mondo* (*Woman of the World*, 1963), ostensibly had a lofty ambition to educate audiences about differing social cultures around the world. In almost all cases they were nothing more than crass exploitation that took advantage of people's fear and distrust of the changing social landscape. Worldwide audiences who had previously enjoyed "gawking" at other cultures via the mondo film in the '60s, changed their tastes in '70s. They became bored with seeing exploitative documentaries and could now see many similar documentaries on television. Producers, in turn, decided to use completely fictionalized stories that involved strange customs and rites of international cultures without changing any of the graphic nature of the material.

Both the cannibal and zombie films are a reflection of man's disruption of the natural order of the world. They are also a reflection of the collective fears of an Italian society going through a social transformation. As mentioned earlier, immigration patterns in Italy had changed by the '70s. A huge influx of immigrants from Asia, North Africa and Eastern Europe had begun to settle in Italy. This fear of societal encroachment, mixed with a new cynicism of western values, created the template for the cannibal film. Audiences from the '60s saw the mondo films as cultural education and marveled at the differences between the modern world and the poor one. Cynical audiences of the '70s saw western man's encroachment on these societies as a bad thing, and this nihilism is reflected into the cannibal subgenre. The Italian cannibal genre proliferated in the era when audiences were clamoring for more adult fare in their movies about the subject of death. Television had begun to air documentaries that were slightly shocking in nature and had even begun playing heavily edited versions of *Mondo cane* (1962) on local television stations.[166] The cannibal film, for all its positive and negative points, offered audiences a barbaric, visceral thrill ride where they could obtain their own catharsis by sitting in a darkened movie theater with others looking for the same release.

Filmmaker Umberto Lenzi (1931–) took a break from filming gialli such as *Sette orchidee macchiate di rosso* (*Seven Blood Red Orchids*, 1972) and *Orgasmo* (*Paranoia*, 1969) to develop the template for the cannibal film. The resulting work, *Il paese del sesso selvaggio* (*Deep River Savages*, 1973), set up all the plot devices that became familiar with the subgenre.[167] Almost every cannibal film from the '70s follows the template to some degree, with an unsavory, morally bankrupt character (often from a large metropolitan area) paired with the occasional scientist/student. They find themselves in either the Amazonian or Asian jungle where they slaughter live animals, terrorize (and often rape) the indigenous tribes, and then are literally cannibalized when the tribes fight back. If a woman is involved (and there is always a woman involved), she is usually stripped and deified, or is so utterly heinous that she is eviscerated. *Il paese* starred Ivan Rassimov as an English photographer on assignment in Thailand and Burma who accidentally kills a criminal, forcing him to escape into the jungle. Captured by a primitive tribe, he is forced to endure a variety of tortures to prove his worth, including being used as a human dartboard and forced to hunt live animals. After all the torture, Rassimov is accepted into the tribe, marries a native girl (Me Me Lai), and becomes the head tribesman.[168] Essentially an action/adventure film, *Il paese* contains all the graphic scenes of rape and torture that one associates with the subgenre. Since no one involved in the filming of any of these exploitation films has come forward to press

The typically lurid poster for Lenzi's *Il paese del sesso selvaggio* (*Deep River Savages*, 1973) which sets up the template for the cannibal film.

charges against the filmmakers (only with the film *Emanuelle in America* was there a case of mental anguish brought against producers), these constructs can go down as simply exploitative subplot. The same cannot be said for the live animal killings that are graphically shown on the screen. Throughout the decade, a variety of turtles, monkeys, snakes, mongooses, crocodiles and other animals were killed on camera for no other purpose than shock value. It's what the cannibal subgenre is known for. Animal snuff magnifies the fictional construct of the human death, giving audiences their closest proximity to the forbidden world of real death.

For directors of the subgenre, the practice of killing live animals didn't seem too extreme; most had no issues with it and thought their actions were justified. This was the era before PETA (People for the Ethical Treatment of Animals) and the mindset was that if the mondo film was legitimized via its documentary-style depiction of animal killings then so would be the cannibal film. These lofty ambitions were also balanced by what filmmakers thought of as the necessity of killing these animals. Lenzi pointed out that no animal suffered unnecessarily if it wasn't to be used as food for the film crews.[169] Ruggero Deodato (1939–), director of the *Ultimo mondo cannibale* (*Jungle Holocaust*, 1977) and the infamous *Cannibal Holocaust* (1980), also defends this practice: "The rats, wild pigs, crocodiles and turtles were killed by the Indios [on the set of *Cannibal Holocaust*] themselves, for food. I simply followed them on the hunts—the equivalent of shooting the butchers at the slaughterhouse." Deodato takes a dim view of animal rights activists, calling them "very inflexible; they make such a fuss about films when so many animals are killed to provide food for us all...."[170] Of course, the idea of shooting animals in peril is bunk. These staged killings were meant for one thing, and that was to create controversy by grossing out the audience. Controversy, the life blood of exploitation films, helped to sell tickets.

The violence directed towards humans was also intense. Lenzi took a decidedly political viewpoint when dealing with critics on this subject:

> Look, my position about cannibal films, films that, should we say, exploit, are all primarily a result of experience I had with a previous film entitled *The Man from Deep River*. The scenes in that film were taken from genuine, authentic rituals that a local anthropologist had explained to us. We should not be surprised by it, if the film contains some violent actions that take place among savage tribes. What I wanted to show primarily is that this violence, even when it's not merely sexual violence, but violence such as killing, mutilation, has been caused above all by a policy, by a long history of third world colonization of the exploitation of savage tribes.[171]

As shocking as these animal killings and human violence were, the controversy over these films created great word-of-mouth, and worldwide audiences flocked to theaters to see them. It must be mentioned that no director of the cannibal subgenre thought he was making artistic statements. Many times, as was the case in almost all exploitation filmmaking, these films were simply a means to keep working. Says Lenzi, "With the exception of Italy, *Deep River Savages* was a great success all round the world. Apart from whatever merit they might have, they were in fact projects made on commission and shot 'cold,' as it were, purely to make a living."[172]

Though *Il paese* was popular, it was five years before the next cannibal movie was produced. The worldwide box-office success of Ruggero Deodato's *Ultimo mondo cannibale* (*Jungle Holocaust*, 1977) was what got the cannibal subgenre rolling. Deodato got the idea from an article in a *National Geographic* magazine which described a tribe of aboriginal cannibals living in a cave on the island of Mindanao (Philippines), and working with that

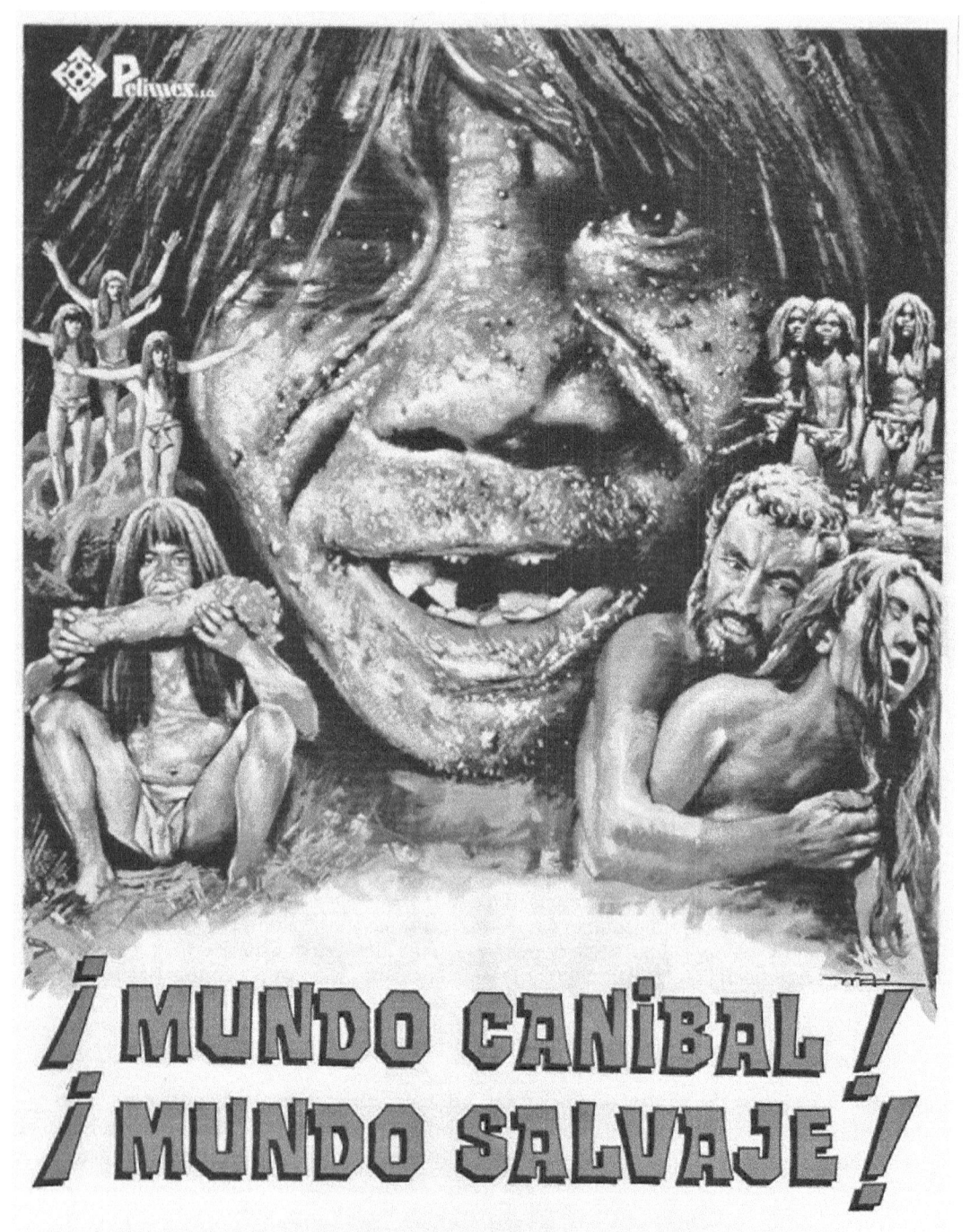

Before he assaulted everyone's senses with *Cannibal Holocaust* (1980), Deodato hit pay dirt with the success of *Ultimo mondo cannibale* in 1977.

idea he developed a screenplay that would posit the entrance of two outsiders (i.e., westerners) into this strange jungle environment.[173] *Ultimo*'s narrative doesn't break away much from the previous *Il paese*, as it follows oil entrepreneur Paul (Massimo Foschi) and anthropologist Rolf (Ivan Rassimov), who become lost in the Philippine jungle. Separated, Paul is captured and imprisoned by a cannibalistic tribe. Stripped of all his clothes, he is abused by the tribe, slung up and down on a large catapult, and forced to eat raw meat from recently dead animals. When he's not being urinated on from above by the local cannibal kids, he is being masturbated by a woman from the tribe (Me Me Lai, appearing in her second cannibal film). If that weren't enough fun for the audience, the exploitative highlight of the film comes when the tribe catches a female member of an opposing tribe and proceeds to rip open her stomach and eat her insides. Add to the film the requisite animal killings and rapes and you have the makings of a film that has little, if no, cultural sensitivity.[174] The beauty for Deodato was that he didn't have to show any sensitivity. This is a film made for westerners and clearly, in Deodato's eyes, western man, regardless of what events happen to him, will eventually take over and lead whatever population he chooses. He may turn into a savage, be urinated on from on high, but he will always end up leading and in this film that is exactly what happens. Western countries around the world, pardon the pun, ate up all of this western dominant ideology and packed theaters to see how these savages can be tamed by western man.

The popularity of *Ultimo mondo cannibale* opened the Italian market for a variety of new cannibal films. First on the list was Aristide Massaccesi's (1939–1999) *Emanuelle e gli ultimi cannibali* (*Emanuelle and the Last Cannibals*, 1977) which was an entry in the popular "Black Emanuelle" (see the Black Emanuelle section) soft-core series of the late '70s. By 1977 the series had begun to run out of fresh ideas for situations into which to place Emanuelle. There were only so many places that she could have sex, as venues like Paris, Venice, Hong Kong, and strangely, Long Island had already been explored, while she had dabbled in such exploitative subject matters as snuff filmmaking, white slavery and bestiality. Massaccesi, seeing the popularity of cannibal films, thought the jungle and its inhabitants would be a perfect foil for our lustful heroine as well as allow him the opportunity to include a variety of gore sequences. When asked in a 1998 interview why he chose to incorporate erotic footage into the cannibal genre, Massaccesi truthfully replied, "Well, you know I'm a real copy-cat and since Deodato's film [*Ultimo mondo cannibale*, 1977] had been so successful we thought about doing something along the same lines commercially."[175]

In the film, intrepid reporter Emanuelle (Laura Gemser) gets wind of a cannibal cult in the jungles of Brazil. She then assembles and leads a group into the Amazon, where they come under attack from the local jungle cannibals. From there the cast is either ripped to shreds, eaten or (because this is a Black Emanuelle film) forced to perform various sexual acts. Knives are thrust between females' legs, breasts are torn off and eaten, and men are gutted, stripped of their intestines, all of this moving the plot forward. Emanuelle manages to survive by painting herself as a water goddess and rowing away, but not before having public sex with a female member of the cast.[176] The film, for all its over-the-top histrionics, plays off the fear of colonialism and the unknown as the outside of the western world is portrayed as a scary place that only a woman with brains and a healthy sexual appetite can conquer.

The combination of the film's hard-core violence and soft-core sex, which began in earnest a year earlier with *Emanuelle in America* (1976), also plays into the fear of sexuality and death. Massaccesi sees both as primal forces of nature and inextricably linked. This is

Popular stars like Ursula Andress couldn't help but get in the Eurocult game, and her stint in *Mountain of the Cannibal God* (1978) adds a touch of class to an otherwise tawdry affair.

obvious in the first 10 minutes of the film as Emanuelle visits a New York hospital to take pictures of a cannibal girl (who looks like she just left a shopping mall in Ohio). The young cannibal manages to bite off the breast of a nurse before begin restrained by hospital officials. Emanuelle gets the story in the only way she knows how: by sneaking into the hospital room and masturbating the girl while she's tied down to the bed. The girls reveals her origins with a pleasurable moan amid her primal grunts. Throughout the film Emanuelle is spared most of the indignities, as it is the rest of the cast that is made to suffer. It is not surprising in these films that protagonists who carry on illicit affairs or incite overt violence are usually subjected to the worst punishments, such as castration or being burned alive, perfectly in line with the genre.[177]

Attempting to give the genre a touch more class was 1978's *La montagna del dio cannibale* (*The Mountain of the Cannibal God*), starring popular international actors Ursula Andress and Stacy Keach. Director Sergio Martino, who like Lenzi was well known for his gialli in the early 1970s, concocted a tepid action/adventure movie that incorporated all the stylings of the cannibal genre. Martino takes his time setting up the story of a woman (Andress) and her brother (Antonio Marsina) search for her missing husband in equatorial New Guinea. With the help of an anthropologist (Keach), Andress is put through the usual cannibal wringer of being attacked by snakes, tarantulas and the assorted piranha before being kidnapped and painted up (à la Laura Gemser in *Emanuelle e gli ultimi cannibali*) by the gut-munching locals.[178] With the exception of the animal killings, which occur throughout the film, Martino saves the true exploitation for the last 15 minutes, when the audience is treated to not only the usual intestine eating, but a young woman graphically masturbating and, in a scene cut from a lot of international prints, a man having simulated sex with a very large, very bored-looking boar! The film does boast some slick production values, belying the fact that a majority of the film was shot in Sri Lanka and Malaysia. Martino had no delusions about the artistic merit of a film such as this. Speaking about the film in 2003, he concluded that the film was a product of its time, relating:

> I decided to begin making cannibal movies because I've always worked for an organization whose main purpose is to make successful movies. At that time, we were working in the "imitation" genre, mimicking successful American genre films at 10 times less cost. The film definitely focused on some images of violence that at times were meant to have a documentary quality. Maybe this movie is a little too violent; I blame myself now because movies this violent are counter-educational. But in those days, to tell you the truth, there were other movies made earlier that are worse in that respect.[179]

The movie that Martino was probably referring was the 1980 release of the most controversial example of the genre, Ruggero Deodato's *Cannibal Holocaust.* Banned, seized, and/or heavily censored in most areas around the world, *Holocaust* has earned the reputation of one of the most frightening films ever, being dubbed by critics as "one of the most extreme and brutal films ever screened."[180] Utilizing a combination of fictional narrative and a documentary style like that of the mondo films, Deodato's film blurs the line between reality and fantasy, creating a cinema verité experience that shocked and disgusted film critics and audiences alike. The precursor to such films as *The Blair Witch Project* (1999) and *The Last Broadcast* (1998), *Holocaust* begins with the departure of a search party hoping to locate a documentary film crew that was lost in Amazon. After trekking through the jungle, the party (led by porn star Robert Kerman[181]) comes across a tribe of "tree" people who hold both the remains of the film crew and their film. Proving their worth via an initiation involving some typical exploitation constructs—eating human flesh, naked bathing by the local girls in the river etc.—the searchers are given the film canisters to take back to New York with them. The remainder of *Cannibal Holocaust* consists of viewing the material found in the canisters depicting the tree people's horrific revenge on the sadistic filmmakers who tortured, raped and humiliated the tribe in order to procure sensationalistic footage for their documentary.[182]

The mixture of mondo-style documentary and fictionalized narrative allows the film to move from one torture sequence to the next. Young native women get their vaginas bashed in by large wooden dildos as punishment for extramarital affairs, a pregnant woman is tied to a stake and given an abortion while being beaten fatally on the head, animals are killed outright, and men are castrated and eaten, all shown in graphic excess on the screen. Even more disturbing is the complete lack of humanity shown by the American documentarists. Lacking any moral compass, the Americans are portrayed as behaving as savagely as the natives, raping, killing and even turning on each other in complete disregard of human and animal life. Deodato went for realism, wanting to dupe his audience into thinking what was on the screen was real, and future lawsuits bear out that's exactly what he accomplished. He masked the production in secrecy so as to not cause untold attention, as well as using unknowns for his actors so there wouldn't be any press attention to the mysterious nature of the film. Deodato believed that the film's subject was so savage that he made the actors sign a release asking them not have any contact with other producers for a year so that the hype surrounding the film would not have a negative impact on their careers. When the film was later confiscated in Italy, Deodato exempted them from the contract when the judge, believing that he actually killed the four actors, threatened him with life in prison. Looking back, actor Luca Barbareschi, commenting in 2004, explained why he believed the controversy about the film is worse today than when it was made: "Probably because of the story, of the violence against animals, especially in an era of political correctness and attention, which is as it should be, based upon respect of nature. You know, a lot has happened in 25 years. Twenty-five years ago, the problem of the environment was not heard of as much as it is today. Today, everything is untouchable to the point that I did a show that made fun of the Green Party. But nature is defended and rightfully so and this is a film that is politically incorrect in that sense."[183]

It isn't just the animal violence that is disturbing in *Holocaust*, but the violence directed towards people, especially women. Gender-affirming characters and situations are not usually found in exploitation — in fact, that's one aspect that usually delineates it from other genres — but Deodato's film is downright disturbing in its portrayal of women. The only two main female characters are the television producer who wants to show the missing film (portrayed as sympathetic, but stupid) and one of the young filmmakers (Francesca Ciardi), whose cruelty throughout the film completely belies her femininity. After the shock of watching a woman killed by a monstrous dildo, as well as the abortion/murder scene, we are treated to the rape of a local tribe woman by the young male filmmakers in the group. It is here that we see the only instance of a heart, as Ciardi freaks out and tries unsuccessfully to put a halt to proceedings. It's a ridiculous moment, asking us to believe that after spending the movie brutalizing and killing man, woman and animal, along with having public sex with her head filmmaker boyfriend, she should suddenly find the concept of rape so offensive.

Deodato and crew aren't afraid to push every single exploitive button in order to secure the controversy that he was looking for. *Holocaust*'s director of photography, Sergio D'Offizi, provided some insight into the mindset of Deodato and others who dabbled in the cannibal subgenre, saying, "When we film, at least speaking for myself, perhaps we distort ourselves. We enter into a way of looking at things that is not the objective one, the correct one of the viewer, who sees something horrifying. We didn't notice. This distortion, let's call it 'professional,' as far as I'm concerned kept me from understanding precisely and objectively what we were doing. So the violence against people was a fake violence, as was recognized later. Less so with the animals, unfortunately, but that's what the scenes called for."[184]

Ready for distribution, *Cannibal Holocaust* (1980) immediately faced the wrath of censors. Pre-sold by United Artists, the film was met with a barrage of criticism on its opening in Italy. Deodato recalled the legal battles: "Perhaps the producer's mistake was to not pre-release it in a small country the way they usually did, to get it confiscated. Instead they immediately attempted, and perhaps it was United Artists that wanted this, to premiere it in Milan. In Milan, there was this terrible aggressive young judge who confiscated it. The film was seized, the film was stopped after it had earned an amount equal to $5 million today after 10 days."

Seizing the film was not the only thing the judge did. Convinced that the filmmakers really did kill people (false) and animals (true) for the making of this film, he ordered a trial. Hiring seven to eight media lawyers, Deodato was able to produce the actors in the film, freeing him from murder charges, though he was found guilty of the animal cruelty charge. Given a suspended sentence of four months and a fine of $300, Deodato was forced

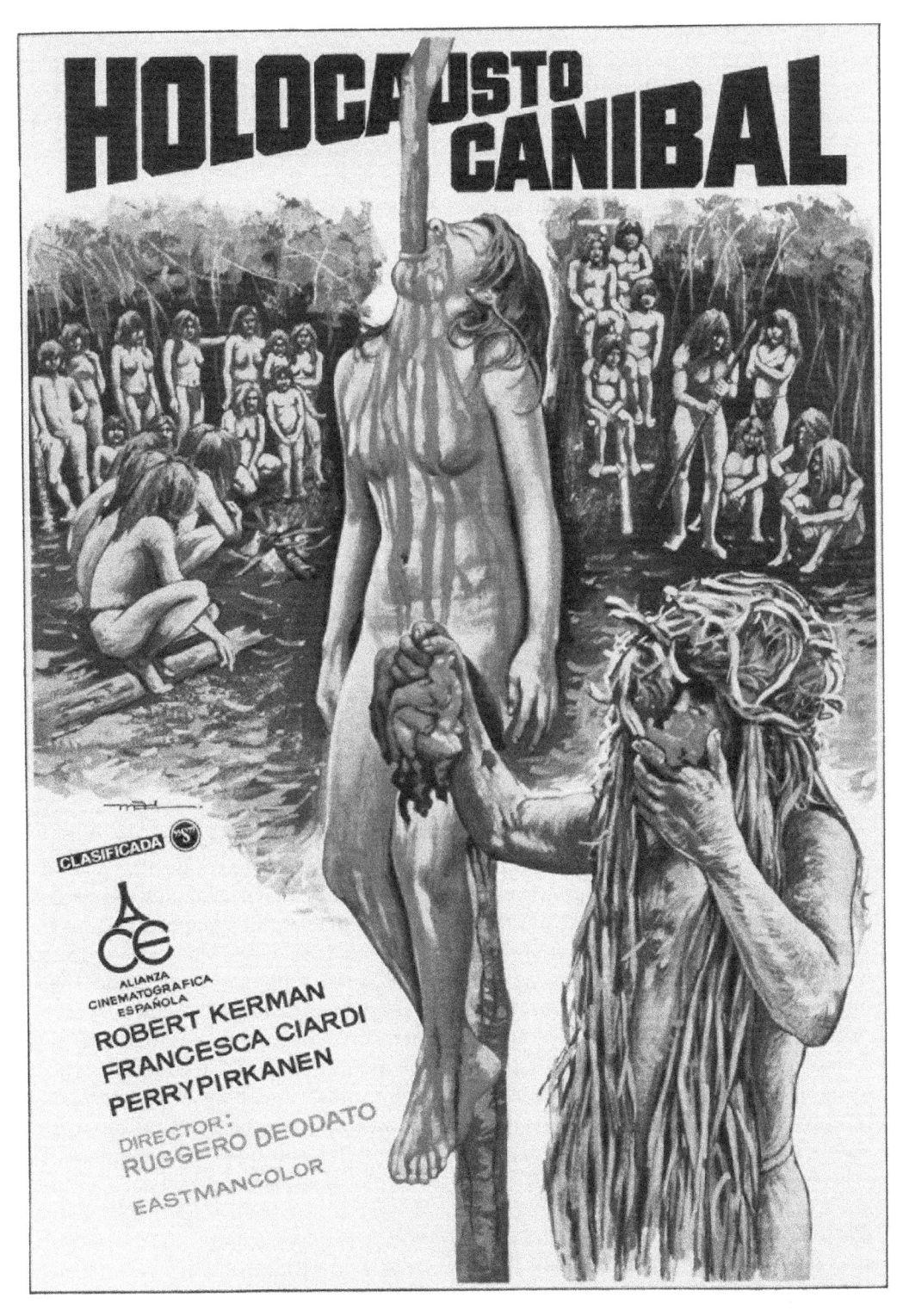

The marketing for *Cannibal Holocaust* (1980), one of the most controversial films ever produced, alerts viewers to exactly what they are going to be seeing.

to find a way to distribute the film. United Artists dropped out early and Deodato found it impossible to sell the film abroad. Three years later (1983) the film was released due to intervention by the Italian Appeals Court.[185] The film still underwent editing dependent upon the country it was playing in. In Britain, the film was banned outright and put on the "video nasty" list, meaning that it could not be viewed at all. Violators could be subject to a fine, confiscation, or in the worse cases, some jail time.[186]

For all of its excessive, exploitative violence and sex, there is something remarkably salient in *Holocaust*. At the time the film was meant to look at western man's savagery and his complete disregard for anything that he deems on an unequal level. Today, while these themes still resonate, it is the mixture of visual reality and drama with our fascination as an audience that really hits home. The film is as timely, if not more so, today as it was during its release. The second portion of the film, which sets up the battle between Kerman, who has watched the tapes and is disgusted by the content, with the television producers who want to show the footage unedited for the ratings is an argument is probably fought within every television network in today's media environment. The rise and popularity of pseudo-reality programming around the world has caused audiences to demand more controversial subject matter. Whether this pushes the boundaries of good taste is a matter for each member of audience to decide, but it's a good guess that had the fictional footage that Deodato shot have existed in real life it would undoubtedly be the number-one downloaded clip on YouTube. The film would actually fit within the parameters of today's online society quite well. It would be interesting to see how he would have marketed a film like *Holocaust* to the social media crowd.

The success and controversy surrounding *Holocaust* spurred other filmmakers to jump on the cannibal bandwagon. The same year, 1980, saw the release of several cannibal-themed movies, most of which deviated slightly from Deodato's film. Trying to steer away from the controversy and perhaps not wishing to indulge in a costly legal battle, directors looked to make their cannibal films more commercial, focusing more on traditional movie narratives.

Mangiati vivi! (*Eaten Alive*, 1980) marked Umberto Lenzi's return to the genre. Filmed before the release of *Cannibal Holocaust*, it was a fictionalized account of the Reverend Jim Jones and the Jonestown massacre. Lenzi opted to use a traditional action/adventure narrative instead of the mondo style of previous cannibal movies. *Mangiati* is the story of a young woman (Janet Agren) searching for her sister (Paola Senatore), who's been abducted by a strange Jim Jones–type cult in the jungles of Sri Lanka. With the aid of a guide (*Holocaust*'s Richard Kerman), she battles cannibals in the jungle and the sexual advances of the cult leader (Ivan Rassimov) before escaping with her life.[187] For the film, Lenzi used previous footage from other cannibal films to supplement the gore. He believed that gore was essential to the success of these films. Lenzi recalls: "The film was a smashing success especially because of the famous scene that I think the audiences will remember — when the Italian actress, it was Paola Senatore, is cut to pieces and eaten alive, still alive, by the cannibals."[188] Whereas Deodato's film was entirely nihilistic, devoid of humanity, Lenzi goes for fun, imbuing his characters with charm that is somewhat reminiscent of the Indiana Jones films that were popular at the time. This more whimsical style of cannibal film didn't last, though, as Lenzi's next cannibal film in 1981, *Cannibal ferox* (*Make Them Die Slowly*), completely eschewed any lightheartedness and was as rough as Deodato's film, resulting in another round of censorship difficulties and bannings.[189]

The cannibal film is one of the most exploitive and most violent in the Eurocult canon.

1. Italy 123

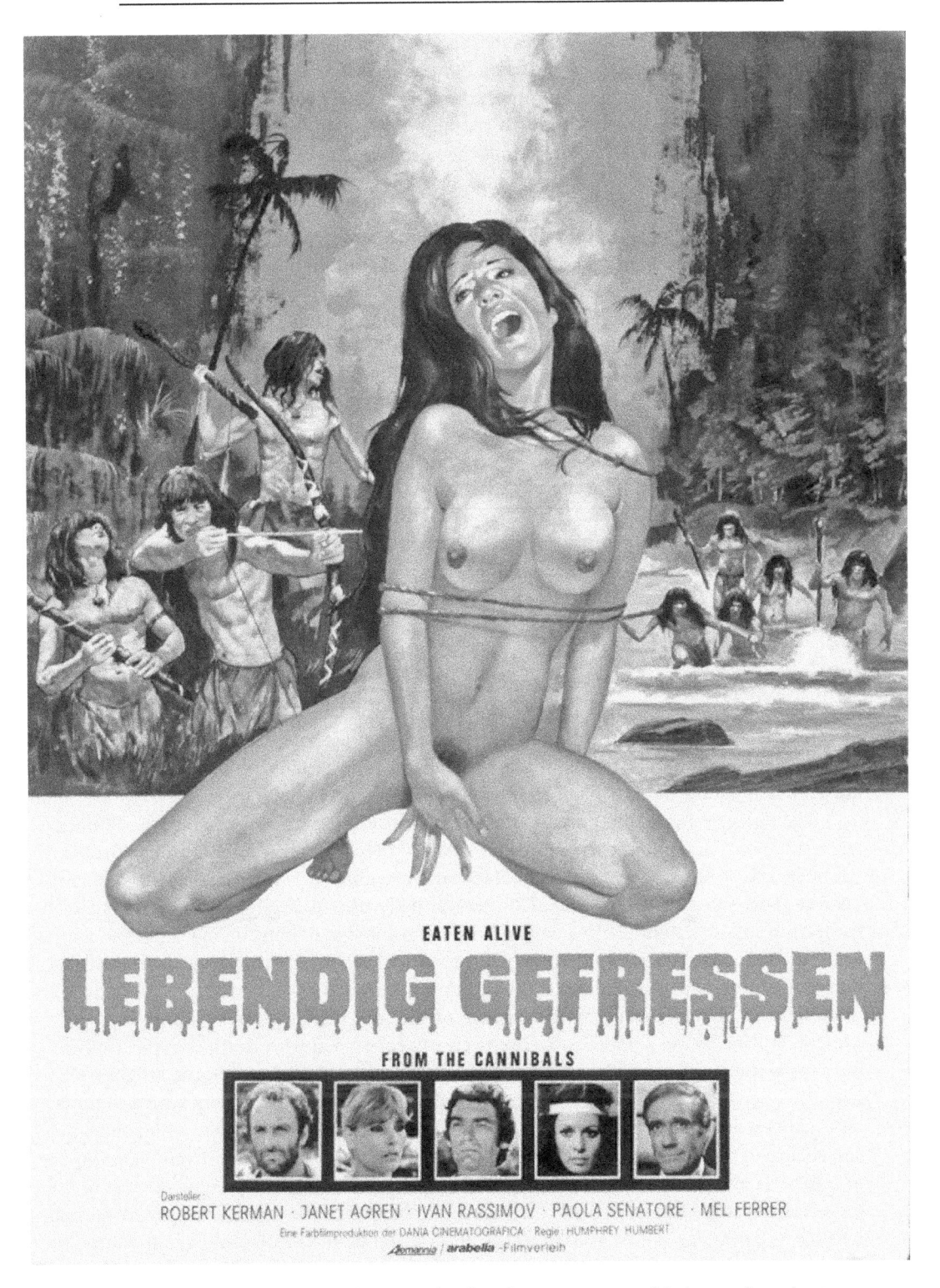

As the '80s began, Eurocult posters began to display almost pornographic images in order to get audiences interested in the films.

Producers who previously exploited the unknown with the mondo film were more than happy to ratchet up the violence and sexuality using fictional narratives. While the mondo film had the "your culture sucks" mindset, the cannibal subgenre was much more nihilistic, with an "every culture sucks" attitude. By the late '70s, Italian producers were just as negative about western society and the effects that the hegemonic leaders had on emerging nations and primitive tribes. Audiences tapered off sharply for Italian cannibal films after 1980 as the rise of the VCR was able to bring films like *Faces of Death* (1978) into homes, as well as the proliferation of cable and satellite television stations which produced more professional brands of documentary entertainment. For exploitation audiences, a steady of diet of cannibal films was a soul-killing experience, as these films seldom had any moments of lightness in them and just bombarded them with graphic negative images. For those who liked their violence hard-core but wanted a little more fictionalized levity, another subgenre was being retooled by the Italians in the late '70s. Related to the cannibal subgenre, this resurgence of an American popular culture monster icon can actually thank the Italians and film director Dario Argento for reintroducing audiences to a subgenre still popular today: the gut-munching zombie film.

Preceded by the cannibal subgenre by a few years, the zombie used a different motif than the cannibal film and was far more good-natured about it. Zombie films usually centered on man's ability to screw up his environment, and much like the "big bug" movies of the '50s, which were a direct result of the environmental uncertainty created by the atom bomb explosions, zombie films reflect the uncertainty of late '70s society with regard to things like nuclear power and medical breakthroughs. Accidents like the nuclear accident at Three Mile Island or the contamination of Love Canal in the United States, as well as European disasters such as the A-1 nuclear spill in Czechoslovakia, added to the Italian imagination that man was somehow screwing up the world. The zombie film is the culmination of that screw-up. With the release of American George A. Romero's *Dawn of the Dead* (1978; *Zombi* in Italy), the cannibal subgenre was replaced by a type of film that didn't make audiences feel morally bad for viewing it.

The Italian zombie film borrows the cannibalistic and nihilist aspects of the cannibal genre and adds an action component that is strictly Hollywood. Though other European countries, most notably Spain, also dabbled in these films, it is in Italy that the subgenre had the most success. Author Stephen Thrower believes that it's not surprising that Italy turned out so many zombie films. He explains, "A zombie in Italian cinema carries an iconoclastic connotation. It is explosive; able to fragment realism by inferring the implacable presence of something supernatural yet stubbornly corporeal. For Christians the body is a mere waste product, exerted by the passage of the soul into heaven."[190] Thrower is onto something here, as the zombie subgenre is clearly concerned with death and the afterlife. Italy made a natural home for this subgenre, being the seat of the Catholic religion. The dogma associated with the religion gave the zombie film fertile territory in which to mine, especially the idea that body is merely a vessel for the soul and only those with souls have any chance of redemption. Zombies have no souls; they have been taken from them, never to return. If one is lured into becoming soulless, he will remain soulless for the rest of his existence, becoming the scourge of Christianity, as they cannot be saved. The ever-increasing numbers of zombies can be seen as eradication of religion and of good moral values, or simply as a depiction of the idea that the world is becoming soulless. Regardless of what a zombie is or isn't, it represents a serious threat to Christianity, which means it needs to be exterminated. Zombies don't go easily, since true evil is always difficult to destroy; the only way to effectively kill them is by the fun task of destroying their brains (this is exploitation, after all) and producers throughout the subgenre have gratified audiences with some of the most outlandish decapitations, gunshots, and smashing of skulls that the censors around the world would stand. By the late '70s, Italians, as well as the rest of the western moviegoing audiences, were predisposed to the idea the "other" is inherently bad and must be mocked (the mondo film) or, even worse, destroyed (the cannibal film). The zombie resonates on the idea that these "others" bring with them disease that will effectively destroy all of society. Whether this disease be this lack of religious conviction, commercialism, globalization, environmentalism, or products of war, the zombie film manifests the fear people have of a changing world. This fear can be eliminated by gleefully gunning down, video-game style, the hordes of zombies that populate the film. Without the burden of humanity that the cannibal subgenre was forced to deal with, the effective eradication of zombies is a simple, mindless pleasure audiences can take part in.

The Italian zombie movement success began with the release of the U.S./Italian co-production *Dawn of the Dead* (1978). Though an American construct in idea and execution, George Romero's sequel to his own cult classic *Night of the Living Dead* (1968) was co-produced and co-financed by Dario Argento and producer/brother Claudio. Speaking of his involvement in the film, Dario commented, "One of my all-time favorite horror films was *Night of the Living Dead* and when I found out George Romero was looking for a co-producer [for the sequel], naturally I was more than a little interested. The Italian film industry was going through another time of crises and I thought investing overseas would be a good way of keeping the wolf from Seda Spettacoli's door."[191]

Romero spent the better part of a year at Argento's apartment in Rome writing the script. After completion of the film, retitled *Zombi* in Italy, Romero ran into some severe censorship roadblocks in the United States. The MPAA wanted to slap an X rating on the film for its violence, which included the usual head explosions, intestine pulling, and a cute little number in which a zombie gets the top of its head cut off by a helicopter rotor. Romero knew that an X rating would essentially kill the film, both because of the rating was associated with pornography and because many theater distributors and marketing avenues such as television had rules forbidding the marketing of X-rated films. He eventually chose to release the film without a MPAA rating, imposing his own "no one under 18 admitted," allowing for both better marketing avenues and controversial interest in the self-imposed rating. While Romero was grappling with these issues in the States, *Zombi* (1978) opened in Italy eight months prior to the U.S. premiere and was a resounding smash success. In order to obtain funding, Romero cut a distribution deal with the Argentos that ironically worked in reverse of the way many of the exploitation films ended up being shown around the world. Most Eurocult films had a variety of distributors around the world that demanded things, like extra nudity or violence, that would appeal to their own home audiences. Directors and producers usually gave free reign to distributors to do whatever they needed to in order to sell their films. American filmmakers were not apt to have some third party come in and change their films, so their distribution contracts were much more concrete. The deal between Argento and Romero, though, stipulated that Argento would have the final cut on all non–English-language versions. By selectively editing down some of Romero's humor, Argento was able to tailor the film to a European sensibility.[192] "When we brought the negative back to Italy for editing," relates producer Claudio Argento, "we created an entirely different version. We made lots of cuts because George's version was too long."[193] Perhaps because of the Argento name, the film had immediate European distribution, in

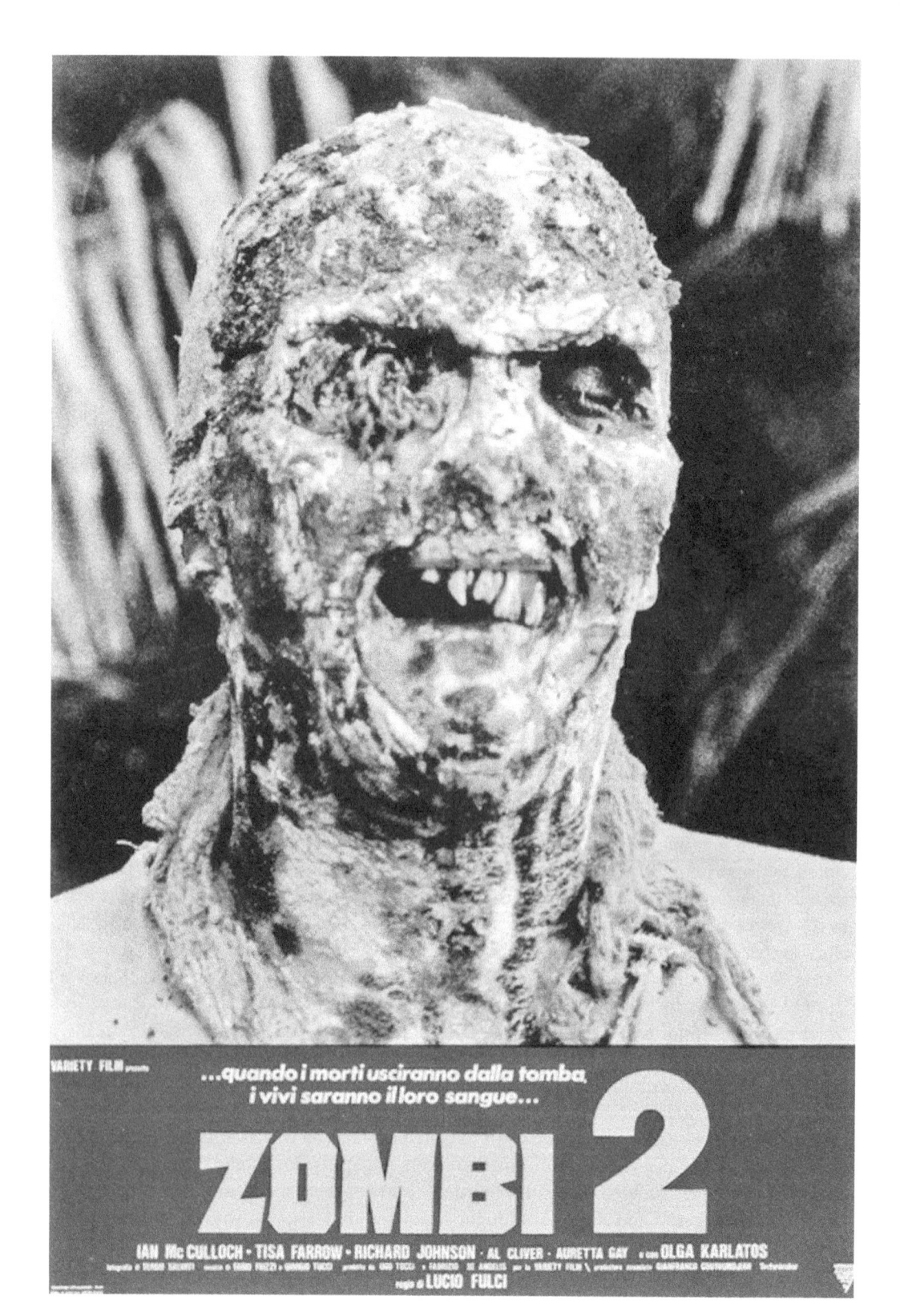

An international success, Fulci's *Zombi 2* (*Zombie*, 1979) out-grossed (both literally and figuratively) George Romero's popular *Dawn of the Dead* (*Zombi*, 1978) in many parts of the world.

contrast to America, where Romero had to go around looking for buyers who were willing to take on such a film.

Romero's film is distinctly American. Aside from some musical cues supplied by Italian band the Goblins, there is very little to denote that its conception may have had a small amount of Italian influence. Argento recognized that Romero's vision for the film, as a scathing indictment of American commercialism, would not play so well in Europe, and he edited down the film to be much more of a straight horror-action story.

The success of *Zombi* (1978) across Europe quickly caught the eye of Italian filmmakers who by now could turn rip-offs into moneymakers with surprising speed. The first of these, Lucio Fulci's classic *Zombi 2* (*Zombie*, 1979) went into production one month after the initial release of the original and quickly became a bigger box-office hit, with receipts topping a billion and half Italian lire.[194] Though it was not technically a sequel, Fulci happily acquired the moniker in order to get audiences into theater seats and quickly distanced himself from any lofty ideas that Romero may have had in the original. Set in both New York and Santo Domingo, with an international cast (American Tisa Farrow, Scottish Ian McCulloch, British Richard Johnson and Italian Al Cliver), *Zombi 2* sees Farrow stars as a young woman in search of her doctor father (Johnson), who has disappeared on an island in the Caribbean. After his boat is found abandoned in New York Harbor, save for one flesh-eating zombie, she travels to the island with reporter McCulloch. From there violence begins with Farrow and her group being terrorized by the hungry undead. Eyeballs are gouged out, blood flows from every orifice, and flesh is torn off the bone, all accompanied by a beating soundtrack from Fabrizo Frizzi that makes the film a truly visceral experience.[195] Fulci plays *Zombi 2* as a straight horror film, echoing such diverse themes as both Tourneur and the popular Italian cannibal film. Like Romero, Fulci doesn't give much explanation for the zombie phenomenon other than perhaps voodoo (though this is never satisfactorily explained). Taking a page from the cannibal film, he posits that it is the natives or the "others" that have caused it, certainly not western man. This is unlike Romero, who saw that it was perhaps man's meddling in outer space via a Venus probe that is responsible for the carnage. Regardless, Romero takes responsibility for the situation; Fulci doesn't, nor does he try to do anything lofty with the material. Gory entertainment is the name of the game here as Fulci simply tries to out-gore and out-action Romero. On a number of occasions he actually succeeds, especially in Naomi's (Olga Karlatos) death by wooden splinter (you'll have to see it to believe it) and her subsequent disembowelment, as well as a pretty exciting fight between an underwater zombie and a shark. Another major difference between the American zombies and European ones is their degree of humanness. Fulci's zombies are not representative of everyday people like Romero's. His zombies, a marvel of late-'70s makeup, are monsters barely resembling anything human, designed to look more like they've been through the shredder. These are the type of zombies meant to scare and disgust little kids, unlike Romero's, who—perhaps due to lack of budget—are showcased as green/blue representations of people bumbling their way through life. So willingly were distributors to have another zombie movie in theaters, *Zombi 2* became one of those Eurocult films that made over a million dollars' profit before it was ever shown in the United States. This was in addition to the millions it brought in around the world after its release in 1979. The film premiered in the United States with the tag line "We Are Going to Eat You" and benefited greatly from Romero's ratings fight over the original *Dawn of the Dead* (*Zombi*, 1978) as Fulci could now bypass the MPAA and release the film without a rating. This became standard practice in the late '70s and early '80s with films such as *Paura nella città dei morti viventi* (*Gates of Hell*, 1980) and *Virus* (*Hell of the Living Dead*, 1983) as European exploitation filmmakers looked to screen their films at large cineplexes without cutting the gore, which was so plentiful that it would have no doubt gotten them the dreaded X rating. By stipulating that there was no explicit sex in the film and self-imposing the rule that only those over 18 were allowed to see it, filmmakers could show their films without the marketing stigma that the X rating carried.

With the financial success of *Zombi 2*, Italian filmmakers jumped on the bandwagon trying to outdo Fulci's masterpiece. Borrowing a page from that successful film, most filmmakers chose to eschew any intellectualism and focus on the blood and guts. First on the list was Marino Girolami's *Zombi Holocaust* (*Dr. Butcher M.D.*, 1980). Utilizing some of the cast of *Zombi 2* as well as the same locales, *Zombi Holocaust* juggles both the zombie genre and the cannibal genre with mixed results. As was becoming increasingly popular, the film begins in New York and follows a policeman (Ian McCulloch) investigating brutal mutilations going on at New York hospitals. After 15 minutes it moves to its tropical setting as our policeman and a beautiful anthropologist (Alexander Delli Colli) end up in Southeast Asia, where they discover a mad doctor (Donald O'Brien) transforming the local natives into cannibal zombies. Though the plot is strictly action-adventure, the gore and sex are pure exploitation. Those expecting another apocalyptic zombie film à la Fulci were probably disappointed as the zombies don't really appear till the end and are fairly secondary to the plot. Those wanting the usual sex and violence were probably quite satisfied, as zombies have boat motors driven into their faces, hands are seen delving into eviscerated bodies with the inevitable intestine pulling, people are impaled on makeshift bamboo traps, and our luscious-lipped heroine manages to show her breasts at 10-minute intervals before getting painted up (à la Ursula Andress or Laura Gemser) and made to become part of the local primitive tribe.[196] Though the original film was enough to appease European audiences, the American distributors believed the film needed a more localized setting in order to be successful, so they incorporated a small amount of footage from American filmmaker Andy Foukes's half-completed film *Tales That Will Tear Your Heart Out* (1979). Ironically, that film had absolutely nothing in common with the original story, which didn't seem to bother U.S. distributors. Sensing a great marketing opportunity, they retitled the film as *Dr. Butcher M.D.*, giving audiences the idea that it was an American film about a doctor run amok in a New York hospital instead of Ian McCulloch running around a jungle looking for zombies. Distributors often blurred the line of production in order to get higher returns at the box office, and happily for exploitation filmmakers, this often meant box-office success.[197]

Italian filmmaker Umberto Lenzi, after successful subgenre turns with both the giallo (*Sette orchidee macchiate di rosso*, 1972) and cannibal pictures (*Mangiati vivi!*, 1980), tried his hand at zombies in 1980. Looking to infuse the subgenre with a little more intellectual bite, Lenzi crafted a zombie movie with a few key differences from most other genre fare. Instead of the recent dead coming back to life, in *Incubo sulla città contaminata* (*Nightmare City*, 1980), Lenzi decided to use the fear of nuclear power that was prevalent in the early 1980s. Lenzi related: "If you ask me what is the biggest threat to society, it is contamination from radiation and chemicals that cause sickness and death. It's not that I wanted a political message, I didn't, but I did want to have an alarm go off."[198]

Political fears aside, *Incubo* plays like exploitation camp! The story of a reporter (Hugo Stiglitz) who witnesses the siege of a large unnamed Italian city by radioactive cannibals is awash in over-the-top sex and violence. The film is a picture postcard of early-'80s kitsch, with Lenzi setting up a zombie attack on the local Italian version of a "Solid Gold"–type video dance/aerobics show (it was 1980 after all). With the camera rolling, we lovely leotard-clad young ladies getting "physical" before being attacked, and getting their nipples ripped out for the viewing public to see.[199] While most of *Incubo* is forgettable, a couple of fun new zombie characteristics are introduced, including getting away from the standard eating of the flesh. In his film, Lenzi is more concerned with contaminated blood (the film was made and released just prior to the AIDS epidemic) than with intestine pulling. What separates Lenzi's film from the other zombie films of the day is that he imbues his zombies with speed. Unlike the rambling, slow dead of both the Romero and Fulci films, Lenzi's zombies are fast and intelligent, and use weapons to destroy their prey.[200] This shift to speed helps deliver more action to audiences and helped influence later filmmakers like Danny Boyle (*28 Days Later*, 2003) and Zack Synder (*Dawn of the Dead* remake, 2004), who both opted for fast-moving zombies in their recent films.

Lenzi's introduction of new elements into otherwise typical zombie movies was not lost on other Italian exploitation directors. Each tried to come up with a different angle that would move a formula that was already becoming stale by 1980. Antonio Margheriti, known for his Gothic horror films of the 1960s, came up with one of the most unusual, *Apocalypse domani* (*Cannibal Apocalypse*) in 1980. Set in Atlanta, Georgia, *Apocalypse* looks at the lives of three Vietnam vets, including American John Saxon and Italian Giovanni Lombardo Radice,[201] who, after undergoing extreme torture during their stints in Vietnam, find themselves lusting after human flesh. It was the political content that most appealed to actor Saxon: "I thought it was interesting, it was a horror film but had a kinda of a metaphor that war or something like war was transmittable like a virus. We were just finishing up the sense of Viet Nam, the problem of the war in Viet Nam and the problem it caused in this country. There was something like kinda a virus, something that made people sick, the idea that something was going on, that was transmitted, was interesting."[202]

Margheriti's film had the lofty idea of exploring a different side of cannibalism, this time through the eyes of a war/horror film. Exploitation film producers looking to ensure an audience saw to it that, though there was a message, the movie also contained large doses of gore. Consequently in *Apocalypse* stomachs are shot out, blood is spilled and the usual amounts of female nudity are all part of the film.[203] Not surprisingly, the censors in both the United States and Britain had a field day with it. In the United States the film was initially shown, slightly trimmed, under the title *Cannibals in the Streets*, without a rating. It was replaced by a massively edited R-rated version, *Invasion of the Flesh Hunters*, which distorted the screenplay to a large extent. In Britain, the film was banned outright, another casualty of the "video nasties" era of the early 1980s.[204]

Another zombie-themed film released in 1980 with much less lofty cinematic goals was Aristide Massaccesi's *Anthropophagus* (*The Grim Reaper*). The story of a group of travelers tormented on a Greek island by a cannibalistic killer (writer Luigi Montefiore, aka George Eastman) was made solely for entertainment and had no artistic pretensions. Written in four days and shot on a shoestring budget, the film works because of its ghost-town setting and because audiences know that the filmmakers were willing to step over any boundaries necessary to create controversy. *Anthropophagus* contained some of the most radical gore sequences to date, including our cannibal protagonist pulling an unborn fetus out of actress Serena Grandi and eating it, and climaxes with the killer eating his own intestines after receiving a fatal knife wound from heroine Tisa Farrow.[205] Montefiore stated that these effects were included as a game to see who, between him and Massaccesi, could come up with the most disgusting scenes.[206] Consequently many of the heavy gore sequences were

He is a depraved, sadistic rapist; A bloodthirsty, homicidal killer. ...and He Makes House Calls!

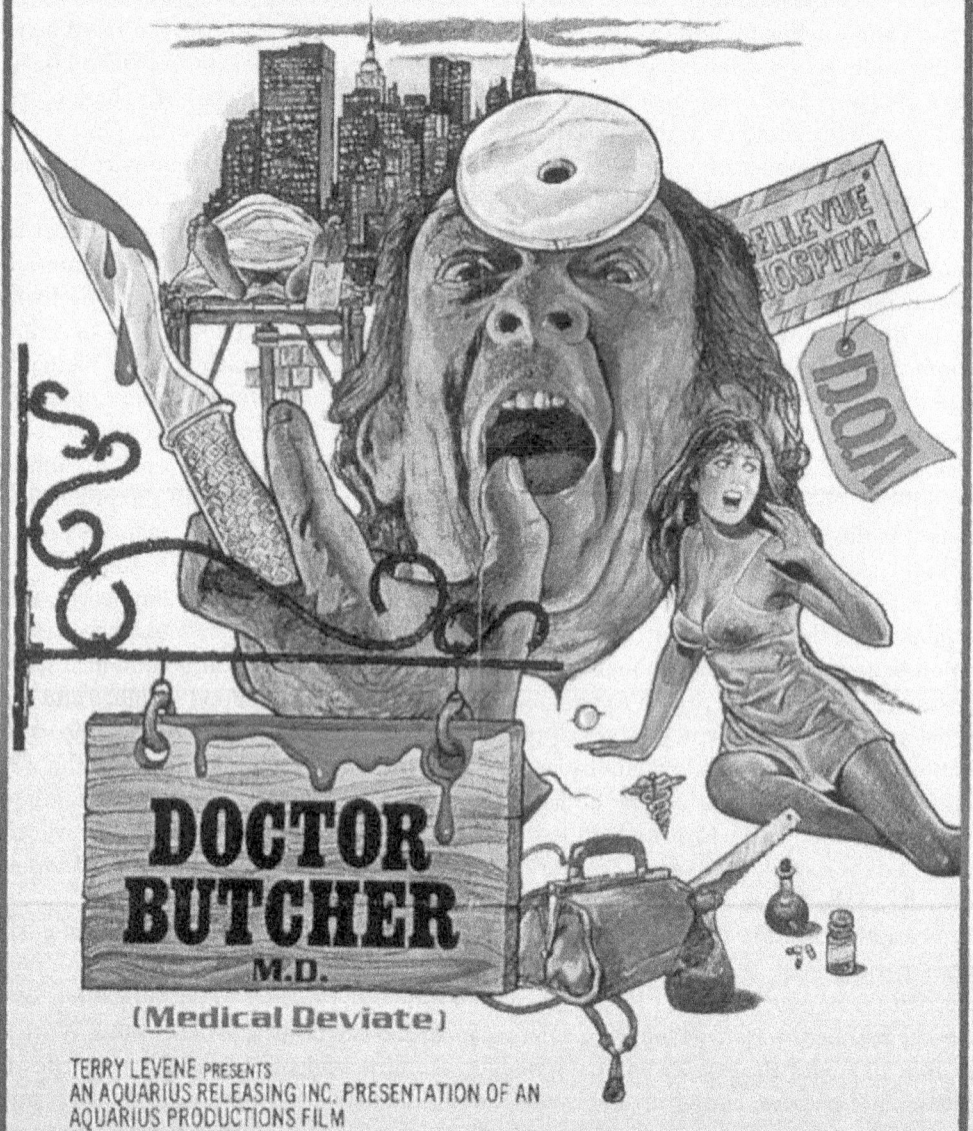

DOCTOR BUTCHER M.D.
(Medical Deviate)

TERRY LEVENE PRESENTS
AN AQUARIUS RELEASING INC. PRESENTATION OF AN
AQUARIUS PRODUCTIONS FILM
Starring IAN McCULLOCH • ALEXANDRA COLE • SHERRY BUCHANAN • PETER O'NEAL and
DONALD O'BRIAN as DR. BUTCHER Music by WALTER SEAR • Executive Producer RON HARVEY
Written and Directed by FRANK MARTIN • Produced by TERRY LEVENE
Prints by TECHNICOLOR®

Opposite and above: Two differing ways of marketing *Zombi Holocaust* (1980): the German distributor focused on the cannibal-type feel of the film, while the U.S. goes for a completely different feel, utilizing new scenes shot for another film.

Margheriti tries a new approach to the cannibal/zombie film with his *Apocalypse domani* (*Cannibal Apocalypse*, 1980). Note that there were numerous titles for nearly all of these films.

edited out of most U.S. and British versions. Retitled *The Grim Reaper*, it was only with the DVD release in 2006 that film was shown in its entirety, uncut, to very little controversy.

If Massaccesi made movie audiences uncomfortable with his aborted-fetus gore tricks, he confounded everyone when he included hard-core pornography within the zombie sub-genre. In 1980 came the release of both *Le notti erotiche dei morti viventi* (*Erotic Nights of the Living Dead*) and *Porno Holocaust*, filmed together in Santo Domingo with the same cast. Massaccesi, who had previously filmed many of the Black Emanuelle films, fuses the two genres together, making for a visceral experience. Both *Le notti* and *Porno Holocaust* focus on a group of businesspeople and/or scientists who reach a deserted island, have sex, and are killed one by one. Bad acting, poor gore effects and unerotic sex make the films an alienating experience, as the merging of hard-core sex and extreme violence is disturbing.[207] In *Le notti*, the juxtaposition between a man having a three-way with two ladies and another man getting his throat torn out is jarring. Another scene in which the hero (Luigi Montefiore) is being orally pleasured, only to have his penis ripped off, confounds an audience's response. Are people supposed to be turned on and excited or scared and disgusted? In *Porno Holocaust* (1980), racist attitudes dominate, as a dark-skinned zombie with a monstrous penis rapes the white female travelers, killing them with his wide girth. In one scene, the zombie forces a woman to fellate him, which inevitably leads to her choking to death.[208] Neither of these films garnered much success. Massaccesi, who endeavored to mingle his two favorite genres, conceded that the public rejected both films.[209]

Though many can argue that the Italian zombie subgenre was exploited for purely financial reasons, the truth is the zombie film was more than that. These films were a manifestation of all the fears society had in the late '70s and the early part of the '80s. Whether it was nuclear, religious, environmental, or political fear, or even a response to increasing globalization, the zombie film forced audiences into facing their fears in a visceral way. In a time when the Italian horror industry needed a hit, the zombie film provided some brief comfort. Though wildly popular in 1980, the zombie craze would only last a few more years. Films such as Fragrasso's *Zombi 4: After Death* (1988) and Bianchi's *Le notti del terrore* (*Nights of Terror*, 1981) pretty much thematically bankrupted the genre with bad effects, lifeless acting and terrible scripts. Only recently, with films such as the English *28 Days Later* (2003) and *28 Weeks Later* (2007), the Spanish *REC* (2007) and *REC2* (2009), and the American remake of *Dawn of the Dead* (2004), as well as the successful comic hybrids *Shaun of the Dead* (2006) and *Zombieland* (2009), has the zombie film experienced a resurgence in popularity. As of 2010 the Italians have opted out of the zombie resurgence, perhaps to return to it when they can put their own indelible stamp on it. Regardless, with the wars in Iraq and Afghanistan, new and frightening medical advances, new diseases emerging, immigration issues and a world increasingly more chaotic, the zombie films will continue to provide fodder for filmmakers around the world to enable audiences to transfer these fears to a mindless foe, just as they did in the late '70s.

Filmography

Anthropophagus, aka *The Grim Reaper*. Prod. George Eastman, Edward L. Montoro, Aristide Massaccesi. Dir. Aristide Massaccesi. Italy, 1980. Shriek Show, 88 min. DVD. Starring: Luigi Montefiori, Tisa Farrow, Saverio Vallone and Zora Kerova.

Ask yourself, is there really a movie where a woman in the ninth month of pregnancy gets her fetus ripped out of her and eaten by cannibal? Yep, it's *Anthropophagus*! Aristide Massaccesi's

Massaccesi mixes hard-core violence with hard-core porn with predictable results in *Le Notti erotiche dei morti viventi* (*Erotic Nights of the Living Dead*, 1980). The poster used Anglicized stage names in order to sell to a U.S. audience. Joe d'Amato is Aristide Massaccessi and George Eastman is Luigi Montefiori. Also note the misspelling of Shannon.

(under his nom de plume Joe D'Amato) masterpiece still manages to disgust viewers decades later. Actually there's a lot to enjoy in the film, which has a group of travelers setting out for a remote Greek island. Things start out poorly when one of the travelers (Kerova), who purports to be a psychic, starts freaking out that something horrible is going to happen. Well, guess what? She's right. The island town is completely deserted except for a very frightened blind girl who warns of a very scary cannibal man (Montefiori also goes by the name George Eastman; yep, he's the producer) who likes to eat his victims. Soon the sun goes down, the storms begin and the cannibal man shows up for dinner. It's up to Tisa Farrow, still battling zombies after Fulci's *Zombie* (1979), to save the day. Though hampered by a low budget, Massaccesi does a masterful job with the setting as the deserted Greek town is a wonderful environment (just like the Spanish island town does in 1975's *Who Could Kill a Child?*). What sets this film apart from other exploitation fodder, though, is the gore. From severed heads in buckets and the infamous abortion scene (which only lately has reappeared after being cut from nearly every print shown), to the finale, which is truly original, *Anthropophagus* goes to the limit with its violence, and what exploitation fan doesn't like that? The film starts off slow, but if you can wade through the first 20 minutes of some rather bad acting, you might find you actually like it. Bon appétit!

Cannibal Apocalypse, aka *Apocalypse domani* (IT). Prod. Maurizo and Sandro Amati. Dir. Antonio Margheriti. Italy/U.S./German, 1980. Image Entertainment, 96 min. DVD. Starring: John Saxon, Elizabeth Turner, Giovanni Lombardo Radice and Tony King.

Cannibal Apocalypse has an interesting premise. What if cannibalism was a social disease? I know it sounds crazy, but if Canadian director David Cronenberg can explore violence via social diseases in such films as his killer herpes movie *Shivers* (1975) or killer armpit movie *Rabid* (1976), certainly Antonio Margheriti, known for his tasteful Gothic horrors, can equate violence as the root problem of our wanting to eat each other. You're right, it's a silly premise, but he gives it a good try. Vietnam war vet John Saxon experiences some terrible situations during the war. Looking for his captured squad, he finds them in a trapped in a hole, where they have resorted to cannibalism. Freeing them, he is bitten on the arm by one of the men. Years later, living in Atlanta, he can't hide this developing hunger he feels. The problem is compounded by his army buddies, who are going through Atlanta spreading cannibalism to the local populace, as well as the little Lolita next door who wants a piece of him ... just not the same piece he wants from her. The movie contains enough blood and gore to make Eurocult fans happy, including some graphic flesh munching, a French-kissing scene that will scare the hell out of you, and a shotgun blast that has to be seen to be believed.

Cannibal Holocaust, aka *Holocaust Cannibal* (IT). Prod. Franco Di Nunzio. Dir. Ruggero Deodato. Italy, 1980. Grindhouse Releasing, 96 min. DVD. Starring: Robert Kerman, Luca Barbareschi, Francesca Ciardi and Perry Pirkanen.

Here it is, folks, the film that will separate the neophytes from the true connoisseurs. One of the most shocking movies of all time that is just as disgusting today as when it was first shown. In fact, I would say it's more shocking today because of it now mirrors our own media tastes as a society and calls attention to just how far we will go in order to entertain. Robert Kerman (the star of many of the '70s biggest pornos like *Debbie Does Dallas*, 1978) stars as a university professor who goes into the Amazon to find a group of filmmakers who have disappeared. After many adventures he manages to track down a primitive tribe that has the film canisters and barters with them (via eating a nice piece of charred flesh) to get them back. Back in New York he develops the film and finds just what lengths the young filmmakers went to and what they did to get this footage. This leads up to a fight between Kerman and a TV company that wants to play the footage unedited for big ratings. So before it airs, Kerman shows them (and us) the footage. Deeply degrading on every level, the film is nevertheless a complete success that will haunt you for a very long time. The violence against both humans (fake) and animals (real) is graphic in the extreme, involving rape with a giant dildo, infanticide, cannibalism (of course), castration along with a long list of other atrocities. The low budget actually works well for the film, as does the amateur acting by the young filmmakers that contributes to the level of believability. This film should be required viewing for anyone studying mass communications as I think it raises some pretty pertinent questions about our media ethics. Deodato was truly ahead of his time. A definite must-see, but be prepared.

Dawn of the Dead, aka *Zombi* (IT). Prod. Claudio Argento and Richard P. Rubinstein. Dir. George Romero. U.S./Italy, 1978. Anchor Bay Entertainment, 118 min. DVD. Starring: David Emge, Scott Reiniger, Ken Foree and Gaylen Ross.

George Romero's *Dawn of the Dead* is a classic of American horror. So what's it doing here? Simple: Dario Argento, who was instrumental in getting the film financed, had final cut approval on the European version, which he released under the name *Zombi*. Argento's version eliminates many of the comedic scenes while extending some shots that were in Romero's original. The outcome is a shorter, more compact film that plays up the action (though for some reason he cuts out the zombie decapitation by helicopter blade scene). Though many of Romero's purists may disagree I actually don't have a problem with the cut, as I think it's a legitimate alternative the original film. Personally I'd like a definitive version that has the all footage from Romero's extended cut, along with Argento's additions to make one big version of the film. I can dream, can't I?

Eaten Alive, aka *Mangiati vivi!* (IT), *Doomed to Die* (U.S.). Prod. Mino Loy and Luciano Martino. Dir. Umberto Lenzi. Italy, 1980. Shriek Show, 87 min. DVD. Starring: Robert Kerman, Janet Agren, Ivan Rassimov and Paola Senatore.

Jim Jones meets stock footage! Lenzi capitalizes on the international interest in the rise and death of cult leader Rev. Jim Jones and pads it with footage from a bunch of other cannibal films for this ridiculous film. In New York City (where all good exploitation begins in the late '70s), it seems that there's some primitives running around shooting people with poison darts and taking them back to the jungle. Not that anyone around would notice; it is New York, after all, and crazy stuff like that happens all the time, right? Regardless, Sheila's (Agren) sister is taken, and via the help of a severely slumming Mel Ferrer, Sheila finds herself on the next flight to New Guinea to find her. After she hooks up with Robert Kerman, they make their way through the jungle, stumbling upon a Jim Jones–type cult run by a Jim Jones–type madman (Rassimov, who was actually quite good at playing these parts). The cult obviously mistakes Sheila for Ursula Andress or Laura Gemser and paints her up in gold, parading her around. Lots of animals get killed for real, courtesy of footage already used in previous cannibal films. The violence, which is pretty graphic, is unfortunately pretty fake.

Emanuelle and the Last Cannibals, aka *Emanuelle e gli ultimi cannibali* (IT), *Trap Them and Kill Them* (U.S.). Prod. Gianfranco Couyoumdjian. Dir. Aristide Massaccesi. Italy, 1977. Shriek Show, 91 min. DVD. Starring: Laura Gemser, Gabriele Tinti, Nieves Navarro and Donald O'Brien.

Oh, Black Emanuelle, you're so crazy. As if busting a male prostitution ring, a snuff filmmaking scam and a prince's harem, or just enjoying the carnal pleasures of, I don't know, an entire young man's field hockey team from your previous films weren't enough for you, you had to go and find yourself some honest-to-goodness cannibals. Forsaking the hard-core footage that had been creeping into the series, Massaccesi starts laying up more of the violence and seems to be having a good time putting poor Gemser in increasingly absurd situations. Beginning in, yes, New York City, our intrepid journalist is called to a local hospital where a nurse had her breast bitten off by a captured cannibal (who looks ironically like she came from New Jersey). Emanuelle is able to get the full account of what happened by masturbating the female cannibal while she is tied down (total rape). From there it's off to the Amazon, where our free-loving heroine finds an anthropologist (real-life husband and series regular Gabriele Tinti) to take her around, and then hooks up with most of the cast. Halfway through, the cannibals come calling, and it's up to Emanuelle to save the day. Do you think at some point she gets painted up nude like Ursula Andress or Janet Agren did in their respective cannibal movies? Yep, you're right. Actually the film is fairly harmless compared to other cannibal films of the time, with the violence coming in the last 20 minutes. Obviously by this time the Black Emanuelle series was pretty much running out of ideas and it definitely shows in this film.

Erotic Nights of the Living Dead, aka *Le notti erotiche de morti viventi* (IT), *Sexy Nights of the Living Dead* (U.S.). Prod. and Dir. Aristide Massaccesi. Italy, 1980. Shriek Show, 112 min. DVD. Starring: Laura Gemser, Luigi Montefiori, Dirce Funari and Mark Shannon.

Mixing hard-core pornography with the zombie film is sorta like mixing watermelon and chocolate milk. It doesn't mix and the outcome could be disgusting. For some reason Massaccesi thought that by adding these two exploitable elements he could create a super-exploitation genre. He may have had success combining porn with another subgenre, say the devil possession films where illicit sex is tied in with the taboo subject, but with the zombie movie it just doesn't work. The plot (yep, there's kind of one of those) begins in a mental hospital where crazy Montefiori is having the fakest sex with a nurse (fake because through the entire film he never takes off his jeans when having sex!). From there we see in flashback that he was a boat captain in Santo Domingo hired to take a slimy businessman (Shannon) to a cursed island for development. Before they go, everyone has sex, Montefiori with a dancer who sure knows how to blow the cork off a champagne bottle, and Shannon with a group of prostitutes, followed by his hotel neighbor. Oh, and there's a zombie there too. Anyway, they get to the island protected by an old man and Black Emanuelle herself, Laura Gemser, looking a little more emaciated than usual. Then come the zombies, people die (fakely), and Montefiori goes crazy. A film like this would work if it were either sexy or scary. Unfortunately, it's neither: the zombies are laughable, and the sex is about as hot as an episode of *Hawaii Five-O*. Probably the scariest thing in the movie is the fact that one of the male actors (not Montefiori, because again, he never takes off his jeans) has a bad case of genital warts for the whole world to see. At least the scenery is pretty, and Gemser, who is way too classy an actress to participate in any of the hard-core action, brings some sense of professionalism to the proceedings. Bad.

Jungle Holocaust, aka *Ultimo mondo cannibale* (IT), *Last Cannibal World*. Prod. Georgio Carlo Rossi. Dir. Ruggero Deodato. Italy, 1977. Shriek Show, 96 min. DVD. Starring: Ivan Rassimov, Massimo Foschi, Sheik Razak Shikur and Me Me Lai.

Deodato's *Jungle Holocaust* is a textbook example of the Italian cannibal subgenre and was an international success, spawning numerous rip-offs. While searching for oil in New Guinea, two men (Rassimov and Foschi) are involved in an airplane crash that leaves them stranded in the jungle. Unfortunately, the jungle is filled with cannibal tribes and when the men become separated, Foschi is captured by one. There he is treated to the warm hospitality of the natives, who strip him, make him fly (via ropes), and for that extra-special service, the tribe has some of their younger members pee on his head. Oh, well, at least he has Me Me Lai to come by and masturbate him through the cell gate on occasion. She takes a liking to him and they escape into the jungle to face even more fun. For those who like their cannibal films with some shock value but are too turned off by *Cannibal Holocaust* (1979) or *Make Them Die Slowly* (1980), *Jungle Holocaust* may be for you. There are the requisite animal killings, which are no fun but are balanced with lots of fake intestine pulling and totally inappropriate nudity. The film is not nearly as nihilistic as later entries and plays much more like an adventure movie than outright exploitation. Don't be fooled, though: this isn't for children.

Make Them Die Slowly, aka *Cannibal ferox* (IT). Prod. Luciano Martino. Dir. Umberto Lenzi. Italy, 1980. Grindhouse Releasing, 93 min. DVD. Starring: Giovanni Lombardo Radice, Lorraine De Selle, Robert Kerman and Zora Kerova.

Lenzi tries to out-gross *Cannibal Holocaust* and nearly succeeds! Another one of those "banned in 31 countries" films, *Make Them Die Slowly* is in some ways more disgusting than Deodato's classic film, but it's less powerful because it doesn't take its subject matter as seriously, choosing only to disgust and entertain rather than tackle serious issues. Young PhD student Gloria Davis (Lorraine De Selle) thinks she knows everything. She's written a dissertation that disproves the existence of cannibals and sets out with some idiot friends to South America to prove she's right. She should have taken some driving lessons because no sooner do they get there than they crash the car and are forced to walk the rest of the way. Fortunately, they run into two guys (Radice and Lucchini) who claim they were victims of a cannibal tribe and are more than happy to help them.

Unfortunately, they are also two of the most depraved humans in existence, and from there the fun begins, including the usual goodies of rape, castration, burning, eye gouging, drug use, stabbing, shooting, animal killing, public humiliation, and much to the chagrin of Gloria, who was out to prove differently, a whole lot of gut-munching. Yes, the film is horribly nihilistic as well as disgusting, repellent and pretty much without any redeeming social value. It showcases human beings at their worst and is not what one would call entertaining. But the acting is so over-the-top and the situations so dramatized that it's very difficult to take this film seriously. Its disgust factor is just as high as *Holocaust* but without any of the intellectual (yes, I'm going to say it) "bite" of the Deodato film.

Mountain of the Cannibal God, aka *La montagna del dio cannibale* (IT), *Slave of the Cannibal God*. Prod. Luciano Martino. Dir. Sergio Martino. Italy, 1978. Anchor Bay Entertainment, 103 min. DVD. Starring: Ursula Andress, Stacy Keach, Claudio Cassinelli and Antonio Marsina.

Ursula Andress may have come a long way since her time with James Bond in *Dr. No.* (1962) but she's stuck in some of the same circumstances. Andress's husband has disappeared and now she and her equally blond brother have to trudge across the jungle to find him. She meets up with Stacy Keach, who is more than happy to help. Soon the beautiful Andress is caught in situations involving large snakes, spiders and the occasional native. Soon (well, not so soon as it takes almost the whole movie to get to this point) she is captured by cannibals and painted completely gold, allowing her get naked once again. Martino's foray into the cannibal genre is for the most part a tame affair. It plays mostly as an adventure story, sort of like an Indiana Jones film (except without all the excitement). The film could have easily retained a PG rating in the United States (the kiss of death for any exploitation film) had Martino not decided to go crazy in the last 20 minutes and show us (in uncut prints) a graphic masturbation scene, some intense intestine pulling, and, most bizarrely, a native in a bad wig, fornicating with a very bored-looking giant boar! I can only imagine what Andress thought when she viewed this scene for the first time. She acquits herself nicely, and Martino slinks out of the cannibal subgenre without too much embarrassment.

Nightmare City, aka *Incubo sulla città contaminata* (IT), *City of the Walking Dead* (U.S.). Prod. Luis Méndez. Dir. Umberto Lenzi. Italy/Spain, 1980. Anchor Bay Entertainment, 92 min. DVD. Starring: Hugo Stiglitz, Mel Ferrer, Laura Trotter and Stefania D'Amario.

Fast zombie time! *Nightmare City* is a fun, rollicking ride that is absolutely terrible in every respect, making it a must-watch for all fans of zombie movies and Eurocult fans alike. Reporter Stiglitz has been assigned to cover a story of a military plane landing under mysterious circumstances. As the world watches, the plane is actually filled with fast-moving zombies who open up a can of whoop-ass on the awaiting army guard. These zombies can not only move fast, they can also use weapons, and soon the unnamed city is overrun with these fast-moving monsters. The ghouls don't exactly eat flesh; they're more into blood, but that doesn't stop them from ripping up the live Italian version of Solid Gold, tearing off those lovely '80s-style leotards of the dancers. It's up to Stiglitz (along with Mel Ferrer, who obviously filmed his role in the span of two days) to save the day, which sends him to the local amusement park (don't ask). Lenzi is out of his mind here and creates an absolutely bizarre movie that is as entertaining as it is bad. Bad acting, bad make-up effects (the zombies look like poorly constructed Muppets), a plot that makes no sense, and inappropriate dance numbers make for one helluva party movie. So grab some popcorn, call some friends and enjoy! C'mon — zombies with machine guns! Can you get any better than that?

Porno Holocaust. Prod. and Dir. Aristide Massaccesi. Italy, 1980. Exploitation Digital, 113 min. DVD. Starring: Luigi Montefiori, Dirce Funari, Annj Goren and Mark Shannon.

Here we go again. As if *Erotic Nights of the Living Dead* (1980) wasn't enough to put a nail in the zombie/hard-core porn subgenre, we get this winner. Actually, Massaccesi was just being financially prudent, as he had completed *Erotic* early and still had most of the cast (luckily for her, Laura Gemser opted out) available. So why not film another movie? I think "why" would be more like it, as this *Porno Holocaust* is even crazier than the previous outing. This time Montefiori plays a scientist while Shannon gets his turn as captain of a boat. It seems that there's an island near Santo

Domingo that is giving off a lot of radiation and it bears examination. Bringing along a bevy of "beautiful" women, the group investigates, soon finding that the radiation has created a zombie with a rather large and deadly endowment. Lots of women die. Again Montefiori keeps his pants on, and again we're treated to another actor's genital warts. Fun.

Zombie, aka *Zombi 2* (IT). Prod. Fabrizio De Angelis. Dir. Lucio Fulci. Italy, 1979. Shriek Show, 91 min. DVD. Starring: Ian McCulloch, Tisa Farrow, Richard Johnson and Al Cliver.

This classic Fulci shocker completely redirected his career and, along with *Dawn of the Dead* (released as *Zombi* in Italy), was responsible for whole slew of rip-offs. Leisurely paced in the middle, this is still a first-rate shocker that is scary, gross and just plain fun. What appears to be a deserted boat is found drifting in New York Harbor. After careful examination and much bloodshed it is discovered that there is a zombie onboard, who is then disposed of in the sea. The boat belonged to the father of Ann (Tisa Farrow, Mia's sister, and later star of the gruesome *Anthropophagus* in 1980), who, with the help of reporter Ian McCulloch, boat captain Al Cliver, and his wife Rosetta Gay, goes and looks for him on a small remote tropical island. The island is being slowly taken over by zombies, and the local doctor (Richard Johnson) is none too thrilled about it. Lots of mayhem results. From its zombie vs. shark fight, to a very graphic murder involving a large wooden splinter, *Zombie* delivers all the exploitation goods as well as a taut, well-produced story. Fulci's zombies are truly a wonder as the make-up effects men go all out creating truly disgusting creatures. Working in all the zombie angles from Romero's perspective to traditional zombie folklore, Fulci covers all his bases here. A definite must-see, the film stands as one of the best zombie films made.

Zombie Holocaust, aka *Zombi holocausto* (IT), *Dr. Butcher, M.D.* (U.S.). Prod. Fabrizio De Angelis. Dir. Marino Girolami. Italy, 1980. Shriek Show, 90 min. DVD. Starring: Ian McCulloch, Alexandra Delli Colli, Peter O'Neal and Donald O'Brien.

Wow, that was fast! Produced on the heels of Fulci's *Zombie* (1979), *Zombie Holocaust* shows how quickly the subgenre degenerated into stupidity. The film fuses both the cannibal genre and the zombie film into an incoherent mess that, while fun in the beginning and end, drags severely in the middle. It seems body parts are disappearing from a local New York hospital. When one of the staff members is seen chowing down on a heart (they probably should have paid him more), reporter Ian McCulloch, along with doctor and student of anthropology Delli Colli (who in many ways is genetically similar in the lips to Angelina Jolie), decides to investigate. It seems that there's a cannibal tribe that may be responsible, so they decide to truck down to the jungle, where they find a doctor performing all sorts of experiments that would not fly with the AMA. Soon the blood is flying, eyeballs are being gouged, and McCulloch is ramming boat propellers into zombies' heads! As a bonus, since this is part cannibal film and Delli Colli is not part of the tribe, she gets to be painted up nude (though admittedly it's not the full body paint Ursula Andress received for her role in 1978's *Mountain of the Cannibal God*, but then again, the budget here is half that of the latter film) and almost sacrificed. A silly film that manages to entertain in short bursts.

The Devil Made Her Do It: Satanic Possession and Nunsploitation

> Naturally if *The Exorcist* had not had been successful, no one would have thought of *L'anticristo*.
> —Italian Director Alberto de Martino[210]

The worldwide success of British director Ken Russell's controversial *The Devils* (1971) and American William Friedkin's *The Exorcist* (1973) helped give Italian filmmakers another subject matter to exploit in the mid–'70s, this one centered squarely on religion. Creating two distinctive subgenres, nunsploitation and devil-possession films, Italian filmmakers

LA WARNER BROS PRESENTA
WILLIAM PETER BLATTY
L'ESORCISTA
WILLIAM FRIEDKIN
ELLEN BURSTYN · MAX VON SYDOW · LEE J. COBB · KITTY WINN · JACK McGOWRAN
JASON MILLER
LINDA BLAIR
WILLIAM PETER BLATTY
NOEL MARSHALL
WILLIAM PETER BLATTY
ARNOLDO MONDADORI EDITORE
DISTRIBUZIONE
From Warner Bros
A Warner Communications Company

were able to successfully exploit the very controversial topic that had rarely been tackled prior to the 1970s, shell-shocking the entire world with these films' gleefully blasphemous spirit.

Italy's strong connection to Roman Catholicism ensured that the church had a powerful influence over the content of Italy's films. Prior to the '60s, anything religious shown on screens had to be vetted in some way through the church for approval. This made it especially difficult for filmmakers to explore controversial themes in religion because the church had a long history of being archaic and traditional in its thinking. The modernization process begun in 1962 with Pope Paul VI and the Second Vatican Council mirrored the social changes that were going on during the era. The changes involved everything from new design for clerics to the choice of language in sermons. This modernization had an effect on films that had religious subjects.[211] Critics and filmmakers could now start to criticize religious themes as well as produce films with mature subject matter, subjects the church would often disapprove of. By the early '70s, though government censorship still had to be dealt with, the Church itself could rarely come up with enough influence to interfere with a film's release.[212] It was in this atmosphere that "Nunsploitation" or "Nasty Nun Sinema" began to proliferate. Rebellion against the decades of repression via the church spilled out on theater screens throughout world. Films such as *Suor omicidi* (*Killer Nun*, 1978) and *Le scomunicate di San Valentino* (*The Sinful Nuns of St. Valentine*, 1973) showcased nuns indulging in the most lewd behavior, whether it was sex outside of marriage, rampant lesbianism or just plain murder. These films' modus operandi was to convey the "truth" of what was perceived to go on behind convent walls as well as looking at forbidden acts within the clergy.[213]

It cannot be overstated how important Russell and Friedkin's films were in changing the exploitation landscape. Russell's *The Devils*, tells the fact-based story of nuns (including Vanessa Redgrave, playing a special-needs sister who's extremely warped) who are driven to psychological and sexual frenzy by the very religion that seeks to eliminate it in 17th-century France. Russell, who was never known for understatement, piles on all the sexual fantasies he can, mixing it with flagellations and violence in such a graphic way that it stunned audiences and got the censor's scissors snapping. The Catholic Church was obviously not happy about the film and worked to get it banned throughout the world. All of this controversy was good enough for Italian exploitation filmmakers, who, seeing that people were shocked yet still coming to theaters to see these films, immediately went about trying to come up with some derivative films that would try to out-blaspheme Russell's film.

Giullio Berutti's *Suor omicidi* (*Killer Nun*, 1978) is as good a representation as any of the subgenre. The first 20 minutes of the film have the morphine-addicted Sister Gertrude (Italian bombshell Anita Ekberg) looking for a fix. Ditching the habit in favor of some provocative Italian fashion, she establishes her fix and decides to seduce a stranger ("I need a man, that one will do") from a local bar. Following him along the streets of Turin, she has sex with him in the hall of some unfamiliar local apartment house. Add to the plot the killings of hospital patients, a young lesbian nun who likes to sleep naked, and Sister Gertrude's further slide out of reality and you have the makings of an exploitation classic. Marketing materials for the film laughingly play up that the film is "A True Story from the Vatican Files!"—which may confirm what audiences may have been looking for in these

Opposite: The popularity around the world of *The Exorcist* (1973) caused Italian exploitation filmmakers to find ways to exploit religion in the mid-'70s.

Italian filmmakers often tried to intermix their genres in order to garner the largest audience possible. Here the mixture of nunspolitation with the popular Black Emanuelle series creates an unbelievable but obviously fun film.

types of films. The cloistered, hierarchical nature of the Catholic Church, along with its social and political past, had left an indelible mark on society, leaving open the possibility of suspicion. Nuns have the perception of being the epitome of virtue, free from sin and noble in their giving their lives to God. The nature of the Church, though, promoted the idea that the behavior of nuns was to be respected regardless of what it may entail. Therefore many people around the world had probably had some serious run-ins with some psychologically damaged nuns. Since in many instances it is impossible to question a nun without some form of retribution, people may have built up some form of animosity that was ready to be exploited. Add to that the intense repressed attitude for natural things like sexuality and emotional feelings, issues that were being explored in the early '70s by societies around the world, and you had a built in audience ready to suspect that something had to be going on behind the closed doors of nunneries.

There were a couple of other factors in understanding why this particular subgenre proliferated in the '70s, mostly concerning the nature of the media and good old-fashioned rebellion. For audiences, especially Christians, it is the ultimate rebellion and taboo to watch the most revered profession performing the most lewd acts imaginable. It satisfies a basic need in some to see women behaving badly in places (churches, nunneries, and other religious environments) that they shouldn't be and allows them to indulge in fantasies they may have always harbored. The media environment also played its part, as the '70s were a free-for-all in terms of what exploitation films could and would show. A wide variety of controversial subject matter (incest, rape, cannibalism, homosexuality, psychosis, etc.) was already being explored, and exploitation filmmakers were finding it more difficult to find that one controversial subject matter that would get audiences talking about a film. For many filmmakers, the dismantling of religion was a final frontier to be pushed. Many of the giallo filmmakers had begun to seriously question religion, like Fulci did in *Non si sevizia un paperino* (*Don't Torture a Duckling*, 1972), but almost without exception they concentrated on the male role (e.g., priest, etc.) in religion and not that of the female. Having women of the cloth masturbating, indulging in lesbian orgies and performing sadistic acts of violence in the name of God garnered the controversy expected from such fare. Censors around the world, as well as religious organizations, were quick to demand edits, rewrites, and in the worst cases, confiscation of the prints they deemed sacrilegious. The controversy over these films naturally led to a modicum of box-office success which, of course, made Italian filmmakers push the envelope as to what these naughty nuns could do. Some like *Flavia the Heretic* (1974) took a more serious approach, trying to fuse women's equality issues with male subjection, but even these had the requisite number of decapitations, disembowelments, or in the case of *Flavia*, horse mutilations. Most nunsploitation is exactly that, exploitation. Director Aristide Massaccesi, known for aborted-fetus feasting in *Anthropophagus* (*The Grim Reaper*, 1980) as well as the "classic" *Porno Holocaust* (1980), was more than happy to include hard-core footage in his *Immagini di un convento* (*Images in a Convent*, 1978), which showcased an audience's willingness to see nuns actually penetrated as they give in to their forbidden lust.

The nunsploitation cycle was a relatively brief one lasting less than a decade. One of the reasons for this may be that the subgenre did not enjoy much box-office success in the United States, which was where the most exploitation filmmakers recouped their investments. The United States has always had a troubled censorship battle with films of this type. *The Devils*, the film that launched the nunsploitation subgenre, had been severely cut by Warner Bros. on its release and has yet to play in any unedited form there. While the public outcry was significant for the film, the subject matter didn't hold much sway with American audiences. It was another subgenre, begun in 1973 and involving women, God and the devil, that they found much more alluring: the devil possession movie.

If the nuns of Italy were sinfully bothered by Satan, then the virginal daughters of pious Italian fathers must have had the same target on them. It was these women that the devil himself liked to possess in a series of *Exorcist* and *Rosemary's Baby* (1969) rip-offs in the mid-'70s. William Friedkin's *The Exorcist* (1973), with its tale of a young girl (Linda Blair) possessed by the Devil, touched a huge nerve with '70s audiences around the world. Friedkin has often stated that he didn't see his film as a horror film, let alone exploitation, and he's probably correct at least in regards to exploitation, as his lofty ambition was to facilitate discussion on the nature of religion and the good and evil forces that are within the universe. With that said, the film definitely does contains exploitive elements: Blair's forcibly masturbating with a crucifix or projectile vomiting would have been not out of place in any Italian exploitation film of the era. *The Exorcist* came along at the right time to appeal to a mass audience that was beginning to question some of the long-standing accepted ideas about religion. Not surprisingly, the film was a huge hit in Italy, sending Italian filmmakers scurrying to find suitable scripts by which to exploit this new and financially lucrative subgenre. These films were a natural for Italians because they not only exploited religion but in most instances took a critical view of modern families, especially with regard to good Italian fathers, absentee or amoral mothers, and their "virginal" daughters. Each of these films showcased young, pious women who were possessed by Satan, or in the case of *Che sei?*, impregnated with his child. The young women in these films are often made to perform a myriad of sexual acts, including those involving family members, young teenage boys, and in some cases even animals.[214] With the requisite green pea soup, and occasional toad, vomiting out of every orifice and cursing that would make a truck driver blush, these films used religious iconography to express a twisted view of the conflicts of sexual freedom. One of the first films in the devil possession subgenre, Alberto De Martino's *L'anticristo* (*The Anti-Christ*) in 1974, is most exemplary of films of this type. It stars Carla Gravina as Ippolita, a young, crippled woman, who under hypnosis becomes possessed by the spirit of her former life, a nasty heretic. She begins reliving her previous life via some disturbing visions of black masses involving her drinking blood and performing analingus on a goat (!). Soon after that she seduces her brother as well as young high school boys, discovers that she can move furniture at will, and develops a Linda Blair–like skin condition before finally being exorcised by an Irish priest (Arthur Kennedy). The film is interesting in its dichotomy between its condemnation of religion, as witnessed in the beginning, in which Ippolita is witness to a group of over-the-top religious zealots who crawl around on the ground as if possessed, and having a religion essentially save her at the end. The dichotomy plays itself out throughout the entire movie. The focus on sexuality is no accident, either, as producer Guilio Berruti saw the film not as an indictment of religion but of sexual frustration, saying, "This film was different because it displayed a sexual frustration that the audience can identify with. My film doesn't have shocks like you would expect from a horror film; the audience does not scream. Instead they see the sexual frustration and understand the feeling."[215] I'm not exactly sure what film Berruti is speaking about here, but *L'anticristo* is definitely designed to shock. While sexual frustration is the main issue here and played out via Ippolita's relationship with her father (Mel Ferrer) and his new, younger wife (played by giallo favorite Anita Strindberg), I'm not sure worldwide audiences would equate sexual frustration with the need to perform oral sex on a goat. Clearly Ippolita

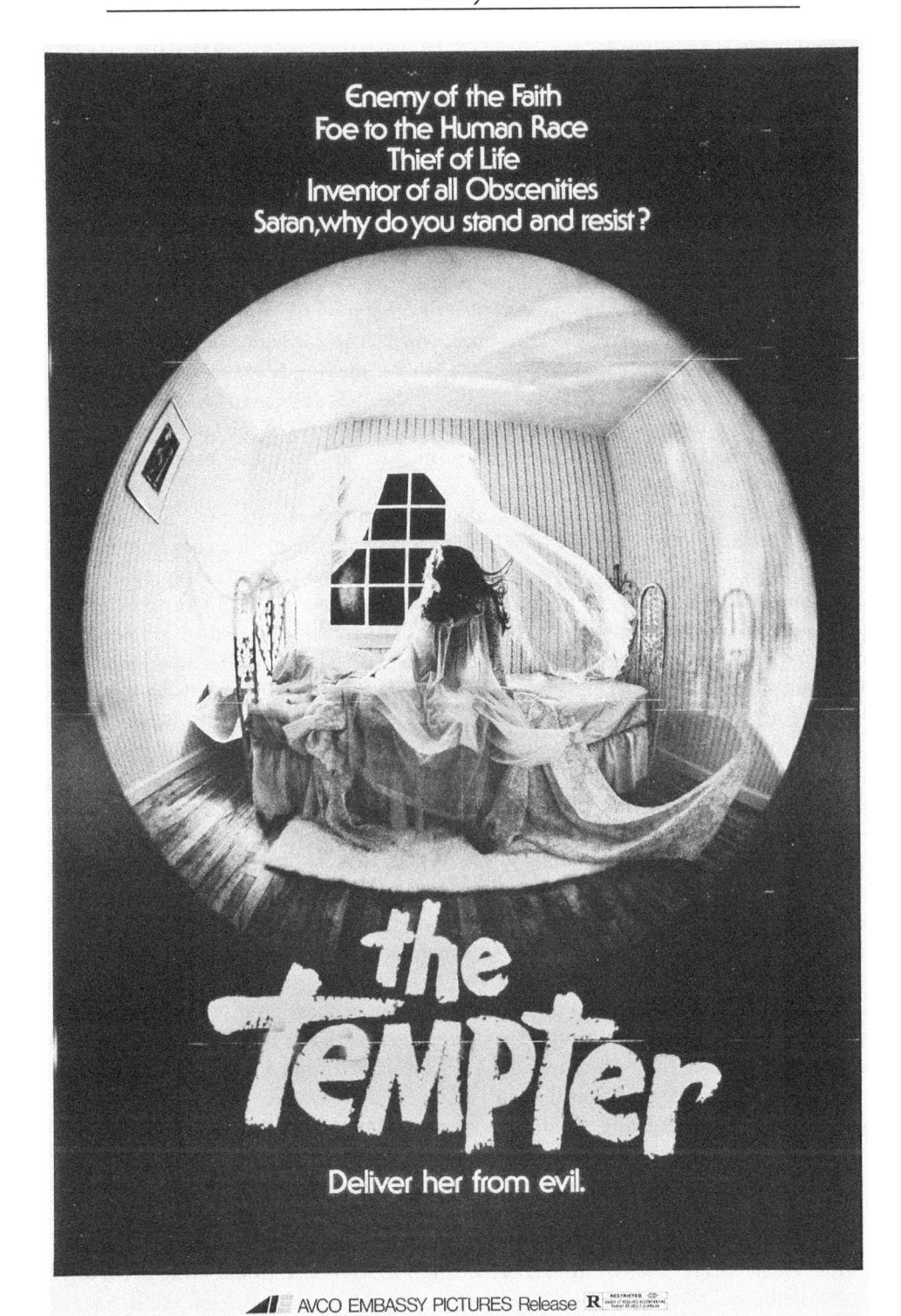

Not sure with what to do with the original Italian film, U.S. distributors try to convey as little as possible about *L'anticristo* (*The Tempter*, 1974).

harbors incestuous feelings for her father which come out during the initial stages of her possession, though this taboo isn't played out with him, but with her brother in a surprisingly unarousing scene, as he was clearly posited as gay throughout the picture. The shocks in the film come with the lurid sex with the young high school boy, followed by his murder, as well as the typical subgenre constructs of projectile vomiting, furniture flying around the room (via some terrible special effects), and the typical flagrant sexual behavior toward the clergy. Clearly the film is about keeping women in their traditionally conservative role within Italian society. Ippolita may be unhappy and repressed in her handicap but at least she's chaste. Once she is possessed and able to leave her wheelchair she exhibits all the signs of a sinner and her freedom must be curtailed, leaving it up to a dominant male priest put her back in her place. Unlike Friedkin's film, where it was obvious he had sympathy for young Regan, de Martino has very little for Ippolita, making her almost as shrewish and bitter before her possession as during. In addition, he doesn't seem to care that this terrible possession is even happening to her, focusing on ramifications of the family instead. In de Martino's world, as in all the rest of the subgenre, woman acts up, woman gets possessed, woman needs man to put her in her place.

Released around the same time as *L'anticristo*, Ovidio Assonitis's *Che sei?* (*Beyond the Door*, 1974) was a surprise worldwide hit that successfully fused elements from both *The Exorcist* (1974) and *Rosemary's Baby* (1968) into one narrative. After taking away the sexuality of a young woman in *L'anticristo*, *Che sei?* looks to take away childbirth as beautiful San Franciscan Jessica Barrett (played by Juliet Mills of TV's *Nanny and the Professor*) finds herself pregnant with her third child. This pregnancy isn't as easy as the other two because the baby happens to be Satan's and is being protected by her ex-boyfriend (Richard Johnson), who is being blackmailed by the Devil to make sure it is born. Her husband (*Profondo rosso*'s Gabrielle Lavia) is understandably upset, as this condition has Jessica eating discarded banana peels off the streets, turning her head 360 degrees, and engaging in the usual projectile vomiting. Though the film had a great marketing campaign that scared many kids at the time, including this author, the plot wasn't meant to mine the fertile field that Friedkin brought to his exploration of religion, but to gross out the audience who wanted to watch a sweet young woman French kissing her five-year-old son. Again, this is male-dominated fantasy, as the woman in peril cannot save herself but needs the help of a wizened white man to save her. Regardless, audiences were anxious to see another *Exorcist*-type film and lined up to see *Che sei?*, resulting in a 15-million-dollar return for a film that cost only $350,000 to make, and adding to the demand of more of these films.

The rush to produce films with a devil-possession motif was on in Italy, and filmmakers jumped at the chance to produce them out of any material they saw fit. Such was the case of Mario Bava's hauntingly beautiful Gothic *Lisa e il diavolo* (*Lisa and the Devil*, 1973; see the Gothic section). Showing the film to an enthusiastic audience in Cannes, producer Alfredo Leone had high hopes that it would be one of Bava's most successful films. Unfortunately, whether it was the non-linear storyline, the lack of true hard-core gore or the intellectual point of view, no one save for a small Asian distributor offered any serious money to distribute the masterpiece. Having sunk a million dollars of his own money in the film, Leone had no choice but to recut the film in a style that would bring in the largest possible audience. Not surprisingly, he chose the popular devil-possession motif. Bava was

Opposite: One of the more successful devil-possession films, *Che sei?* (*Beyond the Door*, 1974) found sweet Juliet Mills possessed by Satan's child.

EVIL GROWS BEYOND THE DOOR!

Beyond this door the most terrifying event in the history of mankind is about to occur!

BEYOND the DOOR

demoniac possession lives, and grows... and grows... and grows... and

JULIET MILLS as Jessica • RICHARD JOHNSON as Dimitri
with ELIZABETH TURNER • DAVID COLIN, Jr.   Directed by OLIVER HELLMAN
Screenplay by RICHARD BARRETT   color by DELUXE
An Edward L. Montoro Presentation of a Film Ventures International Release

initially game, since he wanted to help his friend out of financial trouble, as well as have the world see at least some portion of his film, but this good nature did not last long given the subject of devil possession. *Lisa* was the story of a young woman (Elke Sommer) caught up in a dream and brought to a house with an assorted group of strange characters, including Telly Savalas as the Devil. Leone wanted to use half the footage already shot so as to save the cost of reshoots, but he wanted some new exploitive material with which to secure an audience. So he called back Elke, hired actor Robert Alda (father of *M*A*S*H* star Alan Alda) to play a priest, and reconstructed a monstrosity known as *La casa dell'esorcismo* or *The House of Exorcism* (1975).

All pretense of art is thrown out the window as Elke is no longer lost in a dream but is now demoniacally possessed by one of the characters in Bava's previous film. Instead of being taken into a nightmarish ghost story, Lisa instead spends her time in a hospital completely possessed and out of her mind, walking on the walls like a spider, cursing priests ("Fuck you, you prick," being one of her favorites), and, in a spot of originality with the vomit theme, managing to throw up the occasional toad. The old *Lisa* footage is now recycled as flashback scenes which make absolutely no sense within the narrative. Bava himself was not happy with the shape that his masterpiece was taking and failed to show up to direct many of the more unsavory scenes, though as Tim Lucas cites, it may have been because he was beginning to work on his crime drama *Cani arrabbiati* (*Rabid Dogs*, 1975). Never one to be so blatant, Bava was disgusted by the final outcome and by an industry that was willing to turn art into a cheap, tawdry piece of exploitation. Ironically, for all the bitterness that came out of the revamp, the film made millions around the world, becoming one of Bava's top-grossing films as international audiences were eager to see sexy Elke Sommer behave in the most outrageous manner.

Like all subgenres in the Eurocult canon, it was usually a quick slide down the quality ladder after the first initial rip-off films, and the devil-possession fad was no exception. *L'ossessa* (*The Sexorcist, Eerie Midnight Horror Show*, 1974) tried like *L'anticristo* (1974) to fuse serious topics of religion and religious iconography into the narrative, but like its predecessor it used these lofty ideas as tools with which to showcase some serious exploitation. Art student Daniela (Stella Carnacina) is having some disturbing experiences, including watching her mother indulge in S&M activities with her adulterous lover and being haunted by a cross-shaped statue of a sexually suggestive Jesus-like man (Ivan Rassimov) that she finds in a deconsecrated church. The wooden Jesus-like man becomes alive (sort of), rapes her (sort of) and sets loose a powerful sexual hunger in Daniela. This results in her trying to seduce her father and the local priest (neither of whom is exactly turned off by the idea), masturbating furiously to just about every situation the movie devises, eating large clumps of her own hair, and developing the usual poor skin, day-glow eyes and penchant for spewing out copious amounts of vomit. She is sent to a convent (because that's where all good Italian girls go to iron out their demonic possessions) where she is "sexorcized" back to normalcy. *L'ossessa* tries hard to derive meaning from the power of the Church and its importance, as do most in the devil-possession canon, but often what these Italian films show us is a patriarchal view from a point in time when the roles of women were changing. They showcased the confusion and conflict of an era when female sexual expression was looking for an outlet and Italian men had to adjust.[216] *The Exorcist* (1973) channeled its evil through a young girl

Opposite: Bava's beautiful Gothic ghost story **Lisa and the Devil** (1973) is gutted and remounted as a devil-possession film.

EVERY CORNER OF THE SOUL IS LOST TO THE ICY CLUTCH OF THE SUPERNATURAL!

Alfred Leone presents

Telly Savalas   **Elke Sommer**

in

"THE HOUSE OF EXORCISM"

with Silva Koscina   guest starring Alida Valli and Robert Alda as Father Michael

R RESTRICTED UNDER 17 REQUIRES ACCOMPANYING PARENT OR ADULT GUARDIAN   directed by Mickey Lion an Alfred Leone International Production Color by Movielab A Peppercorn Wormser Release

with the statement that it can reside in the most innocent of youth, but the Italians saw that corruption of youth as a sign of a the burgeoning independence of women. Judging from the content of these films, which go to great lengths to show how unattractive a sexually independent woman can be, Italian men didn't seem to be adjusting too well. Daddy's little girls are meant to be virginal, and it is within this context that the repressed sexuality of these young girls plays out in father/daughter incest scenarios, a recurring theme in almost all devil-possession films. This is only natural, as the father figure in these films is always stalwart and beyond reproach. He acts in a masculine, professional, loving though occasionally stern manner. What is disturbing is that in many of the incestuous moments most of the fathers actually seem torn between their desire and revulsion. Never in these films is it the father's fault that the young girl or new mother, as in the case of *Che sei?*, is possessed; rather, it is the absence or lack of a strong, moral mother. Borrowing a theme present in Friedkin's *The Exorcist* (1973), which had Ellen Burstyn as the working actress mother who spent most of her time away from her family, these patriarchal films are only interested in keeping the traditional role of women in place, completely subservient, meaning that if a daughter and/or mother begins to assert her sexual independence or transcend her ascribed gender role then she can only expect bad things to happen, like having her daughter possessed by Satan. If you look at the devil-possession films, most of the daughters are orphaned (*L'anticristo*; *Il medaglione insanguinato*, aka *The Night Child*, 1974), or have mothers who are morally corrupt and not attentive to the child's needs (*L'ossessa*). For Jessica in *Che sei?*, the root of her problems stems from the fact that she was a bad girl earlier in her life and made some poor dating choices. Looking at this group of films from the mid–'70s viewpoint, it seems to be the last stand for men to take out their psychological angst against the rise of female equality. It's no surprise that the women of these subgenre films are only cured of their sexuality and blasphemy by strong, conservative men. The finale of these pictures is always the same in that after their brush with eroticism and violence, each female character becomes exactly what the male-dominated society demands: a good little girl.

The devil-possession subgenre, like its nunsploitation brother, was short-lived. After the initial shock of seeing good little girls indulging in some nasty, taboo-breaking behavior, audiences quickly soured on the subgenre. Many religious patrons found the films to be offensive simply because they trivialized the role of religion and made a mockery of it. Most exploitation fans rather enjoyed the idea of a sexually provocative female but without all the messy vomit. They found that sexual superwoman in the guise of Eurasian actress Laura Gemser, who was experiencing great worldwide success turning on audiences' exploitation style with another very popular series, the Black Emanuelle films.

Filmography

The Antichrist, aka *L'anticristo* (IT), *The Tempter* (U.S.). Prod. Edmondo Amati. Dir. Alberto de Martino. Italy/Spain, 1974. Anchor Bay Entertainment, 112 min. DVD. Starring: Mel Ferrer, Carla Gravina, Anita Strindberg, Aldila Valli and Arthur Kennedy.

Laughable special effects and a rather slow plot sabotage this, one of the first rip-offs of *The Exorcist* (1973). Carla Gravina stars as Ippolita, a paralyzed young woman with some hidden emotional issues. She's not too happy with her father (Ferrer) for taking up with a much younger woman (Strindberg), she's not happy with her love life (she has none), and she's a little too close to her brother (if you know what I mean). After attending a wacked-out religious happening in which local peasants writhe on the floor, she ends up with a religious artifact and before you can say Linda Blair, she starts doing some crazy things. She visits her past life when she was the star of the show at a ritual and forced to perform analingus on a goat (which is shown), picking up high school boys to have sex with them (she can walk now—it's a miracle!) before murdering them, and seducing her brother, which is kinda odd because he's clearly gay throughout the entire film. Don't even think about inviting her to dinner because the dishes start flying. Understandably her father is upset and sends for the local family priest (Kennedy); then the fake furniture *really* starts flying. Visually stunning, the film takes awhile to get going, but once it does it moves along at a pretty good clip. Unfortunately, de Martino was not blessed with the budget that William Friedkin had for *The Exorcist* and had to use animated furniture which look ridiculous today.

Beyond the Door, aka *Che sei?* (IT). Prod. and Dir. Ovidio G. Assonitis. Italy/Spain/U.S., 1974. Sevrin Films, 109 min. DVD. Starring: Juliet Mills, Richard Johnson, Gabriele Lavia and Elizabeth Turner.

One of the biggest U.S. moneymakers from Italy since Fellini; in fact, it probably made much more than any of his films! Due to some great marketing to audiences looking to get their *Exorcist* on, the film was a smash. Juliet Mills (a long way from the TV series *Nanny and the Professor*) discovers she's pregnant again. She's not altogether happy about it because she keeps vomiting blood and it makes her a little bit moody (enough to eat used banana peels off the street). She's also having dreams about a past love affair that ended badly. He was a devil worshipper; she wasn't. Soon, things get worse and she starts levitating around the house, turning her head 360 degrees and giving her young son hickies. What she doesn't know is that her ex (Johnson) has actually made a bargain with devil to deliver the baby in exchange for his soul. He comes calling and the projectile vomit starts flying. This is a silly picture that makes for perfect Friday-night viewing. Mills plays her role with gusto, going from sweet to sadistic naturally (though when her voice turns deep bass it's completely laughable), and rest of the international cast are passable, with only the kids being annoying. The San Francisco setting is a nice change of pace as well. The uncut version of the film has an extended scene (and I mean extended, as it totally destroys the tension in the film) with actor Lavia walking the streets of San Fran and "enjoying" the local music scene. Fun stuff!

Eerie Midnight Horror Show, aka *L'ossessa* (IT), *The Sexorcist* (INT). Prod. Riccardo Romano. Dir. Mario Garriazo. Italy, 1974. Sinema Diable, 86 min. DVD. Starring: Stella Carnacina, Ivan Rassimov, Luigi Pistilli, Lucretia Love and Gabriele Tinti.

A staple of cable TV in the '80s, *Eerie* is the most sexually flagrant of all the Italian devil-possession movies. It wasn't called *The Sexorcist* in certain areas for nothing. Art student Daniela (Carnacina) is angry at her family. Her handsome father is impotent and refuses to acknowledge that fact that his wife is having an affair with a local lothario (Tinti). After catching her mother indulging in some S&M sex play with her lover (he likes to beat her with thorned roses), she goes back to her office to work out her frustrations on a painting. Lucky for her, the recent crucifixion statue she found at a deconsecrated church is about to come to life and the devil hung on it is quite horny. After dreamlike sex with the sexy devil (Rassimov), Daniela starts coming on to everyone, including her father, before succumbing to the worst of her behavior; chronic masturbation. The self-flagellation is so bad they have to call both a doctor and a priest. Soon she's sent off to convent, where our resident sexorcist (Pistilli) exorcises her. Ironically, the film is meant to be taken seriously. Great fun for the Friday-night crowd, especially in scenes where Daniela is so possessed she starts to eat her own hair, and then, like a cat, starts choking on the hairballs!

Flavia the Heretic, aka *Flavia, la monaca musulmana* (IT). Prod. and Dir. Gianfranco Mignozzi. Italy/France, 1974. Synapse Films, 101 min. DVD. Starring: Florida Bolkan, Anthony Higgins, Claudio Cassinelli and Maria Casares.

Flavia the Heretic is one of those rare exploitation films that wants to accomplish something loftier than just grossing the audience out. That's a nice idea, but this is still nunsploitation, so be prepared for lots of sinful nuns indulging in sex with a spare decapitation and some horse castration thrown in for good measure. Flavia (*Lizard in a Woman's Skin* star Florinda Bolkan) has a crappy life. Her father has locked her away in a convent run by the some very strict nuns and populated with a lot of repressed women. She tries to run away with a male friend after watching a nun being raped by the local duke (in a pigpen, no less) only to be brought back and tortured. Quite unhappy at what she perceives as gender inequity (it is the 1400s, after all), she again escapes and joins a marauding gang of killers called the Tarantulas. Before you can say Helen Reddy, Flavia returns to the convent to deliver a little payback. *Flavia* is a well-done film that is marvelously acted by Bolkan. She brings the same amount of strength here as she did to both Fulci's *Don't Torture a Duckling* (1971) and *Lizard*. Obviously trying to compete with Ken Russell's *The Devils* (1971), *Flavia* is more than happy to add those elements that would make it a hit with the drive-in crowd, like nun nudity and rape. Though the sexual politics are obvious (the horse castration is a signifier, etc.) *Flavia* is one of those rare Eurocult films that don't make you feel like you need a bath after you watch it.

House of Exorcism, aka *La casa dell'esorcismo* (IT). Prod. Alfredo Leone. Dir. Mario Bava. Italy/U.S., 1975. Image Entertainment, 91 min. DVD. Starring: Elke Sommer, Robert Alda, Telly Savalas and Aldila Valli.

Poor Mario Bava! Producers put his beautiful but unsellable classic *Lisa and the Devil* (1973) into the blender and came up with this outrageous, but fun, sacrilege. *Lisa* (see the Italian Gothic section) was a dreamlike nightmare that had Elke Sommer lost in a strange Italian town and a mansion inhabited by strangers, with devilish Telly Savalas running the show. Without any buyers for the film, Producer Leone was forced to retool the picture into something that would sell, so he brought back most of the cast and filmed it as a devil-possession picture! So instead of Elke wandering around a Gothic town, she instead has a full-on Linda Blair attack and starts telling the preacher (Alda) to go fuck himself. It must be admitted that this film is much more successful as an exploitation film than *Lisa*. The sight of beautiful Ms. Sommer spider-crawling up a wall, masturbating and spewing green vomit is a hoot, and she seems to be having a ball! Let's not forget the priest temptation scene that every single devil-possession movie has, which is just an excuse to show some abundant nudity. Bava hated this version of the film and you can't blame him. Instead of just remounting a whole new movie, producers used about an hour of footage from *Lisa*, which adds to the head-scratching hijinks since the two story lines have nothing in common. Many DVDs contain both the *Lisa* and *House* versions on the same disc. Definitely pick it up, as it represents the sacred and the profane of Eurocult.

Images in a Convent, aka *Immagini di un convento* (IT). Prod. and Dir. Aristide Massaccesi. Italy, 1979. Exploitation Digital, 94 min. DVD. Starring: Paola Senatore, Marina Hedman, Paola Maiolina, Maria Rosaria Riuzzi.

Ahh, Aristide Massaccesi (under the name Joe D'Amato) and nunsploitation. The man who mixed hard-core porn and the zombie film in such winners as *Erotic Nights of the Living Dead* (1980) and *Porno Holocaust* (1980), and who gave us many of most exploitive Black Emanuelle films, tackles those naughty nuns and delivers a product that's exactly what you'd predict. Sleazy, with brief flashes of hard-core (in some prints), *Images* stars Senatore as a young woman who is sent to a convent after her father dies. Of course, the convent is filled with the most repressed nuns imaginable, which doesn't get any better when a guest of Satan arrives in the guise of a wounded solider. Obviously a priest is needed to clear up the mess, so Dr. Butcher M.D. himself, Donald O'Brien, is called in. With lots of scenes of nuns fornicating (both soft- and hard-core) as well as the requisite whippings, *Images* is pretty much what the subgenre is about: sleazy, taboo and infinitely interesting.

Killer Nun, aka *Suor omicidi* (IT). Dir. Giulio Berruti. Italy, 1978. Blue Underground, 87 min. DVD. Starring: Anita Ekberg, Joe Dallesandro, Alida Valli and Paola Morra.

From the secret files of the Vatican! Italian bombshell Anita Ekberg starts as Sister Gertrude, your standard Italian nun. She's strong, she possesses a caring heart, and the patients of her hospital mind her without question. Oh, she's also a morphine addict who likes to pick up men in bars and have anonymous sex with them in the hallways of strange apartment buildings, and she may also be a deranged killer (she's not big on false teeth, that's for sure!). Someone in her hospital has an intense hatred of men and is killing them off on a regular basis. It might even be Sister Gertrude when she's wacked out on drugs. With one of the best titles in all of Eurocult, *Killer Nun* has a hint more respectability than most others in the subgenre. This is probably due to the great cast, which also includes Aldila Valli and, rather bizarrely, New York actor Joe Dallesandro, who was regularly appearing in European movies at the time. Blood, nude nuns that climb into bed with anybody, and some very psychedelic drug trips accentuate the film. It's unfortunate that this was Sister Gertrude's only adventure, as it would have been great fun to see her back in more schlock like *Killer Nun and the Cannibals*, or better yet, *Killer Nun meets Black Emanuelle!*

Malabimba, the Malicious Whore, aka *Possession of a Teenager* (INT). Prod. Gabriele Crisanti. Dir. Andrea Bianchi. Italy, 1979. Severin, 98 min. DVD. Starring: Katell Laennec, Mariangela Giordano, Enzo Fisichella and Parizia Webley.

Here's a sick little puppy from the director of *Strip Nude for Your Killer* (1976) and *Burial Ground* (1981) that is both fun and shocking. The Karoli family is experiencing a downturn in fortune. The head of the household (Fisichella) is completely distraught over the death of his wife. Wanting to contact her from beyond, he conducts a séance, but the medium dials the wrong number and summons a sex-obsessed spirit named Lucrezia, who promptly possesses Fisichella's young daughter Daniela (Laennec). Well, as you can guess, the fun starts there as our little darling starts in on seducing both her pointy-nose stuffed elf and a stuffed teddy bear (I'm not kidding) before moving on to members of her family, including her uncle in a very graphic scene. Plus you should just see her party turn at a local family gathering — the girl knows how to party! Soon Sister Sophia (the good-natured Giordano) is justifiably concerned and tries to exorcise the demon from her. Bianchi is not afraid to go all the way in exploiting the subject matter. The film mixes both soft-core and hard-core "inserts" to shocking effect. Laughable in many spots and completely over-the-top, this is a fun film that makes for great weekend viewing with a group of discriminating (and not-so-discriminating) friends.

Nude for Satan, aka *Nude per Santana* (IT). Prod. Reno Angioli. Dir. Luigi Batzella. Italy, 1974. Image Entertainment, 82 min. DVD. Starring: Rita Calderoni, James Harris, Renato Lupi and Iolanda Mascitti.

With a title like this you now exactly what you're getting into. Only in the '70s could you get a narrative like this. A car accident leaves young Susan (Calderoni, back from being reincarnated, I guess) unconscious, but lucky for her there's a traveling doctor (Harris) there to help her. He promptly runs to the nearest fog-shrouded mysterious castle and never comes back. Susan wakes up and heads that way too. At the castle the two strangers are presented with their horny doppelgangers courtesy of one Satan. It seems the Devil is bored and wants to have an orgy. Oh, and Calderoni gets molested by a giant spider. You'll be bored too.

Reincarnation of Isabel, aka *Riti, magie nere e segrete orge nel trecento* (IT), *Black Magic Rites*. Prod. Romolo Forlai. Dir. Renato Polselli. Italy/Spain, 1972. Image Entertainment, 98 min. DVD. Starring: Mickey Hargitay, Rita Calderoni, Christa Barrymore and William Darni.

A psychedelic piece of fluff (meaning it makes no sense whatsoever on a linear level) most notable for Hargitay (Mr. Jane Mansfield and father of *Law and Order*'s Mariska Hargitay) dressed in red spandex with green paint on his face. Isabel (Calderoni) is burned at the stake 400 years previously for being nasty (witch, vampire, whatever; the movie is never quite clear) and her body has been reincarnated as the sexy Laureen. It seems everyone involved in the burning has also been reincarnated as well and now want to resurrect Isabel's spirit because, I don't know, she's more fun than Laureen. Some of the people participating in the reincarnation are vampires, and that's no good for the young naked girls in the local town. If you're expecting this to make sense anytime soon, you're bound to be disappointed. Bad acting, a plot (I use that term loosely) that will leave you shaking your head, and lots of nudity and sex with beautiful women and ugly men, all make this one of those "so-bad-it's-good" treats that Eurocult fans love.

The Sinful Nuns of Saint Valentine, aka *Le scomunicate di San Valentino* (IT). Prod. Gino Mordini. Dir. Sergio Grieco. Italy/Spain, 1974. Image Entertainment, 93 min. DVD. Starring: Françoise Prévost, Jenny Tamburi, Paolo Malco and Franco Ressel.

Oh, this could have been so much more fun! But alas, *The Sinful Nuns of Saint Valentine* is a rather tame affair. Without a director like Massaccesi or Spain's Jess Franco, who reveled in exploiting the possibilities, we're left with a film that is more lofty than profane. Yes, you get some whippings and some lesbian nun groping but the majority of the plot is a love story between a young nun and her wounded boyfriend who is hiding in the local convent. Things take a turn for the worse when the mother superior takes a shine to the young man. The film has all the elements of a good nasty nunsploitation film but never commits to exploiting them. It's a shame.

Sister Emanuelle, aka *Suor Emanuelle* (IT). Prod. Mario Mariani. Dir. Giuseppe Vari. Italy, 1977. Severin, 88 min. DVD. Starring: Laura Gemser, Gabriele Tinti, Vinja Locatelli and Mónica Zanchi.

You just knew it had to happen! Black Emanuelle (Gemser) has renounced her evil ways and has entered a convent! Actually the film is a bit of a cheat as this film has nothing thematically to do with the Massaccesi Black Emanuelle films produced at the same time. Obviously this was meant to be a cheap cash-in on the Emanuelle name, but still it's fun watching Gemser trying to live on the straight and narrow. In our uplifting story of salvation, Emanuelle enters a convent to reform (snicker!) and is quickly tempted by young hussy Monica. After Emanuelle declines her advances, Monica takes in a wounded bank robber (Tinti) and tries to get our heroine to break her vows. While not completely chaste, *Sister Emanuelle* is a far cry from the Massaccesi films that were swiftly moving into hard-core. Director Vari seems uncomfortable with the sex in the film and as a result films it in a relatively unimaginative style. The film's major asset is, of course, Gemser, who is always a remarkable presence regardless of the crazy plot going on around her (just check out *Erotic Nights of the Living Dead*). I just wish Massaccesi had had a crack at this.

Sexploitation — Italia style

> Because that's what it's like to be a woman.
> — Black Emanuelle (Laura Gemser) explaining her reason for leaving the man who loves her. This conversation is just prior to her getting on a train and being gang-banged (with her consent) by a traveling field hockey team in *Emanuelle nera* (*Black Emanuelle*, 1975)[217]

The feminist movement began its ascent in Italy later than in other Western countries. The male-dominated, church-enforced Italian society seemed unable to reconcile the change in women's roles with their long-established patterns of social behavior. In the '60s, Italian feminists began to challenge the rigid Catholic morals of society and a legal system that gave women little defense against male oppression, rape, or even murder. The feminists also challenged the male dominance of politics right across the spectrum, and even within the far-left political movements, and in time their strategies began to sway the public. By the early and mid–'70s, gender dynamics were radically different from what they had been a decade earlier. Divorce was finally legalized in 1970 and confirmed by popular referendum in 1974. Abortion was legalized in 1978.[218] The agitation caused by Italian feminists and the change in attitudes towards women was to have a rather strong impact on the way women were portrayed in exploitation films. But where one would think the roles of women in these films would be enhanced in a positive way, in many instances they became even more stereotypical as Italian filmmakers (i.e., men) took their uneasiness about the shift and transformed it into characters that were independent, yet morally bankrupt.

Italian filmmakers up to the '70s had never been successful in integrating strong, independent women into their films without there being some form of violent catalyst. Roles like Sophia Loren's in *La ciociara* (*Two Women*, 1960) showed the dichotomy of a strong woman in a man's world. These roles were few and far between, though. For Italian filmmakers (men), women were relegated to sexy, kittenish roles in the fun-loving sex comedies that Italians were known for. As the '70s began, exploitation filmmakers began to take advantage of the changing society within Italy and the world; as seen previously, they tried to deal with the new-found sexual revolution by simply saying it was the Devil's work! The devil-possession films clearly posited that any woman behaving badly was surely possessed by the Devil. Case closed. This was an okay arrangement, but after awhile male audience members weren't aroused by women masturbating with religious iconography. A new type of sexually adventurous woman had to be adopted. Lucky for the Italians, the French were successfully introducing a wide variety of sexual females to worldwide audiences, and if the Italians knew how to do anything, it was taking what other countries had done and ripping them off, with the exploitation ramped way up. Under the guise of feminism, these Italian filmmakers began to show female characters being independent and free to explore their lives, their careers and their own sexuality. This was only a guise, though, as the women in these exploitation films are made to suffer for their independence. Raped, abandoned, and even in some cases murdered, the women of this sexually explicit subgenre are exploited completely. This is not to say that the men of these films are honored. Quite the contrary; many times the men of these films are seen as without conscience, evil, and completely focused on dominating women. So, in essence, both sexes are fully exploited for audience satisfaction.

One of the most successful Italian entries of the exploitation market was the *Emanuelle nera* (*Black Emanuelle*) series of soft-core films in the late '70s. Capitalizing on the international success of France's *Emmanuelle* in 1974, Italian producers saw a potential box-office gold mine and tried to come up with a similar product that could be made cheaply. Working around the copyright issues, since the name "Emmanuelle" was copyrighted by the French, by dropping one "m" from the name, Italians were now free to create a series that could provide audiences with the kind of travelogue soft-core porn they seemed to enjoy. Working with lower budgets proved somewhat difficult because the French *Emmanuelle* series adopted an air of sophistication as opposed to the usual bump and grind of other erotic films, and though they were exploitative in their own right (see the France chapter), they dressed up their Eurocult leanings for a more glamorous feel. This forced the Emanuelle nera producers to up their budgets and scout exotic locations around the world in addition to employing expensive clothes in order to maintain the feel of an affluent society.[219]

Using Indonesian actress Laura Gemser in the title role, the Emanuelle nera series created some of the most disturbing mixtures of sex and violence.[220] The first film in the series, *Emanuelle nera* (*Black Emanuelle*, 1975) starts off innocently enough. Playing a newspaper reporter, Gemser sets out for Africa, where she embarks on several sexual conquests including a train full of traveling soccer players and a wealthy husband and wife. Director Bitto Albertini downplays the violence and exploitation and plays up a kittenish, decidedly male-gaze sexuality. For Gemser, filming the erotic content was nothing new as she had played the small part of a masseuse in the French sequel *Emmanuelle, l'antivierge* (*Emmanuelle, The Joys of a Woman*, 1975), and had frequently posed nude for magazine spreads throughout the world. Commenting on her role in one of her last public interviews in 1996, she discussed

Though low on exploitation, the original *Emanuelle nera* (*Black Emanuelle*, 1975) spawned one of the most famous genres in Italian exploitation.

the initial embarrassment of filming erotic scenes for the public: "The first time yes, but in the end you get used to it. Of course, everyone is looking at you stripping! But you treat it like a job and I got paid for doing it."[221] If audiences were thinking that *Emanuelle nera* represented some new transformative way to look at black sexuality, then they were bound to be disappointed. The fact that Gemser is not really black but Eurasian is never satisfactorily answered in any of the films. She is far darker-skinned than, say, German actress Karin Schubert, without question, but she does not register as either African, African American or black in culture or physicality. Her minority status, though, did create opportunities for filmmakers to put her in a variety of distinctly misogynistic situations, much more blatantly and violently than perhaps some of the classical Italian actresses would have been involved in. Clearly Italian exploitation filmmakers knew what they were doing. Sensing a rise in the success of "black" films around the world, and especially in the U.S. with the box-office success of "blacksploitation" films, they created a marketing gimmick that was designed to bring in a larger audience. Their ruse worked, as *Emanuelle nera* was a resounding hit around the world under such titles as *Black Emanuelle* or *Emanuelle in Africa*, prompting producers to come up with a quick sequel.

With *Emanuelle nera: Orient reportage* (*Emanuelle in Bangkok*, 1976), Aristide Massaccesi (Joe D'Amato) replaced Albertini as director and began upping the exploitation factor. Striking a balance between the soft-core sexuality that drew audiences to the first film and the increasingly popular use of shock tactics used in exploitation in the late '70s, Massaccesi began to incorporate mondo filmmaking techniques such as traditional cultural dancing, Thai boxing, cockfighting, and a mongoose and a snake fighting while trapped together in a glass tank, to give audiences more than just a sexploitation picture. He also began to showcase what would be the cruelty and warped ideology of the series which centered on the abusive nature of male/female relationships. In the *Emanuelle nera* series, rape seems to be the only outlet for the typical male/independent female interaction. In *Orient Reportage*, for example, Emanuelle (Gemser) is raped by a large group of military guerrillas, only to conduct a jovial conversation with them when the deed is over. Later, as the film moves to Morocco, she falls in the love with Debbie, the daughter of a U.S. ambassador, prompting jealous rage from her ex-boyfriend Roberto (Gemser's real-life husband, Gabriele Tinti, who appears in all the *Emanuelle nera* films). Catching the young woman masturbating while he and Emanuelle are making love, he is unable to control his rage and tries to force her into performing a ménage à trois with Emanuelle. "You think I'm going to rape the slut? She'd love to be fucked!" he snarls, before casting aspersion on Emanuelle's muddled sexual orientation with, "God, I hate lezzies!"[222] It is this type of interaction that permeates the entire series as Emanuelle happily moves from partner to partner enduring a myriad of torments, all the while spouting a free-sexuality philosophy that the heterosexual men in the audience were sure to respond to.

Massaccesi's next film in the series (and by now they were producing two a year) was *Emanuelle in America* (1976), released strategically during America's Bicentennial. The film incorporated almost every element of exploitation filmmaking, including rape, graphic snuff footage, both hard- and soft-core sex, and bestiality, into one jaw-dropping classic. A synopsis of the film showcases the frenetic narrative that plays out in the series as Emanuelle (Gemser) flits from one outrageous sexual scenario to another at a frenzied pace. Introduced in one scene as a fashion photographer, Emanuelle is first held at gunpoint while driving through New York City by the boyfriend of one of her nude models. The gunman, spouting enough conservative rhetoric to make Glenn Beck blush, plans to murder

Above and right: Emanuelle managed to find herself in exotic locations throughout the world, usually in highly exploitive situations.

Emanuelle in order to purify his girlfriend. When she tries to fellate him so as to persuade him to spare her life, he enjoys it and runs away ashamed. Emanuelle spends the rest of the film going on assignment all over the world, infiltrating a millionaire's personal harem, witnessing an orgy at a high-society party, visiting an exclusive club for women who pay for sex with men while the men are paraded around like cattle, and, just for fun, tracking down a snuff film ring as well as many more misadventures, all designed to satisfy her need for sex.[223]

What makes the film so shocking was Massaccesi's belief that the more he graphically showed the better the film would be. He spared no visual expense whether it was a young woman masturbating a horse or the horrific snuff footage that was screened. Commenting on the inclusion of hard-core sex in the film, Massaccesi said, "During that period we had French distributors and they asked us to put harder material into our films. So if a movie was originally soft-core they asked us to add hard-core. Back then there was just theatrical distribution, we weren't even thinking about TV. Now they are shown on television (edited)."[224] The hard-core sex scenes did not go over so well with Gemser, who refused participate in them. That doesn't mean that her character Emanuelle missed out on any of the action. As Gemser explained, "*Emanuelle in America* contains scenes that I refused to act. They shot scenes with another girl; scenes that I refused to do. I don't know if the scenes were cut from the Italian version but they were put in foreign versions. They were hard-core scenes that I refused to do. They hired body doubles for those scenes."[225]

As if the hard-core sex and horse masturbation weren't enough, the violence of *Emanuelle in America* (1975) is even more shocking. The snuff-footage narrative that Emanuelle is forced to watch near the end of the film includes impalings, acid torture, whippings, breast slicing and rape with large, sharp objects. Massaccesi wanted to pour as much realism into the scene as possible, and having heard that these so-called snuff films, where people were supposedly tortured and eventually killed on camera, were shot in 8mm, he took his 35mm and scratched up the negative so it would appear to have an 8mm look. So good was the effect that most of the audiences believed that they were watching an actual snuff film. This attention to detail not only traumatized the audiences, but had an unintended effect on one of the actresses in the film: Massaccesi was consequently sued by the actress who played in the faked snuff portion of the film. Citing extreme mental cruelty, she tried to take her case to an Italian court. The case was eventually dismissed though with Massaccesi believing that "she only wanted money."[226] She would have a good argument, though, as the footage is some of the strongest in the Eurocult canon. Controversy of any kind is good for Eurocult, and this was no exception: as *Emanuelle in America* was shown to enthusiastic audiences around the world (in a variety of different cuts, of course, as horse masturbation and extreme snuff footage just don't seem to play well in certain countries), ensuring there would be more to follow.

Money was what was being made as series cranked along in the late '70s. Massaccesi put Ms. Gemser into a variety of different and increasingly violent situations. *Emanuelle perché violenza alle donne?* (*Emanuelle Around the World*), which contained scenes just as strong as the earlier *Emanuelle in America* (and also containing both hard- and soft-core sex), with its gritty look at prostitution including a bestiality scene with a rather large German shepherd, and *La via della prostituzione* (*Emanuelle and the White Slave Trade*), which had Emanuelle going undercover to bust a sex slave trade and included scenes of a slave auction taking place at the downtown New York Hilton (!), were both released in 1977. As the '70s wound down, Emanuelle was taking more outlandish steps outside her comfort zone in such exploitive fun as 1978's *Emanuelle e gli ultimi cannibali* (*Emanuelle and the Last Cannibals*, mentioned in the cannibal chapter) which had the sex subgenre mix with the cannibal films to predictable results, and *Suor Emanuelle* (1978), which had her joining a convent!

This conjunction between the sexual freedom of woman and the price she must pay is at the heart of the Black Emanuelle films. Looking at the treatment of Emanuelle in her films, it's clear that most of the violence is directly aimed at her, and because most of the Black Emanuelle films have a mondo feel to them, the violence is magnified. In these films, Black Emanuelle is forced at gunpoint (*Emanuelle in America*, 1976), raped on a train by a field hockey team (*Emanuelle nera*, 1975), gagged, tied up, subjected to animal invasions and almost cannibalized (*Emanuelle e gli ultimi cannibali*, 1978), and beaten to within an inch of her life in prison (*Emmanuelle fuga dall'inferno*, 1983). All of these examples are instances in which the sexual liberation of women is tied to violent acts. Disturbingly, though, violence doesn't seem to be used as the aphrodisiac to get one in the mood, but to actually get one off.[227]

While there were many different Em(m)anuelle films in the late '70s (*Yellow Emmanuelle*, 1977; *Nea, a Young Emmanuelle*, 1977; *Emanuelle in Japan*, 1978; etc.), it was the Italian Emanuelle nera series that worldwide audiences responded to. Gemser retired from the role in the early '80s as the films became staples of American cable television as well as popular VHS and BETA videotapes. As new audiences were experiencing the "joys" of Emanuelle, the series fizzled out. The uncomfortable alliance between sex and graphic violence was no longer in vogue, and the rise of sexually transmitted diseases such as herpes as well as the arrival of the AIDS virus caused a serious re-evaluation of the Italian sexploitation genre.

Filmography

Black Emanuelle, aka *Emanuelle nera* (IT), *Emanuelle in Africa* (U.S.). Prod. Mario Mariani. Dir. Bitto Albertini. Italy/Spain, 1975. Severin Films, 94 min. DVD. Starring: Laura Gemser, Gabriele Tinti, Karin Schubert and Venantino Venantini.

In one of the first rip-offs of the wildly popular French film *Emmanuelle* (1974), Albertini creates a template for one of the most successful series in Eurocult history. Laura Gemser, who had a brief role in the legitimate sequel to the original film, *Emmanuelle, The Joys of a Woman* (1975), stars as a young journalist who sets off around the world in search of good stories and interesting people and finds herself involved in outlandish sexual situations. Using the same free-love themes as the French Emmanuelle ("nothing is wrong if it feels good," etc.), our swinging journalist goes to Nairobi, where she meets up with rich, bisexual Schubert and her lothario husband Gianni (Angelo Infani). Soon she begins an affair with Gianni with the typical outcome. It becomes apparent that Emanuelle must be free to do what she wants, which apparently means she'd rather have sex with an entire trainload of the national field hockey team than pursue a monogamous relationship. Meanwhile we're treated to some rather fetching footage of Emanuelle on safari, where she and Schubert cavort naked taking pictures of themselves, at swanky parties, and lying near waterfalls, all set to some classic kicking music by Nico Fidenco (the soundtrack is included in the Severin DVD box set!). In the scheme of things, *Black Emanuelle* is a very tame movie which never comes near the exploitation heights that Massaccesi took it to a year later. The sex is soft-core and never overtly lurid, the settings are pretty, and Laura Gemser has the natural charisma to carry the role. No matter how much money they poured into these films, though (and it really wasn't that much), there is always something cheap-looking about them. Unlike the three original Emmanuelles (including *Goodbye Emmanuelle*, 1978), which showed their budgets onscreen with amazing settings and locales, Black Emanuelle exhibited to audiences exactly what it was: a fun yet exploitative rip-off.

Emanuelle and the White Slave Trade, aka *La via della prostituzione* (IT). Prod. Fabrizio De Angelis. Dir. Aristide Massaccesi. Italy, 1978. Severin, 89 min. DVD. Starring: Laura Gemser, Gabriele Tinti, Ely Galleani and Venantino Venantini.

One of the last Black Emanuelle films released, *White Slave Trade* is a bit of a comedown from the exploitative highs of *America* and *Around the World*. Massaccesi had by this time simply run out of ideas and spends the movie recycling many of the scenarios from other films in the series. This time around Emanuelle (Gemser) begins in Africa again, looking to interview an international syndicate boss (Venantini). That's right, folks: she's working the organized crime angle here with the help of her goofy stewardess friend Susan (Galleani). After meeting and bedding (in both a two-way and three-way) the boss, she flies to America to view a female slave auction taking place at the downtown Hilton, all of which she captures on her trusty camera that doubles as a cigarette lighter. Soon it's off to Europe to work uncover with Madame Claude (who, for a high-priced madame, looks more like a K-mart check-out clerk) and finds out the real story about this dastardly slave ring. This film is essentially a non-starter: it is neither sexy nor violent; many of the scenes, especially the Africa shots, are possibly taken from the other movies; and the plot is a snooze. Though Emanuelle would go on go to prison and enter a convent (not in that order) this was pretty much the death knell for the series. If you don't believe me, the transvestite bowling brawl in the film should pretty much confirm it.

Emanuelle Around the World, aka *Emanuelle, perché violenza alle donne* (IT). Prod. Fabrizio De Angelis. Dir. Aristide Massaccesi. Italy, 1976. Severin Films, 94 min. DVD. Starring: Laura Gemser, Gabriele Tinti, Karin Schubert and Luigi Montefiori.

Though just a shade less over-the-top than *Emanuelle in America* (1976), this one is a shocker as well as one of the most solid in the series. Focusing in on violence as much as on the sex, Massaccesi treats his viewers to a travelogue of perversity that is not so much fun to actually watch. The "fun" begins in San Francisco, where Emanuelle is having sex in a moving van with her boyfriend after being away on a desert island(?). Her boss decides to send the young journalist to India to find a guru (Luigi Montefiori) who knows how to have a prolonged orgasm. That ends in (of course) a whole cult-like orgy that goes on forever (well, the guru did teach "prolonged"). It's then on to Rome, where things get a little serious: she meets a woman who's been raped, prompting Emanuelle to give up writing about what she deems stupid stuff and start writing about sex slave trades in Hong Kong. These slave trades are no laughing matter: the guys beat and whip women into submission, and as an added bonus, rape them with dogs (yep, fun stuff here, folks). Soon Emanuelle is finding out there are a lot of people in high positions in the government taking advantage of these slave trades. One of the most professionally filmed entries in the entire series, the film manages to shock audiences, much as *Emanuelle in America* did, with its 180-degree turn from lightweight soft-core fodder to hard-core violence and bestiality. Nico Fidenco's score is again here to enjoy, and of course Gemser, who seems to take everything that Massaccesi throws at her in stride, is her usual affable self. Two versions of the film exist; if you're not partial to bestiality, stay away from the XXX cut!

Emanuelle in America. Prod. Fabrizio De Angelis. Dir. Aristide Massaccesi. Italy, 1976, Blue Underground, 100 min. DVD. Starring: Laura Gemser, Gabriele Tinti, Paola Senatore and Roger Browne.

The most notorious film in both the Black Emanuelle series as well as all of Eurocult. Massaccesi throws in everything from hard-core sex to graphic snuff-like film footage to create a sometimes shocking piece of entertainment that often goes over the edge. Our favorite intrepid reporter Emanuelle (Gemser) is back, ready to report on the stories no one else really wants to. After being accosted at gunpoint by a young, repressed Republican who blames her for all the moral decay in the world (he does have a point), she finds herself going undercover in a harem (she gets the job because they need a Virgo!) with a sadistic leader who likes to treat women badly. Emanuelle manages to get the story and meet the bevy of beauties, including one who gets so sexually excited when the stable's horse Pedro whinnies, she just has to go help the horse out (seriously!). It's then on to New Jersey, where she infiltrates a high-class prostitution ring that caters to women before finally having the most fun of all: being drugged by a U.S. congressman and taken to an island to watch the production of a snuff film. Sounds like a typical Black Emanuelle film, with the major difference that Massaccesi is not afraid to show exactly the horrors the early films only intimated (in the uncut versions, at least). Consequently, horse masturbation, hard-core sex with one of the male prostitutes, and worst of all, some of the most disturbing snuff film footage imaginable are all included. Gemser (who never takes part in any hard-core sequences) takes pictures with her trusty hidden camera disguised as a bracelet. How does it wrap up? Like all Black Emanuelle films, it doesn't. No one wants closure; we only want Emanuelle to go on to one perverse situation to another. For someone looking for the model of a '70s Eurocult film you would hard-pressed to find another that delivers the goods like this one.

Emanuelle in Bangkok, aka *Emanuelle nera: Orient reportage* (IT). Prod. Fabrizio De Angelis. Dir. Aristide Massaccesi. Italy, 1975. Severin Films, 91 min. DVD. Starring: Laura Gemser, Gabriele Tinti, Ely Galleani, Venantino Venantini and Ivan Rassimov.

The first successful sequel to *Black Emanuelle* (not counting 1976's *Black Emanuelle 2*, which did not star Gemser nor have anything to do narratively with the first film), and the first to be directed by Massaccesi, begins to show the warped direction he would soon take the series. Playing more like a sexy travelogue, the film begins with journalist Emanuelle on her way to Bangkok with her archaeologist lover Roberto (played by real-life husband Tinti) to interview a Thai king. After dumping her lover ("I've got to be free"), she manages to find a massage parlor to unwind, finds a bellhop willing to give her the five-star service and meets a couple of self-proclaimed obnoxious American Republicans (by their own admission!). Soon, though, Emanuelle's political leanings get her in trouble: someone takes her passport and trashes her room, and she's raped by eight militia men (don't worry, she's obviously fine with it, since she's quite civil with them afterwards). So it's off to Casablanca with one of the female Republicans (both of whom turn quite liberal by the middle of the movie), where she reteams with Roberto, who's suddenly engaged. She then falls in love with a daughter of the U.S. ambassador, all to the strains of some fun and funky music by Nico Fidenco. Though the film is relatively harmless, scenes of violence begin to creep into the narrative. At this point in Italian Eurocult, producers were fascinated by animal killings (see the cannibal section), and Massaccesi throws in a bit of this along with the previously mentioned rape scene. The sex is all fairly tame and perfectly in line with late-night cable TV (which is where this movie played throughout the '80s), with Gemser as always making an interesting and attractive lead.

The Sacred and the Profane: Non-Genre Italian Exploitation

> A strange combination between the art house and the slaughterhouse.
> — Film critic Steve Biodrowski in his review
> of Dario Argento's *Suspiria* (1977)[228]

Not all of the Italian exploitation films of the '60s and '70s belong to a particular genre. Occasionally, Italian filmmakers would come up with an original work that was either too hard to duplicate or simply not successful enough to spawn its own series. Often these films were the most shocking in the Italian canon because audiences had no preconceived idea as to what the formula they would adhere to. Audiences, though, knew to expect the over-the-top gore, perverse sexual situations, strange music and laughable dubbing. On rare occasions they may get something more. Dario Argento's *Suspiria* (1978) was one of those rare occasions.

After the success of *Profondo rosso* (*Deep Red*) in 1975, Argento chose to get away from the gialli that he had help revolutionize in the early '70s. Working with his partner, actress Daria Nicolodi (who broke her ankle prior to filming, resulting in her on-screen absence), he crafted a story that incorporated his love of the stories by H.P. Lovecraft along with the writings of Thomas De Quincy and a ghost story told by Nicolodi's grandmother to conjure up one of the scariest films to come out of Italy. The film, which is long on style and bloodshed and a bit short on narrative, uses the tried-and-true Italian Gothic motif of Mario Bava and combines with Argento's dreamy auteur style of directing to create a film that packs a wallop of scares and exploitation. The plot isn't all that complex, as Suzy Banyon (American actress Jessica Harper) arrives in Germany to attend the prestigious Tanz Akademie. Soon it becomes apparent that the academy is a more than just a dance school; it's the home of a coven of not-so-nice witches who serve at the bidding of one even more terrible monster. Argento wraps his high-brow fantasy in all the excesses of late–'70s exploitation, with the first 15 minutes alone being some of the most evocative and frightening in the Eurocult canon. Suzy arrives in Germany in a blinding thunderstorm while two students of the academy are brutally slaughtered via glass shards and stabbings (in which close-ups of the heart being punctured are provocatively shown). All of this carnage is being set to the loud, pulsing, synthesized music of the Goblins. After the first rash of killings, things settle down a bit for the rest of the film, though Argento still treats his fans to falling maggots, a killer dog, and a very uncomfortable coiled-wire death. But though the violence is over the top, it is all presented in the style of a filmmaker clearly at his peak. In some respects his non-adherence to a substantial narrative means the film can take on a variety of different meanings as viewers could either delve into the mysteries of occultism and mysticism, ponder hegemonic superiority (American Harper seems to be the only person capable of solving the mystery), or enjoy the movie as a throwback to older European horror fables or simply as an exercise in exploitation. So successful was Argento in crafting a story that was visually appealing, controversial and open to interpretation by the widest possible audience, the film secured a major release in most countries. That's not to say that the major studios who distributed the film were proud of it: 20th Century–Fox, who also won the rights to distribute the film internationally, was deeply disturbed by the film's content and embarrassed to release the film in the U.S. under the studio's own name. Consequently they created a special moniker, "International Classics," just in case the outcry of a major studio releasing what essentially was a very high-budget exploitation film had a negative effect. Happily for Fox, the film was a major box office smash in the U.S., though admittedly they still have not reappropriated the film.

If *Suspiria* (1977) represented the high-water mark for Eurocult, most of the other late–'70s exploitation from Italy represented its nadir. With an anything-goes mindset, Italian filmmakers were looking for anything that would shock audiences into a theater. Aristide Massaccesi (Joe D'Amato), who had already tried to fuse pornography with zombie movies in *Porno Holocaust* (1980) and was responsible for showing a man ripping out a fetus and eating it in *Anthrophagus* (*The Grim Reaper*, 1980), decided to use necrophilia to shock audiences that were becoming completely desensitized. Massaccesi was more than happy to show what had only been hinted at during Italy's golden years of Gothic horror in such films as Freda's *L'orribile segreto del Dr. Hichcock* (*The Horrible Dr. Hichcock*, 1964). *Buio omega* (*Beyond the Darkness*, 1980) is a beautiful love story in which rich taxidermist Frankie (Kieran Cantor) decides to stuff his recently deceased girlfriend, keeping her body in his bed for those cold and lonely nights. He becomes more unhinged (if that's possible) and begins to kill most of the women in the film (he's especially handy with the nail clippers!), trusting only his controlling and also unhinged housekeeper (Franka Stoppi, more bizarre than usual), who nicely allows him to breast feed when the mood hits him. Massaccesi adds to the depravity some graphic embalming sequences, a bath full of acid and enough nudity to make happy whomever could get turned on by this. This is one sick puppy that doesn't purport to offer any deep insight other than revulsion, and if the test of good Eurocult is to make the viewer wish he had a bath after watching one of its films, than *Buio omega* would be a classic.

Working on the same necrophilia theme except with fewer parts, Lamberto (Mario's son) Bava's *Macabre* (1980) tells the disturbing tale of recent New Orleans widow Jane (Bernice Stergers), who must come to terms with the decapitation death of her beloved. As the nights pass by, neighbors soon begin to hear sounds of Jane's lovemaking and deduce that

With its necrophilia storyline, Masseccesi's *Buio omega* has the reputation of being one of the most repellent of late–'70s Eurocult films.

she has a secret lover. They are aghast by the end of the movie to find out that she has been keeping her dead husband's head in the icebox by day and making love to it at night. Purportedly inspired by a true story of a New Orleans woman busted in 1965 for keeping her former husband's head in the fridge, Bava seems more interested in letting the storyline shock as opposed to the effects, which shows the pullback that was beginning to happen within the Italian exploitation film industry. The film has its share of bloody fun, but nowhere near the level of the Massaccesi films that were being released during the same period. Still, the sight of Stergers licking a bloody head while naked in bed is enough to give one nightmares for a long time to come. The fascination with necrophilia shows that the Italian exploitation industry had at last explored its final frontier. With nothing left to exploit and audiences now either staying home or returning to American-style blockbusters (e.g., *Star Wars*, 1977; *Close Encounters of the Third Kind*, 1978; and *Raiders of the Lost Ark*, 1981) that were very hard to rip off (though they did try), the subject was the last gasp for Italian filmmakers as the true era of Italian exploitation ended.

Filmography

Baba Yaga, aka *Baba Yaga, Devil Witch* (INT), *Kiss Me, Kill Me* (U.S.). Prod. and Dir. Corrado Farina. Italy/France, 1973. Blue Underground, 83 min. DVD. Starring: Carroll Baker, Luigi Montefiori, Isabelle De Funès and Ely Galleani.

Baba Yaga is an interesting but not altogether successful mix of Guido Crepax's Italian comic book genius and European exploitation. It seems like it would be a perfect mix, though, as Crepax's subject matter, usually involving all sorts of nudity, and its provocative subject centered on lesbian S&M relationships, would make it compatible with Eurocult. Valentina (De Funès in her Amélie-type wig) is a famous fashion photographer who likes to shoot men and women in provocative (i.e., nude) situations. One night after a late-night party she's nearly hit by a car driven by Baba Yaga, a witch (American star Carroll Baker, who's obviously enjoying her time away from Hollywood). Working the lesbian mojo on her, Baba pulls the young Valentina into a world of Nazi fetish dreams, killer S&M dolls that turn into Ely Galleani (*Emanuelle in Bangkok*, 1976; *Emanuelle and the White Slave Trade*, 1978) when the lights go down, and cameras that kill people. It's up to Valentina to resist the temptation of the witch with the help of her boyfriend Arno (Montefiori). The film is never uninteresting and the comic book style in which many of the scenes, especially the sex scenes, are filmed is well handled. Baker is quite good with her yellow pancake makeup and huge wigs covering up her true beauty, and it's nice to see Montefiori in a role that doesn't require him to eat his own intestines (*Anthropophagus*, 1980), but the film seems to be lacking the "spark" that made the comic books so memorable. Still, it's good to have some originality in the Eurocult canon and *Baba Yaga* fits that bill.

Beyond the Darkness, aka *Buio omega* (IT), *Buried Alive* (U.S.). Prod. Marco Rossetti. Dir. Aristide Massaccesi. Italy, 1979. Shriek Show, 91 min. DVD. Starring: Kieran Canter, Franca Stoppi, Cinzia Monreale and Sam Modesto.

The late '70s was a free-for-all in terms of explicitness in Eurocult. The raunchiest, most shocking subject matter was being explored, and unlike the '60s, this plethora of taboo-busting subjects was being graphically depicted onscreen. *Beyond the Darkness* is one of those films that just makes you say "yuck" both in subject matter and in depiction. The heartwarming story depicts a young taxidermist (Canter) traumatized by the death of his fiancée (Monreale). Not happy being on the singles scene, he decides to dig her up, embalm her and plant her as a permanent resident in his bed. This happy-couple scenario is put to the test by Canter's psychological involvement with his absolutely insane maid (Stoppi) as well as his own increasing madness. Soon he's bringing girls home to kill them and giving them an acid bath in the process. All of this comes to a head when his dead girlfriend's twin sister (Monreale again) comes to visit and isn't too thrilled with her cadaver sister's love life. Sick, cheap, depressing, badly acted, and over the top, with many gore sequences that would please the most hardened of fans as well as lots of cadaver nudity, *Beyond the Darkness* is, of course, a must-see for die-hard Eurocult fans!

Blood for Dracula, aka *Dracula cerca sangue di vergine* (IT), *Andy Warhol's Dracula* (U.S.). Prod. Andy Warhol. Dir. Paul Morrissey. U.S./Italy, 1974. Image Entertainment, 103 min. DVD. Starring: Joe Dallesandro, Udo Kier, Stefania Casini and Vittorio De Sica.

Flesh for Frankenstein, aka *Il mostro è in tavola Barone Frankenstein* (IT), *Andy Warhol's Frankenstein* (U.S.). Prod. Andy Warhol. Dir. Paul Morrissey. Italy/U.S., 1974. Image Entertainment, 95 min. DVD. Starring: Joe Dallesandro, Udo Kier Monique van Vooren and Nicholetta Elmi.

The Andy Warhol factory goes to Europe and brings back some funky Eurocult goodness! Filmed in the same period, *Blood for Dracula* and *Flesh for Frankenstein* represent an innovative but completely over-the-top perspective on the Dracula and Frankenstein legends. More coherent than Spanish director Jess Franco's take on the two monsters at the time (and with a much higher budget), Morrissey concocts two tales that are ridiculous and ridiculously entertaining as they revel in enough bloodshed and sex to have originally been slapped with an X rating in the United States. *Frankenstein* has German Eurocult star Udo Kier playing the good doctor. Married to his sister (we're never really quite sure how they're related), the sex addict Monique van Vooren, he plots to find a male companion to his already (loosely) put-together female monster with the aid of his bug-eyed, poorly acted assistant Arno. Finding the perfect head on a local shepherd, Kier decapitates him and begins the process of reanimation. Here that means that he has to mount his cadavers because, as he puts it, "You have to fuck life through the gallbladder." Meanwhile good guy Joe Dallesandro arrives to sleep with van Vooren and find out what happened to his friend, the shepherd. *Flesh for Frankenstein* is the kind of film Ed Wood would have made had he had a big budget. Morrissey goes all out in the gore department, with organs flying all over the place. The film was also shot in 3-D, which adds to the fun as Kier often shows the audience close-ups of the big helpings of internal organs!

Filmed after *Frankenstein*, *Blood for Dracula* is actually a little more subdued, but still crazy fun! Poor Dracula (Kier) has to leave his Romanian castle because there are no more virgins left in his town. See, he can only drink the blood of virgins (or as he pronounces it, "wirgins") to keep him alive, and lately he's looking very pale and not good at all. So he loads up the casket and heads to Italy in search of fresh virgin blood. He comes across a down-on-their-luck aristocratic family (run by famous Italian filmmaker Vittorio De Sica, who must have been shaking his head throughout the filming) who are desperately in need of an influx of cash. They welcome the count into their home and introduce him to their four young daughters, assuring him of their virginity. Unfortunately for Dracula, the handyman of the house is Joe Dallesandro, and the girls are anything but virgins, causing a lot of digestive problems for our intrepid vampire. For all its camp craziness (plus Dallesandro's wooden acting and thick New York accent), there's something beguiling about the film. Kier makes a perfect vampire with his assorted physical ailments, and the film's sets and costumes are beautiful, portraying the decaying Italian aristocracy. It's almost a shame that Morrissey didn't continue this classic-monster series and give us a version of the Wolf Man while he was at it. With Joe Dallesandro ... now *that* would have been fun!

Contamination, aka *Alien Contamination* (U.S.). Prod. Charles Mancini. Dir. Luigi Cozzi. Italy, 1980, Blue Underground, 95 min. DVD. Starring: Ian McCulloch, Louise Marleau, Marino Masé and Carlo De Mejo.

While almost all that Eurocult chose to exploit were things of an earthly nature, once in a great while they looked up and found that space might be just as exploitable as subjects here. The worldwide success of *Alien* in 1979 did not go unnoticed by the Italians. Quickly putting together a story that incorporated elements of the cannibal film with the Ridley Scott classic, Cozzi developed an interesting variation on both that is sporadically fun to watch. The film opens like gangbusters in New York City (surprise!), where a mysterious boat is lodged in the harbor (yes, it sounds a lot like *Zombie*, 1979). This time, though, there are no zombies, but a crew with their stomachs ripped out and a bunch of large eggs. One of the eggs erupts, dousing the nearest man on the search-and-rescue team, and before you can say Sigourney Weaver, his stomach explodes in slow motion! It's up to top federal agent Marleau, who wisely concludes that the eggs must be from outer space, and astronaut McCulloch to save the world by traveling down to Colombia to face the egg-laying predator. *Contamination* could have been a classic with its opening 10 minutes of carnage laying the foundation for a totally enjoyable film. Unfortunately, budgets probably got in the way, and as result the movie drags during the halfway point, becoming more like a spy/cannibal film as our duo makes it down to the wilds of Colombia on their quest. When we do meet the alien it's sadly much more a like a scene from *It Conquered the World* (1956) than from *Aliens* (1986). A great Goblins score is some compensation.

House on the Edge of the Park, aka *La casa sperduta nel parco* (IT). Prod. Franco Di Nunzio. Dir. Ruggerio Deodato. Italy, 1980. Shriek Show, 89 min. DVD. Starring: David Hess, Annie Belle, Giovanni Lombardo Radice and Lorraine De Selle.

Wes Craven's *Last House on the Left* (1972) was a shocking film that showcased rape and violence as an indictment of early–'70s society and showed us the deeper shade of human depravity. Deodato takes out the social commentary and sticks some really bad early–'80s disco music in this *very* depressing story of a group of guys (Hess and Lombardo Radice) terrorizing a young couple. Mechanic, rapist, murderer, take your pick; Hess just wants to party with his mentally challenged friend Radice. Before they can go, however, duty calls in the form of a young rich couple (Belle and Christian Borromeo) who decide, in one of the most ludicrous plot manipulations ever, to invite the guys to a well-to-do party. Big mistake! It seems the guys haven't read *Pygmalion* or at least watched *My Fair Lady* and don't take too well to being made fun of by the rich folk at the party (though Radice's striptease comes pretty close to being a musical number!). Soon the boys' anger explodes and the raping and violence begin, including your standard golden shower scene, unwarranted sex and a very nasty nude slashing scene. Oh yeah, there's a trick ending, too, that completely makes no sense; you'll be scratching your head long after you've turned the movie off and are headed to the shower to clean off the muck left behind from this gem. If nihilistic hardcore exploitation without any conscience or humor is what you want, here it is.

Inferno. Prod. Claudio Argento. Dir. Dario Argento. Italy, 1980. Blue Underground/Arrow, 107 min. DVD/Blu-Ray. Starring: Mitch McCloskey, Irene Miracle, Daria Nicolodi, Alida Valli and Veronica Lazar.

After a two-year hiatus, Argento is back with his sequel of sorts to the classic *Suspiria* (1977). While good in many respects it unfortunately is not on the same level as its predecessor. Rose Elliot (Miracle) finds an occult book she believes provides a clue to some of the bizarre goings-on in her apartment building. Unfortunately for her, one of the dreaded "3 Mothers," Mater Tenebrarum, lives there (it was Mater Suspiriorum in the first film), and like anyone who discovers her existence, Rose finds out she's not all that nice. Soon her brother Mark (American actor Leigh McCloskey) comes to look for her and finds himself embroiled in a demonic nightmare. *Inferno* is not so much a movie as it is a parade of amazing set pieces. With an obvious ode to the filmmaking of Mario Bava (who worked on several key sequences here, to the film's benefit), Argento bathes the film in shadow, utilizing every color of the rainbow. His meticulous attention to the aesthesis comes at the expense of the plot as he goes for a more ephemeral approach here. This is a nightmare movie that at times resembles the logic of one. While it is bound to disappoint those expecting *Suspiria*'s brilliance, gorehounds will enjoy the innovative ways Argento uses graphic violence to bump off his cast, including a rat attack, a rather large piece of shattered glass and an eye-popping gunshot through the keyhole. The Blu-Ray disc available from both Arrow and Blue Underground is amazing: showing off the entire color palette of the film, making it one of the most vibrant films in the Eurocult canon. The "3 Mothers" saga concluded in 2007 with the final chapter, *Mother of Tears*, and starred Argento's and Nicolodi's daughter Asia.

Macabre, aka *Macabro* (IT). Prod. Gianni Minervini and Antonio Avati. Dir. Lamberto Bava. Italy/Britain, 1980. Blue Underground, 90 min. DVD. Starring: Bernice Stegers, Stanko Molnar, Veronica Zinny and Roberto Posse.

Who said you can't have fun in New Orleans? Even though Bernice Stegers lost her beloved husband in a terrible automobile crash that resulted in his losing his head (literally), she has quickly found someone to replace him. At least that's what the neighbors think every time they hear those sexy noises coming from her bedroom apartment every night in the Big Easy. She's not a very quiet woman when it comes to the throes of passion. Now the neighbors are getting suspicious because they never really see her with anyone. It's a baffling mystery. Oh, and it seems that her husband's head has been stolen from the morgue. You'd think she might show a little more concern, but the only thing she cares about is keeping the lock tight on the freezer door. Southern Gothic, Italian style, shows off Lamberto Bava's first film to fairly good effect. Though the plot is pure exploitation goodness, Bava plays down the exploitation (until the end, of course) in favor of a somewhat slow narrative. Not a bad film, with much humor is derived from the depiction of the American South by the Italians.

S.S. Hell Camp, aka *La bestia en calore* (IT). Prod. Xiro Papas. Dir. Ivan Kathansky. Italy, 1974. Exploitation Digital, 86 min. DVD. Starring: Macha Magall, Gino Turini, Edilio Kim and Xiro Papas.

Oh, here's a doozy that's just plain fun. Working off another Eurocult subgenre, the Nazisploitation film (next volume!), *S.S. Hell Camp* is a patchwork of bad editing, bad acting and hilarious plot ideas all designed to entertain. Dr. Ellen Kratsch (German actress Macha Magall) is one mean Nazi. A lieutenant in Hitler's army, she has one of the most sadistic streaks in the Third Reich! She enjoys the art of castration, especially when it allows her to rub her naked body over her victims beforehand, shocking women with electrodes attached to their genitalia, or the simple pleasures of tearing people's fingernails out one at a time. Her favorite trick, though, is throwing naked women into a cage with a large Neanderthal-looking man who likes to rape them to death. You can guess what happens to the good doctor at the end of the film. Oh, and there's a subplot about people fighting off the Nazis in a town: boring. The reason for the subplot? It's because the film is a cheat. Taking a large chunk of footage from a previous war film he directed, Kathansky filmed all the exploitive stuff involving Magall many years later and repackaged the film. The result is a schizophrenic experience, with the Eurocult lover just wishing we'd get back to the beast in the cage.

Suspiria. Prod. Claudio Argento. Dir. Dario Argento. Italy, 1977, Blue Underground, 98 min. DVD. Starring: Jessica Harper, Alida Valli, Joan Bennett, Stefania Casini and Udo Kier.

An instant classic! *Suspiria* is the perfect movie to show people who have never seen any Eurocult. It's bloody, it's scary, it has flying maggots as well as the Goblins blasting the hell out of the soundtrack. Suzy Banyon (American ingénue Jessica Harper) is off to Germany to join the prestigious Tanz Akademie. She should have gone somewhere else, as the school is filled with the nastiest girls, hard-nosed instructors (like Alida Valli), and just for fun, a coven of witches. These aren't the nice witches, either. Dario Argento has created a modern European fairy tale that is one visual revelation after another. From the opening 20 minutes that involve Suzy's arrival on a rain-soaked night and the deaths of two students, Argento's world is a nightmare where anything can and probably will happen. The sets and color palette (I don't care what anyone says, Mario Bava's influence is all over this) only make it more possible to exploit the violence, which is explicit. It would be very difficult to sustain the amount of shock and awe that he manages cram into those opening minutes, and the film does slow down, allowing for more exposition. Harper makes a beguiling heroine who uses her droll American "I can handle whatever you've got and appear bored" personality as well as ingenuity to solve the mysteries that the dance academy hides. She's surrounded by a cast that is obviously having fun, from stone-faced Valli to oh-so-charming-she's-got-to-be-evil Bennett, as the head of the school. There are some critics that don't look at *Suspiria* as being a true exploitation film but as a standard horror fantasy. I say malarkey. Argento piles on enough graphic heart piercings, stabbings, dog attacks and coiled-wire slayings that aren't necessary, to put to rest that idea. A *definite* must-see, but make sure the TV screen is large enough and loud enough to accommodate this classic.

Werewolf Woman, aka *La lupa mannera* (IT). Prod. Diego Alchimede. Dir. Rino Di Silvestro. Italy, 1977. Shriek Show, 98 min. DVD. Starring: Annik Borel, Dagmar Lassander, Howard Ross and Tino Carraro.

    Werewolf Woman is an interesting film in that it begins in a way that leads you to expect it's going to be an out-of-control exploitation experience, and then settles down to give a fairly involving story. Yes, there is still lots of exploitation, and in fact it touches on some important issues (surprise!). The film begins hundreds of years earlier, when a wolfwoman (who resembles a female Chewbacca) is hunted by the local pitchfork-waving townsfolk and destroyed graphically, with the inclusion of *lots* of nudity and gore. We cut to the modern day (well, the '70s anyway) where the wolfwoman's ancestor Daniela (Borel) is dealing with some very serious mental issues. Raped as a youngster, she now carries an intense fear of men, which results in some pretty weird dreams. The arrival of her shifty sister (Eurocult favorite Lassander) and brother-in-law pushes her over the edge. Soon Daniela is thinking she's just like her ancestor and begins experimenting with sex, leading to some very bloody consequences. Don't be fooled: this isn't a typical werewolf movie. Daniela's issues are her rape and her unwillingness to see any man as compassionate (which isn't helped when she's almost raped again later in the film by a guy who ends up very, very sorry), not the full moon. Expect lots of face chewing, full frontal nudity and howling, but if you look below the surface you might find an little interesting psychological twist.

Conclusion

> There's nothing quite like an Italian horror film. As a genre, they constitute the missing link of the cinema world, straddling the fence between cerebral art films and base exploitation.
> — Historian David White[229]

    The early 1980s signaled the demise of the Italian exploitation juggernaut. Though filmmakers like Lucio Fulci and Dario Argento experienced worldwide success and profitable distribution deals with their heavily exploitative *L'aldilà* (*The Beyond*, 1981), *Quella villa accanto al cimitero* (*The House by the Cemetery*, 1981), *Tenebrae* (1982) and *Phenomena* (1985), the industry very quickly dried up as audiences for these films changed. Exploitation films' venues were changing, as the home video market's success effectively made it impossible for many of the theaters and drive-ins that specialized in these films to make a profit. People could now watch a variety of exploitation from home without having to sit in a rundown theater with a group of people they didn't know (and in some cases wouldn't want to know). Also the American horror and exploitation film was still a profitable endeavor, with films such as *Nightmare on Elm Street* (1983) or any one of the *Friday the 13th* or *Halloween* sequels filling up the local Cineplexes. These factors irrevocably changed the Italian market and filmmakers were forced to think of ingenious ways in which to survive. Occasionally there would be a worldwide success with co-productions such as the Dario Argento–produced, Lamberto Bava–directed fun that was *Demoni* (*Demons*, 1985), a film that began its own brief series. But more often than not, a radical decline in general quality was underway, with films like Fulci's *Zombi 3* (1987) being an embarrassing ghost of the rich, historically evocative types of film that Italian exploitation filmmakers had produced in the previous decades. Ironically for a country that was at the center of the Eurocult phenomenon, the recent proliferation of horror and exploitation films coming out of Europe has passed Italy by. While the occasional film by Dario Argento still manages to cause the excited whisper of a return to Italy's greatness, the country has remained relatively quiet, allowing countries like France and Spain to enjoy a resurgence of the films that Italy helped create.

The history of the Italian horror/exploitation film is a fascinating one. It's an example of a truly production-line type of industry. From the early days of the '50s, when it was only possible to come up with product by copying the popular material of the United States and Britain, the industry forged ahead with original new ideas such as the giallo in the mid–'60s, only to lose out to better funded industries in the '70s. These Italian films represent a distinct social, political and economic viewpoint of their era as they pushed the envelope on taste. Regardless of whether one is shocked, titillated, or outraged, Italian exploitation films are the benchmark of their genre. They continue to this day to make a strong impression on new audiences that are viewing these films for the first time.

CHAPTER 2

Spain

> Spanish cinema lives in a state of isolation. It is isolated not only from the world, but from our own reality.
> —Juan Antonio Bardem, 1950s Spanish filmmaker[1]

The Spanish horror and exploitation film has from its inception been a visual art form in which Spanish filmmakers could express their own horror and frustration with the world. This expression had to be carefully sublimated as the political environment and the censorship rules which governed the country in the '60s and '70s were completely different and much more repressive than in Italy. In this politically charged atmosphere, where a disapproved film could send a young filmmaker into exile, Spain produced some of most visually interesting exploitation films which contained fascinating nuggets of the social and political upheavals, if one was looking closely for them. Unlike Italy, who had a more viable film industry and could begin producing copious amounts of exploitation once the environment (i.e., religious and government entities) would allow, the Spanish exploitation film industry began slowly, having only one or two talented filmmakers taking tentative steps into the genre. Beginning with the Jésus (Jess) Franco film *Gritos en la noche* (*The Awful Dr. Orloff*) in 1961, and continuing until today, the Spanish exploitation film initially experienced more success outside its own country before enjoying the popularity it now enjoys in Spain.

The end of General Francisco Franco's dictatorship precipitated the arrival of exploitation filmmaking in Spain and allowed Spanish filmmakers to create environments to frighten or disgust. Until Franco's regime ended, though, government censorship rules forced Spanish exploitation filmmakers to subvert any examples of overt sexuality and violence. As a result, many of these filmmakers had to rely heavily on traditional monsters such as vampires, werewolves and mummies to frighten and titillate. Re-examining these films today it's possible to see that Spanish filmmakers were actually able to express their criticisms of the government and of society by producing films which laid the foundation for audience re-examination at a later date. By isolating and defining many of subgenres within the category of Spanish horror/exploitation cinema and by looking at many of the auteurs involved, such as Jess Franco, Jacinto Molina (Paul Naschy), Amando de Ossorio, etc., one sees a portrait of a film industry that was as culturally significant as its fellow Italian and French exploitation filmmakers.

Though not as prolific as the Italian output, Spanish exploitation films were a popular mainstay for grindhouses, drive-ins and television stations in the late '60s and '70s. Utilizing evocative visual imagery on smaller budgets, the Spanish exploitation industry many times blurred the line between reality and fantasy as a way to escape the persecution the government would have inflicted on them had they been overt. Consequently these filmmakers offered up traditional horror characters like the Wolf Man, Frankenstein and Dracula, infusing them with Spanish sensibilities and increasingly adult themes, as well as creating new types of horrors like the Templar Knights of Amando de Ossorio's *Blind Dead* series that have gone on to become classic icons in their own right around the world. Due to the heavy political pressure, Spanish exploitation was forced to sublimate any criticism of Spanish society giving rise to these films, like Eloy de la Iglesia's *La semana del asesino* (*Cannibal Man*), whose political message was entrenched within the subplot of an exploitation film for only those viewers who had the wherewithal to decipher it.[2] As Spain moved toward democracy in the '70s, the exploitation genre proliferated. The censorship imposed by General Franco waned and a new era of Spanish film emerged, resulting in worldwide exposure and acceptance.[3] These films were able to incorporate nudity, sexuality and violence to a degree that would allow them to compete with the Italians and French in worldwide distribution.

Prior to the oppressive Franco regime, Spain had enjoyed a profitable film industry which dated back to 1886. These films up the mid–'30s had mostly consisted of operettas and literary adaptations and were filmed in a rich visual style that would later become the trademark of Spanish filmmakers. Offering audiences a chance to escape from everyday life, these high-minded offerings became the most popular form of entertainment for Spanish audiences.[4] After Franco took office via a coup d'état in 1939, the Spanish film industry went through a complete transformation. Studios were forced to conform to the extremist nature of the ruling party, which in the film industry was referred to as "Francoist," and which had a strong intolerance towards outside politics and religion. This intolerance led to the official and social banning of sexuality, a key component in exploitation filmmaking.[5]

Due to Franco's strict and sometimes violently enforced codes, the Spanish exploitation film was relatively nonexistent in the '40s and '50s. As other European countries were beginning to explore genres, including exploitation, that were more modern in approach, the Spanish film industry was forced to adhere to Franco's ultra-conservative stance that rendered many of their films passé. Those in the Spanish film industry had no outlet in which to voice their criticisms about the policies of Franco and the effect that they were having on the state of moviemaking in Spain. In 1955, a four-day national conference held in the university town of Salamanca gave Spanish filmmakers the opportunity to deliver a harsh critique of the state of Spanish cinema. Written by filmmaker Juan Antonio Bardem, the conclusion was: "After 60 years of film, Spanish cinema is politically ineffective, socially false, intellectually worthless, aesthetically non-existent, and industrially crippled." This and subsequent conferences began to galvanize Spanish filmmakers into making more quality pictures even while trying to come to grips with the heavy censorship forced on them by the Spanish government.[6]

Things began to slowly change by the mid–'50s. A behind-the-scenes movement was started to move Spain away from its isolationist tendencies and to be reaccepted into the international community. Events like U.S. President Eisenhower's trip to Madrid in 1959, as well as a burgeoning of tourism within Spain, began to break down cultural barriers.[7] In film, this movement of modernization translated into the introduction of outside influences to Spanish audiences. Italian comedies that were slightly more risqué than their Spanish counterparts began to seep through the censors as well as consumer-oriented "holiday" pictures, which featured fashionable sports cars, pop music and the newest fashions.[8]

In addition to the influx of foreign material, the '50s and '60s were also the time Spain began experimenting with coproductions with outside filmmakers. Epic films with strong American and British backing, like *King of Kings* (1960), *El Cid* (1961), *55 Days in Peking* (1963) and *Doctor Zhivago* (1965), brought a new professionalism into the Spanish movie industry, as well as educating them on the newest technologies. The sharing of production costs that these films afforded offered Spain the chance to recoup their financial expenditures with little or no risk. It also opened the door to future collaborations with these outside film industries.[9] These collaborations were to have a profound impact on the exploitation genre in Spain as filmmaker Jess Franco was about to give the world the first true Spanish exploitation film, *Gritos en la noche* (*The Awful Dr. Orloff*, 1961).[10]

Gritos en la noche: Spanish Genre Beginnings

> It [*Gritos*] strikes an underlying harmonic of progress and innovation, heralding a new age of erotic and sado-masochistic permissiveness within the genre. If ever there was such a place as a museum for horror classics, *The Awful Dr. Orlof* (*Gritos en la noche*) would be placed proudly on a pedestal therein.
> — Tim Lucas, liner notes of the 2000 DVD release
> of *The Awful Dr. Orlof* (*Gritos en la noche*)[11]

Unlike Britain, the U.S. or even Italy, Spain does not have a rich historical tradition of horror literature. Though the classic works of Spaniards Miguel de Cervantes and the poet Francisco de Quevedo have slight horrific themes, Spain as a whole did not have the Gothic literature tradition that provided other countries with the rich source material for horror and exploitation films. Because of this, as well as a political system which eschewed violence and sex on screen, horror and exploitation films were virtually nonexistent before 1961.[12]

Those few films that contained horrific elements prior to 1961 relied on fable-type themes, often containing intermixed elements of horror and wonder. Generally considered to be the first Spanish horror film, *La torre de los siete jorobados* (*The Tower of the Seven Hunchbacks*, 1943) relies on a fable/ghost story to weave its tale.[13] Set in 19th-century Madrid and based on a Spanish novel by Emilio Carrere, the film incorporated the style of the Gothic American Universal horror films that were popular at the time. Directed by Edgar Neville, the film tells the story of a ghost (Félix de Pomés) who enlists the aid of a young man (Antonio Casel) to protect his niece from a secret society of counterfeiting hunchbacks hiding in an underground Jewish bunker. The film utilizes a myriad of different horror stereotypes, including ghosts, sinister hunchbacks, secret societies, old abandoned houses, hypnotism and murder, themes that were popular in Gothic horror films from America.[14] The plot device of having the sinister hunchbacks holed up in an underground Jewish bunker is interesting from a historical viewpoint. Though the film makes it clear that it was an abandoned bunker left over from the Inquisition, it is easy to see the correlation between the Spanish mistrust of the Jews and the events happening within Germany and Eastern Europe during wartime in the early '40s. Unlike the standard horror films coming from the United States, though, the film also incorporated humor to soften those violent and horrific themes that Spanish audiences had not been used to. Whether it was this humor, the fact that Spanish audiences weren't predisposed to horror, or simply because the government was not supportive of films of this type, *La torre* was not a huge success in Spain.

Gritos en la noche (The Awful Dr. Orloff) unleashed Jess Franco onto the world film stage in 1961.

The other Spanish films that incorporated some elements of horror in the '40s and '50s included *El crimen de la calle de Boradadores* (1948); also directed by Neville, *El huésped de las tinieblas* (*The Monster of las Tinieblas*, 1948); and *La corona negra* (*The Black Crown*, 1951). All followed the same traditional formula: historically based, with a ghost or monster avenging social wrongs. The horror element in each of these films was played down, as was the violence, with most of murders happening off screen. Most of these films incorporated an historical angle which was meant to soften any criticism state censors may have had. In a device used effectively by the Italians in their Gothic subgenre, setting a story far enough in the past avoided criticism by the government and allowed for a more literary approach to the material, as well as making it seem that it appeared irrelevant to current situations. Regardless, none of the Spanish thrillers garnered much success, which in turn did little to convince Spanish filmmakers to look at the horror genre with anything but indifference. It would take 10 years before Spain discovered a winning formula for the horror/exploitation film and that would be at the hands of Spain's most prolific filmmaker Jésus (Jess) Franco, and a character by the name of Dr. Orlof (also sometimes spelled Orloff).

Released in 1961, *Gritos en la noche* (*The Awful Dr. Orloff*) became the first internationally successful horror and exploitation film from Spain. Following a storyline that was somewhat closely related to Franju's *Les Yeux sans Visage* (*Eyes without a Face*, 1959) as well as gleaned from a popular story from Central America that director Jess Franco knew from childhood, *Gritos* tells the story of Dr. Orlof (Howard Vernon, who would go on to play Dr. Orlof in a variety of sequels), a madman in France whose sole intent is to repair his sister's burned, ravaged face with skin grafts from local young women he's kidnapped.[15] With the assistance of a blind bug-eyed man named Morpho, Dr. Orlof tries to carry out his heinous experiments, torturing these young women before being brought down by a police chief (Conrado San Martin) and his beautiful fiancée (Diana Lorys). Though Franju's film may have had some obvious part in the narrative, it was the British who had a profound impact on Franco with their successful brand of movie monster updates (Dracula, Frankenstein, The Mummy) by Hammer Films. While shooting *Vampiresas 1930* (*Vamps of 1930*, 1960) a big-budgeted homage to the Hollywood musical filmed in the south of France, Franco persuaded his producers to see the British release of *Brides of Dracula* (1960). He related that it was not easy getting them to see it because "it was a new experience for both of them. I had to show the possibilities for them [sic]. They just thought it was some shit they saw when they were children."[16] After screening *Brides* with his co-producers, Franco believed he could make a movie similar to the popular Hammer horror films infiltrating the continent at the time. He recalls: "When the screening [for *Brides*] ended I proposed him [sic] to make a movie in the same vein, but with a different style. He became a little nervous because making a terror movie in Spain, in 1961, sounded like a Surrealist provocation, but I insisted so much that in the end, he agreed to make it with the same French co-producer of *Vampiresas 1930*."[17]

While *Gritos* liberally borrows plot elements of other films of the day that were popular (Brahm's *The Lodger*, 1944; Summers's *Dark Eyes of London*; Ferroni's *Il mulino delle donne di pietra*, 1960; and of course, Franju's *Les Yeux sans visage*, 1959), Franco modernizes his story with liberal doses of violence and, for the first time, nudity. He clearly is willing to give an adult interpretation of what could have been a child's monster movie narrative. From its opening scenes, which show us a very drunk woman of obvious easy virtue being attacked in her apartment by Morpho, to our gold-digging cabaret singer who's more interested in diamonds and booze, Franco is not afraid to get a little dirty. Thanks to him, the good doctor's scared, helpless victims are not only sexualized; they now have their breasts playfully peeking out in order to entice the audience. This teasing kind of nudity, similar to that used in the Italian coproduction *Il mulino delle donne di pietra* (*The Mill of the Stone Women*, 1960) predated the British horror films' use of nudity by nine years. Franco, who was confident the film would be a hit, was much more concerned that censorship difficulties in Spain might stop the film from being made or distributed. In order to accommodate the censors, he produced two versions of the film. One, a complete unedited version, would play in countries like France (under the title *L'horrible Docteur Orlof*) whose society had a higher acceptance of nudity and violence. The second, edited version would play in countries like Spain and England, where nudity was not yet an accepted form of public entertainment. According to Franco, he was worried that the uncut version would have had a disastrous effect with the Spanish censors. When asked about creating a tamer, Spanish version, Franco replied, "If I hadn't they'd have killed me, pushed me out of Spain or something."[18] Franco was also able to do a couple of other things in order to placate censors who may have thought even the edited version of *Dr. Orlof* was too much, including both changing the setting of the narrative and making use of humor. Franco's Spanish censors were concerned with trying to preserve Spain's image, not only within its borders but outside as well, and were adamant that terrible events such as the ones in *Gritos* happen outside of Spain. Con-

Gritos was the first Spanish horror film that was a success internationally, leading Jess Franco to produce more in that vein.

sequently, Franco places his narrative in France, which helps set up the construct that practically every Spanish exploitation film in the '60s adhered to: it doesn't happen here. Much like the Communist propaganda that was floating around the world, Spanish censors happily allowed more violence and sexuality in those films that made other countries look bad. Secondly, in order to not project complete, abject terror throughout the picture, Franco infuses it with a humor. There's something playful about the film: whether it's the introduction of a kitten who happily takes up residence in the police office, the romance between our young inspector and his beautiful fiancée, or the introduction of eccentric townspeople, Franco does all he can to lessen the horror and lighten the film dramatically. This is ingenious because it allows him to make the "dark" parts of the film even more horrifying, offering a balance between the light humor and horror.

Arriving in European markets around the same time as France's *Les Yeux sans visage* (1959) and Italy's *La maschera del demonio* (*Black Sunday*, 1960), *Gritos* was a huge success, especially in France, where the uncut version of the film was met with acceptance and, more importantly, positive box-office receipts. As was typical of the era, the film took awhile to make it to American shores. Retitled *The Awful Dr. Orloff*, the film was released three years later in 1964 as the second half of a double bill with Riccardo Freda's 1962 classic Italian Gothic, *The Horrible Dr. Hichcock*.[19] Because both films had narratives set in the early 19th century, there was little problem with releasing the films much later than they were produced. Had either one been set in the early 1960s, there may have been some problem; society and culture were changing so dramatically in the period between 1961 and 1964, it would have been reflected on the screen. Franco reflects back on the success of the film, stating, "It was a wonderful directorial experience without any problems whatsoever; everything went just right. The critics weren't bad, and the film, from a strictly commercial point of view, was rather successful, since it was somehow distributed all the world over, so much so that, to date, I'm still reading several American magazines where my name is usually reported as Jess 'The Awful Dr. Orloff' Franco."[20]

The success of the Dr. Orlof character meant that Spain could now enjoy its own homegrown villain whom to exploit in a series of films for worldwide distribution. These films were directed by a handful of different directors as well as Franco himself, and became increasingly more lurid throughout the decade.

Dr. Orlof was not the only mentally unbalanced character hanging around Spanish/European soil in the early '60s. In the U.S./Spanish co-production *Fuego* (*Pyro*, 1963), Spanish locales showcase a story of an adulterous American engineer (Barry Sullivan) who breaks off an affair with the mentally unbalanced Laura (Martha Hyer) only to find out that she is a pyromaniac. Sullivan's face is completely burned off while he's trying to save his wife and daughter from a fire set by the jealous Hyer, setting the stage for a murderous confrontation.[21] A precursor to films like Adrian Lyne's *Fatal Attraction* (1987) and Edel's *Body of Evidence* (1993), *Fuego* gives credence to the idea that you will burn (literally) if you commit adultery and that illicit sex between a married man and his mistress must be paid for. It's easy to understand that in a country where, as in Italy, the Catholic Church had historical presence, such a message would be received warmly, as well as being the subject of nightmares for people thinking about indulging in such behavior. One of the interesting things that separates *Fuego* from the other '60s Spanish exploitation films was that it was actually set in Spain and unabashedly Spanish. This is most probably explained by the fact that both protagonists are American and that Spain is not in any way responsible for the disruptive behavior these two cause each other. This could also have been a reason that Spanish censors accepted the rather lurid screenplay without much editing. Also, *Fuego*'s American coproducer, Sidney Pink, very wisely hired a Spanish production company, which cemented good economic will with the Spanish government as well as employing several Spanish supporting actors. One of these was Soledad Miranda, in the role of a naïve carnival worker who helps Sullivan enact his revenge, who would go on to become Jess Franco's most famous muse in a slew of exploitation pictures in 1969 and '70. Pink was no stranger to procuring European production companies to coproduce his exploitation films, and he found the experience of making the film a joy.[22] Unfortunately, the film did little international business; the heads of American International Pictures (A.I.P.), the company distributing the picture, saddled the film with a difficult title to understand (*Pyro*), resulting in poor box-office receipts. In one of his last interviews before his death in 2002, Pink related the joys and pains of exploitation filmmaking, relating, "I would say that *Pyro* is probably one of the best I've ever done. The Spanish cast was absolutely perfect and the backgrounds of Spain were so gorgeous. Everyone loved it, but nobody came to see it. It was a bad title job. Jimmy Nicholson and Sam Arkoff [heads of A.I.P.] gave it that title, and I asked them if you asked 90% of people what the title means they couldn't tell you."[23] Pink's assessment may be a bit optimistic. While the film is certainly entertaining, *Fuego* falls in with the tried-and-true narrative of revenge movies with scarred protagonists, which seemed to be the big thing in the early '60s, with the British version of *Phantom of the Opera* (1962), *Circus of Horrors* (1962) and the Italian *La vergine di Norimberga* (*The Virgin of Nuremberg*, 1963) all having the same general storylines and competing for the same audience attention. Unfortunately for *Fuego*, there was little in the film other than Spanish settings to distance it from the others.

The lack of financial success of *Fuego* in 1963 meant that most Spanish filmmakers would not participate in a genre that was becoming extremely lucrative for their Italian and British counterparts. It would be another four to five years before the Spanish horror boom took off and Spanish filmmakers could profit from this type of entertainment. The one lone exception to this was a Spanish filmmaker who wasn't afraid to explore darker subject matter and who saw the advent of the '60s as time to break free from conventional filmmaking. That filmmaker was Jess Franco.

Filmography

The Awful Dr. Orloff, aka *Gritos en la noche* (SP), *L'horrible Docteur Orlof* (FR). Prod. and Dir. Jesus Franco. Spain, 1961. Image Entertainment, 83 min. DVD. Starring: Howard Vernon, Conrado San Martin, Diana Lorys and Perla Cristal.

One of the first true Spanish horror films and an exploitation classic. Utilizing the familiar themes of old Universal horror films, throwing in a little of Franju's *Eyes Without a Face* (*Les Yeux sans visage*, 1959), and mixing it with some subversive perversity, Jess Franco finds the right combination to prove that there was a worldwide market for Spanish exploitation. Pretty (and often drunk) prostitutes are being abducted in a French town by a bug-eyed man named Morpho. He is just a mindless slave for the man at the bottom of the kidnappings, the evil Dr. Orlof (Vernon), who needs the prostitutes' skin to repair the broken face of his daughter. It's up to the local inspector (San Martin) to figure out the mystery before the next woman dies. What makes *Dr. Orlof* different from the other Eurocult classics at the time (the French *Eyes without a Face*, 1959, or the Italian *Black Sunday*, 1960) is the gutter perversity that Franco almost succeeds in bringing to the surface. The prostitutes, though pretty, are slightly more worn than in other films of the time, and Franco's surprising use of some very tasteful nudity (in a distasteful scene) also contributes to that wonderful dirty feeling you sometimes get watching Eurocult. Taken as a whole, *Dr. Orlof* is a great glimpse into early Spanish filmmaking in a realm where they hadn't gone before. Yes, it's very low-budget;

yes, the acting leaves something to be desired; yes, the monster Morpho is ridiculous; and yes, you should definitely see it!

Pyro: The Thing Without a Face, aka *Fuego*. Prod. Sidney Pink and Richard C. Meyer. Dir. Julio Coll. Spain/U.S., 1963. Troma Team Video, 93 min. DVD. Starring: Barry Sullivan, Martha Hyer, Sherry Moreland and Soledad Miranda.

Pyro is an interesting film. Colorful, melodramatic, reasonably well-acted by a group of American actors, it plays like one of those lurid Hollywood films from the early '60s. The difference, though, is that this is one of those rare films from the era actually shot in Spain with a Spanish crew and Spanish sensibilities. A horror/potboiler, *Pyro* stars Barry Sullivan as an engineer who's working on a project in Spain while also having a "mucho caliente" affair with the super-unstable Laura (Hyer). Guilty about the affair, he decides to end it and go back to his long-suffering wife and children. Sorry, bud, but obviously Laura must have been the biological mother of Glenn (*Fatal Attraction*) Close, and before you can say "dead rabbit," she's burning down the house with his wife and kids in it. Horribly disfigured while trying to save them, Vince goes after her with a vengeance befitting an exploitation film, involving some nifty plastic surgery and a carnival setting. The film, with its twists and turns, is actually fun stuff that makes good use of the Spanish locales and the Spanish supporting players. Soledad Miranda, who would later become the ultimate muse of Jess Franco, shows up as a sweet young girl who unwisely develops feelings for the rage-driven Sullivan.

Jess Franco: El Maestro

> I'm finding myself very comfortable in my skin and I love my work. If there's a minority who doesn't like me, too bad for them.
> — Jess Franco, July 2005[24]

> If exploitation were to have a king, it would have to be Franco. I mean nobody can be as passionate about filth and filmmaking as Franco.
> — Nigel Wingrove, Salvation Films[25]

With more than 200 films to his credit and more being produced every year, Jésus (Jess) Franco is in the Guinness Book of World Records as one of the most prolific filmmakers of all time.[26] Franco's films run the gamut from edgy horror to outright hard-core pornography. No other filmmaker has been as exalted or decried as Franco, whose films have played around the world in a variety of different versions, languages and titles. Critics split on Franco, calling his films everything from "perversely naughty"[27] to "entertainingly bizarre"[28] to "torturously slow and painful to watch."[29] Moving with the social times of the late '60s and '70s, Franco called upon his Spanish upbringing to produce films that were surrealistic, horrifying and erotic. Unfortunately, the devotion to this type of subject matter did not sit well with the Spanish censors, forcing Franco to flee Spain and produce films throughout all of Europe.

Europe's foremost rebel, Jésus Franco Manera was born in Madrid on May 12, 1930. The son of a medical colonel father and a Cuban mother, Franco spent his early life in Spain dealing with the cruelty of General Franco's (no relation) regime. The enforced conformity, extremist ideology, general intolerance for outside politics, heavy-handed religion and repression of sexuality were to have a profound impact on Franco and helped shape his rebellious tendencies.[30]

Franco's only outlet from the oppressive Spanish society of the time was cinema. Relating his early love of cinema, Franco recalled, "I first thought to give myself to cinema when

I was 9. In 1939, I would often imagine myself dressed like the directors used to back then; loose-fitting trousers, peaked cap and megaphone. When I was 11 or 12, my younger brothers and I used to play with newspapers, guessing the names of the movie actors and directors listed within."[31]

Later, as Franco moved through boarding schools and universities, he discovered another love that kept him sustained throughout his entire life: jazz. This love of music became an obsession for him, and Franco learned to play several musical instruments, hoping perhaps to have a career in the field. His restless, rebellious spirit had prevented him from actually graduating from the universities he attended, which included the I.I.E.C., an institute designed to teach aspiring filmmakers the profession, and the Royal Academy of Music in Madrid. Moving through a variety of different jobs throughout the late '40s, bored and unfulfilled, he ended up in Paris in 1952. To Franco, Paris represented all the freedom and culture that were not available in Madrid. Studying at the I.D.H.E.C, the French government's film school, Franco immersed himself in the French, as well as the entire European, culture, learning six languages and becoming knowledgeable of classic literary works.[32]

In 1953, Franco was called back to Spain to work on a film project with Juan Antonio Bardem, a friend he met at school. Working as a second assistant director for the film *Cosmicos* (1953), Franco got his feet wet in a business that would consume the rest of his life. He spent the better part of the '50s working his way up through the industry, directing his first film, a documentary produced for the Spanish Ministry of Industry, *El árbol de España*, in 1957.[33]

After producing more documentaries in the late '50s, Franco decided to make the jump to feature films with the comedy *Tenemos 18 años* (*We Are 18 Years Old*, 1959). The film was a complete departure from his previous efforts, as well as a departure from typical Spanish narratives at the time. Talking about the innovation, Franco has said, "It occurred to me that I could make a film without any storyline. It had to be shot with the basic equipment that I carried with me, that's a van, a small group of people and an electric generator."[34] While this cinéma vérité approach to filmmaking would soon be accepted throughout Europe in the '60s, the film confused the few in the audience who actually saw it, and more seriously ran afoul with the Spanish censors. Citing a scene involving an escaped prisoner, the Spanish authorities slapped the equivalent of an NC-17 rating on it, meaning it could only play in a few areas of Spain. Franco recounts, "They did it just to fuck me up, you know. They didn't like it from the political point of view." So few if any moviegoers saw the film that Franco thought would be a "revolution in cinematic narrative."[35]

After the censorship battles with *Tenemos*, Franco decided to go mainstream, combining his love of cinema with his love of music. He began directing musicals. His first, *La reina del Tabarín* (1960), was inspired by American musicals with its rags-to-riches story and big, brassy musical numbers. His other musical, *Vampiresas 1930* (1961), is even more a throwback to the Busby Berkeley style of musicals from the '30s.[36] Both of these films are diametrically opposed to the Gothic horrors of *Gritos en la noche* (*The Awful Dr. Orlof*) that Franco would direct in 1961 and forever change the course of his work in film.

The worldwide success of *Gritos* did not immediately translate into success for Jess Franco in Spain though. His next three horror productions—*La mano de un hombre muerto* (*The Sadistic Baron Von Klaus*, 1962); the sequel to *Gritos*, *El secreto del Dr. Orloff* (*Dr. Orloff's Monster*, 1964); and *Miss Muerte* (*The Diabolical Dr. Z*, 1965)—were all exercises in fighting a film industry that was not interested in producing the kind of films Franco wanted to make.[37] These films constituted a trilogy to which Franco refers to as "museum pieces," for their old-fashioned style of filmmaking and traditional narratives.[38]

While revenues for *Gritos*, especially in France, were high, the Spanish film industry saw little advantage to producing more in the same genre. As Franco relates, "*El secreto del Dr. Orloff* could have been a good movie, at least as good as *Gritos en la noche*, but the filming was a disastrous experience." Citing the lack of money available, Franco puts the problem squarely on the Spanish filmmakers' mentality, commenting, "It was a cooperative society which wanted to get into cinema and when I proposed to make another 'Orloff,' they asked me, dumbfounded, 'What's that?' As a matter of fact Spanish producers see no other films except their own. It was such a poor production I couldn't even hire back Howard Vernon as the leading character since we didn't even have enough money to pay his air-ticket, much less his cachet."[39] Franco was obviously going through the same financial and production problems that held back most of the Italian and French exploitation filmmakers of the day.

Money problems aside, Franco made each of the films more marketable by pushing the sleaze and sex factor. *La mano de un hombre muerto* (*The Sadistic Baron Von Klaus*, 1962) contains, as historian Tim Lucas puts it, "horror cinema's first sequence of 100-proof erotic horror."[40] The story of a young man (Argentine actor Hugo Blanco) who returns to his haunted family estate for the death of his mother, *Le Mano* spends most of its running time being the standard "is he or isn't he nuts" in a haunted house scenario. The murders for three-fourths of the film are either off-camera or low-key. It's the final 20 minutes where Franco pushes the envelope. Margaret (Gogó Robins/Rojo), the local barhop, is secretly carrying on with Blanco. It's a bad move, since he is a protagonist with a penchant for torturing his victims. In a climactic scene, Blanco takes her, drugged, to his torture chamber, where he undresses her on a bed, kissing and fondling her naked body. He then proceeds to whip her with a large steel chain before tying her up, taking a hot machete and eviscerating her.[41] With the exception of the final gutting, all of this scene's nudity and torture are shown on the screen. This is significant because for the first time it gives audiences a visual representation of violent acts that have only been implied previously.

El secreto, while not as graphic, is just as disturbing. Oddly the film does not focus on Dr. Orloff, but on Dr. Conrad Fisherman (Marcelo Arrotia-Jáuregui) a scientist driven mad by an adulterous affair between his brother and his wife that leads to his brother's demise. Complications arise when Melissa (Agnès Spaak), his niece, comes to spend the Christmas holidays and finds out her father (Hugo Blanco) has been electronically reactivated and his body manipulated via remote control in order to carry out Fisherman's will. This being an exploitation film, his will means killing assorted prostitutes and other not-so-virtuous characters in a variety of violent ways.[42] Again, good old-fashioned guilt is the culprit here, as adulterous affairs must be punished. Dr. Fisherman is especially cruel in his treatment of his wife Ingrid (Perla Cristal), as she is allowed to live under the condition that she suffers guilt and remorse over the affair every second of her life. Her pain is more pronounced than that of her lover as his soul is gone; it is only his body that is reactivated. Franco was able to flesh out some of the screenplay for the film by mining some of the outlandish material from the popular spy dramas that were beginning to catch on in Europe in 1963 and '64. Reminiscent of the early James Bond movies (*Goldfinger* was released around the same time), the film is infused with a science-fiction sensibility, as the victims of the robot must wear a special tracking device embedded in jewelry given to them by the good doctor. This kind of cross-genre hodgepodge enabled a film to be marketed to a variety of different audiences, though ironically, in France where *Gritos* was popular, the film was retitled *Les Maîtresses du Dr. Jekyll* or *The Mistresses of Dr. Jekyll*, though having nothing to do with a Dr. Jekyll or any of his own mistresses, for that matter.

Franco's favorite of his "museum pieces" was *Miss Muerte* (*The Diabolical Dr. Z*) in 1965. Keeping the same framework as his two previous films, a medical thriller with a penchant for gadgetry, a mad scientist and a slew of half-naked women, *Miss Muerte* is the point at which Franco's filmmatic style begins to solidify, setting a template that would play itself out throughout the late '60s and '70s. Changing the protagonist from male to female, Franco explores the story of a revenge-minded surgeon (Mabel Karr) who creates a machine that turns people into her slaves (she must have gotten the blueprint from Dr. Fisherman!). She uses the machine on a young dancer/stripper named Miss Muerte (Estella Blain) to take revenge on the doctors who drove her father to ruin. Muerte kills her victims with poisoned long black fingernails, all the while wearing her dancing outfit, a see-though black lace garment, causing her to look like a spider.[43]

Audiences around the world were now beginning to open themselves up to more provocative material in the mid-'60s and *Miss Muerte* allowed Franco to explore a more sexually adventurous terrain. All the sexiness one needs is found in Muerte's dance in the nightclub, which consists of her slowly moving a across the floor like a spider, the light spots resembling a web, to a male mannequin sitting in the chair. She moves slowly, seductively, until she crawls up the mannequin, straddling it then "killing" it viciously with her long poisoned nails. Erotic scenes like this with varying degrees of explicitness would show up time and time again throughout Franco's filmography. *Necronomicon* (*Succubus*, 1968) opened with a scene similar to this as star Janine Reynauld performs an S&M scene with a male/female couple. *Vampyros lesbos* (1970), *Eugénie de Sade* (1970) and *Exorcism* (1974) all had similar scenes of performance that were meant to signify the danger and sexual allure of these performers. The singers in his films, like Barbara McNair in *Venus in Furs* (1969), would often sing their numbers while lying seductively on the floor. In many of Franco's films to become sexually aroused is to be close to death, and this shows us that perhaps Franco equates these dances of death with female eroticism.

Miss Muerte (1965) was produced during the height of Franco's discontent with the Spanish film industry. When talking about the film Franco comments, "In truth, it was born out of a frustration of mine. *Miss Muerte* shouldn't have even been made. Censorship was causing me troubles."[44] The oppressive Spanish censors were beginning to take a large toll on Franco, whose work was becoming increasingly adult and subversive as the '60s rolled on. In addition, the "business only" side of producers was also a problem to an artist like Franco. Continuing his discussion from a 1991 interview, Franco related the problems that a director had to navigate and the pressures that both producers and censors put on him, saying, "They wouldn't forbid me to do them [stories Franco was intending to film], but they'd impose on me every type of rearrangement. Then I grew obstinate and I told them I refused to change anything. They replied, 'You should compromise, somehow,' and I said to them 'No, I'd rather not make the movie then.'"[45]

The rebellious nature of Franco may be another reason that he was drawn to the exploitation genre. Instead of making requisite changes for the Spanish censors, Franco made horror films as a way to get back at producers, citing that he believed that they thought the movies were silly and non-lucrative.[46] The Spanish government did not appreciate Franco's rebellion toward its policies. They could deal with his not making the movies they had wanted, but couldn't handle the movies he *was* making. Sexuality, explicit or implied,

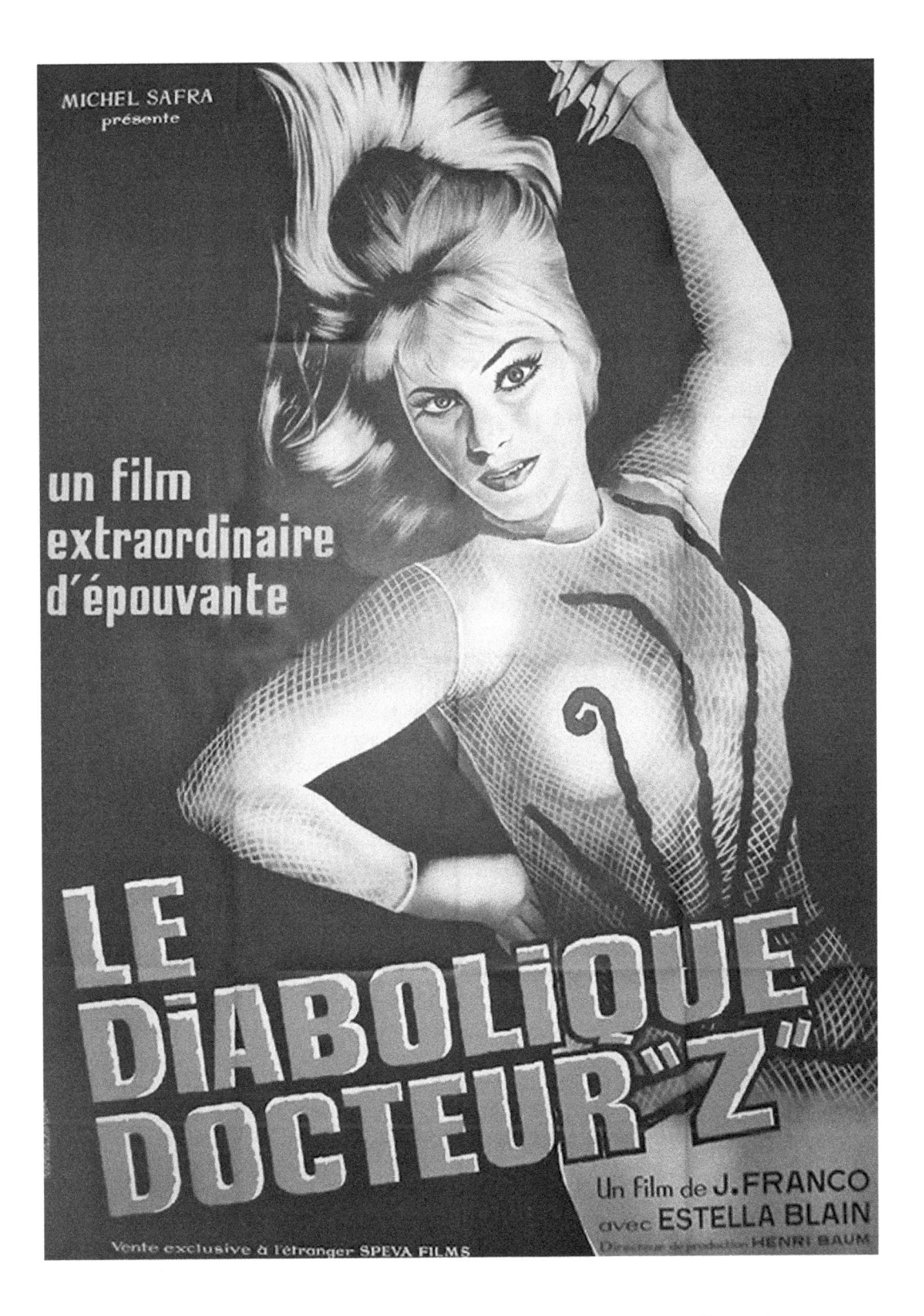

The Jess Franco style really cemented itself with one of his last black and white films, *Miss Muerte* (*The Diabolical Dr. Z*) in 1965.

was still taboo in 1965, and though the rest of the world had begun to loosen censorship, Spain's iron-fisted approach remained. Relates Eurociné's producer Daniel Lesoeur, "You have not to forgot [*sic*] the context of the life at this time in Spain. [With] General Franco, there was no way to say one word to say against the church, no sex. And he [Jess Franco] was one of the first who were able to speak of sex or show a little sex, which at the time it was really something."[47]

Franco's career got a potential boost in mid–'60s when he teamed for a series of projects with the legendary Orson Welles. Welles, like Franco, was a rebel and had built a career on being exacting as to his ideals on filmmaking. Their shared spirit of rebelliousness had alienated many within their respective film industries. By 1963, Welles was unable to raise money for projects in the U.S. and moved to Spain in hopes of filming *Chimes at Midnight* and a version of *Treasure Island*.[48] An assistant to Franco from film school, Juan Cobos, put Franco's name forward as a possible collaborator, and Franco was subsequently hired by Welles as a second-unit director for *Chimes*.[49] The two filmmakers became fast friends and plans were formulated for Franco to direct a version of *Treasure Island* with Welles starring. Unfortunately, the collaboration did not work out as intended due to a series of logistical and financial problems. *Chimes* was completed through immense difficulties and *Treasure Island* was shelved.[50]

The brief collaboration with Welles and the growing discontent over dictatorial Spain began to weigh heavily on Franco in the mid–'60s. He decided that if he were going to make the pictures he wanted, he would have to leave Spain. Connecting again with the French producers of *Miss Muerte* (1965), Franco directed a wacky science fiction film called *Cartas boca arriba* (*Attack of the Robots*) in 1966. This was to be Franco's last black and white film, and it showcased his creativity in the pulp cinema genre, a genre he would continually touch on throughout the rest of his career. Starring Eddie Constantine, *Cartas* rips off the successful James Bond genre in a Euro/Spanish way. Devising it as a satire, Franco tried to invest in the film with all the fun and whimsy that the movies *Goldfinger* (1964) and *Thunderball* (1965) had, but those movies had high budgets not even in the realm of possibility for a Spanish film, so he understood that the film would be prevented from being fully realized.

The lack of finances was dismaying for Franco, so he began to search for international backing. Outside financial backing was essential not only for the extra production money, but more importantly, it provided Franco an opportunity to get past the Spanish censors.[51] With financial backing Franco felt he could explore subject matter that was firmly taboo in Spain but financially viable in other countries; and with the social climate around the world becoming more permissive, Franco felt he understood what would sell. Franco found financial backing with German production manager Karl-Heinz Mannchen in 1966. After producing the fast-paced comic strip concoction *Lucky, el intrépido* (*Lucky, the Inscrutable*) in 1967, Franco came to Mannchen with an eight-page script for a proposed erotic horror feature that would go on to be considered one of his finest films, *Necronomicon*.

Necronomicon, or *Succubus* (1968) as it was called in the United States, would be the film that forever cemented Jess Franco as a premier exploitation filmmaker. Fusing all the ingredients that make up a Franco picture — the haunting jazz score, non-linear narration, and beautiful, exotic women with murderous minds, and targeting an international social

Opposite: *Necronomicon*'s (*Succubus*, 1967) non-linear story line was perfectly in synch with late-'60s audiences, making the film an international hit.

succubus
THE sensual experience of '69

This motion picture is rated adults only, naturally. **X RATING**

"A SEX FANTASY THAT ASPIRES TO A KIND OF CRAZY... SURREAL LITERACY! AN EROTIC HORROR STORY ABOUT A DEMENTED LADY OF BIZARRE SEXUAL TASTES!"
—Vincent Canby, N. Y. Times

"A PSYCHO-SEXUAL DRAMA!"
—Ann Guarino, N. Y. Daily News

"SUCCUBUS" starring JANINE REYNAUD · JACK TAYLOR   Produced by ADRIAN HOVEN   Directed by JESS FRANCO   Screenplay by PIER A. CAMINNECI
A PIER A. CAMINNECI · ADRIAN HOVEN Color Film Production of The AQUILA FILM ENTERPRISES, BERLIN   A TRANS AMERICAN FILMS RELEASE
In COLOR

69/211

clientele that liked to see a little more nudity and a lot more sexual situations—Franco created a film that was true to his vision. The film follows Lorna (Janine Reynaud), an upscale S&M nightclub performer, as she surrealistically slips slowly into madness. Is this madness psychological or is it the result of a pact her manager (Jack Taylor, making the first of many appearances in a Franco film) made with the Devil? The film contains, for the time, a large amount of nudity, murder and public displays of eroticism. For Franco this subject matter was, not surprisingly, a difficult process to get through the Spanish censors. He comments, "I was aware that this film would be harder to make than my other horror films so I was trying to make a film that I liked. Because I had to make co-productions with Spain, but the censors had taken their red pen and crossed everything out, even the title, yes! At the time, all co-productions with Spain, and remember Spain was cut off from the rest of Europe, had the prerequisite that the film had to be shot in Spain. It didn't matter if you had a completely Spanish crew, you had to shoot there and prove that you did or else you wouldn't get the co-production money."[52]

Sensing the film could not be made to his own vision, Franco made a bold decision to forgo Spanish investment and went completely with his German investors. The decision to shoot entirely outside of Spain meant Franco and producer Mannchen would have to scrounge up more money. As is typical with exploitation films, friends, friends of friends, and business acquaintances were scouted and called upon. The process of producing *Necronomicon* offers a good example on how the exploitation films of the '60s and '70s were financed and produced. As Jess Franco puts it, "I started scouting locations in Spain and Berlin and it's there I met my second co-producer of the film because my partner was Adrian Hoven, but he had an associate a co-producer named Pier Maria Caminnecci. He was very rich, the main stockholder in Siemens. So he had quite a bit of money. And he had a magnificent house. And on his bookshelf, I discovered a book entitled *Necronomicon*."[53] Looking for ideas, Franco found a short story in the book that he felt could be translated to film. The problem was the story was only three pages long. Fusing it with a script from a horror movie he'd previously written, Franco came up with a complete screenplay. After securing enough money to begin shooting, he began to look for a lead who could play voluptuous, schizophrenic Lorna. Looking for someone with a strong presence and personality, Franco found this particular muse sitting in a bistro in Rome, when French star Michel Lemoine called Franco to meet his wife, model Janine Reynaud. "I looked up and saw her," related Franco, "and said 'Damn, she's the one!'"[54]

Though she was 37 at the time, Reynaud had only worked in a few films. Having the open mind it took to take part in an adult-themed movie that contained a lot of nudity and violence, Reynaud set about inhabiting the hallucinatory world of a woman who may or may not be a tool of the Devil. Her Lorna is an evil temptress who spends her nights as an S&M performer, Franco's idea of a legitimate dancer, haunted by dreams that she is a tool of the devil. Whether she is or not is left deliberately up to the audience.[55] Reynaud's screen presence is electrifying. She projects an aura of deviant sexuality that is marked with vulnerability, making her sympathetic to the audience. Not only was the public enamored, but she also had same effect on co-producer Caminnecci, resulting in the film's success.

Franco's earlier statement about working with the millionaire Caminnecci, while true, is missing one important component. During the making of the film, the German backers pulled out of the film. Without any capital to finish the film, coproducer Hoven desperately called Caminnecci to see if he'd like to take part. Charging a plane ticket they could not pay for, Hoven and Franco flew him to the set in Lisbon to gain his interest, and as is apt to happen sometimes, his interest was gained not by the film itself but by its star. As an affair developed between producer and star, the money was secured to not only finish the film but to promote it as well.[56] Ironically, Reynaud's husband, French actor Michel Lemoine, did not seem all that bothered by the affair his wife was having with the producer. Lemoine had roles in the three Franco films produced by Caminnecci and by all accounts pretty much kept a low profile during the affair.

Necronomicon (1968) was a smashing success in its initial run. Fusing sexuality with dreamlike violence seemed to be exactly what 1967 audiences were looking for. German auteur Fritz Lang heralded the film at the Berlin Film Festival as an erotic masterpiece and the film was a financial success. Released in the United States as *Succubus*, the film utilized an exploitation marketing approach, offering a phone number curious audience-goers could call if they didn't know the definition of a succubus. The ploy worked and U.S. audiences also flocked to see this very strange non-linear movie. Coming at a time when films like Ahlberg's *I, a Woman* (1966) and Sjöman's *I Am Curious (Yellow)* (1967) were enjoying phenomenal success with the art-house crowds, *Necronomicon* (*Succubus*) rode the wave of sexually explicit international films and allowed American audiences to experience a sex-and-violence scenario without feeling "dirty."

Franco found the process of shooting outside of Spain to be joyous. Commenting on his new independent status, Franco said, "It took me awhile to realize that I was free. Because I wasn't used to being free. When I became aware of this freedom, I decided to adopt a new approach, one different from the point of view of a regular horror film. I tried to broaden the scope. *Necronomicon* was the first opportunity I had to make a film the way I wanted to make it. I'm rather astonished that the film did as well as it did."[57]

Looking to cash in on the success of *Necronomicon* (1967), Franco, Hoven and company produced two back-to-back sexy spy movies under the moniker of "Red Lips" featuring Reynaud, Lemoine and Argentine actress Rosanna Yanni. Both *Sadisterotica* (*Two Undercover Angels*, 1968) and *Bésame monstruo* (*Kiss Me Monster*, 1968) cashed in once again on the comic-strip spy genre (James Bond, Flint, Matt Helm, Diabolik) that was popular in the '60s. Precursors to such shows as *Charlie's Angels*, both films were a hodgepodge of different styles, throwing in elements of horror, action, comedy and sex, as gun-toting, sexy, psychedelic detectives Reynaud and Yanni spend both movies' running time chasing after monsters and dead bodies in a high camp way. Talking in an interview in 2006, Franco related his thoughts about using comic strips as influences for his films: "I don't make films that will be relegated to the history of culture. The director is an entertainer, he is not Pascal. He's just a guy who does something to please the audience. And comic strips are great for that."[58]

Though Franco classifies the films as a comic strips, they are comic strips for adults only. Sexuality is the main weapon that these women use. The two hapless characters are tied up, chased after, and made to do outlandish things in various states of undress. They walk around totally bubbly, saying stupid things (a situation not helped by the awful dubbing the movies received around the world), completely buying into the stereotypical male-gaze portrayal of women in a "man's" job.[59] Unfortunately for Franco, neither film was a financial success, perhaps due to the fact that the spy genre had become oversaturated, and Franco's fun-loving detectives were too silly to be received well by audiences in any country.

The failure of the "Red Lips" films forced Franco to look for another producer. In 1968, he teamed with legendary British movie producer Harry Alan Towers for a series of films which many consider the most consistent of the Franco canon.[60] These nine films produced between 1968 and 1970 utilized both classical literature sources and popular fiction of the time, while providing Franco with some of the highest budgets he would ever have. The films included two Dr. Fu Manchu films, a retelling of Bram Stoker's *Dracula*, a couple of works inspired by the Marquis de Sade, as well as a couple of original films that cemented Franco's career as the ultimate exploitation filmmaker. For the first time, Franco was able to secure bankable stars (Christopher Lee, George Sanders, Klaus Kinski, Jack Palance, Maria Schell, Mercedes McCambridge) to play alongside Franco regulars (Howard Vernon, Jack Taylor, Paul Müller). He was also able to shoot in some of the most exotic locations around the world (Rio de Janeiro, Portugal, Istanbul) and utilize the settings to paint a pretty picture around some not-so-pretty scenarios that were occurring in the narrative.

The result of these films is a weird hodgepodge of classy stylings mixed with exploitation that leaves the viewer feeling slightly disoriented. There's something slightly off in these films with Towers. They have the look and feel of big-budget traditional Hollywood fare, yet they are so seedy in content you can't really believe you're seeing what is on the screen. When else but in the late '60s could you see Oscar winner Mercedes McCambridge (*99 Women*, 1968) overseeing the whipping of half-naked girls in an island prison, Christopher Lee (*Eugenie, the Story of Her Decent into Perversion*, 1970) reading from de Sade as a young girl is drugged, stripped and beaten as a party game for a sadistic brother-and-sister incest combo, or George Sanders cavorting with nude Brazilian women (*The Girl from Rio*, 1968)? The fact that "name" stars would appear in these films is indicative of the change going on in the worldwide film industry as moviegoers had to accept that their beloved stars of yesteryear were now making their livings in the international exploitation market. This situation became necessary in the late '60s as traditional studios were faltering and film actors who had previously been under contract were left to find their own vehicles and appeal to audiences that were radically changing in their tastes.[61] Exploitation offered quick money, short shooting schedules, and worldwide travel opportunities for stars whose box office had dwindled significantly.

The stars as well as the settings for films like Franco's were made possible by producers like Harry Alan Towers, who was infamous in filmmaking circles. Born in 1920, he began producing radio shows during his stint in the RAF in the '40s before moving to television in the '50s, where he produced a slew of unsuccessful series for ITV in Britain. Broke and out of work by the end of the decade, he moved to New York and operated a prostitution ring which was busted in 1961. Fleeing back to Europe to avoid jail, he successfully developed a scrupulous system of financing films involving tax breaks, a system that is now illegal.[62] To finance his films, Towers set up, according to author David McGillivray, "high-class prostitution rackets for politicians or, anyhow, very powerful men, he'd use to close movie financing deals offering to the various co-producers his wife's sexual attractions, the Austrian actress Maria Rohm."[63] It is actress Rohm who is the link between all the films Franco directed for Towers. Starring in eight out of the nine films, *Castle of Fu Manchu* (1969) being the exception, Rohm was able to secure not only star status but have her choice of the best roles in the films. Franco for his part was thrilled because he saw Rohm as a great actress and gave her better parts with each consecutive movie. For someone with a questionable reputation, Maria Rohm actually turned out to be one of the best actresses in the entire Franco filmography. Though many, including Franco himself, argue that Soledad Miranda was his favorite muse, Rohm handled herself superbly in these films, playing a variety of roles each vastly different from the other. From the jailed innocent in *99 Women* (1968), to the Brazilian maid and feminist crime fighter in *The Girl from Rio* (1968), to the vicious, manipulative Juliette in *Justine* (1969), to Wanda, a transcendental ghost in *Venus in Furs* (1969), Rohm played each of these characters with surprising depth not found in most films of these types or in Franco's later films.

The collaboration between Franco and Towers began with *Kiss and Kill* (*The Blood of Fu Manchu*) in 1968. The famous evil Sax Rohmer character had already been played in the cinema many times by such stars as Boris Karloff and Warner Oland. By the '60s, British actor Christopher Lee had donned Asian makeup to play the role in a series of films for producer Towers and Warner Bros. As the films did less and less business, Towers looked to Franco to spice things up a little, and Franco, a fan of Rohmer's books, did just that, incorporating nude scenes and violent situations into what was typically family fare. Having a dungeon cell where the hero and heroine await their fates is not a new concept in the genre. Having that dungeon filled with topless women hanging from their wrists and covered in blood was.[64] This adult approach befuddled many of the stars of the film, including Asian actress Tsai Chin, who portrayed Fu Manchu's evil daughter Ling Tang. She commented, "That was the day all these women were just kinda hanging there and Christopher came in, and Christopher is not a womanizer, bless his heart, and he was so [complete surprise] OH MY GOD WHAT IS THIS? [laughing] And I'm just standing there laughing so much about his reaction. As an actress, you did what you had to do. By the time I did the fourth one, the Fu Manchu films, I didn't really read the script with enormous carefulness."[65]

There is something definitely off kilter in *Kiss* as the mixture of what was family entertainment makes its transformation to exploitation. Interestingly, *Kiss* actually makes Fu Manchu more palatable. The character has always been a negative in regards to portrayal of Asians, but within the context of the exploitation film, where all stereotypes are naturally magnified, it works. That is about all that works in the film, though, as it is obvious that Franco isn't very devoted to the story, which gives him ample opportunity to mine the sci-fi spy medical device. This time it's 10 beautiful women who have the ability to kill with their kiss, an idea that he used effectively earlier in *Miss Muerte* (1965). Needless to say, film critics of the time were just as baffled that such a cultural icon was turning into an exploitation mess, complete with the requisite nude women, but audiences were just interested enough for the film to amass enough money to leave the door open for a future sequel.

After *Kiss*, Franco and Towers went to Rio de Janeiro to shoot *The Girl from Rio* (*La ciudad sin hombres*, 1968). Another comic-strip concoction from Sax Rohmer and starring former Bond girl Shirley Eaton (*Goldfinger*, 1964) as Sumuru, the evil, diabolical mastermind bent on world destruction, *Girl* was Franco's most fun adult film to date.[66] Featuring a bevy of topless women in space-age uniforms, the film is a feminist version of James Bond complete with mythical lairs, exotic locations and gadgetry. Of course, this being 1968, the male protagonist, played woodenly by Richard Wyler, would have the upper hand, soundly defeating Sumuru in her city of women. The film is not meant to be taken seriously, and like the comic books that it was inspired by, it is an obvious male fantasy that may have been the inspiration for many such soft-core Euro porn movies as the German *5 Mädchen blasen zum Angriff* (*2069: A Sex Odyssey*, 1974) and the French *Spermula* (1976).

Star Eaton had some of the same issues with exploitation filmmaking that would later plague Christopher Lee. Actors were very seldom told about a film's distribution deal nor about the demands that other film markets would make on producers for more titillating material. Not told that there were lesbian scenes involving her character in *Girl*, Eaton was surprised and shocked to see a lesbian love scene in the film when she saw it with an audience for the first time. As she puts it in a 2004 interview, "I sorta make love with the leading

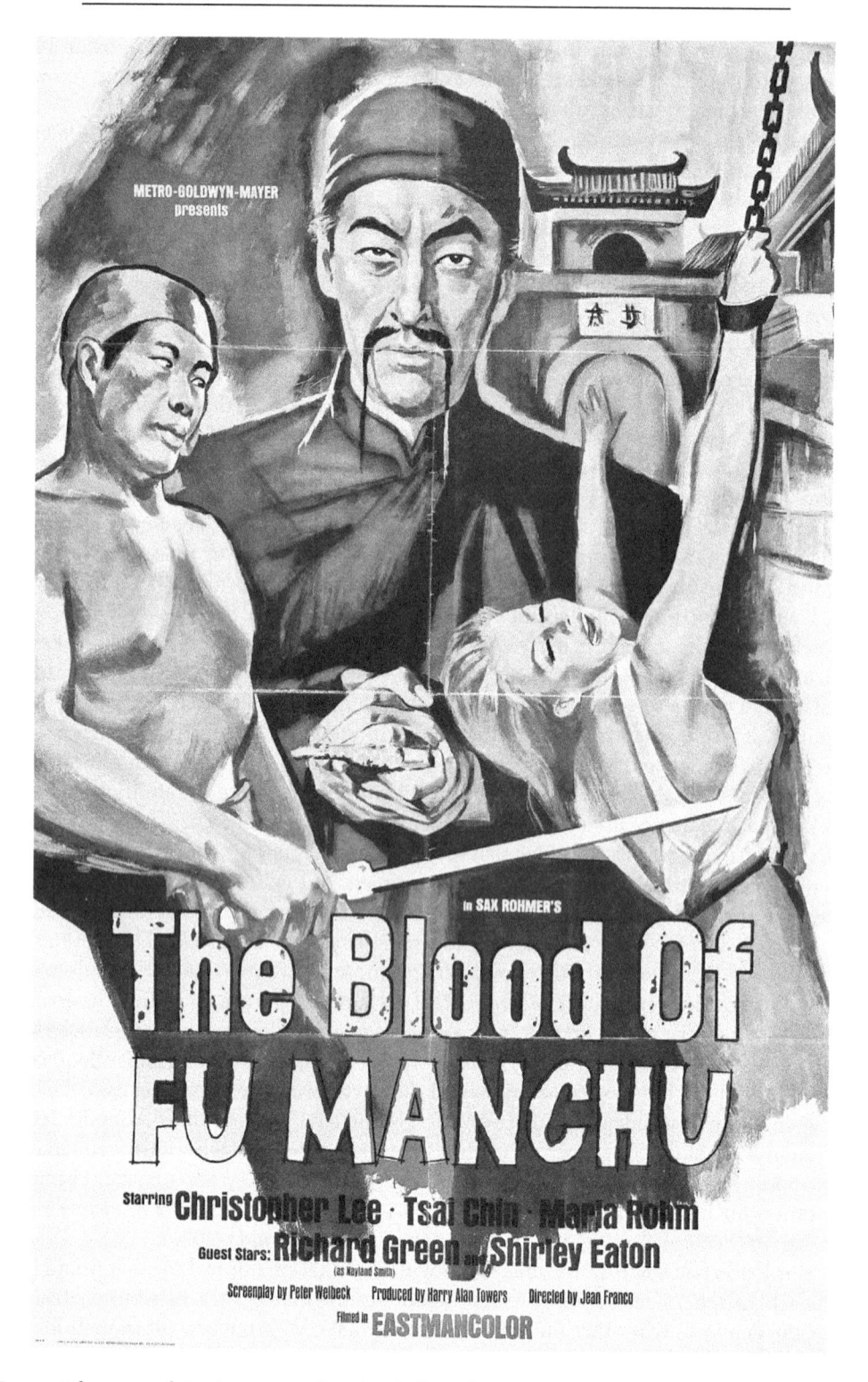

Franco takes an exploitative approach to Sax Rohmer's Fu Manchu character in *Kiss and Kill* (*The Blood of Fu Manchu*, 1968).

man, like a spider catching a fly in her web, as a normal woman, that was fine, there were two little scenes like that. But they managed to shoot a double, obviously cause I knew it wasn't me, from behind, they just had a woman, a blonde, with hair much longer than mine, which was one clue, not the same quality as mine. Then a girl comes in, presumably, for them to have a love scene, you see her face and you just see my character looking up and they begin to embrace and then they cut it. But I was a bit cross about it, I think it's a liberty actually."[67]

Franco's quick shooting style resulted in *Girl*'s being completed well before the anticipated stop date, causing major problems for Towers. Central to the theme of the movie were shots of the Brazilian Carnival, but Franco, being Franco, managed to finish the film about a week before the celebration was set to commence. Not having the luxury that a major studio would have of keeping a crew on paid standby, Franco and Towers had to come up with an idea that would justify paying the crew. Spending the weekend writing, Towers came up with an idea for a script for a women's prison picture called *99 Women* (*99 Mujeres*, 1968) that could go into production immediately.[68] As Franco relates, "We thought, 'what are we going to do during this time?' So I understand the problems of production. I understand it's natural to think, 'Shit! I'm going to have to pay all your salaries during this time.' Harry explained to me that he wanted to make *99 Women*. He gave it to me to read, I read it and thought it was superb."[69]

Using a local Brazilian jungle as a backdrop, Franco shot 25 minutes of film in one week, utilizing some of the same actors (Rohm, etc.) who were in *The Girl from Rio* (1968). He finished *Rio* and returned to Europe while Towers, with the 25 minutes of footage in hand, went about securing funding for *99 Women* (1968). The importance of *99 Women* (1968) cannot be overestimated, as it was the first successful "women in prison" movie, a cinematic staple in the exploitation genre. Previously relegated to a few lower-budget Hollywood exploitation films like *Caged* (1950), for which it must said that actress Eleanor Parker received an Oscar nomination, *Women's Prison* (1955), *Girls in Prison* (1956), and *House of Women* (1962), women in prison movies, or WIPs, appealed to an audience looking for a variety of exploitive themes in their entertainment choices. The interest in this subgenre stems from the fascination for deviant behavior in women, with infamous female gangs like the Baader-Meinhof in Germany and Switzerland capturing the imagination of Europeans in the '70s. One could look at these films from a variety of viewpoints: either as vicarious thrill ride of seeing beautiful "bad" girls punished for forsaking their domesticity in a masculine world, or as vulnerable women forced to contend with all-female environments, or even from a feminist perspective of strong-willed women overcoming their adversity.[70] These films represented a backlash to the gender equality that was occurring in society, with many in the audience attending with a vicarious thrill of seeing what may happen to female activists who go too far.[71] Regardless of the question of why people were attracted to the subgenre, one thing was for sure: they were getting the same thing in every movie of this subgenre. WIP films almost always follow the same formula, and *99 Women* created it. Franco modernized the hackneyed scripts and melodrama of the earlier prison movies and brought in a late–'60s sensibility that included a generous portion of nudity, lesbianism and sadomasochism. Storylines in WIP are often threadbare, being more character-driven. Here Franco presents a story of a nice young woman (Rohm) sent to a Spanish prison island for killing in self-defense the men who gang-raped her. Lorded over by an evil overseer (American actress Mercedes McCambridge) and warden (British actor Herbert Lom), the women are treated terribly, often bound, raped and used by the state's vicious penal system.

One soul hungered to touch another!
WHISPER TO YOUR FRIENDS YOU SAW IT!
From the exciting story by Peter Welbeck
99 WOMEN
...behind bars-without men!
A Commonwealth United Corporation Presentation
STARRING
Maria SCHELL · Mercedes McCAMBRIDGE · Luciana PALUZZI · Herbert LOM
as the Governor
COLOR
Suggested For Mature Audiences
Screenplay by PETER WELBECK · Directed by JESS FRANCO · Produced by HARRY ALAN TOWERS · A Commonwealth United Entertainment, Inc. and Towers of London (Films) Limited Production
Released by Commonwealth United Entertainment, Inc.
69/44

The only for hope for the girls comes from a social worker (Austrian actress Maria Schell) sent to investigate the depraved goings-on. With a haunting title track sung by popular American artist Barbara McNair (soon to be star of Franco's *Venus in Furs*, 1969), the film is never less than entertaining as it quickly races through its running time.[72]

Like the other films in association with producer Towers, *99 Women* has a variety of different international stars to help promote his film, with Oscar winner McCambridge, former Bond girl Luciana Paluzzi (*Thunderball*, 1965) and Austrian actress Schell appearing in various degrees. As in a lot of exploitation films, the appearances of the stars is somewhat deceiving to audiences. Many times "name" actors would appear on set for a day or two and receive top billing, and other times they may not film their scenes until well after the production had been completed. Star Luciana Paluzzi is given third billing in *99 Women*, though she only appears in a total of five minutes; watching the film, it is obvious that her appearance was filmed after principal photography because she is shown only in close-up. When her character has to interact with other players, she is shot from the back and played by an actress who is clearly not Paluzzi. Filming with stand-ins allowed the producers to secure talent at a later date and "drop" them into a film in order to get better marketing traction.

For Franco, the theme of a woman stuck in a female prison appealed to the anarchist in him, giving him a somewhat romantic outlook on the gloomy genre. As he put it, "In a prison film, naturally one is disturbed by defenseless women at the mercy of a group of bastards. It's something that afterwards you may think 'Oh shit, they went too far.' But while you're watching it you're watching something beautiful."[73] Whether one thinks of women behind bars as beautiful, it is a theme that resonates with Franco, as he returns to the subgenre time and time again with such films as *Los amantes de la isla del diablo* (*Devil's Island Lovers*, 1972), *Frauengefängnis* (*Barbed Wire Dolls*, 1976), *Frauen für Zellenblock 9* (*The Women of Cellblock 9*, 1977), *Greta, the Mad Butcher* (*Ilsa, the Wicked Warden*, 1977) and *Sadomania* (1981), each more depraved than the last. Franco must have understood the interest in female incarceration because the film was a phenomenal success. Released around the world in 1968 and '69 with the exploitative teaser "99 women ... without men!," the film received an X rating in the United States from the newly formed MPAA and became the highest-grossing film of Franco's career, topping the *Variety* list of top box-office earners in 1969.[74] Throughout the early '70s the film was shown throughout the world in a variety of different versions, the most notorious being the hard-core version that included "inserts" of characters having sex. These scenes were not shot by Franco and were added after the original release, much to the chagrin of the actresses involved.

The box-office success of *99 Women* (1968) provided the opportunity for Franco and Towers to produce more literary adult entertainment. After finishing the final and much more family-friendly Fu Manchu film, *Castle of Fu Manchu* (1969), they began to look closely at the works of the Marquis de Sade.[75] Relating to Franco that he wanted to make an erotic movie, producer Towers went ahead and wrote a lavish script from one of de Sade's most famous novels, *De Sade — Les Infortunes de la vertu* (*Justine, or the Misfortune of Virtue*, 1791). Franco loved the script but knew the dangers of producing a film based on the works of someone so infamous. "I thought [the script] was very good," related Franco in a 2004 interview, "because it was quite difficult especially back then, you really had to be careful,

Opposite: One of the first "women in prison" films, *99 Women* was a success around the world and led to the proliferation of a subgenre that continues today.

it was like playing with fire."[76] Though the film cost less then 1 million dollars to produce, it was Jess Franco's most expensive film to date, and with a roster of stars like Klaus Kinski (playing the Marquis de Sade in a non-verbal but scene-chewing role), Jack Palance and Mercedes McCambridge, as well as Franco regulars Maria Rohm, Howard Vernon, and Rosalba Neri, Franco went about creating an exploitation spectacle. The outcome was a bit like watching a Cecil B. DeMille film on crack. Watching stars like Palance sexually torturing the heroine Justine, or McCambridge inciting violence in a god-awful prison cell (clearly Franco was making her pay cinematically for her turn as warden in *99 Women*), is a psychedelic mind trip to traditional audiences expecting the typical Hollywood-type epic. For exploitation audiences, *Justine* is far too slow-paced and plodding, and though there is an abundance of nudity it all seems too safe. So in retrospect neither audience was happy.[77] For Franco, the film was an epic, but even he understood that exploitation by nature is almost always a rip-off and that this style of filmmaking was never to be on par with Hollywood. He said, "It was a very costly film because there were an enormous number of costumes, sets, horses, carriages and stuff. It wasn't a real film but it was what the guys at American International at the time called 'a fake big film.' Only we knew it was fake!"[78]

Because of the high budget for *Justine* (1969), some concessions had to be made to foreign distributors. Most notably, the casting of the leading actress in the film, Romina Power, the daughter of American actor Tyrone Power, was forced upon Franco in order to receive funding. Originally casting actress Rosemary Dexter, who had prepared and rehearsed for the role, Franco was stunned when a Hollywood financier announced the change: "All of a sudden the boss in Hollywood proclaimed, 'The time has come for our actors' children.' I said, 'What is that supposed to mean?' 'Romina Power is going to do it.'" recalled Franco, "I said, 'Fuck! I can't do it with Romina Power. I will never be able to do the story of a young girl who gets involved, who becomes a masochist, who starts to truly feel pleasure when being treated so atrociously."[79] Franco's problem with Romina was not only her lack of experience, but a lack of sensuality that the role required. Reframing it as more of an *Alice in Wonderland*–type story, he diluted the essence of de Sade's story, making few fans happy. Acting issues aside, it must also be pointed out that *Justine* may have been produced just a shade too early to be potent. While nudity and sexuality were becoming commonplace in mainstream theaters around the world via the films of Russ Meyer or Radley Metzger, the use of the full-fledged explicit sexuality was still a few years away from 1968. Franco had to be content with the amount of sex and debauchery tolerated by the general public in order to make the film marketable. The result was a beautifully filmed movie that was strangely unerotic. Critics who viewed the film agreed, finding that it lacked personality and was both amateurish and dull.[80]

Franco made sure after the experience with *Justine* that no outside financier would have full control over picking a leading performer if he wasn't convinced the star would be suitable. One actress he was impressed with was Towers's wife, Maria Rohm, and in his next film, the de Sade–flavored *Venus in Furs* (1969), it is her leading performance that elevates the film which many Francophiles believe his best. *Venus* stars American singing and acting idol James Darren as a jazz musician (what else, considering this is a Franco movie?) who finds the body of a woman, Wanda (Rohm), on a beach and is subsequently pulled into a psychedelic world of murder, sex and death.[81]

Opposite: One of Franco's best, *Venus in Furs* (1969) successfully balanced the line between reality and dreams.

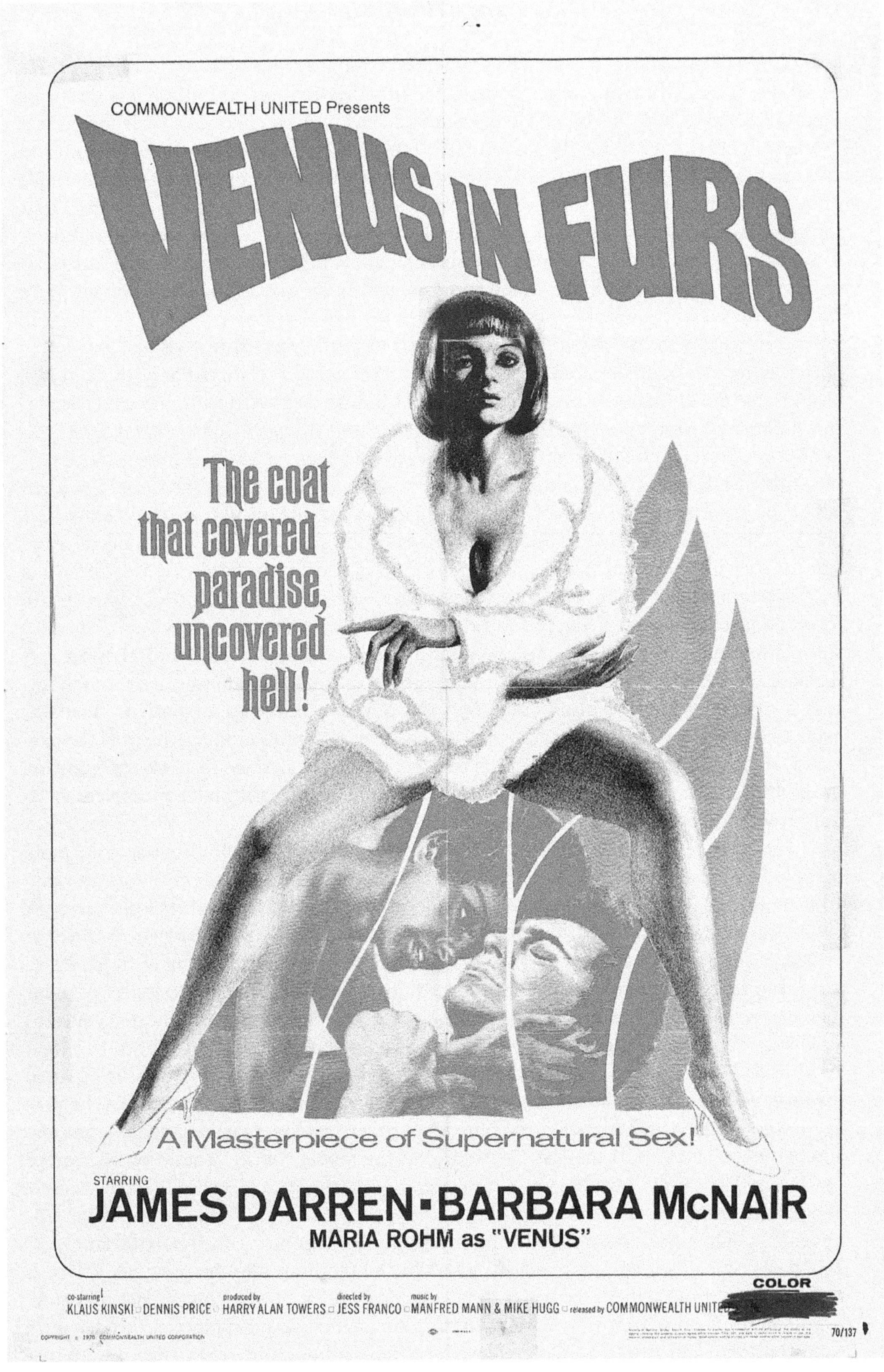

After Franco had worked with Towers on genre films, comic-strip yarns, WIPs, movies based on classical literature, etc., *Venus* is the first film that seems entirely his. From its non-linear storyline to the psychedelic color and slow motion effects, *Venus* is the perfect example of alternative filmmaking in the late '60s. Originally it was called *Black Angel* and conceived as a bi-racial love affair between a black trumpeter and a white woman, but Franco was forced to make some changes to appease U.S. distributors who worried about the racial aspects of the story. Franco confounded and surprised the racist attitudes of American producers, stating, "The producers wouldn't allow it because they said the American public are not ready to see a black man and a white woman in bed. But the thing they were fine with was a white man sleeping with a black woman, but never a black man sleeping with a white woman. Because it's a shame on her race. [disgusted] Impossible!"[82]

Having to rewrite the story, Franco focused on creating a relationship he thought jazz legend Chet Baker might have with one of his black mistresses. African American '60s pop star Barbara McNair, who sang the theme to Franco's *99 Women* (1968), was brought in as James Darren's long-suffering mistress who tries to keep Darren with one foot into reality.[83] One thing he did not change, though, was the non-linear narrative of the film. Like a bad acid trip, *Venus* spins the characters and audience into a dream-like environment where reality is hard to distinguish. The film has many of the same plot devices found in many later movies like Shyamalan's *The Sixth Sense* (1999) and Lyne's *Jacob's Ladder* (1990), as well as playing like a latter-season episode of TV series *Lost* (2005), in which viewers are forced to just give up on trying to solve the mystery and go along for the visual and audio ride. This visual ride has many pleasures, most notably that of Rohm, murdering her way through the cast in various stages of undress while the jazz score permeates throughout. Like his previous *Necronomicon* (*Succubus*, 1968), *Venus* played to an audience that was engrossed in the counterculture. The obsessional love, sex, and sadomasochism of the narrative, along with the jazzy score, were in perfect tandem for a crowd that was experiencing the bitterness of various wars, experimenting with drugs, and dealing with a complete social upheaval that was occurring in the late '60s.

The acceptance of the surrealistic aspects in *Venus in Furs* (1969), along with more permissive rules about nudity, prompted Franco and Towers to push the envelope yet again with another effort by the Marquis de Sade. *Eugenie, the Story of Her Journey into Perversion* (1969) was Franco's most adult film to date. Taken from de Sade's *Philosophy in the Boudoir* (1795), *Eugenie* contained themes, such as the corruption of a minor sexually via violence, drugs and rape, that are even more shocking in the politically correct atmosphere of today then they were in 1969. Starring Swedish actress Marie Liljedahl as Eugenie, the plot concerns a sadistic brother and sister (Maria Rohm, Jack Taylor) who bring young Eugenie to their lavish island estate only to drug and rape her every night.[84] Christopher Lee shows up in the final reel to add more sinister goings on as Dolmance, the de Sadean narrator, who may or may not be the Devil himself. The film is a shocker mostly because Liljidahl looks and acts about 16. She spends the last 10 minutes of the movie rolling around on a deserted beach completely nude, bleeding from the whippings she received earlier in the film. *Eugenie* also carried on the psychedelic approach that Franco mastered in *Venus in Furs* (1969). Is Eugenie's plight a real one or is this innocent young girl capable of such horrific fantasies? To Franco, it's all within the realm of possibility as the film, like the previous *Venus*, is nothing but a dream where the worst things can and probably will happen. He shies away from none of the provocative situations in the film: a father who happily sells his daughter to his mistress, a brother and sister whose incestuous longings involve drugging and tor-

As censorship crumbled in the late '60s, Franco could begin to film even more startling and explicit films. *Eugenie, the Story of Her Journey into Perversion* (1969) was a good example of that new direction.

turing innocent young girls, mute servants who need violence and pain to feel they're doing their jobs, all reside in the screenplay.[85] Beautiful in its execution, the film remains one of Franco's most praised works, with Franco and Eurocult scholar Tim Lucas calling *Eugenie* "intellectual, sensual, transgressive, literate and literal," going on to say that the film is "like nothing else in the annals of horror or erotic cinema."[86]

As literate and respected as the film may be, the subject matter and exploitation process of making the film caught some of the actors off guard. Calling the original text "an atrocious story," Franco knew the subject matter was too explicit to be shot the way de Sade had written it. "We had a hard time adapting the story, not for me but for the actors," said Franco in a 2002 interview, "because back then Shakespearean actors refused to act in *Philosophy in the Boudoir*."[87] One of the actors who had a problem with it was again Christopher Lee, who accepted the film at the last minute when the original actor, Bernard Peters, was killed in a plane crash only days before shooting began. Promised that he did not have to participate in any sex scenes, Lee agreed. Commenting on the proceedings, Lee related:

> So I went out there, put on my red velvet smoking jacket which I wore in *Sherlock Holmes*, a previous film, and I stood there with these people all around me and I did the various speeches and bits and pieces that were required of me over the two-day period in a studio in Barcelona. All the people around me weren't doing anything at all, they were just standing around listening to me. I subsequently discovered, there was a friend of mine who said, "You're on in a cinema on Compton Atreet" [an area in London known for its adult theaters], which shook me slightly, to say the least. "You must be joking." He said "No, no, no, your name is up there starring in this film." And of course I wasn't starring; I did two days. The point is, after I left they reshot my point of view and everybody took their clothes off. So now I guess you can say that I've been in nearly every kind of film one way or the another![88]

What Lee found out, similar to Shirley Eaton's issues with *The Girl from Rio* (1968), was that distributors had the right to cut a film to their preferences, which occasionally meant they would add scenes not produced during initial production. Many times, especially as the '70s progressed, this meant the inclusion of hard-core pornography inserts. *Eugenie* was one the first films to "benefit" from the practice, much to the horror of many of its actors. Because exploitation films are sometimes released throughout the world years after their production, Lee probably did not discover this deception until after he had completed two more films for Franco and Towers, *El conde Drácula* (*Count Dracula*, 1969) and *The Bloody Judge* (1970). Those two films represent the final pictures that Franco would make with Towers. *El conde Drácula* (1969) was an attempt to film an authentic version Bram Stoker's novel, unlike the watered-down sequels Britain was producing at the time with Hammer Studios. By the time *El conde* went into production, Hammer was on its third sequel to the popular *Horror of Dracula* (1958), and Christopher Lee, who had starred in them all (except *Brides of Dracula*, 1960) had grown tired of the role. He accepted the role in Franco's film only because he wanted to see the story done right. Franco assembled the usual cast of actors including Klaus Kinski, Herbert Lom, Maria Rohm, and Paul Müller, as well as an actress who would be closely associated with Franco in the next two years, Spanish actress Soledad Miranda.

Downplaying the exploitative aspects of his previous films (there is no nudity and only one very brief scene of violence), Franco went for a more Gothic approach in keeping with original source material. Unfortunately, the film turned out to be mixed bag both for fans expecting a faithful translation of Stoker's novel and for those expecting an exploitation version from Franco. The biggest problem with the film was the budget. Obvious sets, including a pair of fake rocks that rival anything Ed Wood Jr. could come up with, a lethargic screenplay and overall dullness marred the film. Performances were all over the map as well, ranging from the sublime (Klaus Kinski as Renfield) to the ridiculous (Herbert Lom, playing half the film in a wheelchair). For the first time in his career, Franco seemed bored. The traditional scripts and ideas of Stoker novels or for *The Bloody Judge* (1969), a quickly made rip-off of the German/Italian coproduction *Mark of the Devil*, no longer seem to appeal to the Spaniard who wanted to take his films in the more experimental route of *Venus in Furs*. Audiences, perhaps sensing Franco's detachment from Stoker's material, were not satisfied, and the film ended up a box-office disappointment.[89]

By the end of 1969, Franco began to tire of his association with Towers. After the dullness of *El conde Drácula* (1979), he began to look around for funding of his own brand of films that more deeply explored his non-linear narrative style. One of the first, *Les Cauchemars naissent la nuit* (*Nightmares Come at Night*, 1970) was produced for a reported $20,000 and shot in the down time between *El conde* and *The Bloody Judge* (1970).[90] Starring raven-haired Diana Lorys as a bisexual woman being driven mad by those around her, *Les Cauchemars* allowed Jess to forgo the conventions of traditional film. The plotline of the film was downplayed; long, deliberate pauses by the actors accentuate the dreamlike quality of the film. In addition, full nudity is shown, shot in crazy, psychedelic ways befitting a 1970 film.[91] Even the presence of actress Soledad Miranda, who played a small role in the film, could not ensure its success. The completed film was never shown in most countries around world, playing only in Belgium three years after it was shot.[92] Though not a financial success, *Les Cauchemars* gave a peek at what audiences around the world would find in Franco's films of the '70s.

After *Les Cauchemars*, Franco returned to producer Harry Alan Towers for another big budget exploitation romp. *The Bloody Judge* (1970) was based on exploits of Judge George Jeffreys, a 17th-century British witchfinder. The film was meant to cash in on the success of the British director Michael Reeves's film *Witchfinder General* (*Conqueror Worm*, 1968), as well as the previously mentioned *Mark of the Devil* (1968). Films of this type, period pieces with themes of uprisings and demonstrations, held a special attraction for the young audiences. Referring to *Witchfinder*, scholar Tim Lucas said, "The film resonated with young people because it was a film of righteous youthful rebellion released at a time of righteous youthful rebellion."[93] *The Bloody Judge* (1970) also followed in *Witchfinder*'s, path upping the exploitation factor of the earlier film. Beheadings, nude floggings, forced lesbian jailhouse groping, and people being burned alive followed Franco regulars Christopher Lee, Maria Rohm, Leo Glenn, Maria Schell and Howard Vernon, all of whom acted out the cruelty of 17th-century England. In the film, Franco is able to take some crack shots at the Gen. Franco regime and the general state of Spain as he explores the issue of tyranny and dictatorship within in the context of the story. His conclusion is not an optimistic one as "innocence," in the form of Rohm and her sister (Margaret Lee), finds itself powerless against the dictatorial rule of a government enslaving its population via religious persecution.[94]

The problem distributors had with the picture was that they couldn't define the genre in which they could sell it. Franco asserts that the confusion was because of the distributors themselves. Working with Harry Alan Towers meant for Franco working with a variety of coproducers. Explained Franco:

> The only problem was that he liked to do co-productions with everyone; this was going to be an Anglo/American/German/Spanish/French/Italian co-production. The producers in each country had their comments, especially when it came to what they wanted in the movie. Not

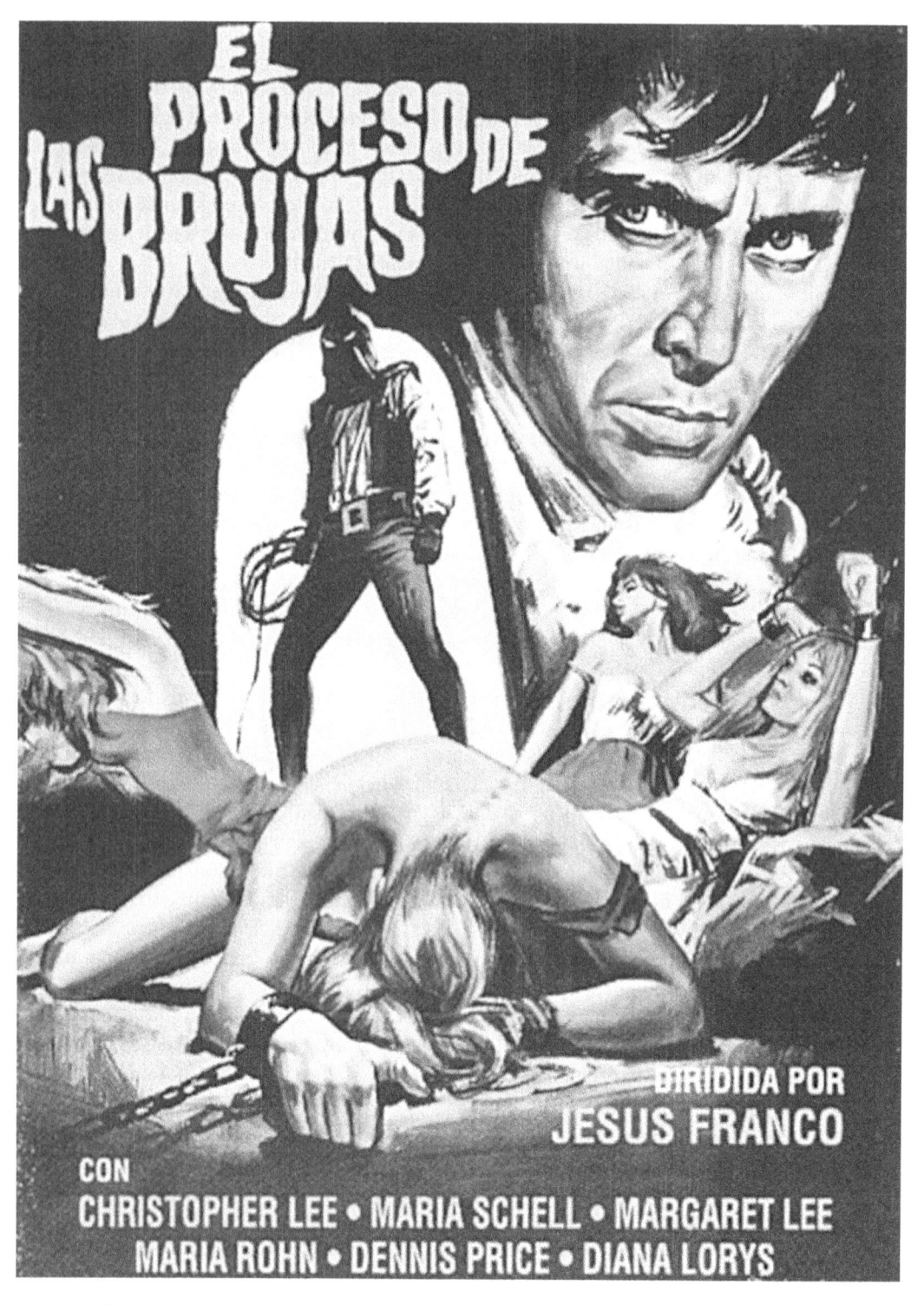

One of Franco's most ambitious films, *The Bloody Judge* (1970) suffered from the fact that distributors couldn't agree on how to market the film. The Spanish artwork focuses in the exploitation factor.

about the things that were not in the movie. There was a certain amount of confusion about the style of the film. At first it was supposed to be a horror film with a historical background. But it became more of a historical film with a background of the Inquisition. Then is became a film primarily about the Inquisition with a harsh negative take on the Inquisition, then an erotic film! And each coproducer wanted something different. These things happen![95]

By 1970, Franco had had enough of the interference and split amicably with Towers. For Franco, the bigger budgets were fine, but it was the loss of creative control that he found too stifling. Rebellious by nature due to his Spanish upbringing, Franco sought out to do his own projects in his own frame of mind.

The international film industry was a lot different in 1970 than it had been even five years earlier, allowing for new perspectives and filming styles. Audiences, no longer content with big-budget Hollywood-style films, were looking for the new thrills that offered nudity, sex and violence regardless of the budget, meaning that independent filmmakers like Jess Franco could now take their cameras out and begin shooting anything under the thread of a simple plotline and have that film shown and distributed in some part of the world.[96]

After leaving Harry Alan Towers, Franco embarked on a series of films starring his most famous muse, Soledad Miranda. It was his work with Miranda that defined the Franco film of the early '70s. With her long black hair, beautiful body, and face that could change from innocence to cruelty in a matter of seconds, she personified all that was female to Franco. Her performances in seven of his films are considered by many critics as his greatest achievements, and she is regarded as a cult heroine, in many respects as the Spanish Barbara Steele, meaning that her appearance in a film alone would make it worthy to view.[97]

Born in Seville, Spain, in July1943, Miranda came from a Spanish acting and singing family. With the acting bug in her soul she moved to Madrid at the age of 16 to pursue her goal. Small parts came her way, including a small cameo in the earlier Franco musical *La reina del Tabarín* (1960) as well as a few Spanish westerns, most notably *100 Rifles* (1968). Many times her appearances would be included solely as a way to show off her incredible figure and big Spanish brown eyes. Her only exploitation film previous to her work with Franco was the American/Spanish coproduction of *Pyro* (1963), where she played a carnival waif in love with a man bent on revenge.

With very few good roles going to her, Miranda decided to settle down and married a Portuguese race car driver. After having a child, she decided to go back to acting, trying out and receiving the role of Lucy in Franco's *El conde Drácula* (*Count Dracula*, 1969). Her performance startled many in the cast, including Christopher Lee, who thought the vampirism scenes with Miranda were some of the most effective of his career.[98] Franco took notice of Miranda's performance and began to formulate a series of films utilizing her, stating, "I told her before leaving [from shooting *El conde*] I probably would be making foreign films, meaning non–Spanish; would you like to play parts more or less good? 'Oh yes, Jess, yes!' So when the moment arrived, I asked for her and she came. I asked her about the problems with nudity and she said, "Woof ... my God, I have no problems.'"[99]

Franco must have been relieved that Miranda had no problems with nudity because her first starring role was full of it. Going back to the works of the Marquis de Sade, which had been fruitful for him and producer Harry Alan Towers, Franco decided to make *Eugenie de Sade* in the winter of 1970. Inspired by de Sade's *Eugénie de Franval* (1800) and cited as one of the most faithful adaptations of a de Sade novel, *Eugénie* is the story of a young girl (Miranda) who seduces her stepfather (Franco regular Paul Müller) and takes part in his sadistic, sociopathic games. As a duo, they travel across Europe killing prostitutes and hitchhikers.[100]

DE SADE 2000

CON
PAUL MULLER • SUSAN KORDA
ANDRES MONALE • FRANCO MANERA

REGIA DI
JESS FRANCO

MUSICHE DI
BRUNO NICOLAI

PRODUZIONE PRODIF FILM   EASTMANCOLOR

From the beginning of the film, in which Miranda seduces her stepfather by lying half naked in the bedroom, to the end where, confessing her sins, she dies in a hospital bed, *Eugénie* is vehicle in which Franco is allowed to let loose all his sexual fantasies. But within these fantasies is no joy and the film is a depressing affair. The kind of obsessive love shared between Miranda and Müller is completely cancerous, and Franco's bleak European winter landscapes only add to the cold, perverse atmosphere of the film.[101] Franco is beginning his long descent into some truly uncharted psychological areas with *Eugenie* that were masked by the high budgets and commercial restraints of the Towers films. Now without the rope of commerciality, Franco was free to explore any forbidden story he chose (including de Sade) and film it in whatever way he wanted. The lack of budget meant that these films had to be done on the cheap, meaning single camera shots (truly Franco's fascination with the zoom shot begins here), hiring actors who would perform for less money, and shorter films were the rule of the day.

In the spring of 1970, Franco embarked with Miranda and crew on *Vampyros Lesbos*, a lesbian vampire movie that personified early '70s filmmaking. Shot in Turkey and awash in long pan shots, slow plot development, sitar music and those zoom lens shots that would become the Franco standard, *Vampyros* is a mind-blowing, yet frustrating assault on the senses. Miranda plays Countess Nadine Carody, a lonely vampire bent on seducing businesswoman Linda Westinghouse (Ewa Strömberg). While this seems like a simple enough synopsis, the film defies such logic as Franco produces it in an almost dreamlike fashion with very little dialogue. Using many of the devices of previous films like the long strip club sequences (*Miss Muerte*, 1965; *Necronomicon*, 1967), the female protagonist (*99 Women*, 1968), etc., Franco paints a surrealistic cinematic portrait of Miranda while she runs around nude in a black cape and red scarf (symbolizing blood) with the rest of the actors, who walk around nearly catatonic.[102] This catatonia of the entire cast is emblematic of Franco's positing everything in his standard dream scenario. By this point in his career he totally invested in exploring different frames of consciousness, having already examined alternative frames of existence in *Venus, Eugenie,* and *Necronomicon*. In Franco's eye there seems to be no reality, only an alternative world where people play up their darkest and most lurid fantasies, which inevitably leads to freeing themselves from moral repression. The outcome of this independence is usually death, but Franco makes no moral judgment calls in the film, instead seeing the liberating of oneself from societal pressures as a good thing. The lesbianism aspect of the film is played up more than in any other previous Franco film, allowing him to express his views of freedom with regards to sexual preference. Eurocult films revel in lesbianism and Franco is one who has exploited this trend throughout his career. The reason for its popularity throughout all of Europe among filmmakers is twofold. First, these films are written and produced with men in mind and the idea of two (or more) women making love is safe male fantasy as long as neither woman becomes possessive and a threat to the male. Also, the male audience does not feel itself in "competition" with the female actor on the screen, foregoing any comparison they may have with them. Second, for filmmakers the choice is also aesthetic as women are easier to film in sexual situations because they need not register real excitement. Two women can perform a sexual scene on camera without feeling any emotional or physical stimulation, while the male sexual response is purely visual and cannot be faked.

Many times Eurocult posters had nothing to do with the actual film. *De Sade 2000*, actually *Eugenie de Sade* (1970), looks like a fun, hip movie instead of the darkly depressing fantasy it really is.

One of the most famous Eurocult films of the early '70s, *Vampyros Lesbos* (1970) was tailor made for its star, Soledad Miranda, and shot a few short months before her untimely death.

Next to the evocative images that Franco created in *Vampyros*, it is the music that is most memorable about the film. Forsaking the typical jazz of his previous films, Franco comes up with a psychedelic sound that is as strange and, it must be said, sometimes as annoying as the events on the screen. European audiences loved the style and ambiguity of the film (plus, with a name like *Vampyros Lesbos* you can't go wrong), making it a big success in Europe when it was released in late 1971. Something about the film has stayed resonant with audiences for the last 40 years. The soundtrack was innovative enough that 20 years after it was first released it became a Top 10 hit on the British alternative music charts.[103]

As in the days of the Harry Alan Towers films, Franco and crew would shoot one film right after the other. Less than a month after wrapping *Vampyros*, they began shooting the revenge picture *Sie tötete en Ekstase* (*She Killed in Ecstasy*, 1971) for German producer Artur Brauner. Again, following plots recycled from his previous films (*Miss Muerte*, 1965; *Venus in Furs*, 1969), Franco took the standard revenge picture to new surrealistic heights. As a woman seeking revenge for the suicide death of her doctor fiancé (Fred Williams), Miranda plays the film with an intensity not seen in her earlier work. She is feral, afraid and utterly destroyed when Williams is killed, yet turns cold and calculating when she begins to put in motion her revenge scenario. In the final scene, she torments her final victim, Dr. Houston (played by Franco) by tying him to a chair, then seducing and stabbing him viciously.[104] The fact that the doctor was played by Jess Franco himself helped blur the line for audiences between reality and fantasy and created the disturbing dichotomy between the two that is his trademark. The film is all Miranda's as she seduces and destroys all the men and women (yes, she seemingly has no troubles switching between the sexes) in the cast, using her steely brown eyes to capture the audience's sympathy.

With no time off, the crew started their next film for Brauner, the third in three months, called *El diablo que vino de Akasawa* (*The Devil Came from Akasawa*, 1970). With *Devil*, Franco took a different approach from that of previous films, cutting back on the horror and going for a more comic-book approach that he perfected in the late '60s. More James Bond than exploitation, the film follows the same pattern as a Matt Helm film with a little *Raiders of the Lost Ark* to balance it out.[105] *Akasawa* is mildly entertaining but its lack of button-pushing subject matter makes the film seem like a comedown from the previous *Lesbos* and *Sie Tötete*. With seven movies in a period of a year and a half, things seemed to be going well for the Franco/Miranda partnership. German producer Brauner was more than willing to sign Miranda up for a five-year extension and her career finally looked like it was going places. Unfortunately, it was not to be: one month after the completion of *Devil*, while traveling with her husband to sign the contract that Brauner had offered, Miranda was killed in an auto accident on August 18, 1970, at the age of 27.

For Franco the loss of Miranda was devastating. He was not only invested in Miranda in a professional sense but in a personal one as well, seeing himself as an uncle of sorts to this whimsical girl. Franco, years after Miranda's death, said, "She was a unique person, she had no knowledge of the stuff [sex and violence scenes] she was doing. She was transformed during the period in which she and I worked, because she loved the parts."[106] With no muse to work with, Franco threw himself into a series of uninspired projects in 1970 and '71 for the German producer Brauner. After completing a couple of action/adventure *Krimi*'s based on the novels of Edgar Wallace and the Dr. Mabuse film *Dr. M. shlägt zu* (1971), Franco and Brauner split, paving the way for his return to the horror/exploitation genre.

Producing for the first time, Franco filmed the surrealistic *Christina, princesse de l'éro-*

The monster motif of this poster belies the true essence of *Christina, princesse de l'érotisme* (*A Virgin Among the Living Dead*, 1971), a strange, non-linear film about death and the afterlife.

tisme (*A Virgin Among the Living Dead*) in 1971.[107] More French in nature than Spanish, the film stars French actress Christina von Blanc as a young woman returning to her ancestral home after the death of her father. Finding her extended family in an extremely dysfunctional state, von Blanc realizes that her family members are ghosts bent on taking her soul. While the narrative sounds distinctly linear and familiar to the Gothic genre, this is a Franco film and retreats into the dreamlike catatonia from the very beginning, filling the screen with surrealistic images that shock and disturb. A beautiful cousin (Britt Nichols) who ties up her blind housekeeper, stabbing her gently while licking the blood from near her pubic region, the "idiot" servant (played by Franco himself) who ambles around the castle sets chopping off the heads of chickens, or the uncle (Howard Vernon) who takes to slapping von Blanc whenever displeased, are among the cast of characters who inhabit this strange, unemotional world.[108] Interpreted by critics as perhaps a reaction to and examination of Soledad Miranda's early death, with its images of the dead cast trying to cross over to the netherworld but being stuck unemotionally in this world, the film begins to showcase a disturbing pattern in Franco's films where his joy as a filmmaker is masked by the joylessness of his productions. Depending on where an audience saw the film, it would be difficult to get Franco's true vision of it, as *Christina* is a prime example of the many Eurocult films that have been shown in a variety of different forms with a slew of names. For example, the French version eliminated the violence in favor of soft-core sex, while Britain edited down the sex and played up the violence. Finally, the film was completely butchered in 1980, at the height of the European zombie film craze, when sequences featuring underwater (?) zombies were added by French horror auteur Jean Rollin, and the film was distributed as a zombie picture.[109]

Franco's next films were among his most strange. Capitalizing on the popularity that fellow Spaniard Jacinto Molina (Paul Naschy) was experiencing by revitalizing traditional Universal monsters (the Wolf Man, Frankenstein, etc.), Franco decided, with French producer Robert de Nesle, to film a string of original stories involving these traditional monsters. These being Franco films, though, any resemblance to the traditional, classic narratives would be thrown out in favor of nudity, violence and surrealistic settings. The films, *Drácula contra Frankenstein* (*Dracula, Prisoner of Frankenstein*, 1972), *La maldición de Frankenstein* (*The Erotic Rites of Frankenstein*, 1972) and *La Fille de Dracula* (1972), though certainly high on originality, were produced with some of the smallest budgets Franco had worked with, which consequently showed on screen. Because of these budgetary constraints Franco is forced to rely on his patented "zoom" camera effect and cheap makeup effects to relay his modern '70s screenplays. This fly-by-night style played havoc with the production crew, and actors had to deal with Franco's wacky style of writing scripts, which he would often do the night before a scene was to be shot, meaning the actors had very little idea how the stories were going to progress. This is probably the reason that Franco developed a small group of dedicated actors (e.g., Howard Vernon, Dennis Price, Lina Romay) who understood how he worked and actually thrived in the dynamic environment. In *Drácula contra Frankenstein* (1972), scripting doesn't matter as the first half hour is almost without dialogue, focusing on an atmosphere that, quite frankly, looks cheap and grainy.[110] While offputting for traditional audiences who wanted to see something akin to Universal's *House of Frankenstein* (1944) or *House of Dracula* (1945), Franco loved the baroque nature of the film. "As a matter of fact," related Franco in a 1991 interview, "the first half hour of *Drácula contra Frankenstein*, until the dialogues begin, is one the parts of my filmography that I like the most."[111] Franco may have had optimistic hindsight when it comes to the film, since it's hard to imagine that audiences understood what he was trying to accomplish. The film is a mess, making no comprehensive sense. Though it was filmed with no budget, it has a sense of visual style. Unfortunately, it's the only thing to recommend about the movie. Actor Dennis Price, in the twilight of his career, not only seems inebriated throughout but also acts as if it were a high school play. The final showdown between the monsters, including a werewolf, is sadly pedestrian.[112]

With its metallic green, horny Frankenstein monster, *La maldición de Frankenstein* (1972) is even stranger than *Dracula (Contra Frankenstein)*. Containing characters like the "birdlady" (Anne Libert), a blind, half-naked woman who screeches like a crow, an evil sorcerer (Howard Vernon), and the usual mad scientist (Dennis Price), *Maldición* threw in all elements of the genre and came out with a psychedelic hodgepodge that mirrors the sanity of a bad comic book plot. With heavy doses of nudity and scantily clad women, the exploitation factor of the film is the only reason to view it.[113]

Utilizing the same cast, musical score and sets as the previous films, *La Fille de Dracula* (1972) fared little better. As a modern updating of Joseph Sheridan Le Fanu's classic lesbian vampire novel *Carmilla* (1872), which served as fodder for a variety of exploitation films in the '60s and '70s throughout Europe, the film contained all of the cheap machinations that plagued Franco's previous outings with De Nesle. Too much time is spent watching the beautiful (you can't say that Franco doesn't have good taste in his choice of leading ladies) Britt Nichols wandering aimlessly around her inherited castle looking wide-eyed in the presence of Dracula (Howard Vernon). The sex includes the typical soft-core heterosexual and lesbian couplings one now expects from his films, though his hold on the linear began to spin out of control as each successive movie became more far-out. Reality held very little place in the story as the films became one outlandish scene of hedonism after another.

As the '70s progressed, Franco alternated between a variety of exploitation subgenres. After his second women-in-prison movie *Los amantes de la isla del diablo* (*Devil's Island Lovers*, 1972), another Dr. Orloff movie, *Los ojos siniestros del doctor Orloff* (*The Sinister Eyes of Dr. Orloff*, 1972), and a semi-sequel to his earlier *The Bloody Judge* (1970), *Les démons* (1973), Franco's material became solely focused on sexuality. The legalization of pornography in Denmark and Sweden in the late '60s as well as the popularization of hard-core pornography in America by such films as *Mona* (1970), *Deep Throat* (1972) and *Behind the Green Door* (1972) offered exploitation filmmakers like Franco an opportunity to take sexuality to its cinematic limits not previously seen in their films.[114] For Franco it allowed him the opportunity to crank out more scripts, as sex scenes serve to "pad" a movie's running time, meaning screenwriters don't have to write as many scenes per movie if they include long lovemaking sessions. It is this era of anything-goes filmmaking that gave rise to the Franco "genital" zoom. From 1972 onward the Franco filmography showcases a fascination with the female sex. Close-ups and zooms of female genitalia constitute a large portion of screen time. Franco admitted his fascination, calling the area "the first place my eye looks."[115]

In order for Franco to fully exploit this obsession with female genitalia, he had to find an actress who would be willing to give herself completely to the Spanish director. He found her in actress Lina Romay. Born Rosa Maria Almirall in Barcelona in 1954, Romay filled the gap in Franco's professional career left by the early death of Soledad Miranda. Similar to Miranda in looks (dark eyes and black hair in keeping with traditional Spanish looks), Romay was far more open about her sexuality than Miranda. This allowed Franco to exploit her willingly and sometimes quite shockingly. In her first starring role, *Les Avaleuses* (*The*

The beautiful Britt Nichols stars in Jess Franco's strange *La Fille de Dracula* (1972).

Female Vampire, 1973) the 18-year-old was cast as the Countess Irina, a vampire who roams around Europe searching for fresh blood. Mute and habitually undressed, save for black cape, she finds nourishment not in the necks of her victims but via the sex organs: she literally blows them to death. Consequently, after she fellates men and performs cunnilingus on women (of course she's bisexual), they die of both pleasure and fluid loss. Only after this draining is Irina then able to achieve her own orgasm via some disturbing necrophilia.[116]

Though it was certainly pornographic by most standards, Franco believed the film more erotic than pornographic.[117] Franco related his thoughts about in-your-face sexuality: "I prefer what a story asks you for, what the scene asks you for. Look at the Japanese film by Oshima [*In the Realm of the Senses*, 1976], for instance, there are lots of hardcore shots, but nobody would say 'Oh, it's a porno film!' No. It's a very important story. I felt in *The Black Countess*[118] I did the same thing. There was a need to show it, like you must show how Dracula sucks the blood, you *need* to show how this Countess sucks the semen."[119] Actress Romay had no problems with showing how that particular procedure was done. Her willingness and belief in Franco catapulted her into becoming Franco's muse throughout the rest of his career: she appeared in over 100 movies for the Spanish director and became his devoted wife in the process. During the '70s she'd been asked to perform every type of possible exploitation throughout her career, from light comedy to hard-core pornography with both men and women. She was Franco's most durable asset who seemed to revel in an exploitative world; as she herself has said in interviews, "If I liked it or was comfortable with it, I did it."[120] A good example of Romay's work with the bizarre fascination with female sexuality can be found in 1973 film *Lorna l'exorciste* (*Lorna*, 1974), in which Romay plays a young Linda Mariel who's about to turn 18. Unfortunately for Linda, her father made a pact with Lorna (aka the Devil) for her soul when she was a child, and Lorna's come to collect. Franco opens the film with an extended lesbian sex scene that threatens to take up the whole first half (which must have saved Franco a fortune in screenwriters), followed by the most bizarre hour and 15 minutes ever committed to film, as Lorna and Linda play out their Faustian pact amid dildo worship, blood sharing, and in the most memorable scene of all, watching black spiders (actually crabs ... which make it more ironic) come crawling out of Romay's mother's (Jacqueline Parent) vagina. The movie is a perverse ode to female genitalia: Franco makes sure to concentrate his camera almost completely on that body part, exposing it as both sensual and powerful (Romay), or as disgusting and decaying (Parent).

Not all of Franco's films in the '70s were completely without artistic merit. *Le Journal intime d'une nymphomane* (*Sinner*, 1973) was seen by some critics as a film that "lies somewhere between trash and social commentary."[121] Exploiting the open sexuality of the '70s and the alienation such behavior caused, *Le Journal* was awash in heavy metal music, outlandish retro clothes and copious amounts of nudity, a factor for which Franco could employ his genital zoom shot. But behind the overtly pornographic film was a stinging indictment of the '70s and the loss of the innocence that was present in earlier decades. The film's predominantly lesbian plot device was used consistently throughout the rest of the decade, while films like *Tendre et perverse Emmanuelle* (*Tender and Perverse Emanuelle*, 1973), *Célestine, bonne à tout faire,* (1974) and *Die Liebesbriefe einer Portugiesischen Nonne* (*Love Letters from a Portuguese Nun*, 1976) all looked at a corruptive sexuality with an eye for the decade it was posited in.

The cinematic and social environment of the mid-to-late '70s allowed Franco to delve into all areas of exploitation. With the popularity and acceptance of hard-core pornography,

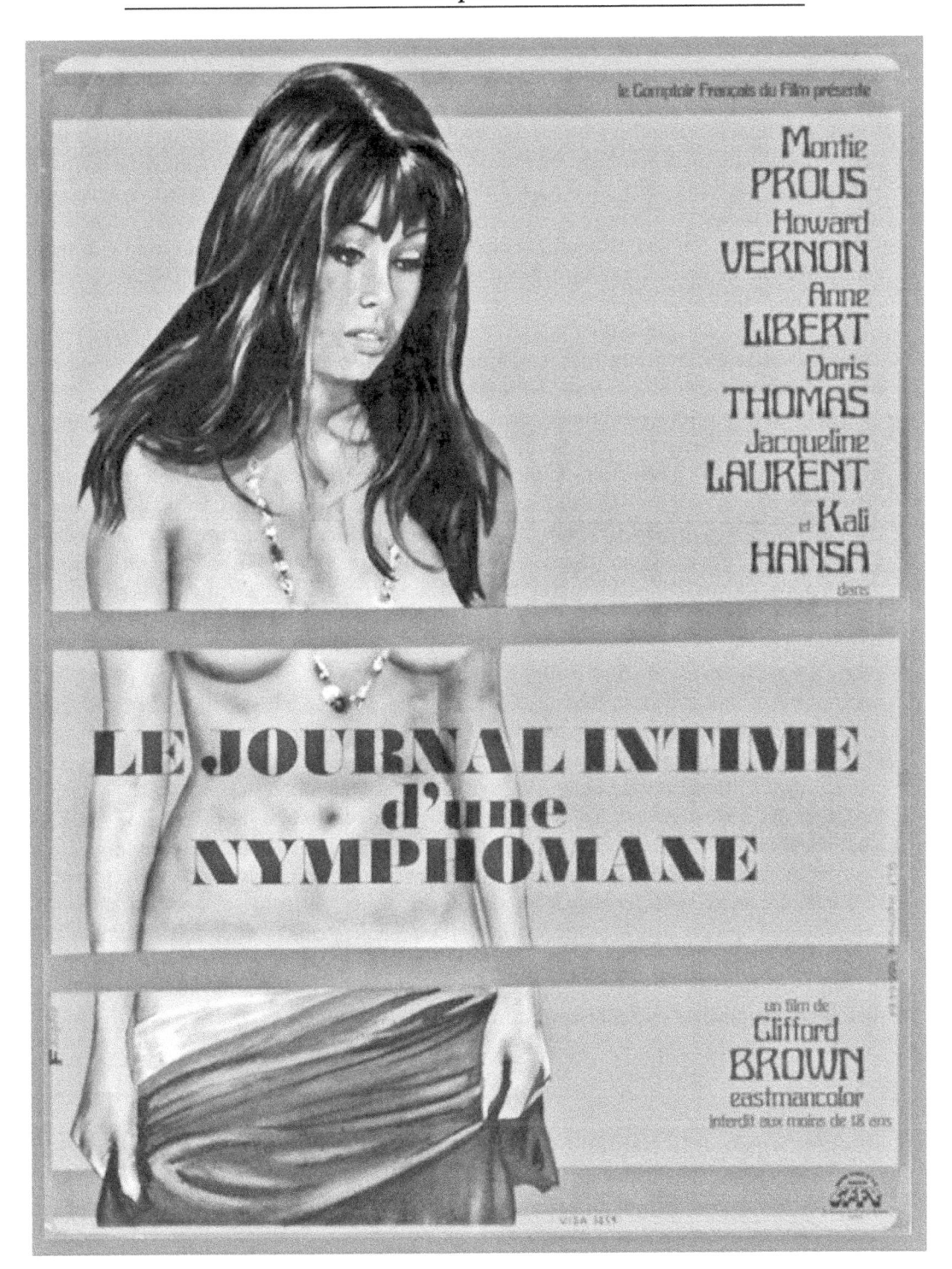

Jess Franco turned out an extraordinary number of films throughout his career in a variety of different genres, including both hard- and soft-core pornography.

he was able to make a successful jump into that realm. The complete abandonment of censorship meant that Franco could now completely indulge in his passions and film degraded things without fear of retribution. Most of this took the form of putting his future girlfriend/wife Romay through a potpourri of exploitive situations, such as making a prisoner perform analingus on her after she uses the toilet in *Greta, the Mad Butcher* (*Ilsa, the Wicked Warden*, 1977) or being whipped mercilessly by a sexually frustrated priest (played by Franco) in *Exorcism* (1974).

Franco spent the rest of the '70s cranking out a huge number of films that run the gamut of every exploitation subgenre available, including nunsploitation (*Die liebesbriefe einer portugiesischen Nonne*, 1976), de Sade remakes (*Juliette*, 1970), standard horror films (*Jack the Ripper — Der Dirnenmörder von London*, 1976), women in prison films (*Frauen für Zellenblock 9*, 1977), and cannibal films (*Mondo Cannibale*, 1979), as well as a slew of hard- and soft-core features, all produced with frightening speed.

Unfortunately, ultra-low budgets, combined with very little participation from major production companies, plus audience indifference or in some cases shock, led to the decline in quality of Franco's productions to the point where many of these films became no better than home movies. For the Spanish Franco, though, none of it mattered. Brought up in an atmosphere of censorship and persecution, he reveled in the idea of creating an art form on a moment's notice without regard to confinement. He continued to produce the movies that he wanted to make throughout the '80s, '90s and into the new millennium where scholars and film critics have begun to re-examine his filmography and his genius. Jess himself is bemused by this re-examination, stating, "After being set aside and scoffed at for so many years, what can I say? ... I find it funny. And, naturally, that pleases me. Even though it reminds me of that glorious phrase by Oteiza: 'After I spent my whole life going through one failure to the next, now these people come along to pay homage to me?!'"[122]

The biggest homage to Franco (and, it must be admitted, to all exploitation filmmakers) was paid by the Spanish Academy of Art and Cinematographic Sciences in 2009 when they bestowed a Goya Award, Spain's highest artistic honor, to him for his lifetime of cinematic dedication. It is the height of irony that the country Franco felt compelled to leave in order to give a free voice to his vision would honor him with such a prestigious award. Commenting on his work with such stars as Orson Welles, Klaus Kinski and Christopher Lee (though I suspect they kept the vagina-spilling-spiders conversation to a minimum), the Spanish film industry rightly bestowed the Goya on a man who wasn't afraid to film the most provocative, entertaining, and scandalous fantasies he had amid an environment that did not appreciate or understand him.

Filmography

Blood of Fu Manchu, aka *Kiss and Kill* (GB). Prod. Harry Alan Towers. Dir. Jesus Franco. Spain/U.S., 1968. Blue Underground, 94 min. DVD. Starring: Christopher Lee, Tsai Chin, Maria Rohm and Richard Greene.

Castle of Fu Manchu. Prod. Harry Alan Towers. Dir. Jesus Franco. Spain/U.S., 1969, Blue Underground, 94 min. DVD. Starring: Christopher Lee, Tsai Chin, Rosalba Neri and Richard Greene.
    Blood and *Castle of Fu Manchu* are an interesting set of films in the Jess Franco canon. One (*Cas-*

Opposite: Capitalizing on the success of the Nazisploitation classic ***Ilsa, She Wolf of the SS*** (1977), Franco's ***Greta, la donna bestia*** (1978) looks to repeat the same formula.

ELITE-FILM presenta

DYANNE THORNE

(Famosa come "ILSA")

in

GRETA
LA DONNA BESTIA

ERIC FALK - TANYA BUSSELIER - LINA ROMAY — regia di JESS FRANCO · EASTMANCOLOR

tle) is more in the action/adventure family (!) vein and very different from the types of films Franco produced for the rest of his career, while the other (*Blood*) represents something that is a lot more akin to his exploitative frame of mind. Can you guess which one I liked better? *Blood* was the second to last film based on Sax Rohmer's culturally suspect character Fu Manchu (and no, 1980's *The Fiendish Plot of Dr. Fu Manchu* doesn't count), and by this time the series was pretty stale. Enter Jess Franco, who decides to throw in some nudity and sex, along with some graphic torture to try to spice things up. Fu Manchu (Lee), with the help of his evil daughter Lin Tang (Chin), kidnaps 10 women and trains them to assassinate people with their kiss via some very interesting snake venom. Fu Manchu's nemesis Nayland Smith (Greene) normally would be thwarting the plot, but he's been poisoned by our bevy of beautiful kissers, and it's up to his sidekick Dr. Petrie (Howard Marion Crawford) to find Fu Manchu's South American hideaway (don't ask me why he's there; obviously budget reasons) and put an end to his diabolical plot. Much maligned by Fu Manchu fans, the film is terrible, with plot holes big enough to drive a truck through, as well as some of the worst ethnic stereotypes of both Asians and Mexicans in film. But it's done in such an obvious way you can't help but enjoy yourself.

The Bloody Judge, aka *Night of the Blood Monster* (INT). Prod. Harry Alan Towers. Dir. Jesus Franco. Ger/Spain, 1970. Blue Underground, 104 min. DVD. Starring: Christopher Lee, Maria Rohm, Margaret Lee, Maria Schell and Leo Glenn.

Coming at the end of the Towers partnership, *The Bloody Judge* is one of the most sumptuous films in the Franco canon. It's also a profound disappointment. With a fantastic cast and lurid subject matter, one would expect an instant classic as Franco mines the terrors laid out by both Reeves's *Witchfinder General* (1968) and Adrian Hoven's *Mark of the Devil* (1968), but sadly comes up way short. Christopher Lee plays the historic Judge Jeffries, one of the most sadistic men of the British Empire, who protected King James II by conducting witch hunts and promoting terror throughout the land. Maria Rohm (the producer's wife) is on hand to tempt Lee and attempt to put an end to the tyranny. Will she succeed or will she meet Franco regular Howard Vernon, who plays the torturer Jack Ketch, and be forced to submit to some naked whipping? What do you think? Overlong and with a bunch of star cameos that add nothing to the script, *The Bloody Judge* is a bloody mess. It's ironic that Christopher Lee is especially fond of this film and his performance.

Count Dracula, aka *El conde Drácula* (SP). Prod. Harry Alan Towers. Dir. Jesus Franco. Spain/Germany/France, 1970. Dark Sky Films, 94 min. DVD. Starring: Christopher Lee, Herbert Lom, Maria Rohm, Soledad Miranda and Klaus Kinski.

This could have been so good! With Christopher Lee on board and excited (for once) to play the Count, Klaus Kinski to play the madman Renfield, the beautiful Soledad Miranda to play Lucy and Jess Franco directing, what could go wrong? It's horrible, and worse, it's boring. After the big-budget excesses of *Justine* (1968) and *The Bloody Judge* (1969), you would think that Towers would invest some money in what could have been an international smash, but it was not to be. Perhaps Franco and Towers were just exhausted by their collaboration of producing nine (!) films in a two-and-a-half-year period to give this the attention that it deserved, but the final outcome is cheap, shoddy and strangely lacking in any emotional base. Even as exploitation it's a failure with an absence of very much blood or sex. You know the story: Jonathan Harker goes on a business trip to Transylvania to help out one Count Dracula, who wants to move to England to update his "winery." Badness ensues, and Dracula gets younger looking as the ladies of England start looking pretty pale. Franco plays around with a bit of the story and that's okay, but his filming techniques here are strangely off kilter, which is not surprising, as in less than a year after filming he would begin the most psychedelic stage of his career. Performance-wise the film runs the gamut from great (Miranda, making a haunting Lucy), to good (Rohm, always engaging) to not-so-good (Lom, who's good in the first half but strangely absent for most of the second).

Devil Came from Akasava, aka *Der Teufel kam aus Akasava* (GER). Prod. Karl Heinz-Mannchen. Dir. Jesus Franco. Spain/Germany, 1970. Image Entertainment, 84 min. DVD. Starring: Fred Williams, Soledad Miranda, Howard Vernon and Ewa Strömberg.

Franco goes back and mines one of his favorite themes, the spy genre, in this cheap but psychedelic little gem. Don't expect James Bond–esque filmmaking here, just a wacky story of the discovery and theft of a mineral (called here the Philosopher's Stone; makes you wonder if J.K. Rowling is a Eurocult fan) that can turn ordinary metals into gold and people into mindless zombies. Enter sexy agent Jane Morgan (Miranda) and Scotland Yard detective Rex Forrester (Williams), who go to the fictional Akasava to get the stone back amid a fun, funky sitar soundtrack. There may be those who wonder where the action is in the movie, but if the sight of Soledad Miranda with a gun and working as an exotic dancer leaves you cold, then the movie wasn't for you in the first place.

Devil's Island Lovers, aka *Quartier de femmes* (FR), *Los amantes de la isla del diablo* (SP). Prod. Arturio Marcos. Dir. Jesus Franco. Spain/France, 1974. Image Entertainment, 80 min. DVD. Starring: Dennis Price, Geneviève Robert, Andrés Resino and Rosa Palomar.

Jess Franco goes back to prison in a film that's nowhere near as interesting as his successful, big-budgeted *99 Women* (1969), but perhaps is just as important as it shows the lingering effects that the Gen. Franco regime had on the filmmaker. Beatriz (Robert) has a problem. She's the sole heir to a family fortune and in love with a rebellious young man (Resino) with known anti-government ties. That's not her problem, though. Her ex-brother-in-law Colonel Mendoza wants the cash, so he frames Beatriz and her beau for murder and throws them into a dirty prison where they await a death sentence. *That's* her problem, and the two don't help matters by trying to escape. Lots of flashbacks accentuate a film that is rather dull in its original form. If you want some extra spice, many of the DVDs have extra footage that add a lot more spice in the form of longer lesbian sex scenes, as well as a much more satisfying ending.

Diabolical Dr. Z, aka *Miss Muerte* (SP), *Le Diabolique docteur* (FR). Prod. and Dir. Jesus Franco. Spain, 1965. Mondo Macabro, 84 min. DVD. Starring: Estalla Blain, Howard Vernon, Guy Mairesse, Mabel Karr and Antonio Jiménez Escribano.

A wonderful film full of wackiness, sex and robots, this is among Jess Franco's very best. A loosely based sequel to the previous Dr. Orlof films, *Dr. Z* involves Dr. Zimmer, who is carrying on the work done by Dr. Orlof and discovers the part of the brain that can control good and evil. Berated by other medical professionals in public, the good doctor dies, leaving his secrets to his dastardly daughter Irma (Karr). She proceeds to control a local exotic dancer named Miss Muerte and begins laying the spider webs of her revenge against those who wronged her father. Those would be literal spider webs, as Miss Muerte (Blain, who's excellent) has a penchant for dancing on her back over a painting of a web, as well as being equipped with some rather long fingernails that transmit poison. With obvious nods to James Bond as well as the German Krimi, Franco concocts a story that is sexy, interesting and fun. With a great jazz soundtrack contributing, *Dr. Z* represents the final chapter of Franco's work within the confines of the Spanish film industry. He would soon join Adrian Hoven for some internationally successful films like *Succubus* (1968) that were increasingly non-linear and psychedelic. For those who only know Franco's work by *Vampyros Lesbos* (1970), *The Diabolical Dr. Z* should erase any doubt that the man could make some very well-crafted movies you don't have to be stoned to enjoy.

Dr. Orlof's Monster, aka *El secreto de Dr. Orlof* (SP), *Les Maistresses de Docteur Jekyll* (FR). Prod. Marious Leseur. Dir. Jesus Franco. Spain/Austria/France, 1964. Image Entertainment, 85 min. DVD. Starring: Hugo Blanco, Agnès Spaak, Perla Cristal and Marcelo Arroita-Jáuregui.

The sequel to *The Awful Dr. Orlof* is an interesting, delightfully sleazy, yet disjointed affair whose problems probably have more to do with the budget and the film environment in Spain than with anything Jess Franco might have done. Working with a lot of adult themes including adultery, *Monster* concerns young student Melissa (Spaak) who visits her uncle's castle (he's named Dr. Jekyll in the French version) for the Christmas holidays. Things aren't so merry around the house as it seems Uncle Conrad killed Melissa's father while he was having an affair with his wife and turned him into a robot zombie. The wife doesn't have it so good either as she is forced to live like a slave with the vengeful doctor. It's just your typical Eurocult Christmas celebration when young Melissa finds out that dad is still around! If you're wondering where Dr. Orlof is in this, he's not! The good doctor doesn't appear at all. Good exploitation relies on the power to get you into the theaters, and a little untrue press agentry and marketing can be forgiven if the movie is sleazy enough. But don't worry: Franco piles on the sexual tension with a bevy of scantily clad dancers who strip down often. Many of the versions today contain a surprising amount of nudity for the time. If you're not into Franco's later psychedelic films, this might make for fun viewing.

Dracula, Prisoner of Frankenstein, aka *Drácula contra Frankenstein* (SP). Prod. Arturio Marcos. Dir. Jesus Franco. Spain/Germany, 1972. Image Entertainment, 82 min. DVD. Starring: Dennis Price, Howard Vernon, Anne Libert and Alberto Dalbés.

The Erotic Rites of Frankenstein (INT). *Rites of Frankenstein*, aka *La maldición de Frankenstein* (France), Prod. Robert de Nesle. Dir. Jesus Franco. Spain/France, 1972. Image Entertainment, 85 min. DVD. Starring: Alberto Dalbés, Dennis Price, Howard Vernon and Anne Libert.

Who needs the legalization of marijuana when we've got Jess Franco? For the cost of a DVD rental (good luck finding one to rent; you're better off buying it), you can get the same effects and without the messy legal entanglements. Both these films are absolutely off-the-wall lunacy, showcasing that Franco was really the king the WTF film! Utilizing the same cast and filming both at the same time, Franco gives us two films that are amazing in their horribleness. *Dracula, Prisoner of Frankenstein* defies description but I'll give it a go. Frankenstein (Price, suffering from chronic alcoholism) wants to create a super army and rule the world. He's got his monster (laughably like a high school version of Boris Karloff's creature), Dracula (Vernon, who hasn't a single line of dialogue), a couple of vampire girls (don't get too excited; there's no nudity in the movie), and even a werewolf! Sounds exciting, eh? It's not, but it is interesting. Dialogue is at a minimum — in fact, no one speaks until well after 15 minutes into the movie — and the effects of the film are in the so-bad-it's funny category. Even the kids will hate this one.

Dennis Price returns briefly as Frankenstein again in the zanier *Rites of Frankenstein*. This time out he's bumped off early by a bird-lady vampire (I'm really not making this up; she has clawed hands) who steals Frankenstein's monster with the help of evil ghost Vernon (who was probably glad that he didn't have to play Dracula again). They proceed to build a wife for the monster so they can begin to make a race of super humans. Interestingly, the Frankenstein monster is gold-colored in this one, looking like Shirley Eaton with a flattop! It's just bad. Both of these films work in direct opposition to fellow countryman Jacinto Molina's (Paul Naschy) successful series of *Hombre Lobo* movies that were showcases for his affection of the old Universal horror films. Franco obviously couldn't care less and goes out of his way to dismantle everything fans held sacred to the original series. It would be interesting to see how Franco would have filmed these had the budgets been there to accommodate some better effects. Would they be more traditional or would his penchant for turning everything upside down win out? My guess would be the second option.

Exorcism; aka *L'Éventreur de Notre Dame* (FR), *Demoniac* (U.S.), *The Sadist of Notre Dame* (INT). Prod. Marius Lesquier & Daniel Lesquier. Dir. Jesus Franco. France, 1974. Synapse Films, 94 min. DVD. Starring: Jess Franco, Lina Romay, Catherine Lafferière and Nadine Pascal.

Jess Franco takes on the devil-possession subgenre? Sorry, no. Franco was never that much of a fan of flying pea soup. Actually, this is a pretty sick ticket in which Franco goes after the church and '70s society will both guns ablaze. Franco himself plays defrocked priest Mathis Vogel, just out of the mental hospital, who spends his time sending S&M stories involving murder to a porno magazine. He becomes increasingly unbalanced and begins to kill "bad" girls throughout Paris. When he finds out his co-worker Anna (Romay) is into performing in fake S&M shows, he sees it as an opportunity to cleanse her soul and rid the world of these "unclean" things. *Exorcism* is one of Franco's most mature films of the '70s. As with all Franco films of the era, you have to get past all the gratuitous nudity and sex as well as the long passages without dialogue to discern what he's trying to do (which is why those uninitiated to Franco's style should *never* watch his '70s films first). There's a lot of sin to get through here, as we are treated to Ms. Romay being tied up naked for long stretches and tortured, extended lesbian trysts, and an orgy scene that borders on hardcore, as well as some very explicit guttings of our defrocked priest's victims. Many versions of this film exist, including some with hard-core inserts. Beware: this is not a feel-good movie and you will definitely feel like you need a bath when it's over.

Eugenie, the Story of Her Journey into Perversion, aka *Eugenie* (SP). Prod. Harry Alan Towers. Dir. Jesus Franco. Spain/U.S., 1969, Blue Underground, 87 min. DVD. Starring: Marie Liljedahl, Maria Rohm, Paul Muller, Jack Taylor and Christopher Lee.

My choice for Jess Franco's best film! With a high budget, great cast and an interesting, kinky adult story that still allows his genius to shine through, *Eugenie* is great example of what could have been a more traditional filmmaking path for Franco. Eugenie (Swedish actress Liljedahl) is a typical 17ish-year-old girl. Her father (Müller) is often away, her mother doesn't understand her, and she is looking for some fun teenage adventure. She's developed a friendship with the older, sexy and exciting Madame de St. Ange (Rohm), who offers to take her to her island home. Little does Eugenie know that her father has already given his permission as payment for his getting to sleep with the beautiful Rohm. So off she goes to the island home inhabited by Rohm, her brother Mirvel (Taylor) and a few mute servants. Sounds harmless enough, right? Wrong, for soon enough, the drugs start to flow, the threesomes start up, and Christopher Lee arrives to monitor Eugenie's "journey into perversion." Dreamy and nightmarish at the same time, *Eugenie* starts out like those wonderful European soft-core films from likes of directors like Radley Metzger, but it soon degenerates into a wild S&M fantasy where the lines between reality and fiction are blurred. Liljedahl makes a perfect heroine as her purity is put up against the depravity of Rohm and Taylor with predictable results. Rohm puts in her strongest performance yet as someone who appears so sweet yet is so evil. The film is everything one expects from a treatment of the Marquis de Sade's work, in that it's sexy, unnerving and occasionally quite provocative. A definite must-see!

Eugenie de Sade, aka *Eugénie* (SP), *Eugenie Sex Happening* (INT). Prod. Karl Heinz Mannchen. Dir. Jesus Franco. Spain/Germany/France, 1970. Wildeast Video, 86 min. DVD. Starring: Soledad Miranda, Paul Müller, Alberto Dalbés and Jess Franco.

A year after directing *Eugenie, the Story of Her Journey into Perversion* (1969), Franco continues to explore some of the same themes with this. Though still based on the works of de Sade, this film has nothing to do with the previous one and is a much more nihilistic portrayal of family values gone awry. Set in winter, this is a terribly depressing film that has Eugenie (Soledad Miranda) trying like hell to seduce her father (Müller), a frustrated writer (later we find out that he's actually her stepfather, so it's okay, I guess). Anyway, she finally gets her dad and the two of them embark on a killing spree that involves finding some loose women in nightclubs, having sex with them and then killing them. Life is good for our little family until Eugenie falls for an artist, which doesn't make Dad too happy. Meanwhile, the local police, led by Franco himself, try to solve the murder problem that seems to be proliferating around Europe. *Eugenie de Sade* is not an enjoyable film; in many ways it's the ugliest of all those that starred Miranda — ugly in both narrative and in environment as the bleak winter landscapes contribute to the complete despondency of the characters. Müller, who was obviously running for Father of the Year after selling the other *Eugenie* (1969) down the river for a good time with Maria Rohm, and here bedding his daughter and giving her an education on the art of carnage, is appropriately pervy. Feel like being depressed? *Eugenie de Sade* will have you running for the Zoloft before the movie is through.

Female Vampire, aka *Les Avaleuses* (FR), *Bare Breasted Countess* (INT), *Erotikill* (GER). Prod. and Dir. Jesus Franco. France/Belgium, 1973. Image Entertainment, 101 min. DVD. Starring: Lina Romay, Jack Taylor, Alice Arno and Jess Franco.

Female Vampire, in any of its incarnations (and there are a lot), is one of Franco's most talked about and viewed films. It's also one of his most hilarious! Here's the plot: Naked vampire (well, she does wear a cape) Countess Irina (Romay) sucks the blood out of men and women via oral sex. After she's done she has sex with the bodies. Her life is pretty bad, though she does get to drive in a cool car that has a flying bat for a hood ornament, and she has an odd-looking mute male butler she likes to masturbate in front of. Some weird guy (Taylor) is also looking for her in order to, I don't know, enjoy the lifestyle that being undead brings. The film is absolutely impossible to take seriously as the production values are the bare minimum. If *Vampyros Lesbos* (1970) alienated you, this is will have you hitting the stop button after 4.5 minutes. The opening scene should alert viewers for the fun that they are in for. We are treated to a view of Romay walking down a mist-covered road, fully naked except for the black cape, the soundtrack playing some variation of "I'm Always Chasing Rainbows." She stops. Franco's camera eyes her up and down with the requisite close-up of her genitalia. She begins to walk alluringly towards the camera again — slowly, slowly — until she hits her head on it and caroms off it! Hysterical stuff!

The Girl from Rio, aka *The Seven Secrets of Sumuru* (GER). Prod. Harry Alan Towers. Dir. Jesus Franco. Spain/U.S., 1968 Blue Underground, 98 min. DVD. Starring: Shirley Eaton, Richard Wyler, George Sanders and Maria Rohm.

If Jess Franco ever had the opportunity and free rein to direct a James Bond movie, I'm guessing it would turn out something like *The Girl from Rio*. One of the larger-budget films he worked on, *Rio* tries hard to be in the vein of Bava's *Diabolik* (1967), but it just ends up being another Jess Franco funfest. The beautiful but evil Sumitra (or Sumuru, take your pick), played by *Goldfinger* beauty Shirley Eaton, is intent on taking over the world with her henchwomen, beautiful soldiers from the lovely land of Femina. Enter Jeff Sutton (Wyler) an American racketeer who makes off with $10 million of other people's money and heads to Brazil, much to the delight of local crime lord (a wryer-than-usual George Sanders) and Sumitra, who all want the money. Hooking up with beautician (yeah, right) Maria Rohm, Jeff is soon taken to Sumitra's lair, which is like Candy Land for adults. With touches of nudity and a look that resembles early-'70s soft-porn, the film is kind of fun, meaning there are worse ways and worse films to spend a Friday night with.

Ilsa, the Wicked Warden, aka *Greta, the Mad Butcher* (INT), *Wanda, the Wicked Warden* (U.S.), *Greta, Haus ohne Männer* (GER). Prod. Erwin C. Dietrich. Dir. Jesus Franco. Spain/Switzerland, 1977. Anchor Bay Entertainment, 94 min. DVD. Starring: Dyanne Thorne, Tania Busselier, Eric Falk and Lina Romay.

One of the most infamous series in exploitation film history gets a crack from Jess Franco! Well, sort of. Not originally conceived as an official Ilsa film, *The Wicked Warden* benefited from the fact that it was filmed with no natural sound. Therefore distributors could change the name of any character in the dubbing process. This film starred Ilsa herself, Dyanne Thorne, who plays a warden in a prison who likes to stick pins into people, so I'm sure they thought, "What the hell, let's just call her Ilsa, the public won't mind!" I'm not sure the public cared, either, but I can bet they were disgusted. Ilsa was the series in which Thorne played an overly endowed, sadistic (putting it mildly) Nazi soldier who enjoyed torturing pretty much everyone. Here she plays a warden in a prison that Abby Phillips (Busselier) has infiltrated to find out what happened to her sister. Big mistake, as the prison is full of lesbians and nymphomaniacs out to exploit Abby, the worst being No. 10 (Romay), who is the warden's lover as well as her human pincushion (you'll see). The lovely warden enjoys filming the torture of the women and selling the footage on the porno market. Soon Abby finds her plan to infiltrate the prison may have been a mistake from which she cannot escape. Graphic, without any redeeming social value, completely exploitative, this is the kind of rough stuff that you expect from late-'70s Franco. If you ever wanted to watch a film where a prisoner is forced to perform analingus on a woman after she used the toilet, this is your film! You've been warned.

Justine, aka *Marquis de Sade: Justine* (IT). Prod. Harry Alan Towers. Dir. Jesus Franco. Spain/U.S., 1969. Blue Underground, 124 min. DVD. Starring: Romina Power, Maria Rohm, Jack Palance, Akim Tamiroff, Mercedes McCambridge and Klaus Kinski.

Probably Jess Franco's most commercial film and one of his least successful. Looking to exploit the changing acceptance of sexual content on the screen, Franco and producer Harry Alan Towers try to resurrect the writings of de Sade, with mixed results. The film opens in a jail cell with the intense de Sade (played by equally intense Klaus Kinski) penning the story of Justine and Juliette. Both Justine (Romina Power, Tyrone's daughter) and Juliette (Rohm) are bounced from their orphanage after their last benefactor dies. Juliette decides to go the tramp route and becomes a prostitute (i.e., she has a great time!), while Justine goes for the more moral approach (i.e., she doesn't). Soon our little heroine is getting ripped off, forced to live a servant's life, and has to put up with a lot sexual harassment, which eventually lands her in jail. In jail she meets the feisty thief Dubois (Mercedes McCambridge, obviously working off her karma from being an evil warden in *99 Women*, 1968), who helps her escape. Ditching the thieves, she has an affair with an artist, but of course that doesn't work out. Running into her sister Juliette, who is now living high on the hog, being a criminal and pretty much enjoying her debauched life, Justine decides she needs to go to a convent to live out her days. Well, unlucky for her the convent is run by Jack Palance (whose performance makes Elizabeth Berkley's *Showgirls* performance seem subtle!), who's not as saintly as one would think. Does it sound like a lot is going on here? It is. The film is entirely too long, and after a while we end up just not caring. It's one of Franco's most beautiful films in terms of cinematography, but the story is cumbersome. The sex, while plentiful, doesn't graduate beyond light soft-core, and the violence is laughable. If you're looking for a better mixture of de Sade and Franco, I'd check out *Eugenie, the Story of Her Journey into Perversion* (1969).

Kiss Me Monster, aka *Besame Monstro* (SP), *Küß mich Monster* (GER). Prod. Adrian Hoven. Dir. Jesus Franco. Spain/Germany, 1967. Blue Underground, 79 min. DVD. Starring: Janine Reynaud, Rosanna Yanni, Adrian Hoven and Michel Lemoine.

Two Undercover Angels, aka *Sadisterotica* (INT). Prod. Adrian Hoven. Dir. Jesus Franco. Spain/Germany, 1967. Blue Underground, 79 min. DVD. Starring: Janine Reynaud, Rosanna Yanni, Adrian Hoven, Michel Lemoine and Jess Franco.

Long before *Charlie's Angels* hit the TV screens of the world, Jess Franco was having a blast with his two ditzy female detectives Diana and Regina in his "Red Lips" films, *Kiss Me Monster* and *Two Undercover Angels*. With their bad dialogue (made even worse by the abysmal English dubbing; try to search out a Spanish version), even more outlandish plots, to say nothing of the fashions, these are good-natured films that are an absolute hoot and very enjoyable. C'mon, who doesn't want to see Reynaud and Yanni running around with guns in their hands, chasing bad guys? In *Angels*, our detective duo (who run an operation called Red Lips Detective Agency) are called in to investigate the disappearances of bridal models. We, the audience, already know they are being kidnapped by a werewolf-type man (Lemoine, husband to actress Reynaud) and using them for realistic art (just let it go). *Kiss Me Monster* is slightly sleazier but even more hard to follow as our funky, fun detectives want to branch out of the investigation business to become striptease artists (!) but find themselves involved in the case of a missing scientist. From there they are chased by a cult, lesbian virgins, and a gay couple with their own studly looking assassins. Reynaud and Yanni are clearly having fun and so will you. When your brain is clamoring for a mental margarita, visit the Red Lips Detective Agency!

Nightmare Comes at Night, aka *Les Cauchemars naissent la nuit* (FR). Prod. Karl Heinz Mannchen. Dir. Jesus Franco. Spain/France/Germany, 1970. Shriek Show, 83 min. DVD. Starring: Diana Lorys, Paul Muller, Jack Taylor and Soledad Miranda.

Not exactly the cinematic equivalent of Ambien, but it sure comes close. Cementing his reputation as the master of WTF films by working the same "dream" aspect that marks so many of his, as well as other Spaniards,' films, Franco is continuing on his path to be the most non-linear filmmaker in existence. Princess turned stripper turned whatever Anna (Lorys, a long way away from her turn as the heroine in Franco's *The Awful Dr. Orlof*, 1961) is having terrible dreams about murdering a man. Though her lesbian girlfriend Cynthia tries to convince her she's not a murderess, she runs off to psychiatrist Müller, who promptly prescribes drugs. We're then treated to a very long flashback with the requisite scenes of Lorys dancing on her back (Franco loves that!), which catches the eye of Cynthia. Back in real-time (though one is never really sure in a Franco film), we find out that perhaps Cynthia doesn't have Anna's best interests at heart, and perhaps the psychiatrist knows a little more than he is letting on. Oh ... and why are Soledad Miranda and her jewel-robbing boyfriend watching her house via binoculars? (Answer: because her scenes were all filmed for another picture and spliced into this one to give it some marketing power.) Lots of nudity, lots of voice-overs, lots of unanswered questions, little resolution.

99 Women, aka *99 Mujeres* (SP). Prod. Harry Alan Towers. Dir. Jesus Franco. Spain/U.S., 1968. Blue Underground, 90 min. DVD. Starring: Mercedes McCambridge, Herbert Lom, Maria Rohm, Rosalba Neri, Maria Schell and Luciana Paluzzi.

Women in prison! Just the mere thought of lovely lasses behind bars sends Eurocult fans into shivers of excitation, and here is one of the first and most successful examples. Maria Rohm is sent to some island prison for killing some men who attempted to rape her. There she meets the usual suspects including the tough, hardened (but of course, sexy) woman (Neri), drug addicts (Paluzzi, who promptly dies after her five minutes on the screen), and a sadistic lesbian warden (McCambridge, so delightfully over-the-top) whose sole purpose it is to terrorize the prisoners. Sweet Maria Schell is sent to investigate the goings-on and befriends Rohm. To add to the fun, there's a male prison on the other side of the island, run by equally scummy Herbert Lom. Soon the violence and mayhem reach a boiling point and the girls try make their escape. With a fairly high budget and a slew of slightly-past-their-prime actors, *99 Women* is the perfect film for those not familiar with the subgenre. While it includes everything you expect from a film of this type—the usual lesbian groping, the torture sequences and provocatively clad women who never seem to lose their makeup while they're losing their dignity—it still tries to maintain an air of dignity (this applies only to the standard cut of the film; beware of the X-rated version floating out there that includes hard-core inserts!) that would soon disappear from the subgenre, to be replaced by total debasement. A huge box-office success, *99 Women* is a fun, engaging movie that is easily one of Jess Franco's most accessible films.

Sadistic Baron Von Klaus, aka *La mano de un hombre muerto* (SP). Dir. Jesus Franco. Spain/France, 1962. Image Entertainment, 95 min. DVD. Starring: Howard Vernon, Hugo Blanco, Gogó Rojo and Fernando Delgado.

Franco's second horror film after the success of *The Awful Dr. Orlof* shows him taking an even larger leap into exploitation. Ludwig Von Klaus (Hugo Blanco) returns home to his Austrian family castle to see his dying father. Once there he is informed of the family curse ("Oh, son, didn't we tell you?") which involves a distant ancestor who went nuts and carved up the family and townsfolk, and whose spirit now haunts the male members of the family. Well, soon enough, the locals start dropping off and it looks like the curse is coming true again. Talky and very much in the spirit of the Italian Gothics that were popular at the time, Franco's film is much more sadistic as he happily spends the last 20 minutes inflicting various torture methods on actress Rojo. Her topless whipping scene, followed by the inevitable hot poker, is one of the most shocking scenes in Eurocult for its time period. A solid film for those who like their Gothics slightly skewed toward sadism.

She Killed in Ecstasy, aka *Sie Tötete in Ekstase* (GER). Prod. Karl Heinz-Mannchen. Dir. Jesus Franco. Spain/Germany, 1970. Image Entertainment, 74 min. DVD. Starring: Soledad Miranda, Fred Williams, Paul Muller and Howard Vernon.

A slight reworking of his earlier film *The Diabolical Dr. Z* (1965), *She Killed in Ecstasy* contains Soledad Miranda's most intense performance of her career. Here she plays the wife of Dr. Johnson (Fred Williams) who has been using a '70s version of stem-cell research in order to increase children's reaction to disease. When his findings are ostracized, he quickly loses his mind and kills himself, depriving Mrs. Johnson of her love. She doesn't react well and soon becomes her own Miss Muerte, seducing and killing each of the doctors (both male and female) who caused her husband's death. Though it contains all the excesses of Franco's filmmaking style—zoom shots, stilted dialogue, scenes that stretch out for extraordinary periods of time—this is still one of Franco's strongest films of the '70s. Miranda is amazing as she becomes a killing machine, utilizing both sympathy and cold-edged resolve to accomplish her tasks (her final collaboration with director Franco is fraught with all sorts of meanings). Franco wisely films her from every advantageous angle available, showcasing her beauty. What makes most of her performances so memorable is that she seems willing do anything for the character, which is essential in exploitation, and seems to trust Franco and his talents. Sadly, as this was one of the last films she completed before her death, we see just what a loss her passing was.

Succubus, aka *Necronomicon* (INT), *Necronomicon: Geträumte Sünden* (GER). Prod. Adrian Hoven. Dir. Jesus Franco. Spain/Germany, 1967. Anchor Bay Entertainment, 76 min. DVD. Starring: Janine Reynaud, Jack Taylor, Adrian Hoven and Howard Vernon.

    The ultimate acid trip and one of those original WTF films! Critics have called *Succubus* everything from brilliant and passionate to mind-numbing and awful. One likened the film to "jazz set to celluloid," which should pretty much tell you what you're in for when watching Jess Franco's first foray into psychedelic cinema. Though the film defies rational description, here goes: Lorna (the evocative Janine Reynaud) is an S&M dancer/performer who acts as a dominatrix on stage, beating and whipping the other performers. It seems these onstage theatrics may be causing poor Lorna to be losing her mind in real life, though. She's constantly in a dream state where she thinks she's being pursued by the Devil (who wears great clothes, by the way), and who makes her do horrible things. Did Lorna sell her soul to the Devil? Is she responsible for the terrible things she dreams of? Are they even dreams? When you figure it out, let me know; I'm still trying to put it together. *Succubus* belongs in that category of pretentious European films that tried to be oh-so-classy but were really just selling situations in which you could watch sex publicly. It's evocatively filmed, and Reynaud is always an interesting actress, but the movie is horrendously, perhaps consciously, slow and feels like what I think a bad trip would feel like. The film was released in the United States with an X rating (probably a light R today) and was a box-office smash, propelling Franco into seriously delving into non-linear filmmaking.

Vampyros Lesbos. Prod. Artur Bauner. Dir. Jesus Franco. Spain/Germany, 1970. Synapse Entertainment, 90 min. DVD. Starring: Soledad Miranda, Ewa Strömberg, Dennis Price, Jess Franco and Paul Müller.

    Cue the sitar — here comes *Vampyros Lesbos*! One of the most exploitable titles in Eurocult is also one of the most well-known films by fans and a Franco classic. A mind-alternating experience, *Vampyros* forces the viewer to put away all preconceived notions of any vampire film (okay, let's be honest: *any* film) away and wander through the recesses of Franco's mind and Miranda's body. German lawyer Linda (Ewa Strömberg) is sent to Istanbul to handle the estate of Countess Carody (Miranda). Before meeting the Countess she and her boyfriend go and visit a club that specializes in erotic dancing (of course). Struck by a beautiful woman performing a bizarre S&M routine with a mannequin (?), Linda is surprised the next day to find that the dancer turns out to be the Countess herself. Soon it's all about the naked swimming, the drugging, and the bloodsucking, as Linda becomes obsessed with the exotic bloodsucker to the tune of some crazy sitar playing. Can Dr. Seward (a very drunk Dennis Price) help her in time to save her soul? *Lesbos* defies logic at every turn. Logic is not the reason you watch it. What Franco does so masterfully is pull you into a world where nothing makes sense, refusing to let you out. Then he springs Miranda on you and suddenly you don't *want* to get out. Her performance is the heart of the film and what separates what would have been another Jess Franco "what-the-hell-was-that-all-about?" film from the piece of art it is today. Franco would go on to revisit some of the same themes a few years later with *Female Vampire* (1973), but to compare the two would be like comparing wine with Coke.

Venus in Furs, aka *Paroxismus* (GB). Prod. Harry Alan Towers. Dir. Jesus Franco. Spain/U.S., 1969. Blue Underground, 86 min. DVD. Starring: James Darren, Barbara McNair, Maria Rohm, Margaret Lee and Klaus Kinski.

    All the elements of Jess Franco's mind come together for this classic piece of late–'60s psychedelia. Like *Succubus* before it, and practically every Franco movie after, *Venus* relies on non-linear storytelling to reel its audience in. Only here, some of Franco's excesses are reined in and everyone is a winner! Jazz trumpeter ('60s teen heartthrob James Darren, playing way against type) finds the naked body of Wanda (Rohm) on a beach in Istanbul. Recognizing her as a woman he saw gang-raped by a group of socialites (including Dennis Price, Klaus Kinski and Margaret Lee), he is spooked enough to hop a trip to Rio. He soon finds out that Wanda is alive, much to the chagrin of Jimmy's soul-singing girlfriend ('60s chanteuse Barbara McNair; and since it's a Franco film, she also has to dance on her back). Soon Jimmy becomes completely obsessed with the iconic Wanda, but not nearly as obsessed as she is with getting revenge against those who wronged her.

Working with a cast of professionals and a screenplay that actually works, Franco uses all the tricks of his trade to draw the audience in. The jazz score is outstanding, the nudity provocative for its time, and the acting, especially by Rohm, is very good (even Dennis Price seems slightly less intoxicated here). Not a happy film by any means, *Venus in Furs* is arguably one of Jess Franco's best films and a very good introduction to his work.

Virgin Among the Living Dead, aka *Christina, princesse de l'érotisme*. Prod. Robert de Nesle. Dir. Jesus Franco. Spain/France/Germany, 1971. Image Entertainment, 79 min. DVD. Starring: Christina von Blanc, Britt Nichols, Anne Libert, Howard Vernon and Jess Franco.

Oh, Jess, you always do this to me. You hand me the most complete drivel and force me to watch, and soon I'm stuck in this nightmarish world and I can't for the life of me gather the strength to push the "stop" button. I want to stop, I know it's crap (and not even well-produced crap), but you always get me with the most outlandish things you do. *Virgin Among the Living Dead* is another one in a long list of dreamlike movies where nothing makes logical sense and the strangest things happen. Christina (von Blanc, delightful; I've always wondered how Franco managed to get the most beguiling heroines for his films) comes back to her home after the death of her father. Her stepmother is adamant that she leave immediately for her own good, but dies herself before she can escort her away. That leaves Christina with the nutcases otherwise known as her family: Crazy Uncle Howard (Vernon), who's like the Liberace of the dead world (only without the style); cousin Carmencé (Britt), whose libido forces her suck blood from the breasts of a blind woman; and Franco himself, who appears as schizophrenic idiot (yep, it's that kind of movie). To make matters worse, the ghost of her father shows up to warn her to leave too! This film isn't for Franco novices; in fact, no film after 1970 really is. Eurocult and Franco fans will find a lot to enjoy, from the gratuitous nudity to the bizarre situations that Christina finds herself in. The ending is predictable but still resonant. Some prints of the film have extra scenes added to it that were directed by French Eurocult artist Jean Rollin, involving zombies rising up from the local pond. Stay away from that version!

The Heart of a Monster: Paul Naschy

> What is the Paul Naschy trademark? Why is it that my movies lasted so long? I believe there is a very powerful reason, which is honesty. I always believed in what I was doing.
> —Spanish actor and writer Paul Naschy[123]

With Jess Franco traversing the continent producing his own outlandish style of exploitation films, Spain was experiencing a financial windfall from an artist who preferred to stay within its sometimes unfriendly borders. Jacinto Alvarez Molina (Paul Naschy) was, along with Spanish director/producer Amando de Ossorio, one of the true auteurs of Spanish exploitation. Staying away from the esoteric concepts that dotted Franco's work, Naschy preferred to use the familiar to shock and delight both Spanish and worldwide audiences. A huge fan of the old American Universal horror films, Naschy used the traditional movie monsters such as the Wolf Man, Dracula and Frankenstein characters to bring a refreshing change to the Spanish filmmaking industry and scare up box-office receipts with a brand of fun, sexy exploitation films. With the worldwide success of his third werewolf film, *La noche de Walpurgis* (*Werewolf Shadow*, 1969), he single-handedly opened the door to exploitation in Spain, creating a genuine horror film character in Waldemar Daninsky and allowing other Spanish filmmakers to experiment with the genre. With over 75 films to his credit, Naschy became one of most successful and visible artists from Spain. His death in late 2009 was a loss to fans around the world who remember the lovable, sometimes troubled Spanish actor who brought both fear and fun into exploitation films.

Born on September 6, 1934, in Madrid, Molina was raised in a traditional Catholic family. His father was a leather and fur cutter whose ambition led him to the top of the industry, while his mother, a huge film buff, would take Molina to the movies on a regular basis, fueling the fantasy life of the child.[124] Like Jess Franco, Molina grew up within the oppressive confines of Gen. Franco's regime where movies with overt horror or adult themes were not permitted to be shown. Lucky for Molina, a few foreign films managed to slip through the government cracks. One of these films, Universal's *Frankenstein Meets the Wolf Man* (1943), was to have a profound impact on the young Molina. The film was an attempt by the studio to cash in on its two biggest moneymakers by pitting them against each other. Less serious than previous entries in the series, the film touched something in the Spaniard, who became somewhat obsessed with the werewolf character and the tragic nature of Larry Talbot (the Wolf Man), someone whose soul was cursed and whose fate was to destroy those he loved the most. It was this duality between hero and villain that most interested the young boy and it was these "fun" monster movies that set in motion his desire to become a filmmaker.[125]

Before embarking on a career in film, though, Molina had to survive his own childhood. When the Spanish Civil War broke out in 1936, the violence left an indelible mark on the young Spaniard. Remembers Naschy, "I can clearly remember a great many things about the time. From the balcony of our summer residence I saw a man's head blown off by a shell and saw how the headless body took a few steps before collapsing in a macabre, twisting heap. Opposite the house, there was a little square with a fountain and a crumbling stone cross. Many unfortunates were executed by firing squad at this place and I remember seeing the rigid, shattered corpses like puppets with broken strings."[126] Molina's own father was faced with a firing squad during the time as well. Accused of having right-wing sympathies and being an avid churchgoer, Enrique Molina was forced to flee on a motorcycle hidden in a haystack while military officials shot the mayor, the local priest and other officials accused of such crimes.[127]

Molina remained fatherless for the next couple of years as his wanted father traveled around Spain securing whatever job would keep him out of the way of the militia. The boy was taught Gothic literature by his tutor, a kindly Austrian-Prussian woman, and indulged in his love for movies and the escape that they offered. By the late '40s, Molina, with his family reunited, began to take not only his creative mind and love of film more seriously but also his body. A lover of sports as a young child, Molina had begun to develop an interest in weight training in his late teens. Blessed with natural quickness and stamina, he segued from gymnastics to wrestling before settling upon weightlifting as his sport of choice.

Working throughout the '50s, Molina became the lightweight champion of Spain in 1958.[128] As a happy consequence, film producers began to take notice of the young Spaniard as he developed a body that rivaled those of the actors in the popular "gladiator" and Hercules films that were coming out of Italy in the late '50s and early '60s. Initially Molina was not looking for a role in front of the camera, as his aspirations were behind it. Taking a cue from his father, he looked at a film set as an artistic endeavor and his initial objective in the movie business was to be a set designer or art director, but producers thought Naschy's body was too good to keep behind the camera.[129] Getting a small role in the mega-budget Hollywood epic *King of Kings* (1960) that was filming in Spain, he could begin to see how quality filmmaking is accomplished. He also formed lifelong professional friendships with cast and crew, including director Nicholas Ray and star Jeffrey Hunter.

While enjoying the experience of *Kings* and the other film he played a small role in at the time, *El príncipe encadenado* (1960), Molina decided to concentrate full time on his bodybuilding career, securing a spot on the Spanish team for the 1964 Olympics. Set to represent his country, Molina was the target of some behind-the-scenes manipulations by Spanish officials who thought he was an inappropriate choice and subsequently forced him out of his position. With his Olympics hopes dashed, he was also growing tired of being a premiere Spanish athlete. The physical as well as political strain of the sport was beginning to take a toll on him. His body and photogenic face still brought in movie and television offers from around the world, and Molina decided to take another shot at filmmaking, this time as a writer.[130] After appearing in a 1966 episode of the popular American television series *I Spy* (1965–1968) with veteran horror film actor Boris Karloff, Molina was determined to write a screenplay that would bring horror cinema into Spain.

Going back to the film that affected him the most, *Frankenstein Meets the Wolf Man* (1943), Molina began to write a script for *La marca del Hombre-lobo* (*Frankenstein's Bloody Terror*, 1968) that encompassed all the fun and thrills he found in such movies as a child. His love for the Wolf Man, along with his realization that the character had never been done in Spain, prompted Molina to construct a homegrown version of the tragic figure. Pushing the limits of his story, he mixed in other famous monster themes as well, such as vampires and mad scientists, into a singular plot. All of these elements could have produced an innocuous, sterile monster movie aimed at squarely at kids had Naschy decided not to incorporate some of the taboos of Spanish society.[131] Immediately, though, Molina was met with resistance within the Spanish filmmaking society. Spanish producer/director Amando de Ossorio, who would later go on to have immense worldwide success with his "Blind Dead" movies, sat the young Molina down and told him point-blank that horror films in Spain just don't work and that he should leave that kind of film to the British. Molina had problems with the government as well. Though the political climate of Spain was not as oppressive in 1968 as it had been earlier in the decade, General Franco still ruled the country with an iron fist, causing problems for anyone who opposed his ideals or his government's. So naturally Naschy ran afoul of Spain censors over *La marca*. Interestingly, it wasn't the subliminal political content that caused them worry (they may not have even picked up on that, as the film seems like frothy fun on a casual viewing), but the main character himself: Spanish censors were not too happy about the idea of a killer being Spanish. Related Naschy, "The character of Waldemar Daninsky was Spanish, I even remember his Spanish name, his name was Jose Bubidorro. I had to change his name because of the Spanish censorship of the time, which was strange and harsh. They told me that if he was a Spanish werewolf I wouldn't be able to do the movie. There were no werewolves in Spain. And if there were, they would never do a movie about a character so sinister."[132]

Naschy was able to circumvent any possible trouble by changing the name and ethnicity of Jose Bubidorro to Waldemar Daninsky, a Polish aristocrat who rambled throughout Europe seeking refuge from his lycanthropy. Molina chose Poland as Waldemar's ethnicity because of his love for the Polish people. But it wasn't just the nationality of the werewolf that worried Spanish censors. They frowned heavily on the mention of cults, witchcraft and other things supernatural and mandated that Molina cut them out. In typical exploitation fashion of the time, he did ... sort of. Believing some of these shots were essential, he shot them regardless, then edited them out of the prints that played in Spain or in any other country in which they might offend.

As filming was set to commence, another problem arose. Who would play the title character? Initially Molina wanted Lon Chaney Jr., who had popularized the character in the United States in the '40s. But by the mid-'60s, Chaney was battling chronic alcoholism and was in no condition to fly to Spain. With no actors interested, producers offered the role to the fit Molina, who was excited by the prospect of living out his childhood fantasy with a character he had invested so much heart and soul into. He happily accepted playing the part.

Molina had one more change to make before the film could be released. The German distributor of the film was unhappy about Molina's name, and fearing that it may be uncommercial, or worse, too ethnic, they asked that he change it. Happy to see the film released, Molina consented. Taking his name from Pope Paul VI and Hungarian weight lifting champion Imre Nagy, Paul Naschy was born.[133]

La marca del Hombre-lobo (*Frankenstein's Bloody Terror*, 1968) sets up the origins of Daninsky and his accursed condition. Bitten by a local werewolf during a hunt, Daninsky is forced to come to grips with his condition. Enlisting the aid of the girl he loves (Dianik Zurakowska) and her ex-fiancé (Manuel Manzaneque), he tries to find a cure. Unfortunately for him, this brings him into contact with a vicious vampire (Julian Ugarte) and his nymphomaniac wife (Aurora de Alba), whose only interest is furthering his lycanthropy. Daninsky spends the rest of the movie not only fighting the vampires but also his own animalistic urges.[134] Shot in widescreen and filled with colorful Gothic images, *La marca*, with its swipes at Spanish class culture, was a modest hit in Spain. Local critics ravaged the picture, but audiences found something sympathetic and nostalgic in Naschy's portrayal: it is obvious that he is having fun and trying to provide the same thrill he had watching these types of films as a boy. There's something playful and benign about the film even though the blood flows often ("gushes" might be more apt term) and the sexual tension throughout the film is palpable. The vampire seduction scenes are among the strongest, especially as de Alba bites down on some of the younger guys in the cast, hinting at the sexual revolution about to take place in Spain. There's no subtlety in *La marca*; Naschy puts everything on the screen with the earnest desire to please, amping the action to keep a new audience interested.

Though *La marca* sold fairly well in Spain, it was the success outside its borders, under the title of *The Mark of the Werewolf*, which caused Spanish filmmakers to take notice that perhaps horror and exploitation could be moneymakers. Though the film retained its werewolf title in most markets around the world, U.S. distributors called the film, laughably enough, *Frankenstein's Bloody Terror* (1968), which is ridiculous, since Frankenstein's creature is the one monster that does not appear in the film. Never one to miss a trick, the distributors wanted a Frankenstein film to sell to American audiences and got one by adding a cartoon of the monster during the short credits, then having a 20-second prologue explaining that through a curse the Frankenstein family had (miraculously!) become wolf monsters and changed the family name to Wolfstein! After the short prologue no other references to Frankenstein are mentioned, which meant a lot of Americans expecting to see a Frankenstein film were severely disappointed.

Riding the modest success of *La marca*, Naschy went immediately into the second Daninsky film, *Las noches del Hombre Lobo* (*Nights of the Werewolf*, 1968). Unfortunately the film, which centered on a Parisian scientist trying to conduct research on Daninsky, was never released in Spain or around the world, prompting some to believe the film was never made. Some stills have been seen, and Naschy insists that the film was impounded after the death of its director, René Govar. The film remains one of true "lost" films of the

NOW - MORE HORROR! MORE SCREAMS! MORE FRIGHT! THAN YOU'D EVER DARE TO DREAM!

FRANKENSTEIN'S BLOODY TERROR

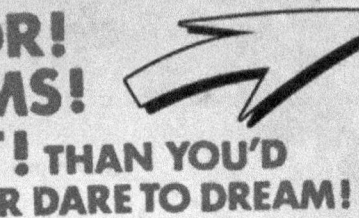

ALL NEW / ALL COLOR

Filmed In
SUPER 70mm
CHILL-O-RAMA

IN EASTMAN COLOR

Released by
INDEPENDENT INTERNATIONAL
Pictures Corp

GP ALL AGES ADMITTED
Parental Guidance Suggested

ONE OF THE BEST HORROR MOVIES YOU WILL EVER SEE!

Eurocult era.[135] Undaunted by the problems of *Las noches*, Naschy filmed a short bit as Daninsky in *Los monstruos del terror* (*Assignment Terror*, 1969), a Spanish-German-Italian co-production of a monster free-for-all that starred American actor Michael Rennie as an alien bent on taking over the earth by using those monsters that strike fear into the population. Resurrecting the traditional Universal monsters from the '30s, Frankenstein, the Mummy, Dracula and, of course, the Wolf Man, Rennie unleashed them on an unsuspecting populace, causing mayhem.[136] While not a big success in Spain, the film sold well enough around the world to prompt Naschy to film a fourth entry in the Daninsky saga. This one would ignite the Spanish exploitation industry and spark the Spanish horror boom of the '70s.[137]

La noche de Walpurgis (*Werewolf Shadow*, 1970[138]), the fourth installment of Naschy's Daninsky's werewolf saga, is generally credited by most scholars to be the film that broke down Spanish resistance to producing horror/exploitation films.[139] Adapting the formula a bit from the previous films, Naschy and fellow writer Hans Munkel enhanced the violence and began to add gratuitous amounts of nudity that would appeal to a worldwide audience. The Spanish were far behind the Italians and French in their expression of sexuality, but by 1970, Spanish censors were starting to cave in to filmmakers who wanted to put adult themes in their films and had begun to allow them, with some very interesting caveats. For Naschy and company to get the extra violence and nudity his films required past the censors, they simply had to change plot locales and make the pretense of dancing around sensitive issues. Explained Naschy, "If a story happened in another country, in Transylvania or wherever, things like lesbianism, as there is *Night of the Walpurgis*, or even sex and violence, it was all okay if it was set in another country. [Though] we shot double versions much of the time, you were subject to luck. But you had to be careful. They were not only cutting nudity and erotic scenes. When you had delicate subjects such as religion, eroticism became more permissible. And they allowed more violence, with limitations of course."[140] These first steps toward a freer Spanish cinema were not done simply to accommodate changing social mores, but were more likely tied to economic reasons. By the late '60s, Italian exploitation was flooding not only Spain but the entire world, and the Spanish film industry, though uncertain on how to produce exploitation, were more than interested in how to make money from it. Censors were beginning to allow some (emphasis on *some*) violence and nudity to creep into these films with the hope that country would receive some financial benefit.

Violence and nudity may have been what got audiences into cinemas, but it was the stories that kept their attention. *La noche* finds Daninsky doing battle with an evil vampire queen (Patty Shepard), a figure dressed in black that moves in an eerie slow motion. As in the other films, he saves the girl he loves (Gaby Fuchs) before being killed, yet again, by a silver cross through the heart.[141] In practically all of the Daninsky films, the character is killed off in some way, only to be resurrected at the beginning of the next one, which could explain why Naschy seemed more distant as each successive film was made. Much like *La marca*, Naschy's fourth werewolf movie is an adult homage to the Universal horror films of the '30s and '40s with over-the-top monster attacks, screaming heroines, and an adherence to horror traditions like silver bullets killing the beasts. The slow-motion camera work

Opposite: *La marca del Hombre-lobo* (*Frankenstein's Bloody Terror*, 1967) was the first major success for a horror film inside Spanish borders. Ironically, the U.S. poster downplays the werewolf story, instead focusing on a Frankenstein one that never actually appeared in the film!

Even more of a box-office success than *La marca*, *La noche de Walpurgis* (*Werewolf Shadow*, 1970) kicked off the huge stream of Spanish exploitation that was produced in the early '70s.

done on the vampire queen is evocative and struck a chord in Spanish audiences, who had enjoyed a long history of nightmarish stories of ghosts. Naschy isn't saying much here in this movie; he doesn't have to. The point here is to entertain and create some nostalgia for the love he shared with fans of those old U.S. horror films.

Unlike the Universal films, though, he also goes for the exploitation factor by leeringly filming an abundance of bare breasts, creating some inappropriately timed sexual scenes, as well as making his werewolf foam or spew an amazing amount of blood. As usual the amount of violence and nudity you see is dependent what print of the film you watch. Naschy and Russian-Argentine director León Klimovsky shot two separate versions of the film, as became the custom throughout their entire stint in exploitation: one with all the nudity and violence intact, the other much more subtle. The difference between the family-friendly version of *La noche* and the adult version can sometimes be startling. If you took away all the sex and hard-core violence, you would have something that could be (and frequently was, in the '70s and '80s) shown on Saturday afternoon television shows. The first female kill is a good example. Escaping into the night (in what was a tradition of simply awful day-for-night photography in Spanish exploitation) after having his silver bullets removed, Daninsky viciously attacks a young woman. In the family-friendly version you see the back of Daninsky's head as he's supposedly ripping out her throat, and after he's finished he runs away. But in the adult version, the body falls, close-ups of the chewed neck are shown, followed by a pan to her ripped-open blouse and rather long close-ups of blood trickling down her exposed breasts. This dual version approach to filmmaking was a boon to Naschy and Klimovsky, as they could sell a market whatever their censors and audiences would allow. Some countries would take the family-friendly version, others the adult, and some would take a mixture of each. This smorgasbord approach has resulted in a variety of versions of this movie, making it difficult for home video audiences, or those who attend reissues, to know exactly what version they are getting.

The nostalgia that Naschy would generate with *La noche* turned out to be resonant. Spanish audiences responded enthusiastically to the film, making it a huge success, the first of its kind for a horror film in Spain. The success of the film worldwide meant that Spain now had a viable commodity which they could exploit and make money, and resulted in a whirlwind of activity for Naschy. Spanish producers soon were begging him to star in their next pictures. Not content that the world had seen the last Waldemar Daninsky, Naschy rushed into *La furia del Hombre Lobo* (*The Fury of the Wolf Man*, 1970) and *Dr. Jekyll y el Hombre Lobo* (*Dr. Jekyll and the Werewolf*, 1971). Unfortunately each of these films was a pale comparison to the previous *La noche*. So intent were producers on getting these films in the theaters quickly, they reused previously seen footage from the earlier Daninsky films to pad the new plots, which meant that, while audiences were getting new stories, they were seeing the same old werewolf footage.[142] To Spanish and worldwide audiences (especially in Spanish-speaking countries like Mexico, where these films were extraordinarily popular), it didn't matter. They wanted to see Naschy running around the European continent (aka Spain) creating terror and bloodshed, and happily made both of these films a success.

Looking to break away for a bit from Daninsky, Naschy wrote *Jack el destripador de Londres* (*Jack the Ripper*) in 1971. Filmed almost entirely in England, the film found Naschy playing a crippled ex–trapeze artist who may or not be Jack the Ripper. With the softening of censorship, the violence of the murders could be exploited, and a gruesome amount of bloodletting is shown, as this Jack the Ripper not only slashes his way through a myriad of prostitutes but also keeps body parts of each as a memento. Happy with his performance

230 PERVERSE TITILLATION

and the success of the film, Naschy threw himself into a slew of projects away from el Hombre Lobo. Two of the most successful were *El gran amor del conde Drácula* (*Count Dracula's Great Love*, 1972) and *El jorobado de la Morgue* (*Hunchback of the Morgue*, 1973).

El gran amor del conde Drácula (1972) is, no surprise, a throwback in story to both the Universal and Hammer horror films of previous decades with a decidedly '70s twist. Naschy

The success of the Daninsky character made it possible for Naschy to play other villains. In *El gran amor del Conde Drácula* (*Dracula's Great Love*, 1972) he takes on the famous Bram Stoker character.

plays Count Dracula, who needs a victim to vampirize in order to resurrect his daughter. The story takes on a strange twist when one of the women (French actress Haydee Politoff) falls in love with Dracula and actually contemplates giving him what he wants. In the end she refuses eternal life, sending Dracula into a strangely suicidal tailspin.[143] Though critics had problems seeing Naschy as Dracula (his physical presence was far too robust to be playing a vampire), the film is a favorite of horror and exploitation aficionados.[144] In addition to a slew of bare-breasted young ladies getting their throats ripped out, and the bloody stakings, Naschy plays up the sexuality of the vampire by having Dracula bring his victims to orgasm prior to death. This more robust sexuality was part of a strategic new direction that he was taking Spain in the exploitation realms and early–'70s audiences around the world loved it. The sensuality of Naschy's films was never overtly lurid; in fact, many times they bordered on optimistic nostalgia. In comparison to exploitation directors like Italian Aristide Massaccesi, who took a very dark, pornographic approach to sex, Naschy's films, while no doubt exploitive, use sexuality as good-natured provocation, nothing more than titillation adding to the enjoyment of the film.

After playing Dracula, Naschy turned his sights on updating Victor Hugo's *Hunchback of Notre Dame* in *El jorobado de la Morgue* (*Hunchback of the Morgue*, 1973) which saw him play Gotho, a hunchback morgue assistant whose murderous deeds are only in response to an unrequited love. When his childhood sweetheart is killed, Gotho looks to Dr. Orla (an obvious Dr. Orlof rip-off, Alberto Dalbes) to resurrect her. Dr. Orla uses Gotho's unrequited love for the woman to make him commit hideous murders. Realizing that he is being used and horrified that the reanimated love of his life is now a monster, Gotho kills himself and his love in an acid pit.[145] The film is yet another example of a monstrous character portrayed sympathetically by Naschy, who manages as always to find a humanistic motive behind the character's action. His performance in the film was one of his most celebrated, winning several awards, including the Georges Méliès Award for best actor at the International Festival of Paris.[146] While the film was winning praise with critics, animal rights lovers would be hard-pressed to find anything positive to say about the film, as many of the live rats, essential for a catacomb piece like *El jorobado*, were actually set on fire for effect, making the film rather uncomfortable to watch.

Following his successful turns as Dracula and the Hunchback, Naschy's films became more and more exploitative. In order for these films to be successful in the early to mid–'70s, a heavy dose of violence and sex had to be included. Censorship in Spain was on its last legs, and while edited versions of films, minus the sex and violence, were shown in Spain, the government now allowed filmmakers to shoot any type of scene as long as they did so discreetly. *El espanto surge de la tumba* (*Horror Rises from the Tomb*, 1973) took advantage of the new system. As per usual, the film was released, like all the other Naschy films, in a "clothed" version which played successfully in Spain and Mexico while varying degrees of violence and nudity were shown throughout Europe. The United States had its own version, which was a composite of both versions, obtaining a PG rating in the end.[147]

The film itself was one of Naschy's most successful, telling the story Alaric de Marnac (Naschy) who comes back as a ghost to haunt the ancestors of those who executed him. He is defeated in the end by a modern-day hero (Naschy again, in a dual role) who sends the evil de Marnac to hell.[148] Much like Amando de Ossorio's Blind Dead films, *El espanto* tapped into the psyche of the Spanish audience, which takes its history seriously. Now that the Franco regime was dying its slow death and new freedoms were creeping in, Spanish

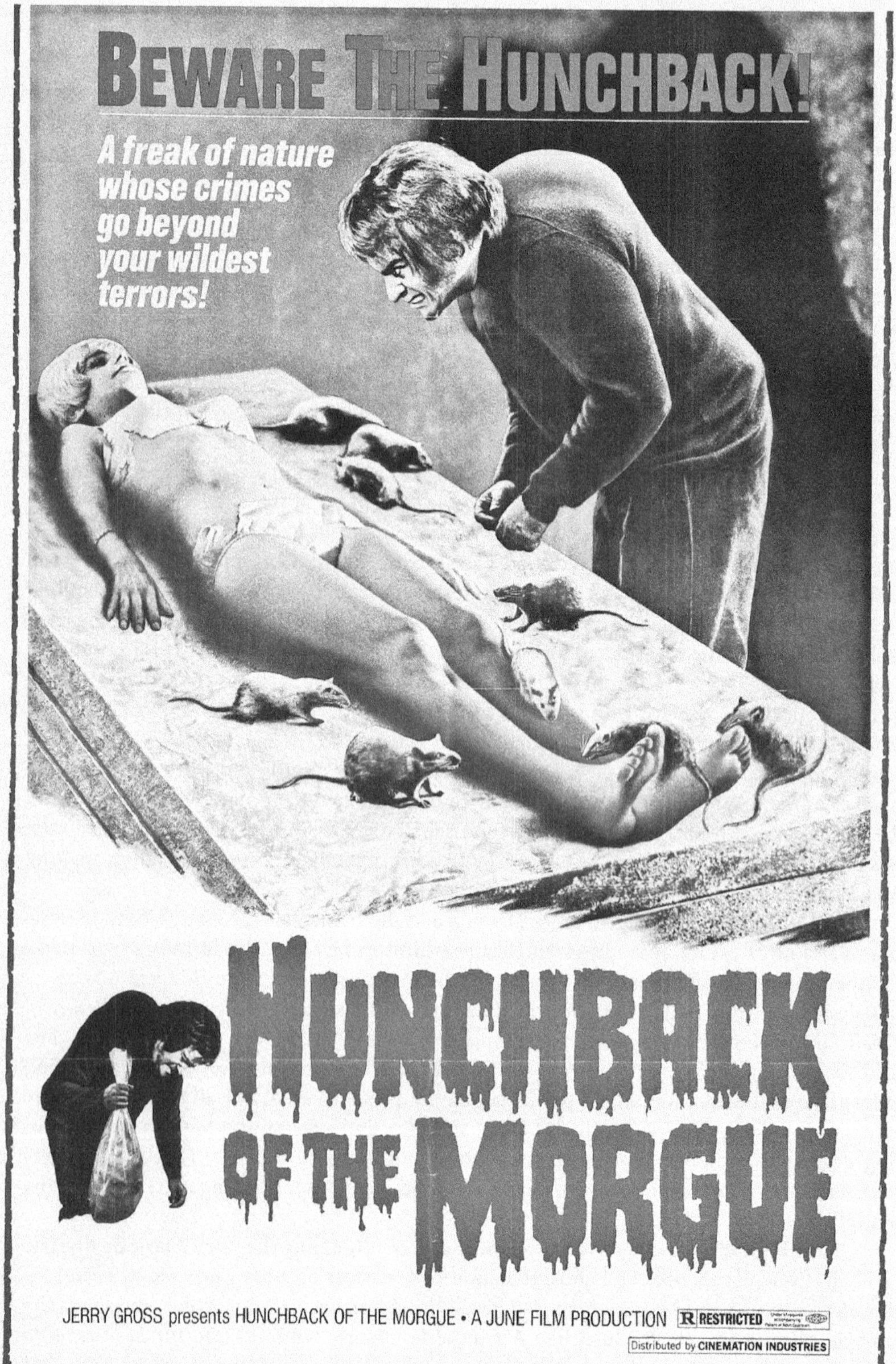
BEWARE THE HUNCHBACK!
A freak of nature whose crimes go beyond your wildest terrors!
HUNCHBACK OF THE MORGUE
JERRY GROSS presents HUNCHBACK OF THE MORGUE • A JUNE FILM PRODUCTION
R RESTRICTED
Distributed by CINEMATION INDUSTRIES

audiences were looking for those subjects that might explain some of the atrocities that were committed in their history. Though not historically accurate by any stretch, the film's bloody decapitations and depiction of the negative effects on a populace by a dictatorial regime resonated strongly with a Spanish audience. The rest of the world were not so interested Spanish history; they just wanted the thrill of watching Naschy tear out and eat the hearts of his victims, not to mention the opportunity of seeing beautiful B-movie Spanish actresses in various stages of undress adorning the screen.

The list of Naschy's mid–'70s films plays like a scorecard for the different subgenres of exploitation as he tried his hand at a variety of projects that were mostly rooted in traditional horror themes. There were the zombie movies, *La rebelión de las muertas* (*Vengeance of the Zombies*, 1973) and *La orgía de los muertos* (1974); Gialli, *Los ojos azules de la muñeca rota* (*Blue Eyes of the Broken Doll*, 1973) and *Una libélula para cada muerto* (1975); mob movies with horrific twists like *Las ratas no duermen de noche* (*Crimson*, 1973); *Exorcist* rip-offs like *Exorcismo* (1975); Inquistion and nunsploitation films like *Inquisicion* (*Inquistion*, 1976), which Naschy directed. He even tackled true sexual exploitation with *El Transexual* (1975) which looked at the life of a transsexual. With all these different subgenres being explored, he still had time to concentrate on the standard movie monsters like the Mummy in *La vengenza de la momia* (*Vengeance of the Mummy*, 1973). This being exploitation, though, instead of slowly chasing the damsel in distress, this Spanish mummy would slit the throats of its naked victims and drink their blood.[149]

While experimenting with all types of exploitation genres, Naschy still wrote and starred in films with his most famous character, Waldemar Daninsky. Not relying on the standard formula of the previous films, Naschy tried to inject the series with new ideas that would take Daninsky on a variety of different adventures. El Hombre Lobo returned in 1973 with *El retorno de Walpurgis* (*Curse of the Devil*), which not only had a thrilling medieval prologue but also explored the Daninsky family and the curse that he passes on to his son. *La maldición de la bestia* (*The Werewolf and the Yeti*, 1975) had the werewolf fighting the Abominable Snowman in the Himalayas. Like his other films of the time, these Daninsky adventures contained ménage à trois scenes, female cannibals, beheadings and torture. *El retorno del Hombre Lobo* (*Night of the Werewolf*, 1980), Naschy's ninth Daninsky film, saw him return to the same themes as the decade's earlier *La noche de Walpurgis* (*Werewolf Shadow*, 1970) with Naschy up against another evil vampire queen, this time Erzabeth Bathory. The film is steeped in Gothic imagery and achieves a high mark for professionalism, which had been lacking in some of the earlier Daninsky-themed films. By 1980 worldwide audiences were more sophisticated and demanded more in terms of professional values and believable plots. Naschy's cute, nostalgic homages to monsters gone by were quite passé by this time with the popularity of the more graphic zombie, slasher and cannibal films easily besting Naschy at the box office.

Naschy's films are a reflection of an imagination that was fueled with fantasy stories as a child, as well as the real violence that surrounded him every day. Without the exploitive violence and sex that were added to appeal to wide audiences, Naschy's films come across as quite harmless and even charming. Unlike Jess Franco, who was also severely influenced by Gen. Franco's regime, Naschy shows a profound affection for the new generation in Spain and a sense of pride in where the country was going. Though his films touch on a

Opposite: In one of his most celebrated performances, Paul Naschy portrays the sympathetic hunchback in *Jorobado de la Morgue* (**Hunchback of the Morgue**, 1973).

Opposite: Naschy played the tragic figure of werewolf Waldemar Daninsky in a number of '70s Spanish exploitation films.

Naschy finally gets to direct his first Daninsky film in *El Retorno del Hombre Lobo* (*Night of the Werewolf*, 1980), the one of last entries in the series.

variety of historically violent situations, they denote a touch of optimism that act as the complete antithesis of Jess Franco's films of the same era.

Naschy continued writing, starring and directing throughout the early '80s. The death of his father in 1984, a heart attack in the early '90s and the shift in Spanish filmmaking away from horror and exploitation films led to serious bouts of depression. This depression was magnified by some of the low-budget movies in which he was forced to appear. Since the advent of DVD, Naschy's films have begun to appear around the world in their original forms, allowing their influence to be felt by a new generation of filmmakers. This had a positive effect on Naschy as he experienced a renaissance, appearing in some more expensive productions such as *Mucha sangre* (2000) and *The Vampyre* (2006) that capitalized on his reputation as Spain's favorite cinematic horror actor.

Naschy died from complications of pancreatic cancer in November 2009. The news saddened fans but offered the chance for further interest and re-examination of his long, distinguished career. Naschy was always sentimental about his career in the genre. He saw himself as a Spanish storyteller carrying on the historic tradition set by his ancestors. As he explained in his 1997 autobiography *Memoirs of a Wolfman* (1997, 2000), "My role has always been like that of some wizened old villager, recounting tales of terror in front of a blazing fire inside a darkened kitchen while the wind howls and screams outside. To quote Lord Dunsany: 'Men tell tales and the smoke rises. The smoke departs and the tales are told.'"[150]

Filmography

Crimson, aka *Las ratas no duermen de noche* (SP). Prod. and Dir. Juan Fortuny. Spain, 1973. Image Entertainment, 89 min. DVD. Starring: Paul Naschy, Silvia Solar, Roberto Mauri and Evelyne Scott.

Naschy gets a brain transplant and the doctor is worried it might cause psychological damage! That's pretty much what you get with this gangster-meets-exploitation piece that is as silly as it is stupid (stupid in a good way). Naschy plays Surnett, who runs the local band of jewelry thieves, and who is shot in the head during a botched robbery. He gets a crooked doctor to help repair the damage and the doctor deduces that the only way to save him would be a fairly common little procedure known as a brain transplant (I'm sure it was an outpatient kind of thing). The gang decides that the best brain would be that of Surnett's worst enemy, affectionately known as "The Sadist." After they remove his head from his body with the help of a local train (don't ask), it's back to the hospital where the surgery takes place. Soon Surnett is up and around and acting out all of the Sadist's perversions (yep, lots of misogynistic nudity here), bedding and beating most of the female cast. Soon, though, the original Sadist's gang comes calling and there's hell to pay. There's always something earnest about a Paul Naschy film. No matter how silly the plots were, he always put his bodybuilding heart into them. *Crimson* is a funky, fun piece of outlandish entertainment that offers Naschy going crazy for half the movie wearing bloody head bandaging. What more could you want?

Curse of the Devil, aka *El retorno de Walpurgis* (SP), *Return of the Werewolf* (INT). Prod. Luís Gómez. Dir. Carlos Aured. Spain, 1973. Anchor Bay Entertainment, 84 min. DVD. Starring: Paul Naschy, Fabiola Falcón, Mariano Vidal Molina and Maritza Olivares.

Naschy's fourth film as the long-suffering Waldemar Daninsky is one of the most self-assured, yet it meanders wildly. We get a little backstory at the beginning as we are transported back in time to see the ancestor of Daninsky (also played by Naschy) destroy the evil Count Bathory, much to the dismay of his wife the Countess. Not to worry, as we know the Countess is a witch and puts a curse on poor Waldemar, effectively stating that if any descendants of his kills one of her descendants (yes, I know, it's getting confusing) then he's going to pay. Centuries later, after inadvertently killing a Gypsy, he pays. Turned into a werewolf, Daninsky must live his life as a recluse because he seems to have this nasty habit of killing all those he loves around him. Lots of bad acting, blood and bare breasts follow. By this time in the series Naschy was perfectly comfortable in the role and is able to wring every ounce of sympathy he can for the poor werewolf. Interestingly, the film, when released in the States, had the tag line: "The Horror of Psycho! The Terror of the Exorcist!" I bet the people who initially paid money for that felt *really* ripped off.

Dracula's Great Love, aka *El gran amor del conde Drácula* (SP), *Cemetery Girls* (U.S.). Prod. and Dir. Javier Aguirre. Spain/Italy, 1972. Sinister Diable, 83 min. DVD. Starring: Paul Naschy, Haydée Politoff, Rosanna Yanni and Ingrid Garbo.

Harmless fun from Naschy has him playing Dracula (unconvincingly, but with great reverence), who is trying to revive his daughter. In order to that, he has to find his one great true love. Since he's not really a man who can travel that much (the daylight hours are really tough on him), he can't easily meet the girl of his dreams. Lucky for him, the all-night bevy of beauties still delivers, and four beautiful women and their tough male chaperone (pimp?) show up on his door due to a broken carriage. Drac must don the disguise of Dr. Wendell, all-around good guy (this is a Paul Naschy film, meaning he's got to play the hero in at least some part of it) to get everyone on his side. After that's accomplished he turns into his batty self, biting and bedding all the pretty lasses. Settling on one, he professes his love. Will she return his affection, which would make it possible for him to revive his daughter? Or will she conclude an eternity with Dracula might not be such a great thing? For those who like their exploitation sexy without nihilistic violence, you really can't go wrong here. The movie is filled with beautiful Spaniards who walk around in low-cut negligees and develop a blood lust for Naschy as well as each other via the typical soft-core lesbian gropings. As usual, Naschy tries to win sympathy for his bad guys via some tears and sentimental narration that are rather misplaced, but make fans of his respect him even more.

Exorcism, aka *Exorcismo* (SP). Prod. and Dir. Juan Bosch. Spain/Italy, 1975. Sinister Diable, 90 min. DVD. Starring: Paul Naschy, Maria Perschy, Grace Mills, María Kosty and Mercedes Molina.

The exorcism bug hits Paul Naschy with laughable results. By 1975, all of Europe was trying to replicate the success that William Friedkin had with *The Exorcist* (1973). The Italians had already produced an abundant number, some of which were successful, such as *Beyond the Door* (1974), and some which weren't, like *The Eerie Midnight Horror Show* (1974). This Spanish entry is much tamer than some others (sorry, folks, no goat analingus scene here!), but still offers a couple of interesting variations from the devil-possession template. Naschy stars as studly Father Adrian, a man suffering from the typical crisis of faith. He's called to the home of an affluent family experiencing some, well, interesting domestic issues. Daughter Leila (Mills) recently had a car accident after returning from a voodoo ritual and really hasn't been the same. Her mother (Perschy) is obviously not cool with it, not only because she's embarrassing at parties and seems to cause a fuss with all the males in the house, but because she's actually possessed by her dead husband, who was a bit of a cad (putting it mildly). It's up to Naschy put a stop to it. Definitely hide the family dog during that procedure. Much more convoluted than Friedkin's film, *Exorcism* tries hard to add something to the subgenre but doesn't quite succeed. The fact the all the projectile vomiting and bad skin don't occur until the last 15 minutes doesn't help. Still, Naschy makes a sympathetic figure (as always), and the film did end up making quite a bit of money around the world.

Frankenstein's Bloody Terror, aka *La marca del Hombre-lobo* (SP), *Mark of the Wolfman* (INT). Prod. Maximilliano Pérez-Flores. Dir. Enrique López Eguiluz. Spain, 1968. Shriek Show, 91 min. DVD. Starring: Paul Naschy, Dyanik Zurakowska, Rosanna Yanni and Manuel Manzaneque.

The first Waldemar Daninsky film is a fun introduction to the long-running series that made Paul Naschy a star. Colorful and exciting, the film is an homage to the Universal horror films of the '30s and '40s with a great bit of '60s eroticism thrown in. A young Gypsy couple (including "Red Lips" star Yanni) decide to spend the night at the local deserted castle of Count Wolfstein. They purposefully remove the gold cross from the count's body, hoping that it will make them rich. Instead it just makes them dead, as the werewolf count rises up and kills them. Soon the count is roaming the countryside, where he is slain by the locals, but not before putting the bite on Waldermar Daninsky, local nobleman. Now knowing he's cursed for eternity, Daninsky's friends try to find a cure. They think they find someone who can help in the person of Dr. Mikhelov (Julian Ugarte) and his beautiful Wandessa. Unfortunately for Daninsky and friends, these two are rather long in the tooth and have a bit of blood lust. *Frankenstein* (and let's be honest: there's no Frankenstein in this movie; it's just some not-so-great marketing to get butts in seats) is a hoot, and Naschy and company throw in everything but the kitchen sink. You want werewolves? You got 'em. Vampires? check. Hot vampire seductions? Double check. Romantic triangles? Uh-huh. Everything that an exploitation audience could be looking for is found here (remember: it is 1968, though so the nudity and violence quotients won't be as high as they would have been in the '70s), and the action moves quickly enough to not allow boredom to sink in. Naschy makes a great anti-hero and his affection for his character is evident from his opening moments. This is the beginning of the true Spanish horror-exploitation era, making this film a must-see!

Horror Rises from the Tomb, aka *El espanto surge de la tumba* (SP). Prod. Modesto Pérez Redondo. Dir. Carlos Aured. Spain, 1972. Mondo Crash, 89 min. DVD. Starring: Paul Naschy, Emma Cohen, Victor Alcázar and Helga Liné.

Horror Rises from the Tomb should be retitled *The Paul Naschy Show*. In the film he plays three different characters, all of differing motivations. There's the evil Alaric de Marnac, a centuries-old man who, convicted with his wife (Liné) for both vampirism and witchcraft, promptly loses his head by executioner's axe (who's doing the chopping? That's right, Naschy himself.) Then there's the more modern Hugo de Marnac, all-around nice guy who has taken to exploring his ancestral home. Looking for artifacts, he finds one: Alaric's severed head, which seems to have a life of its own. Our old warlock/vampire is not happy being a head and works feverishly to get the rest of himself restored intact so he can produce another reign of terror. Lots of nudity and blood-shed involving hearts, the only thing that sustains the evil Alaric, follow. *Horror* plays down many of the humorous situations that are a staple of Naschy's films and plays up the seriousness. Naschy is clearly having a blast playing all of these characters, but his Alaric may be one of his best: he plays the bearded warlock with all the evil and sexuality that he can muster as he beds all the ladies of the cast while killing the rest. True, the film drags around the mid-point, but if you're a Paul Naschy fan, this film is not to be missed.

Night of the Werewolf, aka *El retorno del Hombre Lobo* (SP). Prod. Modesto Pérez Redondo. Dir. Jacinto Molina. Spain, 1980. BCI Eclipse, 93 min. DVD. Starring: Paul Naschy, Julia Saly, Silvia Aguilar and Beatriz Elorrieta.

Naschy begins the '80s where he started the '70s, with Waldemar Daninsky, as he returns to the world of the Hombre Lobo with a new position, director. A semi-remake of *Werewolf Shadow* (1969), *Night* opens like so many of Naschy's movies with a prologue from the past in which Daninsky's archnemesis Countess Elizabeth Bathory (Saly, taking over for Patty Shepard) is sentenced to die a very slow death. Her werewolf slave (Naschy) is put to death quickly via silver cross to the heart. There he stays until three stupid archeologists decide to pull the cross out of his body. Obviously having a werewolf around isn't dangerous enough for one of the girls, so she takes to reviving Bathory as well (in a nifty blood-soaked resurrection). Soon, the countryside is awash in blood, annoying the local townspeople as they, and we, await the inevitable showdown between the monsters. By this time in the series there was probably no person who could direct these films better than Naschy. The investment of time and effort that he had made for his entire career pays off here. Though he does incorporate a little more blood as well as a typical amount of nudity, Naschy is still in homage mode, which makes the film quaint by comparison to the other werewolf movies (*The Howling*, 1981, and *An American Werewolf in London*, 1981) that were released at the time. This is a labor of love and it shows. Recommended.

Vengeance of the Zombies, aka *La rebelión de las muertas* (SP). Prod. Ricardo Muñoz Suay. Dir. León Klimovsky. Spain, 1972. BCI Eclipse, 90 min. DVD. Starring: Paul Naschy, Romy, Mirta Miller and Antonio Pica.

Vengeance of the Zombies was released during the stage when Naschy was trying to cover every single subgenre of the horror industry and inject them with some extra helpings of nudity and violence. Here he and director Klimovsky go after the voodoo crowd in a colorful yet completely insane film. No flesh-eating zombies here; simply the good old-fashioned religious raising of the dead, as London is experiencing some problems with their local dead coming to life. Again, Naschy is playing three roles here, each of which is totally hysterical. First we have the Hindu mystic named Krishna (I'm not kidding); he's the good guy. Then we have his evil, disfigured brother who is raising the zombies—and since this is exploitation, they are mostly beautiful semi-naked women—in order to kill those he believed wronged him. Finally and most hysterically, Naschy plays the horned, goat-legged Satan himself. They should give honorary Oscars for sheer gall! Anyway, the film is laughable, terribly scored, completely misogynistic and yes, incredibly fun.

Werewolf Shadow, aka *La noche de Walpurgis* (SP), *The Werewolf vs. the Vampire Woman* (IT). Prod. Salvadore Romero. Dir. León Klimovsky. Spain, 1969. Anchor Bay Entertainment, 95 min. DVD. Starring: Paul Naschy, Gaby Fuchs, Patty Shepard and Barbara Capell.

Considered one of the classic Hombre Lobo films and a huge financial success all around the world, *Werewolf Shadow* has a lot to recommend it. With that being said, it also has some major problems. Two silly female graduate students (you know the type: they're so smart but they forgot to put gas in the car) are on the hunt for the remains of Elizabeth Bathory, an evil vampire/witch. Running out of gas (see, I told you) they end up at the country estate of Daninsky (Naschy), who just wants to be left alone to live out his days as a werewolf. He takes them in for a couple of days and even helps out finding the grave of Bathory. In one of those "Oh, I cut my hand, let's watch the blood fall into the mouth of the vampire skeleton" moments, Bathory is resurrected and the mayhem begins. Our vampire queen goes slinking around in slow-motion (in some terrible day-for-night sequences) trying to bring Satan back into the world. This sets us up for the exciting conclusion in which Daninsky must face down Bathory. Yet, with all this horror going on, the scariest thing in the movie is that Daninsky is falling for Elvira (Gaby Fuchs), one of the ditzy grad students. Shepard, as the eerie dreamlike villain, is spot-on and scary, and Naschy himself is always solid. But, and it's a big but, the casting of Fuchs drags down the entire film. She gets my vote for one of the top five worst actresses in Eurocult. Her IQ in the film can't be more than 65, and that's being generous. It's impossible to see how Daninsky could even tolerate her silliness for five minutes, let alone fall for her. You expect bad acting in Eurocult—it's part of its charm—but this takes it to a whole new level. When Naschy later remade the film in 1980 as *Night of the Werewolf*, fortunately he left Fuchs out.

Spanish Nightmares: Exploitation 1970s Style

> A country of opposites and extremes, Spain's penchant for sleaze exploitation and polished art house has given it one of most intriguing resumes in the genre.
> — Author Jay Slater[151]

Spain in late '60s and '70s was not only experiencing as much social and political upheaval as the rest of Europe, it was also rapidly becoming a modern industrialized country. The economy had somewhat stagnated during the Franco regime, resulting in the country's being on the tail end of the technological and economic development that was occurring around the world. As was typical of many societies undergoing economic transformation, the shift from rural to urban began in Spain during this time as poverty began to take a toll on the rural, agricultural citizens and they began to migrate to larger cities. As the country moved from a two-fifths rural population in 1960 down to one-fifth by 1976, many residents of Spain's rural population immersed themselves in urban culture. This presented social, economic and cultural conflicts, as internal migration became a major issue in Spain, with traditions and cultures that had prospered in rural areas were now conflicting within a rapidly modernizing country.[152]

Not all members of Spanish society accepted the adjustment to a modern lifestyle. Many of the government's new policies were fiercely resisted by some of the more conservative members who claimed that this form of governance was a surrender to neo-capitalism. Consequently, all attempts at a limited liberalization of the regime by those in reformist wings were blocked by the conservative party, the lone exception being Manuel Fraga's Press Law of 1966, which gave the Spanish press greater freedom and influence.

Regardless of the pressure by conservatives to halt modernization, Spain began to experience huge economic growth that led to both the enlargement of the middle class and a revival of the workers' movement. Workers set up Workers' Commissions (Confederación Sindical de Comisiones Obreras, or CC. OO.) to negotiate wage claims outside the official framework and to call serious strikes. The result of these actions directly affected the Spanish middle class, who were now able to enjoy more freedoms than earlier generations, such as indulging more in their entertainment choices. Spaniards were now spending more on luxury items, taking more vacations as well as enjoying more films. The church, still a major influence in Spanish culture, was sympathetic to claims for greater social justice and responsive to the recommendations of the Second Vatican Council. Indeed, many younger priests were sympathetic to the Workers' Commissions, and although they generally felt that the church should support the regime, they were increasingly aware of the long-term dangers of such an alliance.

All of these new social issues were to influence the generation of Spanish exploitation filmmakers as they grappled with the new society and culture that were emerging in Spain in the '70s. These filmmakers were able to take those issues that the general population feared, just like the Italians and French, and exploit them as entertainment.

As prolific and popular as Jess Franco and Paul Naschy were, they were not the only Spanish filmmakers indulging in exploitation filmmaking. Names such Amando de Ossorio, Jorge Grau, Eloy de la Iglesia, Narciso Ibañez Serrador, and Claudio Guerin Hill were all responsible for producing some of the most bone-chilling, titillating, innovative horror and exploitation to come out of Spain. Each one dealt in his own way with the change in Spain and created original films that have gone on to become classics of the genre. Though their overall input did not rival that of Italy during the '70s, where hundreds of exploitation films were produced, they still managed to make a strong impact on exploitation lovers around the world.

Spain's exploitation boom arrived in 1968, around the same time as in France and a good eight years after the Italians. That year saw the release of the first bona fide successful Spanish horror films. In addition to Paul Naschy's *La marca del Hombre-lobo* (*Frankenstein's Bloody Terror*, 1968), Amando de Ossorio released *Malenka, la sobrina del vampiro* (*Fangs of the Living Dead*, 1968). Born in Coruna, Galicia, in 1918, de Ossorio was raised in a middle-class family whose only dream for their son was to study business and get engaged. Much to their chagrin, de Ossorio loved movies, and fueling his love of film, the young business major would rush to the film studios every day after working in the local bank. At age 30, he decided to relocate to Madrid and indulge his love of filmmaking fulltime. Producing some of the first travelogue Cinemascope films in Spain, de Ossorio quickly mastered moviemaking and began looking for commercial projects that he could direct. His first film, the political *Bandera negra* (*The Black Flag*, 1956), was immediately banned outright by Spanish censors who vehemently rejected the film's critique of the state's death penalty.[153]

Spending another eight years without making a film, de Ossorio began making westerns in the early '60s. Utilizing foreign backing and distribution, he began to see avenues outside of Spain that could fund his projects. As each western became more successful, de Ossorio got the idea of producing a horror film. Securing Swedish actress Anita Ekberg, de Ossorio developed the Gothic vampire drama *Malenka* in 1968. A copy of both the Italian and British vampire movies that were being produced in late '60s, *Malenka* was the story of a woman (Ekberg) who goes back to her ancestral home only to discover that she is the descendant of a vampire witch.[154] The film, much like Naschy's *Le Marca*, which was released in the same year, is almost quaint in its execution. A mixture of Italian Gothic and both Hammer and Universal horror, the film offers very little to offend, outside of Ekberg's heaving bosom; the film has relatively little blood and its violence is cartoon-like. Shot in record time with many scenes being improvised, *Malenka* confounded Spanish audiences, who were not used to the subject matter but quite interested nevertheless. De Ossorio scholar Rafa Calvo summed up issue: "In the '70s, Paul Naschy had great success with a film on werewolves called *La noche de Walpurgis*, because it provided a kind of forbidden pleasure. Can you image that generation of Spanish men watching these types of films, including vampires, lesbians, sadism and many other different elements? It caused long queues at all the cinemas. After this, many people began to produce horror films in Spain."[155]

While *Malenka* was a modest success, probably owing more to Ekberg's presence than anything else, it was de Ossorio's next film, *La noche del terror ciego* (*Tombs of the Blind Dead*, 1971) that really captured the imagination of both Spanish and worldwide audiences. Relying on traditional Spanish history and folklore as well as modern-day influences such as American director George Romero's *Night of the Living Dead* (1968), de Ossorio concocted a story that updated the historic Templar Knights and gave them a narrative that would scare people for the next decade. De Ossorio created a world akin to a terrible nightmare as the group of long-dead, horse-riding, skeletal zombies, dressed in traditional religious garb, that like to eat the flesh of their victims. The historic Templars' slow-motion riding (via the same slow-motion photography that worked so well in Naschy's *La noche de Walpurgis*, 1970) in the dreary, abandoned graveyards denoted a complete sense of isolation and added to the nightmarish concept of the films.

The 1971 film concerns a young girl (Maria Elena) with a lesbian past who runs away from her cheating boyfriend to find herself in an abandoned town overrun by the Templars. After her death, her boyfriend (Cesar Burner) and friend (Lone Fleming) search her out, only to suffer the same fate.[156] For the Spanish, who had grown up with historical stories about the Templars, and who were living under somewhat tyrannical systems of both the government and the church, *La noche del terror ciego* represented the worst of their nightmares. You don't have to look too deeply to see the political dynamics at work in *del Terror Ciego*. The entire film is steeped in the conflict between the "old" conservative Spain and its "new" counterpart. The difficulty is gauging just where de Ossorio sits on this issue. His Templar Knights are ancient, slow, skeletal, eyeless and malefic, yet extraordinarily powerful as they create a presence that is claustrophobic (with the aid of a great musical score which consists of deep bass religious chanting) yet omnipresent. This is in direct opposition to the younger members of the cast, who are full of life and colorful, but dealing with issues like adultery and sexual orientation that run counter to the religious foundation of the church. It's fairly obvious that de Ossorio sees the younger generation as profoundly stupid: they find the most inopportune ways of behaving, whether it's running away (literally) from relationships, cheating with a friend's lover, or thinking they could actually defeat something

One of the most popular exploitation films from Spain, Amando de Ossorio's *La noche del terror ciego* (*Tombs of the Blind Dead*, 1971) introduced the world to his version of the Templar Knights.

as powerful and wise as the Templars. In the film, the Templars make all the sinners (i.e., youngsters) pay for their transgressions. *La noche* and its sequels were not only a link between the religious persecution of the past and the current climate of fear under the dictatorship of General Franco, but were about searching for freedoms both democratic and sexual. This was difficult for Spanish censors to take, and it was also sometimes hard on the Spanish actresses, who had not been exposed to performing in films of this type. The star of the film, Lone Fleming, explained the difficulty in doing some of lesbian love scenes that seem to have been in every Eurocult screenplay in the decade, saying, "Of the two most difficult scenes which I had to do, one was with Helen Harp. It was a scene in which I had to seduce Helen because I was a lesbian schoolgirl. To kiss and touch a woman when you fancy men is quite difficult. So I asked Amando if he could bring us some wine. We drank half the bottle and the scene turned out fantastic!"[157]

Fun, exciting and sometimes genuinely terrifying, *La noche del terror ciego* (1971) was a smash success all over the world. The success of the film led de Ossorio to bring back the slow-riding, bloodthirsty Templar Knights for three other movies throughout the '70s. All of these films were set in different locations and had different plots so as to excite audiences who were constantly looking for new thrills. *El ataque de los muertos sin ojos* (*Return of the Blind Dead*, 1973) saw a town in the midst of an annual festival overcome by the living dead as penance for atrocities committed by their ancestors. *El buque maldito* (*The Ghost Galleon*, 1974) saw the Templars transported to a ghost ship encountered by a group of unlucky boaters (this being exploitation, they're pretty bikini models). The final film, *La noche de las gaviotas* (*Night of the Seagulls*, 1975) found the Templar Knights back on land and conducting periodic sacrifices of the local townspeople to appease their god. All of the Blind Dead films are able tap into the Spanish tradition of ghost stories and folklore. De Ossorio sets up the Templar Knights as the ultimate ghosts: they make no sound, move slowly via their horses, can find you by your breathing (they are blind, after all), and are seemingly indestructible, which means de Ossorio was free to place them in a variety of different settings, e.g., ghost ships (*El buque*), old historic towns (*El ataque*) or by the sea (*Gaviotas*).

De Ossorio's past association with distributors came in handy while filming the series, as all of Blind Dead films had to be shot with the different foreign distributors in mind. De Ossorio himself related the creative and political problems that this could bring: "I was asked by the French producer, 'Why don't they kiss on the lips?' 'Why don't they undress a little bit more?' 'And why doesn't Esperanza Roy appear totally nude?' and things like that. What if they put me in jail? I had to obey. They'd have only shown it in France, not here in Spain. And the German producer was exactly the same. He wanted the horror films to be very erotic. That's how it had to be."[158] De Ossorio's "jail" statement was probably a comment that distributors could have producers thrown in jail for breach of contract if they did not deliver a movie to specifications.

The Blind Dead series was not the only exploitation that de Ossorio contributed. He produced a wide variety of Eurocult throughout the '70s, and though they may have had entirely different themes, each one had the same dreamlike/nightmarish quality that the Blind Dead movies had. *Las garras de Lorelei* (*The Lorelei's Grasp*, 1972) mixed lycanthropy and eroticism as a man falls in love with a murderous reptile woman who consumes human hearts. This time is was the Rhineland of Germany that was home to our buxom, beautiful by day/evil frog-looking creature by night heroine (Helga Liné) in a film that was reminiscent of traditional folklore tales of Europe. *La endemoniada* (*Demon Witch Child*, 1975) was one of the first rip-offs from Spain of *The Exorcist* (1973). De Ossorio's film followed

After two films, de Ossorio moves his Templar Knights from dry land to a ghost ship in *El buque maldito* (*The Ghost Galleon*, 1974).

American director William Friedkin's vision closely, with the twist of having the young girl (Marian Salgado) possessed not by Satan but by an old witch. It would seem that the witch was none too happy that the young girl's father, a politician, had thrown her in jail. Consequently, the little girl starts to develop the standard possession behavior traits of spasms, vomit, and overt, inappropriate sexuality. *La noche de los brujos* (*Night of the Sorcerers*, 1973) combined jungle adventure with pure exploitation as a group of elephant researchers meet a cannibalistic tribe who captures young women and turns them into vampires. All of these films happily exploit the boundaries of good taste and are overflowing with blood and sex. The decapitations of *La noche*, the heart-eating sequences of *Las garras*, or the young girl spitting out sexual profanities in *La endemoniada* were all standard exploitation gimmicks that de Ossorio used to bring in audiences who were looking to be shocked. Though very little in these films was original, he did have his pulse on the things that frightened '70s audiences, and it made him one Spain's most influential writers and directors.

The social and political unrest that was occurring in Spain in the early '70s had a profound impact on the exploitation industry. Directors were using horrific stories to convey subversive thoughts about the government. Violence was the tool within the plots that served as a catalyst for political change. Film Scholar Andrew Wills wrote that violence in Spanish movies brought a potential to operate subversively, flying in the face of Francoist censors who wanted a skewed, wholesome image of the country.[159] One of the first striking examples of this is Uruguayan-born Narciso Ibañez Serrador's *La residencia* (*The House That Screamed*, 1969). Set in an all-girls French (of course, it wouldn't be set in Spain) reform/boarding school run by a militant headmistress (Lilli Palmer), *La residencia* is packed with enough counterculture angst to shine through what appears to be a standard Gothic horror. The film is posited as a negative critique of traditional, repressive authority as the teenage girls of the Academy try to exert their individuality over the excessive dominance of the headmistress. Serrador sees these girls as natural, positive beings who are stunted by the oppression handed out by Palmer. He doesn't see Palmer as evil incarnate, which would be easy to do, but as someone who, because of her fear of the future, is destined to contaminate the next generation. There is some genuine sympathy for her as the final events of the movie play out, and the audience takes a "Well, that's what you get" point of view. Unfortunately for the girls at the school, there also happens to be a vicious killer around who has a habit of slicing them up, graphically, whenever they try to escape from their "prison." Serrador is blatantly indifferent to his victims: it doesn't matter to him if the girl is good or bad, the hegemonic system will kill them all in the end. Using the Gothic motif that was popularized in Italy and Britain, Ibañez Serrador adorns his school with darkest browns and utilizes very light, magnifying the oppressive atmosphere. This is multiplied even more when Palmer orders all the windows and doors of the establishment to be nailed down, encasing both the girls and the audience in the school.

In case one couldn't comprehend the subtext of *La residencia*, Ibañez Serrador's next exploitation film, the anti-abortion tale *¿Quién puede matar a un niño?* (*Who Can Kill a Child?*, 1975) left no room for doubt that he was out to destroy the entire older generation to make a new start in the world. The film depicts a young English couple (Lewis Fiander and Prunella Ransome) on holiday in Spain while awaiting the birth of their child. They decide to visit one of the local islands, where they find that no one is there but children. The couple is stunned to learn that these cute little kids have risen up to butcher all the adults, and that they are next on the list.[160] Serrador's story, which shares a similar theme with Stephen King's *Children of the Corn* (1977), and the reactionary tone of the movie con-

ONE BY ONE THEY WILL DIE!

Only the killer knows **why** and **how** and **who** is next!

THE HOUSE THAT SCREAMED

STARRING **LILLI PALMER**
CRISTINA GALBO · JOHN MOULDER BROWN · MARY MAUDE   DIRECTED BY NARCISO IBAÑEZ SERRADOR
WRITTEN BY LUIS VERÑA PEÑAFIEL   MUSIC BY WALDO DE LOS RIOS   AN ANABEL FILMS PRODUCTION   IN PANAVISION® COLOR BY MOVIELAB   released by AMERICAN INTERNATIONAL Pictures

GP ALL AGES ADMITTED

71/88

stitute a response to what he sees as the contamination and suffering (as witnessed in the opening credits) of our children by the ruling classes. He wisely gives no logical reasoning behind the children's change of behavior, allowing audiences to frightfully contemplate their own responsibility for such situations. It's clear that Ibañez Serrador wants a societal "do-over" in which children will cleanse the world of their elders. He also takes a very strong position on abortion with the film; he seemingly equates it with infanticide, as is obvious by the title of the film alone. In the film, the children's only emotions are evoked when they confront the very pregnant Evelyn (Ransome) and are shown to be amazed and awed by her condition. Serrador takes the stance that nothing should stop the baby from being born and that abortion is nothing short of child-murder, a position that is not surprising, as Spain is heavily Catholic and the ingrained resistance to such procedures is taught by the church from day one.[161] But this being an exploitation film, he puts in the idea that once a woman wants to get rid of her baby, the unborn child will eventually kill her for such thoughts.

Pregnancy also figures into Carlos Puerto's *Escalofrío* (*Satan's Blood*, 1976). Another pregnant young couple (José María Guillén and Mariana Karr) decides to take a break in the country via an invitation from friends they don't remember. Not wishing to seem ungrateful, they end up in the dark castle of their friends, who head up a group of Satanists and may have their own plans for their unborn baby.[162] Forsaking many of the political overtones of Ibañez Serrador's film, *Escalofrío* prefers to pile on heapings of very explicit sex and violence from orgies (in a very erotic scene) to our Satanists' annoying habit of eating flesh without using their hands. Where Puerto does get political is in his mistrust of everyone in the film. From the next-door neighbors, to the couple who our hero cannot remember, to each representative partner, Puerto shows his increasing agitation of the modern world by positing that no one is to be trusted. Again, this is a "dream" movie wherein the unfolding events make very little sense in a rational world. So he hedges his bets, making it possible to change the outcome of increasing modernization, thereby perhaps, changing the nihilistic outcome this film ends on.

Eloy de la Iglesia's *La semana del asesino* (*Cannibal Man*, 1972) is much more obvious in expressing his desire to carefully examine controversial social issues within the context of an exploitation film. Here Iglesia takes full advantage of subversive narratives, presenting a story of a man, Marcos (Vicente Parra), driven insane by the cultural and political situation in Madrid. A butcher by trade, Marcos is an outcast in a society that is firmly run by the police. Losing his temper, he accidentally kills a man, which sets off a murderous rampage in which Marcos kills most of his friends and family.[163] The wonderfully exploited title is actually a misnomer as Marcos doesn't himself crave human flesh, but disposes of the bodies he kills in the meat grinder at the butcher shop, sending the flesh out with the rest of the meat. Iglesia is giving us something more than typical exploitation here as he contrasts Marcos's life with that of an acquaintance, Nestor (Eusebio Poncela), an affluent man who is clearly posited as homosexual. Ironically, the homoeroticism between the two characters is seen as the only thing that brings Marcos any peace, which is not surprising, given Iglesia's own homosexuality. If showcasing the difference between classes weren't radical enough, presenting a homoerotic subplot to an audience that valued male machismo was groundbreaking, though the typical '70s association of homosexuals with murders somewhat stereotypical. But *La semana* is careful to show that these outcasts are born out of a flawed

Opposite: Spanish Gothic reigns in Narciso Ibañez Serrador's *La residencia* (*The House That Screamed*, 1969).

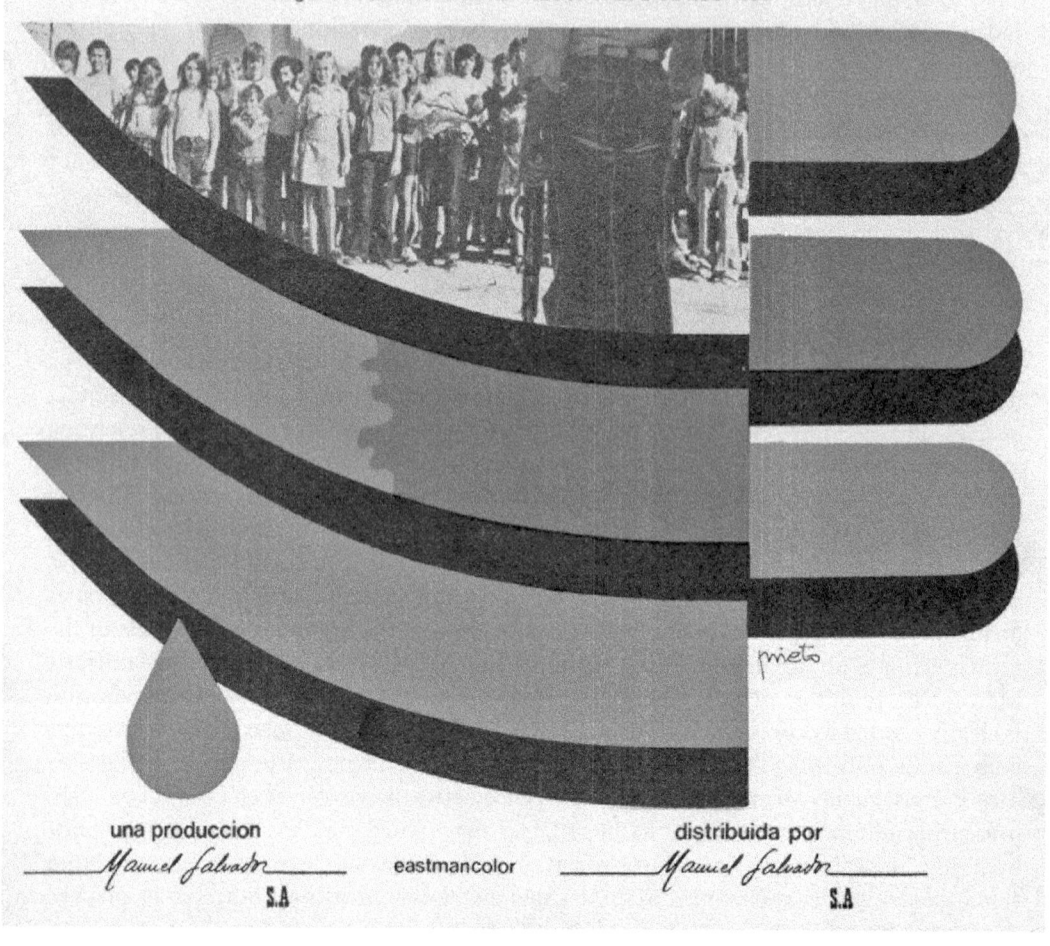

Not all Spanish exploitation centered on movie monsters, as Ibañez Serrador's *¿Quién puede matar a un niño?* (*Who Can Kill a Child?*, 1975) proves.

society and not a flawed personality. Not surprisingly, and perhaps due to the homoerotic nature of the screenplay, the film was not a success during its initial run. Audiences who were enjoying a steady stream of Spanish werewolves and vampires didn't know what to make of this attempt to paint Spanish society as something malefic.

It wasn't just male-male relationships that were undergoing examination in Spanish exploitation. Vicente Aranda's *La novia ensangrentada* (*The Blood Spattered Bride*) focused more on the changing dynamic between men and women. Another story based on Sheridan Le Fanu's *Carmilla* (1872), it focuses on a young married couple who are haunted by the ghost of Mircalla, a lesbian with a severe hate for men. As the new wife (Maribel Martin) struggles to accept her new role, she finds herself drawn to the alluring Mircalla. With dreams of being raped haunting her, she resorts to violence as Mircalla's spirit engulfs her.[164] Written by Aranda, the film is full of subversive feminist ideology that seems that it could have been penned by any of the leading feminists of the early '70s, but with a few very strong caveats. It's disingenuous for a film that purports to have a strong female perspective to have its male protagonist (Simón Andreu), who has behaved in a chauvinistic manner throughout most of the film, turn out to be the eventual hero, surviving by tearing out the hearts of our two lesbian heroines. Also at issue is Martin's frigidity, which seems to be directly correlated to her lesbian impulses and is shown to be catalyst for the events that take place. Obviously the relationship is a direct threat to masculinity, therefore the lesbian triangle has to be put to an end, and the heart extraction is a not-so-subtle signifier of that. Though fairly entertaining, the constant rape of Martin by her husband and the heavy dose of male gaze throughout make *La novia* more a peek at the burgeoning gender roles in Spain than an actual examination.

Family relationships also underwent examination as Claudio Guerin Hill's *La campana del infierno* (*A Bell from Hell*, 1973) examined the outcome of dysfunctional Spanish families. Returning home after some time spent in an insane asylum, John (Renaud Verley) sets out to destroy his remaining family, Aunt Marta (American actress Viveca Lindfors) and three beautiful cousins (Maribel Martin, Nuria Gimeno, Christine Betzner). The heavy mixture of incest, insanity and violence culminates in John's hanging his naked young cousins on meat hooks before going after the man he most wants, the wealthy neighbor next door.[165] Director Hill utilizes the bleak winter landscape to add to the somber feel of the proceedings as he films a story of youth alienation and a family's disintegration into violence.[166] If you were to judge the state of Spanish families from this film you'd be left with the idea that they are more dysfunctional than most, as jealousy over money takes precedence here. Interestingly, though, Hill never exposes the true villain of the piece until the end. He accomplishes this by portraying everyone in the film as malicious. The "pranks" that Juan plays on his family are not funny; stinging may be a better word. Is he the real protagonist or not? Hill lets the audience decide, though he himself never actually heard any feedback from his masterpiece. Haunted by his own personal demons, he was killed prior to end of the shoot when he fell (jumped?) off the scaffold that held the church bell of the title.

In 1973 and 1974 the Spanish film industry produced 29 horror/exploitation films, far more than any other period in its existence.[167] The worldwide acceptance of these films gave Spanish filmmakers the opportunity to travel outside of Spain with a full Spanish crew, learning new procedures and experimenting with novel narratives. Not all horror/exploitation movies coming out of Spain in the '70s were as serious as the works of Hill, Serrador and Iglesias; in fact, most Spanish exploitation used a variety of monsters that were ridiculous, though fun in their execution. *Necrophagus* (*Graveyard of Horror*, 1971) found a young man returning home to find his scientist brother has turned himself into a fish-looking monster with a desire for human flesh. With an assorted cast of oddball characters, the film is severely hampered by a low budget; the fish-brother is only seen briefly at the end, looking like Kermit the Frog with teeth.

Zombies were the subject in director Jorge Grau's seminal film *The Living Dead at the Manchester Morgue* (*No profanar el sueño de los muertos*, 1974). The Spanish government had allowed its filmmakers to shoot abroad, and Grau took full advantage of the evocative English countryside. Taking George Romero's initial concept and updating it with a '70s perspective, Grau blames the raising of the dead on man's dependence on technology. The story concerns a rebellious young artist (Italian Ray Lovelock) who leaves a polluted London for some rest and relaxation. Meeting a young woman (Christina Galbo) who inadvertently runs over his motorcycle, the young couple find themselves fighting for their lives against flesh-eating zombies. Accidentally mobilized by supersonic sounds emitting from a new piece of farm equipment, the living dead munch their way through the cast.[168] Though purely meant for entertainment, Grau tries to tackle environmental woes such as overpopulation and pollution, as evidenced during Lovelock's opening motorcycle ride through '70s London, as one of the major culprits of zombie reanimation. Like the American "big bug" movies of the '50s, Grau seems to think that if we mess with nature, nature will surely come fighting back. His political leanings are also on display here via the inclusion of a very fascist police detective, played by Arthur Kennedy, who goes off the deep end several

La semana del asesino (*Cannibal Man*, 1972) was a serious attempt to look at the social problems occurring in modern Spain. The title shown on the poster is one of the many release titles

Silliness reigns in *Necrophagus* (*Graveyard of Horror*, 1971), in which the monster on the poster is far scarier than the one in the actual film.

DIESE "FRÖHLICHEN" GESELLEN WERDEN JHNEN 90 MINUTEN GÄNSEHAUT BEREITEN
Eastmancolor
Das Leichenhaus der lebenden Toten
(THE LIVING DEAD AT THE MANCHESTER MORGUE)
ARTHUR KENNEDY, Ray Lovelock, Christine Galbo, William Lyton
Regie: George Grau
Produktion: Flamina Cinematografiche S.R.L. / Profilm

times in the movie lamenting the moral decay of the younger generation with "their faggot hair and clothes." Kennedy's hatred for the younger generation pits our heroes not only against the horde of zombies but the establishment as well. Grau's summation of the generation gap is very much in tandem with other provocative exploitation coming out of Spain, and this film, like the others, is a model of the chasm between traditional and modern attitudes. Regardless of the high-mindedness, though, this is still a zombie picture and Grau spares no expense, with the requisite intestine-pulling scenes, realistic zombies (more in the Fulci vein than Romero's), and utter carnage. Thought by critics to be one the most effective zombie movies, *The Living Dead* was well received around the world in various incarnations and titles, most notably in the United States, where it was released with the great exploitation title *Don't Open the Window*, utilizing the same market approach as Wes Craven's *The Last House on the Left* (1972): "To avoid fainting, keep repeating, it's only a movie, it's only a movie, etc." The film showed that zombies still resonated with audiences, perhaps paving the way for the success of the Romero/Argento *Zombi* (*Dawn of the Dead*) four years later.[169]

Also in 1974 came José Ramón Larraz's ultra-erotic *Vampyres*. Like *The Living Dead at the Manchester Morgue* (1974), the film was shot in the rain-soaked English countryside. Turning up the sex and violence factor, Larraz presented the story of two bisexual vampires (Marianne Morris and Anulka) who pick up men, seduce them, and then drink their blood.[170] Awash in blood, the ladies' bloodletting activities as well as sexual proclivities are filmed in close-up as the film pushes the soft-core limits of the genre. *Vampyres* was well received by mainstream critics. *Playboy* magazine said the film "had more sex appeal than any other Dracula film."[171] Not a surprising review from *Playboy*, as the film is nothing but a male fantasy that plays both as sexual one, with the inclusion of the lesbian female vampire, and as an illustration of the male fear of strong women, the bloodsucking aspect. Another reason for success of the film was Larraz's insistence that the film be shot in English in order to better sell it to the lucrative U.S. market. Just like the Italian film industry, Spain did not use natural sound for its films until the '70s, allowing actors to speak whatever language they wanted during the filming. Many of the exploitation films made in the late '60s and early '70s were mostly performed in English but suffered through some unbearable dubbing. By the mid-'70s natural sound had begun to creep into films like *Vampyres*, making them much more attractive to Great Britain and the United States, so much so that many mistake the film's point of origin to be one or the other of those countries. Unfortunately, the process of filming in English doesn't always work effectively if you have actors that can't speak English well, as was the case with *The Living Dead*: though it was filmed in English, lead Ray Lovelock's Italian accent didn't work for his very British/Scot character. Consequently, he had to be dubbed in what turned out to be one of the worst Cockney or Scot (we're never quite sure) accents ever committed to film! For both British U.S. audiences watching both *The Living Dead at the Manchester Morgue* (1974) and *Vampyres* (1974), the cognitive dissonance that goes along with watching a foreign film was kept at a minimum, consequently opening the door for more distribution.

Opposite: One of the seminal zombie films of the '70s, Jorge Grau's *The Living Dead at the Manchester Morgue* (*No profanar el sueño de los muertos*, 1974) combined English settings with Spanish sensibilities.

LAS
HIJAS de
DRACULA
MARIANNE MORRIS
ANULKA
MURRAY BROWN
Director: JOSEPH LARRAZ
COLOR
CLASIFICADA
"S"

Filmography

A Bell from Hell, aka *La campana del infierno* (SP). Prod. and Dir. Claudio Guerin Hill. Spain, 1973. Pathfinder Home Entertainment, 92 min. DVD. Starring: Renaud Verley, Viveca Lindfors, Alfredo May and Maribel Martín.

For those who think that Spanish exploitation consists only of Paul Naschy monster mashes or a Jess Franco mind meld, I give you *A Bell from Hell*, a slow-moving but nevertheless fascinating film about greed and dysfunctional families. John (Verley) is a troubled young man who's been released from the local asylum and into the care of his aunt (American actress Lindfors) and his three female cousins at the family estate. The estate was inherited by John but his aunt is the executor; see where this is going? The problem is we don't know if John is still disturbed or sane due to his proclivity to play some really nasty jokes on people (those with a phobia of bees might want to opt out). His job at a slaughterhouse doesn't engender confidence, either, especially when he starts setting up his basement to look like one. Proud of his accomplishment, he invites the relatives over to take a look. Moody, evocative, depressing, *A Bell from Hell* is not a fun experience, but there is richness behind its melancholy as the film says a lot about family relationships. While there are no chainsaws in the film, exploitation lovers will enjoy the last 20 minutes, when John gets to show off his newly created slaughterhouse. Recommended.

Blood Spattered Bride, aka *La novia ensangrentada* (SP). Prod. and Dir. Vicente Aranda. Spain/Italy, 1972. Anchor Bay Entertainment/Blue Underground, 101 min. DVD. Starring: Simón Andreu, Maribel Martin, Alexandra Bastedo and Deal Selmier.

Sheridan LeFanu's *Carmilla* has been the subject of many, many horror and exploitation films. From the French *Blood and Roses* (1962) to Britain's *The Vampire Lovers* (1970), there's something about the lesbian vampire Carmilla that makes exploitation filmmakers take notice; go figure. Here comes another modern (for 1972) approach that is generally entertaining stuff. Susan (Maribel Martin, a year before she was hung up by her cousin in *A Bell from Hell* (1973), is experiencing some major problems in her emotional life. She just got married to rich hunk Andreu and thinks she should be the happiest person in world, but she keeps having these dreams of being raped by a guy that are unromantic, to say the least. Arriving at her husband's home, she begins to be haunted by a young woman who looks exactly like her husband's grandmother, Mircalla (an anagram of Carmilla), who murdered her grandfather during their honeymoon. Susan's justifiably annoyed new husband starts exhibiting some violent tendencies, which doesn't do anything to help Susan's mental condition. Soon, the vampire/ghost is telling Susan to kill her husband and the blood starts flowing. *Blood* is a lesbian fantasy that tries to have it both ways. It wants to be aggressively feminist with its stance that the violent rape dreams are only due to mistrust of men, but then, in its conclusion, which involves a casket and an embrace, it is the man who puts a stop to the ruckus. Best to put aside the politics of this and to concentrate on Martin losing her mind as well as her soul. It's a vampire movie, so the blood is plentiful and the nudity abundant.

Cannibal Man, aka *La semana del asesino* (SP). Prod. Jose Truchado. Dir. Eloy de la Iglesia. Spain, 1971. Anchor Bay Entertainment, 98 min. DVD. Starring: Vicente Parra, Eusebio Poncela, Emma Cohen and Charly Bravo.

The early '70s was an amazing time for subversion and socially conscious exploitation in Spain. With *The Blood Spattered Bride* (1972) which looked at male/female relationships and sexual orientation, and *A Bell from Hell* (1973), which looked at greed within the constructs of an extended family, Spanish filmmakers were tackling subjects that were resonating within their society. *Cannibal Man* is no different, with its gritty look at urban life in a country that was dealing with radical changes. The film is a classic not only of exploitation but of Spanish cinema; plus, it may even turn you into a vegetarian! Slaughterhouse employee Marcos (Parra) is your typical working man trying to get ahead in life. He wants to work, eat his meat, make a little money, enjoy his girl-

Opposite: Obviously audiences had no problem figuring out what the main theme of José Ramón Larraz's *Vampyres* (1974) was about.

friend, etc. One night he and his girlfriend get into a fight with a taxi driver that results in the driver's death. His hysterical girlfriend wants him to go to the police, but Marcos knows he'll never get a fair trial and kills her too. With his small apartment racking up the body count, Marcos decides to use his job in his favor. All of these proceedings are being watched by his new gay affluent friend Nestor (Poncela), and soon their relationship becomes the focal point of their lives. You may be wondering where the zombies are, but happily in this case there are none (unless you want to argue that Spanish working-class man is a zombie, etc., but we'll save that for another time). True, flesh is eaten, and in a very ironic way, and yes, the killings are nasty, but *Cannibal* is one of those rare films that examines the roles people have in society and how those roles sometimes make us a little crazy. If you like Hitchcock, you'll like *Cannibal Man*.

Fangs of the Living Dead, aka *Malenka* (SP). Prod. and Dir. Amando de Ossorio. Spain/Italy, 1968. Brentwood Home Video, 88 min. DVD. Starring: Anita Ekberg, Gianni Medici, Diana Lorys and Rosanna Yanni.

One of the first vampire movies to originate in Spain, *Fangs of the Living Dead* is pretty much a knock-off of the British Hammer films with a bit of Italian Gothic thrown in. The lovely Anita Ekberg (long before she became *Killer Nun!*) stars as a youngish model who finds out her mother has died (bad) but left her a stately castle in the country (good!). Leaving her fiancé behind, she sets off to see her uncle and her inheritance. Upon arrival she is upset to learn that her uncle doesn't get out of bed till 10 P.M. and the house is full of a lot of weird people. Much to her chagrin, she also finds out that Uncle just wants her body to resurrect his wife Malenka, a vampire who died awhile back. Lucky for Ekberg, her fiancé is not too cool with her hanging out with vamps and he comes to rescue her. She resists at first ("It's my birthright"), but soon gets her head together and joins in the vampire slaughter. Silly, harmless fun from de Ossorio, who would have later success with his thrilling Blind Dead films.

Ghost Galleon, aka *El buque maldito* (SP), *Ship of Zombies* (INT). Prod. J.L. Bermudez Castro. Dir. Amando de Ossorio. Spain, 1974. Anchor Bay Entertainment, 90 min. DVD. Maria Perschy, Jack Taylor, Bárbara Rey and Carlos Lemon.

Ever wonder where John Carpenter might have gotten some of his inspiration for *The Fog* (1979)? Look no further. The third in the popular Blind Dead series has a great premise, but unfortunately bad pacing, and some of the worst special effects imaginable, sabotage it. Leaving behind the old Spanish town locales, the film uses an abandoned ghost ship as the residence for our blind Templar Knights (yep, that means no horses here). Sports gear producer Howard (Taylor) comes up with the worst idea for selling a new powerboat: Put two vacuous models on the boat, send it out to sea with no gas, then take pictures of them getting rescued and show that the boat can take it. Well, Einstein is not too happy when they can't find the girls, and he sends out a rescue party including the friend of one of the models (okay, in reality she's kidnapped to go along), a professor who is researching a story about a ghost ship, and a couple of other bikini-clad models. They get to the ghost ship (the very fake ghost ship, the *very* fake "let's put a model in the bathtub and shoot it" kind of ghost ship) and the fun begins. The problem with the film is that it takes forever to get to the good stuff. Before the arrival of the Templars we're treated to a kidnapping plot as well as a lot of senseless arguing with characters we don't care about and some amazingly bad special effects (see above). When the Knights arrive on the scene, the movie picks up immensely, as de Ossorio's creatures are the stuff of nightmares and the ship's atmosphere, with rolling fog, genuinely enhances the chilling effect they have. De Ossorio wisely put his Templar Knights back on land for the final installment, *Night of the Seagulls* (1975).

Graveyard of Horror, aka *Necrophagus* (SP), *The Butcher of Binbrook* (INT). Prod. Tony Recoder. Dir. Miguel Madrid. Spain, 1971. Image Entertainment, 86 min. DVD. Starring: Bill Curran, Catherine Ellison, Victor Isreal and Beatriz Elorrieta.

Wow, this is bad, and what's worse is you don't know how bad it is until you're halfway through it and you realize, wow, this is bad. Then you see the monster responsible for this and words can't explain how bad this is. Michael Sharrington (Curran), returning to his castle (because everyone in Eurocult has one) after a long business trip, finds that his wife and unborn child have died. No one in the family will talk about it and he himself was not able to view the body. What's worse is his wife's sister is starting to put the designs on Mike and there are some graverobbers stealing corpses to feed to something. When you find out what that something is, you'll want your 86 minutes back, as this is definitely low-budget horror at its worst.

The House That Screamed, aka *La residencia* (SP), *The Boarding School* (GB). Prod. Arturo González. Dir. Narciso Ibáñez Serrador. Spain, 1969. 99 min. Starring: Lili Palmer, Christina Galbo, John Moulder-Brown and Maribel Martin.

Think *The Prime of Miss Jean Brodie* meets *Friday the 13th*! Taking its cue from the Gothic subgenre in Italy, *The House That Screamed* is a well-done movie with enough intimated perversity to make exploitation film lovers happy. Cristina Galbo stars as Theresa, a young girl of questionable upbringing sent to a French reform school run by the very prim Madame Fourneau (Lilli Palmer). Madame runs the school with a strict hand and does not put up with insolence very well, which accounts for the secret room where she whips the bad girls into submission (she also makes them take showers with their clothes on, which should tell you where her mind is). That's right, we've got a battle brewing here between conservative values of Fourneau versus the freedom of our trashy juvenile delinquent girls. We've also got a killer on the grounds who starts hacking up the young girls, especially the ones who want to get the hell out of the school. Who could it be? The gardener? Fourneau herself or her young son who lives with her? I wouldn't dream of giving it away as this is one of those films you don't want to know too much about before watching. It doesn't move fast but it's always engaging, thanks to a fine cast, and if you stick around long enough you'll find it time well spent. The ending is pure exploitation gold!

Let Sleeping Corpses Lie, aka *No profanar el sueño de los muertos* (SP), *The Living Dead at the Manchester Morgue* (GB), *Don't Open the Window* (U.S.). Prod. Manuel Pérez. Dir. Jorge Grau. Spain/Italy, 1974. Anchor Bay Entertainment, 92 min. DVD. Starring: Ray Lovelock, Christina Galbo, Arthur Kennedy and Aldo Massasso.

Let Sleeping Corpses Lie (or whatever the particular name is of the version of this film you're watching) is one of the seminal zombie films of the '70s and perhaps all time. Filmed and released after Romero's *Night of the Living Dead* (1968) and three years before *Dawn of the Dead* (1978), *Sleeping Corpses* carries on the violent tradition of modern zombie films while inputting an environmental and social lesson. Artist George (Italian Ray Lovelock, with one of the worst dubbed voices in Eurocult) is tired of the dirt and grime of London and goes for a motorcycle weekend spin in the country. Unfortunately, his bike is damaged by Edna (Christina Galbo), who is hurrying to see her heroin-addicted sister and brother-in-law in the country as well. Little does Edna know that her sister is under attack from the walking dead. They've killed her brother-in-law and are populating the countryside. As usual in films like this, there's a detective (Kennedy) who doesn't believe them until it's much too late. Could the dead be rising because of a new pesticide machine that sends out high-frequency waves designed to bring things out of the ground? Could be. *Sleeping Corpses* works for many reasons. The environmental message of the film may be a little heavy-handed but still resonates, and let's be honest, it is original. The English countryside is meticulously filmed and colorful, especially on the Blu-Ray edition, providing a great Gothic feel, especially around the graveyards. Lovelock and Galbo make an attractive pair, the zombie make-up is quite good, and the blood and entrails are suitably disgusting. What more could you want? Word of warning, though: this is not a fast-paced zombie movie. The pacing is sluggish in the beginning, but stay with it; the payoff is worth the trip.

Night of the Seagulls, aka *La noche de las gaviotas* (SP). Prod. Francisco Sanchez. Dir. Amando de Ossorio. Spain, 1975. Anchor Bay Entertainment, 89 min. DVD. Starring: Victor Petit, María Kosty, Sandra Mozarowsky and José Antonio Calvo.

The final installment of de Ossorio's Blind Dead series is usually cited as a step up from the previous *Ghost Galleon* (1974). From an exploitation standpoint, I'm not sure I agree, but neither one can compare to the original. Dr. Stein (Petit) and wife Joan (Kosty) arrive in a small beach town to practice medicine. The locals are not thrilled to see them and treat them accordingly, with warnings not to leave their house at night, etc. It seems the townies have a secret that involves sacrificing seven girls (virgin alert) on seven nights every seven years to appease the bloodthirsty wrath of the Templar Knights, our galloping band of hooded undead. It's up to the doc to figure out what's going on (we already know) and put a stop to it, if he can. Sadly, the series ends up at a bit of a low point. A lot of the sex and violence is toned down in order to make the film more of a folk tale than an actual horror film. The attention to atmosphere is admirable with the seashore making an attractive setting for the Templars' slow-motion romps (aided by the seagulls who announce the Templars' arrival, hence the name of the film), but the high-mindedness of the film takes away from the exploitation factor. No lesbian gropings here, and the violence is played down. Still, if you like to see the Blind Dead work their mojo one more time (and who doesn't?), pop *Night of the Seagulls* into the machine and be glad you don't live in that town.

Return of the Blind Dead, aka *El ataque de los muertos sin ojos* (SP). Prod. Ramon Plana. Dir. Amando de Ossorio. Spain, 1973. Anchor Bay Entertainment, 91 min. DVD. Starring: Tony Kendall, Fernando Sancho, Esperanza Roy and Lone Fleming.

The sequel to the popular *Tombs of the Living Dead* (1971) may take awhile to get going, but once it does it's a fun-filled ride. Deviating slightly from the original, *Return* has the skeletal Templar Knights returning to the small Spanish town of Berzano that once a year celebrates the fact that their ancestors burned out the eyes of Knights during their reign of terror (you can imagine the parade banners for that one). This year is a little bit different as the Templars come back, thanks to the sacrificing of a young woman (again we're thinking virgin here) by the local hunchback. Let's just say this year's celebration will be one for the record books as the indomitable Templars crash the party in their slow-motion style, forcing the party guests to barricade themselves into their homes or churches. *Return* has all the same ingredients as the first film but manages to have a more cohesive flow. De Ossorio has full command of his Templar Knights, and his positing them in a real town (as opposed to their ruined one of the first film) helps move the action along. The comparisons to Romero's *Night of Living Dead* (1968) are obvious but only add to the fun. De Ossorio would tire of the town setting after this, and looking for new environments to exploit, would set the next film *Ghost Galleon* (1974) on a ghost ship!

Satan's Blood, aka *Escalofrio* (SP), *Don't Panic* (GB). Prod. Juan Piquer Simón. Dir. Carlos Puerto. Spain, 1977. Mondo Macabro, 82 min. DVD. Starring: Ángel Aranda, Sandra Alberti, Mariana Karr and José María Guillén.

Now here's an interesting piece of nonsense that defies logic but still manages a good jolt of exploitation goodness. Taking pieces of *Rosemary's Baby* (1968), *The Exorcist* (1973), and a bunch of coven porn from the early '70s, Puerto gives us the far-fetched story of Andy (Arnada) and Anna (Alberti) a cute young couple from Madrid who are expecting their first baby. Deciding to go out on a Sunday afternoon, they run into another couple (Guillén and Karr) who swear they know them. Accepting an invitation to their home, which in true exploitation fashion turns out to be a sprawling chateau in the middle of nowhere, the young couple soon realize that these two are a little more malefic than friendly as the Ouija boards come out, the orgies begin and the hosts keep popping off into the kitchen to eat something that results in blood on their lips. Can our young couple escape? Do they even want to? *Satan's Blood* is an exasperating movie that keeps shifting its concentration. First it's a pregnancy horror film, becoming a pretty hot soft-core porno film before finally becoming one of those "we can't escape from this dream" films that the Spanish excelled at. Plot points like the pregnancy are completely dropped by the movie's end, while the "shock" ending is implausible, to say the least, and seems tacked on. This is definitely one of those, "oh, I was just attacked in the kitchen by a stranger, we've got to get out of here, but let's first have a fireplace orgy with the other couple" kind of films. The movie contains a ton of frontal nudity and enough eviscerated dead dogs to keep Eurocult lovers happy. An interesting example of Spanish filmmaking at a time when censorship in Spain had finally been eliminated.

Tombs of the Blind Dead, aka *La noche del terror ciego* (SP). Prod. José Antonio and Perez Giner. Dir. Amando de Ossorio. Spain/Portugal, 1971. Anchor Bay Entertainment, 97 min. DVD. Starring: Lone Fleming, César Burner, Maria Elena Arpón and José Thelman.

    A Spanish classic! True, the film is relentlessly slow and takes forever to get going, but the introduction of the horse-riding, skeletal, hooded Templar Knights makes this film a definite must-see. Poor Virginia (Arpón), she's just not happy. Her boyfriend Roger (Burner), whom she's traveling with in Portugal, is a total jerk. To make matter worse, Betty (Fleming), a girl she had a brief lesbian affair with in Catholic boarding school (a standard practice, judging from Eurocult) shows up, much to the delight of Roger, who definitely has some lust in his eyes. Virginia is not so ready to march in the Rainbow Pride parade and certainly doesn't want to see Betty and Roger hook up, so she jumps off a train (literally) and heads to the closest abandoned monastery. Unfortunately for her, this one is haunted by the Templar Knights, who, though slow-moving and blind (they have some *great* hearing, though), can eat a mean piece of flesh. Noticing Virginia's disappearance and feeling guilty about their flirtation (but not *that* guilty, obviously), Betty and Roger head to the monastery to find her. Let's just say only one makes it back and is completely out of his or her mind. *Tombs* is a colorful little exercise that gave this author some goodly sized nightmares when younger. Many years later the Templar Knights still make for some pretty effective nemeses, accentuated by the deep bass chanting musical soundtrack that de Ossorio adds. Not overly well acted, and the characters are too stupid to care about, but the film is nevertheless a classic in atmosphere and execution.

Vampyres, aka *Vampyres: Daughter's of Darkness* (GB). Prod. Brian Smedley-Aston. Dir. José Ramón Larraz. Spain/Britain, 1974. Blue Underground, 88 min. DVD. Marianne Morris, Anulka Dziubinska, Murray Brown and Brian Deacon.

    Sexy, sultry, bloody good fun from England via Spain. Larraz's *Vampyres* is exactly the type of film for those who enjoy a lot of sex and nudity with their bloodsucking. Fran and Miriam (Morris and Anulka) are two beautiful vampires living in the English countryside who spend their days posing as hitchhikers in order to pick up men, bring them back to their stately home (because they have to have one of those, though this one needs a bit of a dust), have sex with them (both at the same time, of course), and then drink their blood. Two complications, in the form of a vacationing couple who hitch their trailer on the vamps' property, and Ted, a victim that Fran has taken a liking to, threaten to break up our happy lesbian vampire home. This is the one of those perfect exploitation films whose sole ambition is to titillate; it's not scary per se but it is damned sexy. The English setting is a complete contradiction to the sexy goings-on. The lesbian sex scenes, along with requisite soaping up in the shower afterward, are shown not in the light, playful way that is standard in Eurocult, but in an animalistic style reminiscent of hard-core pornography. There is a lot of bloodletting, but it's more in the "let me lick it off your wound in your arm" manner than actual slicing and dicing. Larraz wisely plays down many of the vampire clichés — teeth, bats, etc.— and plays up the sexual frenzy that these ladies get from drinking blood. If you're in the mood for a night of sexy bloodletting, you can do worse than *Vampyres*.

Who Can Kill a Child?, aka *¿Quién puede matar a un niño?* (SP), *Island of the Damned* (U.S.). Prod. and Dir. Narciso Ibáñez Serrador. Spain, 1975. Dark Sky Films, 93 min. DVD. Starring: Lewis Fiander, Prunella Ransome, Antonio Iranzo and Miguel Narros.

    One of the best, most thought-provoking films from Spain in the mid–'70s, *Who Can Kill a Child?* packs a wallop. Everything Stephen's King's *Children of the Corn* should have been is here in a much more suspenseful film that mirrors Ibañez Serrador's take on social issues such as abortion and infanticide. Englishman Tom (Fiander) and his stressed-out pregnant wife Evelyn (Ransome) decide to take a trip to the Spanish coast and to the island of Almanzora because Tom believes it would be a great place to unwind. Obviously he didn't read any of the brochures, because arriving at the island, they discover that there are no adults, only kids (sounds like hell to me!). They do manage to spot an adult in the deserted village, but not before he is bludgeoned to death by a little girl. It seems the kids have killed all the adults, and now, with the arrival of two more adults, they have something to do. Can our couple actually kill children in order to survive? Ibañez

Serrador's film pulls out all the stops, from beginning archival footage (cut from many prints) about the infanticide during war, to the chilling way he deals with Evelyn's baby. This is one of those films that hangs a noose around your neck and pulls it tighter and tighter with every second. Well acted, though it must be admitted that Ransome's hysterics (though justified) got on my nerves, and nicely filmed. The core of this story is a serious attempt to explore the idea of what happens if we don't take care of our children. Highly recommended!

Conclusion

> In 1977 with the abolishment of censorship, the fuse was lit for an explosion of exploitation.
> — Author Jay Slater[172]

It never happened.

In 1975, General Franco died, leaving an uncertainty within the Spanish filmmaking community and the country itself. There were no sweeping reforms; instead, the country's censorship policies remained in limbo. After decades of iron rule, there seemed uncertainty about how to proceed with modernizing, bringing the country up to the same standards as the other European countries. Many of the Spanish-produced exploitation films of the period were trying to be commercially popular, which meant the elimination of the political underpinnings that had marked so many of the genre's films, basically emasculating it.

By 1976, the horror/exploitation industry in Spain had waned considerably. Output dropped from 29 films produced in '73–'74 to 15 in '76–'77 to 8 in '78–'79, as horror films no longer held allure for Spanish producers as they did in the beginning of the decade.[173] With Italy and the United States producing the bulk of exploitation, the Spanish film industry moved into what was called the "destape" or stripping era, which saw the rise of risqué comedies in place of cheap horror.[174] Censorship was finally abolished in Spain in 1977. A new system of classification was established, similar to the MPAA in the United States "Clasificada S" was the rating given to those films that had strong violence, horror or sex.[175] Given the freedom to now produce all types of adult fare, many Spanish producers chose to forsake horror and move to the lucrative sex film. This movement had a severe effect on the genre essentially shutting down the market in Spain for the next decade and a half. By the mid–2000s this began to change with the release of whole new set of violent films by such Spanish directors as Nacho Cerdà, Alejandro Amenábar, Agustí Villaronga and Álex de la Iglesia that began to show a resurgence in Spanish exploitation that fans have been waiting for. The release of such worldwide successes as *REC* (2007) and its sequel *REC 2* (2009) ensures that the exploitation spirit has not been lost in Spain, while other films like *El orfanato* (*The Orphanage*, 2007) continue the Spanish tradition of eerie, dreamlike ghost stories designed to haunt those who love them. The dreamlike narratives, though, now take a different form as they no longer need to be used to cover up the discontent that Spanish filmmakers had with the Franco government. The new Spanish filmmakers will create a new niche of gory, ultra-violent exploitation that will forever put its stamp on future generations, but the glory days of Jess Franco, Paul Naschy and Amando de Ossorio have sadly disappeared, like the dictatorship that helped give them birth.

CHAPTER 3

France

> The problem with the French is they don't trust their own language [when it comes to horror]. American horror movies do well, but in their own language, the French just aren't interested.
> — French director Alexandre Aja[1]

From its inception, the French exploitation film was never really as devoted to dialogue as it was to the physical body. From its beginning with films like Georges Franju's film *Les Yeux sans visage* (*Eyes Without a Face,* 1959) to the films of Jean Rollin, French exploitation's focus was on the body and everything one can do in order to exploit it. While they may not have trusted their instincts on the pure horror aspects of exploitation during the '60s and '70s, French filmmakers were able to contribute more than their fair share of exploitation by producing films with a subject matter they were most comfortable with: sex. Fusing hard-edged exploitive narratives with soft, erotic, sensual visuals, the French contributed to the boom of European exploitation films that were popular throughout the world during the '60s and the '70s. Instead of focusing on extreme violence like the Italians or relying on traditional monsters and folklore like the Spanish, the French exploited the crumbling of world censorship rules that had governed sensuality on the screen and created exploitation movies that were novel and daring. What made most French exploitation different from its other European counterparts was its distinctive look, as France was able to package many of its exploitation films in the most delicious of wrappers. For the French exploitation filmmakers it was the "look" of a film that was paramount to success rather than its content.

Films like Just Jaeckin's *Histoire d'O* (*The Story of O,* 1974) or the entire output of Jean Rollin's films of the '60s and '70s all played up the sexuality of the characters while dealing with the same themes of violence and exploitation as their European counterparts. By isolating and defining the subgenres within the category of French horror/exploitation cinema and by looking at some of the auteurs involved — Rollin, Jaeckin, Mario Mercier, etc. — we see that France was just as major a player in Eurocult films as Italy and Spain, using its distinctive identity to thrill and shock audiences around the world.

Though its film industry made France the leading European filmmaking country in quantity and quality between 1960 and 1993, French producers seldom saw exploitation as a legitimate form of the profession.[2] Traditional French audiences had been used to a nationalized cinema system that promoted a degree of state control over the industry. This control, though, did not have a serious effect of the quality of French films, as audiences enjoyed adventures and dramas with such French superstars as Jean Gaban, comedies with the likes of Jacques Tati, and costume dramas with Michèle Morgan. What made the French film industry different from its Italian and Spanish neighbors was its readiness far earlier to explore subjects that were more adult in nature. Films like Becker's *Casque d'or* (1950), with its story of prostitutes and pimps, and Audry's study of a lesbian relationship in *Olivia* (1950), showcased the willingness of French auteurs to tackle the seamier side of life.[3] Though many of these adult themes played out subliminally in the frameworks of grand epics, some played overtly in the gritty poetic realism genre from filmmakers like Carné and Renoir. Audiences did not have to look as hard in French films to find subplots and images that were nowhere to be seen in other films from around the world.

Another area of difference between French exploitation and that of its Italian and Spanish counterparts was that France's censorship of many of these types of films actually worked in opposition to that of those other countries. While the rest of the world was relaxing standards in the '70s, France was actually taking governmental steps to enforce them. Ironically, it wasn't for reasons of morality, religion or fear of subversive material, as it was for Italy and Spain, but for the protection of art! For the French, exploitation wasn't dangerous for political reasons but aesthetic ones, as critics saw the genre, as well as the pornography genre, as a cancer on the good name of French film and worked hard via the government channels to suppress it. The vehemence the critics shared about the exploitation genre often times led to their "ganging up" on those auteurs like Jean Rollin. They frequently wrote the most inflammatory pieces on both the films and filmmakers in order to ostracize them out of making films. To send a clear message to these filmmakers, they simply refused to see their films or review them in their publications, effectively freezing them out of any press that might lure an audience to the film. These film critics and patrons of the arts looked to the French government to help them censor the offending material.

The one commonality that France shared with some of its European counterparts was the control over its industry by the government. Though not nearly as oppressive as Franco's control in Spain, the French film industry still had to grapple with the demands of a fluctuating government that looked to not only control the industry but to ensure its prosperity as well. As Hollywood became the main competitor to French films in the early '30s, the French filmmakers looked to the government for help in keeping U.S. films out of France, or at least controlling how many films could legally be shown. Realizing at the time that there wasn't much the government could do about the importing of these films, French filmmakers began to concentrate on making films that would appeal directly to the very nationalistic French people. Consequently, those films that embraced the French culture and language proliferated in the '30s and were among the most successful of the decade.[4]

German occupation in the early '40s had a profound impact on the industry. Contemporary and adult-themed films that may have once been considered intellectual were sidelined, while American and British films were banned outright. French filmmakers, finding that environment completely nonconducive to making films, left France for the United States or Britain. During the war, the establishment of the Comité d'Organisation de l'Industrie Cinématographique (COIC) under the Vichy government attempted to reverse the decline in profitability that inevitably occurred with Nazi occupation. Establishing yearly quotas that limited the number of French films produced, it required that the French government approve all film financing. These quotas, combined with guaranteed financing for approved projects, virtually assured the profitability of French movies as the French government was allowed to finance up to 65 percent of cinematic projects that were deemed worthy by the COIC, usually at very low interest rates.[5] After liberation, the Centre National de la Cinématographie (CNC) was founded to carry on what the COIC had begun. A degree of state control, a tax at the box office, an assist to independent or non-commercial cinema, and the rebuilding of the nations cinemas were all a part of getting the French film industry back on its feet after World War II.[6]

By the late '50s, though, French cinema was growing increasingly stale. It had nothing to do with box office, as audiences were turning out in record numbers (400 million in 1957). Instead, there was a general malaise in the industry creatively.[7] This lethargy manifested itself in a string of French films that seemed slightly too safe, too traditional, and too much like the film industry in the United States. In the late '50s there was a rebellion brewing. Many young French filmmakers were beginning to re-examine and rebel against long-held customs of the industry, and ushered in the new, modern age of cinema known as the "New Wave" in 1959. All of this coincided with the arrival of de Gaulle and the Fifth Republic government, which took a more active role in funding French cinema than the previous administration had. The French government began to levy a small tax on each ticket that was bought, to be put into a general fund. French filmmakers could then petition the government for these funds to make their films. This process allowed young unknown filmmakers to have access to money they wouldn't normally have.

The New Wave grew out of more than just government regulation. It was reaction by filmmakers to the stale, formulaic offerings that were doled out by French studios. Young filmmakers wanted to see important, political works that showcased the true spirit of what was happening in France, not big-budgeted, empty epics. Spearheaded by such filmmakers as François Truffaut and with a literary outlet for the philosophy found in the respected *Cahiers du Cinéma*, the New Wave ushered in true auteur filmmaking. Directors began to feel free to experiment with subject matter that was complex, rebellious and adult. Films by Chabrol, Resnais and Rivette revealed a darker side to French society that played out during the tumultuous '60s.[8]

In 1959, one of these New Wave directors, Georges Franju, created one of the first and most influential examples of exploitation/horror the world cinema had seen, *Les Yeux sans visage* (*Eyes Without a Face*, 1959). Not only would the film be France's first true foray into the exploitation market, but would go on to leave an indelible mark on all European exploitation films for the next 20 years. Though French critics were apt to ravage any French filmmaker for producing exploitation, which they deemed to be an inferior genre, causing most film artists of the time to shun it, the French contribution to the exploitation market in '60s and '70s was sizable and, without a doubt, influential.

Grand Guignol et Les Yeux: French Genre Beginnings

> To return to what I said about the fantastic, the spectacle. I don't like it. It doesn't interest me. It doesn't move me and I don't believe it.
> — Georges Franju discussing his film *Les Yeux sans visage* (1959) and his abhorrence of its inclusion in the horror (fantastic) realm.[9]

The French distaste for violence, horror and exploitation has been historically balanced by their interest in the subject. Classic French fairy tales, *Les Contes de fées*, like *Sleeping Beauty*, *Cinderella*, and *The White Deer*, were all conceived in France as tales for adults, with many of these classic stories involving a mixture of death and mayhem. Like their cinematic exploitation counterparts of the '60s and '70s, these fairy tales often relied on subverted texts to get past court censors. Works by Madame d'Aulnoy, Countess de Murat and Marie-Jeanne L'Héritier de Villandon all contained themes present in the authors' own lives, which many times included sex, murder and a variety of assorted debaucheries. As would be the case later with exploitation films, these stories were considered vulgar and suitable only for the local peasants, although members of the upper classes often heard such tales via their own nurses and servants.[10] This disapproval of controversial material would continue throughout the centuries and form the foundation for criticism against exploitation films in France.

As the popularity of fairy tales faded, first being relegated in edited form to the cheap popular press and then disappearing back into oral tradition, the French found new, vicarious thrills at the end of the 19th century in the Grand Guignol. Opening in 1897, Le Théâtre du Grand Guignol specialized in violent, bloody horror shows. Audience members would come to see beheadings, stabbings, and acts of infanticide and insanity played out on a stage for the world to see. Reveling in their fears, audience members would be treated to the first plays that featured an actual prostitute or pervert character that would then be either raped or guillotined. With occasional sex farces thrown into the mix, the Grand Guignol threw French audiences into a tailspin, creating an atmosphere of uncertainty where what started out as a sexy play would end with a horribly graphic murder, all with the help of local butchers who supplied the blood needed for the productions.

Not surprisingly, French censors were appalled by the material and sought to have the theater closed down on many occasions. Unfortunately for critics, censors and the police, the Grand Guignol became a huge success in Paris with audiences from around Europe coming to see the bloody goings-on onstage. Efforts to close the theater only resulted in more interest by a populace looking to escape the realities of real life and indulge in a little vicarious bloodletting.[11] Though the Grand Guignol somehow managed to keep its doors open, its touring productions were seldom allowed to be shown. What was chic in Paris didn't always translate into other areas, as local censors from around Europe were successful in barring many of the Guignol's productions from appearing in their local theaters.

Coinciding with the rise of the Grand Guignol was the beginning of France's film production, as the first film shown in France was by the Lumière brothers in 1895.[12] Among its earliest pioneers, Georges Méliès produced some of the first films that showcased the fantastic in cinema. Never overtly exploitative, Méliès nevertheless founded the French horror movement with his "trick" films of the late 1800s. These films would rely on camera tricks that showed audiences things like a woman turning into skeleton (*Escamotage d'une dame au théâtre Robert Houdin*, 1898) or a bat turning into the devil himself (*Le Manoir du diable*, 1896). These early films with an emphasis on the fantastic were to have an impact on the future French filmmakers who were to take the genre one step further with longer narratives.

One of those filmmakers inspired by the work of Méliès was Louis Feuillade. The founder of the suspense thriller, Feuillade created a series of serials in the early 1900s that utilized supernatural themes and balanced them with modern-day French society. Serials such *Fantômas* (1913–14) and *Les Vampires* (1915–16) created dreamlike worlds where superheroes thwarted the evil geniuses preying on unsuspecting French families. While these serials were somewhat popular with the French audiences, they were not with French critics, who were beginning to look at film as an art form: where they wanted to see intellectual statements from film, they were not finding it in the comic-book styling of *Les Vampires*.

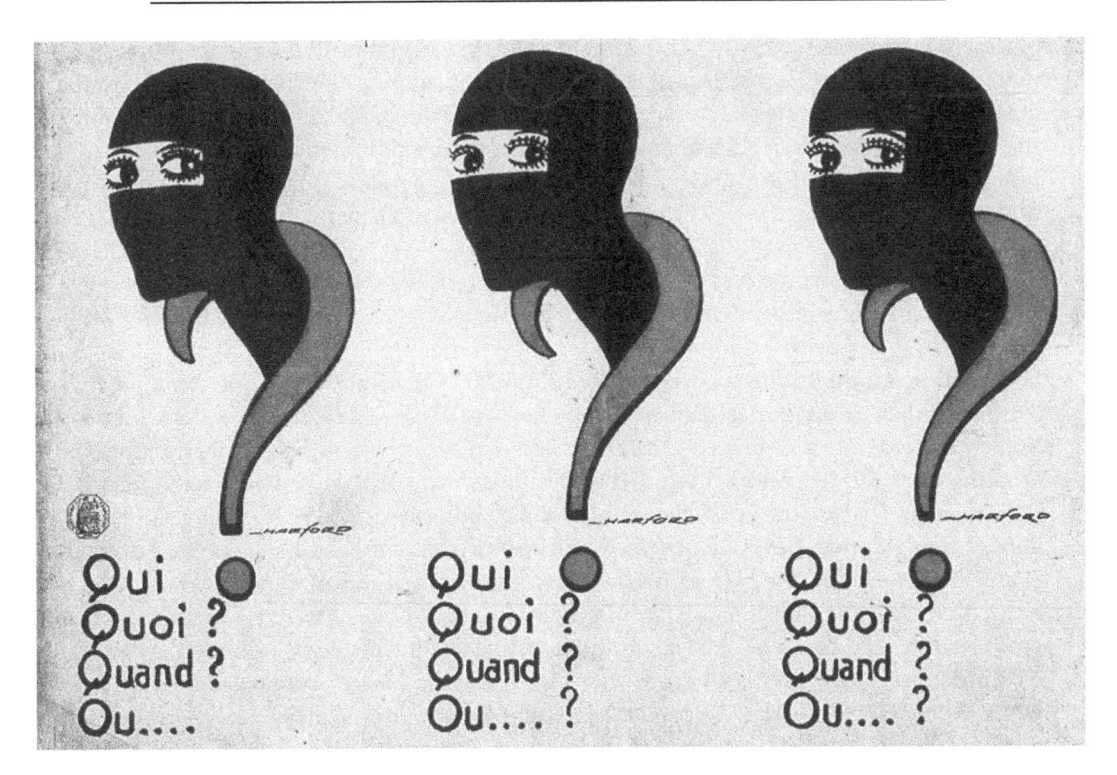

Classic French serials like *Les Vampires* (1915) had an effect on exploitation filmmakers 50 years after their initial premieres.

Feuillade for his part saw himself in the role of entertainer. Wanting to keep his audience happy, he composed those storylines that would appeal to a mass audience. The critics were not impressed and dismissed his work outright. It wouldn't be until the dawn of the New Wave in the early '60s that his work would be revisited and find favor.[13]

Very little horror/exploitation was produced in France from 1920 to 1959. With no historical tradition in Gothic, the popular horror genre of the time, the French went about creating a formidable film industry with genres they were familiar with. Though they developed a strong resistance and mistrust of the exploitation/horror genre, a few of their filmmakers tried their hands at it. Using classical literature, films such as Epstein's *La Chute de la maison Usher* (*The Fall of the House of Usher*, 1928) or Duvivier's *Le Golem* (*The Golem*, 1936) tried to find audiences by creating visual works of art to cover up the horror aspects. Unfortunately, neither French audiences nor critics were buying it, and in each case, the filmmakers received such a critical lambasting that their careers suffered from the effects for years.[14]

In order to have some success in the horror/exploitation genre, French filmmakers had one of two choices they could make. They could either leave France completely or gloss over the horror to please the French audience. Jacques Tourneur, who created some of the '40s' best horror films (*Cat People*, 1942; *I Walked with a Zombie*, 1943), chose to shoot his films within the confines of Hollywood, knowing that it was necessary if he was to have any success with them. His father Maurice tried his hand at the genre in France with *Le Main du diable* (*The Devil's Hand*, 1942). The resulting film, involving a hand that gives its owner great manual dexterity at the price of one's soul, is so watered down and completely lacking in horror that it's hard to classify it as one. Maurice toned down all the horror elements because of his intense fear of a French critical drubbing.[15] Perhaps it was due to the atrocities of the war or just to cultural disposition that many French films of the '40s muted the horrific tones in their screenplays. One good example of this is Cocteau's *La Belle et la bête* (*Beauty and the Beast*, 1945), which retained the cinematic wonder begun with such filmmakers as Méliès, as well as the subliminal themes of ancient fables, but downplayed any overt horror aspects.[16]

The international success of Alfred Hitchcock in the late '40s and '50s inspired French filmmakers to refine the suspense thriller. To the French, Hitchcock was an artist, and while his films were not overt exploitation, the lurid mysteries and murderous situations would be played up in the future by exploitation filmmakers throughout Europe. Using a style similar to that of the poetic realism filmmakers, new talent began to dig deep into the French cultural fabric and expose a seamy side that was ready to be exploited, while the working class of France was interested in seeing subjects that resonated. Henri-Georges Clouzot's *Les Diaboliques* (*Diabolique*) in 1955 helped usher in the period. The story of an abused young woman (Vèra Clouzot) who concocts a plan to murder her lecherous husband (Paul Meurisse) with the help of her husband's mistress (Simone Signoret) shocked and riveted not only the French audience but an international one as well.[17] The film is a first glimpse into what could have been a rather exciting avenue for French filmmakers. Intertwining supernatural events with a tawdry plot involving murder and mystery could have opened the door for a series of bankable French exploitation thrillers. Sadly, this did not come to pass, but the Italians took up the gauntlet a couple of years later with the Giallo.

France, like the rest of Europe, was changing considerably in the '50s. By the time Charles De Gaulle's government came in 1959, making sweeping political and economic reforms, France had undergone a metamorphosis. A long series of crises, including the German occupation, had unnerved the nation since 1930 and had left a deep imprint on French attitudes. The routines and the values of the French people had been shaken up and subjected to challenge by a generation of upheaval. As a result, there was much less public complacency as many of the men and women emerged from the Resistance movement into political life, business posts, or the state bureaucracy and worked hard to build a new perspective as well as to renovate and reassert France's lost greatness.[18]

Georges Franju was one new French director who was looking to help propel France forward by pointing out some of its own internal flaws. Known primarily for his work in documentaries, Franju was no stranger to showcasing the rougher side of life in his films, and his intense and angry views of society seeped through his camera lens. His first documentary, *Le Sang des bêtes* (*The Blood of Beasts*, 1948), showed the insides of a Parisian slaughterhouse. Not shying away from any of the actual violence that occurs in these establishments, Franju subjected his audience to extreme animal slaughter.[19] Using animal slaughter as a metaphor for human waste and corruption, he continued directing socially responsible documentaries, spending most of the '50s creating nihilistic stories of society with such topics as abandoned dogs (*Mon Chien*, 1955), worn-down veterans' hospitals (*Hôtel des invalides*, 1952) and corruptive modernization (*En passant par le Lorraine*, 1950).[20]

By the late '50s, Franju decided to branch out into fictional films. Looking to tap the same anger and attention to violence that marked his documentaries, he began toying with the idea of creating a suspense thriller. The opportunity arrived when French producer Jules Borken presented Franju with the rights to a novel written by Jean Redon that focused on a mad scientist who kidnaps local girls and tries to graft their faces onto his scarred daughter. Stories such as this had never been attempted in France, but the success of Britain's *Curse of Frankenstein* (1957) and *Revenge of Frankenstein* (1958) across the European continent gave Borken hope that a film such as this could be a commercial prospect in France.

Before the film could be shot, though, Franju had to strictly adhere to Borken's request that certain subjects be shied away from. Recalled Franju, "When I made the film the producer told me, 'You're going to make a horror film. I want a horror film, but no blood, that would cause problems with the French censors. No animals tortured — that would cause problems with English censors. No mad doctors — that would cause problems with the German censors because it brings back bad memories.'"[21] Promising to adhere to these standards, Franju hired the screenwriters of Clouzot's *Les Diaboliques* (1955) to give the film a little extra kick. They began by taking Borken's request and slightly altering the characters and situations to appease the worried producer. Dr. Génessier (Pierre Brasseur) would not be just a mad scientist but a man wracked with guilt for causing the disfigurement to his daughter, Christiane (Edith Scob). Blood would only be used within the confines of surgery and not as a violent act within the story, and no animals would be harmed at all. With the producer satisfied, Franju went about a creating his suspense/horror drama from scratch, as he had no previous template to work with.

The final product shocked and thrilled audiences while confusing French critics. Filmed in black and white, *Les Yeux* begins on a dark, cold night as Louise (Alida Valli) drives recklessly to a remote part of the Seine to dump a body whose face has been surgically removed by Dr. Génessier, a world-famous surgeon. It seems the good doctor is looking to find a suitable candidate for a skin graft to replace his daughter's face, who lost hers in an automobile accident caused by the doc. In the meantime, daughter Christiane is becoming more depressed, sadly gliding through the doctor's chateau wearing an emotionless white mask.[22] Released in 1959, the film packed a wallop and either entertained or disgusted the viewing public. To the French, not only was the subject matter extraordinarily distasteful, but the fact that Franju refused to turn his camera away from the horrific surgery performed was an affront to good taste. He craftily made good on his promise that he would not show any violent bloodletting within the context of the plot, but he went for broke during the surgical procedures, which were wincingly real. Franju showed the unsuspecting audience what a real facial graft surgery might look like, showing the entire procedure by using a realistic-looking dummy and a variety of chocolate syrups for blood. Not surprisingly, the surgery scene caused a huge uproar throughout Europe. At the Edinburgh Film Festival, seven viewers fainted, provoking Franju to testily proclaim: "Now I know why Scotsmen wear skirts."[23] In the United States, where the film was released with the highly exploitive title *The Horror Chamber of Dr. Faustus*, the censors demanded cuts to the scene and insisted the film be marketed as an art film in order to scare away young children. This was ironic, since U.S. distributors double-billed the film with the Japanese exploitation classic *The Manster* (1960), which laughably featured a man growing another head on his body and was marketed to and for children directly. Luckily for Franju, he had filmed in black and white: the use of color in this scene like this would have probably led to its complete omission from the final print, as black and white is often a much tamer way of showcasing blood. Both George Romero's *Night of the Living Dead* (1968) and Quentin Tarantino's *Kill Bill* (2003) benefited ratings-wise from filming graphic, extreme gore sequences in black and white because audiences (or at least ratings boards) don't perceive black as the color of blood to be real, and because the amount of it is usually diminished by shadow.

Georges Franju's classic *Les Yeux sans visage* (*Eyes without a Face*, 1959), whose centerpiece was a very gory facial skin graft.

If the worldwide audience reaction to the film was strong, it was nothing compared to the intensity of the French critics. With a clear bias against anything resembling a horror film, and without any previous entries in the genre by which to ascertain quality, French critics immediately tore into the film. Criticizing for its exploitation factor, its subject matter and its daring, most French critics of the time tried to deny the film's existence, let alone its artistic merits, and those who found the film evocative had to reclassify it to another genre just to feel confident in giving it praise. *Cahiers du Cinéma* critic Michel Delahaye argued that *Les Yeux* must actually be a noir film rather than a horror film since "it was beyond question that no serious artist would lower himself by making a horror picture."[24]

Make no mistake, *Les Yeux* is not only a horror film and a damn good one at that, it was also the catalyst for all European exploitation in the '60s and '70s. Predating both Italy's *La maschera del demonio* (*Black Sunday*, 1960) and Spain's *Gritos en la noche* (*The Awful Dr. Orlof*, 1961, with which it has much in common thematically), *Les Yeux* predicates itself on the idea that the quest for physical beauty, a very French trait, is in itself an illness causing great moral lapses. The characters of Franju's film do despicable things in order to restore this much sought-after physical beauty. This plays out in the character of Christiane, whose increasing mental illness is in contrast to the chilling, expressionless white mask she is forced to wear (this type of mask was used just as efficiently 20 years later when John Carpenter incorporated one for serial killer Michael Myers in the classic *Halloween*, 1978). With her sinewy, anorexic body and ballet-type movement (actress Scob studied ballet), she is the epitome of perfection, the perfect supermodel 30 years before their assault on mainstream consciousness. The fact that she is a sad, pathetic figure should bring audience sympathy, but in fact, she truly frightens as her lapse into mental illness becomes more pronounced, culminating in murder. Franju seems to say that once beauty is lost it can never be regained, and though it may appear rejuvenated (via both Christiane and Louise), underneath it is still marred. No one seems to understand this except in the end but Christiane: she decides to escape, freeing all things she's loved in the process. Her final waltz out of her father's laboratory amid barking dogs and flying doves is a classic cinematic moment of any genre that will stay with you long after the film has ended.

The success of *Les Yeux* could have opened the doors for new types of French horror and exploitation, but sadly, it didn't. Though it had an enormous and lasting effect on other European filmmakers like Jess Franco and Antonio Margherti, it did nothing to jump-start a genre in an industry that wanted no part of it. Some films that were exploitive by nature and theme did manage to slip through. In 1961, French director Roger Vadim, who had previously directed the smash international hit *Et Dieu … créa la femme* (*And God Created Woman*, 1956), catapulting sex goddess (and ex-wife) Brigitte Bardot to stardom, brought one of the earliest incarnations of lustful female vampires to world audiences. *Et mourir de plaisir* (*Blood and Roses*, 1961) was based loosely on Sheridan Le Fanu's vampire classic *Carmilla* (1871). Unlike the in-your-face realism of Franju's *Les Yeux*, *Et mourir* took a decidedly softer approach, preferring to film in classy surroundings and strong colors. A cross between the Hammer Dracula films of Britain and the classy epics of France, *Et mourir* toned down all the violence, making it more a psychological film than a horror film. The film involves a young woman, Carmilla (another of Vadim's ex-wives, Annette Vadim), who's haunted by the ghost of the female vampire, Mircalla. Driven by jealousy at her cousin's (Mel Ferrer) upcoming wedding, she becomes a pawn of the murderous spirit and finds herself committing unspeakable acts of violence.[25] Though the lesbian subtext of novel

The Gothic settings of Roger Vadim's *Et mourir de plaisir* (*Blood and Roses*, 1961) are evident in this poster, as is the lesbian subtext.

is played down, Vadim still manages to create a highly charged sexual air that was shocking to many in the early '60s. The sexual tension between Carmilla and her cousin Leopoldo, as well as her attraction to his fiancée (Elsa Martinelli), is palpable, and Vadim plays this out as much as censors would allow. In addition, by playing up the psychological aspects of the story instead of the outright horror (is there really a vampire or is it all just in Carmilla's head?), Vadim is able to walk the line between the French film critics who eschew the horror genre and the worldwide audiences that love it.[26]

Between 1963 and 1967, the French film industry was content to coproduce outside productions of horror and exploitation movies. Working with Italians like Mario Bava (*La frusta e il corpo*, 1963; *Sei donne per l'assassino*, 1964) and Spaniards like Jess Franco (*Miss Muerte*, 1965), French filmmakers showed very little inclination to produce their own brand of exploitation. This may have continued indefinitely had not a youth rebellion taken place in Paris in 1968 and a young filmmaker from the suburbs of Paris had the guts to produce wildly experimental exploitation films, causing furor and distain with the French critics.

Filmography

Blood and Roses, aka *Et mourir de plaisir* (FR). Prod. Raymond Eger. Dir. Roger Vadim. France, 1962. Paramount Home Video, 74 min. VHS. Starring: Mel Ferrer, Elsa Martinelli, Annette Vadim and René-Jean Chauffard.

A watered-down yet beautiful rendition of Sheridan Le Fanu's lesbian vampire tale *Carmilla*. Vadim makes the perfect French horror film by toning down the violence, not big with French audiences, and turning up the romance. Karnstein Castle in Italy is in the midst of an engagement celebration. The beautiful Georgia Monteverdi (Martinelli) has come from Austria to marry the head of the Karnstein family, Leopoldo. Leopoldo's cousin Carmilla (Vadim's second ex-wife at the time, Annette) isn't so happy, as she wanted the dashing Count for herself (yes, I know they're cousins, but why quibble?). Her loss adds to her mental instability. Soon she becomes obsessed with the Karnstein history, which wasn't so "rosy" and involved an evil vampire named Mircalla (Vadim again). The celebrations continue at the castle, and the setting off of some fireworks in honor of the engagement sets off a chain of events that allow the spirit of Mircalla to rise and take possession of Carmilla. From then on it's lesbian subplot and some very artistic uses of blood. Thanks to Vadim's sense of style, *Blood and Roses* comes off an artistic horror/exploitation film. It's still a lesbian vampire film but it's a damn good-looking one, gorgeous in every manner from its cast to its evocative set pieces, which combine French artistry with Italian Gothic. Vadim uses blood as though it were paint, weaving it around like a tapestry. Though there is no graphic sex, the lesbian subplot is pretty pronounced and much more erotic in tone, making the film a landmark in its adult themes. If any film cries out for Blu-Ray rendition that's uncut (many U.S. prints are truncated), it is this film.

Diabolique, aka *Les Diaboliques* (FR). Prod. and Dir. Georges-Henri Clouzot. France, 1955. Criterion Collection, 116 min. DVD. Starring: Simone Signoret, Véra Clouzot, Paul Meurisse and Charles Vanel.

Not exactly an exploitation film, *Diabolique* is a tense, Hitchcockian thriller that was the model for so many exploitation films (most of those obviously being associated with the Italian Giallo) in Eurocult. A little implied lesbianism, a lot of implied violence and a whole lot of tension mark the story of first-class misogynist Michel Delasalle (Meurisse), who abuses both his long-suffering wife (Clouzot) and his mistress (Signoret) to the point where the two want to kill him. The two ladies develop a symbiotic relationship and put their plan into action. Not everything works the way they'd hoped. Again, *Diabolique* is not as exploitative as many of the films that followed over the next two decades, but for those looking for a starting point in which the projection of the seamier side of life is played out via death and murder, this classic French film should be for you.

Eyes Without a Face, aka *Les Yeux sans visage* (FR), *The Horror Chamber of Dr. Faustus* (U.S.). Prod. Jules Borkon. Dir. Georges Franju. France, 1959, Criterion Collection, 90 min. DVD. Starring: Pierre Brasseur, Alida Valli, Edith Scob and Juliette Mayniel.

Though preceded by Riccardo Freda/Mario Bava's classic *I vampiri* (1956), this is the classic French film that was the starting point for the entire Eurocult phenomena! *Eyes* is a taut, spooky, lyrical and ultimately sad film that still makes audiences shudder and avert their eyes. World-renowned surgeon Dr. Génessier (Brasseur) is well thought of around the world. One wonders if the world would think so much of him if they knew that he had been responsible for an automobile accident that severely disfigured his daughter (the very thin Scob) and was now killing the young girls of Paris for their skin to repair her face. Lucky for the good doctor, he has a loyal assistant (Valli, who would go on to star in a number of Eurocult films throughout her illustrious career) who not only dumps the faceless bodies of his victims into the Seine, but happily procures the girls and brings them back to Génessier's mansion. Hopefully, it looks like his latest operation is a success, which is good in that his daughter doesn't have to float around the mansion in her expressionless white mask. Karma, though, is not so forgiving. With the exception of a fast-moving plot, *Eyes* has everything one could hope for in an exploitation movie in the late '50s–early '60s. A *very* scary-looking "ghost" (in the guise of Christiane, his daughter), very evocative black and white photography, a simple soundtrack that runs the gamut between artistic and annoying, and mostly some good old-fashioned bloodletting like the surgery scene, which is as potent today as it was when it was so wildly criticized by critics around the world. What Franju does so masterfully here is to inject some sympathy into every character. His Christiane is a character to be pitied, as is Valli's character of Louise. These are horrible people, yet Franju makes us care about them, which is a testament to his commitment to the material. Any fan of Eurocult should not miss this one.

Les Pensées de Sang: The Psychedelic Cinema of Jean Rollin

> Some people say I'm a genius, others consider me the greatest moron who ever stepped behind a camera. I have heard so many things said about me and my films, but these are just opinions. I am perfectly happy with what I do.
> — Jean Rollin[27]

Probably the most prolific and controversial auteur in French exploitation, Jean Rollin was born on November 3, 1938, in the Paris suburb of Neuilly-sur-Seine. With his father a theater director and actor, and his younger brother a painter, it was only natural that Rollin found himself attracted to the arts. His art was not on the stage or a canvas, but on film, which had an indelible effect on the young dreamer. It was the first film he remembers seeing, Gance's *Le Capitaine Fracasse* (1942), that had a profound effect of him as the film's sequences of storms on the ocean solidified the aspiring filmmaker's desire to "become an orchestrator of storms, creator of images."[28] This love of the sea and water was to translate into a lifelong fascination, some would say obsession, for Rollin. Said Rollin of his early inspiration: "My first short film was an evocation of Corbiere on a beach near Dieppe. I was young, no money, no material, etc. But I was there, on a strange beach covered in stones deserted with the 'falaise' [cliff] and the seagulls."[29]

Rollin's love of the tragic irony within the French landscape explains his fond affection for filmmakers Luis Buñuel and Georges Franju. He compares Buñuel to an artist like Trouille, who paints people and objects in a realistic, some would say ultrarealistic, manner. It is the imagery in Buñuel's films, independent of the story, that leaves Rollin full of exaltation. In addition, Rollin completely admires Franju's *Les Yeux sans visage* (*Eyes Without a Face*, 1959) which he refers to as "greatest film in the genre." It's no surprise that Rollin was a fan of the film: with its haunting, atmospheric visuals combined with a tragic plot and horrific overtones, *Les Yeux* mined the subjects of dreams, nightmares, poetry and madness, subjects that Rollin gravitated to over and over again through his works.[30]

After finishing school, Rollin became increasingly political and aligned himself with anti–Franco groups from Spain who were looking for someone to produce propagandist documentaries. Working as a TV and sound editor at the time, Rollin eagerly took up the challenge and headed to Madrid to shoot the film. Immediately the Spanish police got wind of the endeavor and began to hunt down the young filmmakers. After 10 days of cloak-and-dagger maneuvering, the young filmmakers fled back to Paris to edit their movie. The resulting film, *Mourir à Madrid* (*To Die in Madrid*, 1962), was shown during anti–Franco conferences and meetings around Europe.[31] By 1966, Rollin had begun to associate himself with some of the avant-garde intellectuals surrounding Parisian-based Eric Losfeld. The group was beginning to fall under the influence of the burgeoning hippie movement, in which Rollin saw as a way to indulge his revolutionary spirit and break free from the conventions of the French critics, who he believed were enforcing their own antiquated beliefs on the arts. Indulging in his love for the fantastic, and under the influence of Losfeld, Rollin began to write comic books. These comics were in the spirit of Feuillade; they were strongly sexual and contained a lot of his revolutionist ideas, ideas that were shocking to mainstream audiences. For Rollin, though, these comics were a temporary diversion from his real love, cinema. Hooking up with American expatriate producer Samuel S. Selsky, he decided to create a short film that would serve as a second feature to distributor Jean Lavie's rerelease of *Dead Men Walk* (1943). Assembling a small crew of enthusiastic young filmmakers and a budget of 100,000 francs ($15,000), Rollin wanted to create an avant-garde style of film that was primarily composed of images from artists who had had an impact on him. Realizing that it couldn't be done on such a low budget, Rollin instead concocted a sexy horror story that would take place in his most inspirational locale, the beach.[32]

It is this beach near Dieppe where a majority of Rollin's first film would be shot. Filmed in black and white, *Le Viol du vampire* (*The Rape of the Vampire*, 1968) is an ethereal look at the vampire legend and was proclaimed as the "first Vampire movie in France."[33] Shot in two parts, the film is actually a serial of sorts, à la *Les Vampires* (1915) or *Judex* (1916), as it is actually two short films combined to make a longer one with only a small thread of continuity. *Le Viol* serves as homage to the adventure serials that had a profound effect on Rollin as a child. Rollin relates, "When I was about 13 or 14 I became really obsessed with American serials. The cinema and comic books were our whole lives! We were playing them, talking about them, living them. I remember *Jungle Jim* (1948) with Johnny Weissmuller, also *The Shadow* (1940) and *The Mysterious Dr. Satan* (1940). These were serials, always to be continued next week, so once an episode was over, nothing mattered but getting through the next week as quickly as possible! The serials were not just a special piece of culture; they also had a real spirit to them, which changed our lives and attitudes."[34]

The effect of these serials, in addition to the classic Feuillade French serials *Les Vampires* (1915) and *Judex* (1916), had influenced Rollin as an auteur: "I certainly know that these events are the source for most of the ideas that recur throughout my films. The spirit, structure and contents of the serial is the key to my type of cinema. I work from childhood memories, and even if I sometimes cannot name a film in particular, I know that all my ideas originated from that time."[35]

Though he may have nostalgic memories of childhood, the first section, "Le Viol" is pure college-student angst and deals with four vampire sisters residing in a dilapidated chateau and hounded by the local peasants. When three headstrong college students (Bernard Letrou, Marquis Polho, Catherine Deville) arrive, love, passion and some '60s revolutionary idealism collide, with inevitable results. The initial film ran only 38 minutes and when it was screened, the producer was sufficiently impressed to ask if Rollin would go back and film enough footage to make it a complete picture. Instead for continuing with the original narrative, Rollin filmed the second part of the film, titled "Les Femme Vampire," dealing with a society of vampires on the beach. In an ode to serials of his childhood, they are ruled by an African queen, as the departure from the first story plays up the comic-strip aspects that had first attracted him.[36]

The style of the film is only a partial success, though, as overall, *Le Viol du vampire* was a patchwork of concepts and execution that didn't quite fit the serial milieu. There's an element of fun involved in a serial, and that fun is missing for most of the running time of *Le Viol*. In addition, '60s audiences had long given up watching serials; they were not used to the split narrative style, and were confused by it.

Unfortunately, *Le Viol du vampire* was not released during an idyllic, relaxed period where serial-type escapism mixed with erotic horror could be enjoyed. The film was released in May of 1968, during the social and political revolution that was taking place throughout Paris. Student unrest at universities in Paris exploded on May 3, when a rally of student radicals at the Sorbonne became violent and was broken up by the police. This minor incident quickly became a major confrontation which resulted in street fighting breaking out, police barricading the Latin Quarter, and the Sorbonne's being occupied by student rebels, who converted the university into a huge commune. The unrest spread to other universities and then to the factories, resulting in a wave of wildcat strikes that rolled across France. Several million workers were involved, virtually paralyzing the nation. Prime Minister Pompidou ordered the police to evacuate the Latin Quarter and concentrated on negotiations with the labor union leaders.[37]

This political unrest had an unexpected consequence for Rollin. With the lack of new films in the theaters at the time, critics came out to view Rollin's experimental film. They were universal in their opinion. The French newspaper *Le Figaro* wrote that film was made "by a team of drunks who had escaped from the mental asylum."[38] *Midi-Minuit Fantastique*, a respected magazine devoted to fantastic cinema, found it awful, as did every other critic in France. Adding to the discord, 1968 French audiences were in no mood to put up with experimental cinema in a genre unfamiliar to them. The effects the 1968 revolution on the filmgoing audience may never be known, but the scandalous impact that it had on Rollin as well as his film career has not abated. Commenting on the initial reaction, Rollin has said "People were really mad when they saw it. In Pigalle, they threw things at the screen, the principal reason was that nobody could understand the story. But there was a story, I swear it! The audience knew only Hammer vampires and my film disturbed their classical idea of what such a film should be. And outside it was the revolution, so people were able to exteriorize themselves. The scandal was a terrible surprise for me. I didn't know I had made such a 'bizarre' picture."[39] It was the "succes de scandale" of the film that forever pegged Rollin as a maker of sexy vampire films.

Though the film was blasted for belonging to genre unsuitable for French filmmakers, it did have a decidedly political sensibility (the three university students represented the new generation of the populace looking to banish outmoded superstitions). In a 1995 interview with Peter Blumenstock, Rollin expresses his ideas about the mixture of politics with the intricacies of the horror genre. Said Rollin, "The fantastic cinema is always a good vehicle for discussing certain political ideas in the form of symbols and metaphors. In general, the fantastic cinema is always political, because it is always in the opposition. It is subversive and it is popular, which means it is dangerous. I made films with sex and violence at a time when censorship was very strong, so that was certainly a political statement as well, although again, not a conscious one. I just happen to have an imagination, which doesn't correspond with those of certain conservative people."[40]

Le Viol also served as Rollin's initial foray into a modern poetic realism structure, which was very much a French film construction. The film is poetic in practically all of its manifestations of French culture. The townspeople, gripped in terror by their fears; the students and their abhorrence to status quo but most importantly the four "vampire" sisters: as shot by Rollin, these characters take on the sadness of those who are persecuted by society yet forced to warily live in it. Filmed as white ghostly visions (long, flowing white gowns, pale white skin), these women represent purity in an atmosphere decaying, ancient, and cold. Even the sea is of no comfort as our main characters are shot along the sandy shore. The black and white filming offers no warmth to the audience with the water appearing icy as the waves break, which is not surprising, as Rollin filmed the movie in winter. France's first vampire film was indeed an alienating affair much in the same way that French audiences distanced themselves from popular films like *Le Jour se lève* (1939). Perhaps they were not prepared to see an accurate, albeit fantastic portrayal of their beloved society.

With the complete lambasting of his first film, Rollin continued his work as sound editor for the newsreel company. When the company folded in the late '60s, he decided to pursue his dream of filmmaking again, with a few big differences. This time the film he chose would be shot in color, professional actors would be used, and the serial structure would be abandoned. One thing that would not change would be his use of nudity and sex. Even from his first film Rollin was always interested in portraying unabashed sexuality, commenting in a 2006 interview, "When I was making my first film [*Le Viol*] my producer thought it would be great if I could somehow find a way to put a naked girl in the film. I said, 'Why not!?' These kinds of films were becoming increasingly popular in America and in Europe, so I did it. For my next picture I decided to explore vampirism and again put in some naked girls.... It worked for me, I liked it."[41]

Rollin's second film, *La Vampire nue* (*The Nude Vampire*, 1969), continued the trend of telling strange, ephemeral, non-linear vampire stories. With *Nue*, Rollin set out to introduce fantastic elements into the everyday world and push the normal until it becomes supernormal. *Nue* concerns a suicide cult run by the Master, who has a dimensional gap into another universe. The film, like its predecessor, shuns classical Hollywood narrative, as Rollin's style is very reminiscent of Feuillade and his "cinema of attractions" approach to story telling. This approach is characterized by the spectator, who is external to the story space, an effect created by tableau staging, which uses long takes and the essential autonomy of each shot. The overall strategy of this technique is one of showing.[42] Though more technically proficient than *Le Viol*, Rollin's style and non-linear approach was again alienating to audiences. That is not to say that the film does not contain hidden comments on French society of the time. The film borders on science fiction and is very much in the style of the popular French comic books of the day. The "vampire" girl (Caroline Cartier), signifying again the outcast in society, is actually, in addition to being an alien, the next link to a higher, more evolved human. Rollin seems fascinated by this dichotomy, stating, "After *Le Viol*, I had to make a more classical film. So in place of the delirious images of *Le Viol*, I tried to put some mystery into *La Vampire nue* (1969)—mystery of the strange people, the

Jean Rollin's second feature, *La Vampire nue* (*The Nude Vampire*, 1969), was his first color film and continued his style of non-linear narratives.

strange girl who is not really a vampire, and mystery with the locations in Paris I found."[43] *La Vampire nue* utilized Rollin's idiosyncratic style to build his film around the idea of enigma, mystery. This played out not only in elements of the text but with Rollin's mise en scène. Rollin explained, "Places had great importance for me in that film. For example, I like the strange meeting in the beginning between the girl and the boy under the pale light. Nothing special, only elements of everyday, except the girl with her strange costume, but the bizarre atmosphere is there. Why? Which? What? I don't know but the mystery is there."[44]

The mystery for most of the audience was figuring out exactly what the film was about. Rollin exploits his use of color photography to the extreme as the late '60s explode via some of the most psychedelic set pieces in French film, which coincide with the dreamlike narrative that he follows. The film also begins Rollin's trademark of using twins (the Castel twins here) in key roles. The role of twin or of a young female duo resonates in the majority of his films. In almost all cases these girls are either over-sexualized in the extreme or complete virgins. Rollin doesn't take the middle ground here, working out some fetish issues that usually have the girls shooting or screwing their way out of outlandish situations. Though not a huge success at the box office, Rollin's decision to make his vampire films more linear caught the eye of some distributors and producers. After viewing a cut of *La Vampire nue*, female producer Monique Natan found Rollin's view of female vampirism unique. After meeting Rollin, she agreed to produce another film that would be even more appealing to French audiences.

Written over the course of one weekend, *Le Frisson des vampires* (*The Shiver of the Vampires*, 1970) was Rollin's most assured and commercial film to date. Like his others films, elements become more important to the viewer than actual plot development, and Rollin's use of mise en scène took on a fascinating context within the film. He is as focused in his films on the environment as he is on his actors. Much in the style of European softporn master Radley Metzger, who was experiencing worldwide popularity at the time, the décor is a character all in itself. He achieves a bizarre world in his films where pulp aesthetics are mixed with art aesthetics to create a surrealistic nightmare.

Though interested in décor, it is from the "hippie" movement of the early '70s that he derives most of his ideology. What begins as a typical horror movie device—newlyweds forced to spend the night in a haunted castle—becomes a manifesto for youth culture as the lead vampire (Nicole Naciel) spends half the movie spouting off about the history of religion in Europe.[45] Again, decaying decadent castles, filled with the souls of the undead, is the theme, but mining the rebellious nature of France's youth in the early 1970s is where Rollin takes his inspiration. With the '70s ushering in a new permissiveness in representations of sexuality, he really begins to explore the sexual liberation: scenes of semi-nude female vampires (with extraordinarily large teeth) rising out of grandfather clocks was a clear signal that Rollin believed the youth of France was waking up. To help this along, and perhaps give the film a little more commercial success, he bathed the film's soundtrack in free-form progressive rock, including everything from guitars to organs and flutes.[46]

Le Frisson did achieve some commercial success in France and was one of his first to find distribution abroad. French critics, though, were not pleased that a new Rollin film had been released and subsequently refused to even review the film. Producer Natan, happy with the film's popular acceptance, immediately began to formulate another vampire movie with Rollin. Unfortunately, she was killed in an automobile crash in late 1970. As a result, Rollin returned to Sam Selsky, who had produced *Le Viol* and *La Vampire nue*, and with a

Les distributeurs associés présentent :

LE FRISSON DES VAMPIRES

Un Film de Jean Rollin. Production Films Modernes et Films A.B.C

Sandra JULIEN · DOMINIQUE · Nicole NANCEL · Jean-Marie DURAND
Michel DELAHAYE · Jacques RIBIOLLES · MARIE-PIERRE et KUELAN

INTERDIT AUX MOINS DE 18 ANS

EASTMANCOLOR

little success under his belt he tried to create a film that would explore both the commercial side of filmmaking and his own personal concerns.

The resulting film, *Requiem pour un vampire* (*Requiem for a Vampire*, 1971), was like getting a peek inside Rollin's mind. Like all of Rollin's films, dialogue is kept to the barest minimum, with the first real words not spoken in the film for 40 minutes. "I wanted to create the ultimate naive film, to simplify story, direction, cinematography, everything. Like a shadow, an idea of a plot," said Rollin.[47] This "idea" of a plot concerns two sexy young women on the run in a stolen car who are forced to stay in a "typical" Rollin castle inhabited by vampires. The narrative is filmed poetically, where one situation melds into the next situation without attention to linear development. Though the on-camera sex is played down a bit in *Requiem*, the exploitation factor is still high because of our two main protagonists, Marie-Pierre Castel and Mireille D'argent, who look like they just came out of a Quentin Tarantino version of *Lolita*. These young, pigtailed, adolescent criminals ooze sexuality, and their freedom with their bodies is very much in line with Rollin's ideas about the freedom of sexual expression in French youth. Their sexuality is represented very much in comic-book style: the situations in which they find themselves inevitably have the young pixies appearing wide-eyed, in various stages of undress and completely open to new experiences. For Rollin, this type of sexuality was important to the horror aspects of the story, not for titillation effect alone. He has eschewed the idea that these vampire films are sex films saying, "I don't think my horror and fantasy films are sex films, I think they are erotic. I think of them as a kind of poetry, fantastic and sad. For example, an image that I have used often (and one that resonates in *Requiem*) is that of an old graveyard with cold grey stones and so on. By having a beautiful nude woman walking through that graveyard, through the crosses and statues, perhaps holding a torch or lantern, she is a symbol of light and beauty in the dark. Very poetic."[48]

Most genre authors agree that *Requiem* remains a consolidation of the experimental Rollin period.[49] His craftsmanship solidified, he begins to incorporate standardized commercial forms of film with the integration of more personal concerns. Not surprisingly, these concerns focus on the decaying social structure not only of France but of Europe. Looking at his first four vampire films of the late '60s and '70s, one can see the completion of the war that was waging within society. From impossible odds in *Le Viol du vampire* (1968), where society in the form oppressed villagers and historical precedent win out, to *Requiem pour un vampire* (1971), where the head vampire is old, dying and looking to pass along his power, the films complete a progression. That the object of his transference is two young nubile French girls, who happen to be criminals, is significant in itself. These girls represent the future of horror: young, pretty, yet complaisant about death or violence. They are French Lolitas who are vicious in their self-indulgence and who represent a modern-day revamping (no pun intended) of the "femme fatale." It is in these girls' hands that Rollin places the future of France.

Requiem pour un vampire (1971) became the first Rollin film to receive distribution in the United States. Distributor Harry Novak saw some potential in the drive-in and grindhouse circuit for the film. Unfortunately this partnership didn't work out. Taking exception with the film's being retitled *Caged Virgins* (1972), producer Selsky thought the film was marketed all wrong. Quipping sarcastically that "Americans probably don't know what

---

Opposite: Rollin continued to use avant-garde–style marketing to alert his audience that perhaps they could be seeing something different from the usual vampire film.

One of the few Rollin films to obtain release in the United States, Rollin's *Requiem for a Vampire* (1971) actually seems coherent in this poster. Audiences of the time thought otherwise after viewing the film.

requiem means anyway," he watched one of the few Rollin films to receive distribution in the American market fizzle to vast indifference.[50]

In 1972, French filmmakers were beginning to find another source of inspiration for their films: pornography. The release of *Deep Throat* (1972) and *Behind the Green Door* (1972) in the United States interested the French insofar as they could see a big return on a small investment. Added to that, the French producers felt fairly comfortable with the subject of sex. By the early '70s, French producers had already begun to "splice" in bits of hard-core to liven up their soft-core features. Censorship rules around France, as well as Europe, were already being challenged, and the popularity of hard-core made any form of censorship difficult. Distributors now began offering international buyers two versions of films depending on the censorship rules in a particular country, one with the hard-core added, one without.

Jean Rollin was one of the first to make movies that allowed this practice to flourish. His first attempt at a non-vampire/sex film was *Jeunes filles impudiques* (*Schoolgirl Hitchhikers*) in 1973. He was unsure if he could make a straight-ahead sex picture. Related Rollin in 1995, "Lionel obliged me to put some sex scenes in *Requiem* [*Pour un vampire*, 1971] during the dungeon sequence. I told him that I wasn't too fond of that kind of thing, and he answered: 'But you do that kind of thing very well. If we made an entire film like that, I bet it would be successful. You may not like it, but you know how to do it.' 'Okay, I'll do it, but I won't invest any of my own money into it.' Well, he raised the money, we made the film, and he was right. The two sex films I made, *Jeunes* and *Tout le monde il en a deux* [*Bacchanales sexuelles*, 1974] were very successful."[51]

The budgets for these soft-core films were even lower than for his vampire films, resulting in cheap, amateurish visuals, but it didn't seem to bother Rollin. He found inspiration in the film serials of old, weaving the tale of two female hitchhikers who get involved with jewelry thieves. The girls in the film hop from one bed to the next with a carefree sexual abandon that was fairly standard in early '70s soft-core. Fearing that his non-hard-core films may suffer, he adapted the pseudonym Michel Gentil for this and his subsequent sex pictures. Rollin's second soft-core film, under the Michel Gentil moniker, was *Tout le monde il en a deux* (*Bacchanales sexuelles*) in 1974. This film is nothing more than a comic-book romp. French beauty Joëlle Coeur stars as Malvina, the leader of a gang of hedonists who live in an elegant French chateau. Wearing outfits that look like a sexualized version of a Batman costume, members of Coeur's gang slink around comically trying to kidnap a young woman (Marie-France Morell) whose cousin has some incriminating evidence about the sex cult.[52] Executed as an outlandish comedy, the film pushed the boundaries of soft-core, which Rollin found surprisingly difficult to direct. As he put it, "It's strange, but it was much more embarrassing for me to shoot my first [sic] soft-core film, *Tout le monde*. I walked off the set one day, because I just couldn't direct phony lovemaking. When it became real, I had no problem at all. I really don't know why. Maybe because in soft-core films, the only person revealing his obsessions is the director, because he has to call the shots while the actors simply do as they are told. In porno, both the actors and director are in the same position. One reveals his obsessions, and the actors live them out, so there is nothing to be ashamed of."[53]

Tout le monde performed fairly well in French theaters, even securing a release in the United States with the name *Fly Me the French Way*, though the film was edited down from 102 minutes to 77 to make it perfect for grindhouse viewing. Its relative success propelled Rollin to write another horror movie, this time without vampires. *Les Démoniaques* (*The*

Schoolgirl Hitchhikers

with GILDA STARK
MARIE HELENE REGNE
FRANCOIS BRINCOURT

Sex Kittens who stop at nothing

R | ADULTS ONLY

A SUNSET INTERNATIONAL RELEASE

EASTMANCOLOR

Demoniacs, 1974) allowed him to incorporate his love of the Hollywood swashbuckler and pirate film into an exploitation film. *Les Démoniaques* is a story of revenge: two young girls (again working on themes present in all of his films) are raped and murdered by a group of shipwrecked pirates led by Tina (played by *Tout le monde*'s Joëlle Coeur). After making a pact with the devil, the two girls return as ghosts to inflict some payback on the evil crew.[54] Even more "out there" than his other films, *Les Démoniaques* relies on the expressionistic way that Rollin shoots the film. Dialogue and characterization take second place (no surprise, as none of his films are dialogue-heavy) as the atmosphere is played up.

Though Rollin had intended the film to be larger in scope, the budget problems and outside meddling from coproducers caused some radical reshuffling of ideas. Shooting exploitation pictures during the early-to-mid-'70s relied on ingenuity and tenacity. According to Rollin, "Even with the Belgian money involved, we were close to leaving it unfinished. There was one week of shooting ahead of us, and we had absolutely no money left. We were in despair and really didn't know how to go on. So, we all went into a little bar where the director of photography got drunk every night. They were selling lottery tickets there, and that night, they had only one ticket left. Lionel, the producer, bought it, just for fun, and he won about 100,000 francs! We were saved!" Budgets weren't the only problems an exploitation filmmaker had to deal with. Reputation of both the genre and filmmakers could have a large effect on the proceedings. Explained Rollin, "I also had a lot of problems with two actresses who were supposed to play the leading parts. We found two very attractive, young girls who worked in an office near mine, and I offered them the parts. Everything was fine until somebody told them that, if they made a film with me, I would make them walk the streets as prostitutes to raise money for the film's financing! And they believed it! I never found out who did it. As you can see, I had a very bad reputation at that time, and my films were also infamous, which certainly did not help."[55]

Feeling dismayed by the lack of respect for his films, Rollin looked to escape the exploitation genre entirely and create a thought-provoking film about two people lost in a strange environment. *La Rose de fer* (*The Iron Rose*, 1974) was his attempt to present to French audiences something different. Without any horror or sex involved, financial backers shied away, causing Rollin to put up his own funds to get the film made. Typical exploitation troubles aside (problems with locations, actors, etc.), Rollin did manage to show the completed film to a group of horror fans at the second Convention of Cinéma Fantastique in Paris. Critics as well as fans were horrified. French magazine *Cinématographe* recounted gleefully how Rollin at been booed by the audience "in a way that the writer had ever seen a director booed in his life."[56] Rollin was completely devastated. Not only had he sunk a substantial financial investment in the film, he saw it as a way to branch out of the exploitation genre. The French critics would have none of it and were unimpressed.

Forced to work for financial reasons, Rollin relegated his filmmaking talents primarily within the hard-core porn industry, producing 12 films under the name Michel Gentil. Rollin has always stated that for him it was easier to shoot a hard-core sex film than a softcore one. He goes on to say: "Movies like *Deep Throat* (1972) became very popular in Paris and distributors were free to screen it wherever they wanted." Rollin stated, "So, all the little cinemas that would show my vampire films immediately stopped showing them

Opposite: Most of Jean Rollin's films were never shown in the United States, and when they were, they received the barest, most childish marketing, designed to appeal to the local drive-in movie crowd.

because they were too tame and instead showed only porno films. So in order to live, I started making X-rated films. I did what I had to do, as did many other small European filmmakers at the time."[57]

Of the 12 sex films he produced between '74 and '78, only one was strong enough to warrant his real name, *Phantasmes* (*The Seduction of Amy*, 1975). Trying to successfully blend horror and porn, he again felt the wrath of French critics. Now that Rollin was doing porn, the critics felt they had a scapegoat on whom to blame a rapidly changing French film industry. So vehement was their ire that one magazine, *Écran*, blamed Rollin himself for the whole wave of French porno that was being produced thanks to the abolishment of censorship in 1975, claiming that it was his "half dozen turds a year" that led to the proliferation of a genre that was killing the indigenous French film industry.[58]

Rollin's final three vampire-themed films, *Lèvres de sang* (*Lips of Blood*, 1976), *Les Raisins de la mort* (*The Grapes of Death*, 1977), and *Fascination* (1979), were all filmed in between his porn projects. Each one had the typical, lyrical female who in some way was forced to confront the unnatural state of being a vampire, or in the case *Les Raisins*, a contaminated zombie. Each film piled on more nudity and gore than his other previous non-porn films. In addition, each film attempted to branch out into new avenues of introspection about French culture and society in a way that had always marked Rollin's work. By the late '70s, France had adjusted to the new film landscape and freer sensuality standards, and Rollin's films of the era showcased this freedom. While the films had commercial aspirations, they still were deeply invested by his quixotical mind and his use of color and imagery to promote the kind of vision of what he saw within the French social culture.

Working as a "beautiful macabre poem," *Lèvres de sang* is considered by many, including Rollin, to be his best.[59] Frédéric (Jean-Lou Philippe) is obsessed with discovering the location of a castle that he remembers from his childhood. At a party, he is surprised to see a photograph that looks surprisingly similar to the castle, setting up an investigation that leads him to his destiny and a few vampires loose on the streets of Paris.[60] The film is an obvious homage to Rollin's youth, and although the plot reads like simple horror melodrama, what he was really looking at is the subversion of rational order to boyhood fantasies and romantic longings. Film scholars such as Doug Sparks who have reexamined the film find that that confusion and terror, the two predominant emotions in the film, can (when related to a downtrodden existence) evoke a childlike simplicity or even romance in the traditional sense.[61] It's an interesting concept as Rollin, for all his sentimentality, sees this obsessive longing for one's childhood as having terrible consequences for the future, not just for Frédéric but for those around him (via some vampire action set loose on the populace of Paris because of his quest to find his castle). Also interesting to see is that he views his adult characters as nothing more than manifestations of their childhood fears. This statement can also describe Rollin himself, who sees each of the fears of childhood manifested in the simplicity of his films.

Rollin's next non-porno film was an entry into the zombie movie genre. The zombie film was enjoying much popularity in Europe with films like Jorge Grau's *The Living Dead at the Manchester Morgue* (1974) and Dario Argento's European version of *Zombi* (*Dawn of the Dead*, 1978) playing to full audiences around Europe. Surprisingly, it wasn't the zombie film but the American disaster movie that first enticed Rollin to film *Les Raisins de la mort* (*Grapes of Death*, 1977). The success in the early and mid–'70s of disaster films like *The Towering Inferno* (1974) and *Earthquake* (1974) had interested European producers who were looking for a quick buck. Rollin determined that a disaster movie of any quality could

Lèvres de sang (*Lips of Blood*, 1976) was one of Jean Rollin's most personal films.

not be achieved with such low budgets and began to focus his ideas on a biological disaster. Looking to find some horror in everyday life, he developed a story that took the French national beverage (wine) and deviously turned it into a device to drive the local country folk mad.

Les Raisins is Rollin's ode to poetic realism. In his hands it becomes exploitative. As he summed up the movie in 1995, Rollin replied, "The key to my story is the guy who cuts off the head of his girl with an axe, yet he says, 'I love you' in doing that, because he is conscious."[62] Forsaking the traditional vampire storyline, *Raisins* instead deals with a young woman, Elizabeth (Marie-Georges Pascal), trying to escape the French countryside that's been overrun with decaying, infected locals who've been poisoned by pesticides in the wine.[63] Nevertheless, the themes still remain the same with the purpose of assimilation. Rollin shoots the entire film against the dead, depressing backdrop of the volcanic mountain region of Cévennes in southern France. The delineation between Rollin's foggy oppressive atmosphere and, say, the dark harbor town of *Le Quai des brumes* (1938) is slight. Like *Quai*, Rollin fills the screen with the trappings of lower-class life. Suicide, desertion, flight, alcoholism and incestuous longings are set patterns in the existence of the villagers. Their contamination only seeks to magnify their yearnings as well as their hidden animosity against the ruling establishments.

Yet, for all their madness, Rollin sees this group of zombies as happy. They do not kill each other; in fact, their condition liberates them to those emotions that remained under the surface. They are able to free these emotions up so they can express more love, hate, and desire. It is only for those not contaminated that they harbor violent feelings. Said Rollin, "The idea was to do a 'living dead' film with the horrors you would in a Romero film, but with a different story. Romero's style is claustrophobic.... I tried a contrary approach; people are running in the vast countryside area, and, more importantly, my zombies are part of the living, with consciences, they know what they are doing but can't stop themselves. So the sequence where the actor becomes mad and cuts off the head of his girlfriend, telling her at the same time that he loves her, is very dramatic!"[64]

Clearly Rollin is again taking out his angst against the government and, much like the Spaniard Grau, blaming man's technological advancement for poisoning the natural order of things. The idea that Rollin uses French wine as the catalyst for madness is delicious, since it is also a metaphor for the purity of all things French. The subsequent contamination by the government is a direct lob at the power structure of French society. It is they who have poisoned the wine, it is they who must suffer. Suffer they do as the film contains some graphic gore and sex sequences to showcase the violent nature of his "zombies," including a pretty nifty decapitation, as well as the sight of an increasingly naked porn star turned legit actor, Brigitte Lahaie (who would go on to star in numerous Rollin films), as she roams the town literally falling apart. The film is easily one of Rollin's most coherent, with a linear story line that is often quite frightening. Unfortunately, while the film is his most accessible, it did not create the box-office punch to erase the poor reputation he had in France.

Filmed in just two weeks, *Fascination* (1979) signaled a return to a somewhat more traditional vampire narrative. True, there are no fangs or bats, and the blood drinking was done in wine stalls by the nouveau riche, but it nevertheless uses a vampire motif to convey a story of longing by those oppressed. Marc (Jean-Marie Lemaire), a petty thief on the run from the law, finds himself within the confines of an elegant castle inhabited by a group of well-to-do women who, unfortunately for him, feast off the blood of local inhabitants.[65] The story serves as Rollin's take on the class warfare raging within France. Marc represents

Squeezing the life out of French culture was the aim of Rollin in his zombie classic *Les Raisins de la mort* (*The Grapes of Death*, 1977).

the poor man whose presence among the French elite drags down the atmosphere. Clearly, he does not belong and must pay a price for his intrusion. Yet, the longing is still there. In the beginning he pushes his way through the castle doors, manhandles the beautiful French maid (Lahaie again), and prepares to take control of the domain. The arrival of the rich blood-drinkers puts Marc in his place. He is from the lower class and his desire to reach above his station will never be fulfilled.

Rollin had to constantly battle his producer during the making of the film. "My co-producer wanted me to make a very explicit sex film — straight exploitation fare without too much emphasis on the fantastical elements— so we had a constant battle during the shooting (which I won eventually, much to the disappointment of my 'enemy') [laughs]!"[66] For Rollin, *Fascination* (1979) was considered another one his finest achievements.[67] Making good use of his porn-star cast and working with what little written script he had, he used his decade of producing exploitation films to create a piece of art that he could be proud of.

Life for Rollin did not get any easier. Though he produced some evocative films in the early '80s (*La Nuit des traquées*, 1981; *La Morte vivante*, 1983), Rollin's reputation had tarnished him, separating him completely from legitimate French filmmakers. After producing films of lessening quality, Rollin gave up on the film industry in the late '80s, returning to it in 1993. In recent years there has been something of a Rollin renaissance, as evidenced by his numerous awards, such as the 2007 Lifetime Achievement award from the Fantasia Festival, one of the largest genre film festivals. With the release of his films on DVD/Blu-ray there has been deep renewed interest in his works. It seems what was once considered far out and unredeeming socially now seems evocative and deep, not only in a historical sense but in a filmmaking one as well. Rollin's films stand out among Eurocult's most artistic efforts: the fangs may look phony, the dialogue (what dialogue there is) may be incoherent, and the attention many times is only on sex, but Rollin framed each film in a tapestry of color and light in a way that could only be executed by a true artist.

The death of French filmmaker Jean Rollin on December 15, 2010, was sadly a low-key event that garnered no major headlines, no large obituaries, and very little in the way of casual fan remembrances. For the true fan it should come as no surprise that the cinematic legacy of Rollin has remained as obscure and esoteric as his subject matter often was.

Filmography

Bacchanales sexuelles, aka *Tout le monde il en a deux* (FR), *Fly Me the French Way* (INT). Prod. Lionel Wallmann. Dir. Jean Rollin. France, 1973. Synapse Films, 102 min. DVD. Starring: Joëll Coeur, Marie-France Morel, Brigitte Borghese, Marie-Pierre Castel and Catherine Castel.

I'm sure everyone has at one time or another watched a film and wondered at the end of it, "What the hell was that all about?" You can see where I'm going with this. *Bacchanales* is just the kind of craziness that one expects from a Jean Rollin film, but instead of voluptuous vampires we get a crazy cult in bat leotards! Anyway, it's wall-to-wall sex here, pretty much the closest you'll get to hard-core without its actually being hard-core. So here's the plot with the sex included. Valerie (Coeur) gets to stay at her cousin's apartment in Paris while he's in New York. She invites a female friend over for SEX. After SEX the friend gets kidnapped by the bat people. Understandably annoyed, she gets her male friend to drop by, and they have SEX before they investigate. They find some SEXY photos and conclude that her friend has been kidnapped by a SEX cult, which would be right, because the girl is becoming a SEX slave. A maid comes to visit Valerie and her male friend, and they all have (you guessed it) SEX. Once they find the cult leader, they head on over to the mansion where they all have, yes, SEX. In case you couldn't tell, there's a lot of sex in this movie. Not much else but really funky '70s fashions, a lot of amateur actors and no budget to speak of (and for some reason everyone looks cold). This is bottom-of-the-barrel stuff that is so outlandish that it forces you to watch from start to finish.

The Demoniacs, aka *Les Demoniacs* (FR), *Curse of the Living Dead* (U.S.). Prod. Lionel Wallmann. Dir. Jean Rollin. France, 1974, Image Entertainment, 95 min. DVD. Starring: Joëll Coeur, John Rico, Lieva Lone and Patricia Hermenier.

The story of some nasty karmic revenge finds Rollin back where he feels most comfortable, the beach. A group of pirates led by the Captain (Rico) and the *very* evil Tina (Coeur) make their living by getting local ships to crash on the rocks near shore (they're more successful at it than you think) so they can pilfer the wreckage. This time their plans work, but the wreckage produces two lovely survivors (Lone and Hermenier), who are then promptly raped and left for dead by our band of thieves. It doesn't take a rocket scientist to figure out what happens as the girls may not be so dead and are looking for a little payback. They head to the local monastery to find a spirit who just might help them with their vengeance plans. With lots of typical long dialogue-free passages and huge, gaping plot holes, the film will not be to everyone's taste, especially those who want a lot of action. But no one watches a Rollin film for its linear story lines (*Grapes of Death* and *Fascination* excepted); what they watch for is the poetic, surrealistic ways he carries out his stories. *Demoniacs* doesn't disappoint, and the film is very avant garde in his outside settings, both at the beach and in the monastery. In addition, the film boasts one of the most outlandish fun performances in all Eurocult with Coeur's crazy, over-the-top performance as Tina, the evil pirate woman. An absolute screaming sadist capable of anything, her character and performance are so devilishly campy it makes the film worth watching regardless of Rollin's script.

Fascination. Prod. Joe de Palmer. Dir. Jean Rollin. France, 1979, Image Entertainment, 80 min. DVD. Starring: Brigitte Lahaie, Franca Mai, Jean-Marie Lemaire and Fanny Magier.

One of Rollin's most linear movies (along with the *Grapes of Death*) and one of his best. Twelve years of working with minuscule budgets in both exploitation and pornography culminated in this fine film, which has his vampires moving up the social scale. Vampire is actually a misnomer here, as these female bloodsuckers aren't of the undead variety, but more from Beverly Hills chic society. Petty thief Marc (Lemaire) double-crosses his partners, causing him to go on the run. Needing shelter, he very luckily (he thinks) runs into a beautiful château whose only residents are two beautiful young servants (Lahaie and Mai). It's obvious that the women are having a sexual relationship but one of them takes a shine to Marc, causing obvious friction. The women seem to be waiting for something or someone. That someone is a group of elite women from around the country who come for a little premium wine tasting once a year. Except, as you can imagine, it's not wine they're going to drink, and you can guess which male they want to drink from. Not altogether that violent, though there is a great scene involving Lahaie and a sickle. Most of the movie's adult content is derived from the abundance of nudity that Rollin uses to showcase Marc's seduction. Word of warning to those expecting lots of action: this film is a slow burn, but the outcome is definitely worth it.

Grapes of Death, aka *Les Raisins de la mort* (FR). Prod. Claude Guedi. Dir. Jean Rollin. France, 1978. Synapse Films, 90 min. DVD. Starring: Marie-Georges Pascal, Félix Marten, Serge Marquand and Brigitte Lahaie.

Rollin enters the zombie arena with some pretty spectacular results! Okay, so it's not the living dead per se, it's the residents of the French countryside who were slowly poisoned by pesticides in the wine (somewhere in the universe, Betty Ford is smiling). The poisoning is leading to some pretty psychopathic behavior including uncontrollable anger that may result in random decapitation, stabbings with garden shears or the ever-popular eye gouging. In addition, long-term exposure will lead to severe dermatological damage as rural folk literally begin to fall apart, and I haven't even mentioned the sexual side effects that make families prone to incest. Élisabeth (Pascal) is on her way to the country to visit her fiancé when she's attacked on the train. Abandoning the train, she is forced to make her way through the countryside as it becomes increasingly populated with sick farmers. Even those who don't like or understand, or are just plain confounded by, Rollin's films will enjoy this as it's one of the few that offers a truly linear storyline that's fun, scary and horribly ironic (c'mon ... poisoning the French with wine — you can't get any more ironic than that!). Pascal makes a wonderfully sensitive heroine who's completely bewildered by the events, and Rollin throws in a slew of wonderful supporting characters (like Lahaie, who again uses her combination of sexuality and menace to great effect) that keep the movie flowing. This is as close as France ever got to classic zombie cinema, so you owe it to yourself to see it.

Lips of Blood, aka *Lèvres de sang* (FR). Prod. Jean-Marie Ghanassia. Dir. Jean Rollin. France, 1975. Image Entertainment, 87 min. DVD. Starring: Jean-Loup Phillipe, Annie Belle, Nathalie Perrey and Martine Grimaud.

Lips of Blood is a strange film that is oddly reminiscent of many of the films of Spaniard Jess Franco. Its dreamlike ambiance and nonlinear plot structures make it a heavy slog, though it is one of Rollin's most personal films. The film is about childhood fantasies and dreams and their effects on an adult's life. Frederic looks to recreate his childhood, when he met a strange little girl at a castle when he was young. Seeing the castle again in a picture, he stumbles into a nightmarish world of vampires and ghosts that end up taking him to, no surprise, the beach. Before he gets there, though, he manages to let out a few color-coded vampires who bite their way through Paris. *Lips of Blood* is very much like *Twin Peaks* meets *Dark Shadows* (except without Barnabas Collins) in its execution. It's a beautiful film that Rollin shoots with great care and amazing color, though I do wish Rollin would have spent a little more money on vampire teeth or lose them entirely, as his penchant for using those long teeth really bring down the believability in these films (perhaps in this case, since it's not entirely a vampire film, that's his point). Those attracted to films that are dreams within dreams will find some good stuff here; those who are looking for some traditional vampire action will want to look elsewhere.

The Nude Vampire, aka *La Vampire nue* (FR), *Desnuda entre las tumbas* (SP). Prod. Jean Lavie. Dir. Jean Rollin. France, 1969. Redemption, 90 min. DVD. Starring: Olivier Martin, Maurice Lemaître, Caroline Cartier, Catherine Castel and Marie-Pierre Castel.

When you're watching Eurocult, the standards that apply to those things that make a film "good" are changed. You simply can't judge the films of a Jess Franco or Jean Rollin the same way you'd judge those from Godard or Renoir. The French probably didn't understand that when they first saw films like *The Nude Vampire*. This is definitely one of those WTF films that were seemingly cranked out at regular intervals in the late '60s and early '70s that make absolutely no sense, are badly acted, and are laughable for all the wrong reasons. Caroline Cartier is the nude vampire (not nude, actually, but wearing an orange see-through negligee throughout the film) who is kidnapped by a cult that likes to wear animal heads (don't ask). They see her as sort of a god. Before her kidnapping she managed to put some sort of romantic mojo on Olivier Martin, who goes to investigate the cult. Imagine his surprise when he finds out his father is the head of it, trying to scientifically explain the secrets of eternal life. Oh, did I mention there's some time-shifting in the film as well? Look, I'm going to level with you, there's very little plot, and what there is really, really bad, but that's not why you watch a Jean Rollin film. It's about perspective and the thrill of watching an artist (yes, I said artist) transcend all the negative things like low budget and bad press to create a vision. The film, like the rest in the Rollin canon after this, is colorful and bursting with excitement. Though there's very little sex in the film, Eurocult fans will enjoy the nudity as well as the fun bloodsucking by the Castel twins. Turn the brain off and let the art overcome you.

The Rape of the Vampire, aka *Le Viol du vampire* (FR). Prod. & Dir. Jean Rollin. France, 1968. Image Entertainment, 91 min. DVD. Starring: Solange Pradel, Bernard Letrou, Catherine Deville and Ursule Pauly.

Jean Rollin's first film is an interesting, thought-provoking hodgepodge of different elements that don't always make one cohesive whole. Filmed in evocative black and white, *Rape* is actually two different stories combined into one film. In the first story three college kids Marc, Thomas and Brigitte, come across a house inhabited by four sisters who believe they are vampires. The locals are more than convinced they are, and are ready to burn the house around them. College kids being what they are, they try to convince the villagers they are just being petty and bourgeois and that there's no such thing as vampires. They may be wrong. The second story is not so high-minded and concerns a vampire queen who raises some of the vampires from the first part (the only thread between the two stories) and tries to take over the world via her beach location. Funky, amateuresque, but with a certain style, this is independent filmmaking at its most interesting. The camerawork may require viewers to pop some Dramamine before viewing, but that's all part of the charm. Very little sex and actual violence are on display here, which may turn off some people looking for a little more perverse titillation, but since this one of the very first examples of French Eurocult it definitely needs to be watched.

Requiem for a Vampire, aka *Vierges et vampires* (FR), *Caged Virgins* (U.S.). Prod. Sam Selsky. Dir. Jean Rollin. France, 1971. Image Entertainment, 86 min. DVD. Starring: Marie-Pierre Castel, Mireille Dargent, Phillipe Gasté and Dominique.

Requiem for a Vampire is probably is one Rollin's strongest yet strangest of all his early–'70s vampire films. It takes silly-looking vampires (with the requisite overlarge teeth) and pits them against two sexy outlaws, which had me thinking this would be the perfect movie for Quentin Tarantino to remake. Outlaw Lolitas Castel and Dargent are involved in an automobile shootout in the middle of the French countryside (all dressed in clown attire, no less). Escaping, they manage to find themselves in a castle inhabited by an old vampire and his dying race of minions. Okay, to be honest, I'm paraphrasing here for the sake of space, since it takes them a good 20 minutes to get to the castle because ... well, there's really no good reason why. Rollin just seems to drag out the screenplay in order to have our pig-tailed sexpot little thieves tool around in graveyards, almost get buried alive, casually seduce a local food truck vendor, etc., all without much, if any, dialogue. Anyway, back to the castle, where our girls are forced by the vampires (laughably, because they are virgins; I guess all that lesbian sex the two have doesn't count) to find victims to help the vampires to carry out their legacy. That's pretty much it. *Requiem* is a comic book without the dialogue. The girls are cute as they race around in their miniskirts, shooting their guns at vampires to no effect, and the scenery is shot with pure affection as is the norm in a Rollin film. So if you like to see renegade Barbie and crazy Pippi Longstocking taking on the vampire king in a film that really makes no sense, this is for you.

The Shiver of the Vampires, aka *Le Frisson des vampires* (FR), *Strange Things Happen at Night* (INT). Prod. and Dir. Jean Rollin. France, 1970. Image Entertainment, 96 min. DVD. Starring: Sandra Julien, Jean-Marie Durand, Jacques Robiolles and Marie-Pierre Castel.

Another "WTF" film from Rollin, which finds him in a pontificating mode. A young couple, Isa and Antoine (Julien and Durand), travel to a small town to see the wife's cousins. Upon their arrival they are told that both cousins have died. Bummed from the news, they decide to spend some time in the gloomy chateau, which is inhabited by two very strange semi-nude servants. If the couple had taken a closer look at the grandfather clock, they would have found the vampire living there too (they really are worse than mice). That's not so good, as Isa finds herself more and more attracted to the chateau and Antoine just wants to leave. Soon we find out that the cousins are alive and quite prepared to give extensive monologues to anyone who will listen; unfortunately, as audience members we have no choice. Can Antoine save Isa from her family fate? Will you even care by the time the film is over? Again, it's important to remember that you don't watch a Jean Rollin movie for plot. It's an exercise in style, and truth be told, the man has style. His lighting and framing are as innovative as they are evocative, and his use of sexuality is very erotic in its movement. Does it sound like I'm critiquing a painting or sculpture? That's how to critique a Rollin film. If you're looking for plot and substance, may I suggest any one of the Hammer films from the era.

Le Sexe Terrible: The Devil and Emmanuelle

> So what if they're just B films? These guys with their shoestring budgets have created incredible films. Just because they loved cinema, they were mad for it. They didn't care about being rich. They just loved what they did.
> — French actor and director Michel Lemoine[68]

Though Jean Rollin had made inroads in French exploitation film with his lusty vampires, the French film industry as a whole was unimpressed. Very few avenues for exploitation were made available to those French filmmakers who wanted to compete with Argento, Fulci and Franco. Without any previous historical precedent, the French were not acclimated to take traditional horror film characters like Frankenstein, the Mummy or the Wolf Man and exploit their potential in film like the Spaniards did. Nor were they predisposed to the Gothic horror traditions that the Italians and English mined in the '60s and '70s. Proud and original, they also never felt the need to rip off popular movies from abroad, the basis of a majority of exploitation films. For the French there were only two horrific characters that appealed to them: the vampire and the witch. Both characters resonated with something in common which was extremely appealing to the French public: sex.

Jean Rollin had mined the vampire territory by focusing on the erotic nature of vampires. His vampires played up their sexuality via nudity, erotic movements and beauty. To the French, the vampire signified a perverse eroticism. The character of the witch is not traditionally known as an erotic character, but in the hands of French filmmakers, witchcraft became a sexy exploitation gimmick that was mined with some modestly successful results.

In the social revolution of the early '70s, groups of young people were forming communes around Europe. Like those in the United States, these communes were sources of mistrust with leaders of government as well as society. The cult murder of actress Sharon Tate by Charles Manson and his commune, along with the influx of Gypsies into Europe, resonated strongly, leading to both the interest and distrust that people developed. Without knowing what really went on in these mysterious groups, people used their active imaginations to vilify the residents, and exploitation filmmakers were more than happy to take advantage of this mistrust to exploit these groups, proliferating stereotypes and giving mainstream audiences exactly what they wanted.

Bruno Gantillon's *Morgane et ses nymphes* (*Girl Slaves of Morgana Le Fay*) in early 1971 began a short but prolific period of sexual witchcraft movies in France. Shot in six weeks, the film is more linear than a Rollin picture, but only slightly. The opening scene sets up what viewers can expect: a young naked girl is tormented by a handicapped dwarf (Alfred Baillou, in blue eye shadow, no less) and a slew of middle-aged ladies who wish to make her a sexual slave. It seems the girl has offended the queen of witches, Morgane (Dominick Delpierre), and must pay for her insurrection with her youth. The rest of the film involves two young girls (Michèle Perello, Mireille Saunin) who become unwilling slaves to the witch and her libidinous desires.[69] The film is a complete male lesbian fantasy, with the emasculated dwarf as the only male, and one who does not participate in any of the sex. For director Gantillon, whose previous work included a stint co-directing the popular French television show *Dim dam dom* (which was a trailblazing TV magazine show in France that attracted stars like Jimi Hendrix and the Rolling Stones while also containing burlesque-type numbers), the change to do an erotic horror film was exciting and challenging.[70] "I wanted to do a movie that we don't see very often. Only women and a dwarf,"

Gantillon told film scholar Pete Tombs. About the process of filming an erotic movie with exploitive undertones, he said, "We wrote it without thinking that we will do this because there is this book or there is this painting or theatrical play. We write it as we wanted to see this ... nice ... story ... with only women and a dwarf. I saw a lot of girls, and of course when I say some of them there is nudity, they say NO. Okay. So I find only people that were not ashamed. And I loved to film them. I loved to direct the younger student actors. But it was soft and tender and not vulgar and this is what I wanted to do."[71]

Soft and tender as the film may be, French censors still had problems with the film's sexuality and demanded cuts.[72] Gantillon got his wish: he made a film with only women and dwarf that is absolutely what Eurocult audiences expected. Using the Gothic-castle motif, he develops a film that is absolutely beautiful to behold but completely lacking in any logical sense. Like the majority of French exploitation, it simply doesn't matter what happens in the plot as long as the violence is downplayed and the sex is ramped up in an erotic fashion. A bevy of beautiful French girls (and some not-so-beautiful elderly women) parade around in colorful see-through fabric while our two heroines decide if they want to become love slaves to our lesbian protagonist or spend their lives enjoying bondage fun in the dungeon, giving Gantillon the opportunity to lovingly film his actresses in the most beneficial ways possible. The film is a fantasy, of course, and regardless of the violent undertones, the moral of the story (for men, anyway) is that a lifetime of damnation might not necessarily be a bad thing.

Mario Mercier's *La Goulve* (*Erotic Witchcraft*, 1972) and *La Papesse* (*A Woman Possessed*, 1975) also mined the erotic witchcraft themes. *La Goulve* revolves around a young man (Hervé Hendrickx) who, being raised by a sorcerer, taps into magic to win the love of a local girl. Unfortunately, calling on the Goulve, a witch with power over snakes, brings a terrible price.[73] Shot with no budget and utilizing amateur actors who happily cavort in the nude, the film plays like a French version of an Ed Wood film, clumsily handling the sexual fulfillment angle, and resembling an amateur high school production complete with topless models. That's not to say there's nothing going on here, though, as there's something playful about the way that Mercier teases out his fable; though technically nowhere near the professional level of *Morgane*, the film does retain the type of charm of a very adult fairy tale. Mercier, who previous to this film had published a completely censored short story called *La necrophiliac* about the last days of a haunted necrophiliac, seems to be trying to out-obscure fellow countryman Jean Rollin, which is no easy feat. French critics, who hated exploitation films and did not even entertain notions that French filmmakers could dare produce them, refused to review the picture and consequently the film was failure.

La Papesse (*A Woman Possessed*, 1975) is a bit more conventional, with emphasis on the words "a bit." Using real witches from a local sect, it is the story of a young woman (Lisa Livane) who is haunted by strange occurrences that seem to be connected with her selfish writer husband. She's not wrong, as he has become involved with a ritualistic witch coven and sort of promised her to the coven.[74] Though easier to comprehend then *Goulve* (when I say comprehend, I mean that there are at least two scenes that make sense when put back to back), the film retains all the violence and nudity of Mercier's earlier film. Naked men and women are tied to stakes in the wilderness and beaten into unconsciousness. Blood rituals, including the requisite orgies, are all performed ably by the amateurs who spout enough meaningless nonsense to make most of the film incomprehensible. Not surprisingly, the film ran into huge censorship problems in France. By 1974, a move was underway by French filmmakers and the Ministry of Culture to start banning exploitation and pornographic films in France. *La Papesse* was caught in the middle as the Commission's statement that the film was "nothing but an uninterrupted succession of scenes of sadism, torture and violence, and a total and permanent disregard for humanity, displayed in a crude and revolting fashion," initially sealed the fate of Mercier's original vision. Though there were televised assurances by the French president d'Estaing that no films would be censored, Mercier was asked to remove controversial footage.[75] This type of censorship was not equitable across the board, though. While Mercier was having to fight censorship battles with his own country, imported films like *The Exorcist* (1973) were scaring up big box office in France without interference. This dichotomy may have more to do with production values and good old-fashioned francs: Warner Bros. delivered a quality product and had the cash to effectively promote it, unlike Mercier, who was just lucky to have a theater that would consent to play his movie. Though audiences showed some interest in *La Papesse*, the French critics were, as usual, merciless. *Écran*, the magazine so critical of Jean Rollin, found a comparison between the two. Reviewing *La Papesse*, they decried, "Rollin, you are not alone! [Mercier] is a disciple of this Master in the creation of a pompous naiveté and genuine French camp." For Mercier, the critical drubbing was too much to bear for someone who considered himself an artist. Not having the thick skin that Rollin had, Mercier, after *La Papesse*, quit the movie business to refocus on his writing.[76]

In addition to witches, there were a few examples of other types of exploitation coming out of France in the early '70s, all with an emphasis on sexuality. *Mais ne nous délivrez pas du mal* (*Don't Deliver Us from Evil*, 1972) was one of the more shocking. Based on the same true story that inspired Peter Jackson's *Heavenly Creatures* (1994), the film looks at two young girls (Jeanne Goupil, Catherine Wagener) in a Catholic boarding school whose cruelty and detachment spiral out of control. Influenced by erotic novels, they delight in seducing older men and inflicting torture on the nuns of their school. Soon the girls tire of their mundane pranks and the plot turns murderous.[77] Director Joël Séria's script plays up all the exploitation angles. A student himself of a strict religious school in France, Séria invests all the torment that he felt during his youth into the film arriving at his shocking story of youth gone bad. He doesn't shy away from the fact that these girls are monsters and that organized religion is probably to blame for that. Of course, that did not sit well with French censors, and from the beginning Séria had problems getting the film made. He stated, "People who read the script were shocked by it. In France we have to send scripts to the National Cinema Centre. They wrote back a terrible letter. They said that if we made this film it would be banned. So we were unable to get any money from the distributor."[78]

Getting money from friends and business acquaintances, Séria was able to begin filming. When it was completed, the French censors were even more convinced that the public should not see the film. In addition to the blasphemy, the most shocking images of the film revolve around the girls themselves. Goupil and Wagener look like 15-year-olds (both were over 18) and the scenes with them seducing an older shepherd bordered on child pornography. As the girls literally go up in smoke in the end, so too went Séria's chance to have the film released: due to censors' interference the film was banned completely for eight months. Even worse, French authorities would not allow the film to be exported, meaning no money could be made from distribution.[79] Forced to take financial stock, Séria acquiesced and made some cuts to the film, allowing it to be shown. Séria did learn a valuable Eurocult lesson, though, in that audiences have a built-in interest in those films that are forbidden. *Mais ne nous délivrez pas du mal* ended up becoming a huge hit in both England and Germany, due primarily to its "banned in France" notoriety, which distributors happily exploited.

Another film banned outright in France was Michel Lemoine's *Les Weekends maléfiques du Comte Zaroff* (*Seven Women for Satan*) in 1974. Lemoine, an actor who was able to utilize his very intense face to great success, had been appearing in Eurocult films for about 15 years appearing in a variety of films by Jess Franco (along with his wife at the time, Janine Reynaud), Mario Bava and Antonio Margheriti. By the mid–'70s he began to turn his sights to directing with an idea for a horror film that borrows heavily from both the Giallo films of Italy and the Krimi's from Germany. Lemoine came up with idea for the film when walking along the Champs Elyseés with one of the founders of *Midi-Minuit Fantastique*, France's premier horror journal. Commenting that it's difficult to get inside people's minds and that anyone could be thinking murderous thoughts at any time, he constructed the story of Count Zaroff (Lemoine playing the lead), an affable man who rapes, tortures and murders women on his family estate. Explains Lemoine, "I always wanted to make a horror film. Sadly, when I started to direct, it was hard to make such a film here. The idea of a French horror film is not really accepted. One day I found a producer, showed her some scenes I'd shot in an old castle, and managed to convince her to put up half the money for *Zaroff*."[80]

Mais ne nous délivrez pas du mal (*Don't Deliver Us from Evil*, 1972) was far too explicit for the French government, which promptly banned the film. The Japanese took a more romantic approach to marketing the film.

Much like Séria's film two years earlier, Lemoine's finished film was immediately banned by the French censors. Citing the uneasy blend of unabashed eroticism mixed with hardcore violence, the censor board made it impossible for Lemoine to show the film for years after its completion. It's rather inexplicable in this day why French censors would be up in arms over the film, as it plays out like your standard run-of-the-mill evil killer story. The nudity and sex are no worse than any other middling Eurocult film of the era; in fact, they're much lighter than, say, any of the Italian cannibal films or Spaniard Jess Franco's pornography. There would be a silver lining for Lemoine, as the banning of the film could be a marketing tool to get a curious audience into the theater. Eventually the film was shown in England with extensive cuts and ironically won the silver medal at the 1977 Sitges Festival of Horror Cinema in Barcelona Spain.

Les Week-ends was one of the last true horror/exploitation films to be produced in France in the '70s. By the mid–'70s French filmmakers were already switching their perverse eyes to the soft-core sex industry that was rapidly competing with the rise of hard-core pornography. France has always been a country that was synonymous with romance and sexuality. Historically from literature, culturally by nature, eroticism was naturally a big part of the nation's film industry. Beginning with Roger Vadim's *Et Dieu ... créa la femme* (*And God Created Woman*) in 1956, French films were the outlet for the world's foray into sexuality. Both the art house *and* grindhouse audiences accepted the romantic, eroticism of them. Worldwide audiences came to expect some unabashed sexuality when viewing these films. Filmmakers from around Europe began to film their productions in France in order to tap some of the erotic spirit of the country. Bernardo Bertolucci's *Last Tango in Paris* (1973) became a worldwide hit in the early '70s from just such an expecting audience. Unashamedly erotic, the film reaped major acclaim from film critics who found it deep and introspective, though for audiences the attraction was the thought of seeing Marlon Brando in an X-rated film.[81] Movies like *Tango* made it respectable to attend adult films. So long as they weren't overtly pornographic and had artistic merit, early to mid–'70s audiences were open-minded to the possibility of erotic works of film. This is where the French film industry excelled. They were the masters of taking tawdry subjects and filming them in beautiful surroundings. Soft lighting, beautiful women and men, and haunting classical music were all tools the industry used to export palatable erotic product around the world.

Exploitation audiences had already discovered the attraction of France as filmmakers like Radley Metzger (*Dirty Girls*, 1964; *Therese and Isabelle*, 1968; *L'Image*, 1973) were already regularly shooting in Paris to give their erotic films an air of respectability, and international audiences ate them up. There was something safe about watching an erotic film from France because it didn't require its audience to feel guilty about their own culture's view on sexuality. Audiences could feel guilt-free watching sex acts they never would have seen in films produced in their own country because they believed, "Well, that's just the way the French are." For the most part, these sex films were fairly low in violent content. Most involved the awaking of (usually) a young woman to her sexuality and contained happy scenarios wherein the main protagonist is liberated by no longer being a virgin. Very much playing into the rise of the Women's Liberation movement that was beginning to sweep the world during this period, these films offered a distinctly male-gaze view of female sexuality.[82] Though most of the sexually charged material coming out of France was fairly tame, by the mid–'70s a disturbingly violent trend was beginning to creep into the films. While still giving the impression that they were about the discovery of sexuality, they were employing devices that exploitation filmmakers around Europe were using in horror films to get people into the theaters. One of these subliminally violent movies happened to be one of the most successful, Just Jaeckin's *Emmanuelle* (1974).

Based on the scandalous novel by Emmanuelle Arsan (nom de plume for Marayat Rollet-Andriane, though there is some dispute as to whether the actual author of the book was she or her husband), a Eurasian/French actress who was the wife of a diplomat, *Emmanuelle* caught the imagination of the French, as well as the world. The simple story of a young girl who indulges in sexual adventures in Paris and Bangkok on her quest for sexual liberation was a controversial scandal when released in Paris in 1957. President Charles DeGaulle condemned the book as an "outrage" and convicted the publisher, Eric Oldfield, for offending public morality, sending the book into banned purgatory until 1967. Regardless of its banned status, the book was a huge hit on the underground circuit, creating a massive cult following. Loosening censorship and a change of publishers allowed the book to be distributed in the mainstream, where it immediately grossed millions.[83] A sequel, *Emmanuelle: L'antivierge*, was released a year later, making the original even more successful.

An initial film version, *Emmanuelle* (1968), was unsuccessfully produced by Jean-

Pierre Thorn, but the story was too erotically charged for late–'60s audiences, resulting in a version that was too watered-down for an audience expecting some graphic titillation from the highly pornographic novel. By the mid–'70s, events made producers believe the time was right to mount a more accurate version of the book. The rise of hard-core pornography and the success of Bertolucci's *The Last Tango in Paris* (1973) showed producers that there was a market for adult material and that audiences could be persuaded to come to theaters without embarrassment. In addition, the social mores of the world were changing too. Commenting on the culture that made *Emmanuelle* (1974) a success, feminist writer Polly Toynbee commented, "A lot of things came together in the '70s. You had a whole new generation that had money. Money to be free. To buy things like motorbikes, to go to other places, to be free of their parents' houses. And with freedom came, inevitably, a moment of sexual liberation. For a brief time it looked like you could have pleasure without responsibility, sex without consequences."[84] Producers thought that *Emmanuelle* would fit perfectly into this new sexualized popular culture.

Looking for an "intellectual alibi," producer Yves Rousset-Rouard bought the rights to *Emmanuelle* in 1972 and immediately began looking for the right director who could give a classy look to the film. He offered the job to photographer and artist Just Jaeckin. Jaeckin, who had never directed a feature film before, was shocked and daunted by the project. "I read the novel and said, 'My goodness, what can I do with a book like that?'" He called Rousset-Rouard to beg out, but they developed a compromise: "So we decided to do something soft and beautiful with a nice story."[85] After coming up with a scenario that was suitably erotic yet not hard-core, the filmmakers next had to find a suitable actress to play the part. Casting sessions were held throughout Europe with no luck. Many actresses were justifiably suspicious of creating a role that was based primarily on sex and were unsure exactly what would be demanded of them. After viewing a short film by a European director, the producers came upon 21-year-old, Dutch actress Sylvia Kristel. Convent educated, Kristel had the innocence and elegance that producers were looking for, as well as an obvious sensuality important to the type of film. Kristel herself described the initial meeting with director Jaeckin, saying, "I met with Just and I did some things for the camera. And since he told me there would was nudity involved I had a dress with spaghetti tie ups and, um, in this one movement, I didn't even have to touch it and the entire dress just fell to my waist and I just went on talking, where I lived, my hobbies, why I could do this film, da da da, and Just said, 'I want to do some nude photography,' and that was fine. It was fun and he could see that I would have no problems with the nudity."[86]

With the cast set, the producers worked feverishly to get the film ready to premier in Paris in June 1974. Filming at locales throughout Thailand with the interiors done in Paris, they knew they had a property that could exploit the sexual permissiveness of the times and bring in big box office. The film tells the story of Emmanuelle (Kristel), the 21-year-old wife of an open-minded diplomat Jean (Dan Sarkey). Jean, interested in his wife's emotional growth, propels the young girl to sexual affairs with his male and female friends. Eventually she allows herself to be taught the true spirit of eroticism by an elderly gentleman, Mario (Alain Cuny).[87] *Emmanuelle* begins as a fairly straightforward travelogue soft-core sex film. It's fairly harmless in its execution and beautiful to look at. It is only halfway through the film that it swerves off into exploitation, as hidden behind the beauty of Jaeckin's photography is what eventually ends up to be the ugliness of the story. Rape, racial discrimination and misogyny all play out within the plot to varying degrees. The film is a dichotomy of images and values. For example, Emmanuelle's first tender love scene with

One of the most popular films of all time, *Emmanuelle* (1974) put a pretty picture on exploitation.

Jean under a mosquito-netted bed is beautiful, soft and romantic. It is intercut with scenes of a male servant chasing a maid through the Thai jungle and forcibly raping her, which of course she ends up enjoying as the violence brings her to orgasm. Later in the film, Emmanuelle herself is forcibly raped by two drugged natives in a Bangkok opium den on her quest to discover the "joys" of sexuality. Kristel herself was not happy with the scene or with the way that it was produced. Commenting on the exploitative aspects of filming the scene, she said, "I couldn't see how a rape would be pleasurable. These two Thai people were not actors. I really had to fight for my life there. They were rough. It seems like they enjoyed what they were doing. And I kept my underwear on because I knew otherwise things would go absolutely berserk. I really had no choice. Thank God he's a really good director and used many different cameras. I only had to do that scene once and I came out black and blue."[88] Kristel wasn't the only one taken aback by exploitation filming techniques, as Jaeckin had his own surprises for him as director. In one of the film's most talked-about scenes, Jean is in a Thai bar where the main attraction is a young Thai girl whose talent is smoking a cigarette out of her vagina. The scene seems somewhat out of place in the film and Jaeckin has since denied any involvement with shooting the scene. In the true spirit of exploitation filmmaking, it seems that producer Rousset-Rouard shot the short clip without Jaeckin's knowledge to add some "spice" to the film. Jaeckin claims that he first saw the scene while sitting in the theater. That may well be, but the debasement of Emmanuelle herself in the last 20 minutes was as harsh and unerotic as our "smoking" hooker.

By the summer of '74, *Emmanuelle* was ready to be shown in France. Because the book garnered such extreme controversy, both government and society kept a close eye on its production. The Pompidou government, in the midst of change itself, was trying to control the onslaught of sexually explicit material that was beginning to infiltrate the French market. The government had believed that they done a good job censoring the likes of Jean Rollin and Mario Mercier, and in their eyes, *Emmanuelle* looked like the perfect film for Pompidou to make an example of. The government refused to grant the film a certificate allowing it to be shown, but the ban was fortunately lifted after the death of Pompidou in April of '74. Luckily for Jaeckin and company, the end of the Pompidou government signified some dramatic changes in French censorship laws. With the blessing of the government, *Emmanuelle* was now ready to open. Capitalizing on the public's desire to see sexually explicit material, the film was an instant smash in France. Coproducer Alain Sirtzky recalled the first-week excitement of the film: "I peeked my head around the corner on the Champs D'Elysees and all of a sudden I saw there is a crowd. So, I ran to the lobby of the theater and said to the cashier what was going on. She said 'Oh everything is fine, we're almost full.' So I ran back the restaurant and knew we had a success on our hands."[89]

Almost instantly upon release, the name Emmanuelle became synonymous with French sexuality. The picture struck a chord throughout the world and a myriad of different international distributors immediately expressed interest in marketing the film to their own audiences. Columbia Pictures in the U.S. decided that the social and economic climate was right for them to take a chance and release *Emmanuelle* as its first X-rated film. Using the market ploy that "X was never like this," the company took a highbrow approach in selling their exploitive gem. The gamble paid off, and even with the critical drubbing received by U.S. critics (film critic Roger Ebert, who loved the film, being one of the lone exceptions), *Emmanuelle* became one of the biggest foreign film blockbusters in the United States. So successful was the film that it helped Columbia recoup most of its costs for the big-budgeted G-rated remake of *Lost Horizon* (1973), which was a huge financial failure for the company.

The film was a success all over the world, especially in Asia, where many women saw it as a liberating piece, focusing on the power and strength of Emmanuelle and not her exploitation.

The success of *Emmanuelle* opened up the floodgates to a variety of knockoffs.[90] For French producers, the pressure was on to create another film that pushed the boundaries even more. *Emmanuelle: L'antivierge* (*Emmanuelle, the Joys of a Woman*, 1975) had to be more explicit and more daring than the previous outing to beat all the worldwide competitors. For producer Rousset-Rouard, getting financing for the film was easy. Sylvia Kristel would return to the role, as her initial contract called for a three-picture deal playing the title character. The film had Emmanuelle Arsan's second novel as literary inspiration, and a built-in audience had already been established. The only problem was that director Jaeckin did not want to film the second installment. Not wishing to be a series director, he had been approached to film another classic of erotic literature, Pauline Reage's *Histoire d'O* (*The Story of O*, 1974), and was interested in what he could do for that film. Roussett-Rouard took Jaekin's advice and hired French fashion photographer Francis Giacobetti. Giacobetti, like Jaeckin, had not directed a feature film before and was known more for his mise en scène than for his work with actors.[91]

Filmed in Hong Kong, the film follows the further adventures of Emmanuelle and her husband Jean (now played by Italian actor Umberto Orsini) as they sleep their way through their friends and strangers. Like the first film, there's a strong exploitation factor. In the film, Emmanuelle is given an exotic acupuncture that leads to sexual fulfillment. She has brutal intercourse with a severely tattooed polo player (Venantino Venantini) as well as dressing up as a prostitute and having group sex.[92] For Kristel, the exploitation aspects of the plot seemed overplayed by director Giacobetti. She said, "It definitely had something to do with Giacobetti's tastes, particularly the scene in the brothel. I don't know, at the time I didn't question it lot because I go along with ideas of my director and with the script. I thought it was here and there more misogynist. I felt more used in number two than in number one."[93]

If the first *Emmanuelle* film had problems with the censors, the second film's battle was even more intense. In April of 1975, the first hard-core porno film was released in Paris to thunderous success. This had a chilling effect on members of the government and film community who did not want to see the French film industry go down the path that the German film industry went down in the early '70s, when a large majority of films were nothing but erotic comedies.[94] They tried to develop ways to put a stop to French filmmakers' doing the same thing. Though the censor board passed *Emmanuelle II* (1975) by saying it was erotic, not pornographic, the government declared the movie unsuitable. This was a problem for producer Rousset-Rouard because erotic movies could be shown in any movie theater in France, while films with a porn designation could only be shown in small designated venues, usually in the seedy parts of town. Angered by the government's interference, Rousset-Rouard boldly decided to sue the government and not show the film in France. Looking to teach the government a lesson, he released the film around the world to a smashing success. Even in countries that were more restricted about sexuality, the film played to packed audiences. In the U.S. Paramount pictures outbid Columbia and released *Emmanuelle II* (1975) as a "legitimate X-rated movie" (though they one-upped Columbia's marketing

Opposite: Even more beautiful than its predecessor, *Emmanuelle II* (*Emmanuelle, The Joys of a Woman*, 1975) continued the exploitive story of a young woman finding her sexual identity.

Nothing is wrong if it feels good.

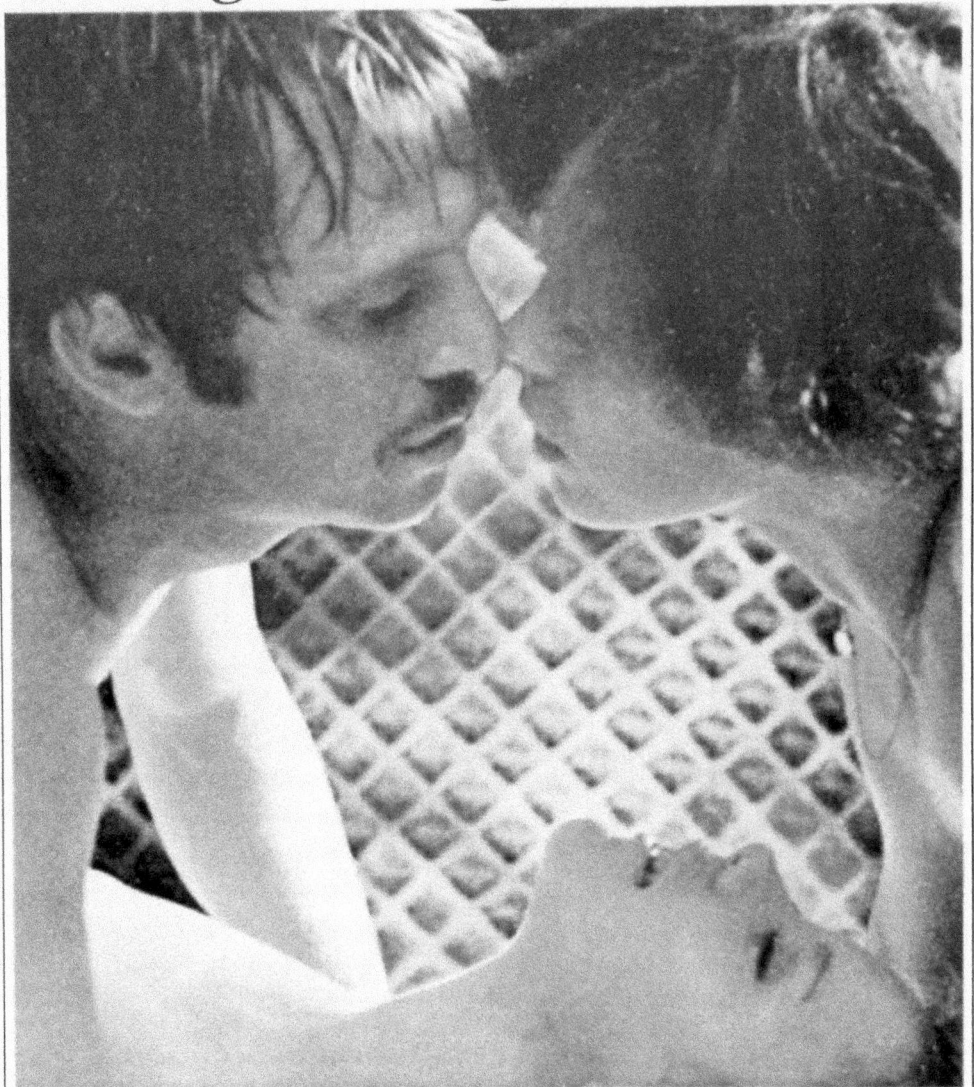

Paramount Pictures presents

Emmanuelle
The Joys of a Woman

X NO ONE UNDER 17 ADMITTED

EMMANUELLE THE JOYS OF A WOMAN

by having the slogan "Nothing's wrong if it feels good!" adorn the film). Two years later, after its international success, Rousset-Rouard won his suit against the French government and was able to release the film. By then standards had been put in place that made it easier to delineate between erotic and pornographic. The long delay to show the film resulted in disappointing box-office receipts from France, though producers were quick to add that those people who wanted to see the movie on its initial run had simply crossed the borders to neighboring Spain, Italy, Germany, etc., in order to attend the movie.

With new measures in place to separate pornography from more highbrow erotic films, producers looked for adult material that they could exploit. One of the biggest film successes to take advantage of the delineation was the film Just Jaeckin chose to direct instead of *Emmanuelle II* (1975), *L'Histoire d'O* (*The Story of O*, 1974). Released later in the same year

Opposite and above: Two distinctly different marketing techniques for the S&M fantasy *L'Histoire d'O* (*The Story of O*, 1974).

as the popular novel *Emmanuelle* and based on another scandalous book by Pauline Reage (aka Anne Desclos, though again the true authorship is a matter of conjecture), *O* cemented France's reputation for literate, pretty exploitation. Looking within the confines of a sadomasochistic relationship, *O* tells the story of a young woman, O (Corinne Cleary, who later became a Bond girl in *Moonraker*, 1979), who allows her boyfriend (exploitation regular Udo Kier) to take her to a strange castle where she is made to submit to torture and debasement in order to prove her love. Whipped, beaten, forcibly raped, O emerges a stronger woman who surrounds herself with those who believe that punishment is the best proof of love.[95]

Make no mistake, *O* is hard-core exploitation. Women are made to walk around barebreasted, whipped viciously, branded and made to wear harnesses for instantaneous subjection to men. It is only its presentation that defies the exploitation label, as Jaeckin shoots the film like it was a *Vogue* cover shoot. Beautiful elegant women, opulent locales, soft pretty lights and an evocative score, all the things that made *Emmanuelle* (1974) a successful film with middle-class society, were perfected in the film. For Jaeckin, the coarse, exploitative nature of the story was tempered by the fact that he saw the film as an adult version of *Alice in Wonderland*, stating, "It is an imaginary story that could have started with anything. It is important to remember this because *The Story of O* is a fantasy. It's an imaginary story and absolutely not in the first degree but the third degree. It's the power of imagination, it's a fantasy, at no time can this story be taken to the first degree. That would be catastrophic. It's a wonderful love story."[96]

Regardless as to whether the audience thought of *O* as *Alice in Wonderland* in chains, the film fascinated both European and U.S. audiences. Though Radley Metzger's *L'Image* (*The Image*, 1973), another cult literature classic dealing with a sadomasochistic ménage à trois, was filmed a year earlier in Paris and contained a more realistic depiction of this type of relationship, it was *O* that captured the audience's imagination.[97] It's actually a shame, as Metzger's film looks seriously at the mechanics of a sadomasochistic relationship and the emotional toll it takes on those involved, while Jaeckin's film is shallow, with no emotional depth and much more misogynistic; he just wants everything to look good. And look good it does: as one the best-looking exploitation films from the era (even more assured than his previous *Emmanuelle*), *O* is a treat for the eyes for those viewers who wouldn't be caught dead watching something like *Morgane et ses nymphes* (*Girl Slaves of Morgana Le Fay*, 1971) and who were tricked into believing they were watching something other than exploitation. The steel rings glisten, the outfits are outlandish yet tasteful, the heavy soft blur of the camera gives the film an air of fantasy, all confirming that the French, for all their protests, were just as much connoisseurs of exploitation as anyone else in Europe. They just wanted it to look pretty.

Filmography

Don't Deliver Us from Evil, aka *Mais ne nous délivrez pas du mal* (FR). Prod. Bernard Legargeant. Dir. Joël Séria. France, 1971. Mondo Macabro, 102 min. DVD. Starring: Jeanne Goupil, Catherine Wagener, Bernard Dhéran and Gérard Darrieu.

Completely inappropriate stuff, which of course means you need to see this! Catholic boarding school again screws up more of its flock as two little girls, Anne (Goupil) and Lore (Wagener), begin to rebel against their strict religious upbringing and in the process become infatuated with each other. Though these two are the picture of innocence, they represent anything but as their relationship brings out their most evil impulses. It starts out with the typical smoking, drinking and imagining their posturing priests in the nude, and turns into something much darker as the girls explore seduction and death (keep your pet birds away from these girls) before giving their souls to Satan in a ritual performed with some of the religious artifacts they stole from their own church! Bad girls! If some of this sounds familiar it's because it was based, very loosely, on the same murder trial (Parker-Hulme) that Peter Jackson used as the basis for the successful *Heavenly Creatures* (1994). It's a deeply fascinating and extraordinarily controversial film, its success predicated on the fact that we believe the two actresses can effectively portray the age range, which is about 16. No problems here as Goupil and Wagener scarily look that age, only adding to the forbidden nature of the film. Their seduction of a feeble farmer borders on child pornography and is way past the point of good taste. This is a character study and a well-produced one at that, so don't expect the boom-chicka-boom of porn music for our underage evil nymphets, but a serious study of the effects that organized religion may have on us.

Emmanuelle. Prod. Yves Rousset-Rouard. Dir. Just Jaeckin. France, 1974, Anchor Bay Entertainment, 94 min. DVD/Blu-Ray. Starring: Sylvia Kristel, Daniel Sarky, Marika Green and Alain Cuny.

Ahh, Emmanuelle! There's been no one quite like her in the annals of film. She's been ripped off, aged, given many different cultures (black, yellow, etc.), she's been around the world so many times — hell, she's even fought Dracula and been in space! You just can't bring a good girl down, and here is Just Jaeckin's hugely successful starting point for our intrepid heroine of eroticism. Based on the bestselling novel, *Emmanuelle* follows the lovely Sylvia Kristel as she jets to Bangkok with her husband Jean (Sarky) and learns to become a true woman. Of course, the version of a true woman that Jaeckin and company would have you believe is that of an insatiable sexpot. So amid the beautiful Thai scenery, Emmanuelle has public sex on a plane with two different strangers, gets seduced on the squash court by her bisexual friend Ariane, and falls is love with the beautiful lesbian Bee (Green), all under the watchful eye of her husband, who believes she is free to do what she wants (oh, except fall in love; he's not too happy about that). All of this before getting a true education by aging lothario Mario (Cuny) which entails a night of getting high and being raped by natives in an opium den! Finally, her lessons complete, Emmanuelle sits in front of a mirror and piles enough makeup on to make Tammy Faye Baker proud. Voila! She's now a woman! The lesson behind *Emmanuelle* is an ugly one, but you would never know it from watching this, as it's expertly produced and absolutely beautiful to watch. Kristel is one of most beguiling characters to ever grace the screen: she comes across as believable in both her innocence and her carnality. The sex is soft-core and actually quite light compared to other films in the genre, so it really doesn't offend (unless, of course, you're a cigarette smoker). Beautiful, dopey and completely politically incorrect, *Emmanuelle* takes us back to a bygone era, before the advent of AIDS, where "nothing's wrong if it feels good." See it.

Emmanuelle: L'antivierge, aka *Emmanuelle, the Joys of a Woman* (U.S.). Prod. Yves Rousset-Rouard. Dir. Francis Giacobetti. France, 1975, Anchor Bay Entertainment, 91 min. DVD. Starring: Sylvia Kristel, Umberto Orsini, Catherine Rivet, Frédéric Lagache and Laura Gemser.

She's back and better than ever! The phenomenally successful Emmanuelle returns in the first sequel that's in some ways better than the original. After the lessons learned from the first film, Emmanuelle (Kristel again, in a much more self-assured performance) is off to meet her husband Jean (this time played by Italian Umberto Orsini) in Hong Kong. From there it's a series of sex-capades that involve some sexy acupuncture, group sex in a brothel, and a very intense Chinese massage experience, as well as tattooed fun at a local polo match, all culminating in the deflowering of the only virgin in the film, Anna-Marie (Rivet), by Emmanuelle and Jean themselves. All of this is set to some of the most classically romantic music by Francis Lai. *Emmanuelle: L'antiverge* works on many levels, easily making it one of the best films of its type. The photography is simply gorgeous as Giacobetti lovingly films both the Chinese exteriors and the nouveau-riche interiors with exquisite care. Most of all, we don't have to see Emmanuelle debase herself as she did in the first picture, as producers wisely made her a much stronger character in charge of her own destiny, therefore making her much more likable. The sex is hotter than in the first film (though still soft-core) and still highly exploitive, while the cast is more than attractive. This represents the pinnacle of the series. Kristel and company would return for one more sequel, 1977's *Goodbye Emmanuelle*, which eschewed the exploitative aspects of the story and found Emmanuelle falling in love with a French filmmaker and leaving her husband and his life of debauchery behind for a monogamous one!

Girl Slaves of Morgana Le Fay, aka *Morgane et ses nymphes* (FR). Prod. and Dir. Bruno Gantillon. France, 1971. Mondo Macabro, 86 min. DVD. Starring: Dominique Delpierre, Alfred Baillou, Mireille Saunin and Ursule Pauly.

Naked women and midgets: what more could a Eurocult fan want? It's impossible to think of *Girl Slaves of Morgana Le Fay* and not smile as the film is an absolute treasure trove of exploitation goodness. Françoise (Saunin) and Anna (Michéle Perello) can't seem to get it together. They are driving through the French countryside and are lost. Stopping at a local pub, they are spied upon by Gurth (Baillou), a dwarf who makes Liberace look conservative in his green mascara and his purple pants. Soon the lucky lasses are back on the road where they, yep, run out of gas. Finding shelter in a local barn (cue porn music), they settle down for a warm night of snuggling. In the morning Françoise awakens alone and the dwarf makes a reappearance, bidding her to follow him to a mist-shrouded castle on the water. It's all downhill from there as the castle belongs to Morgana (Delpierre), one of the famous students of the magician Merlin, who likes to keep a castle full of naked women of all ages (and we're talking about a *lot* of women here of differing ages) to have a big lesbian love fest. Françoise is then given the choice to either join the lesbian express or spend her days down in the dungeon, which I can tell you is not a very fun place to be. You have to say this about French exploitation: it may be as silly as any other country's in terms of plot, but its aesthetics are beyond reproach. Morgana looks great! Whether it's the eerie castle or the final lesbian orgy (you knew there was going to be one of those), the film is awash in bright colors and utilizes some pretty evocative framing. The story? Does it matter? Believe me, *Girl Slaves of Morgana Le Fay* is not about story, it's about beautiful women (and some not so beautiful, as a bevy of elderly women are also included in the naked mix; after all, Morgana has been around a long time) indulging in a lot of heterosexual male fantasy. It's as simple as that and so is this movie.

La Goulve, aka *Erotic Witchcraft* (FR). Prod. Bepi Fontana. Dir. Mario Mercier. France, 1972. 86 min. Starring: Hervé Hendrickx, César Torres, Anne Varèze and Marie-Ange Saint Clair.

For those who think Jean Rollin's films are unwatchable due to the ephemeral nature of their stories, may I present Mario Mercier, another master of WTF filmmaking. Mercier's brand of non-linear story and truly confusing dialogue will have you running for the nearest insane asylum. Though the style borders on camp (okay, let's be honest: it doesn't border on camp, it sets up a big maison of camp right in the middle of your brain and forces you to not take his material seriously), his stuff his fascinating in a car-crash sort of way. You can't stop watching it. *La Goulve* is a fairy tale, a kind of hippie fairy tale, that has Hendrickx as Raymond who, as a young boy, had to endure the stigma of his father killing his mother and then committing suicide. He was raised by a wizard who taught him magic, and he discovered the Goulve (Saint Clair), a rather nasty female spirit that inhabits people and things, as well as acting as Raymond's other face (yes, I know it's complex, but I'm trying). With the death of the wizard the Goulve begins inhabiting other people and things, like Raymond's incestuous cousin Agnes, as well as making women have sex with dead trees. It's now after Raymond too. This is surrealist filmmaking at its most intense. How good or bad it is (and if you're not a film fan of amateurish acting, you'll opt for the second choice) is completely up to you. Its wall-to-wall nudity will have some fans into it, and French film scholars will want to study it as a great example of early–'70s independent film, but the general public should steer clear.

Seven Women for Satan, aka *Les Week-ends maléfiques du Comte Zaroff* (FR). Prod. Denise Petit-diddier. Dir. Michel Lemoine. France, 1974. Mondo Macabro, 84 min. DVD. Starring: Michel Lemoine, Nathalie Zeiger, Howard Vernon and Joëlle Coeur.

What? Satan gets only seven?? Well, actually, Satan doesn't really make an appearance here; only the diabolical-looking Michel Lemoine in a dual role. Lemoine, who had been working for a variety of Eurocult directors like Jess Franco throughout Europe, tried to bring exploitation to French filmmaking with only a modicum of success. It's still fun, though, as Lemoine plays both the older Count Zaroff and Boris, who spends his most of his time attracting lovelies to his house to kill them off. The descendant of a true nutcase, Boris seems to have inherited the genetic trait for torture and murder, as he loves to indulge his fantasies of hunting women for sport à la an erotic *The Most Dangerous Game* scenario. With the help of his trusty and completely unbalanced servant Karl (Eurocult regular Howard Vernon), Boris lives the life of an entitled mass murderer until a ghost (Coeur) from generations past materializes and some young, stupid travelers barge in on his fun. *Seven Women* is an effective time killer. Lemoine has learned well from his Eurocult past, as he's able to manipulate his way around a rather hackneyed script. Wisely he fills the screen with actors such as Vernon, who could perform their roles in their sleep. Exploitive enough, with an abundance of nudity and violence (his doing doughnuts on one of his victims is not to be missed) to make this a legitimate viewing.

The Story of O, aka *L'Histoire d'O* (FR). Prod. Roger Fleytoux. Dir. Just Jaeckin. France, 1974. Sommerville House Releasing, 100 minutes. DVD/Blu-Ray. Starring: Corinne Cleary, Udo Kier, Anthony Steel and Jean Gaven.

Imagine the most horrifically misogynistic story you can and film it in the most beautiful way possible, throw in some gorgeous music to go over it, hire some very beautiful and talented actors, and voila, you have *The Story of O*. Another scandalous novel (by Pauline Reage) is given the French film treatment by *Emmanuelle* director Jaeckin, who again manages to beautify the ugliness of the material. O (Cleary) is sent by her boyfriend Rene (Eurocult favorite Kier) to undergo some sort of test to prove her love at Roissy, the local chateau. This test involves her learning how to be completely submissive to her partners, which has her being chained up at night, whipped three times a day, forced to submit to any of the men at the castle when they want, and to never look a man in the eyes or talk to him. Worse, the women at the chateau are made to wear the most inappropriate garments that look like they came out of an S&M daily catalogue. After spending a three-day final test that has her chained and whipped, she is released back into public. Rene decides to share her with Sir Stephen (Steel), the Mr. Big of this little S&M circle, and a strange and very brutal relationship develops involving piercing, branding and burning, all to prove their love for each other. Whatever. *The Story of O* is one of those films you'll want to watch with your feminist friends, as you would get the chance to watch their heads explode. Jaeckin, who really can't be faulted because the material was this way in the first place, subverts the ugliness of the story by filming it as if it were a fashion photo shoot, in very much the same style he did with *Emmanuelle* (1974). It's a truly stunning film to watch with its soft blur and beautiful sets and music. It's just a shame the beauty of the film doesn't mute the revulsion you'll feel for the story.

A Woman Possessed, aka *La Papesse* (FR). Prod. Robert Pallardon. Dir. Mario Mercier. France, 1975. Pathfinder Video, 95 min. DVD. Starring: Jean-Francois Delacour, Geziale, Lisa Livane and Erika Maaz.

Mercier's second film (after his hippie fairy tale *La Goulve*, 1972) may be one step improved in the filmmaking department, but it's still a confounding experience when trying to put it together narratively. It's a true WTF experience, and this is the best I can make out: An unhappily married couple, Laurent (Delacour) and his emotionally unstable wife Aline (Livane), are having some marriage issues. He's an artist and just not really inspired, so he's now involved with this satanic cult. This involves his being buried up to his head and having snakes poured on him, or being savagely whipped. He now wants to get his wife involved and because she can't live without him, she agrees. So we next move on to ritual night, when the cult, run by French hippies, try to make Aline one of their own. They rape her, beat her, wall her into a rock quarry (where she's violated by Satan or some green-looking, long-fingernail-wearing copycat), and throw her into a pig sty naked, all the while they are wildly dancing around nude. Will Laurent finally have pity on his poor wife and do something to stop it? Will Aline lose what little mind she has left? Did this synopsis make sense? If so, I'm glad, because nothing in this film does. It's completely out there on another realm. Much has been written that the current DVD copy of the film is badly subtitled. It's true that large portions of it are not subtitled at all. Can you imagine the poor translator who had to sit through this and try and put it to words in another language? I'm thinking medal! *Woman* is something you want to put on late at night when you can't get to sleep. This should do the trick: your mind will think it's dreaming.

Conclusion

> *Emmanuelle* could not cause a tingle in the Achilles tendon of a celibate scoutmaster. Why it is turning on the French is a matter of the most melancholy sociological conjecture.
> —*Time* magazine movie reviewer Jay Cocks[98]

The success of both *Emmanuelle* (1974) and *L'Histoire d'O* (1974) opened the floodgates for French filmmakers to make adult erotic films. The world market was flooded with sexually charged films with one-word female named titles like Guy Casaril's *Emilienne* (1975), *Felicity* (1978), *Nea, a Young Emmanuelle* (1976), and *Laure (Forever Emmanuelle*, 1977), which was, ironically, written, directed and co-starred in by Emmanuelle Arsan herself. This influx caused a strain on the French government both morally and financially. In October of '76, the so-called X Law was passed by the French legislature. The law, actually a finance bill, was designed to limit the production of sexually explicit films, stating that producers of sexually explicit material could no longer petition the government for funds in creating their pictures. Worse, those who made sex pictures had to pay into a tax that was meant to fund "legitimate" films. Filmmakers were quick to catch on and not push the limits of sexuality any further. The third and final installment of the original *Emmanuelle* saga, *Goodbye Emmanuelle* (1977), is a good reflection of this period. In the film Emmanuelle (Kristel) finally tires of her hedonistic husband (played again by Orsini) and lifestyle and finds monogamous love with a French filmmaker. *Goodbye* eschews everything that the previous Emmanuelle films philosophized about—free love, sexual ambiguity—and plays up the attractiveness of romance and monogamy. All of this allowed the film to play down its graphic sexuality to such a degree that no censor had trouble with the film and even in the United States, the film, despite its typically provocative genre, was given an R rating.

The X law effectively killed what little exploitation filmmaking was being done in France. With the exception of the films by Jean Rollin, and a handful of fun spoofs that combined standard exploitation with *Emmanuelle*-type sexiness, no other exploitation movies were produced. The French, with their complete mistrust and artistic snobbery toward the genre, were content to spend the next two decades criticizing exploitation films that were produced abroad.

For a country that has historically been critical (to say the least) of exploitation films, it is ironic to find that France has suddenly become one of the hottest producers of exploitation in the world. Since the release of films like Delplanque's *Promenons-nous dans les bois* (*Deep in the Woods*, 2000) and the internationally successful *Haute tension* (*High Tension*, 2004), it has been on the cutting edge of some of the most violent exploitation in the world. Films like *À l'intérieur* (*Inside*, 2007), which takes abortion to a whole new level, *Frontière(s)* (*Frontier[s]*, 2007) which re-examines "typical" French families, and *Martyrs* (2008), which gives new definition to the words "torture porn," the French have seemingly become comfortable with issues they tried for decades to eschew. As if making up for decades of suppression, young French filmmakers have taken violence to the extreme, creating films that are intense, nihilistic and completely pornographic in their execution of this violence, the complete antithesis of earlier French exploitation from the '60s and '70s. These young filmmakers, who have grown up with a plethora of available home videos and DVDs of Eurocult, have taken their love of exploitation and made it culturally relevant to a country that has always done its best to avoid it.

A Euro-Conclusion

The Eurocult phenomenon is coming up on its 50-year anniversary and yet, it is only now that we are beginning to compile a complete history of the genre. Issues of intellectual snobbism, a distaste for much of the subject matter, and a limited exposure to the relevant primary sources have stunted the exploration of this topic. Recently, academic acceptance of Eurocult as a legitimate art form, the new global economy, and the advent of home entertainment technologies such as DVD and Blu-Ray have made Eurocult a viably commercial prospect, as well as an legitimate field of study. Examining European exploitation films from 1960 to 1980 serves an important role in helping us understand some of the social concerns, political history and cultural upheavals that were occurring in Western society at that time.

Looking at Eurocult from a cultural-studies standpoint, or even an entertainment standpoint, is not always an easy task. Not only is the subject matter frequently distasteful, the chronic low budgets with which these films were made hamper a natural viewing experience. Whether it's the dubbing, which is often atrocious, poor sets, really bad acting or simple stories, Eurocult is easy to dismiss as irrelevant or amateurish. Examination of this genre is difficult because of the investment it takes by an audience member to understand its meaning. Eurocult viewers must make a stronger investment in a film, navigating its contents more thoroughly than mainstream films. The modern-day viewer may view a film like *La Semana del Asesino* (*Cannibal Man*, 1971) as simply a story of a murderous man who takes his victims to the slaughterhouse where he works and makes meat pies of them. But under examination, the film is a statement on the class warfare that was raging in Spain in the '70s. Without a proper history to put these films in context, the messages carried within them may be lost.

One of the most important conclusions that this work has unearthed is the true multinational spirit in which these films were created. Long before there was a European Union or before cinema developed into the multi-production/distributional business it has become today, Eurocult films were being made through cooperation between varying countries with completely different social, political and moral standards. Nowhere in recorded film history is the standard of production so varied and multinational. This is important because it speaks to mutableness of culture, especially cultures that were experiencing profound transformation, as many in Europe were in the '60s and '70s. Those traits which make a film integral to a particular country or culture—for example, a film by Truffaut in France or Fellini in Italy—traditionally resonate strongly within that country while acting outside its borders as an educational opportunity for understanding the country of origin. Eurocult operates differently. Its production is designed from the beginning to appeal to as many different populations and cultures as possible in order to ensure its success. It's difficult to image auteurs like Antonioni being made to edit their films according to different countries' tastes, cast non–Italian-speaking outsiders for ensured success, or hand over rights to distributors with no input on the final versions shown. With Eurocult films, these were standard demands that were happily met in order for excited exploitation film directors to continue indulging their passion for film production. The outcome of this is a hodgepodge of perspectives that is not French per se, nor Spanish, but European as a whole. Their patchwork production denies the cultural imperialism that is found in each individual country's film industry and settles for a broad, overarching identity that is European.[1]

Social scientists with an eye to cultural studies often examine the ideology behind cultural products like film. Every film carries, either explicitly or implicitly, ideas about how the world is, how it should be, and how both men and women see themselves in it. Author Terri Corrigan states, "Movies are never innocent visions of the world," and this study shows that Eurocult films and their specific sub-genres are indeed strongly political texts.[2] Each country's film output shares a common rebellion against its traditional government as well as society. This rebellion is usually manifested in violence. In Spain traditional notions of family life are obliterated in films like *La campana del infierno* (*A Bell from Hell*, 1972) and *¿Quién puede matar a un niño?* (*Who Can Kill a Child?*, 1975), where brothers hang their sisters up on meat hooks and children kill all their parents. In Italy, mistrust of religion, a powerful influence in Italian politics, produced films in which nuns behaved in overtly sexual acts (*Suor omicidi*, 1978) or with priests abusing and then killing young boys (*Non si sevizia un paperino*, 1971). France paid the price for traditionalism as its social, cultural artifacts (local wine) decimated the country turning normal people into mindless killers (*Les Raisins de la mort*, 1978).

This study also concludes that the political atmosphere of Europe in the '60s and '70s had an untold effect on those producing exploitation films. Many of the auteurs of the genre were shaped by the events in their own countries, and most rebelled against what they viewed as dictatorial governments and conservative social pressures. Spaniard Jess Franco grew up in Francoist Spain and literally had to leave the country in order to escape persecution. Frenchman Jean Rollin spent his youth working against Franco, then premiered his first film in Paris in May of '68 to universal condemnation. Italians Aristide Massaccesi (Joe D'Amato) and Dario Argento spent their early lives under the tutelage of their filmmaker fathers, as was the social structure in Italy, before rebelling and producing their own extremely violent shockers that scandalized the world.

All the European exploitation filmmakers of the era had to successfully navigate the challenges to censorship that were occurring during the period. In 1960, very little explicit gore could be shown, and nudity, in European versions only, would consist of brief breast shots that were only meant to titillate. By 1980, everything was permissible, from hard-core violence to hard-core pornography. Each exploitation filmmaker had to adapt to changes in some way. Traditional filmmakers like Italian Mario Bava, who eschewed much of the blood and gore of the early '70s, poured it on in an explicit, sarcastic way in *Ecologia del delitto* (*Twitch of the Death Nerve*, 1972) or simply left it to others to shoot material he found offensive. Spaniard Jacinto Molina (Paul Naschy) incorporated more nudity and outlandish violence in his traditional werewolf films that managed to be both homages to the Universal Pictures monster movies of the past as well as modern retellings. Some auteurs like Italian Lucio Fulci completely embraced the lax censorship codes and produced ultra-violent films that shocked and disgusted audiences. What they all had in common was a responsibility to bring in an audience for their producers. Whether they enjoyed pushing the envelope (Italian Aristide Masseccesi) or were uncomfortable with overtly violent and sexual themes (French Georges Franju), the directors of Eurocult did what they had to do in order to produce a product that fans would want to see.

Unfortunately, Eurocult directors found that the subject matter of their films was at the mercy of overzealous censors that were under governmental control. This forced many of them to sublimate their message into the confines of a plot of a silly monster movie or sexual comedy. The initial reaction to these films by critics and the mainstream filmmakers was swift and negative. Many Eurocult directors found themselves completely ostracized (France's Jean Rollin) by their countrymen, or worse, the target of criminal investigations (Italian Ruggero Deodato). These filmmakers were not reproducing Shakespeare and most of them knew it, but they did, however, have a respect for their craft and for their product. With very few exceptions Eurocult filmmakers have taken pride in their accomplishments, delivering a product that has stood the test of time. They have withstood the initial critical lambasting and are now experiencing a positive revision that looks at these films as important to history and culture.

This study is only the beginning of a very long road of research and discovery. Though Italy, Spain and France were some of the most prolific producers of European exploitation films, they were by no means the only ones. A truly comprehensive history would need to cover those remaining European countries that contributed to the Eurocult phenomenon. The largest of these would be Germany. Though German exploitation producers gained most of their Eurocult credentials by coproducing many other countries' films, they still managed to produce a large variety for themselves. Whether is was violent crime/adventure stories based on the works of Edgar Wallace (Krimis) or pure horror/sexploitation like *Ein toter hing im netz* (*Horrors of Spider Island*, 1959), German contributions to the genre bear future examination. Sweden contributed a staggering array of erotic films that frequently crossed the line into exploitation. Directors such as Joe Sarno (1921–) produced sexy softcore features like *Inga* (1967) that predated the *Emmanuelle* (1974) phenomenon by seven years. In addition, countries such as Belgium, Denmark, and Greece all made forays into the field. These, along with filmmakers who were so multinational they carry no national influence, such as U.S. Radley Metzger (1929–) and Polish-born Walerian Borowczyk (1923–2007), need to be examined for their influence.

The purpose of this book was not to develop an understanding as to why people watch Eurocult, but to understand the environment from which these films came. Many studies have been conducted on why people watch horrific, violent or sexually explicit material. Uses and gratifications research, entertainment theory, or even theories like catharsis can help us understand the need we have to watch some controversial subject matter. The Eurocult phenomenon requires the same type of examination, helping us answer questions not only about our responses to such material, but also about topics of cognitive dissonance, cultural imperialism and interpersonal relationships. Future studies with either experimental, survey or ethnography research should be conducted both in the country of origin and outside to gauge reactions. Also of importance is age of participants. Are those who were living within the time of this study more predisposed to certain reactions than those younger? This would aid in understanding if the reactions of a moviegoing audience change with time, or if simple horrors/titillation transcend both time and geography.

Eurocult has been frequently criticized, as well as the horror genre itself, as being extraordinarily misogynistic. While that may be true for a sizable number of films, future research should look at the roles that women and minorities played in these films. Did they perpetuate negative stereotypes or did they offer something more substantial than mainstream European or U.S. filmmakers were producing? Using either a content or textual analysis and applying a legitimate theory, for example feminist theory, answers to these questions may be found. In addition to women and minorities, these films took a rather jaded view of the cultures around the world. Future research should include some in-depth analysis on issues of cultural hegemony and how these films visually represent that divide.

In addition to gender roles, a more thorough examination of the genre's influence on modern-day society needs to be addressed. This study attempts to put a history to the phenomenon and showcases a few examples of modern-day filmmakers who have stated their love of Eurocult and the influence of Eurocult films on their own works. More research is needed to see exactly how deep this genre is ingrained on the psyche of modern-day filmmakers. Also, how has the genre affected our modern daily entertainment life? This study shows that certain subgenres have mutated into other forms of entertainment. Using a content or textual analysis, it is possible to make the correlations between, for example, the Italian mondo films of the early '60s and the reality-based television of today. This type of study would be advantageous because of its historical value.

Another very important study would be an analysis of the promotional material that accompanied these films. This book has provided some colorful examples of the way Eurocult has been promoted throughout the world. Eurocult has had a worldwide audience that required each film to be advertised in a different way for each country. Some films like *Zombi* (*Zombie 2*, 1979) or *Profondo rosso* (*Deep Red*, 1975) were shown in all European countries, barring a few in Eastern Europe, and throughout the United States and Asia. Each country had a different advertising scheme, sometimes resulting in over 25 different posters or ads for one movie alone. A content analysis would allow researchers to look at the different signifiers and iconography in the ads, perhaps shedding some light on the culture itself or dispelling any cultural assumptions that are not true.

Regardless of what direction you want to take your research, as either an academic or as fan, the history of Eurocult is fascinating one. Filmmakers, focusing on subject matter that had never been explored so publicly before, have provided a fascinating and sometimes frightening look at the human psyche. Though these films often focus on themes most people shy away from, the subject itself is pure enjoyment, and future filmmakers from Europe as well as around the world will continue to pay homage as they create their own exciting brand of Eurocult. Whether it be demons, witches, vampires, evil children, sexually perverse dwarfs, naughty nuns or flesh-eating zombies, these new generations of filmmakers will no doubt shock and disgust future generations just as their filmatic forefathers did 30 and 40 years ago. Pushing all the buttons of fear, revulsion, and excitation that make audiences flock to films, they have given all those around the world a platform to visually indulge in their perverse titillations.

Chapter Notes

Introduction

1. Adrian Luther Smith, *Blood and Black Lace*, Introduction (Liskeard, UK: Stray Cat Publishing, 1999). The word "giallo" means "yellow" in Italian. The term was originally used to describe the mystery thriller novels published in Italy with yellow covers.
2. Steve Fentone, *Antichristo: The Bible of Nasty Nun Sinema and Culture* (London: Fab Press, 2003), 5.
3. Cathal Tohill and Pete Tombs, *Immoral Tales: European Sex and Horror Movies 1956–1984* (London: Primitive Press, 1995), 42.
4. Douglas Kellner, "Cultural Studies, Multiculturalism and Media Culture," in *Gender, Race and Class in Media*, 2nd ed., ed. Gail Dines and Jean Humez (Thousand Oaks, CA: Sage Publications, 2003), 10.
5. Stephen Jay Schneider and Tony Williams, *Horror International*, Introduction (Detroit: Wayne State University Press, 2005), 3.
6. Alexander Olney, *Playing Dead: Spectatorship, Performance and Euro-horror Cinema* (Ph.D. diss., University of Nebraska, 2003).
7. Geoffrey Nowell-Smith, *The Oxford History of World Cinema* (New York: Oxford Press, 1996), 486.
8. Bill Landis and Mike Clifford, *Sleazoid Express* (New York: Fireside Publishing, 2002), 5.
9. Interview with Amando de Ossorio, Blind Dead Collection DVD (Blue Underground, 2007). Interview conducted in 2000.
10. Tohill and Tombs, 66.
11. Pete Tombs, "A Note about *French Sex Murders*," DVD supplement, *French Sex Murders* DVD (Mondo Macabro, 2005).
12. Smith, 17.
13. Steven Thrower, *Beyond Terror: The Films of Lucio Fulci* (London: Fab Press, 2002), 17.
14. Jay Slater, *Eaten Alive!: Italian Cannibal and Zombie Movies* (London: Plexus Press, 2002), 102.
15. Troy Howarth, *The Haunted World of Mario Bava* (London: Fab Press, 2002), 32, 73, 86.
16. Tim Lucas, *Black Sunday* DVD Audio Commentary (Image Entertainment, 1999).
17. Catriona MacColl, *The Beyond* DVD Audio Commentary (Anchor Bay Entertainment, 2000).
18. Richard Harlan Smith, *Your Vice Is a Locked Room and Only I Have the Key*, DVD Liner Notes (NoShame films, 2005).

Chapter 1

1. Luca Palmerini and Gaetano Mistretta, *Spaghetti Nightmares* (Key West, FL: Fantasma Books, 1996), 147.
2. Louis Paul, *Italian Horror Film Directors* (Jefferson, NC: McFarland, 1995), 33.
3. Palmerini and Mistretta, 9.
4. Tim Lucas, *Black Sunday* DVD liner notes (Image Entertainment 1999).
5. Tohill and Tombs, 33.
6. Peter Hutchings, *The Horror Show* (Harlow, UK: Pearson Longman, 2004), 71.
7. Howarth, 16.
8. Howarth, 149.
9. Alan Jones, *Profondo Argento* (London: Fab Press, 2004), 7.
10. *Entertainment Weekly*, October 25, 2000.
11. Tim Lucas, *Mario Bava: All the Colors of the Dark* (Cincinnati, OH: Video Watchdog), 171.
12. Gerald Mast, *A Short History of the Movies* (Indianapolis: Bobs-Merrill Press, 1981), 285.
13. Mary Wood, *Italian Cinema* (New York: Berg Publishing, 2005), 16.
14. Wood. 17.
15. Though sexuality and violence were cropping up in Italian films, they were fairly suppressed. The Catholic Church acted as supreme censor until the late 1960s.
16. Luigi Barzini, *The Italians* (New York: Touchstone Press, 1964). Also quoted in Tim Lucas's audio commentary on *Blood and Black Lace* (2000), VCI DVD.
17. Thrower, *Beyond Terror*, 153.
18. Keala Jewell, *Monsters in the Italian Literary Imagination* (Indianapolis: Wayne State University Press, 2001), 12.
19. Tim Lucas, *I vampiri* DVD liner notes (Image Entertainment, 2001).
20. Nowell-Smith, 586.
21. Nowell-Smith, 358.
22. Lawrence McCallum, *Italian Horror Films of the 1960s* (Jefferson, NC: McFarland, 1998), back cover.
23. Lucas, *I vampiri* DVD liner notes, 2.
24. Howarth, 16.
25. Lucas, *op. cit.*, 2.
26. Lucas, *op. cit.*, 3.
27. Lucas, *op. cit.*, 3.
28. Howarth, 17.
29. Howarth, 319.
30. Thrower, 17.
31. Slater, 102.
32. John Sirabella. *Zombi 2* DVD liner notes (Shriek Show, 2005).
33. Howarth, 32, 73, 86.
34. Lucas, *Mario Bava*, 265.
35. Tim Lucas, *Mobius Home Video Forum* (http://www.mhvf.net/ Accessed: May 15, 2007).

36. Steven Thrower, *Eyeball: Compendium 1989–2003* (London: Fab Press, 2003), 126.
37. Cynthia Henderson, *I Was a Cold War Monster: Horror Films, Eroticism and the Cold War Imagination* (Bowling Green, OH: Popular Press, 2001), 1.
38. Elizabeth McKeon and Linda Everett, *Cinema Under the Stars: America's Love Affair with the Drive-In Movie Theater* (Nashville: Cumberland House, 1998), 65–67.
39. *Tempi duri per i vampiri* (*Uncle Was a Vampire*), prod. and dir. Mario Cecchi Gori, Italy, 1960. Christopher Lee's poor dubbing was a sore spot for the actor. After being poorly dubbed again in Mario Bava's *La frusta e il corpo* (*The Whip and the Body*, 1963) Lee contractually asked that he provide all the dubbing for his international pictures himself.
40. *Il mio amico Jekyll* (*My Friend, Dr. Jekyll*), prod. and dir. Marino Girolami, Italy, 1960.
41. McCallum, 216.
42. *Playgirls and the Vampire* (*L'ultima preda del vampiro*), prod. Tiziano Longo, dir. Piero Regnoli, Italy/Germany, 1960. Regnoli was also one of the writers for *I vampiri*. With his stints in both *L'amante* and *L'ultima*, Walter Brandi became one of the first de facto stars of Italian horror/exploitation. Though never as popular as a Christopher Lee, Barbara Steele or Peter Cushing, Brandi continued to act in genre films through the sixties in films such as *La strage dei vampiri* (1964) and *Cinque tombe per un medium* (1965).
43. C. McGee, A. Martray, J. Norrs, and S. Unsinn, "Goth in Film," Ithaca College Senior Seminar web site (www.ithaca.edu/keg/seminar/gothfilm.htm 2002. Accessed March 13, 2006).
44. Gary Johnson, "The Golden Age of Italian Horror 1957–1979," *Images Journal* web site (www.imagesjournal.com/issue05/infocus/intr02.htm. Accessed March 13, 2006).
45. John Stanley, *Creature Features: The Science Fiction, Fantasy, Horror Movie Guide* (New York: Boulevard Press, 1997), 48.
46. McCallum, 38.
47. Howarth, 29.
48. Lucas, *Mario Bava*, 308.
49. Lucas, *Black Sunday* liner notes. In the U.S., the age prohibition stood even though the film was severely edited.
50. Gary Johnson. *Black Sunday* DVD review, *Images Journal* web site (www.imagesjournal.com/issue10/reviews/mariobava/blacksunday.htm).
51. McGee et al.
52. Clive Barker, *Clive Barker's A–Z of Horror* (New York: Harper Prism, 1996), 126.
53. Pete Tombs, *Mill of the Stone Women* DVD liner notes (Mondo Macabro DVD, 2004). Though the film was shot in color in 1960, the practice of shooting Gothics in color didn't really catch on until 1963. Color at the time was saved for epics and action films.
54. Johnson.
55. Tohill and Tombs, 37–38.
56. Andrew Mangravite, "Once Upon a Time in a Crypt," *Film Comment* (January 1993): 29.
57. Barker, 128.
58. Glenn Erickson, "*The Horrible Dr. Hichcock*: Women on the Verge of a Gothic Breakdown," *Images Journal* web site (www.imagesjournal.com/issue05/infocus/hichcock.htm, 2000).
59. Barker, 128.
60. It also has the character married to a Dr. Hichcock, but the movie never explains if it's supposed to be the same character as in the earlier film.

61. *Horrible Dr. Hichcock* (*L'Orribile segreto del Dr. Hichcock*), prod. Ermanno Donati, dir. Riccardo Freda, Italy, 1962.
62. The film was released two years later (1964) in America, along with Mario Bava's *Ercole al centro della terra* (*Hercules in the Haunted World*), filmed in 1961.
63. Between 1960 and 1966, Barbara Steele appeared in more than 8 Italian Gothic or horror films.
64. *Castle of Blood* (*Danza macabra*), prod. Marco Vicario, dir. Antonio Margheriti, Italy/France, 1964.
65. Tim Lucas, *Castle of Blood* DVD liner notes (Synapse Films, 2002).
66. Palmerini and Mistretta. 73.
67. *Virgin of Nuremberg* (*La vergine di Norimberga*), prod. Marco Vicario, dir. Antonio Margheriti, Italy, 1963.
68. *Black Sabbath* (*I tre volti della paura*), prod. Paolo Mercuri, dir. Mario Bava, Italy, 1963.
69. Tim Lucas, *Black Sabbath* DVD liner notes (Image Entertainment, 2000). In the original European version, the stories were in the order of *The Telephone*, *The Wurdulak*, and *The Drop of Water*. The producers believed that *The Drop of Water* was entirely too scary to end the movie on and *The Telephone* wasn't strong enough. In the American version (*Black Sabbath*), the stories' order was *The Drop of Water*, *The Telephone*, and *The Wurdulak*.
70. Howarth, 86.
71. Howarth, 84.
72. Howarth, 310.
73. *The Whip and the Body* (*La frusta e il corpo*), prod. Frederico Natale, dir. Mario Bava, Italy/France, 1963.
74. Howarth, 91.
75. McCallum, 61, 66–67. The film never did receive a proper American theatrical release. It was bought by AIP for the straight-to-television market.
76. Paul, 96.
77. Leon Hunt, "A (Sadistic) Night at the *Opera*," in *The Horror Reader*, ed. Ken Gelder (London: Routledge, 2000), 332.
78. Howarth, 145.
79. Thrower, *Beyond Terror*, 144–145. Gothic made a comeback in the early 1980s with a trio of successful films by Lucio Fulci. Though these films were modern and set in the U.S., Thrower insist that they were "southern Gothic" and adhered to the same standards as earlier Italian Gothic with only the places and time changed. These films included *L'aldilà* (*The Beyond*, 1981), *Quella villa accanto al cimitero* (*The House by the Cemetery*, 1981), and *Paura nella città dei morti viventi* (*Gates of Hell*, 1980).
80. Palmerini and Mistretta, 73.
81. Phil Hardy, *The Overlook Film Encyclopedia: Horror* (Woodstock, NY: Overlook Press, 1995), 263.
82. *Baron Blood* (*Gli orrori del castello di Norimberga*), prod. Alfredo Leone, dir. Mario Bava, Italy/Germany, 1971.
83. Howarth, 276.
84. *Lisa and the Devil* (*Lisa e il diavolo*), prod. Alfredo Leone, dir. Mario Bava, Italy, 1973. The use of a lollypop for the Telly Savalas character predates the lollypop sucking he enjoyed in his CBS-TV show *Kojak*. Originally the character of the Devil was supposed to be chewing gum, but Savalas believed that using a lollypop would be to more dramatic effect.
85. Tim Lucas, *Lisa and the Devil/House of Exorcism* DVD liner notes (Image Entertainment, 2000).
86. Lucas, *Lisa* liner notes.

87. Giovanni Simonelli, interview, *Seven Deaths in a Cat's Eye* DVD (Blue Underground, 2005).
88. Thomas Jane, *The Mondo Cane Film Collection* DVD review, DVD Maniacs web site (www.dvdmaniacs.net/Reviews/M-P/mondo_cane.html, November 6, 2003).
89. Bill Gibron, *The Mondo Cane Film Collection* DVD review (PopMatters web site, www.popmatters.com/film/reviews/m/mondo-cane-collection.shtml, October 28, 2003).
90. "Italy," *Encyclopædia Britannica* Online (May 2007).
91. Nowell-Smith, 592.
92. "Exploitation Film." Dr. John Grohl's Psych Central web site (http://psychcentral.com/wiki/Exploitation_film, April 12, 2005).
93. Peter Goldfarb, *Mondo Cane* movie review, *Film Quarterly* 17, no. 1 (Autumn 1963): 46–47.
94. Tombs, 31.
95. David Gregory, *The Godfathers of Mondo* DVD documentary (Blue Underground, 2003).
96. Gregory.
97. Gregory.
98. *Mondo cane*, prod. and dir. Paolo Cavara, Italy, 1962.
99. Gibron.
100. Gregory.
101. Gregory.
102. *Mondo cane 2*, prod. Mario Maffei and Giorgio Cecchini, dir. Gualtiero Jacopetti and Franco Prosperi, Italy, 1964.
103. Gregory.
104. *Africa addio*, prod. Angelo Rizzoli, dir. Gualtiero Jacopetti and Franco Prosperi, Italy, 1966.
105. Gregory.
106. Landis and Clifford, 168.
107. *Africa addio* DVD liner notes (Blue Underground, 2003).
108. Landis and Clifford, 165.
109. Gilbert and Sullivan, 164.
110. *Mandingo* was a popular exploitation novel in the early '70s that was about a slave and his sexual exploits on a plantation in the South prior to the Civil War. Full of illicit sex and violence, the novel was turned into a box-office success in a 1975 exploitation film starring Ken Norton, Susan George and James Mason.
111. *Goodbye Uncle Tom (Addio Uncle Tom)*, prod. and dir. Gualtiero Jacopetti and Franco Prosperi, Italy, 1971.
112. Gregory.
113. Jones, 10.
114. Mikel Koven, *La Dolce Morte: Vernacular Cinema and the Italian Giallo* (Lantham, MD: Scarecrow Press, 2006).
115. Gary Needham, "Playing with Genre: An Introduction to the Italian Giallo," *Kinoeye* 2, no. 11 (June 10, 2002).
116. Smith, 5.
117. Windslow Leach, "Spaghetti Slashers: Italian Giallo Cinema," http://members.aol.com/grindhousesite/giallo.html (April 12, 2005).
118. Tim Lucas, *The Girl Who Knew Too Much*, DVD liner notes (Image Entertainment, 2000). Many of the unsavory aspects were cut for the American print. American International Pictures (who had distributed *Black Sunday* the year before) had held the picture back a year. Released under the name *The Evil Eye*, the film was rescored, the name of the main character was changed, and the aforementioned drug use was deleted.
119. Howarth, 67.
120. *The Girl Who Knew Too Much (La ragazza che sapeva troppo)*, prod. Lionella Santi, dir. Mario Bava, Italy, 1962.
121. Gary Needham, "Playing with Genre: Defining the Italian Giallo," in *Fear Without Frontiers: Horror Cinema Across the Globe*, ed. Steven Jay Schneider (London: Fab Press, 2003), 136.
122. Needham, *op. cit.*
123. *Black Sabbath (I tre volti della paura)*, prod. Paolo Mercuri, dir. Mario Bava, Italy, 1963 (DVD, Image Entertainment, 92 min.).
124. Lucas, *Black Sabbath* DVD liner notes.
125. Howarth, 337.
126. Needham, "Defining," 143.
127. Smith, 1, 110.
128. The names of many of Baker's gialli can be confusing. *Orgasmo* (1968) was retitled *Paranoia* for international audiences. Her next film with Lenzi was given the Italian title of *Paranoia* (1969) but called *A Quiet Place to Kill* outside of Italy.
129. Baker's full-body nude scene in Corrado Farina's *Baba Yaga* (1973) was so shocking that Italian censors cut it out completely. It has since been included as an outtake in Blue Underground's DVD.
130. *Twitch of the Death Nerve (Ecologia del delitto)*, prod. Giuseppe Zaccariello, dir. Mario Bava, 1971.
131. Jones, 22.
132. Dario Argento, *Cat o' Nine Tails* 30-second ad. *Cat o' Nine Tails* DVD (Anchor Bay Entertainment, 2000).
133. *The Bird with the Crystal Plumage (L'uccello dalle piume di cristallo)*, prod. Salvatore Argento, dir. Dario Argento, Italy, 1970.
134. Jones, 20.
135. Jones, 27.
136. An example of the American version of this style of gritty filmmaking would be Pakula's *Klute* (1971), which showcased many of the same giallo filmmaking techniques that were being used in Italy.
137. *Cat o' Nine Tails (Il gatto a nove code)*, prod. Salvatore Argento, dir. Dario Argento, Italy, 1971.
138. Paul, 41.
139. *4 Flies on Grey Velvet (Quattro mosche di velluto grigio)*, prod. Salvatore Argento, dir. Dario Argento, Italy/U.S., 1972.
140. Jones, 38.
141. The film was picked up in the U.S. by Paramount, hoping to cash in on the success of Argento's earlier works.
142. Jones, 55.
143. *Lizard in a Woman's Skin (Una lucertola con la pelle di donna)*, prod. Edmondo Amati, dir. Lucio Fulci, Italy/Spain/France, 1971.
144. John Sirabella, *Shedding the Skin*, DVD documentary, *Lizard in a Woman's Skin* DVD (Shriek Show, 2004).
145. Thrower, *Beyond Terror*, 70.
146. *Don't Torture a Duckling (Non si sevizia un paperino)*, prod. Renato Jaboni, dir. Lucio Fulci, Italy, 1972.
147. Thrower, *Beyond Terror*, 98. It is easy to posit the Father Avoline character as a repressed homosexual taking out his sexual and anger frustrations on the young boys.
148. The flashback "Dies Irae" theme is so effective it was later recycled as Michael Madsen's theme for *Kill Bill, Vol. 2* (2004).
149. Nathaniel Thompson, *The Strange Vice of Mrs. Wardh* DVD review, DVD Maniacs web site (www.mondo-digital.com/torso.html. Accessed on April 13, 2006).

150. Smith, *Your Vice* liner notes.
151. *All the Colors of the Dark* (*Tutti i colori del buio*), prod. Mino Loy and Luciano Martino, dir. Sergio Martino, Italy/Spain, 1972.
152. John Sirabella, interview with Sergio Martino, *All the Colors of the Dark* DVD (Shriek Show, 2004).
153. *I corpi presentano tracce di violenza carnale* (*Torso*), prod. Carlo Ponti, dir. Sergio Martino, Italy/France, 1973.
154. Smith, 36.
155. One could make the argument that Ercoli did not like putting his real-life wife and girlfriend into situations that would make her appear weak, but no interview or reference material substantiates this argument.
156. Jones, 63.
157. *Deep Red* (*Profondo rosso*), prod. Salvatore Argento, dir. Dario Argento, Italy, 1975.
158. Julian Grainger, "Deep Red," in *Art of Darkness: The Cinema of Dario Argento*, ed. Chris Gallant (London: Fab Press, 2000), 115.
159. Federico Galanetto and Vittorio Cristiano, "An Interview with Michele Soavi," in *Flesh and Blood: A Compendium*, ed. Harvey Fenton (London: Fab Press, 1996), 350.
160. Nowell-Smith, 594–596.
161. Travelotica web site (http://www.travelotica.com/travelguide/180/italy/the-1970s-and-1980s-33225.htm. Accessed: May 23, 2007).
162. "Italy." *Encyclopaedia Brittanica*.
163. Nowell-Smith, 314.
164. Nowell-Smith, 594. This would fall even further to 165 million in 1983. By 1992 it would be down to 90 million.
165. Slater, 22.
166. Landis and Clifford, 165.
167. Slater, 44.
168. *Deep River Savages* (*Il paese del sesso selvaggio*), prod. Ovidio G. Assonitis, dir. Umberto Lenzi, Italy, 1973.
169. Slater, 46.
170. Palmerini and Mistretta, 42.
171. John Sirebella, interview with Umberto Lenzi, *Jungle Holocaust* DVD (Shriek Show, 2001).
172. Palmerini and Mistretta, 69.
173. Palmerini and Mistretta, 42.
174. *Jungle Holocaust* (*Mondo cannibale*), prod. Georgio Carlo Rossi, dir. Ruggero Deodato, Italy, 1977.
175. Manilo Gomarasca and Davide Pulici, "Joe D'Amato Competely Uncut," *Nocturno Cinema*, 1998.
176. *Emanuelle and the Last Cannibals* (*Emanuelle e gli ultimi cannibali*), prod. Gianfranco Couyoumdjian, dir. Aristide Massaccesi, Italy, 1977.
177. Xavier Mendik, "Black Sex, Bad Sex: Monstrous Ethnicity in the Black Emanuelle Films," in *Alternative Europe: Eurotrash and Exploitation Cinema Since 1945*, ed. Ernest Mathijs and Xavier Mendik (London: Wallflower Press, 2004), 156.
178. *Mountain of the Cannibal God* (*La montagna del dio cannibale*), prod. Luciano Martino, dir. Sergio Martino, Italy, 1978.
179. Gino Vitacane, "Legacy of the Cannibal God: DVD interview with Sergio Martino," *Mountain of the Cannibal God* DVD (Blue Underground and Anchor Bay Entertainment, 2001).
180. Slater, 108.
181. Kerman, who under the pseudonym R. Bolla appeared in such porn films as *Debbie Does Dallas* (1978) and *Amanda by Night* (1981), would go on to appear in such films as Lenzi's *Cannibal ferox* (1981), as well as such mainstream films as *Spider-Man* (2002).
182. *Cannibal Holocaust* (*Ultimo mondo cannibale*), prod. Franco Di Nunzio, dir. Ruggero Deodato, Italy, 1980.
183. Alan Young, "The Making of Cannibal Holocaust," *Cannibal Holocaust 25th Anniversary* DVD (Grindhouse Releasing, 2005).
184. Young.
185. Young.
186. Jay Slater, "The Forbidden Era," *Rue Morgue* 47 (July 2005), 30. The "video nasties" were films banned in the early 1980s by the Thatcher administration, who believed these films led to the burgeoning violence that was plaguing England during that time.
187. *Eaten Alive* (*Mangiati vivi*), prod. Mino Loy and Luciano Martino, dir. Umberto Lenzi, Italy, 1980.
188. John Sirabella, interview with Umberto Lenzi, *Eaten Alive* DVD (Shriek Show Entertainment, 2002).
189. Bill Landis, liner notes, *Make Them Die Slowly* DVD (Grindhouse Releasing, 2000).
190. Thrower, 22.
191. Jones, 97.
192. Jones, 103–104.
193. Perry Martin. *The Dead Will Walk*, DVD documentary, *Dawn of the Dead Ultimate Edition* (Anchor Bay Entertainment, 2004). There would be three versions of *Dawn of the Dead*: the U.S. theatrical version at 127 minutes; the extended version at 139 minutes; and Argento's European version at 118 minutes.
194. John Sirabella, "Building a Better Zombi," *Zombi 25th Anniversary Edition* (Media Blasters, 2005).
195. *Zombie* (*Zombi 2*), prod. Fabrizio De Angelis, dir. Lucio Fulci, Italy, 1979. The death of Olga Karlatos by a wooden splinter to the eye is considered to be one of the most shocking deaths in the zombie canon. Fabio Fabrizzi, the film's composer, would go on to produce many electronic scores for Fulci in films such as *Aldila* (*The Beyond*, 1981) and *Lo Squattore de New York* (*New York Ripper*, 1983).
196. *Zombie Holocaust* (*Zombi Holocaust*), prod. Fabrizio De Angelis, Dir. Marino Girolami, Italy, 1980.
197. John Sirabella, interview with Roy Foukes, *Zombie Holocaust* DVD (Shriek Show, 2002). The M.D. in *Doctor Butcher M.D.* stood for Medical Deviate.
198. David Gregory, *Tales from a Contaminated City*, DVD interview with Umberto Lenzi (Anchor Bay Entertainment, 2002).
199. *Nightmare City* (*Incubo sulla città contaminata*), prod. Luis Méndez, dir. Umberto Lenzi, Italy/Spain, 1980.
200. This type of fast zombie was recently resurrected in both Danny Boyle's *28 Days Later* (2002) and the 2004 remake of *Dawn of the Dead*.
201. Radice was busy in 1980 making 3 of the most infamous Italian exploitation films — Fulci's *Paura nella città de morti viventi*, Lenzi's *Cannibal ferox*, and Margheriti's *Apocalypse domani* — in the span of a year.
202. *Cannibal Apocalypse Redux*, Cannibal Apocalypse DVD (Image Entertainment, 2003).
203. *Cannibal Apocalypse* (*Apocalypse domani*), prod. Maurizo and Sandro Amati, dir. Antonio Margheriti. Italy/U.S./Germany, 1980.
204. Travis Crawford, "The Butchering of *Cannibal Apocalypse*," *Cannibal Apocalypse* DVD (Image Entertainment).
205. *Anthropophagus*, prod. George Eastman, Edward L. Montoro, Aristide Masseccesi, dir. Ariside Massaccesi, Italy, 1980. The effect used was a skinned rabbit to take the place of the fetus.

206. John Sirabella, interview with Luigi Montefiore, *Anthropophagus* DVD (Shriek Show, 2006).
207. The sexual scenes can be considered a turnoff because lead actor Mark Shannon clearly had genital warts, which were fully on display.
208. Jamie Russell, *Book of the Dead: The Complete History of Zombie Cinema* (London: Fab Press, 2005), 134–135.
209. Palmerini and Mistretta, 77.
210. Alberto De Martino interview, *The Antichrist* DVD (Anchor Bay Entertainment, 2002).
211. M. Bertonlino and E. Ridola, *Vizietti all'italiana: L'epoca d'oro della commedia Sexy* (Florence, Italy: 1999).
212. Tamao Nakahara, "Barred Nuns: Italian Nunsploitation Films," in *Alternative Europe: Eurotrash and Exploitation Cinema Since 1945*, edited by Ernest Mathijs and Xavier Mendik (London: Wallflower Press, 2004).
213. Nakahara, 129–130.
214. Troy Howarth, DVD review of *The Antichrist*, DVD Maniacs web site (www.dvdmaniacs.net/Reviews/A-D/anti_christ.html. April 25, 2002).
215. "Raising Hell: Interview with Guilio Berruti," *The Antichrist* DVD (Anchor Bay Entertainment, 2002).
216. Nakahara, 132.
217. *Emanuelle nera*, prod. Mario Mariani, dir. Bitto Albertini, Italy/Spain, 1975.
218. "Italy," *Encyclopaedia Brittanica*.
219. David Flint, *The Emanuelle Phenomenon*, DVD supplement, *Emanuelle in America* DVD (Blue Underground, 2003).
220. Mendik, 147.
221. Manilo Gomarasca and Davide Pulici, audio interview with Laura Gemser, *Nocturno Cinema*, 1996.
222. *Emanuelle in Bangkok* (*Emanuelle nera: Orient reportage*), prod. Fabrizio De Angelis, dir. Aristide Massaccesi, Italy, 1975.
223. *Emanuelle in America*, prod. Fabrizio De Angelis, dir. Aristide Massaccesi, Italy, 1976.
224. Gomarasca and Pulici, 1999.
225. Gomarasca and Pulici, 1996.
226. Gomarasca and Pulici, 1999.
227. Mendik, 146–156.
228. Steve Bodrowski, *Suspiria: A Nostalgic Review*, Cinefantastique Online (http://cinefantastiqueonline.com/2008/06/nostalgia-suspiria-1977/).
229. David White, "History of the Italian Horror Film, pt. 1" (www.horror-wood.com/italianhorror1.htm).

Chapter 2

1. Cathal Tohill and Pete Tombs, *Immoral Tales* (New York: St. Martin's Griffin, 1994), 63.
2. *Cannibal Man* (*La semana del asesino*), prod. Jose Truchado, Dir. Eloy de la Iglesia, Spain, 1971.
3. Marsha Kinder, "Spain After Franco," in *The Oxford History of World Cinema* (London: Oxford University Press, 1997), 596.
4. Jay Slater, "Hispanic Horror: A Brief History," *Rue Morgue*, July 2005, 26.
5. Carlos Aguilar, *Jess Franco: El Sexo del Horror* (Rome: Glittering Images, 1999), 23.
6. Kinder, 597.
7. Tohill and Tombs, 63.
8. Tohill and Tombs, 63. In addition, westerns, spy dramas and comedy thrillers also were popular staples of the Spanish moviegoer.
9. These international collaborations would continue into the 1970s with such high-profile films as *Nicholas and Alexandra* (1971) and many westerns.
10. David Kalat, "French Revolution: The Secret History of Gallic Horror Movies," in *Fear Without Frontiers*, ed. Steven Jay Schneider (London: England, Fab Press, 2003), 277.
11. Tim Lucas, *The Awful Dr. Orloff* (*Gritos en la noche*) DVD liner notes (Image Entertainment, 2000).
12. Alan Jones, "Spain," in *The Rough Guide to Horror Movies* (New York: Rough Guides, 2005), 245.
13. Jones, 245.
14. *La torre de los siete jorobados* (*The Tower of the Seven Hunchbacks*), prod. Luis Judez, dir. Edgar Neville, Spain, 1943.
15. Lucas, *The Awful Dr. Orloff* liner Notes. The name of Dr. Orloff comes from the Edgar Night novel *The Dead Eyes of London*. Howard Vernon would go on to become Franco's most prolific actor, starring in over 35 films for the Spanish director. Born in Baden, Switzerland, in 1914 to an American father and a Swiss mother, Vernon grew up in the U.S. before returning to Europe to finish high school. Specializing in playing German officers during the early 1950s, Vernon became well known later by playing shady, smooth characters like Dr. Orloff. In addition to his work for Franco, Vernon worked with such talent as Orson Welles, Rita Hayworth, Fritz Lang, Woody Allen and Michael Powell. Vernon died in Paris in July 1996.
16. Andy Starke and Pete Tombs, *The Diabolical Mr. Franco*, DVD documentary (Mondo Macabro, 2001).
17. Aguilar, 154.
18. Tohill and Tombs, 84–85.
19. Lucas, *The Awful Dr. Orloff*.
20. Aguilar, 154.
21. Sullivan's death as a result of a fall from a Ferris wheel is symbolic of the European fascination with, yet mistrust of, traveling carnivals.
22. Previous to *Pyro*, he co-produced two Danish science-fiction films, *Journey to the Seventh Planet* (1962) and *Reptilicus* (1962), Denmark's answer to the Godzilla films.
23. Sam Sherman, interview with Sidney Pink, *Pyro* DVD (Troma Team Video, 2001). In England the original name, *The Phantom of the Ferris Wheel*, was used. AIP changed the title to the more lurid *Pyro* for American audiences.
24. Chris Alexander, "Spain's Sweet Sadist: Interview with Jess Franco," *Rue Morgue*, July 2005, 21.
25. Starke and Tombs, *The Diabolical Mr. Franco*.
26. Starke and Tombs, *The Diabolical Mr. Franco*.
27. *Succubus* review by Vincent Canby of the *New York Times* (Blue Underground DVD, 2006).
28. *All Movie Guide* review, *Two Undercover Angels* and *Kiss Me Monster* (Blue Underground DVD, 2006).
29. James Marriott, *Horror Films* (London: Virgin Press, 2004), 66.
30. Aguilar, 22–23.
31. Aguilar, 23.
32. Tohill and Tombs, 80.
33. Aguilar, 23.
34. Tohill and Tombs, 81.
35. Tohill and Tombs, 81.
36. *Les Vampiresas 1930*, prod. Marius Lesoeur, dir. Jess Franco, Spain, 1962.
37. The name Dr. Orlof transformed to Dr. Orloff in the sequel *El secreto del Dr. Orloff* (1964) and its subsequent sequels.
38. *Dr. Orloff's Monster*, DVD liner notes (Image Entertainment, 2001).

39. Aguilar, 154.
40. Tim Lucas, *The Sadistic Baron Von Klaus* DVD liner notes (Image Entertainment, 2001).
41. *Sadistic Baron Von Klaus* (*La mano de un hombre muerto*), dir. Jesus Franco, Spain/France, 1962.
42. *Dr. Orloff's Monster* (*El secreto del Dr. Orloff*), prod. Marius Lesoeur, dir. Jesus Franco, Spain/Austria/France, 1964.
43. *Diabolical Dr. Z* (*Miss Muerte*), prod. and dir. Jesus Franco, Spain, 1965.
44. Aguilar, 154.
45. Aguilar, 154.
46. Starke and Tombs, *The Diabolical Mr. Franco*.
47. Starke and Tombs, *The Diabolical Mr. Franco*.
48. Welles had had some success getting funding in Spain previous to this with the film *Mr. Arkadin* (1955). Unfortunately, the film labored in post-production for years and did not find a distributor until 1962.
49. Tohill and Tombs, 86–87.
50. Aguilar, 54–56. Welles did appear in a version of *Treasure Island* in 1972 directed by both Italian Andrea Bianchi, who directed such exploitation classics as *Le notti del terrore* (*Burial Ground*, 1981), and British director John Hough.
51. Tohill and Tombs, 93.
52. David Gregory and Bill Lustig, "From *Necronomicon* to *Succubus*: Interview with Jess Franco," *Succubus* DVD (Blue Underground, 2006).
53. Gregory and Lustig. Adrian Hoven was both an actor and producer. A matinee star in Germany before working with Franco, he would later go on to produce one of the most successful European exploitation films, *Mark of the Devil*, in 1969.
54. Gregory and Lustig.
55. *Succubus* (*Necronomicon*), prod. Adrian Hoven, dir. Jesus Franco, Spain/Germany, 1967.
56. Tohill and Tombs, 94.
57. Gregory and Lustig.
58. David Gregory and Bill Lustig, "The Case of the Red Lips: Interview with Jess Franco," *Two Undercover Angels* and *Kiss Me Monster* DVD (Blue Underground, 2006).
59. *Two Undercover Angels* (*Sadisterotica*), prod. Adrian Hoven, dir. Jesus Franco, Spain/Germany, 1967. Dubbing can destroy any intricacies of pitch and intonation in an actor's original performance, disposing of any wit that the writer intended.
60. Peter Nelhause, "Saturday Night with Jesus (Franco)" (www.coffeecoffeeandmorecoffee.com/archives/2005/09/saturday_night.html. September 4, 2005; accessed October 17, 2006).
61. Joe Bob Briggs, *Profoundly Erotic: Sexy Movies that Changed History* (New York: Universal Publishing, 2005), 9.
62. Aguilar, 69–70.
63. David McGillivray, "Harry Alan Towers," *Film and Filming*, no. 400, January 1988.
64. *Blood of Fu Manchu*, prod. Harry Alan Towers, dir. Jesus Franco, Spain/U.S., 1968.
65. David Gregory, "The Fall of Fu Manchu: Interview with Tsai Chin," *The Castle of Fu Manchu* DVD (Blue Underground, 2003).
66. The name of Eaton's character is somewhat confounding. She is called both Sumuru and Sumitra throughout the film.
67. David Gregory, "Rolling in Rio: Interviews with Jess Franco, Harry Alan Towers and Shirley Eaton," *The Girl from Rio* DVD (Blue Underground, 2004). Whether Franco really believed that he was putting one over on the audience is open to debate. The body double looks nothing like Eaton and the lesbian scene seems more like an afterthought that adds nothing to the film.
68. Harry Alan Towers wrote film scripts under the *nom de plume* of Peter Welbeck.
69. Gregory, "Rolling in Rio."
70. Ann Morey, "The Judge Called Me an Accessory," *Journal of Popular Television and Film*, Summer 1995.
71. Tohill and Tombs, 115.
72. *99 Women* (*99 Mujeres*), prod. Harry Alan Towers, dir. Jesus Franco, Spain/U.S., 1968.
73. David Gregory, "Jess' Women: Interview with Jess Franco," *99 Women* Unrated Director's Cut DVD (Blue Underground, 2004).
74. Gregory, "Jess' Women."
75. *Castle* was the least acclaimed entry in the Fu Manchu series. A strangely watered-down plot that took away any of the previous films' exploitation factor, as well as a patchwork of scenes from different films, effectively killed the franchise.
76. David Gregory, "The Perils and Pleasures of Justine: An Interview with Jess Franco and Harry Alan Towers," *Marquis de Sade's Justine* DVD (Blue Underground, 2004).
77. *Justine*, prod. Harry Alan Towers, dir. Jesus Franco, Spain/U.S., 1969.
78. Gregory, "The Perils and Pleasures of Justine."
79. Gregory, "The Perils and Pleasures of Justine."
80. Matthew Coniam, "The Trouble with De Sade," in *Necronomicon, Book 4: The Journal of Horror and Erotic Cinema*, ed. Andy Black (Hereford, UK: Noir Publishing, 2001), 123.
81. *Venus in Furs*, prod. Harry Alan Towers, dir. Jesus Franco, Spain/U.S., 1969.
82. David Gregory, "Jesus in Furs: Interview with Jess Franco," *Venus in Furs* DVD (Blue Underground, 2005).
83. McNair had some minor chart success in the mid-'60s with such songs as "Honeymoonin'" (1962) and "You're Going to Love My Baby" (1965). She was one of the first African-American artists to have her own television series (1969) and appeared on such shows as *Hullabaloo* and *Toast of the Town*. She can also be heard singing the theme song to Franco's *99 Women* (1968).
84. Marie Liljedahl was no stranger to adult-themed movies, having starred in Joe Sarno's Swedish classic soft-porn *Jag en Oskuld* (*Inga*, 1967) and its sequel *Någon att älska* (*The Seduction of Inga*, 1970).
85. *Eugenie, the Story of Her Journey Into Perversion* (*Philosophie du boudoir*), prod. Harry Alan Towers, dir. Jesus Franco, Spain/U.S., 1969.
86. Tim Lucas, *Eugenie, the Story of Her Journey Into Perversion* DVD liner notes (Blue Underground, 2002).
87. David Gregory and Bill Lustig, "Perversion Stories: Interview with Jess Franco, Marie Liljedahl and Christopher Lee," *Eugenie, the Story of Her Journey Into Perversion* DVD (Blue Underground, 2002).
88. Gregory and Lustig, "Perversion Stories." Producer Towers concurred in a later interview that they probably did deceive Lee in order to secure his accepting the role.
89. *Count Dracula* (*El conde Drácula*), prod. Harry Alan Towers, dir. Jesus Franco, Spain/Germany/France, 1970.
90. Alain Petit, *Jess Franco's Eugenie de Sade* DVD liner notes (Wild East Productions, 2001).
91. *Nightmares Come at Night* (*Les Cauchemars naissent la nuit*), prod. Karl Heinz Mannchen, dir. Jesus Franco, Spain/France/Germany, 1970.

92. Lucas Balbo, *Nightmares Come at Night* DVD liner notes (Shriek Show/Media Blasters, 2004).
93. Tim Lucas, *The Bloody Judge* DVD liner notes (Blue Underground, 2003).
94. *The Bloody Judge*, prod. Harry Alan Towers, dir. Jess Franco, Spain/Germany/France/Italy/U.S./Britain, 1970.
95. David Gregory and Bill Lustig, "Bloody Jess: Interview with Jess Franco," *The Bloody Judge* DVD (Blue Underground, 2003).
96. Briggs. 9.
97. Tim Lucas, *Vampyros lesbos* DVD liner notes (Synapse Films, 1999).
98. Lucas, *Vampyros lesbos*.
99. Reuban Arvizu, interview with Jess Franco, *Nightmares Come at Night* DVD (Shriek Show/Media Blasters, 2004). One thing that Miranda did request was that her original name not be used in those versions that would show nudity. She and Franco settled on the name Susan Korda as a moniker for the more adult versions of their films.
100. Petit, 1.
101. *Eugenie de Sade*, prod. Karl Heinz Mannchen, dir. Jesus Franco, Spain/Germany/France, 1970.
102. *Vampyros lesbos*, prod. Artur Bauner, dir. Jesus Franco, Spain/Germany, 1970.
103. Lucas, *Vampyros lesbos*, 3.
104. *She Killed in Ecstasy* (*Sie tötete in Ekstase*), prod. Karl Heinz-Mannchen, dir. Jesus Franco, Spain/Germany, 1970.
105. *Devil Came from Akasava* (*Der Teufel kam aus Akasava*), prod. Karl Heinz-Mannchen, dir. Jesus Franco, Spain/Germany, 1970.
106. Arvizu.
107. Though many sources state that Franco did indeed produce the film himself, some French money was also used, explaining why the film was shot in French.
108. *A Virgin Among the Living Dead* (*Une Vierge chez les morts vivants*), prod. Robert de Nesle, dir. Jesus Franco, Spain/France/Germany, 1971.
109. Tim Lucas, *A Virgin Among the Living Dead* DVD liner notes (Image Entertainment, 2002).
110. Things aren't helped by the fact that Franco recycles much of the music from previous films. *Drácula contra Frankenstein* (1971), for example, uses the same score as *Justine* (1969) and *El conde Drácula* (1970).
111. Aguilar, 155.
112. *Dracula, Prisoner of Frankenstein* (*Drácula contra Frankenstein*), prod. Arturio Marcos, dir. Jesus Franco, Spain/Germany, 1972.
113. *Rites of Frankenstein* (*La maldición de Frankestein*), prod. Robert de Nesle, dir. Jesus Franco, Spain/France, 1972. This depends on what version you see. The 2006 Image Entertainment DVD titled *The Rites of Frankenstein* omits all the sexuality of the film, leaving only the violence and the plot. Fortunately, the erotic scenes are included as a supplement.
114. David Flint, *Babylon Blue: An Illustrated History of Adult Cinema* (London: Creation Books, 1998), 18.
115. Tohill and Tombs, 113.
116. *Female Vampire* (*La Comtesse noire*), prod. and dir. Jesus Franco, France/Belgium, 1973.
117. Harvey Fenton and Bill Lustig, "A Conversation with Jess Franco," in *Flesh and Blood: A Compendium* (London: Fab Press, 1996). Franco believed the difference between the two genres is camera point of view. In an "erotic" film the camera shoots from above; a "porno" film is shot in close-up.
118. Another one of the many names for *Les Avaleuses* (1973).
119. Fenton and Lustig, 240.
120. Lina Romay, interview, August 13, 2009 (http://dimensionfantastica.blogspot.com/2009/08/entrevista-exclusiva-lina-romay.html).
121. Tohill and Tombs. 113.
122. Aguilar, 159.
123. Gary Hertz, "An Interview with Paul Naschy," *Werewolf Shadow* DVD (Blue Underground, in association with Anchor Bay Entertainment, 2002).
124. Paul Naschy, *Memoirs of a Wolfman*, trans. Mike Hodges (Baltimore: Luminary Press, 2000), 229.
125. Todd Tjiersland, "Cinema of the Doomed: The Tragic Horror of Paul Naschy," in *Fear Without Frontiers* (London: Fab Press, 2003), 69.
126. Naschy, 16.
127. Naschy, 17–19.
128. Naschy, 78.
129. Hertz.
130. Naschy would continue his love affair with weight lifting throughout the '60s, retiring from the sport in 1971.
131. John Sirabella, "Interview with a Werewolf," *Frankenstein's Bloody Terror* DVD (Media Blasters/Shriek Show, 2005).
132. Sirabella, "Interview with a Werewolf."
133. Naschy, 92.
134. *Frankenstein's Bloody Terror* (*La marca del Hombre-lobo*), prod. Maximilliano Pérez-Flores, dir. Enrique López Eguiluz, Spain, 1968.
135. Tjiersland, 70.
136. *Assignment Terror* (*Los monstruos del terror*), prod. Jamie Prades, Dir. Hugo Fregonese, Spain/Germany/Italy, 1969.
137. Tjiersland, 71.
138. As with most exploitation films, different titles were used in different countries. *La noche de Walpurgis* was also known as *The Werewolf vs. the Vampire Woman*, *Night of the Walpurgis* and *Blood Moon*.
139. *Werewolf Shadow* liner notes (Anchor Bay Entertainment, 2002).
140. Hertz.
141. *Werewolf Shadow* (*La noche de Walpurgis*), prod. Salvadore Romero, dir. León Klimovsky, Spain, 1969.
142. Naschy, 103.
143. *Dracula's Great Love* (*El gran amor del conde Drácula*), prod. and dir. Javier Aguirre, Spain/Italy, 1972.
144. Burrell and Brown, 12.
145. *Hunchback of the Morgue* (*El jorobado de la Morgue*), prod. Carmelo Bernaola, dir. Javier Aguirre, Spain, 1973.
146. Naschy, 114.
147. Mirek Lipinksi, *Horror Rises from the Tomb* DVD liner notes (Mondo Crash Entertainment, 2004). The American DVD contains all the differing clothed and unclothed releases.
148. *Horror Rises from the Tomb* (*El espanto surge de la tumba*), prod. Modesto Pérez Redondo, dir. Carlos Aured, Spain, 1972.
149. *Vengence of the Mummy* (*La venganza de la momia*), prod. and dir. Carlos Aured, Spain, 1973.
150. Naschy, 229.
151. Slater, 26.
152. "Spain," *Encyclopaedia Britannica* Online.
153. Kose Zapata, *Amando de Ossorio: The Last Templar*, DVD documentary, The Blind Dead Collection (Blue Underground, 2005).

154. *Fangs of the Living Dead* (*Malenka*), prod. and dir. Amando de Ossorio, Spain/Italy, 1968.
155. Zapata, *Amando de Ossorio: The Last Templer*.
156. *Tombs of the Blind Dead* (*La noche del terror ciego*), prod. José Antonio and Perez Giner, dir. Amando De Ossorio, Spain/Portugal, 1971.
157. Zapata.
158. Zapata.
159. Andrew Wills, "The Spanish Horror Film as Subversive Text," in *Horror International* (Detroit: Wayne State University Press, 2005), 166.
160. *Who Could Kill a Child?* (*¿Quién puede matar a un niño?*), prod. Manuel Salvador, dir. Narciso Ibáñez Serrador, Spain, 1975.
161. Nigel J. Burrell and Paul J. Brown, *Hispanic Horrors* (Huntington, UK: Midnight Press, 2005), 42.
162. *Satan's Blood* (*Escalofrio*), prod. Juan Piquer Simón, dir. Carlos Puerto, Spain, 1977.
163. *Cannibal Man* (*La semana del asesino*), prod. Jose Truchado, dir. Eloy de la Iglesia, Spain, 1971.
164. *Blood Spattered Bride* (*La novia ensangrentada*), prod. and dir. Vicente Aranda, Spain/Italy, 1972.
165. *A Bell from Hell* (*La campana del infierno*), prod. and dir. Claudio Guerin Hill, Spain, 1973.
166. Tombs and Tohill, 66.
167. Mirek Lipinski, "Castilian Crimson: The Spanish Horror Film," Latarnia web site (www.latarnia.com/castiliancrimson.html).
168. *Let Sleeping Corpses Lie* (*Non si deve profanare il sonno dei morti*), prod. Manuel Pérez, dir. Jorge Grau, Spain/Italy, 1974.
169. Slater, "Hispanic Horrors," 27.
170. *Vampyres*, prod. Brian Smedley-Aston, dir. José Ramón Larraz, Spain/Britain, 1974.
171. *Vampyres* DVD liner notes (Blue Underground Entertainment, 2003).
172. Slater, "Hispanic Horrors," 26.
173. Lipinski, "Castilian Crimson."
174. Tombs and Tohill, 67.
175. Pete Tombs, "About the Film: DVD Notes," *Satan's Blood* DVD (Mondo Macabro, 2006).

Chapter 3

1. Jones, *Rough Guide*, 226.
2. Peter Graham, "New Directions in French Cinema," in *The Oxford History of World Cinema* (London: Oxford University Press, 1997), 576.
3. Ginette Vincendeau, "The Popular Art of French Cinema," in *The Oxford History of World Cinema*, 352.
4. Vincendeau, 345, 347.
5. Tyler Cowen, "French Kiss Off: How Protectionism Hurt French Films," *Reason* Online, July 1998 (www.reason.com/news/show/30691.html). Accessed Jan. 3, 2007).
6. Vincendeau, 349.
7. Vincendeau, 350.
8. Graham, 576–577.
9. "Interview with Georges Franju, Le Fantastique ep. Ciné-parade," *Eyes Without a Face* DVD (Criterion Collection, 2004).
10. Terry Windling, "Les Contes de fées: The Literary Fairy Tales of France," Realms of Fantasy web site, 2002 (www.endicott-studio.com/rdrm/forconte.html. Accessed Jan 13, 2007).
11. Agnes Peirron, "House of Horrors," *Grand Street*, Summer 1996 (www.grandguignol.com/history.htm Accessed Jan 14, 2007).
12. David Kalat, "French Revolution," 265. The film was a series of shorts that the Lumière brothers created utilizing the new medium.
13. Kalat, 267.
14. Kalat, 269.
15. *The Devil's Hand* (*La Main du diable*), prod. and dir. Maurice Tourneur, France, 1942.
16. Kalat, 268.
17. *Diabolique* (*Les Diaboliques*), prod. and dir. Henri-Georges Clouzot, France, 1955.
18. "France," *Encyclopaedia Britannica* Online.
19. *Le Sang des bêtes*, prod. and dir. Georges Franju, France, 1948.
20. "Georges Franju," *All Movie Guide*, 2007 (http://movies2.nytimes.com/gst/movies/filmography.html?p_id=90345&mod=bio. Accessed. Jan 20. 2007).
21. "Interview with Georges Franju."
22. Horror film director John Carpenter has stated that his inspiration for the mask of Michael Myers in *Halloween* (1978) was Franju's film. It is easy to see the similarities, as both masks are haunting, white, devoid of any emotion and utterly terrifying in their execution.
23. David Kalat, "The Unreal Reality," DVD liner notes, *Les Yeux sans visage* (Criterion Collection, 2004).
24. Kalat, 1.
25. *Blood and Roses* (*Et mourir de plaisir*), prod. Raymond Eger, dir. Roger Vadim, France, 1962.
26. Vadim would return to erotic horror in 1967 when he directed one of the stories in *Histoires Extraordinaires* (*Spirits of the Dead*). In Vadim's episode, *Metzengerstein*, based on the Edgar Allan Poe story, he cast his then-wife Jane Fonda as a countess in lust with her cousin, played by real-life brother Peter Fonda.
27. Peter Blumentstock, "An Interview with Jean Rollin," Shocking Images web site, May 1995 (www.shockingimages.com/rollin/interview.htm. December 2006.)
28. Blumenstock.
29. Andy Black, "Clocks, Seagulls, Romeo and Juliet," *Kinoeye* 2, no. 7 (www.kinoeye.org/02/07/black07.php. Accessed on April 2, 2006).
30. Black.
31. Tohill and Tombs, 138.
32. Tohill and Tombs, 140–141.
33. Marc Morris, *The Rape of the Vampire* DVD liner notes (Redemption Video, Image Entertainment, 2002).
34. Blumenstock.
35. Blumenstock.
36. *The Rape of the Vampire* (*Le Viol du vampire*), prod. Sam Selsky, dir. Jean Rollin, France, 1968.
37. "France," *Encyclopaedia Britannica* Online.
38. Tohill and Tombs, 14.
39. Black, 3.
40. Blumenstock.
41. Chris Alexander, "Sinema of Flesh and Blood," *Rue Morgue*, April 2006, 17.
42. Colin Odell and Michelle Le Blanc, "Jean Rollin: Le Sang d'un Poète du Cinéma," in *Alternative Europe: Eurotrash and Exploitation Cinema Since 1945*, ed. Ernest Mathijs and Xavier Mendik (London: Wallflower Press, 2004), 151–159.
43. Black, 4.
44. Black, 4.
45. *The Shiver of the Vampires* (*Le Frisson des vampires*), prod. and dir. Jean Rollin, France, 1970.
46. Tohill and Tombs, 145. The film's heroine, the virginal bride, was played by Sandra Julien, who had starred in 2 of Max Pécas's most famous Euro soft-porn films, *Je suis une nymphomane* (*I Am a Nymphomaniac*,

1970) and *Je suis frigide ... pourquoi? (I Am Frigid, Why?,* 1972).
47. Black, 5.
48. Alexander, 17–18.
49. Tohill and Tombs, 149.
50. Tohill and Tombs, 148.
51. Blumenstock.
52. *Bacchanales sexuelles (Tout le monde il en a deux),* prod. Lionel Wallmann, dir. Jean Rollin, France, 1973.
53. Blumenstock.
54. *The Demoniacs (Les Démoniaques),* prod. Lionel Wallmann, dir. Jean Rollin, France, 1974.
55. Blumenstock.
56. Tombs and Tohill, 152.
57. Alexander, 18.
58. Tombs and Tohill, 155.
59. Blumenstock.
60. *Lips of Blood (Lèvres de sang),* prod. Jean-Marie Ghanassia, dir. Jean Rollin, France, 1975.
61. Doug Sparks, "The Romance of Childhood," *Kinoeye* 2, no. 7 (www.kinoeye.org/02/07/sparks07.php. Accessed on Jan 15, 2007).
62. Nigel J. Burrell, *The Grapes of Death* DVD liner notes (Synapse Entertainment, 2001).
63. *Grapes of Death (Les Raisins de le mort),* prod. Claude Guedi, dir. Jean Rollin, France, 1978.
64. Black, 58.
65. *Fascination,* prod. Joe De Lara, dir. Jean Rollin, France, 1979.
66. Blumenstock.
67. Kalat, 278.
68. Andy Starke and Pete Tombs, "Formidable: The Michel Lemoine Story," *Seven Women for Satan* DVD (Mondo Macabro, 2003).
69. *Girl Slaves of Morgana Le Fay (Morgan et ses nymphes),* prod. and dir. Bruno Gantillon, France, 1971.
70. Pete Tombs, "About the Movie: DVD Notes," *Girl Slaves of Morgana Le Fay* DVD (Mondo Macabro, 2005).
71. Pete Tombs, interview with Bruno Gantillon, *Girl Slaves of Morgana Le Fay* DVD (Mondo Macabro, 2005).
72. The film was able to find foreign distribution, being shown in both Spain and Britain in its severely edited forms.
73. *Erotic Witchcraft (La Goulve),* prod. Bepi Fontana, dir. Mario Mercier, France, 1972.
74. *A Woman Possessed (La Papesse),* prod. Robert Pallardon, dir. Mario Mercier, French, 1975.
75. Frédérick Durand, "Sorcellerie *La Goulve,*" http://frederickdurand.blogspot.com/2007/06/aujourdhui-je-vous-parle-de-la-goulve.html
76. Tohill and Tombs, 61. Mercier became even more notorious with his books. Both *Le Journal de Jeanne (Jeanne's Journal,* 1998) and *Le Nécrophile* caught the ire of French censors, with *Le Nécrophile* being banned outright.
77. *Don't Deliver Us from Evil (Mais ne nous délivrez pas du mal),* prod. Bernard Legargeant, dir. Joël Séria, France, 1972.
78. Pete Tombs, interview with Joel Séria, *Don't Deliver Us from Evil* DVD (Mondo Macabro, 2006).
79. Tombs, interview with Joel Séria.

80. Michel Lemoine, Interview. *Seven Women for Satan* DVD (Mondo Macabro. 2007).
81. Briggs, 271.
82. It must be seriously noted that many feminist and film theorists (Linda Williams, etc.) believe these films to be just as exploitative as the other films in this study. Though I believe that there is much relevance in that statement, the focus of this work is on a more violent sexual exploitation. Many a dissertation could be and has been written about the exploitative tendencies of porn films.
83. Garrett Chaffin-Quiray, "Emmanuelle Enterprises," in *Alternative Europe: Eurotrash and Exploitation Cinema Since 1945,* ed. Ernest Mathijs and Xavier Mendik (London: Wallflower Press, 2004), 136.
84. Jan Wellmann, *The Dark Side of Porn—Hunting Emmanuelle* (Firecracker Films, Channel 4, London, 2006).
85. Wellmann.
86. Wellmann.
87. *Emanuelle,* prod. Yves Rousset-Rouard, dir. Just Jaeckin, France, 1974.
88. Wellmann.
89. Wellmann.
90. The most successful of these were the Black Emanuelle films from Italy, discussed in depth in chapter 2.
91. This would end up being Giacobetti's one and only film.
92. *Emmanuelle: L'antivierge,* prod. Yves Rousset-Rouard, dir. Francis Giacobetti, France, 1975.
93. David Gregory, "The Joys of *Emanuelle pt. 2,*" The Emanuelle Collection (Anchor Bay Entertainment, 2003).
94. Tohill and Tombs, 55.
95. *The Story of O (Histoire d'O),* prod. Roger Fleytoux, dir. Just Jaeckin, France, 1975.
96. Just Jaeckin, director's commentary, *The Story of O* DVD (Somerville House Releasing, 2000).
97. Radley Metzger was the premiere filmmaker for erotic films in the late '60s and '70s. *L'Image (The Image,* 1973) was his first foray into more hard-core material. Less misogynistic than *Histoire d'O,* the film is considered to be the classic S&M movie. In many instances the film was released in Europe after *Histoire,* causing some to think of it as rip-off.
98. Danny Peary, *Cult Movies* (New York: Delta Press, 1981), 80.

A Euro-Conclusion

1. It must be mentioned that some exploitation films from France eschewed this overarching identity, preferring to remain a decidedly French product. Soft-core erotic films like *Emmanuelle* (1974) were successful based on the assumption they were from France and not Europe as a whole. These were exceptions to the rule, though, as most French exploitation filmmakers were happy to settle for any identity to ensure success.
2. Corrigan, 98.

Bibliography

Africa addio DVD liner notes. Blue Underground, 2003.

Aguilar, Carlos. *Jess Franco, El Sexo del Horror*. Florence, Italy: Glittering Images, 1999.

Alexander, Chris. "Sinema of Flesh and Blood." *Rue Morgue*, April 2006.

———. "Spain's Sweet Sadist: Interview with Jess Franco." *Rue Morgue*, July 2005.

Argento, Dario. *Cat o' Nine Tails* 30-second ad. *Cat o' Nine Tails* DVD. Anchor Bay Entertainment, 2000.

Arvizu, Reuban. Interview with Jess Franco. *Nightmares Come at Night* DVD. Shriek Show/Media Blasters, 2004.

Balbo, Lucas. Liner notes. *Nightmares Come at Night* DVD. Shriek Show/Media Blasters, 2004.

Barker, Clive. *Clive Barker's A–Z of Horror*. New York: Harper Prism, 1996.

Barzini, Luigi. *The Italians*. New York: Touchstone Press, 1964.

Bertonlino, M., and E. Ridola. *Vizietti all'italiana: L'Epoca D'oro Della commedia Sexy*. Florence, Italy: 1999.

Black, Andy. "Clocks, Seagulls, Romeo and Juliet." *Kinoeye* 2, no. 7. www.kinoeye.org/ 02/07/black 07.php (February 2007).

Blumentstock, Peter. "An Interview with Jean Rollin." Shocking Images web site. May 1995. www.shockingimages.com/rollin/interview.htm (December 2006).

Bodrowski, Steve. *Suspiria: A Nostalgic Review*. Cinefantastique Online. http://cinefantastique online.com/2008/06/nostalgia-suspiria-1977.

Briggs, Joe Bob. *Profoundly Erotic: Sexy Movies That Changed History*. New York: Universal Publishing, 2005.

Brode, Douglas. *Sinema: Erotic Adventures in Film*. New York: Citadel Press, 2003.

Brottman, Mikita. "Eating Italian." In *The Bad Mirror*, edited by Jack Hunter. London: Creation Books, 2002.

Burrell, Nigel J. Liner notes. *The Grapes of Death* DVD. Synapse Entertainment, 2001.

———, and Paul J. Brown. *Hispanic Horrors*. Huntington, UK: Midnight Press, 2005.

Chaffin-Quirey, G. "Emmanuelle Enterprises." In *Alternative Europe: Eurotrash and Exploitation Cinema Since 1945*, edited by Ernest Mathijs and Xavier Mendik. London: Wallflower Press, 2004.

Cherry, Brigid. "The Universe of Madness and Death." *Kinoeye* 2, no. 7. www.kinoeye.org/02/07/cherry07.php (January 2006).

Coniam, Matthew. "The Trouble with De Sade." In *Necronomicon, Book 4: The Journal of Horror and Erotic Cinema*, edited by Andy Black. Hereford, UK: Noir Publishing, 2001.

Cook, Pam, and Mieke Bernink. *The Cinema Book*. 2nd ed. London: BFI Publishing, 1999.

Corliss, Richard. "Aristocrat of the Erotic." *Film Comment*, January 1973.

Cowen, Tyler. "French Kiss Off: How Protectionism Hurt French Films." *Reason* Online. July 1998. www.reason.com/news/show/30691.html (January 3, 2007).

Crawford, Travis. "The Butchering of *Cannibal Apocalypse*." Liner notes, *Cannibal Apocalypse* DVD. Image Entertainment.

Cultural studies website. Main page. www.jahso nic.com/Cultural_studies.html (October 2006).

Erickson, Glenn. "*The Horrible Dr. Hichcock*: Women on the Verge of a Gothic Breakdown." *Images Journal* web site. infocus/hichcock.htm, 2000 (November 2006).

"Exploitation Film." Dr. John Grohl's Psych Central web site. http://psychcentral.com/ wiki/Exploitation_film. April 12, 2005.

Fenton, Harvey, and Bill Lustig. "A Conversation with Jess Franco." In *Flesh and Blood: A Compendium*. London: Fab Press, 1996.

Fentone, Steve. *Antichristo: The Bible of Nasty Nun Sinema and Culture*. London: Fab Press, 2000.

Flint, David. *Babylon Blue: An Illustrated History of Adult Cinema*. London: Creation Books International, 1998.

———. *The Emmanuelle Phenomenon*. DVD supplement. *Emmanuelle in America*. Blue Underground, 2003.

"France." *Encyclopaedia Britannica* Online (May 2007).

Gallant, Chris, ed. *The Art of Darkness: The Cinema of Dario Argento*. London: Fab Press, 2000.

Gibron, Bill. *The Mondo Cane Film Collection* DVD Review. PopMatters web site. www.popmatters.com/film/reviews/m/mondo-cane-collection.shtml (October 28, 2003).

Goldfarb, Peter. *Mondo Cane* movie review. *Film Quarterly* 17, no. 1 (Autumn 1963): 46–47.

Gomarasca, Manilo, and Davide Pulici. Audio interview with Laura Gemser. *Nocturno Cinema*, 1996.

_____. "Joe D'Amato Completely Uncut." *Nocturno Cinema*, 1998.

Goodall, Mark. *Sweet and Savage; The World through the Shockumentary Film Lens*. London: Headpress, 2006.

Gregory, David. "The Case of the Red Lips: Interview with Jess Franco." *Two Undercover Angels* and *Kiss Me Monster* DVD. Blue Underground, 2006.

_____. "The Fall of Fu Manchu: Interview with Tsai Chin." *The Castle of Fu Manchu* DVD. Blue Underground, 2003.

_____. "From *Necronomicon* to *Succubus*: Interview with Jess Franco." *Succubus* DVD. Blue Underground, 2006.

_____. *The Godfathers of Mondo*. DVD documentary. Blue Underground, 2003.

_____. "Jess' Women: Interview with Jess Franco." *99 Women* Unrated Director's Cut DVD. Blue Underground, 2004.

_____. "Jesus in Furs: Interview with Jess Franco." *Venus in Furs* DVD. Blue Underground, 2005.

_____. "The Joys of *Emmanuelle pt. 2*." The Emmanuelle Collection. Anchor Bay Entertainment, 2003.

_____. "The Perils and Pleasures of *Justine*: An Interview with Jess Franco and Harry Alan Towers." *Marquis de Sade's Justine* DVD. Blue Underground, 2004.

_____. "Perversion Stories: Interview with Jess Franco, Marie Liljedahl and Christopher Lee." *Eugénie, the Story of Her Journey Into Perversion* DVD. Blue Underground, 2002.

_____. "Rolling in Rio: Interviews with Jess Franco, Harry Alan Towers and Shirley Eaton." *The Girl from Rio* DVD. Blue Underground, 2004.

_____. *Tales from a Contaminated City*. DVD interview with Umberto Lenzi. Anchor Bay Entertainment, 2002.

_____, and Bill Lustig. "Bloody Jess: Interview with Jess Franco." *The Bloody Judge* DVD. Blue Underground, 2003.

Hardy, Phil. *The Overlook Film Encyclopedia: Horror*. Woodstock, NY: Overlook Press, 1995.

Hawkins, Joan. "Sleaze Mania, Euro-Trash and High Art: The Place of European Art Films in American Low Culture." *Film Quarterly* 53, no. 2 (Winter 1999–2000): 14–29.

Henderson, Cynthia. *I Was a Cold War Monster: Horror Films, Eroticism and the Cold War Imagination*. Bowling Green, OH: Popular Press, 2001.

Hertz, Gary. "An Interview with Paul Naschy." *Werewolf Shadow* DVD. Blue Underground, in association with Anchor Bay Entertainment.

Howarth, Troy. *The Haunted World of Mario Bava*. London: Fab Press, 2002.

_____. DVD review of *The Antichrist*. DVD Maniacs web site. www.dvdmaniacs.net/Reviews/A-D/anti_christ.html (December 2002).

Hunt, Leon. "A (Sadistic) Night at the *Opera*: Notes on the Italian Horror Film." In *The Horror Reader*, edited by Ken Gelder. London: Routledge, 2000.

Hutchings, Peter. *The Horror Show*. Harlow, UK: Pearson Longman, 2004.

"Interview with Georges Franju: Le Fantastique ep. Ciné-parade." *Eyes Without a Face* DVD. Criterion Collection, 2004.

"Italy." *Encyclopaedia Britannica* Online (May 2007).

Jaeckin, Just. Director's commentary. *The Story of O* DVD. Somerville House Releasing, 2000.

Jane, Thomas. *The Mondo Cane Film Collection* DVD review. DVD Maniacs web site. www.dvdmaniacs.net/Reviews/M-P/mondo_cane.html (November 2006).

Jewell, Keala. *Monsters in the Italian Literary Imagination*. Detroit: Wayne State Press, 2001.

Johnson, Gary. *Black Sunday* DVD review. *Images Journal* web site. www.imagesjournal.com/issue10/reviews/mariobava/blacksunday.htm (October 2006).

_____. "The Golden Age of Italian Horror 1957–1979." *Images Journal* web site. www.imagesjournal.com/issue05/infocus/intr02.htm (March 13, 2006).

Jones, Alan. *Profondo Argento*. London: Fab Press, 2004.

_____. *The Rough Guide to Horror Movies*. New York: Rough Guides, 2005.

Kael, Pauline. "Circles and Squares." *Film Quarterly* 16, no. 3 (Spring 1963): 12–26.

Kalat, David. "French Revolution: The Secret History of Gallic Horror Movies." In *Fear Without Frontiers: Horror Cinema Across the Globe*, edited by Steven Jay Schneider. London: Fab Press, 2003.

_____. "Horror and Eroticism in French Horror Cinema." *Kinoeye* 2, no. 7. www.kinoeye/02/07/kalat07.php (February 2007).

_____. "The Unreal Reality." DVD liner notes for *Les Yeux sans visage*. Criterion Collection, 2004.

Kellner, Douglas. "Cultural Studies: Multiculturalism and Media Culture." In *Gender, Race and

Class in Media. 2nd ed. Edited by Gail Dines and Jean Humez. Thousand Oaks, CA: Sage Publications, 2003.

Koven, Mikel J. *La Dolce Morte: Vernacular Cinema and the Italian Giallo Film*. Lantham, MD: Scarecrow Press, 2006.

_____. "The Film You Are About to See Is Based on Fact: Italian Nazi Sexploitation Cinema." In *Alternative Europe: Eurotrash and Exploitation Cinema Since 1945*, edited by Ernest Mathijs and Xavier Mendik. London: Wallflower Press, 2004.

Landis, Bill. Liner notes. *Make Them Die Slowly* DVD. Grindhouse Releasing, 2000.

_____, and Mike Clifford. *Sleazoid Express*. New York: Fireside Publishing, 2002.

Leach, Windslow. "Spaghetti Slashers: Italian Giallo Cinema." http://members.aol.com/ grindhouse site/giallo.html (April 2006).

Lipinski, Mirek. "Castilian Crimson: The Spanish Horror Film." Latarnia web site. www.latarnia.com/castiliancrimson.html (December 2006)

_____. Liner notes. *Horror Rises from the Tomb* DVD. Mondo Crash Entertainment, 2004.

Lucas, Tim. Liner notes. *The Awful Dr. Orloff* (*Gritos en la noche*) DVD. Image Entertainment, 2000.

_____. Liner notes. *Black Sabbath* DVD. Image Entertainment, 2000.

_____. Liner notes. *Black Sunday* DVD. Image Entertainment, 1999.

_____. Liner notes. *The Bloody Judge* DVD. Blue Underground, 2003.

_____. Liner notes. *Cannibal Holocaust 25th Anniversary Collector's Edition* DVD. Grindhouse Releasing, 2005.

_____. Liner notes. *Castle of Blood* DVD. Synapse Films, 2002.

_____. Liner notes. *Eugénie, The Story of Her Journey into Perversion* DVD. Blue Underground, 2002.

_____. Liner notes. *The Girl Who Knew Too Much* DVD. Image Entertainment, 2000.

_____. Liner notes. *I vampiri* DVD. Image Entertainment, 2003.

_____. Liner notes. *Lisa and the Devil/House of Exorcism* DVD. Image Entertainment, 2000.

_____. Liner notes. *The Sadistic Baron Von Klaus* DVD. Image Entertainment, 2001.

_____. Liner notes. *Vampyros lesbos* DVD. Synapse Films, 1999.

_____. Liner notes. *A Virgin Among the Living Dead* DVD. Image Entertainment, 2002.

_____. *Mario Bava: All the Colors of the Dark*. Cincinnati, OH: Video Watchdog, 2007.

Mangravite, Andrew. "Once Upon a Time in a Crypt." *Film Comment*, January 1993.

Marriott, James. *Horror Films*. London: Virgin Press, 2004.

Martin, Perry. *The Dead Will Walk*. DVD documentary. *Dawn of the Dead Ultimate Edition*. Anchor Bay Entertainment, 2004.

Mast, Gerald. *A Short History of the Movies*. Indianapolis: Bobs-Merrill Press, 1981.

McCallum, Lawrence. *Italian Horror Films of the 1960s*. Jefferson, NC: McFarland, 1998.

McDonagh, Maitland. *Broken Mirrors/Broken Minds: The Dark Dreams of Dario Argento*. Minneapolis: University of Minnesota Press, 1994.

McGee, C., A. Martray, J. Norrs, and S. Unsinn. "Goth in Film." Ithaca College Senior Seminar web site. www.ithaca.edu/keg/seminar/gothfilm.htm (March 2006).

McGillivray, David. "Harry Alan Towers." *Film and Filming* no. 400, January 1988.

McKeon, Elizabeth, and Linda Everett. *Cinema Under the Stars: America's Love Affair with the Drive-In Movie Theater*. Nashville: Cumberland House, 1998.

Mendik, Xavier. "Black Sex, Bad Sex: Monstrous Ethnicity in the Black Emanuelle Films." In *Alternative Europe: Eurotrash and Exploitation Cinema Since 1945*, edited by Ernest Mathijs and Xavier Mendik. London: Wallflower Press, 2004.

_____, and Ernest Mathijs. *The Cult Film Reader*. Berkshire, UK: McGraw-Hill, 2008.

_____, and Graeme Harper. *Unruly Pleasures: The Cult Film and Its Critics*. London: Fab Press, 2000.

Morey, Ann. "The Judge Called Me an Accessory." *Journal of Popular Television and Film*, Summer 1995.

Morris, Marc. Liner notes. *The Rape of the Vampire* DVD. Redemption Video, Image Entertainment, 2002.

Mulvey, Laura. "Visual Pleasure and Narrative Cinema." In *Visual and Other Pleasures*. London: Macmillan Publishing, 1975.

Nakahara, Tamao. "Barred Nuns: Italian Nunsploitation Films." In *Alternative Europe: Eurotrash and Exploitation Cinema Since 1945*, edited by Ernest Mathijs and Xavier Mendik. London: Wallflower Press, 2004.

Naschy, Paul. *Memoirs of a Wolfman*. Translated by Mike Hodges. Baltimore, MD: Luminary Press, 2000.

Needham, Gary. "Playing with Genre: An Introduction to the Italian Giallo." *Kinoeye* 2, no. 11 (June 10, 2002).

_____. "Playing with Genre: Defining the Italian Giallo." In *Fear Without Frontiers: Horror Cinema Across the Globe*, edited by Steven Jay Schneider. London: Fab Press, 2003.

Nelhause, Peter. "Saturday Night with Jesus (Franco)." www.coffeecoffeeandmorecoffee.com/archives/2005/09/saturday_night.html (October 2006).

Newman, James. *Lips of Blood* DVD review. *Images Journal* web site. www.imagesjournal.com/search.htm (January 2007).

Nowell-Smith, Geoffrey. *The Oxford History of World Cinema*. New York: Oxford Press, 1996.

Odell, Colin, and Michelle Le Blanc. "Jean Rollin: Le Sang d'un Poète du Cinéma." In *Alternative Europe: Eurotrash and Exploitation Cinema Since 1945*, edited by Ernest Mathijs and Xavier Mendik. London: Wallflower Press, 2004.

Olney, Alexander Ian. "Playing Dead: Spectatorship, Performance and Euro-horror Cinema." Ph.D. diss., University of Nebraska, 2003.

Palmerini, Luca, and Gaetano Mistretta. *Spaghetti Nightmares*. Key West, FL: Fantasma Books, 1996.

Paul, Louis. *Italian Horror Film Directors*. Jefferson, NC: McFarland, 1995.

Peary, Danny. *Cult Movies*. New York: Delta Press, 1981.

Peirron, Agnes. "House of Horrors." *Grand Street*, Summer 1996. www.grandguignol.com/history.htm (January 2007)

Petit, Alain. Liner notes. *Jess Franco's Eugénie de Sade* DVD. Wild East Productions, 2001.

Russell, Jamie. *Book of the Dead: The Complete History of Zombie Cinema*. London: Fab Press, 2005.

Schaefer, Eric. *Bold! Daring! Shocking! True! A History of Exploitation Films, 1919–1959*. Durham, NC: Duke University Press, 1999.

Schneider, Steven Jay. *100 European Horror Films*. London: British Film Institute, 2007.

_____, and Tony Williams. "Introduction." *Horror International*. Detroit: Wayne State University Press, 2005.

Sherman, Sam. Interview with Sidney Pink. *Pyro* DVD. Troma Team Video.

Simonelli, Giovanni. Interview. *Seven Deaths in a Cat's Eye* DVD. Blue Underground, 2005.

Sirabella, John. "Building a Better Zombi." *Zombi 25th Anniversary Edition*. Media Blasters, 2005.

_____. "Interview with a Werewolf." *Frankenstein's Bloody Terror* DVD. Media Blasters/Shriek Show, 2005.

_____. Interview with Luigi Montefiore. *Anthropophagus* DVD. Shriek Show, 2006.

_____. Interview with Roy Foukes. *Zombie Holocaust* DVD. Shriek Show, 2002.

_____. Interview with Sergio Martino. *All the Colors of the Dark* DVD. Shriek Show, 2004.

_____. Interview with Umberto Lenzi. *Eaten Alive* DVD. Shriek Show, 2002.

_____. Interview with Umberto Lenzi. *Jungle Holocaust* DVD. Shriek Show, 2001.

_____. Liner notes. *Zombi 2* DVD. Shriek Show, 2005.

_____. *Shedding the Skin*. DVD documentary. *Lizard in a Woman's Skin* DVD. Shriek Show, 2004.

Slater, Jay. *Eaten Alive! Italian Cannibal and Zombie Movies*. London: Plexus Books, 2002.

_____. "The Forbidden Era." *Rue Morgue* 47, July 2005.

_____. "Hispanic Horror: A Brief History." *Rue Morgue* 47, July 2005.

Smith, Adrian Luther. *Blood and Black Lace: The Definitive Guide to Italian Sex and Horror Movies*. Liskeard, UK: Stray Cat Publishing, 1999.

Smith, Richard Harlan. Liner notes. *Your Vice Is a Locked Room and Only I Have the Key* DVD. NoShame Films, 2005.

Southworth, Wayne. *Emanuelle in Bangkok* film review. The Spinning Image web site. www.thespinningimage.co.uk/cultfilms/displaycultfilm.asp?reviewid=889 (April, 2006).

"Spain." *Encyclopaedia Britannica* Online (May 2007).

Sparks, Doug. "The Romance of Childhood." *Kinoeye* 2, no. 7. www.kinoeye.org/02/07/sparks07.php (January 2007).

Sparks, Glenn G., and Cheri Sparks. "Violence, Mayhem and Horror." In *Media Entertainment: The Psychology of Its Appeal*, edited by Dolf Zillman and Peter Vorderer. Mahwah, NJ: Lawrence Erlbaum, 2000.

Stanley, John. *Creature Features: The Science Fiction, Fantasy, Horror Movie Guide*. New York: Boulevard Press, 1997.

Starke, Andy, and Pete Tombs. *The Diabolical Mr. Franco*. DVD documentary. Mondo Macabro, 2001.

_____. "Formidable: The Michel Lemoine Story." *Seven Women for Satan* DVD. Mondo Macabro, 2003.

Stevenson, Jack. *Fleshpot: Cinema's Sexual Myth Makers and Taboo Breakers*. Manchester, UK: Critical Mission, 2002.

Thompson, Nathaniel. *The Strange Vice of Mrs. Wardh* DVD review. DVD Maniacs web site. www.mondo-digital.com/torso.html (April 2006).

Thrower, Steven. *Beyond Terror: The Films of Lucio Fulci*. London: Fab Press, 2002.

_____. *Eyeball: Compendium 1989–2003*. London: Fab Press, 2003.

Tjiersland, Todd. "Cinema of the Doomed: The Tragic Horror of Paul Naschy." In *Fear Without Frontiers Horror: Cinema Across the Globe*, edited by Steven Jay Schneider. London: Fab Press, 2003.

Tohill, Cathal, and Pete Tombs. *Immoral Tales: European Sex and Horror Movies 1956–1984*. London: Primitive Press, 1995.

Tombs, Pete. "About the Film: DVD Notes." *Satan's Blood* DVD. Mondo Macabro, 2006.

_____. "About the Movie: DVD Notes." *Girl Slaves of Morgana Le Fay*. Mondo Macabro, 2005.

_____. Interview with Bruno Gantillon. *Girl Slaves of Morgana Le Fay* DVD. Mondo Macabro, 2005.

_____. Interview with Joel Séria. *Don't Deliver Us from Evil* DVD. Mondo Macabro, 2006.

_____. Liner notes. *Mill of the Stone Women* DVD. Mondo Macabro, 2004.

_____. "A Note About *French Sex Murders*." DVD supplement. *French Sex Murders* DVD. Mondo Macabro, 2005.

La Torre de los siete jorobados movie review. *New York Times*. movies2.nytimes.com/ gst/movies/movie.html?v_id=137552 (September 2006).

Vitacane, Gino. "Legacy of the Cannibal God: DVD interview with Sergio Martino." *Mountain of the Cannibal God* DVD. Anchor Bay Entertainment, 2001.

Wellmann, Jan. *Finding Emmanuelle: The Dark Side of Porn*. Firecracker Films, Channel 4, 2006.

White, David. "History of the Italian Horror Film, pt. 1." Horror-Wood web site. www.horror-wood.com/italianhorror1.htm (March 2006).

White, Dennis. "The Poetics of Horror: More than Meets the Eye." *Cinema Journal* 10, no. 2, Spring 1971.

Williams, Linda. *Hard Core: Power, Pleasure and the "Frenzy of the Visible."* Los Angeles: University of California Press, 1989.

Wills, Andrew. "The Spanish Horror Film as Subversive Text." In *Horror International*, edited by Steven Jay Schneider and Tony Williams. Detroit: Wayne State University Press, 2005.

Windling, Terry. "Les Contes de fées: The Literary Fairy Tales of France." Realms of Fantasy web site. www.endicott-studio.com/rdrm/forconte (January 2007).

Wood, Mary. *Italian Cinema*. New York: Berg Publishing, 2005.

Young, Alan. "The Making of *Cannibal Holocaust*." *Cannibal Holocaust 25th Anniversary* DVD. Grindhouse Releasing, 2005.

Zapata, Kose. *Amando de Ossorio: The Last Templar*. DVD documentary. The Blind Dead Collection. Blue Underground, 2005.

Zillman, Dolf. "The Coming of Media Entertainment." In *Media Entertainment: The Psychology of Its Appeal*, edited by Dolf Zillman and Peter Vorderer. Mahwah, NJ: Lawrence Erlbaum, 2000.

_____, and Jennings Bryant. "Entertainment as Media Effect." In *Media Effects: Advances in Theory and Research*, edited by Jennings Bryant and Dolf Zillman. Mahwah, NJ: Lawrence Erlbaum, 1994.

Žižek, Slavoj. *Looking Awry: An Introduction to Jacques Lacan through Popular Culture*. Cambridge, MA: The MIT Press, 1992.

Index

À l'intérieur 308
Addio zio Tom 68–70
Africa addio 8, 61, 66–9
Africa, Blood and Guts see Africa addio
Agren, Janet 122, 136
Aja, Alexandre 261
Al tropico del cancro 80
Albertini, Bitto 155, 157, 160
Alda, Robert 148, 152
L'aldilà 13, 54, 88, 169
Alfonsi, Lidia 73
Alien 166–67
Alien Contamination see Contamination
Aliens 167
All the Colors of the Dark see Tutti i colori del buio
L'amante del vampiro 30–1
Los amantes de la isla del diable 193, 208, 215
Amanti d'oltretomba 48, 57
American Werewolf in London 238
And God Made Woman see Et Dieu … créa la femme
Andress, Ursula 118–19, 128, 136, 138–39
Andreu, Simón 249
Anthropophagus 129, 133, 135, 143, 163, 165
The Antichrist see L'antichristo
L'antichristo 144–46, 150–51
Anulka 253, 259
Apocalypse domani 8, 129, 132, 135
Aranda, Vicente 249
El árbol de España 180
Arden, Mary 77
Argento, Asia 167
Argento, Claudio 125
Argento, Dario 7, 20, 53, 71, 80–8, 90, 95, 98, 101–5, 109–10, 125, 127, 136, 162–63, 167–69, 284, 311
Argento, Salvatore 82
Arrotia-Jáuregui, Marcelo 181
Arsan Emmanuelle 296, 300
L'assassino è costretto ad uccidere ancora 106–7
Assignment Terror see Los monstruos del terror

Assonitis, Ovidio 146
El ataque de los muertos sin ojos 243, 258
Attack of the Robots see Cartas boca arriba
Auger, Claudine 81, 101
Autopsy see Macchi solari
Les Avaleuses 208, 210, 217–18, 221
L'avventura 5
The Awful Dr. Orloff see Gritos en la noche

Baba Yaga 165
Bacchanales sexuelles see Tout le monde il en a deux
Bach, Barbara 108
Baillou, Alfred 292, 306
Baker, Caroll 80, 165
Baker, Chet 196
Baker, Tammy Faye 305
Bandera negra 240
Barbareschi, Luca 120
Barbed Wire Dolls see Frauengefängnis
Bardem, Juan Antonio 171, 180
Bardot, Brigitte 269
Baron Blood see Gli orrori del castello di Norimberga
Bartok, Eva 75
Barzini, Luigi 21
Basic Instinct 88, 107
Bava, Lamberto 17, 163, 165, 168–69
Bava, Mario 11, 20, 22–9, 33–7, 44–54, 56, 58–9, 72–81, 85, 90, 102, 104–6, 152, 167, 271–72
Baxter, Les 75
Bay of Blood see Ecologia del delitto
Beauty and the Beast (1945) see La Belle et la bête
Beck, Glen 157
Behind the Green Door 208, 281
A Bell from Hell see La Campana del Infierno
Belle, Annie 167
La Belle et la bête 266
Bennett, Joan 168
Berkely, Elizabeth 58, 219
Berruti, Guilio 144
Bertolucci, Bernardo 296

Berutti, Giullio 141
Bésame monstruo 187, 219
La bestia en calore 8, 168
La bestia uccide a sangue freddo 108
Betti, Laura 81, 106
Beyond the Darkness see Buio omega
Beyond the Door see Che sei?
The Beyond see L'aldilà
Bianchi, Andrea 109, 133, 153
Bird with the Crystal Plumage see L'uccello dalle piume di cristallo
Birkin, Jane 50, 58
Black Belly of Tarantula see Tarantola dal ventre nero
Black Cat (1981) 53
The Black Crown see La corona negra
Black Emanuelle see Emanuelle nera
Black Sabbath see I tre volti della paura
Black Sunday see La maschera del demonio
Blain, Estella 215
Blair, Linda 151–2
Blair Witch Project 119
Blanc, Erika 56
Blanco, Hugo 181, 220
Blood and Black Lace see Sei donne per l'assassino
Blood and Roses see Et Mourir de plaisir
Blood for Dracula see Dracula cerca sangue di vergine
The Blood of Beasts see Le Sang des bêtes
The Blood of Fu Manchu 189–90, 212, 214
The Bloodstained Bride see La novia ensangrentada
Bloodstained Shadow see Solamente nero
The Bloody Judge 199–201, 208, 214
Blue Eyes of the Broken Doll see Los ojos azules de la muñeca rota
Blumenstock, Peter 274
Body of Evidence 107, 177
Böhme, Herbert 39

Bolkan, Florinda 89–92, 107, 151–52
Borel, Annik 169
Borken, Jules 266–67
Borowczyk, Walerian 312
Bouchet, Barbara 11, 90, 101
Boyle, Danny 129
Brandi, Walter 31, 58
Brandon, Michael 84–5, 87, 105
Brasseur, Pierre 267, 272
Brice, Pierre 39
Brides of Dracula 175
Bruner, Artur 205
Buio omega 1, 41, 163–65
Buñuel, Luis 272
El buque maldito 243–44, 256
Buried Alive see *Buio omega*
Burner, Cesar 241
Burstyn, Ellen 150

Caen, Michel 42
Caged (1950) 191
Caged Virgins see *Requiem pour un vampire*
Cahiers du Cinéma 263, 269
Calderoni, Rita 153
Caltiki, il mostro immortale 24–6, 29, 33
Camille 2000 2
Caminnecci, Pier Maria 186–87
La campana del infierno 249, 255, 311
Campbell, Ramsey 29
Canale, Gianna Maria 22, 29
Cani arrabbiati 148
Cannibal Apocalypse see *Apocalypse domani*
Cannibal ferox 122, 137–38
Cannibal Holocaust 8, 112, 115, 119–22
Cannibal Man see *La semana del asesino*
Cantáfora, Antonio 51
Cantor, Kieran 163
Capolicchio, Lino 102
Capponi, Pier Paolo 93
Le Capitaine Fracasse 272
The Card Player see *Il cartaio*
Carmilla 208, 249, 255, 269, 271
Carnacina, Stella 148, 151
Carpenter, John 98, 256
Carrel, Dany 39, 57
Carrere, Emilio 173
Il cartaio 98
Cartas boca arriba 184
Cartier, Caroline 275
La casa dalle finestre che ridono 7, 106
La casa dell'esorcismo 53, 146, 148–49, 152
Casaril, Guy 308
Case of the Bloody Iris see *Perche quelle strane gocce di sangue sul corpo di Jennifer*
The Case of the Scorpion's Tale see *La coda dello scorpione*
Casel, Antonio 173
Casini, Stefania 102
Casque d'or 262

Cassidy, Joanna 17
Castel, Marie-Pierre 279, 291
Il castello dei morti vivi 48
Castelnuovo, Nino 98, 109
Castle of Blood see *Danza macabra*
Castle of Fu Manchu 193
Castle of the Living Dead see *Il castello dei morti vivi*
Cat o' Nine Tales see *Il gatto a nove code*
Cat People (1942) 265
Les Cauchemars naissant la nuit 199, 219
Cavara, Paolo 61–3
Célestine, bonne à tout faire 210
Cervantes, Miguel de 173
Chaney, Lon, Jr. 225
Charlie's Angels (TV) 187, 219
Che sei? 1, 144, 146–47, 150–51, 237
Checci, Andrea 33
Chi l'ha vista morire? 110
Un Chien andalou 15
Children of the Corn 245, 259
Chimes at Midnight 184
Chin, Tsai 189, 214
Christie Agatha 71, 77, 80
Christina, princesse de l'erotisme 205–7, 222
La Chute de la maison Usher (1928) 265
Ciano, Mario 48
Ciardi, Francesca 120
El Cid 173
Cinque bambole per la luna d'agosto 46, 80–1, 92, 104–5
La ciociara 155
Circus of Horrors (1962) 178
La ciudad sin hombres 189, 191
Clark, Bob 19
Cleary, Corinne 304, 307
Cliver, Al 127, 139
Close, Glenn 179
Clouzot, Véra 266, 271
La coda dello scorpione 71–2, 92, 102
Coeur, Joëlle 281, 283, 288–89
Cold Eyes of Fear see *Gli occhi freddi della paura*
El conde Drácula 198–99, 201, 214
Contamination 166–67
Les Contes de fées 263
La corona negra 175
I corpi presentano tracce di violenza carnale 80, 93–4, 109
Corrigan, Terri 311
La corta notte della bambole di vetro 108
Cosa avete fatto a Solange? 110
Cosí dolci ... cosí perversa 80
Cosmicos 180
Cotten, Joseph 51
Count Dracula (1969) see *El conde Drácula*
Count Dracula's Great Love see *El gran amor del conde Drácula*
Countess du Murat 264
Cozzi, Luigi 73, 106, 166–67

Craven, Wes 100, 167
Crepax, Guido 165
El crimen de la calle de Boradadores 175
Crimson see *Las ratas no duermen de noche*
Crispino, Armando 41
Cristal, Perla 181
Cronenberg, David 5, 135
Crowther, Bosley 63
Cunningham, Sean 98
Cuny, Alain 297, 305
Curran, Bill 256
Curse of Frankenstein 33, 267
Curse of the Devil see *El retorno de Walpurgis*

Dabes, Alberto 231
Dalí, Fabienne 37
Dallesandro, Joe 153, 166
D'Amato, Joe see Massaccesi, Aristide
Damon, Mark 46
Dante, Joe 41
Danza macabra 42, 50, 55
Dargent, Mireille 279, 291
Dark Eyes of London 175
Darren, James 194, 196, 221–22
Dawn of the Dead (1978) 124, 253, 257, 284
Dawn of the Dead (2004) 129, 133
Dead Men Walk 273
Dead Ringers 5
De Alba, Aurora 225
De Angelis, Maurizio 93
Death in Haiti see *Al tropico del cancro*
Death Walks at Midnight see *La morte accarezza a mezzanotte*
Death Walks in High Heels see *La morte cammina con i tacchi alti*
Debbie Does Dallas 135
Deep Red see *Profondo rosso*
Deep River Savages see *Il paese del sesso selvaggio*
Deep Throat 208, 281, 283
De Funès, Isabelle 165
Delahaye, Michel 269
De la Iglesia, Eloy 172
Delli Colli, Alexander 128, 139
Delpierre, Dominick 292
Del Toro, Guillermo 7
De Martino, Alberto 139, 144
Demon Witch Child see *La endemoniada*
Demoni 169
Les Démoniaques 281, 283, 289
Demons see *Demoni*
Les démons 208
de Nesle, Robert 207–8
Deodato, Ruggero 115, 119–22, 137, 167, 312
de Ossorio, Amando 15, 171, 224, 231, 240–45, 257–59
De Palma, Brian 5
De Selle, Lorraine 137
De Sica, Vittorio 166
Devil Came from Akasawa see *El diablo que vino de Akasawa*

The Devils 139, 141, 143, 152
The Devil's Commandment see *I vampiri*
Devil's Island Lovers see *Los amantes de la isla del diable*
Dexter, Rosemary 194
El diablo que vino de Akasawa 205, 214–15
Diabolical Dr. Z see *Miss Muerte*
Diabolik 89, 218
Les Diaboliques (1955) 266–67, 271–72
Dialina, Riki 37
Diary of a Nymphomaniac see *Le Journal intime d'une nymphomane*
Di Paolo, Dante 77
The Dirty Girls 296
Do Not Deliver Us from Evil see *Mais ne nous délivrez pas du mal*
Do You Like Hitchcock? see *Ti piace Hitchcock*
Dr. Butcher M.D. see *Zombi Holocaust*
Dr. Jekyll and the Werewolf see *Dr. Jekyll y el Hombre Lobo*
Dr. Jekyll y el Hombre Lobo 229
Dr. M. shlägt zu 205
Dr. Orloff's Monster see *Secreto del Dr. Orloff*
Doctor Zhivago 173
La dolce vita 5
Dominici, Arturo 33
La donna nel mondo 61, 64–6, 70, 113
Don't Look Now 110
Don't Open the Window see *No profanar el sueño de los muertos*
Don't Torture a Duckling see *Non si sevizia un paperino*
Douglas, Michael 111
Drácula cerca sangue di vergine 166
Drácula contra Frankenstein 207–8, 216
Dracula, Prisoner of Frankenstein see *Drácula contra Frankenstein*
Dracula's Daughter 35
Dressed to Kill 5, 71
Durand, Jean-Marie 291

Earthquake 284
Eastman, George see Montefiore, Luigi
Easy Rider 82, 112
Eaten Alive see *Mangiati vivi!*
Eaton, Shirley 189, 191, 198, 216, 218
Ebert, Roger 299
Ecologia del delitto 46, 77, 80–1, 93, 109–10, 311
The Eerie Midnight Horror Show see *L'ossessa*
Ekberg, Anita 11, 105, 141, 153–54, 241, 256
El Cid 173
Elmi, Nicoletta 51, 104, 110
Emanuelle and the Last Cannibals see *Emanuelle e gli ultimi cannibali*
Emanuelle and the White Slave Trade see *La via della prostituzione*
Emanuelle Around the World see *Emanuelle perché violenza alle donne*
Emanuelle e gli ultimi cannibali 8, 93, 117–18, 159
Emanuelle in America 8, 115, 157–59, 161
Emanuelle in Bangkok see *Emanuelle nera: Orient reportage*
Emanuelle in Japan 160
Emanuelle nera 7, 154–57, 160
Emanuelle nera: Orient reportage 157
Emanuelle perché violenza alle donne 8, 159, 161
Emilienne 308
Emmanuelle 2, 10, 155, 296–300, 305
Emmanuelle: L'antivierge 155, 300–2, 305–6
Emmanuelle, the Joys of Woman see *Emmanuelle: L'antivierge*
En passant par le Lorraine 266
La endemoniada 17, 243, 245
Ercole al centro della terra 44
Ercoli, Luciano 93, 103
Eric, the Conquerer see *Gli invasori*
Erotic Nights of the Living Dead see *Le notti erotiche dei morti viventi*
The Erotic Rites of Frankenstein see *La maldición de Frankenstein*
Erotic Witchcraft see *La Goulve*
Escalofrío 247, 258
Escamotage d'une dame au théatre Robert Houdin 264
El espanto surge de la tumba 231, 233, 237
Et Dieu ... créa la femme 269, 296
Et mourir de plaisir 269–71
Eugénie de Sade 182, 201–3
Eugenie, the Story of Her Descent into Perversion 8, 196–98, 217
Exorcism (Jess Franco, 1974) 182, 216–17
Exorcism (Paul Naschy, 1975) see *Exorcismo*
Exorcismo 237
The Exorcist 1, 53, 112, 139, 144, 148, 150, 243, 258, 294
Eyes Without a Face see *Les Yeux sans visage*

Faces of Death 59, 124
Faces of Death II 59
Falk, Rossella 104
Fallaci, Oriana 64
Fangs of the Living Dead see *Malenka, la sobrina del vampiro*
Fantômas 264
Farmer, Mimsy 85, 101, 105

Farrow, Tisa 127, 129, 135, 139
Fascination 284, 286, 288–89
Fatal Attraction 177
Le fatiche di Ercole 33
Felicity 308
Felisatti, Massimo 98
Fellini, Fredrico 310
The Female Vampire see *Les Avaleuses*
Femina ridens 105
Fenech, Edwidge 92–3, 98, 100, 102, 104, 108–9, 111
Ferrer, Mel 138, 144, 150, 269, 271
Ferroni, Giorgio 39
Fiander, Lewis 245, 259
Fidenco, Nico 160–61
The Fifth Cord see *Giornata nera per l'ariete*
La Fille de Dracula 207–9
Five Dolls for an August Moon see *Cinque bambole per la luna d'agosto*
Flavia, la monaca musulmana 7, 143, 151–52
Flavia the Heratic see *Flavia, la monaca musulmana*
Fleming, Lone 241, 243, 259
Flemyng, Robert 41, 56
Flesh for Frankenstein see *Il mostro è in tavola Barone Frankenstein*
Fly Me the French Way see *Tout le monde il en a deux*
The Fog (1979) 256
Forbidden Photos of a Lady Above Suspicion see *Le foto probite di una signora per bene*
Forsyth, Stephen 106
Foschi, Massimo 117, 137
Le foto probite di una signora per bene 72, 93, 105
Foukes, Andy 128
Four Flies on Grey Velvet see *Quattro mosche di velluto grigio*
Fragrasso, Claudio 133
Francis, Connie 63, 105
Franciscus, James 84–6, 102
Franco, Jess 15, 37, 39, 53, 154, 171, 175–222, 255, 269, 271, 290, 311
Franju, Georges 261, 263–64, 266–69, 312
Frankenstein (1931) 35
Frankenstein Meets the Wolfman 223–24
Frankenstein's Bloody Terror see *La marca del Hombre-lobo*
Frauen für Zellenblock 9 212
Frauengefängnis 193
Freda, Ricardo 14, 17, 22–7, 37, 39–41, 272
Freidkin, William 5, 144, 151, 245
French Sex Murders see *La Maison de rendez-vous*
Friday the 13th (1980) 2, 71, 93, 98, 109
Friday the 13th Pt. 2 98
Frightened Woman see *Femina ridens*

Le Frisson des vampires 277–78, 291
Frizzi, Fabrizio 127
Frontière(s) 308
La frusta e il corpo 44, 47–8, 58–9
Fuchs, Gaby 227, 239
Fuego 177–79, 201
Fulci, Lucio 7, 13, 14, 53, 55, 88–92, 104, 112, 126–28, 139, 169
La furia del Hombre Lobo 229
Fury of the Wolfman see *La furia del Hombre Lobo*

Gaban, Jean 261
Gabel, Scilla 37, 57
Gainesborg, Serge 50, 58
Galbo, Christina 250, 257
Galleani, Ely 160, 165
Gantillon, Bruno 292–93, 306
Las garras de Lorelei 243
Gates of Hell see *Paura nella città dei morti viventi*
Il gatto a nove code 7, 84–6, 102
Gemser, Laura 117–18, 128, 136–38, 154–62
Gentil, Michel see Rollin, Jean
The Ghost see *Lo spettro*
The Ghost Galleon see *El buque maldito*
Giacobetti, Francis 305
Giannini, Giancarlo 101
Giordano, Mariangela 153
Giornata nera per l'ariete 104
The Girl from Rio see *La ciudad sin hombres*
Girl Slaves of Morgan Le Fay see *Morgane et ses nymphes*
The Girl Who Knew Too Much see *La ragazza che sapeva troppo*
Girls in Prison 191
Glenn, Leo 199
The Goblins 95, 168
Gogol, Nikolai 33
Goldfinger 181, 184
Le Golem 265
The Golem (1936) see *Le Golem*
Goodbye Emmanuelle 306, 308
Goodbye Uncle Tom see *Addio zio Tom*
Gorini, Adrana 77
La Goulve 293, 306
Goupil, Jeanne 294, 304–5
Govar, René 225
El gran amor del conde Drácula 230–31, 237
Grandi, Serena 129
Granger, Farley 80
Grapes of Death see *Les Raisins de la mort*
Grau, Jorge 240, 250, 252–53, 284
Graveyard of Horror see *Necrophagus*
Gravina, Carla 144, 150–51
Greta, the Mad Butcher 193, 212–13, 218
The Grim Reaper see *Anthropophagus*
Grindhouse 5

Gritos en la noche 37, 39, 171, 173–81
Gross Jerry 68
Guillén, José María 247

Halloween (1978) 2, 71, 93, 98, 109, 269
Hargitay, Mariska 153
Hargitay, Mickey 153
Harp, Helen 243
Harper, Jessica 162–63, 168
Harris, James 153
Hatchet for the Honeymoon see *Il rosso segno della follia*
Haute Tension 308
Heavenly Creatures 294, 305
Hell of the Living Dead see *Virus*
Hemmings, David 95, 97, 103–4
Hendrix, Jimmy 292
Hercules (1958) see *Le fatiche di Ercole*
Hercules in the Haunted World see *Ercole al centro della terra*
Hess, David 167
Hill, Claudio Guerin 240, 249
Hilton, George 93, 102, 106–8
Histoire d'O 2, 7, 261, 300, 302–4, 307
Hitchcock, Alfred 72, 266
Holden, Gloria 35
The Horrible Secret of Dr. Hichcock see *L'orrible segreto del Dr. Hichcock*
Horror Chamber of Dr. Faustus see *Les Yeux sans visage*
Horror of Dracula 31, 33
Horror Rises from the Tomb see *El espanto surge de la tumba*
Horrors of Spider Island see *Ein Toter hing im Netz*
Hôtel des invalides 266
The House by the Cemetery see *Quella villa accanto al cimitero*
House of Dracula 207
The House of Exorcism see *La casa dell'esorcismo*
House of Frankenstein 207
The House That Screamed see *La residentia*
The House with the Laughing Windows see *La casa dalle finestre che ridono*
Hoven, Adrian 186, 214–15
The Howling 238
El huésped de las tinieblas 175
The Human Centipede 1
Hunchback of the Morgue see *El jorobado de la morgue*
Hunter, Jeffrey 223
Hyer, Martha 177, 179

I, a Woman 187
I Am Curious Yellow see *Jag är nyfiken — en film i gult*
I Walked with a Zombie 265
Ibañez Serrador, Narcisco 240, 245–48, 259–60
L'iguana dalla lingua di fuoco 71, 80

The Iguana with the Tongue of Fire see *L'iguana dalla lingua di fuoco*
Ilsa, the Wicked Warden see *Greta, the Mad Butcher*
L'Image 296, 304
The Image see *L'Image*
Images in a Convent see *Immagini di un convento*
Immagini di un convento 143, 152
In the Realm of the Senses 210
Incubo sulla città contaminata 128–29, 138
Inferno 167
Gli invasori 44
The Iron Rose see *La Rose de fer*
It Conquered the World (1956) 167

Jack el Destripador de Londres 229
Jack the Ripper (1971) see *Jack el destripador de Londres*
Jack the Ripper — Der Dirnenmörder von London 212
Jackson, Peter 294, 305
Jacob's Ladder 196
Jacopetti, Gualtiero 61–70
Jaeckin, Just 7, 15, 297, 304
Jag är nyfiken — en film i gult 5, 187
Jeunes filles impudiques 281–82
Johnson, Gary 37
Johnson, Richard 127, 151
Jolie, Angelina 139
El jorobado de la Morgue 230–32
Le Jour se lève 275
Le journal intime d'une nymphomane 210
Judex (1916) 273
Jules et Jim 5
Julien, Sandra 291
Juliette 212
Jungle Holocaust see *Ultimo mondo cannibale*
Jungle Jim 273
Justine 193–94

Kael, Pauline 59
Karlatos, Olga 127
Karloff, Boris 13, 46, 54, 216, 234
Karr, Mabel 215
Karr, Mariana 247
Keach, Stacy 118–19, 138
Kendell, Suzy 82, 93–4, 101, 108–9
Kennedy Arthur 144, 151, 250, 253
Kerman, Robert 119, 121–22, 135
Kier, Udo 166, 302, 304, 307
Kill Baby Kill see *Operazione paura*
Kill Bill 5, 267
Killer Fish 50
The Killer Must Kill Again see *L'assassino è costretto ad uccidere ancora*
Killer Nun see *Suor omicidi*
King, Zalman 5
King of Kings 173, 223
Kinski, Klaus 108, 188, 198–99, 212, 214, 218, 221

Kiss and Kill see *Blood of Fu Manchu*
Kiss Me Monster see *Bésame monstruo*
Klimovsky, León 229, 239
Koscina, Sylva 53
Kristel, Sylvia 297–301, 305–6, 308

Lado, Aldo 110
Lahaie, Brigitte 286, 288–90
Lai, Me Me 113–14, 116–17, 137
Lamaire, Jean-Marie 286, 289
Larraz, José Ramón 253, 259
Lassander, Dagmar 93, 105–6, 169
The Last Broadcast 119
The Last House on the Left (1972) 112, 167, 253
Last Tango in Paris 296–97
Laure 308
Lavi, Daliah 37, 47–8, 59
Lavia, Gabriele 95, 104, 146
Lavie, Jean 273
Lazenby, George 110
Lee, Christopher 13, 31, 44, 47–8, 58–9, 188–90, 196, 198–201, 212, 214, 217
Lee, Margaret 199, 221
Le Fanu, Sheridan 208, 255, 269, 271
Leigh, Janet 72
Lemaire, Jean-Marie 286
Lemoine, Michel 186–87, 219, 292, 295, 306–7
Lenzi, Umberto 80, 107–8, 113–15, 128–29, 137–38
Leone, Alfredo 51, 53, 146, 152
Leone, Sergio 82
Leroy Philippe 48
Lesoeur, Daniel 184
Lèvres de sang 284–85, 290
Libert, Anne 208
The Lickerish Quartet 2
Die Liebesbriefe einer portugiesischen Nonne 210
Liljedahl, Marie 196–98, 217
Lindfors, Viveca 249, 255
Liné, Helga 243
Lips of Blood see *Lèvres de sang*
Lisa and the Devil see *Lisa e il diavolo*
Lisa e il diavolo 51, 53, 146
Livane, Lisa 293
Living Dead at the Manchester Morgue see *No profanar el sueño de los muertos*
Lom, Herbert 191, 198, 214, 220
The Long Hair of Death see *I lunghi capelli della morte*
The Lorelei's Grasp see *Las garras de Lorelei*
Loren, Sophia 63, 155
Lorna l'exorciste 210
Lorys, Diana 175
Lost (TV) 196
Lost Horizon (1973) 299
Love Letters from a Portuguese Nun see *Die Liebesbriefe einer portugiesischen Nonne*

Lovelock, Ray 101, 250, 257
Lucas, Tim 15, 27, 148, 173, 181, 198–99
Una lucertola con la pelle di donna 7, 12, 71, 88–90, 107
Lucky, el intrépido 184
Lumière Brothers 264
I lunghi capelli della morte 37, 42
La lupa mannera 169
Luxardo, Elda 82

Macabro 41, 163, 165, 167–68
Macchie solari 41, 101
Madame d'Aulnoy 264
Magall, Macha 168
Mais ne nous délivrez pas du mal 7, 8, 294–95, 304–5
Maison de rendez-vous 11, 105
Make Them Die Slowly see *Cannibal ferox*
Malabimba, the Malicious Whore 153
Malden, Karl 84–6, 102–3
La maldición de Frankenstein 207–8, 216
La maldición de la bestia 233
Malenka, la sobrina del vampiro 240–41, 256
The Man Who Knew Too Much 72
Mandingo 68, 70
Mangiati vivi! 122–23, 136
Mannchen, Karl-Heinz 184, 186
La mano de un hombre muerto 181, 220
Le Manoir du diable 264
Manson, Charles 292
The Manster 267
La marca del Hombre-lobo 224–26, 237–38, 240
Margheriti, Antonio 37, 42–4, 50–1, 55, 58, 129, 135, 269
Marielle, Jean-Pierre 88, 105
Mark of the Devil 199, 214
Martin, Maribel 249, 255
Martin, Oliver 299
Martinelli, Elsa 271
Martino, Sergio 14, 80, 92–3, 100, 108–11, 138
Martyrs 1, 308
La maschera del demonio 11, 26, 33–6, 55, 72, 177
Mask of Satan see *La maschera del demonio*
Massaccesi, Aristide 41, 117–18, 129, 133, 135, 137–39, 143, 152, 154, 157–62, 163–65, 311
McCambridge, Mercedes 188, 191, 193–94
McCloskey, Mitch 167
McCulloch, Ian 11, 26, 127–28, 139, 167
McNair, Barbara 193, 196, 221
Il medaglione insanguinato 17, 150
Méliès, Georges 264
Mell, Marissa 89, 107
Memoirs of a Wolfman 236
Mercier, Mario 15, 293–94, 299
Mercier, Michèle 73
Méril, Macha 95

Metzger, Radley 2, 217, 277, 296, 304, 312
Meyer, Russ 66
Midi-Minuit Fantastique 274, 295
Milian Tomas 104
The Mill of the Stone Women see *Il mulino delle donne di pietra*
Mills, Juliet 146, 151
Il mio amico Jekyll 31
Mio caro assasino 107
Miracle, Irene 167
Miranda, Isa 81
Miranda, Soledad 178–79, 198–99, 201–5, 214–15, 217, 219–21
Miss Muerte 180, 182–84, 189, 203, 215
Mitchell, Cameron 77
Molina, Jacinto 15, 171, 207, 216, 222–39, 255, 311
Mon chien 266
Mona 208
Mondo bizarro 66
Mondo cane 8, 59, 61–4, 70, 113
Mondo cane II 61, 64, 70
Il mondo di notte 61
Mondo teeno 66
Mondo Topless 66
The Monster of las Tinieblas see *El huésped de las tinieblas*
Il mostro di Venezia 57
Il mostro è in tavola Barone Frankenstein 166
Los monstruos del terror 227
La montagna del dio cannibale 118–19, 138
Montefiore, Luigi 129, 133, 135, 137–39, 161, 165
Morell, Marie-France 281
Morgan, Michèle 262
Morgane et ses nymphes 292–93, 304, 306
Morricone, Ennio 84–5, 105
Morris, Marianne 253, 259
Morrissey, Paul 166
La morte accarezza a mezzanotte 93, 95, 103
La morte cammina con i tacchi alti 93, 95, 103
La morte vivante 288
Mountain of the Cannibal God see *La montagna del dio cannibale*
Mourir à Madrid 273
Mucha sangre 236
Il mulino delle donne di pietra 37–9, 57, 175–76
Müller, Paul 188, 198, 201, 217, 219
The Mummy (1959) 33
Munkel, Hans 227
Musante, Tony 82–4, 88, 101
My Bloody Valentine (1982) 2, 100
My Dear Killer see *Mio caro assasino*
The Mysterious Dr. Satan 273

Naciel, Nicole 277
Naschy, Paul see Molina, Jacinto
Natan, Monique 277

Navarro, Nieves 93, 100, 103, 105
Nea: A Young Emmanuelle 160, 308
Necronomicon 182, 184–87, 196, 203, 221
Necrophagus 249–51, 256–57
Needham, Gary 73
Nella stretta morsa del ragno 50
Neri, Rosalba, 11, 108, 194
Nero, Franco 104
Neville, Edgar 173
Nichols, Britt 207, 222
Nicolodi, Daria 98, 103–4, 162, 167
The Night Child see *Il medaglione insanguinato*
Night of the Living Dead (1968) 1, 112, 241, 257, 258, 267
Night of the Seagulls see *La noche de las gaviotas*
Night of the Sorcerers see *La noche de los brujos*
Night of the Werewolf see *El retorno del Hombre-Lobo*
Nightmare Castle see *Amanti d'oltretomba*
Nightmare City see *Incubo sulla città contaminata*
Nightmares Come at Night see *Les Cauchemars naissent la nuit*
Nights of the Werewolf see *Noches del Hombre Lobo*
Nights of the World see *Il mondo di notte*
99 Women 191–93
No profanar el sueño de los muertos 250, 252–53, 284
La noche de las gaviotas 243, 257–58
La noche de los brujos 245
La noche de Walpurgis 222, 227–29, 239, 241
La noche del terror ciego 11, 241–43, 259
Noches del Hombre Lobo 225, 227
Non si sevizia un paperino 8, 88, 90, 92, 104, 143, 311
Le notti del terrore 133, 153
Le notti erotiche dei morti viventi 133–34, 137
Novak, Kim 73
La novia ensangrentada 7, 8, 249, 255
Nude for Satan see *Nude per Satana*
Nude per l'assassino 98–100, 109, 153
Nude per Satana 153
The Nude Vampire see *La Vampire nue*
La Nuit des traquées 288

O'Brien, Donald 128, 152
Gli occhi freddi della paura 103
Los ojos azules de la muñeca rota 233
Once Upon a Time in the West 82
100 Rifles 201
One on Top of the Other see *Una sull'altra*
Operazione paura 27–8, 48–50, 56

Orano, Alesso 53
El orfanato 260
La orgia de los muertos 233
Orlandi, Nora 92
The Orphanage see *El orfanato*
L'orrible segreto del Dr. Hichcock 8, 10, 37, 39–41, 56, 177
Gli orrori del castello di Norimberga 9, 51, 54
Orsini, Umberto 300–1, 305, 308
Ortolani, Riz 63
L'ossessa 148, 151, 237

Il paese del sesso selvaggio 113–15
Palance, Jack 188, 194, 219
Palmer, Lilli 245, 257
Paluzzi, Luciana 193
La Papesse 293–94, 307–8
Paranoia 80, 113
Parent, Jacqueline 210
Parra, Vecente 247
Pascal, Marie-Georges 286, 289–90
Paura nella città dei morti viventi 1, 26, 53, 55, 127–28
Perchè quelle strane gocce di stangue sul corpo di Jennifer? 102
Pericoli, Emilio 63
Perkins, Anthony 72
Perversion Story see *Una sull'altra*
Peters, Bernard 198
Phantasmes 284
Phantom of the Opera (1962) 178
Phenomena 169
Philippe, Jean-Lou 284
Philosophy in the Boudoir 198
Pigozzi, Luciano 51
Pink, Sidney 178
Pistilli, Luigi 81, 92, 111
Pit and the Pendulum 42
Planet of the Vampires see *Terrore nello spazio*
Playgirls and the Vampires see *L'ultima preda del vampiro*
Podesta, Rosana 44
La polizia chiede aiuto 110
Pomés, Félix de 173
Poncela, Eusebio 247
Porno Holocaust 133, 138–39, 143, 163
Power, Romina 194, 218
Power, Tyrone 194, 218
Preiss, Wolfgang 37
Price, Dennis 207–8, 216, 221–22
Primus, Barry 101
El príncipe encadenado 224
Profondo rosso 8, 85, 88, 95, 97–8, 103–4, 162, 313
Prom Night (1981) 71
Promenons-nous dans les bois 308
Prosperi, Franco 61–70
The Psychic see *Sette notte in nero*
Psycho (1960) 72
Puerto, Carlos 247
Pyro see *Fuego*

Le Quai des brumes 286
Quattro mosche di velluto grigio 8, 71, 84–5, 87–8, 105

Quella villa accanto al cimitero 53, 169
Quesada, Milo 75
¿Quién puede matar a un niño? 245, 247–48, 259–60, 311

Rabid 135
Rabid Dogs see *Cani arrabbiati*
Radice, Giovanni Lombardo 129, 137, 167
La ragazza che sapeva troppo 11, 26, 72–3, 82
Les Raisins de la mort 7, 284, 286–87, 289–90, 311
Rambaldi, Carlo 90
Ransome, Prunella 245, 259–60
Rape of the Vampire see *La Viol du vampire*
Rascel, Renato 31
Rassimov, Ivan 92, 100, 108, 113–14, 117, 122, 136–37, 148, 151
Las ratas no duermen de noche 233, 236
Ray, Nicholas 223
Reage, Pauline 300, 302, 304
Rear Window 72
La rebelión de las muertas 233, 238–9
REC: Dissecting the Norm?: Plastic Surgery, Deviant Bodies, and the Politics of the Monstrous in Nip/Tuck 7, 133, 260
REC 2 133
Redgrave, Vanessa 141
Redon, Jean 266–67
Reeves, Michael 199, 214
La reina del Tabarín 180, 201
Reincarnation of Isabel see *Riti, magie nere e segrete orge nel trecento*
Rennie, Michael 227
Renzi, Eva 84, 101
Requiem pour un vampire 279–81, 291
La residencia 245–46, 257
El retorno de Walpurgis 233–34, 236
El retorno del Hombre Lobo 233, 235, 238
Return of the Blind Dead see *El ataque de los muertos sin ojos*
Revenge of Frankenstein 33, 267
Reynaud, Janine 102, 185–87, 219, 221
Richardson, John 33
Righi, Massimo 77
Riti, magie nere e segrete orge nel trecento 153
Rivière, Georges 44
Robins/Rogo, Gogó 181
Robsahm, Margrete 42
Roeg, Nicolas 110
Rohm, Maria 188–91, 194–96, 214, 217–18, 220–22
Rohmer, Sax 189, 212, 214
Rollin, Jean 15, 222, 262, 272–92, 294, 299, 311
The Rolling Stones 292
Román, Letícia 72, 74, 76, 106

Romay, Lina 207–8, 210, 216–18
Romero, George 112, 124–26, 136, 267, 286
Roots 70
La Rose de fer 283
Rosemary's Baby 93, 112, 146
Rossi-Stuart, Giacomo 48
Il rosso segno della follia 8, 46, 106
Roth, Eli 19
Rousset-Rouard, Yves 297, 299–300, 302
Russell, Ken 139

Sabato, Antonio 107
Sacchetti, Dardano 26
Sacchi, Robert 11
Sade, Marquis de 193
Sadisterotica 187, 219
The Sadistic Baron Von Klaus see *La mano de un hombre muerto*
Saly, Julia 237
Sanders, George 188, 218
Le Sang des bêtes 266
San Martin, Conrado 175
Sarky, Daniel 297, 305
Satan's Blood see *Escalofrio*
Savage Man, Savage Beast see *Ultime grida dalla savana*
Savalas, Telly 53, 56, 148, 152
Saxon, John 72, 74, 76, 106, 129, 135
Schell, Maria 188, 193, 220
Schneider, Steven Jay 9
Schoolgirl Hitchhikers see *Jeunes filles impudiques*
Schubert, Karin 156–57, 160
Scob, Edith 267–69, 272
Le scomunicate di San Valentino 141, 154
Score (1972) 2
Scorsese, Martin 5
Scott, Ridley 7, 166
Scott, Susan see Navarro, Nieves
El secreto del Dr. Orloff 10, 180–82, 215–16
The Seduction of Amy see *Phantasmes*
Sei donne per l'assassino 10, 46, 75, 77–80, 101–2
Selsky, Samuel S. 273, 277
La semana del asesino 172, 247, 249–50, 255–56, 310
Senatore, Paola 122, 152
Séria, Joël 294–5, 304–5
Sette notte in nero 88
Sette orchidee macchiate di rosso 107–8, 113
Seven Bloodstained Orchids see *Sette orchidee macchiate di rosso*
Seven Deaths in the Cat's Eye 50–1, 58
Seven Women for Satan see *Les Week-ends maléfiques du Comte Zaroff*
The Shadow (1940) 273
Shannon, Mark 137, 138
Shaun of the Dead 133
She Killed in Ecstasy see *Sie tötete en Ekstase*

Shepard, Patty 227, 238
The Shiver of the Vampires see *Le Frisson des vampires*
Shivers 135
Short Night of the Glass Dolls see *La corta notte della bambole di vetro*
Sie tötete en Ekstase 205, 220
Signoret, Simone 266, 271
The Sinful Nuns of St. Valentine see *Le scomunicate di San Valentino*
Siniestros del Doctor Orloff 208
Sinister Eyes of Dr. Orloff see *Los Ojos siniestros del Doctor Orloff*
Sinner see *Le Journal intime d'une nymphomane*
Sirtzky, Alain 299
Sister Emanuelle see *Suor Emanuelle*
The Sixth Sense 196
Slater, Jay 239, 260
Slaughter Hotel see *La bestia uccide a sangue freddo*
Slaughter of the Vampires see *La strage dei vampiri*
Snyder, Zack 129
So Sweet ... So Perverse see *Cosi dolci ... cosi perversa*
Soavi, Michele 111
Solamente nero 102
Sommer, Elke 51–4, 56–7, 146, 148, 152
Sorel, Jean 89–90, 107–8
Sorente, Sylvia 42
The Sound of Music 111
Spaak, Agnès 181
Spaak, Catherine 103
Sparks, Doug 284
Spasmo 108
Spermula 189
Lo spettro 41, 55
S.S Hell Camp see *Bestia en calore*
Steele, Barbara 33–7, 41–3, 55–6
Stergers, Bernice 163, 165, 168
Stewart, James 73
Stiglitz, Hugo 128, 138
Stoppi, Franka 163
Storraro, Vittorio 84
The Story of O see *Histoire d'O*
La strage dei vampiri 58
La strana morte del signor Benson 71
The Strange Vice of Mrs. Wardh see *Lo strano vizio della signora Wardh*
Lo strano vizio della signora Wardh 92, 108–9
Strindberg, Anita 89, 92, 102, 107, 110–11, 144
Strip Nude for Your Killer see *Nude per l'assassino*
Strömberg, Ewa 203, 221
Succubus see *Necronomicon*
Sullivan, Barry 177, 179
Suor Emanuelle 142
Suor omicidi 141, 143, 152–53, 311

Suspiria 6, 7, 162–63, 168
Sutherland, Donald 48

Tales That Will Tear Your Heart Out 128
Tarantino, Quentin 5, 19, 267, 279
Tarantola dal ventre nero 101
Tate, Sharon 292
Tati, Jacques 262
Taylor, Jack 186, 188, 196, 217, 256
Tempi duri per i vampiri 31
10 Little Indians 80
Tendre et perverse Emanuelle 210
Tenebrae 88, 169
Tenemos 18 años 180
Terrore nello spazio 16, 20
Testi, Fabio 110
Therese and Isabelle 296
Thorne, Dyanne 218
Thulin Ingrid 108
Thunderball 184
Ti piace Hitchcock 98
Tiffin, Pamela 104
Tinti, Gabriele 136, 151, 154, 157, 162
Tognazzi, Ugo 31, 42
Tohill, Cathal 15
Tombs, Pete 15, 293
Tombs of the Blind Dead see *La noche del terror ciego*
Torre de los siete jorobados 173
Torso see *I corpi presentano tracce di violenza carnale*
Ein Toter hing im Netz 312
Tourneur, Jacques 265
Tourneur, Maurice 265–66
Tout le monde il en a deux 281, 288–89
The Tower of the Seven Hunchbacks see *La torre de los siete jorobados*
Towering Inferno 284
Towers, Harry Alan 187–201, 205, 214, 218
Toynbee, Polly 297
El transexual 233
I tre volti della paura 13, 26, 44–6, 54, 73, 75
Treasure Island (1965) 184
Truffaut, François 310
Il tuo vizio è una stanza chiusa e solo io ne ho la chiave 72, 92, 110–11
Turner, Kathleen 111
Tutti i colori del buio 80, 93, 100
28 Days Later 129, 133
28 Weeks Later 133
Twitch of the Death Nerve see *Ecologia del delitto*
Two Undercover Angels see *Sadisterotica*
Two Women see *La Ciociara*

L'uccello dalle piume di cristallo 2, 10, 82–5, 88, 95, 101
Ugarte, Julian 225, 238
L'ultima preda del vampiro 31–2, 57–8

Ultime grida dalla savana 69
Ultimo mondo cannibale 115
Una sull'altra 88–9, 107
Uncle Was a Vampire see *Tempi duri per i vampiri*
Ungarno, Francesca 77
Ustinov, Peter 66

Vadim, Annette 269, 271
Vadim, Roger 269–71
Valeri, Valero 48–50
Valli, Alida 53, 56, 153, 168, 267, 272
Vampire and the Ballerina see *L'amante del vampiro*
The Vampire Lovers 255
La Vampire nue 275–77, 290
Les Vampires 264–65, 273
Vampiresas 1930 175
I vampiri 14, 19, 22–6, 29, 33, 272
Vamps of 1930 see *Vampiresas 1930*
The Vampyre 236
Vampyres 253–54, 259
Vampyros lesbos 182, 203–5
Van Beeber, Jim 112
Van Vooren, Monique 166
Venantini, Venantino 300
Vengeance of the Mummy see *La vengenza de la momia*
Vengeance of the Zombies see *La rebelión de las muertas*
La vengenza de la momia 233
Venus in Furs 182, 194–96, 221–22
La vergine di Norimberga 42–4, 58, 178
Verley, Renaud 249, 255
Vernon, Howard 11, 175, 178, 188, 194, 199, 207–8

Vertigo 72, 88, 107
La via della prostituzione 160–61
The Vig 33
Le Viol du vampire 10, 273–75, 290–91
Virgin Among the Living Dead see *Christine, princesse de l'erotisme*
The Virgin of Nuremberg see *La vergine di Norimberga*
Virus 128
Von Blanc, Christina 207, 222

Wagener, Catherine 294, 305
Walker, Pete 10
Wallace Edgar 71, 205
Wan, James 19
War of the Roses 111
Warhol, Andy 166
We Are 18 Years Old see *Tenemos 18 años*
Weaver, Sigourney 167
Les Week-ends maléfiques du Comte Zaroff 295, 306–7
Wells, Orson 184, 212
The Werewolf and the Yeti see *La maldicón de la bestia*
Werewolf in a Girls Dormitory 29
Werewolf Shadow see *La noche de Walpurgis*
Werewolf Woman see *La lupa mannera*
What Have They Done to Solange? see *Cosa avete fatto a Solange?*
What Have They Done to Your Daughters? see *La polizia chiede aiuto*
The Whip and the Body see *La frusta e il corpo*
White, David 169

Who Can Kill a Child? see *¿Quién puede matar a un niño?*
Who Saw Her Die? see *Chi l'ha vista morire?*
Williams, Fred 205, 220
Williams, Tony 9
Wingrove, Nigel 179
Witchfinder General 199, 214
The Wolf-Man (1941) 35
A Woman in a Lizard's Skin see *Una lucertola con la pelle di donna*
A Woman Possessed see *La Papesse*
Women in Prison 191
Women of the World see *La donna nel mondo*
Wood, Ed 293

Yanni, Rosanna 187, 219, 237
Yellow Emmanuelle 160
Les Yeux sans visage 15, 175, 178, 261, 263, 267–69, 272
Your Vice Is a Locked Room and Only I Have the Key see *Il tuo vizio è una stanza chiusa e solo io ne ho la chiave*

Zombi see *Dawn of the Dead* (1978)
Zombi 2 2, 7, 88, 112, 126–28, 139, 166, 313
Zombie see *Zombi 2*
Zombie 4: After Death 133
Zombie Holocaust 128, 130–31, 139
Zombie 3 169
Zombieland 133
Zurakowska, Dianik 225